SOCIAL SECURITY IN DEVELOPING COUNTRIES

T0323374

WIDER

Studies in Development Economics embody the output of the reseach programmes of the World Institute for Development Economics Research (WIDER), which was established by the United Nations University as its first research and training centre in 1984 and started work in Helsinki in 1985. The principal purpose of the Institute is to help identify and meet the need for policy-oriented socio-economic research on pressing global and development problems, as well as common domestic problems and their inter-relationships.

Social Security in Developing Countries

Edited by

Ehtisham Ahmad, Jean Drèze, John Hills,
and Amartya Sen

CLARENDON PRESS · OXFORD

OXFORD
UNIVERSITY PRESS

Great Clarendon Street, Oxford, OX2 6DP,
United Kingdom

Oxford University Press is a department of the University of Oxford.
It furthers the University's objective of excellence in research, scholarship,
and education by publishing worldwide. Oxford is a registered trade mark of
Oxford University Press in the UK and in certain other countries

This volume is published in association with STICERD

The moral rights of the authors have been asserted

First published 1991
Reprinted 2011
First published in paperback 2020

Published in the United States of America by Oxford University Press
198 Madison Avenue, New York, NY 10016, United States of America

British Library Cataloguing in Publication Data
Data available

Library of Congress Cataloging in Publication Data
Data available

ISBN 978–0–19–823300–8 (Hbk.)
ISBN 978–0–19–886015–0 (Pbk.)

FOREWORD

The insecurity in which a large proportion of the world's population lives presents one of the greatest problems and challenges facing mankind. Analysis of the initiatives which have been taken in developing countries in different parts of the world to promote the security of their citizens, and of the potential of new strategies, therefore has great potential value.

The Suntory Toyota International Centre for Economics and Related Disciplines (STICERD) at the London School of Economics supports research in a wide range of areas, two of its largest programmes being concerned with development economics and with welfare policies. The principal purpose of the World Institute for Development Economics Research (WIDER) in Helsinki is to help identify and meet the need for policy-oriented socio-economic research on pressing global economic problems, particularly those impacting most directly on developing countries. The two institutions were therefore very pleased to be able to support the Workshop on Social Security in Developing Countries at which early versions of the papers included in this volume were presented.

The Workshop, which took place in June 1988 at the London School of Economics as part of the tenth anniversary activities at STICERD, brought together not only the authors of the various papers but also a distinguished group of other participants for two days of intensive discussion. It built on the continuing programmes of work on social security in developing countries at both institutions.

As the contents of the book will demonstrate, there is no single approach which can guarantee the security of living conditions which so many people desperately lack. There is, however, much that can be done and many important lessons to be drawn from a wide variety of approaches which have been taken. Disseminating such lessons is one of the key roles of both our institutions and we are delighted that thanks to the editors of the book, who also arranged the original workshop, and to the Oxford University Press these can now reach a wider audience.

Lal Jayawardena
Director, World Institute for
Development Economics
Research

Nicholas Stern
Chairman, Suntory Toyota
International Centre for
Economics and Related
Disciplines

January 1990

PREFACE

In the literature on development issues, it has often been assumed (explicitly or by implication) that developing countries are too poor to be able to 'afford' social-security systems. There are good reasons, however, to question this assumption. It is true that the complex and expensive programmes of social insurance and income maintenance that now form the backbone of social-security systems in the richer countries would be difficult to replicate in poorer countries. But there is no reason why these particular schemes should be seen to represent a universally relevant model of social-security provision. Public involvement in direct support to the vulnerable sections of the population (going beyond simple reliance on economic growth and market mechanisms) can take a wide variety of forms, and many of them have already been used with considerable success in some of the poorest countries of the world. The collection of papers included in this book explores the scope for immediate expansion of social-security systems in developing countries.

In this book, a broad view is taken of what 'social security' is about. We have not attempted to provide a 'new' definition of the term, nor is there a rigidly uniform characterization of the notion of social security in the different contributions. It may, however, help to clarify what we see as the common concern of the collection of papers included in this book, and how this concern relates to conventional notions of social security.

In attempting to define the scope of our subject, we have to guard against two distinct dangers. One danger is that of excessive specificity. 'Social security' has often been defined in terms of the specific instruments of intervention that have been found important in the historical experiences of particular developed countries, including, *inter alia*, unemployment insurance, old-age pensions, and invalidity benefits. While the general relevance of these means of intervention is a topic of great importance (and there is a substantial literature on this question), this approach to the definition of social security is not altogether useful when developing countries are the centre of our interest. We have to go into the objectives underlying these instruments, rather than concentrating on their specific and contingently chosen forms.

The other danger is that of excessive generality. Instead of seeing social security as being concerned with specific means, for instance, we could simply define social security in terms of the broad objective of removing deprivation, and regard anything that contributes to that objective as being—by definition— part of the social-security system. This alternative approach would not seem satisfactory either. Indeed, human well-being is influenced by many economic and social factors that have little to do with 'social security' in any plausible sense of the term. For instance, it would be absurd to describe a reduction of poverty in a particular country due to a change in world prices or to a discovery of natural resources as the result of social-security measures.

In this book, social security is viewed neither exclusively in terms of means, nor exclusively in terms of objectives. Broadly speaking, our concern is with the direct role that public action can play in reducing human deprivation and eliminating vulnerability in developing countries. The focus is on the use of a class of means (broadly, public action) to pursue a category of objectives (broadly, the reduction of deprivation and vulnerability). It is important to take a fairly comprehensive view of the means that are relevant to the pursuit of social security in this sense, and the different contributions to the book investigate a wide range of possibilities—including employment generation, public provisioning of health care and education, land reform, food subsidies, social insurance, among others. We should also stress that 'public action' does not exclusively refer here to the activities of the State. It also includes the role that other social institutions can play, both in directly providing some important forms of public support and in influencing State action in the direction of greater involvement in social-security measures.

For convenience, the term 'formal social security' is occasionally used in this book to refer to the conventional notion of social security, covering State-administered schemes of social insurance and social assistance (Mesa-Lago discusses the content of this conventional notion in greater detail). The paper by A. B. Atkinson and John Hills explicitly focuses on the experience of 'formal social security' in developed countries, and similarly Carmelo Mesa-Lago's discussion of social-security systems in Latin America deals specifically with the 'formal' components of these systems. The other chapters explore a broader range of avenues of action.

The book is divided into two parts, respectively devoted to 'general issues' and 'case-studies'. We shall not attempt, in this brief introduction, to provide anything like a 'summary' of the chapters included in the book. However, it may be helpful to underline some of the more important themes that emerge from these investigations.

The introductory chapter by Jean Drèze and Amartya Sen addresses some foundational and strategic issues of social security, including the nature and forms of human deprivation, the distinction between 'protective' and 'promotional' objectives, the interconnections between economic growth and public support, the influence of the market mechanism, and the relationship between State action and public action. They also argue, on the basis of economic analysis as well as empirical evidence, that public support has an irreplaceable role to play in removing deprivation and vulnerability, and that this role can be played quite effectively even at an early stage of development.

A similar conclusion is reached, along somewhat different lines, by Robin Burgess and Nicholas Stern. Building on the insights of modern public economics, Burgess and Stern provide a systematic analysis of the content of social security, the motivation for public support, the possible contributions of different agents, and the dilemmas that public action has to face. The authors find strong grounds for extensive public involvement in the field of social security, and attempt to sort out some of the strategic issues that arise in devising practical programmes of action.

A. B. Atkinson and John Hills investigate the relevance of the experiences of developed countries to the strategy of social security in developing countries. They bring out how the social-security systems of developed countries have evolved along quite different routes, in response to country-specific objectives, constraints, and pressures. The authors argue that, given the significantly different circumstances applying in developing countries, the relevance of these experiences does not take the form of providing rigid blueprints for policy. Rather, they see the main 'lessons' as being related to methods of analysis, and their chapter contains a rich discussion of what can be learnt in this respect from past research on social security in developed countries.

Aside from the experience of developed countries, one may also ask whether there are lessons to learn from 'traditional' systems of social security. This is the theme of Jean-Philippe Platteau's contribution to the book, which extensively draws both on anthropological studies and on economic reasoning. As Platteau argues, guaranteed access to productive resources and mutual insurance have been the chief ingredients of social security in traditional societies. But the author also notes some important limitations of these mechanisms, connected *inter alia* with problems of population pressure, incentives, and covariate risks. An effective system of social security must go beyond an exclusive reliance on traditional institutions, without neglecting the contributions they can make.

In the last chapter of the first part of the book, Bina Agarwal investigates some aspects of the relation between public action and family relations in the provision of social security. This takes her into an examination of the survival strategies of vulnerable households (drawing largely on empirical material relating to India), with special attention to issues of intrahousehold inequalities. Among other things, her analysis brings out the close connection between the 'external' and 'internal' vulnerabilities of the members of a household. The greater the 'external' vulnerability of particular household members (specifically women) to deprivation in the event of a breakdown of family relations, the greater their 'internal' vulnerability to inequitable treatment. This insight suggests that public action to support more vulnerable individuals may, in some ways, strengthen rather than weaken the support that these individuals get from the family. This possibility throws important new light on the contrasting—and more common—view that social-security measures have adverse effects on family support.

The second part of the book deals with regional experiences in the provision of social security. It begins with an investigation of China's historical experience, by Ehtisham Ahmad and Athar Hussain. This analysis clearly reveals the main ingredients of post-revolutionary China's outstanding success in substantially protecting the population from deprivation in spite of a relatively low level of aggregate opulence. Guaranteed access to land in the rural areas, guaranteed employment in urban areas, and public provisioning of basic commodities and services appear to have been the pillars of this success. The 'reforms' initiated at the end of the 1970s have posed major new challenges to this foundation of China's social-security system, which Ahmad and Hussain discuss in some detail.

Land reform, employment generation, and public provisioning are also the main instruments of action considered in Siddiq Osmani's study of social security in South Asia. In sharp contrast with China, the experience of this region with each of these three routes to the reduction of insecurity has been, so far, rather unproductive. The author also considers the prospects for guaranteeing minimal living standards to be severely limited by economic constraints and political circumstances. He takes a particularly sceptical view of what is likely to be achieved through land reform, and also regards the provision of greater security through generation of employment to require a radical transformation in the conception and planning of employment schemes. However, there seems to be much greater scope for enhancing living conditions through the public provision of basic needs, and in this field there have, in fact, already been remarkable achievements in some parts of the region (notably Kerala and Sri Lanka).

While China and South Asia already have a rich experience of State involvement in social security and public support, it is fair to say that so far the involvement of African States in this field has been more limited. This relates partly to the relative weakness of administrative and political structures in that region. As Joachim von Braun emphasizes, however, sub-Saharan Africa is rich in community institutions, and the potential contribution of some of these institutions to social-security programmes is by no means negligible. This makes it particularly important to study the interconnections between State-based and community-based social-security systems, and von Braun's contribution brings some interesting empirical material to bear on this question. *Inter alia*, the author highlights the contrasting nature of social-security problems in land-scarce and land-abundant economies within sub-Saharan Africa.

A more detailed study of part of sub-Saharan Africa is contained in Richard Morgan's paper on the nature and impact of social-welfare programmes in the nine 'Southern African Development Co-ordination Conference' (SADCC) countries. The author examines policy responses in these countries in relation to both persistent deprivation and short-run crises (resulting from climatic or economic shocks). A particular focus of study is the effect which war and destabilization—military and economic—have had on living standards within the region.

While 'formal' social-security systems similar to those existing in developed countries have tended, in the greater part of Africa and Asia, to cover only a minor (and rather privileged) proportion of the population, the situation is quite different in the relatively urbanized economies of Latin America and the Caribbean, where such systems are comparatively well developed. In his contribution to the book, Carmelo Mesa-Lago describes and assesses the functioning of formal social-security systems in these countries, and also discusses the prospects for reform. The author emphasizes the limitations of the 'Bismarckian model' based on contributory and occupation-specific social insurance provisions, and shows in particular how this model has often led to huge financial deficits as well as to a regressive pattern of public support strongly biased in favour of the more vocal and influential sections of the population. Achieving greater 'uniformity' and 'universality' of provisions is a major challenge to face if these systems are to play a more effective role in preventing deprivation. While some countries have already made substantial progress in that direction, the prospects for reform appear to be severely constrained in many others. This points once again to the need for innovative departures from the models of social security that have developed in industrialized countries.

The chapters of this book were initially presented as papers at a Workshop on Social Security in Developing Countries, held at the London School of Economics in July 1988 with the joint sponsorship of STICERD and WIDER. We are grateful to both institutions for their support. The encouragement and advice of Lal Jayawardena and Nicholas Stern have been especially useful. The organizational assistance of Kerrie Beale and Jacky Jennings has also been extremely helpful.

The contributions to this book have been extensively revised after the workshop, and the revisions have been greatly helped by the comments and suggestions of the participants and discussants, including Pranab Bardhan, Christopher Bliss, Robert Cassen, Angus Deaton, Meghnad Desai, S. Guhan, Margaret Hardiman, Barbara Harriss, Akiko Hashimoto, Lal Jayawardena, Emmanuel Jimenez, Julian Le Grand, Gus Ranis, Shlomo Reutlinger, Bernt Schubert, Chris Scott, Max Steuer, and Frances Stewart. We are especially indebted to Michael Lipton for very detailed comments on each of the presentations.

October 1989   E.A.
                                                                        J.D.
                                                                        J.H.
                                                                        A.S.

CONTRIBUTORS TO THIS VOLUME

BINA AGARWAL is currently a Bunting Fellow at Radcliffe College, Harvard University, and Professor of Agricultural Economics at the Institute of Economic Growth, Delhi. She has written on technological change in agriculture; the political economy of the fuelwood and environment crisis; poverty; and the position of women in India. Her books include *Mechanisation in Indian Agriculture*, and *Cold Hearths and Barren Slopes: The Woodfuel Crisis in the Third World*. She is currently working on a book on gender and property rights in South Asia.

EHTISHAM AHMAD is Director of the Development Economics Research Programme at the London School of Economics, at time of completion on leave of absence at the World Bank as Senior Economist on the 1990 *World Development Report* Core Team. He has written in the areas of fiscal policy, poverty, and income distribution, and is co-author (with N. Stern) of *The Theory and Practice of Tax Reform in Developing Countries*.

A. B. ATKINSON is Thomas Tooke Professor of Economic Science and Statistics at the London School of Economics. He has written extensively on taxation and social security, including *Lectures on Public Economics* (with J. E. Stiglitz), *Social Justice and Public Policy*, and *Poverty and Social Security*.

ROBIN S. L. BURGESS, is on the research staff of the Development Economics Research Programme at the London School of Economics. During 1989–1990 he was at the World Bank as a consultant to the 1990 *World Development Report*. His main research interest is in development micro-economics, especially the role of public policy in the determination of the standard of living.

JEAN DRÈZE, formerly Lecturer in Development Economics at the London School of Economics, is now an Associate of the LSE. He is co-author of *Hunger and Public Action* (with Amartya Sen), and co-editor of *The Political Economy of Hunger* (also with Amartya Sen). He has also written a number of papers on development issues, with special reference to India.

JOHN HILLS is Senior Research Fellow and Co-Director of the Welfare State Programme at the London School of Economics. His main research interests are housing finance, the Welfare State, and taxation. Publications include *Changing Tax: How the Tax System Works and How to Change It*, and *The State of Welfare: The Welfare State in Britain Since 1974* (editor).

ATHAR HUSSAIN is Director of the Development Economics Research Programme at the London School of Economics and Reader in Economics at the University of Keele. His current research interests include the price and enterprise reforms, consumption patterns, and rural and urban social welfare in China. He is the co-author of *Marx's Capital and Capitalism Today, Marxism and the Agrarian Question*, and *Michel Foucault*, and the co-editor and contributor to *Paths of Capitalist Development in Agriculture, The Chinese Economic Reforms*, and *Transforming China's Economy in the Eighties* (vols. 1 and 2).

CARMELO MESA-LAGO is Distinguished Service Professor of Economics and Latin American Studies at the University of Pittsburgh. His major research interests are economics of social security and health care; economic development; and comparative economic systems. His extensive publications include *Ascent to Bankruptcy: Social Security Financing in Latin America*; *The Crisis of Social Security and Health Care: Latin American Experiences and Lessons*; and *Social Security in Latin America: Pressure Groups, Stratification and Inequality*.

RICHARD MORGAN is Senior Programme Officer with the United Nations Children's Fund (UNICEF) in Namibia. His main research interests are household vulnerability and coping ability in southern Africa, and the responses of governments to drought and population displacement in southern Africa. Publications include *Children on the Front Line* (with R. Green and others), 'Coping with Drought in Botswana: an African Success' (with J. Holm in *Journal of Modern African Studies*, 1985), and 'From Drought Relief to Post-Disaster Recovery, the case of Botswana' (*Disasters*, 1986).

S. R. OSMANI is Research Fellow at the World Institute for Development Economics Research in Helsinki, Finland. His current research interests include: the economics of nutrition; the theory of rural labour markets; and a comparative study of growth and poverty in South Asia. Publications include *Economic Inequality and Group Welfare*, and (as co-author) *Pricing and Subsidy Policies for Bangladesh Agriculture*.

JEAN-PHILIPPE PLATTEAU is Professor of Economics at the Facultés Universitaires of Namur (Belgium). His main research interests are development economics and the history of economic thought and institutions. His books include *Les économistes classiques et le sous-développement*; *Technology, Credit and Indebtedness in Marine Fishing* (co-author); and *Land Reform and Structural Adjustment in Sub-Saharan Africa: Controversies and Guidelines*.

AMARTYA SEN is Lamont University Professor at Harvard University. His books include *Choice of Techniques*; *On Economic Inequality*; *Poverty and Famines*; *Choice, Welfare and Measurement*; and *On Ethics and Economics*.

NICHOLAS STERN is Sir John Hicks Professor of Economics and Chairman of the Suntory Toyota International Centre for Economics and Related Disciplines at the London School of Economics. His main research interests are development economics and public finance. Related publications include *The Theory of Taxation for Developing Countries* (with D. M. G. Newbery), *Palanpur: The Economy of an Indian Village* (with C. J. Bliss) and 'The Economics of Development: A Survey' (*Economic Journal*, September 1989).

JOACHIM VON BRAUN is Director of the Food Consumption and Nutrition Policy Program at the International Food Policy Research Institute, Washington, DC. His current research interest is in famine prevention, public works, technical change and poverty alleviation, with studies located in Ethiopia, The Gambia, Sudan, and Rwanda. Publications include *The Effects of the Egyptian Food Ration and Subsidy System on Income Distribution and Consumption* (with H. Alderman); *An Analysis of Policies for Food Security in Developing Countries: The Case of Egypt* (in German); and *Irrigation Technology and Commercialization of Rice in the Gambia: Effects on Income and Nutrition*.

CONTENTS

PART I

General Issues

1

Public Action for Social Security: Foundations and Strategy*

Jean Drèze
Amartya Sen

1. INTRODUCTION

'As you all know,' said Hecate, the mistress of the witches in *Macbeth*, 'security is the mortals' chiefest enemy.' His exaggerated sense of security certainly did not help Macbeth, but the 'chiefest enemy' that the majority of humanity face is the almost total *absence* of security in their fragile and precarious existence. The lives of billions of people are not merely nasty, brutish, and short, they are also full of uncertain horrors. An epidemic can wipe out a community, a famine can decimate a nation, unemployment can plunge masses into extreme deprivation, and insecurity in general plagues a large part of mankind with savage persistence.

It is this general fragility, on top of chronic and predictable deprivations, that makes the need for social security so strong and palpable. That recognition is part of the background of this chapter, but not the whole of it. The case for public action in this field requires us to go beyond the negative diagnosis of what isn't there, to the positive identification of what can, in fact, be achieved through a programme of social security. The motivation here is to investigate what the problems are, why some special actions are needed, what forms such actions should take, and in general how we should think about devising public action for social security.

It is useful to distinguish at the outset between two different aspects of social security—what we may call respectively 'protection' and 'promotion'. The former is concerned with preventing a decline in living standards in general and in the basic conditions of living in particular. The problem of protection is paramount in the context of famine prevention, and also in dealing with other kinds of sudden economic crises and sharp recessions.

This contrasts with the objective of enhancing the normal living conditions and dealing with regular and often persistent deprivation. This promotional aspect of social security is, in a sense, more ambitious, in wanting to eradicate

* Several sections of this chapter draw substantially on our recent book *Hunger and Public Action* (Drèze and Sen 1989). We are most grateful to John Hills and Nicholas Stern for helpful comments on an earlier draft, and to Asad Ahmad, Peter Lanjouw and Shantanu Mitra for research assistance.

problems that have survived thousands of years. The strategic issues involved in promotional social security may differ very considerably, as we shall see, from those in protective social security.

It may be useful to make three clarificatory remarks to prevent misunderstanding of the distinction and in particular of the terms chosen. First, while both 'promotion' and 'protection' have superficially a somewhat paternalistic ring, the terms refer in fact to the objects of the exercise, rather than to the agency that may bring about those objects. As we shall argue, public action for social security is neither just a matter of State activity, nor an issue of charity, nor even one of kindly redistribution. The activism of the public, the unity and the solidarity of the concerned population, and the participation of all those who are involved are important features of public action for social security. There is no assignment of any paternalistic role to the State—or to any other body—in clarifying the plurality of the objectives involved.

Second, the contrast between protection and promotion arises in different contexts in our analysis. For example, we may be concerned with the distinction in the context of the generation of incomes, and we may then distinguish between the promotion of incomes (changing persistently low incomes) and the protection of incomes (preventing sharp declines). The distinction may apply, similarly, in the context of entitlements, living standards, and so on. There will then be a need to differentiate between entitlement promotion and entitlement protection, between the promotion of living standards and the protection of those standards, and so forth. The protection–promotion distinction has to be integrated with other discriminations that will be used in this chapter.

Third, while the objectives of protection and promotion are distinct, the pursuits of these objectives are not, of course, independent of each other. Nor is the importance of one independent of the achievement of the other. For example, success with the promotional objectives may make protection easier (for example, individual insurance may be less difficult when one's normal level of prosperity is higher). It can also make protection less intensely crucial (for example, a decline from a higher standard of living may cause hardship but not the kind of starvation and extreme deprivation that a fall from a lower—more precarious—level would entail). There are other interdependences between the two aspects of social security and their respective pursuits. It is perhaps as important to note the interdependences as it is to clarify the distinction.

The plan of this chapter is something like this. In Section 2, we discuss the nature of well-being and deprivation and try to characterize the focus variables underlying the analysis of social security. This section deals with the normative foundations of the problem, and asks the question: what is the object of the exercise? In Section 3, we examine whether the desired results can be achieved through normal economic and social processes, without needing to devise systems of social security as such. Why do we specifically need social security? The next section discusses a central problem of protective social security, namely, the prevention of famines through public action. What can be done to make communities safe from famines? In Section 5, the attention is shifted to the prevention of chronic deprivation. How can promotional social-security programmes combat regular and persistent hunger and hardship?

In Section 6, the nature of public action for social security is examined, and the role of the public in public action is analysed. We also discuss the problem of integration of State activities with those of the public in general and of non-governmental institutions in particular. Some concluding remarks are made in Section 7.

2. WELL-BEING, DEPRIVATION, AND SECURITY

The basic idea of social security is to use social means to prevent deprivation, and vulnerability to deprivation. What counts as deprivation is, of course, a matter of valuation, and the values involved can be characterized in different ways.

2.1. *Utility versus Objective Deprivation.*

The utilitarian notion of value, which is invoked explicitly or by implication in much of welfare economics, ultimately sees value only in individual utility, itself defined in terms of some mental condition, such as pleasure, happiness, desire-fulfilment. This subjectivist perspective has been extensively used, but it can be very misleading, since it may fail to reflect a person's real deprivation. A thoroughly deprived person, leading a very tough life, might not appear to be badly off in terms of the mental metric of utility, if the hardship is accepted with non-grumbling resignation. In situations of long-standing deprivation, the victims do not go on sighing all the time, and very often make great efforts to take pleasure in small mercies and to cut down personal desires to modest—'realistic'—proportions. A person's deprivation, then, may not at all show up in the metrics of pleasure, desire-fulfilment, and so on, even though he or she may not have the ability to be adequately nourished, comfortably clothed, minimally educated, and so on.[1]

This issue, aside from its foundational relevance, may have some immediate bearing on practical public policy. Smugness about continued deprivation and vulnerability is often made to look justified on grounds of lack of strong public demand and forcefully expressed desire for removing these impediments. For example, the persistence of massive illiteracy in India, especially among

---

[1] On this subject, see Sen (1985*b*).

women (the proportion of the literate among all Indian women above 5 years of age is still only around 28 per cent according to the last census), is often 'rationalized' in terms of the absence of a clamouring demand (especially among rural women) for elementary education. At a more removed—but still fairly immediate—level, similar arguments are used about the quiet tolerance of endemic undernutrition in many parts of the world, including India. These demand-centred arguments tend to hide the enormity of actual social deprivations.

2.2. *Commodities, Incomes, and Quality of Life*

An alternative approach is to focus on a person's 'real income', or command over essential commodities. This concrete perspective need not be subjectivist in the way utilitarian valuation is, since it is not exclusively dependent on the mental metrics of utility. Indeed, this type of 'non-psychological' accounting has been enormously influential in the recent literature on economic development, largely through the use of the 'basic needs' approach, which concentrates on the requirement to provide some specified minimal amounts of necessary goods (such as food, clothing, shelter) to all.[2]

The approach has, however, the disadvantage that commodities—and therefore income and wealth—are *means* to well-being, rather than *constituent elements* of it. In fact, the conversion of commodities into personal achievements may vary greatly between one person and another, and also between communities. For example, the calorie requirement for being well-nourished varies greatly with metabolic rates, body size, sex, pregnancy, age, parasitic ailments, climatic conditions, and so on, and an interpersonal comparison of deprivation or of poverty cannot be adequately performed just in terms of comparing commodity commands.[3]

Focusing only on incomes for analysing poverty and deprivation—as is frequently done—is problematic on two counts. The value of income lies in its use for commanding commodities, and therefore the variability in the relation between commodities and the quality of life applies also to that between incomes and the quality of life. But on top of that there are additional problems in the conversion of incomes into commodities. There are variations in the power of income to establish command over goods and services, because of market limitations in such forms as imperfect competition, presence of externalities, and the unavailability of certain goods in particular markets (for example, the

---

[2] See Streeten *et al.* (1981).

[3] The variability of the relation between commodities possessed and personal states is discussed in Sen (1980, 1985*b*). The 'basic needs' literature, which has played an enormously important and creative part in development economics, has also increasingly focused its evaluative attention on living conditions (being nourished, being disease-free, etc.) rather than on needs defined in terms of command over essential commodities as such (food, health services, etc.). See Streeten (1984) and Stewart (1985, 1988).

absence of educational services on offer in the rural markets of many developing economies). Therefore the problem of conversion of commodities into living standards is compounded by the problem of conversion of incomes into commodities.[4]

2.3. *Living Standards and Capabilities*

If neither the subjectivist utilitarian view, nor the means-oriented (commodity or income) view, is adequate, we need some other focus variable for analysing quality of life in general, and deprivation and poverty in particular. One approach, which has been explored recently, focuses on the capability to perform certain basic functionings.[5] The foundations of the approach go back, in a particular form, to Aristotle. Aristotle examined the problem of 'political distribution' in terms of his analysis of 'the good of human beings', and this he linked with his investigation of 'the function of man' and his exploration of 'life in the sense of activity'.[6] The Aristotelian theory is, of course, a very specific one, and involves elements (such as objectivity of valuation, a particular reading of human nature, and so on) that may or may not be compelling to all of us. But the argument for seeing the quality of life in terms of valued activities (and the ability to choose these activities) has much broader relevance and application.[7]

If life is seen as a set of 'doings and beings' that are valuable, the exercise of assessing the quality of life takes the form of evaluating these functionings and the capability to function. This valuational exercise need not be performed by simply counting pleasures or desires (as in the utility-based accounting), or by focusing on commodities or incomes instead of doings and beings (as in the commodity-based accounting). The task is that of evaluation of the importance of the various functionings in human life, going beyond what Marx called

[4] See Sen *et al.* (1987), with the 1985 Tanner Lectures at Cambridge by Amartya Sen (1987*b*), and comments by Muellbauer (1987), Kanbur (1987), Hart (1987), Williams (1987), and Hawthorn (1987). See also Schokkaert and van Ootegem (1989).

[5] See Sen (1982, 1985*a, b*).

[6] Aristotle (1980: bk 1, pp. 12–14). Note that Aristotle's term 'eudaimonia', which is often misleadingly translated simply as 'happiness', stands for fulfilment of life in a way that goes well beyond the utilitarian perspective. Though pleasure may well result from fulfilment, that is a consequence rather than the cause of valuing that fulfilment. For an examination of the Aristotelian approach and its relation to recent works on functionings and capabilites, see Nussbaum (1988).

[7] Among the classical political economists, both Adam Smith and Karl Marx explicitly discussed the importance of functionings and the capability to function as determinants of well-being; see Smith (1776: particularly 351–2) and Marx (1844). Marx's approach to the question was closely related to the Aristotelian analysis (and indeed was apparently directly influenced by it, on which see de Sainte Croix 1981, and Nussbaum 1988). One part of the Marxian reformulation of the foundations of political economy is clearly related to the importance of seeing the success of human life in terms of fulfilling the needed human activities. Marx (1844) put it thus: 'It will be seen how in place of the *wealth* and *poverty* of political economy come the *rich human being* and *rich human need*. The rich human being is simultaneously the human being *in need of* a totality of human life-activities—the man in whom his own realization exists as an inner necessity, as *need*.'

'commodity fetishism'.[8] The functionings themselves have to be examined, and the capability of the person to achieve them has to be appropriately valued. The evaluation is a reflective activity, and not a matter of identifying valuation with some mental metric or other, such as pleasure or desire.[9]

2.4. Poverty and Deprivation

The approach of focusing on capabilities and functionings can be used in a variety of evaluative problems.[10] In the case of studying poverty, it is the failure to have the capability to achieve minimal levels of certain basic functionings that would occupy the centre of the stage. The capabilities to be adequately nourished, to be comfortably clothed, to avoid escapable morbidity and preventable mortality, and so on, become the appropriate focus variables. This general approach yields a policy perspective that takes us well beyond an income-centred or a commodity-centred analysis, and also forces us to abandon smugness based on socially conditioned, unreflected acceptance of traditional inequities, deprivations, and vulnerabilities. The practical import of this reflective foundation, built on evaluating human functionings and capabilities, becomes clear as strategic problems in devising social-security programmes are seriously considered.[11]

Seeing poverty as capability failure may, at first sight, appear to be quite a departure from the traditional idea of poverty, which is typically associated with a shortage of income. The poor are taken to be those whose incomes fall below a certain specified level, namely, the so-called 'poverty line', and there is an extensive literature on (1) how the poverty line may be fixed, and (2) how the conditions of the different people below the poverty line may be put together to provide an aggregate measure of poverty.[12] However, the motivation under-

---

[8] Marx (1887: chap. 1, sec. 4, pp. 41–55). See also Marx (1844).

[9] It is sometimes presumed that to depart from a person's own pleasures or desires as the measuring rod is to introduce paternalism into the evaluative exercise. This view overlooks the important fact that having pleasure and desiring are not themselves valuational activities, even though the latter (desire) can often result from valuing something, and the former (pleasure) can often result from getting what one values. A person's utility must not be confused with his or her own valuations, and thus tying the evaluative exercise to the person's own utility is quite different from judging a person's success in terms of the person's own valuation. On these and related issues, see Sen (1985a).

[10] See Sen (1980, 1982, 1985a,b, 1987b); Culyer (1985); A. Williams (1985); Helm (1986); Kakwani (1986); Brannen and Wilson (1987); Hart (1987); Hawthorn (1987); Hossain (1987); Kanbur (1987); Muellbauer (1987); Osmani (1987); B. Williams (1987); Griffin and Knight (1988). See also the related literature on social indicators and general development goals, e.g., Adelman and Morris (1973); Sen (1973); Adelman (1975); Griffin and Khan (1978); Morris (1979); Streeten (1981, 1984); Stewart (1985); Dasgupta (1986); Lall and Stewart (1986).

[11] See, for instance, Drèze and Sen (1989) on the implications of the capability approach for public action aimed at removing nutritional and related deprivations.

[12] Some of the conceptual problems in the identification and aggregation of poverty, with suggested solutions, are discussed in Sen (1976a, 1981a); Atkinson (1983); Foster (1984). Foster in particular provides an extensive critical review of the literature.

lying the concern with deprivation of income is indeed the likely impact of income shortage on the lives that people can lead. The income view of poverty is derivative, related to the effects of income on people's basic capabilities to lead minimally acceptable lives. The ultimate concern of poverty analysis has to be with the deprivation of living conditions, for example, lack of nourishment (rather than of the income to buy nutrients), exposure to preventable diseases (rather than inability to buy medicine), and so on.

The concentration on income in the poverty literature, while ultimately justifiable only derivatively, happens to be quite helpful, up to a point, for the analysis of policy issues, since the shortage of real income (appropriately defined) is one of the most visible and crucial factors restricting the basic capabilities of many people. It is because of the recognition of this important fact that the very idea of poverty has got associated with a shortfall of income rather than with a failure to have the ability to achieve certain basic functionings (such as being adequately nourished, minimally sheltered, and so on). That causal connection is an important one to keep constantly in view, and in particular contexts—such as famine prevention—the creation of income may indeed be the crucial policy instrument to use.

But it is precisely because income shortage and poverty *seem* so inseparably tied that we ought to be careful about those cases in which the ties are qualified by other factors which may also have significant policy relevance. First of all, the deprivation of particular members of a family may have a close but somewhat variable relation with total family income, since the intrahousehold distribution may itself vary. No analysis seriously concerned with poverty can leave the matter of, say, child poverty merely to the size of the family income available to support the children, ignoring altogether how that family income is, in fact, used to support the lives that the members of the family—children and adults—can lead. Similarly, no serious poverty analysis can fail to take note of the important needs of women, related to social as well as biological factors, including of course pregnancy. There are also other parameters of age and ability, of health and disease, and so on that must be considered in determining the relationship between income and the capability to lead adequate lives.

While in devising policy strategies note must obviously be taken of the crucial and far-reaching role of income in providing the means of minimally acceptable living conditions, the subtler aspects of policy choice may well be lost unless we also see the importance of income as being ultimately derivative and contingent. Once an adequately comprehensive view of poverty and deprivation has been taken, it is possible to make good use of the diagnosis of income shortage and of the instrumental importance of income creation without losing sight of the ends in the anxiety about the means.

3. WHY SOCIAL SECURITY?

The basic problems that call for social-security programmes are of two different general types. There is, first of all, the problem of widespread, persistent deprivation, and there is also the issue of fragility of individual security.

3.1. *Persistent Deprivation*

Much of humanity has come to terms with systematic denials of decent living conditions, and experiences failures of elementary capabilities. The overall picture is one of extreme deprivation across the world. The 'under-5 mortality rate', which is 13 per thousand in the USA, 11 in the UK, 9 in Switzerland and Japan, and 7 in Finland and Sweden, is more than 50 in eighty countries in the world, more than 100 in sixty countries, and more than 200 in twenty-three countries (among those for which data have been processed by UNICEF 1988). These are average figures, including the rich and the poor, the urban and the rural, and mortality rates for the rural poor would far exceed even these astonishingly high figures.

   While life expectancy at birth is more than 75 years in many of the countries of Europe and North America, the corresponding figure is below 60 years for most poor countries, below 50 years for a great many of them, and even below 40 years for some.[13] Similarly, the incidence of avoidable mortality is incomparably higher in many of the poorer developing countries than in the richer nations of the world. The failure of actual basic capabilities, compared with what is potentially possible, is remarkably widespread and intense.

3.2. *Vulnerability and Fragile Living Conditions*

In addition to the problem of persistent deprivation, there is also the issue of vulnerability. The average experience of the poorer populations understates the precarious nature of their existence, since a certain proportion of them undergo severe—and often sudden—dispossession, and the threat of such a thing happening is ever-present in the lives of many more. The decline may result from changes in personal circumstances (such as illness or death of earning members of the family), or from fluctations in the social surroundings (such as a crop failure, a general recession, or a civil war).

   There are two different, but interrelated, problems raised by this feature of human existence. There is, first, the problem of how to counter the effects of the decline in the lives of those who experience it. And there is, second, the

---

[13] UNICEF (1988).

problem of how to increase the security in the lives of all, so that people do not live in constant fear of a calamity visiting them. The phenomenon of sudden decline affects the interests not only of those who succumb to it, but also those of others who are made to live diminished lives as a result of the ever-present threat (even though they may, in the event, not succumb to it).

3.3. *Opulence, Public Support, and Capability Expansion*

How can we deal with these problems of (1) persistent deprivation, and (2) fragility of individual security, involving irregular declines and persistent vulnerability? What, in particular, is the role of social security in encountering these challenges?

The latter question can be put in a different—and somewhat negative—way also. Why can't these problems be dealt with through standard channels of economic growth and social progress? It could be argued that the rich economies avoid most of these problems simply because of the average level of their opulence. That surely is the way to go? Or, at least, the need for taking the social-security route has to be established by showing the inadequacy of the more non-interventionist, traditional path.

In fact, the basic premises of this 'negative' view are themselves far from sound. Improvements in living standards in the rich economies have often been the direct result of social intervention rather than of simple economic growth. The expansion of such basic capabilities as the ability to live long and to avoid preventable mortality has typically gone hand in hand with the development of public support in the domains of health, employment, education, and even food in some important cases. The thesis that the rich countries have achieved high levels of basic capabilities simply because they are rich is, to say the least, an oversimplification.

The point can be illustrated by looking at the time pattern of expansion of longevity in Britain and in Japan. Table 1.1 presents the increase in life

Table 1.1. Increase in life expectancy in England and Wales per decade (years)

Decades	Male	Female
1901–11	4.1	4.0
1911–21	6.6	6.5
1921–31	2.3	2.4
1931–40	1.2	1.5
1940–51	6.5	7.0
1951–60	2.4	3.2

Source: Based on data presented in Preston *et al.* (1972: 240–71). See also Winter (1986) and Sen (1987a).

expectancy at birth in England and Wales in each of the first six decades of this century (starting with a life-expectancy figure that was no higher than that of most developing countries today). Note that while the increase in life expectancy has been between one to four years in each decade, there were two decades in which the increase was remarkably greater (around seven years approximately). These were the decades of the two world wars, with dramatic increases in many forms of public support including public employment, food rationing, and health care provisions.[14] The decade of the 1940s, which recorded the highest increase in British life expectancy during the century, was a decade of enormous expansion of public employment, extensive and equitable food rationing, and the birth of the National Health Service (introduced just after the war).

The Japanese figures come in less regular intervals, but a similar picture emerges of accelerating increase in life expectancy during the decade of the Second World War and post-war reconstruction (see Table 1.2). This was, again, a period of rapid expansion of public support.[15] These are suggestive

Table 1.2. Increase in life expectancy in Japan (months)

Period	Male		Female	
	Total	Per year	Total	Per year
1908–40	55.2	1.73	87.6	2.74
1940–51	136.8	12.44	144.0	13.09
1951–64	100.8	7.75	123.6	9.51

Source: Based on data provided in Preston *et al.* (1972: 420–39).

[14] See Winter (1986) for an illuminating analysis of the effects of the First World War on public distribution and public involvement, and their impact on living conditions in Britain. The experience of the Second World War is discussed in great detail by Titmuss (1950: chap. 25), who examined the evidence indicating a strong relationship between the surprisingly good health conditions of the British population during the war (including a rapid improvement of the health status of children) and the extensive reach of public support measures in that period. As Titmuss put it, 'by the end of the Second World War the Government had, through the agency of newly established or existing services, assumed and developed a measure of direct concern for the health and well-being of the population which, by contrast with the role of Government in the nineteen-thirties, was little short of remarkable' (p. 506). According to Titmuss, the most influential part of social policy during the war related to employment provision and food rationing. This conclusion is strongly corroborated by Hammond's detailed study of the 'revolution in the attitude of the British State towards the feeding of its citizens' which took place after 1941 (Hammond 1951). On these issues, see also Marrack (1947); McKeown and Lowe (1966: 131–4); McNeill (1976: 286–7); Szreter (1988).

[15] In Japan, it seems that the years of most rapid expansion of longevity were those immediately following the Second World War. Indeed, according to census estimates, the expectation of life for males leaped from 50 in 1947 to 60 in 1950–2, and that for females from 54 to 63 (unpublished figures from the Ministry of Health and Welfare). We are grateful to Akiko Hashimoto for helpful

facts, even though any detailed analysis of cause–effect relations would have to take into account other associated factors (such as the significantly increased tempo of medical innovation during the wars). No matter how exactly the credit for expansion of longevity during the war and post-war years is divided, it is extremely unlikely that the role of public support and social intervention could be shown to be inconsequential. There is more to the expansion of life expectancy than the simple story of economic growth and increased average opulence.

3.4. *Distribution, Provisioning, and the Quality of Life*

The association between the average prosperity of a nation (given by such indicators as GNP per head) and the basic capabilities enjoyed by its population is substantially weakened by a number of distinct factors: (1) inequalities in the distribution of incomes; (2) variations over time of incomes of any person; and (3) the dissonance between personal incomes and individual capabilities.

The first issue has been much discussed in the development literature. There can be remarkable disparities in the sharing of the fruits of economic growth. Even the presumption that there must be substantial 'trickle down' effects has been contradicted by the actual experience of a number of countries.[16] Enhancing the average income level is, thus, an undependable route to the promotion of living standards. Average income is also a capricious variable for protecting entitlements of the population, since different occupation groups can go to the wall and perish even when average income rises, and indeed several major famines have occurred in overall boom situations. The need for social security thus remains strong even when a country is successful in its attempt to generate economic growth.

The second problem concerns variations of income over time even for a given person. A person's earnings may change not merely with age (with little income when one is very old or very young), but also with business fluctuations, international slumps, crop failures, agricultural seasonality, and so on. The time pattern of earnings may not at all match the time pattern of needs. Indeed, sometimes the needs are maximal precisely when incomes tend to be minimal (for example, when a person is seriously ill). This intertemporal mismatch would not matter greatly if capital markets were 'perfect', allowing adjustment of expenditure to needs even without altering the pattern of earnings. The

discussions on the empirical evidence relating to this observation. On the demographic transition in Japan, and its relation to public support, see Taeuber (1958); Shigematsu and Yanagawa (1985); and Morio and Takahashi (1986).

[16] The problem of unequal sharing of economic expansion was extensively discussed by Griffin and Khan (1977, 1978). There have been in recent years several empirical studies on the sharing issue, and while sharing has been, evidently, more equal in some cases than others, altogether 'trickle down' is clearly an unreliable means of reducing poverty.

problem of unexpected fluctuations could similarly be encountered if insurance markets were versatile and efficient. But capital markets and insurance markets are frequently non-existent or feeble (especially in developing countries). Social security has a special role in these circumstances.[17]

The roots of the third problem have already been discussed in earlier sections of this paper. The conversion of commodity holdings into personal capabilities depends on a number of contingent circumstances (for example, the relation between nourishment and food intake can vary greatly with age, sex, pregnancy, climate, and many other factors). Furthermore, often the vital commodities needed for the protection or promotion of living conditions (such as public-health provisions) cannot easily be individually owned, and the public sector may well be able to deliver them more efficiently than the market. Thus, the relation between individual income and individual capabilities is weakened not merely by the influence of variables other than commodities (as was discussed earlier), but also by the importance of delivery mechanisms (this issue will be further examined in Section 5).

The last point indicates that the unreliability of GNP as a guide to living conditions must not be seen merely as a problem of distributional inequality of the aggregate GNP. The problem of the delivery mechanism and the related questions of converting incomes into capabilities require us to go well beyond the usual concern with income distribution as a supplement to the GNP and other aggregate measures.[18]

These factors put together indicate why economic growth alone cannot be relied upon to deal either with the promotion or with the protection of living standards. The strategy of public action for social security has to take adequate note of the problems that limit what aggregate expansion can do in enhancing living conditions. In the next section we turn to an acute problem of protection of entitlements and living standards, namely, the conquest of famines, and in Section 5 we move on to the more diverse problem of promotion of living standards to combat the persistent deprivation that has been the lot of much of humanity for much of history. Which way should the strategy of public action for social security take us in facing these momentous challenges?

[17] On this general question, see Chap. 2 below.

[18] To illustrate the point, the Indian State of Kerala has one of the lower GNP per head among the different Indian States, but has remarkable achievements in generating a high quality of life (e.g., a life expectancy in the upper 60s—far above that of any other Indian State). If the crude aggregate measures of GNP per head are corrected by taking note of distributional inequalities, Kerala's relative position does not go up very much, and it still remains one of the poorest Indian states in terms of distribution-adjusted real incomes (on this see Sen 1976b, and Bhattacharya et al. 1988). It is in the public delivery of health, food, and education that we have to seek an answer to Kerala's achievements in living standards. On Kerala's experience of public support, see the literature cited in Sec. 5.3 below.

4. FAMINE PREVENTION

Starvation is clearly among the most acute forms of deprivation, and famine prevention must, therefore, be—explicitly or implicitly—one of the most elementary functions of social security systems. At the same time, the social-security perspective itself can, as we shall see, throw fresh light on famine prevention issues. While exploring these interconnections, much of our attention will focus on sub-Saharan Africa. This is natural enough, since famine vulnerability afflicts this part of the world more than any other.

4.1. *Famines and Public Action*

In the short term, preventing famines is essentially an *entitlement protection* exercise. In the long term, much more is involved, including entitlement promotion, aimed at a durable elimination of vulnerability—through greater general prosperity, economic diversification, and so on. But even within a long-term perspective, the task of setting up reliable entitlement protection systems remains a central one. Indeed, in most cases it would be very naïve to expect that efforts at eliminating vulnerability could be so successful as to allow a country to dispense with distinct and specialized entitlement protection mechanisms.[19] While entitlement protection does not subsume all aspects of famine prevention, it is undoubtedly the most vital part of the problem.

Any particular exercise of entitlement protection is intrinsically a short-term one. But it should not be confused with the popular notion of 'famine relief' which conjures up the picture of a battle already half lost and focuses the attention on emergency operations narrowly aimed at containing large-scale mortality. The task of devising planned, coherent, effective, and durable entitlement protection mechanisms is a much broader one. Entitlement crises have many repercussions on the rural economy and on the well-being of affected populations, and a comprehensive strategy for dealing with the scourge of famine must seek to ensure not only that human beings have secure lives but also that they have secure livelihoods.

---

[19] The entitlements that need to be protected in a famine situation naturally relate, to a large extent, to food itself. Indeed, the initiation of famine mortality typically follows enfeeblement caused by hunger as well as other destitution-related phenomena such as population displacements. However, given the prominent role often played by water contamination and epidemic diseases in the propagation of famine mortality, measures also have to be taken to guarantee adequate access to basic health care and safe water supply. Many empirical studies have shown that simple measures for the protection of entitlements to staple food and basic public services can lead to a dramatic reduction of excess mortality in famine situations. For some examples (historical as well as contemporary) see Valaoras (1946); Ramalingaswani *et al.* (1971); Berg (1973); Krishnamachari *et al.* (1974); Binns (1976); Smout (1978); Will (1980); Kiljunen (1984); Otten (1986); Drèze (1988); and de Waal (1989) among others.

This is not just a question of immediate well-being, but also one of development prospects. Consider, for instance, the so-called 'food crisis in Africa'.[20] The current débâcle of agricultural production in much of sub-Saharan Africa has, not without reason, been held partly responsible for this region's continued vulnerability to famine. But it is also legitimate to wonder how farmers who are condemned every so often to use up their productive capital in a desperate struggle for survival can possibly be expected to save, innovate, and prosper. Improved entitlement protection systems in Africa would not only save lives, but also contribute to preserving and rejuvenating the economy of this continent. The alleged dilemma between 'relief' and 'development' is a much exaggerated one, and much greater attention has to be paid to the *positive* links between famine prevention and development prospects.

Seeing famine prevention as an entitlement protection problem draws our attention to the plurality of available strategies for dealing with it. Just as entitlements can be threatened in a number of different ways (which may or may not involve a decline in the overall availability of food), there are also typically a number of feasible routes for restoring them. Importing food and handing it over to the destitute is one of the most obvious options. The overwhelming preoccupation of the journalistic and institutional literature on famine prevention in Africa has been with the logistics of food aid, reflecting the resilient popularity of this approach.[21] But there is a good case for taking a broader view of the possible forms of intervention, and indeed the historical experience of famine prevention in different parts of the world actually reveals an impressive variety of approaches to the protection of food entitlements.

At a general level, a reliable system of famine prevention can be seen to consist essentially of two distinct elements. The first is a mechanism to ensure that an early decision to act is taken by the responsible authorities in the event of a crisis. This part of the system has, inevitably, an important political dimension. The second indispensable element of a famine prevention system is of a more administrative nature, and involves an intelligent and well-planned intervention procedure, ensuring that the political decision to act translates into effective action for the protection of entitlements. In the remainder of this section we shall investigate both aspects of the problem of famine prevention.

[20] For analyses of the main issues involved, see Berry (1984); IDS Bulletin (1985); Rose (1985); Eicher (1986, 1988); FAO (1986); Whitehead (1986); Mahieu and Nour (1987); Mellor *et al.* (1987); Rukuni and Eicher (1987); Platteau (1988); Drèze (1989).

[21] International agencies, it must be said, bear some responsibility for the perpetuation of archaic intervention strategies. For instance, the persistent reluctance of the international donor community to undertake multi-year food aid commitments, or to allow the 'monetization' of food aid, have been an important factor of rigidity in famine prevention policies.

4.2. *Early Warning and Early Response*

Effective entitlement protection calls, *inter alia*, for early and decided action in the event of a crisis. The advantages of early intervention are of course well recognized, even from the narrow point of view of saving human lives. Extraordinary difficulties are encountered with containing mortality once large-scale population displacements have been allowed to begin. The penalties of reluctant or apathetic response to a crisis are dramatically visible in the disastrous human toll of unrelieved famines, such as the Bengal famine of 1943 and the Chinese famines of 1959–61.[22]

The blame for delayed action is often put on inadequately detailed *information* about the existence, or the exact character, of a crisis. There has, in fact, recently been a surge of interest and involvement in so-called 'early warning systems'.[23] However, it would be hard to see a central part played by formal early warning techniques in the recent experiences of successful famine prevention, whether in India, Botswana, Zimbabwe, or Cape Verde.[24]

Indeed, most often the warnings of imminent dangers have tended to come from general reports of floods or droughts or economic dislocations, and from newspaper coverage of early hardship and visible hunger. In countries with relatively pluralistic political systems (such as India and Botswana), open channels of protest have also helped to direct forcefully the attention of the authorities to the need for preventive action without delay. Varieties of administrative, journalistic, and political communications have served the 'early warning' role in the absence of elaborate systems of famine prediction or of formal procedures of early warning.

Of course, informal ways of anticipating famine threats can sometimes mislead. But so can formal systems of early warning, which are often based on some rather simple model (explicitly invoked or implicitly presumed), paying attention to a few variables and ignoring many others. There is undoubtedly scope for improving famine-warning systems based on economic analysis.[25] But there is little chance that a formal model can be developed that would be practically usable (with all the necessary data inputs being obtainable at the required speed) and that would take adequate note of all the variables that may well be relevant in the wide variety of cases that can possibly

---

[22] On the inadequate nature of government response in these events, and the political factors involved, see Sen (1981a, 1983); Peng (1987); Brennan (1988).

[23] One study finds the current situation of duplication and heterogeneity of independent efforts to be quite 'surrealistic' (CILSS 1986: 67). That study, which is not meant to be exhaustive, identifies no fewer than 39 different early-warning systems in the Sahel alone, of which 14 are engaged in primary data collection and 25 'recycle' information collected by 'more or less competing agencies' (p. 69).

[24] On this see Drèze and Sen (1989: chap. 8).

[25] On different lines of possible improvement, see e.g. Cutler (1985b); Desai (1986); Borton and York (1987); Autier (1988); Walker (1988); Autier et al. (1989); Swift (forthcoming).

arise. The supplementation of formal economic models by more informal systems of communication and analysis is, to a great extent, inescapable.

It would, moreover, be a mistake to see the problem of early warning only in terms of the gathering and analysis of information. The informational exercise has to be seen in the broader context of the need to trigger early and resolute action on the part of the concerned authorities. Indeed, most cases of unmet famine threats reflect not so much a lack of knowledge that could have been remedied with more reliable systems of prediction, but negligence or smugness or callousness on the part of the non-responding authorities.[26] In this context it is important to note that such informal systems of warning as newspaper reports and public protests carry not only information that the authorities *can* use, but also elements of pressure that may make it politically compelling to respond to these danger signals and do something about them urgently. It is no accident that the countries that have been most successful in famine prevention in the recent past have typically had relatively pluralistic politics with open channels of communication and criticism.

Official tolerance of political pluralism and public pressure in many African countries is, at the moment, quite limited. The opposition is often muzzled. Newspapers are rarely independent or free. The armed forces frequently suppress popular protest. Further, to claim that there are clear signs of change in the direction of participatory politics and open journalism in Africa as a whole would be undoubtedly premature. However, there is now perhaps a greater awareness of the problem and of the need for change. The long-term value of creative dissatisfaction should not be underestimated.[27]

4.3. *Cash Support and Employment Provision*

As was discussed earlier, an effective system of famine prevention requires not only a mechanism to ensure early response in the event of a crisis, but also a sound procedure of entitlement protection. One factor which has frequently accounted for belated and somewhat unsuccessful famine prevention efforts is the dependence of entitlement protection measures on the timely arrival of food aid, and generally on the complicated logistics associated with the direct delivery of food to potential famine victims. The greater use of 'cash support' to protect the entitlements of vulnerable groups is an important option to consider in remedying this problem.

Cash support is not a new idea. It has, in fact, a rich history covering many

---

[26] This applies, *inter alia*, to the famines in Bengal in 1943 and in China in 1959–61, mentioned earlier. In the case of the African famines of 1983–5, too, it has been observed that 'early warnings were given in almost all instances' (World Food Programme 1986: 4).

[27] On the role of the press and adversarial politics in the context of African famines, and the emerging signs of change in some countries, see Yao and Kone (1986); Mitter (1988); Reddy (1988); Drèze (1989).

parts of the world.[28] But the suggestion that it has a contribution to make to famine prevention strategies in Africa today is often met with resilient suspicion. This suspicion cannot reasonably arise from the belief that the conversion of cash into food might prove impossible in a famine situation. Indeed, a plethora of recent sudies have shown that the acquisition of cash (for subsequent conversion into food through the market) is now one of the most important survival strategies of vulnerable populations in famine-prone countries.[29] But there is a deeper problem. If it is clear enough that cash can almost always help an *individual* to acquire food and avoid starvation, it is less obvious that cash support can improve *collective* security. After all, one person's ability to command food through cash support may adversely affect other people's entitlements—for example, by exerting an upward pressure on prices. The merits of cash support do, therefore, require careful scrutiny.

Assessing the likely impact of entitlement protection measures backed by cash rather than by food involves a careful consideration of market responses.[30] Indeed, an immediate effect of cash-based entitlement protection is to exert an upward pressure on food prices (since the effective demand for food increases), and this in turn can have complicated repercussions on the allocation of food in the economy. Needless to say, this increase of prices has altogether different implications from the sort of inflationary pressure that might result from, say, speculative hoarding or a boom in the urban economy. In this instance, the increase of prices has its origin in the greater purchasing power of the needy and is part of the process of improving (rather than undermining) their command over food. In order to assess the precise impact of a cash-based entitlement protection strategy on the allocation of food in the economy, one must examine carefully the effects it is likely to have, via the price mechanism, on (1) the net *aggregate* amount of food consumed in the region under consideration, and (2) the *distribution* of consumption between different sections of the population.

Price increases are likely to lead to an improvement in the availability of food in the affected region through changes in production, trade, and storage. The potential for reducing the forces of famine by inducing interregional food movements towards severely affected regions through the channel of private trade is particularly important to consider.

[28] Cash relief has a long history both in India (Loveday 1914; Drèze 1988) and in China (Mallory 1926; Will 1980; Li 1987), and has also been an important feature of famine prevention in a number of African countries more recently, including Botswana (Hay *et al.* 1986), Cape Verde (van Binsbergen 1986), Tanzania (Mwaluko 1962), and Ethiopia (Kumar 1985; Padmini 1985).

[29] See Drèze and Sen (1989: chap. 5), and the literature cited there.

[30] Our concern here is with the wisdom of cash-based entitlement protection measures that are carried out *without* a corresponding amount of food being released on the market by the relief system. This 'cash injection' issue has to be distinguished from what one might call the 'cash medium' issue, which is concerned with comparing the merits of giving food directly with those of giving cash *with* a corresponding amount of food being released on the market. See Drèze and Sen (1989: chap. 6), for further discussion of this distinction, and of the cash medium issue itself.

In the common international perception, connected largely with the nature of media reports, African famines are often seen in terms of acute and more or less uniform 'shortages' of food everywhere in the affected country or countries. This is, however, largely a myth, and in fact the scope for interregional food movements to alleviate the intensity of distress is often considerable. Large variations in food output between different regions are common in Africa, and frequently a marketable surplus does remain in or near the famine-affected territory. There is also considerable evidence that private trade in Africa is alive to economic opportunities when it is allowed to operate without bureaucratic restrictions. Of course, sharp contrasts exist between different countries in these respects, and it may well be that in some places a major reliance on the operation of private food trade to respond to the demands generated by cash support would be problematic. There are, however, no serious grounds for general pessimism in this respect.[31]

Despite the possibly important effects of cash support on the total supply of food in the affected region, it is very likely that the increase in food availability will fall short of the increase in the consumption of those receiving cash support. Indeed, the same price rise which has an expanding effect on supply will also have a contracting effect on the demand for food of those who do not receive cash support but now face higher prices. To that extent, a *redistribution* of consumption towards the protected groups will take place.

The prospect of dealing with the threat of famine partly by inducing a redistribution process operating within affected areas strikes terror in the heart of many observers. They see this as a failure to respond to the 'real problem' of 'shortage', and as an attempt 'to transfer food from one victim to another'. It must be remembered, however, that large inequalities are a pervasive feature of most famine-prone societies. There is, moreover, considerable evidence that the consumption patterns of even relatively privileged households are quite responsive to price changes in situations of economic adversity.[32] The scope for redistribution from these groups to the most vulnerable may therefore be far from negligible. When direct delivery of food through the public relief system is hampered or slowed down by administrative and logistic difficulties, redistribution through selective cash support may be a crucial option.

The success of the redistributive strategy, however, depends to a great extent on the ability of the relief system to provide preferential support to the entire vulnerable population. If substantial numbers of vulnerable people are excluded from entitlement protection measures but have to take the consequences of price increases, the overall vulnerability of the population could conceivably be exacerbated rather than diminished by the relief system.[33] An

---

[31] For further discussion of this issue, and of the evidence, see Drèze and Sen (1989: chap. 6).

[32] The evidence is discussed in Drèze and Sen (1989: chap. 5).

[33] It should, however, be mentioned that some of the excluded groups could gain from *derived benefits* obtained from the income support provided to other groups. For instance, a reduction of

important question therefore concerns the need to cover all the major vulnerable groups, while continuing to exclude the more privileged in order to preserve the redistributive bias on which the success of the strategy of cash support depends.

In this respect, much can be said in favour of a strategy of open-ended employment provision. The element of 'self-selection' involved in this strategy makes it possible to carry out comparatively large transfers to vulnerable households, while at the same time imparting a strong redistributive bias to the entitlement protection process.

In fact, often the only effective and politically acceptable method of providing large-scale cash support is precisely that of employment provision with cash wages. The case for this strategy receives added strength from a number of other advantageous features of employment-based entitlement protection. These include: (1) being compatible with intervention at an early stage of a subsistence crisis (when affected people are looking hard for alternative sources of income but do not yet suffer from severe nutritional deprivation); (2) obviating the necessity of movements of entire families to feeding camps; (3) at the same time, obviating the necessity of taking food to every village (as in a system of decentralized distribution), to the extent that the work-seeking adult population is mobile; (4) inducing positive market responses in the form of an upward pressure on local wages; (5) providing women (who are, very often, a majority of the work-force on public-works programmes) with an independent source of income and thereby increasing their bargaining power within the household.[34]

Cash support and employment provision have strong and mutually reinforcing advantages, which have been well illustrated in a number of recent experiences of famine prevention, both in Africa and in South Asia.[35] These advantages deserve greater recognition, even though it is also important not to fall into the trap of assuming the existence of a universally attractive model of public intervention in famine situations.

---

distress livestock sales on the part of those who receive support could substantially benefit vulnerable livestock owners outside the relief system by arresting an impending collapse of livestock prices. The increased purchasing power of those who do receive support can also have helpful 'multiplier effects', e.g., through their purchases of labour services from other vulnerable groups.

[34] For further discussion of these and other advantages of employment provision as a strategy of entitlement protection, see Drèze and Sen (1989: chaps. 6, 7).

[35] See Drèze (1988, 1989); and Drèze and Sen (1989: chap. 8), for case-studies of famine prevention in India, Botswana, and Cape Verde. Of course, the provision of employment has to be supplemented by measures of unconditional relief for those who are not able to work and cannot rely on the support of able-bodied dependants. Such measures have been part of the entitlement protection systems of each of these three countries. Also, highlighting the contribution that cash support and employment provision can make to the protection of entitlements should not be seen as dismissing the role of food supply management. The latter can be important too, but it need not be *tied* to income generation measures, as in systems of direct feeding or 'food-for-work'.

5. CONFRONTING DEPRIVATION

We noted earlier (in Section 3) the possible dissonance between the average opulence of a country and the basic capabilities of its population. Despite this possible dissonance, there are good grounds for expecting a positive *general* association between the two. This is partly because the increased private incomes associated with greater general affluence do indeed offer the opportunity to obtain command over a number of commodities which are crucially important to basic capabilities, such as nutritious food, sound shelter, and adequate fuel. But, in addition, greater opulence provides resources for extending public support in areas such as health, education, employment, food distribution, and social insurance. While some of the best things in life may not be purchasable in the market, and while the command over them may depend to a great extent on public provisions made by the State, it is also true that what the State can provide may, in turn, be much facilitated by greater general opulence.

5.1. *Alternative Strategies: Growth-Mediated Security and Support-Led Security*

Given the distinct, though interconnected, roles played by overall opulence and public support in enhancing capabilities, it is possible in principle to distinguish two contrasting approaches to the removal of precarious living conditions. One approach is to promote economic growth and take the best possible advantage of the potentialities released by greater general affluence, including not only an expansion of private incomes but also an improved basis for public support. This may be called the strategy of 'growth-mediated security'. Another alternative is to resort *directly* to wide-ranging public support in domains such as employment provision, income redistribution, health care, education, and social assistance in order to remove destitution without waiting for a transformation in the level of general affluence. Here success may have to be based on a discriminating use of national resources, the efficiency of public services, and a redistributive bias in their delivery. This may be called the strategy of 'support-led security'.

The possibility of success through either approach is credible enough in principle. But there have been, in fact, serious detractors questioning the viability of each of these avenues of action. The merits of the respective strategies have to be assessed against the actual experiences of different countries in the world. Intercountry comparisons of performance may, of course, be quite misleading, but they do provide a preliminary and suggestive bias for noting certain elementary relationships and possibilities.

We shall examine briefly the comparative performance of different countries in terms of one particular indicator, namely the observed percentage reduction in combined infant and child mortality (hereafter 'under-5 mortality') between 1960 and 1985.[36] The ten best performers among the developing countries according to this criterion are the following: Hong Kong, United Arab Emirates, Chile, Kuwait, Costa Rica, Cuba, China, Singapore, Jamaica, and South Korea.[37] The actual figures are presented in Table 1.3.

Table 1.3. Proportionate reduction in under-5 mortality rates: the top ten countries (1960–1985)

Country	% reduction in U5MR (1960–85)	% growth rate of GNP/capita (1965–85)	GNP per head in US$ (1985)	Level of U5MR (1985)
Hong Kong	83	6.1	6 230	11
Chile	82	−0.2	1 430	26
United Arab Emirates	82	n.a.	19 270	43
Costa Rica	81	1.4	1 300	23
Kuwait	80	−0.3	14 480	25
Cuba	78	n.a.	n.a.	19
Singapore	76	7.6	7 420	12
China	75	4.8	310	50
Jamaica	72	−0.7	940	25
South Korea	71	6.6	2 150	35

Note: Excluded from the comparison are the countries of Eastern and Western Europe, Japan, New Zealand, Australia, USA, USSR, and Canada.

Sources: UNICEF (1987: Table 1); World Bank (1987: Table 1).

On the basis of the information contained in Table 1.3, and of what is known about the experiences of the countries involved, it is possible to divide these ten countries into two distinct groups. Growth-mediated security has clearly been an important part of the experiences of Hong Kong, Singapore, South Korea, Kuwait, and the United Arab Emirates. These countries have experienced outstandingly high rates of economic growth between 1960 and 1985, and their remarkable success in reducing under-5 mortality has been much helped by their rising opulence.[38] Thus, a half of the ten highest performers in terms of

[36] The information on under-5 mortality rate (U5MR) for 130 countries, on which this exercise. is based, appears in table 1 of UNICEF (1987). The nature of the U5MR index is explained in UNICEF (1987: 126). This index must not, of course, be interpreted as an overall indicator of the quality of life, but it clearly relates to a very important aspect of it.

[37] North Korea was excluded from the initial list because we learned from the statistical agencies involved that the figures for North Korea were not independently obtained but simply assumed to be the same as those for South Korea.

[38] The first three of these countries have been among the five fastest-growing countries during the period under consideration (World Bank 1987: table 1). The last two (Kuwait and the United

percentage reduction of under-5 mortality seem to have resorted to a strategy of growth-mediated security, of one sort or another.

On the other hand, the other five countries (namely, Chile, Costa Rica, Cuba, China, and Jamaica) have had quite different experiences. Their growth rates have been comparatively low. Moreover, as we shall see shortly, these countries stand out sharply in having achieved far lower mortality rates than most other countries at a comparable income level. The basis of their success does not seem to rest primarily in rapid income growth, and suggests the possibility of support-led security.[39]

There is, in fact, considerable evidence that direct public support has indeed been the driving force behind the success of each of these five countries.[40] We shall return to this question in Section 5.3.

5.2. Economic Growth and Public Support: Interconnections and Contrasts

The distinction made in the preceding section between growth-mediated security and support-led security reflects an important strategic aspect of public action, but it can also be easily misunderstood. A few remarks may help in clarifying the precise nature of the contrast.

First, the distinction involved is definitely not a question of activism versus disengagement on the part of the State. The governments of the countries which have pursued a strategy of growth-mediated security have, in fact, often been extremely active both in bringing about economic growth and in disseminating its fruits. The constructive role of the State in these countries has in varying extents included: (1) promoting economic growth through skilful planning; (2) facilitating wide participation of the population in the process of economic expansion, particularly through the promotion of skills and education and the maintenance of full employment; and (3) utilizing a substantial part of the resources generated by rapid growth for extensive public provisioning of basic necessities. This applies even to countries such as South Korea or Singapore, which are often presented as examples of the fecundity of 'laissez-faire', but whose experiences are in fact rich illustrations of the diverse roles that State activism can play within a strategy of growth-mediated security.[41]

Arab Emirates) have not experienced high growth rates of GNP over that period in terms of conventional measures, but this is mainly because the phenomenal increase in their incomes that has in fact taken place as a result of changes in relative prices (in this case involving oil) is not well captured in the growth rate of the real *quantity index* of GNP per capita (see World Bank 1984b).

[39] The Chinese growth rate appearing in Table 1.3 is quite impressive, and might be seen as suggesting that the basis of China's success may well lie as much in economic growth as in direct public support. It can be shown, however, that (1) China's growth rate during the period of interest has been much exaggerated, and (2) economic growth has *followed* rather than preceded the wide-ranging measures of public support which must be seen as the main source of China's success. On this question, see Drèze and Sen (1989: chap. 11).

[40] See the case-studies in Drèze and Sen (1989: chaps. 11, 12), and the literature cited there.

[41] See the case-studies in Drèze and Sen (1989: chap. 10).

Second, the contrast we have pursued is also not a simple one of market versus State provisioning. The masses can gain a share in general opulence not only through the increase of private incomes, but also through wide-ranging public provisioning. A striking example is provided by Kuwait, where rapid growth has created the material basis for what is clearly one of the most munificent 'Welfare States' in the world,[42] The general notion that one of the important fruits of economic growth can be to facilitate public support is also visible from other successful experiences of growth-mediated security. These experiences contrast sharply with those of countries such as Brazil where there has been little effort to combine rapid growth with social provisioning, and where, as a result, living conditions remain shockingly poor for a large part of the population.[43]

Third, the distinction made in the last section has little to do with the dilemma that has sometimes been construed between the pursuit of 'growth' and the fulfilment of 'basic needs'. A strategy of 'growth-mediated' security is not at all the same thing as the pursuit of economic growth *tout court*, or what might be called 'unaimed opulence'. The former need not conflict with the satisfaction of basic needs—indeed it is an approach to their satisfaction. Conversely, support-led security does not imply surrendering the goal of economic growth. In fact, sometimes improvements in the quality of human life (for example, through better health and education) also enhance the productivity of the labour-force. And economic growth can be crucial to the sustainability of a strategy based on generous public support. The interconnections and contrasts between the two strategies are more extensive and more complex than would be captured in a simple dichotomy between growth and basic needs.

The real source of the contrast lies in the fact that the countries that have made substantial use of the strategy of support-led security have not *waited* to grow rich before resorting to large-scale public support to guarantee certain basic capabilities. The contrast is a real one, but it should not obscure the complementarities that exist between economic growth and public support— and in particular, the prominent role played by public support in the strategies of growth-mediated as well as support-led security.

Despite these complementarities, dilemmas can arise in seeking a balance between the two strategies. Both growth-oriented measures and support-oriented measures make substantial claims on public resources as well as on public administrative capabilities. There are choices to be made in public policy-making, and nothing is gained in obscuring the conflicts involved.

---

[42] On the extensive nature of public provisioning in Kuwait, see Ismael (1982), who describes this country as 'a total service society with almost every human need from the cradle to the grave serviced by institutional arrangement' (p. 105). It should be mentioned, however, that the welfare state in Kuwait discriminates sharply between Kuwaiti citizens and non-Kuwaiti residents.

[43] On this experience of 'unaimed opulence' in Brazil, see Sachs (1986).

5.3. *The Strategy of Support-Led Security*

In Section 5.1 we noted how a number of countries (including China, Costa Rica, Jamaica, Chile, and Cuba) have achieved outstanding success in reducing under-5 mortality rates in spite of unremarkable rates of growth of GNP per head. We have also suggested that these experiences can be seen as illustrative of a strategy of 'support-led security', which consists of embarking on ambitious programmes of public support at an early stage of development.

The causal links between public efforts and social achievements in these as well as other countries have received a good deal of attention in the recent development literature.[44] The investigations have taken different forms. One group of studies has been concerned with examining similarities in the nature of public support efforts in *different countries* (each with good records in mortality reduction and other achievements), and the commonalities involved in their respective efforts have been assessed, especially in contrast with the experience of other countries.[45] A second group of studies has been concerned with *interregional* comparisons within single countries, comparing the achievements of regions which have greater or lesser involvement in public support.[46] A third set of studies has presented *intertemporal* comparisons within single countries of public efforts and social achievements.[47] A fourth set of studies has examined the direct impact of public support measures, such as health and nutrition programmes, at the *micro* level.[48] The causal links between public support provisions and social achievements have been clearly brought out in different ways in these diverse empirical investigations.

Public support can take various forms, such as public health services, educational facilities, food subsidies, employment programmes, land redistribution, income supplementation, and social assistance, and the respective country experiences have involved various combinations of these measures. While there are significant contrasts in the relative importance of these different forms of public support in the different country experiences, the

---

[44] In addition to the 5 countries mentioned above, two further experiences of successful support-led security deserve special mention here: those of Sri Lanka, and of the State of Kerala in India. In the case of Sri Lanka, the main expansion took place *prior* to 1960, and this country is thus not included in the list of top performers for 1960–85 in Sec. 5.1. Kerala, on the other hand, did not appear in this list because it is not a country but only a State in a federal country (India). On these two experiences of support-led security, see Isenman (1980); Halstead *et al.* (1985); Basu (1986); Caldwell (1986); Anand and Kanbur (1987); Kumar (1987); Sen (1987a); Drèze and Sen (1989), among others. See also Chap. 7 below.

[45] See e.g. Sen (1981b); Flegg (1982); Halstead *et al.* (1985); Stewart (1985); Caldwell (1986).

[46] See e.g. Castaneda (1984, 1985), Jain (1985), Nag (1985), Prescott and Jamison (1985), Morrison and Waxler (1986), Kumar (1987), Mata and Rosero (1987).

[47] See e.g. Castaneda (1984, 1985) on Chile, Anand and Kanbur (1987) on Sri Lanka, and Mata and Rosero (1987) on Costa Rica.

[48] See e.g. Gwatkin *et al.* (1980); Harbert and Scandizzo (1982); Garcia and Pinstrup-Andersen (1987); Berg (1987); Mata and Rosero (1987).

basic commonality of instruments is quite striking (especially in view of the great diversity of the political and economic regimes).[49] Underlying all this is something of a shared approach, involving a public commitment to provide direct support to raise the quality of life, especially of the deprived sections of the respective populations.

The empirical investigations cited earlier also throw some useful light on the resource requirements (and affordability) of the kind of public support measures that have been found crucial to the strategy of support-led security. Scepticism regarding the feasibility of large-scale public provisioning in a poor country often arises precisely from the belief that these measures are inordinately 'expensive'. Several experiences of support-led security (particularly those that have succeeded in spite of a low GNP per capita, as in China, Sri Lanka, and Kerala) suggest that this diagnosis is, at least to some extent, misleading.

Indeed, the costs of social-security programmes in these countries have been in general astonishingly small. This applies, in particular, to public provisioning of health care and education. It has been estimated, for instance, that in China the percentage of GDP allocated to public expenditures on health has been only around 2 per cent. Moreover, only about 5 per cent of total health expenditure has tended to go to preventive health care, which has been one of the major influences behind the fast retreat of infectious and parasitic diseases.[50] There are similarly striking figures for other experiences of support-led success.[51]

The relatively inexpensive nature of public provisions in the domains of health and education in developing countries is partly a reflection of the low level of wages. Aside from this, several considerations would tend to reduce the real burden of public support in these countries. First, financial costs are not always a good reflection of social costs, and in particular a good case can often be made for regarding the social costs of labour in labour-surplus economies as being lower than the market wage.[52] Second, the opportunities for raising revenue are not independent of the existence of a social-security system. For instance, the scope for resorting to exacting indirect taxation may be much

---

[49] See the case studies presented in Drèze and Sen (1989: chaps. 11, 12).

[50] Bumgarner (1989). On this general question, see also World Bank (1984a) and Jamison (1985).

[51] The percentage of GDP allocated to public expenditures on health in Sri Lanka in 1981 was barely 1% (Perera 1985: table 8). The corresponding figure for Cuba was around 2.7% (Muniz et al. 1984: tables 6.1 and 6.6). In Kerala, per capita government expenditure on health is not much greater than in the rest of India (Nag 1985: table 16). For further evidence and discussion of the scope of low-cost public provisions in the domain of health, with special reference to China, Costa Rica, Kerala and Sri Lanka, see various contributions in Halstead et al. (1985), and also Caldwell (1986).

[52] On the distinction between financial costs and social costs, see Drèze and Stern (1987), and the literature reviewed there.

larger when vulnerable groups are protected from possibly severe deprivation. Third, there is an element of investment in public provisioning (for example, through the relation between health, nutrition, education, and productivity). This reduces the diversion from investment opportunities that is apparently involved in a programme of public support.

Resource constraints should not be overlooked, but it would be a mistake to regard these constraints as the most important obstacle to be overcome in attempts to provide social security through direct public support in developing countries. The distinction of China, Kerala, Sri Lanka, or other countries with a distinguished record of support-led security does not lie in the size of financial allocations to particular public provisions. Their real success seems to be based on creating the political, social, and economic conditions under which ambitious programmes of public support are undertaken with determination and effectiveness, and can be oriented towards the deprived sections of the population.

It is not enormously surprising that efforts to provide extensive public support are rewarded by sustained results, and that public sowing facilitates social reaping.[53] Perhaps what is more remarkable is the fact that the connections studied here are so frequently overlooked in drawing up blueprints for economic development. The temptation to see the improvement of the quality of life simply as a consequence of the increase in GNP per head is evidently quite strong, and the influence of that point of view has been quite pervasive in policy-making and policy-advising in recent years. It is in the specific context of that simple growth-centred view that the empirical connections between public support measures and the quality of life deserve particular emphasis.

6. THE NATURE OF PUBLIC ACTION

Before closing this chapter we must address some general issues regarding the strategy of public action for social security. These issues are implicit in many of the discussions that we have already presented, but there is a case for addressing them separately and explicitly.

Public action must not be confused with State action only. Public action includes not merely what is done *for* the public by the State, but also what is done *by* the public for itself. We have to recognize *inter alia* the role of non-governmental organizations in providing social security (particularly in times

---

[53] Hunger and deprivation are, to a large extent, social conditions that cannot be seen only in isolated individual terms. There are strong interdependences and so-called 'externalities' involved in health (e.g. through the spread of diseases), education (e.g. through influencing each other), and nutrition (e.g. through food habits being dependent on social customs). The importance of social intervention in ensuring adequate entitlements to 'public goods', and in dealing with externalities generally, has been well recognized for a long time in economics (see Samuelson 1955; and Arrow 1963).

of distress), and the part that social, political, and humanitarian institutions can play in protecting and promoting living conditions.

Among the actions that can be undertaken by the public, the political role of pressuring the government to act is a particularly important one. As was discussed earlier, there is considerable evidence, for instance, that early action in preventing famines has often been precipitated by newspaper reports of early cases of starvation and by pressure from political and social organizations demanding action.[54] Public involvement and activism may have the role both of drawing the attention of the government to problems that may otherwise be neglected and of forcing the hands of the government by making it politically impossible—at least unwise—for it to ignore impending threats.

While this informational and adversarial role of action by the public operates through the government, there are other non-governmental, public activities that directly contribute to the support of entitlements and living conditions of the vulnerable population. The problem of integration of governmental and non-governmental activities is an important one in a programme of public action for social security.[55]

There is also an important problem of integrating State actions in supporting living conditions with what emerges from the market mechanism. While it is true that the need for State action partly arises from the failure of the market to provide adequate protection and promotion of living conditions, it does not follow that State action for social security must dispense altogether with reliance on the market. In so far as the market mechanism contributes to economic expansion, provides effective means of matching supplies to demands, and yields widespread entitlement generation (particularly through employment creation), it can be a very significant ally in providing social security through public action.

A purist strategy—relying only on the market or only on State action—can be awfully short of logistic means. The need to consider the plurality of levers and a heterogeneous set of mechanisms is hard to escape in the pursuit of social security. In the context of discussing famine prevention, we had the occasion to discuss both the possible failure of the market mechanism to provide adequate guarantee of entitlements and the possibly helpful role of markets in meeting demands generated by public relief programmes (Section 4). Similarly, in discussing the elimination of systematic and persistent deprivations and the promotion of living standards in general, we had the opportunity to discuss the part that economic growth—even when promoted by market-related processes —can play provided that the fruits of growth are sensibly used for the purpose of social security (Section 5).

---

[54] See Sec. 4.2. See also Sen (1983); Ram (1986); Drèze (1988); Drèze and Sen (1989); Reddy (1988).

[55] For further discussion of this issue, with special reference to sub-Saharan Africa, see Chap. 9 below.

In this context we have to guard against two rather disparate and contrary dangers. One is to ignore the part that the market mechanism can play in generating growth and efficiency (despite its various limitations as an allocative device), with the State trying to do it all itself through administrative devices. The other is to be over-impressed by what the market mechanism can do and to place our reliance entirely on it, neglecting those things that the government can effectively undertake (including various policies for the promotion of health and education).

The Chinese success during the pre-reform period (that is, prior to 1979) in enhancing the quality of life, despite its low GNP per head, illustrates the important role that the State can play in the direct promotion of social security. But it also shows how easily inefficiencies can be bred and how the engine of economic growth can be rigidly constrained by an over-reliance on administration and a severe neglect of the market. The remarkably fast economic expansion (particularly in agriculture) since the reforms, including the reinstatement of many markets and market-type institutions, brings out the part that the market can creatively play. And yet, there is evidence that there has been some set-back in the sharp decline of mortality rates and related features of the quality of life since the reforms of 1979, and that this may be connected with some withdrawal from public provisioning (especially communal health delivery in the rural areas).[56] In emphasizing the problem of integration, our aim is to warn against both types of problems (namely, over-reliance on as well as neglect of markets).[57]

7. PUBLIC ACTION FOR SOCIAL SECURITY

This chapter has been concerned with foundational as well as strategic issues involved in public action for social security. We began by distinguishing between two different but interrelated challenges, namely, the *protection* of living standards from serious declines (for example, by preventing famines), and the *promotion* of these standards to permanently higher levels (for example, by eliminating endemic hunger, chronic hardship, and rampant morbidity). Social security is concerned with both these challenges (Section 1).

---

[56] See Sen (1987a, 1988); Hussain and Stern (1988); and Drèze and Sen (1989: chap. 11). Some of the reported increases in mortality rates have other explanations (e.g., changes in reporting bias, changing age composition of the population) but some part of the increased mortality rates does seem to be both (1) real, and (2) related to declining arrangements of public provisioning.

[57] The Chinese experience is, in fact, a storehouse of important lessons for social-security planning. In drawing attention to the problems faced, we must not, of course, ignore the basic fact that public action in China has achieved remarkable results in improving various aspects of the Chinese quality of life to levels that are totally unusual in countries with comparably low per-capita income. On this see particularly Riskin (1987), and also Chap. 6 below.

Second, a foundational issue concerning the whole idea of social security is the choice of 'evaluative space', that is, the variables in terms of which the success or failure of social security is to be judged. We have argued in favour of using a suitably adapted version of an old evaluative tradition (associated with the works of Aristotle, Smith, and Marx, among others) which focuses on the capability that people have—based on their individual as well as social characteristics—to achieve valuable functionings (doings and beings). This provides a useful way of interpreting the standard of living and the positive freedom to achieve valued living conditions. This focus contrasts with purely subjective criteria such as utility-based accounting (used in mainstream welfare economics), and also with various criteria that focus only on *means* that are useful in living a good life (such as real incomes, entitlements, Rawlsian 'primary goods', Dworkinian 'resources') rather than on the nature of that life and the freedom to lead a less deprived life. The means are, of course, helpful in achieving ends, and thus the strategy of social security must pay attention to them, but ultimately the successes and failures of social security would have to be judged in terms of what it does to the lives that people are able to lead (Section 2).

Third, another foundational issue concerns the question as to why we need a separate and explicit policy for social security, rather than expecting that it will be taken care of by general economic growth and overall expansion. The popular belief that it is through economic growth as such that the rich countries of today have overcome their own inheritance of massive deprivation can be shown to be a gross oversimplification, and conscious public efforts to enhance living conditions have played a substantial part in that achievement. Even among the poorer countries today, some have achieved a great deal more than others through deliberately planning social security and expanding public support. Any reliance on GNP per head either as a means of protection, or as a vehicle of promotion, can be extremely treacherous, partly because of distributional inequalities but also because of the limitations of private markets in generating good living conditions (Section 3).

Fourth, as far as the protective aspect of social security is concerned, we analysed the phenomenon of famines and experiences in controlling and eradicating them. The prevention of famines has to be sought in entitlement protection rather than only in the marshalling and distribution of food. Public action has to be geared to the variety of economic and social influences that determine the ability of people (particularly vulnerable groups) to command and use food. The study of actual experiences of famine prevention in different countries brings out particularly the importance of both (1) an administrative system that is systematically aimed at recreating lost entitlements (when these are disrupted by droughts, floods, wars, economic slumps, or whatever), and (2) a political system that can act as the prime mover in getting the administrative system to work as and when it is required.

Various specific lessons were also discussed, including (1) the advantages of cash support as a method of quickly recreating lost entitlements (without waiting for prior food movements through bureaucratic channels); (2) the crucial role of employment creation in a comprehensive anti-famine strategy; (3) the power of informal communication channels and political activism in precipitating early action, in comparison with formal 'early warning' techniques; and (4) the need to see famine prevention as a matter not just of containing excess mortality, but also of minimizing hardship, avoiding loss of capital and productive resources through distress disposal, and preventing a lasting disruption of economic and social systems (Section 4).

Fifth, we then shifted our attention from the urgent imperatives of entitlement protection to the more general problem of the promotion of living standards. In this context, we discussed the effectiveness of different kinds of policies, and distinguished in particular between two general approaches, which we respectively called 'growth-mediated security' and 'support-led security'. A comparison of the contrasting performances of different countries brings out the plurality of routes through which living standards have been promoted, in some cases involving the achievement of elevated GNP per head (as in Hong Kong, Singapore, South Korea, the United Arab Emirates, Kuwait) and in others without remarkable increase in GNP per head (as in China, Costa Rica, Cuba, Chile, Jamaica, Sri Lanka). The experience of the latter group of countries brings out the possibility of not waiting for GNP expansion before achieving substantial breakthroughs in guaranteeing minimal living standards to all. This strategy of 'support-led security' involves public action in a particularly crucial and indispensable way.

On the other hand, the experience of the former group suggests that growth too can be an engine of promotion of social secuirty, if the fruits of growth are skilfully used for social objectives. It is, in fact, the misuse of the opportunities provided by enhanced opulence that has been the cause of the most severe disappointments with the route of economic growth (for example, in Brazil). Here too there is a positive role for public action in ensuring productive use of the fruits of growth in enhancing living conditions and in achieving social security (Section 5).

Finally, we discussed some general issues regarding the nature of public action for social security (Section 6). It is particularly necessary to distinguish between actions undertaken *for* the public and *by* the public. The former are, of course, important in achieving social security, but can be both incomplete (requiring integration with efforts of the public in general and non-governmental institutions in particular), and in need of a political push (requiring an informed and active role of public pressure groups). In both these respects, public action for social security has to be seen in a much wider perspective than that of State action only.

References

Adelman, I. (1975), 'Development Economics: A Reassessment of Goals', *American Economic Review*, Papers and Proceedings, 66.

—— and Morris, C. (1973), *Economic Growth and Social Equity in Developing Countries*. Stanford: Stanford University Press.

Anand, S., and Kanbur, R. (1987), 'Public Policy and Basic Needs Provision: Intervention and Achievement in Sri Lanka', mimeo, to be published in Drèze and Sen (1990).

Aristotle (1980), *The Nicomachean Ethics* (trans. W. D. Ross). Oxford: Clarendon Press.

Arrow, K. (1963), 'Uncertainty and the Welfare Economics of Health Care', *American Economic Review*, 53.

Atkinson, A. B. (1970), 'On the Measurement of Inequality', *Journal of Economic Theory*, 2; repr. in Atkinson (1983).

—— (1983), *Social Justice and Public Policy*. Brighton: Wheatsheaf, and Cambridge, Mass.: MIT Press.

—— and Bourguignon, F. (1982), 'The Comparison of Multi-Dimensional Distributions of Economic Status', *Review of Economic Studies*, 49; repr. in Atkinson (1983).

Autier, P. (1988), 'Nutrition Assessment Through the Use of a Nutritional Scoring System', *Disasters*, 12.

—— d'Altilia, J. P., Delamalle, J. P., and Vercruysse, V. (1989), 'The Food and Nutrition Surveillance System of Chad and Mali: The "SAP" After Two Years', mimeo, European Association for Health and Development, Brussels.

Basu, K. (1986), 'Combatting Chronic Poverty and Hunger in South Asia: Some Policy Options', paper presented at a Conference on Food Strategies held at WIDER, Helsinki, 21–5 July 1986; to be published in Drèze and Sen (1990).

Berg, A. (1973), *The Nutrition Factor*. Washington, DC: Brookings Institution.

—— (1987), *Malnutrition: What Can be Done?* Baltimore: Johns Hopkins University Press.

Berry, S. S. (1984), 'The Food Crisis and Agrarian Change in Africa: A Review Essay', *African Studies Review*, 27/2.

Bhattacharya, N., Chatterjee, G. S., and Pal, P. (1988), 'Variations in Level of Living across Regions and Social Groups in India', in Srinivasan and Bardhan (1988).

Binns, C. W. (1976), 'Famine and the Diet of the Enga', *Papua New Guinea Medical Journal*, 19.

Borton, J., and Clay, E. (1986), 'The African Food Crisis of 1986', *Disasters*, 10.

—— and York, S. (1987), 'Experiences of the Collection and Use of Micro-level Data in Disaster Preparedness and Managing Emergency Operations', *Disasters*, 11.

Brannen, J., and Wilson, G. (eds.) (1987), *Give and Take in Families*. London: Allen & Unwin.

Brennan, L. (1988), 'Government Famine Relief in Bengal, 1943', *The Journal of Asian Studies*, 47.

Bumgarner, R. (1989), 'China: Long-Term Issues in Options for the Health Sector', mimeo, The World Bank, Washington, DC.

Caldwell, J. C. (1986), 'Routes to Low Mortality in Poor Countries', *Population and Development Review*, 12.

Castaneda, T. (1984), 'Contexto Socioeconomico y Causas del Descenso de la Mortalidad Infantil en Chile', Documento de Trabajo No. 28, Centro de Estudios Publicos, Santiago.

——(1985), 'Determinantes del Descenso de la Mortalidad Infantil en Chile 1975–1983', *Cuadernos de Economia*, 22.

CILSS (Comité Permanent Interétats de Lutte Contre la Sécheresse dans le Sahel), (1986), *La Prévision des situations alimentaires critiques dans les pays du Sahel: Systèmes et moyens d'alerte précoce*. Paris: OECD.

Cornia, G., Jolly, R., and Stewart, F. (eds.) (1987), *Adjustment with a Human Face*. Oxford: Clarendon Press.

Culyer, A. J. (1985), 'The Scope and Limits of Health Economics', *Okonomie des Gesundheitswesens*, 1985.

Cutler, P. (1985a), 'Detecting Food Emergencies: Lessons from the 1979 Bangladesh Crisis', *Food Policy*, 10.

——(1985b), 'The Use of Economic and Social Information in Famine Prediction and Response', report prepared for the Overseas Development Administration. London: Overseas Development Administration.

Dalby, D., Harrison Church, R. J., and Bezzaz, F. (eds.) (1977), *Drought in Africa 2*. London: International African Institute.

Dasgupta, P. (1986), 'Positive Freedom, Markets and the Welfare State', *Oxford Review of Economic Policy*, 2.

Desai, M. (1986), 'Modelling an Early Warning System for Famines', paper presented at a Conference on Food Strategies held at WIDER, Helsinki, 21–5 July 1986; to be published in Drèze and Sen (1990).

de Sainte Croix, G. E. M. (1981), *The Class Struggle in the Ancient Greek World*. London: Duckworth.

de Waal, A. (1989), *Famine That Kills: Darfur 1984–1985*. Oxford: Oxford University Press.

Drèze, J. P. (1988), 'Famine Prevention in India', Discussion Paper No. 3, Development Economics Research Programme, London School of Economics; to be published in Drèze and Sen (1990).

——(1989), 'Famine Prevention in Africa', Discussion Paper No. 17, Development Economics Research Programme, London School of Economics; to be published in Drèze and Sen (1990).

——and Sen, A. K. (1989), *Hunger and Public Action*. Oxford: Clarendon Press.

——(eds.) (1990), *The Political Economy of Hunger*, 3 vols. Oxford: Oxford University Press.

——and Stern, N. (1987), 'The Theory of Cost-Benefit Analysis', in A. Auerbach and M. Feldstein (eds.), *Handbook of Public Economics*. Amsterdam: North-Holland.

Eicher, C. K. (1986), 'Transforming African Agriculture', The Hunger Project Papers, No. 4, The Hunger Project, San Francisco.

——(1988), 'Food Security Battles in Sub-Saharan Africa', paper presented at the VIIth World Congress for Rural Sociology, Bologna, 25 June–2 July 1988.

FAO (Food and Agriculture Organization), *African Agriculture: The Next 25 Years*. Rome: FAO.

Flegg, A. T. (1982), 'Inequality of Income, Illiteracy and Medical Care as Determinants of Infant Mortality in Underdeveloped Countries', *Population Studies*, 36.

Foster, J. (1984), 'On Economic Poverty: A Survey of Aggregate Measures', *Advances in Econometrics*, 3.

—— (1986), 'Inequality Measurement'. In H. P. Young (ed.), *Fair Allocation*, vol. 33 of Proceedings of Symposia in Applied Mathematics. American Mathematical Society.

Garcia, M., and Pinstrup-Andersen, P. (1987), 'The Pilot Food Price Subsidy Scheme in the Philippines: Its Impact on Income, Food Consumption, and Nutritional Status', Research Report No. 61, International Food Policy Research Institute, Washington, DC.

Glantz, M. (ed.) (1987), *Drought and Hunger in Africa: Denying Famine a Future*. Cambridge: Cambridge University Press.

Grant, J. (1978), *Disparity Reduction Rates in Social Indicators*. Washington, DC: Overseas Development Council.

Griffin, K., and Khan, A. R. (eds.) (1977), *Poverty and Landlessness in Rural Asia*. Geneva: International Labour Organization.

—— (1978), 'Poverty in the World: Ugly Facts and Fancy Models', *World Development*, 6.

—— and Knight, J. (1988), 'Human Development in the 1980s and Beyond', report for the United Nations Committee for Development Planning.

Gwatkin, D. R., Wilcox, J. R., and Wray, J. D. (1980), *Can Health and Nutrition Interventions Make a Difference?* Washington, DC: Overseas Development Council.

Halstead, S. B., Walsh, J. A., and Warren, K. S. (eds.) (1985), *Good Health at Low Cost*. New York: Rockefeller Foundation.

Hammond, R. J. (1951), *History of the Second World War: Food*. London: HMSO.

Harbert, L., and Scandizzo, P. (1982), 'Food Distribution and Nutrition Intervention: The Case of Chile', World Bank Staff Working Paper No. 512, The World Bank, Washington DC.

Hart, K. (1987), 'Commoditisation and the Standard of Living', in Sen *et al.* (1987).

Hawthorn, G. (1987), 'Introduction', in Sen *et al.* (1987).

Hay, R., Burke, S., and Dako, D. Y. (1986), 'A Socio-Economic Assessment of Drought Relief in Botswana', report prepared by UNICEF/UNDP/WHO for the Inter-Ministerial Drought Committee, Government of Botswana, Gaborone.

Helm, D. (1986), 'The Assessment: The Economic Borders of the State', *Oxford Review of Economic Policy*, 2.

Hossain, I. (1987), 'Poverty as Capability Failure', mimeo, University of Stockholm.

Hussain, A., and Stern, N. (1988), 'On the Recent Increase in Death Rates in China', mimeo, London School of Economics.

IDS (Institute of Development Studies) Bulletin (1985), *Sub-Saharan Africa: Getting the Facts Straight*, special issue, 16/3.

Isenman, P. (1980), 'Basic Needs: The Case of Sri Lanka', *World Development*, 8.

Ismael, J. S. (1982), *Kuwait: Social Change in Historical Perspective*. Syracuse, NY: Syracuse University Press.

Jain, A. K. (1985), 'Determinants of Regional Variation in Infant Mortality in Rural India', *Population Studies*, 39.

Jamison, D. (1985), 'China's Health Care System: Policies, Organization, Inputs and Finance', in Halstead *et al.* (1985).

Kakwani, N. (1986), 'On Measuring Undernutrition', Working Paper No. 8, WIDER, Helsinki.

—— (1987), *Analysing Redistributive Policies*. Cambridge: Cambridge University Press.

Kanbur, R. (1987), 'The Standard of Living: Uncertainty, Inequality and Opportunity', in Sen *et al.* (1987).

Kiljunen, K. (ed.) (1984), *Kampuchea: Decade of the Genocide*. London: Zed.

Krishnamachari, K. A. V. R., Rao, N. P., and Rao, K. V. (1974), 'Food and Nutritional Situation in the Drought Affected Areas of Maharashtra: A Survey and Recommendations', *Indian Journal of Nutrition and Dietetics*, 11.

Kumar, B. G. (1985), 'The Ethiopian Famine and Relief Measures: An Analysis and Evaluation', mimeo, UNICEF, New York.

—— (1987), 'Poverty and Public Policy: Government Intervention and Levels of Living in Kerala', D.Phil. thesis, University of Oxford.

Lall, S., and Stewart, F. (eds.) (1986), *Theory and Reality in Development: Essays in Honour of Paul Streeten*. London: Macmillan.

Li, L. M. (1987), 'Famine and Famine Relief: Viewing Africa in the 1980s from China in the 1920s', in Glantz (1987).

Loveday, A. (1914), *The History and Economics of Indian Famines*. London: A. G. Bell and Sons; repr. New Delhi: Usha Publications, 1985.

McKeown, T., and Lowe, C. R. (1966), *An Introduction to Social Medicine*. Oxford: Blackwell.

McNeill, W. H. (1976), *Plagues and People*. Garden City, NY: Anchor Press.

Mahieu, F. R., and Nour, M. M. (1987), 'The Entitlement Approach to Famines and the Sahelian Case: A Survey of the Available Literature', mimeo, WIDER, Helsinki.

Mallory, W. H. (1926), *China: Land of Famine*. New York: American Geographical Society.

Marrack, J. R. (1947), 'Investigations of Human Nutrition in the United Kingdom During the War', *Proceedings of the Nutrition Society*, 5.

Marx, K. (1844), *Economic and Philosophic Manuscripts of 1844*. English trans. Moscow: Progress Publishers, 1977.

—— (1887), *Capital*, i, trans. S. Moore and E. Aveling. London: Sonnenschein; repub. London: Allen & Unwin, 1946.

Mata, L., and Rosero, L. (1987), 'Health and Social Development in Costa Rica: Intersectoral Action', document prepared by the Instituto de Investigaciones de Salud (INISA), University of Costa Rica.

Mellor, J. W., Delgado, C. L., and Blackie, C. L. (eds.) (1987), *Accelerating Food Production in Sub-Saharan Africa*. Baltimore: Johns Hopkins University Press.

Mitter, S. (1988), 'Managing the Drought Crisis: The Zimbabwe Experience, 1982–1983', undergraduate essay, Harvard University.

Morio, S., and Takahashi, S. (1986), 'Socio-Economic Correlates of Mortality in Japan', in Ng Shui Meng (ed.), *Socio-Economic Correlates of Mortality in Japan and ASEAN*, National Institute for Research Advancement, Japan, and Institute of Southeast Asian Studies, Singapore.

Morris, M. D. (1979), *Measuring the Conditions of the World's Poor: The Physical Quality of Life Index*. Oxford: Pergamon.

Morrison, B., and Waxler, N. (1986), 'Three Patterns of Basic Needs Distribution within Sri Lanka: 1971–1973', *World Development*, 14.

Muellbauer, J. (1987), 'Professor Sen on the Standard of Living', in Sen *et al.* (1987).

Muniz, J. G., Fabián, J. C., and Mauriquez, J. C. (1984), 'The Recent Worldwide Economic Crisis and the Welfare of Children: The Case of Cuba', *World Development*, 12.

Mwaluko, E. P. (1962), 'Famine Relief in the Central Province of Tanganyika, 1961', *Tropical Agriculture*, 39.

Nag, M. (1985), 'The Impact of Social and Economic Development on Mortality: Comparative Study of Kerala and West Bengal', in Halstead *et al.* (1985).

Nussbaum, M. (1988), 'Nature, Function and Capability: Aristotle on Political Distribution', *Oxford Studies in Ancient Philosophy*, supplementary volume.

Osmani, S. R. (1982), *Economic Inequality and Group Welfare*. Oxford: Clarendon Press.

—— (1987), 'Nutrition and the Economics of Food: Implications of Some Recent Controversies', Working Paper No. 15, WIDER; to be published in Drèze and Sen (1990).

Otten, M. W. (1986), 'Nutritional and Mortality Aspects of the 1985 Famine in North Central Ethiopia', mimeo, Centre for Disease Control, Atlanta, Ga.

Padmini, R. (1985), 'The Local Purchase of Food Commodities: "Cash for Food" Project', mimeo, UNICEF, Addis Ababa.

Peng, X. (1987), 'Demographic Consequences of the Great Leap Forward in China's Provinces', *Population and Development Review*, 4.

Perera, P. D. A. (1985), 'Health Care Systems of Sri Lanka', in Halstead *et al.* (1985).

Platteau, J. P. (1988), 'The Food Crisis in Africa: A Comparative Structural Analysis', Working Paper No. 44, World Institute for Development Economics Research, Helsinki; to be published in Drèze and Sen (1990).

Prescott, N., and Jamison, D. (1985), 'The Distribution and Impact of Health Resource Availability in China', *International Journal of Health Planning and Management*, 1.

Preston, S., Keyfitz, N., and Schoen, R. (1972), *Causes of Death: Life Tables for National Populations*. New York: Seminar Press.

Pyatt, G. (1987), 'Measuring Welfare, Poverty and Inequality', *Economic Journal*, 97.

Ram, N. (1986), 'An Independent Press and Anti-Hunger Strategies', paper presented at a conference on Food Strategies held at the World Institute for Development Economics Research, July 1986; to be published in Drèze and Sen (1990).

Ramalingaswami, V., Deo, M. G., Guleria, J. S., Malhotra, K. K., Sood, S. K., Om, P. and Sinha, R. V. N. (1971), 'Studies of the Bihar Famine of 1966–1967', in G. Blix *et al.* (eds.), *Famine: Nutrition and Relief Operations in Times of Disaster*. Uppsala, Sweden: Swedish Nutrition Foundation.

Ravallion, M. (1987), *Markets and Famines*. Oxford: Clarendon Press.

Reddy, S. (1988), 'An Independent Press Working Against Famine: The Nigerian Experience', *Journal of Modern African Studies*, 26.

Riskin, C. (1987), *China's Political Economy: The Quest for Development since 1949*. Oxford: Clarendon Press.

Rose, T. (ed.) (1985), *Crisis and Recovery in Sub-Saharan Africa*. Paris: OECD.

Rukini, M., and Eicher, C. K. (eds.) (1987), *Food Security for Southern Africa*. Harare: UZ/MSU Food Security Project, Department of Agricultural Economics and Extension, University of Zimbabwe.

Sachs, I. (1986), 'Growth and Poverty: Lessons from Brazil', paper presented at a Conference on Food Strategies held at WIDER, Helsinki, 21–5 July 1986; to be published in Drèze and Sen (1990).

Saenz, L. (1985), 'Health Changes During a Decade: The Costa Rican Case', in Halstead *et al.* (1985).

Samuelson, P. A. (1955), 'Diagrammatic Exposition of a Theory of Public Expenditure', *Review of Economics and Statistics*, 37.

Schokkaert, E., and van Ootegem, L. (1989), 'Sen's Concept of the Living Standard Applied to the Belgian Unemployed', Public Economics Research Paper No. 1, Centre for Economics Studies, Leuven.

Sen, A. K. (1973), 'On the Development of Basic Income Indicators to Supplement GNP Measures', *Economic Bulletin for Asia and the Far East*, 24.

——(1976a), 'Poverty: An Ordinal Approach to Measurement', *Econometrica*, 44; reprinted in Sen (1982).

——(1976b), 'Real National Income', *Review of Economic Studies*, 43; reprinted in Sen (1982).

——(1980), 'Equality of What?', in S. M. McMurrin (ed.), *Tanner Lectures on Human Values*, i, Cambridge: Cambridge University Press; reprinted in Sen (1982).

——(1981a), *Poverty and Famines*. Oxford: Clarendon Press.

——(1981b), 'Public Action and the Quality of Life in Developing Countries', *Oxford Bulletin of Economics and Statistics*, 43.

——(1982), *Choice, Welfare and Measurement*. Oxford: Blackwell; and Cambridge, Mass: MIT Press.

——(1983), 'Development: Which Way Now?', *Economic Journal*, 93.

——(1984), *Resources, Values and Development*. Oxford: Basil Blackwell.

——(1985a), 'Well-being, Agency and Freedom: The Dewey Lectures 1984', *Journal of Philosophy*, 82.

——(1985b), *Commodities and Capabilities*. Amsterdam: North Holland.

——(1986), 'India and Africa: What do we Have to Learn from Each Other?', C. N. Vakil Memorial Lecture delivered at the Eighth World Congress of the International Economic Association, New Delhi, Dec. 1986.

——(1987a), *Hunger and Entitlements*. Helsinki: WIDER.

——(1987b), 'The Standard of Living', in Sen *et al.* (1987).

——(1988), 'Food and Freedom', Sir John Crawford Memorial Lecture, The World Bank; to be published in *World Development*.

—— *et al.* (1987), *The Standard of Living* (ed. G. Hawthorn). Cambridge: Cambridge University Press.

Shigematsu, I., and Yanagawa, H. (1985), 'The Case of Japan', in J. Vallin and A. Lopez (eds.), *Health Policy, Social Policy and Mortality Prospects*. Liège: International Union for the Scientific Study of Population.

Smith, A. (1776), *An Enquiry into the Nature and Causes of the Wealth of Nations*. Repub. Oxford: Clarendon Press, 1976.

Smout, T. C. (1978), 'Famine and Famine-Relief in Scotland', in L. M. Cullen and T. C. Smout (eds.), *Comparative Aspects of Scottish and Irish Economic History 1600–1900*. Edinburgh: Donald.

Srinivasan, T. N., and Bardhan, P. K. (eds.) (1988), *Rural Poverty in South Asia*. New York: Columbia University Press.

Stewart, F. (1985), *Planning to Meet Basic Needs*. London: Macmillan.

——(1988), 'Basic Needs Strategies, Human Rights and the Right to Development', Luca d'Agliano–Queen Elizabeth House Development Studies Working Paper No. 2, Queen Elizabeth House, Oxford.

Streeten, P. (1981), *Development Perspectives*. London: Macmillan.

——(1984), 'Basic Needs: Some Unsettled Questions', *World Development*, 12.

et al. (1981), *First Things First: Meeting Basic Needs in Developing Countries*. Oxford: Oxford University Press.

Swift, J. (forthcoming), 'Planning Against Drought and Famine in Turkana: A District Contingency Plan', to be published in T. E. Downing *et al.* (eds.), *Coping with Drought in Kenya: National and Local Strategies*. Boulder, Colo.: Lynne Rienner.

Szreter, S. (1988), 'The Importance of Social Intervention in Britain's Mortality Decline c.1850–1914: A Re-Interpretation', *Social History of Medicine*, 1.

Taeuber, I. B. (1958), *The Population of Japan*. Princeton: Princeton University Press.

Titmuss, R. M. (1950), *History of the Second World War: Problems of Social Policy*. London: HMSO.

UNICEF (United Nations Children's Fund) (1987), *The State of the World's Children*. New York: UNICEF.

——(1988), *The State of the World's Children*. New York: UNICEF.

Valaoras, V. G. (1946), 'Some Effects of Famine on the Population of Greece', *Milbank Memorial Fund Quarterly Bulletin*, 24.

van Binsbergen, A. (1986), 'Cape Verde: Food Aid Resource Planning in Support of National Food Strategy', paper presented at a Conference on Food Aid for Development, Abijan, Sept. 1986.

Walker, P. (1988), 'Famine and Rapid Onset Disaster Warning Systems: A Report by the International Institute for Environment and Development for The Red Cross', mimeo, International Institute for Environment and Development, London.

Whitehead, A. (1986), 'Rural Women and Food Production in Sub-Saharan Africa', paper presented at a Conference on Food Strategies held at WIDER, Helsinki, 21–5 July 1986; to be published in Drèze and Sen (1990).

Will, P. E. (1980), *Bureaucratie et famine en Chine au 18e siècle*. Paris: Mouton.

Williams, A. (1985), 'Economics of Coronary Bypass Grafting', *British Medical Journal*, 3 Aug.

——(1987), 'What Is Health and Who Creates It?', mimeo, University of York.

Williams, B. (1987), 'The Standard of Living: Interests and Capabilities', in Sen *et al.* (1987).

Wilson, G. (1987a), *Money in the Family: Financial Organisation and Womens' Responsibility*. Aldershot: Avebury Publishers.

——(1987b), 'Patterns of Responsibility and Irresponsibility in Marriage', in Brannen and Wilson (1987).

Winter, J. M. (1986), *The Great War and the British People*. London: Macmillan.

Wyon, J. B., and Gordon, J. E. (1971), *The Khanna Study*. Cambridge, Mass.: Harvard University Press.

World Bank (1984a), *China: The Health Sector*. Washington, DC: World Bank.

——(1984b), *World Development Report*. Washington, DC: The World Bank.

——(1987), *World Development Report*. Washington, DC: The World Bank.

World Food Programme (1986), 'Lessons Learned from the African Food Crisis', mimeo, World Food Programme, Rome.

Yao, F. K., and Kone, H. (1986), 'The African Drought Reported by Six West African Newspapers', Discussion Paper No. 14, African Studies Center, Boston University.

2

Social Security in Developing Countries: What, Why, Who, and How?

Robin Burgess
Nicholas Stern

1. INTRODUCTION

Millions in developing countries suffer severe and chronic deprivation. This is compounded by general uncertainty with respect to livelihood and life which threatens an even wider section of the population. Short-term, often acute downward fluctuations in living standards are superimposed upon longer-term, persistent deprivation associated with generally low standards of living. The accumulated evidence based on a wide range of indicators strongly suggests that the incidence of these problems is widespread and the consequences severe (World Bank 1986, 1988a; Cornia *et al.* 1987; Drèze and Sen 1989; UNICEF 1989; United Nations 1987; Pinstrup-Andersen forthcoming). This is in contrast to the situation in most developed countries where deprivation and adversity are less prevalent and the implications less severe—though even in developed countries deprivation is common and unpleasant (Atkinson 1989; Danziger and Weinberg 1986; Sawhill 1988; Harvard School of Public Health 1985; Murray 1984).

Part of the reason for this contrast lies in government social-security programmes. Most developed countries have government-operated or -supported programmes to provide all or most of the following: old-age pensions; unemployment benefit; family income support; facilities for the infirm or disabled; education; and health services (Atkinson 1989; Barr 1987). The mechanisms, eligibility, entitlements, coverage, administration, and levels of benefits vary greatly, but nevertheless there is a considerable degree of support for those who may suffer deprivation or adversity. Concern and support for the deprived and destitute is by no means a modern phenomenon and to a large extent current levels of support reflect a long history of social action (Atkinson 1989).

The position for most developing countries is very different. Unemployment insurance and State pensions rarely cover more than a minority, generally a small minority (see Chaps. 3 and 8, below; also Midgley 1984). Health care, whilst often subsidized, may be thinly and haphazardly spread, State support for the infirm and disabled is generally negligible, and education seldom extends beyond primary school (Halstead *et al.* 1985; Caldwell 1986; Schultz

1988). These differences in the level, coverage, and effectiveness of State provision of social security partly reflect acute resource constraints in developing countries (see Chaps. 3 and 7 below; also Ahmad 1989; Midgley 1984). The supply of social security is also restricted by the low level of institutional development of a kind which may help to facilitate effective provision of resources to the poor and vulnerable (Lewis *et al*. 1988). On the demand side, the role of the public in exerting pressure for social security through social, legal, and political processes is hindered by the relative powerlessness of those in need in developing countries (see Chap. 1 above; also Drèze and Sen 1989, 1990).

Greater incidence and severity of deprivation, a low degree of development of formal social-security systems, limited or inappropriate coverage of public support, resource constraints, low levels of institutional development for social-security provision, and the relative powerlessness of the poor and vulnerable are all factors which combine to make the problems of social security in developing countries both important and difficult. The problems are conceptual, ethical, and theoretical as well as empirical, practical, and administrative. Our purpose here is to help clarify some of the problems and issues raised by attempts to understand and alleviate the deprivation and fragility associated with the lives of so many people.

We begin in Section 2 by explaining what we mean by social security. For developing countries we shall define the term with respect to objectives. This contrasts with definition by reference to the programmes and institutional mechanisms designed to deliver support, which is the approach generally used when defining the subject matter for developed countries where extensive programmes are already in existence. One should not be overly rigid, however, in insisting on a definition either through ends or through means. In thinking about social security, what we are considering is public action for the removal or reduction of deprivation or vulnerability. An examination of which social means are effective or appropriate with respect to this objective is clearly central. Writers on social security for developing, as well as for developed, countries quite clearly have both ends and means in mind (see Chap. 3 below; also Atkinson 1989; Drèze and Sen 1989; Midgley 1984).

We go on to ask (Section 3) why the State should be involved in social security and investigate various general reasons for intervention which may be relevant to entities other than government. We examine arguments concerning market failure and income distribution which arise within the standard economic theory of policy and then look more widely at questions concerning rights of individuals, at notions of State obligations, and at the concept of standard of living and the role of the State in improving it. In Section 4 we pose the question of who should carry responsibility for social security. Should it be the central government, the local government, the village, trade unions, the religious community, the family, or some other entity? Section 5 contains a preliminary analysis of the mechanisms for providing social security. We ask how provision may be made and what problems arise. Questions of budget constraints, administration, fraud, and incentives are briefly addressed. Concluding comments are provided in Section 6.

2. WHAT IS SOCIAL SECURITY?

Deprivation and vulnerability are integral to the lives of many in poor countries. In developed countries unfavourable outcomes in economic activity frequently mean real hardship but in poor countries they often lead to death or destitution. For many, severe deprivation is not a matter of an unfortunate fall from a previously more comfortable position but is a chronic state arising, for example, from the absence of any asset or resource that can ensure adequate livelihood. A crucial policy issue is therefore how lives and livelihoods can be made more secure against adversity and deprivation. Accordingly, we define the objective of social security as being the prevention, by social means, of very low standards of living irrespective of whether these are the result of chronic deprivation or temporary adversity. The term 'social security' may then be viewed as a measure of success in meeting this objective. It should, however, be made clear from the outset that we will be restricting the set of means under consideration by examining only those social means which have a direct bearing on deprivation and vulnerability. This restriction is twofold. First, the restriction to social means excludes a wide range of other factors (for example, climatic change, industrialization) which may contribute to our objective but which none the less cannot be considered primarily as part of a social-security agenda. Second, the restriction to those social means which directly influence deprivation and vulnerability further focuses us on a limited set of measures which include direct interventions, alterations in market functioning, and redistributive policy. We are using 'direct' here to distinguish from 'indirect' measures, in which we include the general development of the economy and society. There is no doubt that such developments can contribute to greater security, but that is not our main subject matter. In essence our approach is to focus attention on the role of public action at the State, community, and family level in improving social security.

Our approach contrasts with that of developed countries where social security is generally seen in terms of specific public programmes involving social assistance, social insurance, and redistribution (see Chap. 3 below; also Atkinson 1989; Kotlikoff 1987). For developing countries, the fact that few programmes of this type exist, and those that do often have low or poorly directed coverage (Midgley 1984; Puffert 1988), suggests that a definition along these lines would be too narrow. Increases in social security may arise in ways which are not simply enacted or imposed by government. A definition based on State programmes fails to take into account household and community contributions and their interactions with State provision, and may miss the important role of public pressure (Drèze and Sen 1989; Bardhan 1988; Lewis *et al.* 1988). Even within the sphere of State action, there is no clear indication that social security in developing countries should take the same form as it has taken in developed countries (see Chap. 3 below). Given the greater problems of insecurity, limited administrative resources, and tightness of budget constraints in developing countries, doubts have been expressed as to whether conventional social security measures are operationally tenable or financially viable (see Chap. 7 below). For example, it might be argued that there is a case for more emergency prevention and relief measures at one extreme and for the diversification of economic activity and the improvement of market functioning at the other.

As a result, an analysis of achievement or commitment to our 'social-security objective' in terms of types and levels of expenditure on State social-security programmes is likely to be misleading. This assertion is strengthened by the fact that some State programmes may in fact be regressive and contribute negatively or negligibly to the security of the very poor. This appears to have been the case in some important examples in Latin America (see Chap. 8 below; also Mackenzie 1988; de Oliviera *et al.* 1987; Jimenez and Puffert 1988).

We do not wish to say that choice of the mechanism of delivery is unimportant, but rather to place emphasis, in the analysis, on outcomes instead of confining the subject matter to certain means. The nature and extent of the problems would seem to dictate a wider perspective. Means must, however, play a central part in the discussion, and the diversity of measures implemented across developed and developing countries shows that an analysis of the actual and potential outcomes of programmes should take a broad view of the possibilities (see Chaps. 1 above and 3 below; also Atkinson 1989; Drèze and Sen 1989). Given the various shortcomings outlined above it is imperative that governments view the problem of social-security provision in a framework which is more extensive than that limited to conventional social-security measures.

In defining ends we have avoided specifying goals with respect to poverty lines or safety nets despite the fact that this approach to deprivation has been standard in the literature for many years. Poverty alleviation, typically, requires the definition of a poverty line, usually seen as an income cut-off, and the problems of definition can lead to real confusion both conceptually and in applied work. One cannot simultaneously define poverty as the minimum for survival and then record how many are surviving below the minimum. And given the scope for substantial differences in the choice of line, it is discomforting that the distribution of the population around proposed lines is typically very dense, so that small movements in the line cause big changes in the numbers in poverty (see, for example, Bardhan and Srinivasan 1974; Bliss and Stern 1978). The definition of income itself, generally unavoidable when a poverty line is invoked, raises difficulties which are much more severe in developing countries (than developed) where statistics and administration are much poorer—these include the choice of time period, the treatment of inputs in own-account productive activities, and the specification of unit (household, family, individual—see, for example, Deaton 1988). It is perhaps not surprising that discussions of numbers in poverty in developed countries often focus on State-defined levels for the receipt of benefit, or on how the poverty line has moved over time or with respect to some other level (Atkinson 1989). Further, the focus on a line can divert attention from the distribution below the line which is generally of considerable importance—the number and conditions of the very poor, however defined, will be of as much, or greater significance, as those for the poor (Lipton 1988). Brave, interesting, and important attempts at definition have been made (see, for example, Townsend 1979, 1985; Sen 1976, 1985; Atkinson 1987) but the conceptual and practical basis is not sufficiently strong to lead one to define social security with respect to poverty lines.

Related problems arise with the notion of 'safety net'. Safety nets are supposed to catch anyone who might fall (those designed to save only the most valuable or good-looking members of the troupe would be both impractical and repugnant), and to catch them before they fall below some particular level. This would appear to imply a formula that is both universal and specific. Minimum levels for all types of individual, family, or household (which may, of course, be different for different people depending on the formula) must be specified, together with means by which they may be universally achieved. There may be a case for providing 'safety nets' to individuals who become subject to specific types of identifiable sources of hardship (for example, widowhood, physical disability). Nevertheless it is the universality of coverage of programmes combined with the need to define justifiable minima for each category that make the notion of safety net less than satisfactory as an analytical or administrative tool.

We do not therefore find the language either of poverty lines or of safety nets to be useful for a definition on which to base either analytical enquiry or policy measures. We would suggest that the one we have used is less ambitious, more practical, and carries less danger of misdirection. The objective of preventing deprivation and adversity can be pursued in many different ways from widows' pensions to food for work programmes, and including improved sanitation, water supply, education, and so on. These are not easily incorporated into notions of poverty lines or safety nets. Also, in order to facilitate measurement of poverty lines there is a tendency to concentrate on income as the main welfare criterion and hence ignore other important influences.

The definition of social security suggested here includes public action at the household, community, and State level to remove or reduce deprivation and vulnerability. The breadth of the definition leads to inclusion of the study of possible interactions (for example, between State provision and family support —see Section 5.3) and emphasis on the role of public pressure in facilitating provision. Comprehensiveness of scope must not, however, be taken to imply that all influences are of equal importance. We shall try to retain our focus on those measures which have a direct bearing on deprivation and adversity. The challenge then becomes to identify the most important and fruitful avenues of policy influence and we trust that the studies in this book make some contribution.

We place special emphasis on uncertainty, as developing countries suffer particularly from dependence on risky agriculture, susceptibility to macro shocks, high morbidity, and so on. Separate from the issue of uncertainty is the fact that persistently low standards of living themselves carry negative consequences in the sense of long-term or chronic deprivation. Whilst these may be less visible than those associated with short-term failures, their incidence and persistence suggest that they are perhaps of greater importance. The raising of living standards then becomes an issue that falls within the domain of social security, but it is used here in the narrow sense involving essentially the use of social mechanisms to mitigate the adverse consequences of low levels of living as opposed to the general sense which involves essentially the whole of development economics. Specific measures such as government provision of pensions or subsidization of food-grains would fit into this category, as they are concerned with raising the living standards of the deprived irrespective of whether or not the focus is on uncertainty. One should, however, also note that fluctuating climatic conditions and commodity prices can limit the design of effective social-security schemes in that policy-makers cannot be sure of the environment in which they are operating. Relative price changes induced by the introduction of programmes also constrain policy design.

It is important not to dissociate the chronic deprivation and temporary adversity issues as there are significant complementarities involved and effective policy instruments often influence both simultaneously. In particular, if the probability or consequences of adverse outcomes are reduced or mitigated with little or no change in the probability or consequences of favourable outcomes, then the mean standard of living is raised. More broadly, the probability of occurrence of extreme hardship would generally be reduced if the mean income (or standard of living) is raised, provided the distribution (in the appropriate sense) is not widened. This reminds us that there are broad complementarities between risk reduction and the sustained promotion of living standards, which should be exploited in the design of policy. The dynamics of social-security provision also need to be kept firmly in mind as effects are not limited to the current period. Policies which involve direct provisioning, human-capital formation, and economic growth will influence deprivation over different time scales. There may be important trade-offs between protecting individuals in the short run and providing greater incomes and security in the longer term.

3. WHY SHOULD GOVERNMENTS INVOLVE THEMSELVES IN SOCIAL SECURITY?

The theory of economic policy is usually based on the idea that individuals consistently pursue well-defined objectives which can also be interpreted as their own well-being. We first consider the reasons why governments should involve themselves in social security which arise within this standard framework. In this context there are essentially two reasons for government intervention. The first is that the markets in which individuals trade may not work efficiently in the sense made precise in the theorems of welfare economics. Some markets may not exist, markets which do exist may not be competitive, and there may be externalities. For these reasons an equilibrium (if one exists) may not be Pareto-efficient (where Pareto efficiency is defined in the usual sense that it is impossible to make one person better off without making another worse off—and better off is defined with respect to individual objectives). The second reason for governments to involve themselves in social security within this framework is the improvement of the distribution of welfare. Whether or not an equilibrium is Pareto-efficient, the government might regard the distribution of welfare as unsatisfactory and may see scope for improving it, and a responsibility to do so. In Section 3.1 we consider these two reasons and analyse what they imply for the potential for government intervention.

In Section 3.2 we examine reasons for government involvement in social security which lie outside the standard framework. First, a government may believe that individuals are not the best judges of their own self-interest. Second, a government may have goals which cannot be specified in terms of the objectives of agents, together with an aggregate across agents, which we often term social welfare. Thus a government may have views of individual and social states, and of the processes which generate them, which cannot simply be defined in terms of the usual economic language of individual utility, Pareto efficiency, and social welfare. This leads us to consider what is important about an individual's state for public policy, including capabilities and rights.

Third, the public, or at least sections of the public, may desire the provision of social security. One can then take the view that the provision of social security has some justification from the viewpoint of democracy. The reasons the public might desire social security may well overlap with those we have already mentioned, but it is the fact that they may wish it that we are emphasizing here. The usual qualification to the democratic argument, namely, that it should not interfere with basic rights, would apply here. Note that this normative question is distinct from the positive one which points to the role of public pressure in eliciting a government response (see Section 3.3). We shall not pursue the 'democratic' justification for social security in any further detail here.

Political economy considerations are stressed throughout. What is clear is that the role played by institutions and the interaction between interest groups are critical in determining whether, and to what extent, social security is provided. It should be noted that though we have phrased our approach in terms of government intervention, many of the reasons mentioned apply more generally.

3.1. *The Standard Framework of Welfare Economics*

3.1.1. *Market Failure*   In the standard framework of welfare economics, each agent is assumed to be able to compare and rank economic states which are defined in terms of his or her own consumption and supplies and those of other agents (here households and firms). Individuals are then assumed to act in their own self-interest as defined by this ranking, finding the best outcome for themselves subject to whatever constraints they may face. We are to think of goods delivered at different times as being different goods. We should also think of goods which occur in different states of nature as being different goods (for example, a cold beer when it is drizzling is a different good from a cold beer when it is hot and sunny). The two basic theorems of welfare economics are the following. First, a competitive equilibrium is Pareto-efficient, if there are no externalities. The assumption that there are no externalities means that one agent's action does not directly affect the welfare or opportunities of another. Note that a competitive equilibrium here involves the assumption that all markets exist and are perfect in the sense that any individual acts as if he or she can buy or sell as much as is desired without affecting the market price.

The second theorem states that a given Pareto-efficient allocation can be achieved as a competitive equilibrium, provided again that there are no externalities, and further, that production is convex (constant or decreasing returns to scale), that preferences are convex (constant or diminishing marginal rates of substitution), and that the government can make lump-sum transfers and levy lump-sum taxes. The definition of lump-sum here is that there is no action an individual can take to alter the transfer or the tax. We consider reasons, in the context of social security, why the Pareto efficiency of the first theorem may not be achieved and the problems of redistribution which may be associated with the failure of the assumptions in the second theorem.

There are many reasons why a competitive equilibrium may fail to exist. As we have seen, if one does exist the only reason that it can fail to be Pareto-efficient is that there are externalities. We focus here on the problems of establishing a competitive equilibrium with particular reference to those which may be associated with social security. We then comment briefly on externalities in this context. There are three markets where failures are of particular importance for the security of the less well-off: capital markets, insurance markets, and labour markets. We consider them briefly in turn.

Capital markets allow people to transfer spending power from one period to another, thus freeing them from being constrained in a period by the income which they receive in that particular period. Someone who has low income in a particular week or month may borrow and repay in a period when income is high. This allows the individual to remove fluctuations in the sense of allowing the consumption stream to be independent of the income stream, subject to the overall constraint that loans must be repaid, that is, a long-term budget constraint. Capital markets may therefore prevent a severe disruption for an individual in one period when the individual's overall resources in the long term are indeed sufficient to sustain a higher standard of living. Well-functioning capital markets also allow individuals to save in a productive way for their retirement, an extended period of low or zero earned income. Given high volatility of incomes (for example, through seasonal variations) and general uncertainties surrounding livelihoods, the consumption-smoothing and insurance potential of capital markets would appear to be of considerable importance (see Deaton 1989; Gersovitz 1988).

We must ask ourselves, then, why it is that capital markets may not work properly in the sense that an individual who is likely to be able to pay back may not be able to borrow (at 'reasonable' market rates) to carry himself or herself through a period of crisis. A basic problem is that the lender may not be prepared to take the risk of default or may find it too costly to ensure that the interest and debt are repaid. This consideration tells us that there is a fundamental reason why capital markets can never be perfect. An individual cannot expect to borrow as much as he or she desires at the going price (interest rate), since lenders will regard a higher indebtedness of a particular borrower as a sign that repayment will be more uncertain and may therefore wish to alter the terms of the loan, if indeed there is any preparedness to offer further sums. In addition to this problem it may also happen that higher interest rates attract less dependable borrowers. As a result some degree of credit-rationing may ensue (Stiglitz and Weiss 1981; Braverman and Guasch 1986). The government will therefore never be able to ensure that capital markets are perfect in the sense that is generally used in economics.

On the other hand, capital markets can work more or less well and the government may take action to improve them. We must then ask ourselves what the government can do that the markets without government intervention cannot. The government may, in principle, be able to take bigger risks than the market, since it can pool risks from different sources. This is an argument of size which, however, is not compelling since private banks (or insurance companies) may be large. It may be argued, however, that the government should take the lead, given the limited coverage of private banks and the scarcity of private credit in general in many developing countries (Bell 1988; Braverman and Guasch 1989).

The government may have better information since, for example, it gathers data on individuals for legal and fiscal reasons. A large body of evidence, however, suggests that local institutions and individuals have an informational advantage especially with regard to the crucial issue of ability to repay (Binswanger *et al.* 1985; von Pishke *et al.* 1983; Bhende 1983; Bell 1988, 1989). Governments may have powers of enforcement which are not open to private individuals or local institutions. However, the very high default rates reported for a wide range of geographically distinct government credit programmes, juxtaposed with substantially better recovery rates for localized private credit, would suggest that such measures, if they exist, may not operate effectively (Braverman and Guasch 1989; von Pishke *et al.* 1983). The issue of government provision of credit hinges on the enforcement problems which clearly exist but which none the less must be seen against a background of high interest rates and extreme credit-rationing for the most needy in the local informal market (Ryan and Walker, forthcoming; von Pishke *et al.* 1983). From the perspective of social security it may be that governments have a greater role to play in (1) reducing the cost of private credit through investment in infrastructure and the like (Bell 1988); (2) fostering and financing local institutions which encourage participation by the poor and implement innovative mechanisms such as joint liability in order to enforce repayment (Huppi and Feder 1989; Braverman and Guasch 1989; Hossain 1986; Bell 1989).

While capital markets may allow an individual to borrow in difficult circumstances, insurance markets can protect the individual against those outcomes. Similar kinds of problems to those which constrain the satisfactory functioning of capital markets may arise. There are real difficulties of monitoring, moral hazard, and adverse selection. An insurance company has to monitor in the sense that it has to be in a position to ascertain whether the outcome against which insurance has been bought has actually occurred. Moral hazard arises where this outcome may have been made more likely by the action (inattention, indolence, negligence, or worse) of the insured. Adverse selection arises where insurance arrangements attract bad risks.

Given the magnitude of these difficulties it is not surprising that there is little insurance against unemployment, disease, disability, or widowhood in developing countries. Even predictable life-cycle events such as ageing or the costs associated with child-bearing are not generally covered by government programmes in developing countries. Some protection against these types of events is provided by governments in developed countries in the form of social insurance (see Chap. 3 below; also Atkinson 1989). Government social-insurance schemes are not widespread in developing countries, and where they exist coverage does not normally include the poor (see Chap. 8 below; also Mackenzie 1988; Puffert 1988; Ahmad 1989; Midgley 1984). Apart from their potential for insurance, these schemes could introduce an important element of redistribution into government policy, though both these aspects remain largely unexploited. Given the importance of the events they are designed to protect against, this may represent an area where properly designed government intervention may carry substantial benefits (see Chap. 6 below and Ahmad 1989 for a discussion).

Selling labour is the main source of income for many or most of the poor in developing countries, and it is in the operation of the labour market that government action may be most effective in directly providing social security. Private employers may not be willing or able to take on employees at difficult times because they themselves may be credit-constrained, or uncertain about their ability to sell output, or unwilling to take the risk of hiring labour and producing for future sale. There are many reasons to suppose that employment may fluctuate a great deal and there is ample empirical evidence that loss of employment is indeed an important phenomenon affecting the welfare of the needy worldwide (Rosenzweig 1988a; Drèze and Sen 1989; Srinivasan and Bardhan 1988; de Janvry et al. 1986). Agriculture, an activity in which many of the rural poor are employed, is inherently risky and involves seasonal variation in employment (Chambers et al. 1981; Longhurst et al. 1986; Ravallion 1988). Unemployment and underemployment are regular features of the informal sector in which many of the urban poor are found (Fields 1980). Employment prospects in all sectors are also highly dependent on international commodity prices and the demand for exports, both of which may fluctuate widely (Newbery and Stiglitz 1981).

The provision of employment on public works has been shown, in a number of geographical and historical contexts, to be an effective means of protection both against short-term risk, such as that associated with drought, as well as against longer-term chronic deprivation, as is the case with the Employment Guarantee Scheme in Maharashtra (see Chaps. 7 and 9 below; also Drèze 1988a, 1989; Drèze and Sen 1989; Dandekar 1983). Part of this success may be attributed to an element of self-targeting introduced by offering a wage so low that only the truly needy apply (Ravallion 1989a). Identification of deserving beneficiaries is in general both imperfect and costly (see Section 5.1), and reliance on a self-targeting mechanism can significantly improve targeting and reduce demands on local administrative capabilities and resources, thus enhancing cost-effectiveness. Public work schemes may be used to complement longer-term productivity-raising measures (for example, credit provision) by effectively addressing the issue of how to protect the incomes and living standards of the poor and vulnerable which are regularly threatened by events such as drought or seasonal loss of employment.

Informational constraints such as the lack of reliable data on income

(Glewwe 1989), a lack of resources, and problems of moral hazard and adverse selection may help to explain why means-tested benefits of the kind common in developed countries as well as general insurance against the consequences of unemployment remain extremely rare (see Sections 5.2 and 5.3). Public work schemes have a crucial role to play in protecting the assets of the rural poor, such as livestock, which otherwise might be sacrificed in order to ensure short-term survival. In this way short-term protective measures (for example, public work schemes during droughts) may carry strong positive benefits for the livelihood of the community in the longer term (see Chap. 9 below; Drèze 1988a, 1988b, 1989).

With respect to chronic deprivation, the processes of wage determination are important in determining whether the working poor have incomes which allow them to escape destitution. In this context, wage bargaining, unionization, and the form of interlinked transactions, if any, are all relevant (Drèze and Mukherjee 1987; Datt and Ravallion 1988; de Janvry et al. 1986; Rosenzweig 1988a; Bell 1988). In general, bargaining and conflict between groups over the terms of transactions (for example, wages, prices) profoundly affect the level of security enjoyed by a particular community or occupation group, and the government may see some role in influencing security through this mechanism by such measures as minimum wage laws or tenancy regulations. However, in their desire to protect, governments do not always think through the consequences of market regulation. For example, tenancy regulations may limit the availability of land for leasing, and minimum wages may reduce employment (particularly for the less productive labourers).

Finally, we ask whether externalities provide a reason in this context for government intervention for social security. In order to illustrate the issues we consider only two cases—the environment and relative incomes. Environmental degradation arising from the actions of one group may have dramatic effects on the security of others. For example, it is argued that deforestation and consequent soil erosion in Nepal contribute significantly to the silting of rivers and thus the size and probability of floods in Bangladesh. One cannot expect the market to cope with externalities on this scale. Not even the most fervent devotees of the 'Coase theorem' would suggest that the current (and future) peasants and landless labourers of Bangladesh, recognizing the potential for a Pareto improvement, would seek out their counterparts in Nepal and negotiate on side payments to reduce the amount of silt flowing down from the rivers. Even at the local level, exploitation by individuals of resources on which a community may depend can pose a serious threat to social security. However, at the local level co-operation may be more feasible, as has been shown by the literature on the management of common property resources (Runge 1986; Sugden 1986). Though government may see itself as having a role in preventing or controlling access to large natural resource bases (marine fisheries, for example), evidence would suggest that at a more micro level, such as communal grazing, it may be more effective to support local initiatives and institutions. The greater familiarity in the locality with the complexity of the issues involved can lead to the evolution of mechanisms which may cope adequately with the problems and which are not easily replaced by regulatory mechanisms imposed from outside (Wade 1988; Sugden 1986; Runge 1986; World Bank 1988b; Lewis et al. 1988; Rao et al. 1988).

The second illustration of the problems posed by externalities involves relativity in the determination of welfare. There are those who consider relative income to be an influential aspect of individual welfare. Some individuals may become, or be perceived as, poor not because their absolute income has fallen, but because the income of others is higher whereas theirs has stayed the same, or not risen as much. In this sense the increasing income of others has lowered the welfare of the less well-off. The government may then feel some obligation to compensate those who have not gained. The status of this argument is far from straightforward, and has been the object of some controversy (see Sen 1983; Townsend 1985; Runciman 1966, for a discussion). Notice that it is the negative relation between the perceived welfare of one individual and the income or welfare of another that causes a competitive equilibrium to fail to be Pareto-efficient. Winter (1969) shows how a positive relation between the utility of one individual and that of another will not generally disturb the conclusion that a competitive equilibrium is Pareto-efficient.

3.1.2. *Redistribution*   Whether or not markets are perfect the government may regard the outcomes as unattractive, unsatisfactory, or unjust from a distributional point of view. In these circumstances it may attempt to introduce mechanisms for the redistribution of income, wealth, or assets. The standard theory of welfare economics tells us that the most efficient way to redistribute is through lump-sum taxes and transfers. There are fundamental problems here. It is not because lump-sum taxes and transfers cannot be invented. One could, in principle, have taxes on sex or height, bases which could be changed only by drastic and unusual action. The problem is rather that the desirable set of lump-sum taxes and transfers cannot be implemented without their ceasing to be lump-sum. We may wish to redistribute from rich to poor. This means that the taxes and transfers will be related to income and wealth. Such taxes cannot be lump-sum since individuals will realize the basis of assessment and can then adjust their income and wealth through changes in work or accumulation.

We therefore immediately run into the problem of incentive compatibility. The issue then becomes, in theory, one of trading off efficiency and equity. This has become the subject of a standard literature (see, for example, Atkinson and Stiglitz 1980, or Newbery and Stern 1987), a large part of which builds on the seminal work of Mirrlees (1971). A simple version of the government's problem in these theories can be expressed formally as the maximization of social welfare, subject to the constraint that a given amount of revenue is raised. This revenue constraint will have as a crucial ingredient the responses of individuals to taxation. For example, revenues from indirect taxes depend on consumer demands and from income taxes on factor supplies. These responses we group under the heading of incentives and they can take many different forms depending on the context. Attention has mainly been focused on commodity demands and labour supply but some contributions (for example, Diamond 1977) also examine intertemporal transfers within and between generations.

There are crucial examples, however, where the incentive problems may be of less significance and where focus on them might divert attention from more important issues. Many of these would arise from chronic deprivation. For example, severe disability, such as loss of arms or legs, would be obvious grounds for State support. The relevant personal incentive to self-maim or take less care to prevent accidents is unlikely to be a serious consideration. Similarly widows' pensions are unlikely to lead to a serious rise in the homicide of husbands. The effect of State support on the support provided by others is a different issue to which we return in Section 5.

Given the incentive and administrative problems associated with taxation, a highly uneven distribution of assets (such as land), together with deprivation associated with lack of assets (say, landlessness) may lead a government to consider straightforward redistribution as an alternative. Attempts in this direction, such as those involving land reform, have generally met with strong and often insurmountable opposition (King 1977; Powelson and Stock 1987). The specific examples of land reform and wage bargaining bring into sharp focus the constraints and importance of group bargaining and conflict between interest groups in the determination of social security. Economic and political power is strongly related to ownership, occupation, class, gender, and race and there is thus inherent conflict over control of resources, the outcome of which will largely determine the security of a particular group or individual. The government can thus influence social security by changing the distribution of assets or the conditions of bargaining. The prospects for such interventions, however, are often limited because those who have power tend to be the most able to influence government policy and block redistributive reforms. Serious redistributive measures have typically taken place only in countries which have also witnessed a significant political transformation (see, for example, Chap. 6 below on the crucial importance of land reform for China's social-security system).

3.2. Reasons Outside the Standard Framework for Government Involvement in Social Security

3.2.1. Are Individuals the Best Judges of Their Own Interests?   The preceding theory assumed that individuals are indeed the best judges of their own interests, and the hackles of many economists and others are raised when the contrary is suggested. This irritation is often couched in accusations of paternalism, of violation of liberty, of interference, and so on. There are, however, many examples where individuals do not appear to be, or society does not act as if they are, taking wise decisions from their own standpoint. An obvious example is children (hence the word paternalism). Adults often act to constrain the immediate desires of children, not simply because they may be offensive or destructive, but also because they may be damaging to the future of the child. The argument is that the individual does not understand, or does not act as if he or she understands, that the current action is not in his or her best interests. Society may take analogous action to prevent someone who wants to use drugs and has the money to buy them from actually using them. Important examples where this type of argument appears to have been influential concern compulsory insurance or pension schemes. It is quite common in countries around the world for employment insurance, health insurance, and contributions to pensions to be compulsory (Atkinson 1989). It is not clear that this compulsion can always be justified by invoking the arguments of market failure, which we have discussed above. It seems that the government believes that it has a responsibility to prevent the individual from doing something which might be regarded as short-sighted or irresponsible, and which the individual may subsequently regret. In this sense the government might be seen as acting to reinforce the higher or more responsible self in an individual who may have more than one strand in his or her attitudes and behaviour.

It is not obvious that this kind of compulsion should be regarded as dictatorial or unacceptable. Individuals, for example, when they vote may consciously vote for a government that would impose this compulsion on them because they think they may wish to be protected from themselves. Similarly someone may contract with a slimming or alcohol clinic to be prevented from consuming food or alcohol in the quantity that he or she would wish in the short term.

3.2.2. The Standard of Living   The language and argument of welfare economics suggest individual utility as the object of study (which then may or may not be aggregated into social welfare) and that the level of utility which is achieved by an individual is constrained (and thus determined) by the prices and incomes that individuals face. Hence much of the literature on defining poverty and standard of living focuses on incomes and price indices. The term 'standard of living' can encompass a broader perspective. The ability to be adequately nourished, to avoid preventable morbidity, to escape premature mortality, and so on are obvious candidates for inclusion in the determination of standard of living as perceived by an individual (Sen 1987). Accordingly, indicators of nutritional status, morbidity, and mortality take on special relevance and are frequently used to reflect the conditions of life within a country (see, for example, UNICEF 1989; United Nations 1987; World Bank 1988a). These are not features which are embodied in standard utility analysis as based on revealed preference and market choices. Lives may become adjusted to deprivation. Mechanisms to escape basic deprivations may not be available either through the market mechanism or at the community or household level. Factors such as undernutrition, disease, and poor sanitation may threaten standards of living independently of the level of real income. The government may, then, see itself as having a fundamental role to play in raising the standard of living through various types of direct or indirect interventions which influence nutrition, health, and other constituents of human well-being. The notion of standard of living, and its importance for public policy, are discussed in greater detail in the contribution by Drèze and Sen to this volume (see also Sen 1987, and Drèze and Sen 1989).

3.2.3. Rights   The membership of society may be seen as involving both duties and rights. The duties may involve observance of the law, certain customs of behaviour, military service, amongst others. The rights may involve voting, protection of the law, basic education, health, and housing, and so on (some of these rights may be confirmed in constitutions). The belief that, as members of society, we are entitled to certain fundamental rights is widespread even though the set of rights which are regarded as fundamental may vary. This viewpoint has great practical significance both in terms of the rhetoric and reality of government policy as well as for the perceptions and demands of the citizen.

   A number of aspects of government policy, viewed from the perspective of rights, may be seen as emanating from notions of liberty and equality, and justification for the provision of social security as a basic right may flow from these two ideas. Liberty to pursue one's own life and income opportunities may conflict with ideas of equality of outcomes but for social security the conflict is not so clear. One might argue that equality should operate in the sense of everyone having the right to some basic position from which to pursue the opportunities provided by the liberties while being accorded equal protection against deprivation and adversity. This would appear to be a common theme in Western democracies. Asserted rights might include: the ability to escape serious deprivations (for example, hunger); to live without shame or fear; or to practise important liberties (such as freedom of religion and speech). Important elements of social security might then be regarded as part of the protection of fundamental rights. By fundamental here we mean that it would be wrong for the government to deny these rights even if it were in the general interest to do so.

The assertion of rights involves a basic departure from the objective of maximizing general interest or welfare as embodied in a social welfare function of the type familiar in welfare economics. The objective of treating citizens with equal concern and respect has been expressed in terms of rights to equal treatment and the right to treatment as an equal (Dworkin 1977). Utilitarian arguments (interpreted here in the broad sense which would include the use of a Bergson–Samuelson social welfare function) which might suggest constraints on liberty may violate this conception of equality. Personal preferences and interpersonal judgements, embodied in the Bergson–Samuelson approach, do not provide grounds for distinguishing between individuals if one adopts the viewpoint of rights. If critical weight is attached to these Bergson–Samuelson aspects then the right of everyone to be treated with equal concern and respect may be prejudiced.

3.2.4. *Public Pressure*   The public can exert pressure on the government to provide social security. One can regard this pressure both as a normative justification for social security (if, for example, it embodies a majority) or as a positive exploration of why governments do in fact provide social security. We concentrate on the latter here.

There may be a strong perception on the part of the public that they are entitled to certain basic rights. The consequences of short- or long-term inability to provide for social security can be politically damaging. The survival of a government may depend on its record with regard to the protection of living standards. Even those not directly affected by deprivation or adversity may have motivations which go beyond their own well-being and hence they may rally in support of the deprived. Pressure from individuals, communities, and social or political organizations may provide one of the strongest (positive) reasons for government provison of social security (see Chap. 1 and Drèze and Sen 1989, 1990).

The public may be active both in the dissemination of information to heighten awareness of breaches in social security and in the exertion of pressure to correct them. Drèze (1988a) and Ram (1986) both highlight the role of the press in ensuring early and concerted State action by drawing attention to potential famine situations. It has been argued that some of the differences in success in dealing with Indian and African famines may be traced in part to differences in the freedom to gain access to and disseminate information, and in the ability to exert social and political pressure once alerted (Sen 1988). In a longer-term perspective, success in protecting populations may be traced to the existence of democratic forms of government which make political survival contingent on the maintenance of an adequate standard of living. Violent reactions to the reduction or removal of subsidies seen in countries as diverse as Egypt, Tunisia, Zambia, Bangladesh, and Argentina illustrate the political forces which may be unleashed (Hopkins 1988; Bienen and Gersovitz 1986). People accustomed to a given standard of living may react strongly if the standard becomes threatened. It should, however, be pointed out that political clout does not generally correspond to need, and hence though government action may be elicited (and maintained) it may well be in favour of those not experiencing the most serious deprivation (such as the military or public employees). This appears to be at least partly true, for example, for public food distribution systems in South Asia (see Chap. 7 below; also Sobhan 1986), for food subsidies in Egypt and elsewhere (Alderman 1988a,b; Pinstrup-Andersen 1988) and for formal social-security systems in Latin America and elsewhere (see Chap. 8 below; also de Oliviera et al. 1987; Ahmad 1989; Midgley 1984).

From the perspective of both preventing temporary adversity and removing chronic deprivation it then becomes critical that the needy or threatened have access to institutions or channels of influence by which dissent can be expressed and action instigated (Lewis et al. 1988; Drèze and Sen 1989). The nature and influence of the institutions which exist in a given country, whether they be political (such as opposition parties), social (for example, grass-root organizations) or legal (for example, labour unions), are critical in determining whether the pressure for provision of social security is effective. The empowerment of the poor and their participation in the process of development appear to have been of crucial importance in countries which have had some success in the provision of social security (see Chap. 5 below; also Drèze and Sen 1989; Caldwell 1986; Lewis et al. 1988).

4. WHO SHOULD PROVIDE SOCIAL SECURITY?

The discussion in the preceding section has suggested that there are a number of reasons, many of them strong, for social intervention in the provision of social security. But who should carry out that intervention? Should it be the family (extended or nuclear), the village, the social or religious group, the firm, the city, the province, the national government, or some other entity? Different societies have answered the question in different ways. One part of the answer should be associated with how social security can be most efficiently supplied —different groups have different information, different organizing abilities, different financing capabilities, and different sanctions. Another part of the answer concerns where obligations to help should lie. A number of the questions of efficiency and incentives are taken up in this section and the discussion will be continued in Section 5 when we consider how social security can be provided.

In some Muslim countries charitable provision by religious groups can be of great importance for health, education, and for the alleviation of destitution (see Qureshi 1985). In China the firm and commune have been providers of social security across the board, though this system has undergone fundamental transformation in recent years with the introduction of the 'responsibility system' (see Chap. 6 below and Hussain and Liu 1989). In Israel the trade unions play a major role in providing health services and pensions for a very wide section of the population. In the UK the major responsibility has been taken by the central government, local authorities (concerned with education and some social services) being controlled and heavily subsidized by central government in the provision of services they do supply (Barr 1987). The concept of 'looking after one's own people' appears to be common in a number of communities from supporters of Liverpool Football Club to the Freemasons. Finally, in most countries, the family is for many the first place to turn. Which of these should carry the obligation and which of these can discharge it most efficiently?

Intrahousehold and interhousehold transfers between related or proximate individuals constitute a basic form of social security in developing countries. To a large extent the family or community serves many of the roles carried out by formal institutions in developed countries. As we have noted, information problems and resource constraints make formal institutions difficult to establish or operate effectively in low-income settings (Rosenzweig 1988b). Transfers between related or proximate individuals, for example, have been shown to serve the purposes of risk mitigation, insurance against income shortfalls, support for the elderly in retirement, help during illness, unemployment insurance, educational loans, and financing of rural–urban migration (see Chap. 4 below; also Cox and Jimenez 1989a; Ravallion and Dearden 1988; Rosenzweig 1988b). These transfers represent an important component of household income and expenditure both in traditional village and rural households as well as in urban households (see Chap. 4 below; also Cox and Jimenez 1989a; Kaufman and Lindauer 1984).

The rationale for such provision is unclear, though a greater degree of altruism between related or proximate individuals has been traditionally put forward as an explanation (see Chap. 4 below; also Becker 1974; Cox 1987; Ravallion and Dearden 1988; Sugden 1986). More recently it has been argued that transfer behaviour may result from repeated interactions of self-interested individuals or households in a risky environment, whereby current generosity ensures future reciprocity (Coate and Ravallion 1989). Recent findings in Peru and elsewhere suggest that private transfers are not substituted on a one-for-one basis by public transfers (Cox and Jimenez 1989b). Transfers to those unlikely to reciprocate, such as the disabled, and the finding of an inverse relationship between household income and receipt of transfers in El Salvador and rural Java, where the poorest families tend to be the primary recipients of transfer income, would suggest a strong element of altruism in certain situations (Kaufman and Lindauer 1984; Ravallion and Dearden 1988). Positive relationships have been found by other studies (Cox and Jimenez 1989*b*; Lucas and Stark 1985), and both motives are probably important with self-interested reciprocation increasing in importance as relatedness declines, though clearly the fact that individuals are related or proximate helps to generate trust and facilitates enforcement, thus making sustained reciprocation much more feasible.

It may be argued that a person has special responsibilities toward family members. This may be more than simply the statement that family members are in a position to supply help more efficiently than others. One could reason that being a good member of a family involves much stronger obligations towards others than being a good neighbour, which in turn involves much stronger obligations towards others than being a good member of a village or firm. Further, some bonds may arise from a common religion, occupation, or interest.

The general finding then is that private transfers are significant, do help smooth consumption, and are directed towards the poor, the young, the old, women, the infirm, and the unemployed (Cox and Jimenez 1989*a*). One must then ask how such family and community provisions overcome the difficulties which prevent the establishment or limit the effectiveness of general social-security programmes. It may be argued that the ties of heritage, common background, and altruism which may exist amongst related or proximate persons help to transcend the information problems which confront impersonal markets (Rosenzweig 1988*b*). The immediate family or community may be well placed to judge whether an individual really has fallen on hard times, and thus to deal with the question of fraud, and whether that individual has been careless or indolent in bringing about the difficulties. Further, the sanction of social opprobrium which may arise from fraud or neglect can be very strong within the family or community. From this point of view local entities may be the most efficient suppliers of social security.

Though the family or local community may possess an informational advantage and may thus be able effectively to deal with problems of moral hazard, adverse selection, and the like, insurance and risk-spreading considerations go the other way (see Chap. 4 below). The fact that members of a household or community will tend to be affected by adverse phenomena at the same time (covariate risk, such as drought) places severe constraints on the effectiveness of social-security provision at this level (see Chaps. 4 and 5 below; also Rosenzweig 1988*b*). Insurance is generally most efficiently supplied if the income of the person being insured is not positively correlated with the income of those providing the insurance. Thus if the community falls on bad times it should look for support from outside the community. Rural–urban migration and modernization, which are commonly seen as threats to traditional social-security arrangements, can carry substantial risk-spreading benefits. Diversification of rural activity (for example, into cash crop production or rural industry) and migration (for example, to cities by labourers looking for work, or by women to marry) may both help to mitigate income risk and facilitate consumption-smoothing in agricultural environments characterized by covariate risk (Rosenzweig and Stark 1989; Lucas and Stark 1985; Drèze and Sen 1989).

A second argument for making the provision more distant from the individual concerns the stigma attached to an application for help. It may be much more humiliating for an individual to go to the local group than to a more anonymous body. These more anonymous groups, however, because their information may be poorer, generally involve substantial amounts of administration (see Chap. 6 below).

Given the various difficulties and shortcomings presented so far concerning the provision of social security both at the State and the household or community level, one should consider the role of 'grass-roots' organizations in providing support to the poor and vulnerable. Such organizations, which generally arise from local initiatives, are often oriented towards helping the poor and needy. They also carry the advantage of being able to draw on local information by directly involving the poor, and are often large enough to deal to some extent with covariate risk (see Chap. 5 below for some Indian examples).

Questions of incentives and fraud are usually discussed from the point of view of the individual. However, where several groups may be involved in social security we must ask how the provision by one group may affect the provision by another. This type of incentive is rather different from the individual incentives which have received such prominent analysis in the theoretical and empirical literature for developed countries.

In some circumstances the net effect of State provision may simply be a transfer payment to the entities that would otherwise have provided the assistance. For example, if the State takes over responsibility from a church organization this may act like a transfer payment from the general taxpayer to the church. There may, of course, be other effects in terms of real resources employed in providing the assistance, incentives to the individual, and distributional implications. An assessment of the distributional aspects of this type of incentive will be influenced not only by the incomes of those who would otherwise provide the assistance, but also by the view of who carries the moral obligation for the assistance.

The accumulated empirical evidence, most of which has appeared only recently, strongly suggests that provision of assistance from the State does not result in the complete replacement of the assistance provided by the family or community, though partial displacement is observed (Cox and Jimenez 1989*a,b*). If the State provides a special means of transport for a disabled person this does not mean that the family or local community will automatically cease providing help to that individual. They will probably provide a little less help, but the individual will get a net increase in transport services available to him or her. The government may indeed wish to look for schemes which do provide net additional help to those to whom the scheme is directed, as well as relieving others of the burden of provision. These 'group incentives' should be a crucial element in the design of any scheme. On balance it would seem that there is a role for social provision both at the household or community level and at the government level, especially given the evidence that the different levels are most effective and efficient in insuring against different types of events and that they do not completely displace one another. Again, social and political organizations which provide support somewhere between these two levels would appear to be important both in providing a voice for the poor and vulnerable as well as in serving as an effective alternative source of support which does not depend on the whims or machinations of State bureaucracy.

5. HOW SHOULD SOCIAL SECURITY BE PROVIDED AND WHAT ARE THE PROBLEMS?

5.1. *Costs and Targeting*

Government budgets and the costs of programmes impose severe constraints on what can be achieved by social-security programmes in developing countries. The position is less favourable than for developed countries not only because GNP per capita is low. In addition, raising revenue is more difficult due to the limitations of tax instruments, and often calls on revenue are strong. Both these factors constrain the ability to finance sustained provision of social security at the government, community, and household levels and highlight the importance of self-financing components of different schemes. Further, the problems of low and uncertain standards of living in developing countries affect a very large proportion of the population. The scope and levels of provision seen in developed countries are clearly infeasible (see Chaps. 3 and 7 below).

Examination of costs has led people to consider the importance and role of alternatives, and targeting of limited government resources would appear to be inescapable. Though such arguments have some validity they do evade considerations which should be made explicit. First, how tight in fact is the budget constraint? Does the 'impossibility' of formal social security for all those in need not partly reflect a low priority being attached to such an objective? Could resources, for example, not be transferred out of higher-priority budgets such as defence? Clearly the allocation of government funds is not fixed and may be affected by changes in the perceptions both of government and citizens as to what the priorities of development are. Second, the issue of policy-switching under a fixed budget constraint to improve effectiveness is avoided. Certain programmes (for example, immunization, primary health care) are cost-effective whilst some of the components of formal social-security programmes may simply be inappropriate in developing countries. Third, placing all the onus on the family and community to provide resources for support ignores the important role that government may have in strengthening local institutions which support the poor (see, for example, Lewis *et al.* 1988). Resource constraints are important but there is considerably greater flexibility and scope for innovation than ardent proponents of minimal government would have us believe.

The tightness of existing government budget constraints and the limited opportunities for self-financing schemes do suggest that there will be a high pay-off from making full use of alternative channels of influence. The relative effectiveness of family and community provision of social security (discussed earlier) must be examined and the limitations assessed. Private provision of insurance or of services such as health care represents another mechanism by which dependence on limited government revenue may be avoided. However the association between ability to pay and participation in such schemes casts doubt over whether they would be effective in reaching the truly needy. At worst such schemes may, by reducing contributions or participation by the better-off, divert funds away from public schemes which serve the vulnerable in a more effective manner (for example, private health care). The size of the resource base is critical and for this reason it is essential to examine how different social-security schemes interact with the tax system, other governmental programmes, and informal support (see Chaps. 3 and 9 below; also Ahmad 1989). Despite numerous calls for formal and informal social-security systems to reinforce each other (for example, Midgley 1984), there is little research on the relationship between the two. (See Section 5.3 and Cox and Jimenez 1989*a*, for a review of the available literature on the scope for beneficial co-operation.)

Targeting has recently come to be seen as a major mechanism by which costs can be contained whilst still providing government assistance to those in need (World Bank 1986, 1988*b*), and a spate of mainly theoretical papers reflect the perceived importance of this issue (for example, Besley and Kanbur 1988; Besley 1989; Glewwe 1989; Kanbur 1988; Nichols and Zeckhauser 1982; Ravallion and Chao 1988). Irrespective of the measure which a government chooses to adopt (see Ahmad 1989; Weisbrod 1988, for an examination of some options), it is confronted by a basic dilemma which arises when it tries to provide assistance. If, on the grounds of equity with respect to some particular service, or on the grounds of rights, it tries to make the service available to all people then the costs are likely to be very high and there will be a number of 'non-deserving' beneficiaries. On the other hand if a stringent selection procedure is imposed this will increase the probability that deserving individuals are excluded. Targeting refers to procedures designed to concentrate provision on those individuals who are deserving or needy. The justification for targeting derives in a straightforward manner from a consideration of costs in terms of the attempt to achieve the greatest economy of resources in reaching those for whom support is intended by excluding individuals who do not 'need' the benefit. The success of targeted programmes is intimately linked to how successful the selection procedure is in excluding non-deserving individuals who try to obtain the benefit (for example, rich people receiving an income transfer). This is made difficult by the fact that welfare characteristics are generally unobservable. It is thus important that schemes be incentive-compatible so that potential recipients reveal truthfully such information as they have which is relevant to the policymaker (see Besley 1989; Hammond 1979; and Section 5.3 below).

There is an important sense, however, in which an excessive emphasis on targeting can be dangerous. It may divert our attention from the need to reach all those in need. Weisbrod (1969), for example, has emphasized two aspects of targeting efficiency by examining not only the proportion of needy amongst beneficiaries but also the extent to which the needy are reached.

The arguments against targeting are, in addition to ideas of universal entitlement (for example, to education), also based on administrative costs, 'take-up', and stigma. Many targeting procedures involve substantial administrative costs. The inaccuracy or unreliability of administrative procedures and the dislike by individuals of submitting themselves to testing for eligibility by a bureaucracy can lead to low take-up rates (see Atkinson 1989: Chap. 11). Various authors, following the thinking in the English Poor Laws, see such ordeals as an effective mechanism by which to increase targeting efficiency as those not in need would object to being subjected to a demeaning selection test (Nichols and Zekhauser 1982). However, so might those in need and an important fraction may be deterred. The weaker criterion of the labour test in rural public works programmes would appear to be a more effective form of targeting without the side-effect of low take-up rates although such programmes may be of little help to the most needy who are unable to work—especially the aged, the infirm, and the disabled (Drèze 1988a, 1989).

Self-selection (the central feature of the labour test) does not represent a viable option in a large range of public intervention schemes and the problem then becomes one of targeting with respect to available information. In this context income-testing has often been the main criterion for selection. Important examples include the targeting of subsidized credit, social services, and food. However, maladministration can entail large leakages and has often reduced significantly the effectiveness of such schemes. Given these constraints there is a growing consensus that targeting should not be based solely on income-testing. Regular life cycle contingencies like maternity, sickness, disability, age-related and seasonal undernutrition, unemployment, and old age might be used as more reliable and less costly indicators of the probability of being in need (see Chap. 3 below; also Ahmad 1989). Targeting of benefits may also be based on location of residence or on ethnic identity where deprivation is location- or race-dependent (Garcia and Pinstrup-Andersen 1987; Besley and Kanbur 1988; Anand 1983). In order for there to be significant improvements in targeting performance it is essential that better information on the specific attributes and characteristics of the indigent be gathered (see Drèze 1988b). This requires a better understanding of the processes which lead to deprivation and vulnerability.

There are also important arguments for and against targeting which are based on the need to gather political support for particular programmes. Though targeting assistance to the very needy would appear to carry the greatest moral weight it may be necessary to target benefits to the non-needy who have the political power to force the effective and sustained implementation of any given scheme (for example, the urban élite). In general, any form of targeting may be opposed by those not receiving benefit and this can lead to arguments for universal entitlement. What is clear is that targeting is often based on criteria other than need. In the case, for example, of food subsidies, political clout would appear to be a major consideration in some important examples (Hopkins 1988; Bienen and Gersovitz 1986; Alderman 1988a).

5.2. Administration

In this subsection we comment briefly on two related constraints which often severely limit the implementation of social-security schemes, namely incomplete information and maladministration.

5.2.1. Incomplete Information   Considerations of cost and redistribution lead naturally to targeting of benefits. Given incentives to misrepresent status, administrative selection procedures should be based on observable indicators which are not easily manipulated. Information on the welfare status of individuals, however, is usually highly imperfect (Glewwe 1989). The fact that information on the incomes of all individuals within a population is seldom available limits the scope for means-tested benefits. If the agencies involved have to collect their own data and if the pool of potential claimants is large and the administrative infrastructure needed to collect such information is weak, then the cost of the exercise may escalate to the extent that the potential benefits of the programme are vitiated. Though the problems of incomplete information and limited administrative capability do cloud the prospects for effective provision of social security, various methods for trying to cope with these drawbacks have been devised.

First, household surveys (such as the National Sample Surveys in India and World Bank Living Standard Surveys for various countries) can be used to generate detailed micro-data for a representative sample of households. Close analysis of the sample can then suggest which characteristics provide useful indicators of deprivation, as well as insights into its determinants (Deaton and Case 1987; Cox and Jimenez 1989a). Household micro-data of this type is also essential for the design and testing of tax-benefit models. By examining the interactions between different forms of social security, taxation, and other government programmes within the sample, such models can help policy-makers assess the viability of different schemes and the scope for policy change (see Chap. 3 below; also Ahmad 1989). Household survey data collected over several years can also be used to assess the behavioural responses of households to changes in the form or level of social-security provision (see Section 5.3).

Second, attributes which are 'fixed', costlessly identifiable, and perfectly co-ordinated with poverty represent an ideal choice with respect to both targeting efficiency and administrative capability. To a lesser extent attributes such as landlessness, geographic location, demographic structure, or age can be used effectively to limit coverage and to escape having to collect information on the population as a whole.

Third, problems associated with administrative selection may be by-passed by the use of 'self-targeting' systems, such as a work requirement, to screen out non-needy individuals (see Section 5.3). Subsidies to foods which are consumed mainly by the poor could provide another mechanism of targeting, although it is likely to be less precise.

5.2.2. Diversion by Administration   Though the decisions of policy-makers may aim at the removal of deprivation or protection from adversity, there is no guarantee that this objective is shared by the agency which actually implements the policy. Information on, and control of, the performance of the intervening agency is limited. Hence there may be considerable scope for corruption or misappropriation by agency officials who hold their interests above those of the target group and whose wages will not usually depend on performance in reaching the needy. One might improve incentive compatibility by devising contracts which make the agents' wage dependent on an indicator of targeting performance (Ravallion 1989b), although this system itself could, no doubt, be manipulated.

There may be a less attractive version of 'self-targeting' inherent in administrative behaviour. An obvious and empirically important example of this concerns the case where formal social-security benefits are linked to employment in formal-sector enterprises. Such employees are typically better off than the poor, many of whom are either self-employed in the informal sector, or unemployed, and the system can be both ineffective in reaching the poor and regressive (see Chap. 8 below; also Mackenzie 1988; Midgley 1984). Because the administration holds the purse strings and because internal political support for such measures can be strong and entrenched, there is a tendency not only for such practices to survive but also for them to proliferate so that in addition to social-security payments they also cover life insurance, pensions, food rations, and so on (see Chap. 8 below; also Midgley 1984). The fiscal consequences of this form of 'capture' by non-deserving beneficiaries can be severe (see Ahmad 1989).

5.3. *Incentives*

We consider here three types of incentives: group incentives; the incentive to cheat; the incentive to reduce effort. The first involves the relationship between government support and other forms of support. The second concerns the problem of fraudulent claims for support and the third concerns the possible reduction of effort or care as a result of the insurance or promise of support if things go wrong.

5.3.1. *Group Incentives* In an investigation of the relation between government and other forms of support, a first step is an analysis of the extent, nature, and determinants of household or community provision of social security. This task is complicated by the fact that such forms of support are numerous and poorly documented. Further, many may be specific to certain circumstances. Comprehensiveness cannot be expected and we will have to proceed by examining a few important examples. We look at just two here, one is the support of the elderly, and the other is single-lineage villages in South China.

Old age is for most or many a period of low or zero private income and increased health risks. Support for the elderly has been one of the main elements of social-security programmes in developed countries (see Chap. 3 below; also Atkinson 1989). In developing countries State support for the indigent elderly is generally lacking and the elderly are supported mainly by the family or community (Ahmad 1989; Guhan 1988; Midgley 1984). Evidence on transfers gleaned from survey data for Malaysia (Butz and Stan 1982), Java (Ravallion and Dearden 1988), and Kenya (Knowles and Anker 1981) strongly indicates that significant transfers flow, within the family or community, from the young to the old (see Cox and Jimenez 1989a, for a review). In addition to income support, families also represent the main source of health care for the elderly (Cox and Jimenez 1989a; Hussain and Liu 1989). Provision for those indigent elderly who do not receive family support is often the responsibility of the community, as is largely the case with *wubao* relief in China (see Chap. 6 below; also Hussain and Liu 1989). Provision for the elderly by the family or community may be limited by factors such as urbanization, the breakup of extended families, and increased dependency ratios arising from the ageing of populations.

In the design of policy for supporting the elderly one should know what effect State provision of social security might have on support by the household or community. Households could, for example, reduce support for the elderly if the sole criterion for transfers is the perceived welfare of recipients. If the reduction were one-for-one with public provision of benefits, the effect on the well-being of the elderly might be negligible (see Becker 1974; Barro 1974). Attention would still need to be given to households who receive no support initially. Note that this displacement may not be inconsistent with the achievement of other policy objectives such as population control, that is to say, if individuals can rely on the State for support in their old age they may have fewer children (Nugent 1985). If, however, support for the elderly partly represents some form of intertemporal exchange of services or resources then a complete displacement would not be expected and state provision of social security would carry a net benefit to the elderly (Cox and Jimenez 1989b). Recent evidence from Peru suggests that provision of social security or public health benefits to elderly households does reduce their chance of receiving transfers from other households but such displacement is by no means sufficient to neutralize public policy (Cox and Jiminez 1989b). Those who design schemes for support should look for transfer mechanisms which avoid the withdrawal of help by others (for example, one would favour, ceteris paribus, support for the elderly which kept them within their own communities). On the other hand, if those who would otherwise provide support are also very poor then relieving them of a burden would itself reduce deprivation.

Single-lineage villages (all sharing the same family name) were, and still are, fairly common south of the Yangtze, especially in South-East China. Prior to liberation in 1949, lineages held a certain amount of common property, which was used for the support of corporate activities. These corporate activities consisted of the building and the maintenance of ancestral temples, organizing ancestral rites, providing schooling for the children of the lineage, and occasionally helping the poor members of the lineage. Following the take-over of power by the Communists, the corporate substructure of lineages was disbanded. The social welfare activities financed by the common property of the lineage became the responsibility of the village. Parish and Whyte (1978) point out that during the era of collective agriculture, communal social welfare provisions such as rural health insurance and education were better organized and more extensive in single-lineage villages than in multi-lineage villages. Although lineage organizations were disbanded, lineage continued to exercise influence during the collectivist era. Following the shift to household farming, lineage organizations have revived, and in Guangdong and Fujian the expatriate members of lineages have financed the rebuilding of temples, hospitals, and schools in their ancestral villages. The web of allegiance between lineage members thus not only appears to have enhanced the effectiveness of State intervention in the collectivist period but has also proven to be a viable alternative to State support both prior to the gaining of power by the Communist Government in 1949 and after the recent economic reforms (1979). (For further details see Freedman 1965, 1966 and Parish and Whyte 1978—we are grateful to Athar Hussain for this example.)

5.3.2. *Cheating*   Any system can be fiddled. However, some systems may be more easily fiddled than others and it may be important to consider the potential problems in this direction when social-security systems are designed. Certainly this is a common question which is asked of any tax system. For example, it is often suggested that the value added tax (VAT) has an administrative advantage in that the claim for credit for tax paid on inputs can be checked against the declaration, or lack of it, of tax collected on output supplied by the firm providing the inputs.

There are a number of mechanisms which might be designed to avoid fraud. First, there may be a cost in meeting the requirement for eligibility. An obvious and important example concerns public works programmes. An individual has to present himself or herself and be available for labour at a certain place. Those who are better off, or with a higher value of time, may not be prepared to claim payment in such circumstances. Second, the form of benefits transferred to the needy may be designed to avoid fraud. Examples might include medical treatment and food for the malnourished. Third, we may look for cross-checks of the kind mentioned in the case of the VAT. One may, for example, try to construct a system of records which prevents two separate children claiming assistance for support of an elderly parent. Fourth, one may try to base the eligibility for assistance on certain characteristics which are fairly easily identified. Examples may be widowhood or physical disability. Fifth, one may depend more strongly on local bodies which are in a better position to detect fraud.

Whilst one should look for systems which will reduce the risk of fraud it is clear that this will remain a substantial problem. If eligibility requires a piece of paper, then pieces of paper can be produced. And those administering the system may be in a position to divert funds. As a partial check one may want to compare assistance given against the overall number of people in the locality with certain characteristics, that is, a macro or statistical scrutiny. But these figures can be misrepresented and in any case funds within a correct aggregate total can be misused.

We must ask ourselves, however, how far these problems of fraud undermine the case for particular social-security measures. The answer surely depends on the magnitude and type of fraud. If all funds intended for the poor and insecure are going to the rich and secure (possibly at the expense of the former) then presumably the abolition of the system would represent an improvement. But how much diversion, and to whom, would justify an argument for abandonment of the system? There cannot be general answers to such questions and careful evaluation of schemes *ex ante* and *ex post* is required.

5.3.3. *Reduction of Effort, Care, or Savings* In many Western countries it is argued that unemployment insurance makes people work less hard whilst on the job (because they are less worried about losing it), and put less effort into finding a job, than would be the case if there was no support at all for the unemployed. The empirical literature is hard to evaluate (Atkinson 1989), but in theory the possibility is real and many have claimed that the problems of incentives in practice have been very substantial. Similar arguments have been made concerning sick pay, where it is argued that those who receive pay are sick more often and take longer to return to work (Krueger 1990). These problems of incentives have to be traded off against the equity and protection benefits provided by the insurance. This is essentially the standard problem of optimal policy which has been the concern of the literature on optimal taxation. (It is not possible to provide an extended discussion here but see Mirrlees 1971; Atkinson and Stiglitz 1980; Newbery and Stern 1987; Stern 1984). That literature focuses on the equity–efficiency trade-offs and typically ignores the administrative problems which loom even larger in developing countries than they do in developed.

These incentive problems have, in many respects, dominated the econometric literature on social security for developed countries (Atkinson 1989; Katz and Meyer 1990; Krueger 1990; Moffitt 1990). Empirical work for developing countries has been much less substantial. A major reason for this is lack of data. The kind of data that are necessary for detailed analysis of these problems are the most unlikely to be available. It takes a sophisticated and reliable household survey to provide real information on how receipt of benefit affects various aspects of household behaviour. Recent initiatives to collect this type of data by organizations such as the World Bank and by national governments should help to shed some light on this complex subject. The other possible source is official data from those authorities which are administering social-security schemes such as unemployment benefit or health insurance. As there are so few schemes of this type data is not generally available. It is very difficult, therefore, for those designing schemes for developing countries to form a judgement on the extent of these incentive problems. Also different types of incentives may be of greater significance in developing countries. For example, one might want to account for behavioural responses to the relative price effects of social-security schemes in the design of policy. One conclusion one might draw is that it would be prudent to start with a few experiments in which these problems can be evaluated first, rather than embarking on major economy-wide programmes. At the same time one has to draw what lessons might be available from the empirical work on developed countries and see how they might be applied to developing countries (see Chap. 3 below).

6. CONCLUDING COMMENTS

This paper examined a number of basic issues related to the provision of social security in developing countries. In particular, we have attempted to clarify what social security means, why public action in this field is important, who is best placed to carry out different types of social-security measures, and how social-security programmes can be implemented in practice. We hope that elements of the analysis we have provided for these difficult questions, taken together, constitute a useful framework for the study of social security in developing countries.

6.1. *What*

We have defined our subject as the contribution of public action, be it at the household, community, or State level, to the prevention of very low standards of living. This represents a departure from the government programme-based approach which is standard in the developed country literature (see Chap. 3 below; also Atkinson 1989), and which has been adopted for various developing countries (see Chap. 8 below; also Midgley 1984). A number of aspects of the problem in developing countries, which include the greater severity and pervasiveness of threats to living standards, the lack of conventional social-security programmes, severe resource constraints, a low degree of institutional development, and the relative powerlessness of the poor and vulnerable, would seem to indicate the desirability of a broader approach centred on objectives. Given the restricted prospects for government intervention, the State should not be viewed as the sole provider of social security. Contributions of the household and community assume considerable importance as do interactions between groups which have some responsibility for the provision of social security.

6.2. *Why*

The first major set of arguments concerned market failure. Most people depend to some degree on markets for their livelihood (through labour, for example) and for protection against adversity (for example, through credit). Deprivation and vulnerability may thus result where these markets do not exist or do not function well. The theory of market failure led us to identify several important ways in which governments may intervene in market functioning to improve social security. Given that insurance markets are generally missing in developing countries we saw that the provision of credit or employment may be useful in serving a similar function. Interventions in capital markets can provide the needy with the ability to smooth consumption. Greater access to credit may also allow the poor to engage in productive activities and asset accumulation which may entail long-term benefits as regards levels of living. Interventions in the labour market, such as through the guarantee of employment on public work schemes or through the promotion of non-farm employment opportunities, can provide basic security to those who are able to work. Direct transfers could then be directed mainly at those unable to work (such as the disabled or infirm).

The correction of externalities which are detrimental to social security (such as environmental degradation) may constitute a rationale for government intervention. In the case of environmental externalities, however, the scope for intervention was seen to be limited by difficulties associated with attempts to impose cooperation.

Governments may also wish to alter highly uneven distributions of income, wealth, or assets. Redistribution and the raising of revenue via taxes and transfers raise problems of information, administration, and fraud as well as those of incentives to work, save, and so on. More straightforward redistribution (for example, through land reform) often leads to conflict, political turmoil, and the abandonment of reform.

Another major set of arguments for governments to provide social security included paternalism, the distinction between utility and living standard, and the concept of basic human rights. These may lead governments to acknowledge a duty to provide individuals with protection against certain basic deprivations (such as hunger) and access to certain opportunities (such as education). Exertion of pressure by the public in demanding these rights constitutes a major mechanism by which State action may be elicited and maintained. Institutions which facilitate the expression of popular dissent can help sustain a reallocation of resources towards the poor.

We noted that the democratic process can provide a justification for social security if that is what a majority desire. As ever, one has to check that this argument does not cut across basic rights. The normative argument involving democracy should be distinguished from the positive one which points to the role of public pressure in generating and sustaining government response.

6.3. *Who*

It is neither feasible nor desirable for the State to be the sole provider of social security. Other agencies, family, community, firm, religious group, and so on will have roles to play, and complementarities and trade-offs between State support and other sources of social security require careful examination. An important question here relates to which groups can provide particular types of security most effectively or efficiently. Issues of information, incentives, and risk-pooling are relevant in this context. Generally individual security depends greatly on support by the family and community. We examined the ways in which proximate or related individuals and local institutions might provide workable mechanisms for overcoming the information and incentive problems which confront government agencies. Local institutions may also be more able to stimulate and to respond to local initiatives and to allow the indigent poor to be active agents in the implementation of policy. On the other hand we note that larger bodies such as central government have the ability to deal with collective risks and possess greater resources and potential for redistribution. A combination of efforts to deal effectively with the various types of risk affecting the indigent is thus desirable.

6.4. *How*

Given the different forms which social security might take, the different reasons why it might be proposed or demanded, and the different agencies by whom it could be delivered, it is clear that the answer to the question 'how' cannot be general. We focused our discussion on the many problems of social security in practice, including information and administrative costs, fraud by the bureaucracy, cheating by claimants, and disincentives to individual initiative or care. Limited revenues and high costs mean that sources of finance and the efficient use of resources should be central. The criteria for the assessment of interventions would include administrative feasibility, incentive effects, cost, effectiveness in reaching the needy, political acceptability, and so on. If extra benefits are to be provided then the incidence, coverage, and potential for extra taxation at the central and local level must be considered if the overall impact of any scheme on incomes and welfare is to be evaluated.

We emphasized that criteria for the eligibility of beneficiaries should, as far as possible, be clear in principle, easily measured or identified in practice, and closely correlated with the incidence of hardship. In this sense they should be well targeted. At the same time, we pointed to the dangers of an excessive emphasis on targeting in that large numbers of the needy might be overlooked or excluded. Important examples of groups which might be targeted are those who may find it difficult to work such as the disabled, infirm, or widows. For those who can work, self-targeting mechanisms such as employment guarantee schemes at 'subsistence' wages can be effective.

The nuts and bolts of social-security provision require a great deal of further attention, and we hope that the case-studies included in the second part of this book provide useful clues as to the most important areas of practical enquiry.

6.5. *When*

We have seen that the arguments for social security are strong and the problems in provision severe. It is surely a topic of fascination and importance for research. Having asked 'what, why, who, and how', it is perhaps obvious that we have left out 'when'. The severity and extent of deprivation surely dictate a very prompt response and, whilst intellectual enquiry should inform action, this may be an outstanding example where we shall have to do our learning by doing.

References

Ahmad, S. E. (1989), 'Social Security and Poverty Alleviation: Issues for Developing Countries', mimeo, World Bank, Washington, DC.

Alderman, H. (1988a), 'Do Food Subsidies Reach the Poor?', mimeo, International Food Policy Research Institute, Washington, DC.

—— (1988b), 'Food Subsidies and State Policies in Egypt', in A. Richards (ed.), *Food, States and Peasants: Analysis of the Agrarian Question in the Middle East*. Boulder, Colo.: Westview.

Anand, S. (1983), *Inequality and Poverty in Malaysia: Measurement and Decomposition*. Oxford: Oxford University Press.

Atkinson, A. B. (1987), 'On the Measurement of Poverty', *Econometrica*, 55.

—— and Stiglitz, J. E. (1980), *Lectures in Public Economics*. New York: McGraw Hill.

—— (1989), *Poverty and Social Security*. Hemel Hempstead: Harvester Wheatsheaf.

Bardhan, P. K. (1988), *The Economic Theory of Agrarian Institutions*. Oxford: Clarendon Press.

—— and Srinivasan, T. N. (eds.) (1974), *Poverty and Income Distribution in India*. Calcutta: Statistical Publishing Society.

Barr, N. (1987), *The Economics of the Welfare State*. London: Weidenfeld & Nicolson.

Barro, R. J. (1974), 'Are Government Bonds Net Wealth?', *Journal of Political Economy*, 82.

Becker, C. S. (1974), 'A Theory of Social Interactions', *Journal of Political Economy*, 82.

Bell, C. (1988), 'Credit Markets and Interlinked Transactions', in H. B. Chenery and T. N. Srinivasan (eds.), *Handbook of Development Economics*, i. Amsterdam: North-Holland.

—— (1989), 'Credit and Saving', mimeo, World Bank, Washington, DC.

Besley, T. (1989), 'Targeting Taxes and Transfers: Administrative Costs and Policy Design in Developing Economies', paper presented at the World Bank Conference on Agriculture, Development Policies, and the Theory of Rural Organization, Washington, DC.

—— and Kanbur, R. (1988), 'Food Subsidies and Poverty Alleviation', *Economic Journal*, 98.

Bhende, M. J. (1983), 'Credit Markets in the Semi-arid Tropics of Rural South India', Economics Programme Progress Report No. 56, ICRISAT, Hyderabad.

Bienen, H., and Gersovitz, M. (1986), 'Consumer Subsidy Cuts, Violence and Political Stability', *Comparative Politics*, 19/1.

Binswanger, H. P., Balaramaiah, T., Rao, V. B., Bhende, M. J., and Kashirsagar, K. V. (1985), 'Credit Markets in Rural South India: Theoretical Issues and Empirical Analysis', Research Report ARU 45, Agriculture and Rural Development Department, World Bank, Washington DC.

Bliss, C. J., and Stern, N. H. (1978), 'Productivity, Wages and Nutrition, Part I: The Theory' and 'Part II: Some Observations', *Journal of Development Economics*, 5.

Braverman, A., and Guasch, J. L. (1986), 'Rural Credit Markets and Institutions in Developing Countries: Lessons for Policy Analysis from Practice and Modern Theory', *World Development*, 14.

Braverman, A., and Guasch, J. L. (1989), 'Rural Credit in Developing Countries', Population Planning and Research Working Paper No. 219, World Bank, Washington, D.C.

Butz, W. P. and Stan, P. J. E. (1982), 'Household Compensation and Inter-Household Exchange in Malaysia', *Population and Development Review*, 8.

Caldwell, J. C. (1986), 'Routes to Low Mortality in Poor Countries', *Population and Development Review*, 12.

Chambers, R., Longhurst, R., and Pacey, A. (eds.) (1981), *Seasonal Dimensions of Rural Poverty*. London: Francis Pinter.

Coate, S., and Ravallion, M. (1989), 'Repricocity Without Commitment: Characterization and Performance of Non-Cooperative Risk Sharing', mimeo, World Bank, Washington, DC.

Cornia, G., Jolly, R., and Stewart, F. (eds.) (1987), *Adjustment with a Human Face*. Oxford: Clarendon Press.

Cox, D. (1987), 'Motives for Private Income Transfers', *Journal of Political Economy*, 95.

—— and Jimenez, E. (1989a), 'Social Objectives through Private Transfers: A Review', mimeo, Public Economics Division, World Bank, Washington, DC.

—— (1989b), 'The Connection between Social Security and Private Transfers in Peru', Public Economics Division, World Bank, Washington, DC.

Dandekar, K. (1983), *Employment Guarantee Scheme: An Employment Opportunity for Women*. Pune: Orient Longman.

Danziger, S. H., and Weinberg, D. H. (eds.) (1986), *Fighting Poverty*. Cambridge, Mass.: Harvard University Press.

Datt, G., and Ravallion, M. (1988), 'Wage Bargaining and Income Distribution in India: Measuring Unequal Power', mimeo, Department of Economics, Australian National University.

Deaton, A. (1988), 'Household Behavior in Developing Countries', Occasional Paper No. 1, Economic Growth Center, Yale University.

—— (1989), 'Saving in Developing Countries: Theory and Review', paper presented at the First Annual World Bank Conference on Economic Development, 27–8 Apr. 1989, Washington, DC.

—— and Case, A. (1987), 'Analysis of Household Expenditures', Living Standards Measurement Study No. 28, World Bank, Washington, DC.

de Janvry, A., Sadoulet, E., and Wilcox, L. (1986), 'Rural Labour in Latin America', mimeo, Rural Employment Research Programme, World Employment Programme, Geneva.

de Oliviera, F., Henriques, M.-H., and Beltrao, K. I. (1987), 'The Brazilian Social Security System', mimeo, World Bank, Washington, DC.

Diamond, P. A. (1977), 'A Framework for Social Security Analysis', *Journal of Public Economics*, 8.

Dworkin, R. (1977), *Taking Rights Seriously*. London: Duckworth.

Drèze, J. P. (1988a), 'Famine Prevention in India', Discussion Paper No. 3, Development Economics Research Programme, London School of Economics; to be published in Drèze and Sen (1990).

—— (1988b), 'Social Security in India', paper presented at a Workshop on Social Security in Developing Countries held at the London School of Economics, July 1988.

—— (1989), 'Famine Prevention in Africa', Discussion Paper No. 17, Development Economics Research Programme, London School of Economics.

—— and Mukherjee, A. (1987), 'Labour Contracts in Rural India: Theories and Evidence', Discussion Paper No. 7, Development Economics Research Programme, London School of Economics.

—— and Sen, A. K. (1989), *Hunger and Public Action*. Oxford: Clarendon Press.

(eds.) (1990), *The Political Economy of Hunger*. Oxford: Oxford University Press.

Fields, G. (1980), *Poverty, Inequality and Development*. Cambridge: Cambridge University Press.

Freedman, M. (1965), *Lineage Organization in Southeastern China*. London: Routledge & Kegan Paul.

—— (1966), *Chinese Lineage and Society*. London: Routledge & Kegan Paul.

Garcia, M., and Pinstrup-Andersen, P. (1987), 'The Pilot Food Price Subsidy Scheme in the Phillipines: Its Impact on Income, Food Consumption and Nutritional Status', Research Report No. 61, International Food Policy Research Institute, Washington, DC.

Gersovitz, M. (1988), 'Saving and Development', in H. B. Chenery and T. N. Srinivasen (eds.), *Handbook of Development Economics*, i. Amsterdam: North Holland.

Glewwe, P. (1989), 'Targeting Assistance to the Poor: Efficient Allocation of Transfers when Household Incomes are Unobservable', mimeo, World Bank, Washington, DC.

Guhan, S. (1988), 'Social Security in India: Looking One Step Ahead', *Bulletin of the Madras Development Seminar Series*, 18.

Halstead, S. B., Walsh, J. A., and Warren, K. S. (eds.) (1985), *Good Health at Low Cost*. New York: Rockefeller Foundation.

Hammond, P. J. (1979), 'Straightforward Individual Incentive Compatability in Large Economies', *Review of Economic Studies*, 46.

Harvard School of Public Health (1985), *Hunger in America: The Growing Epidemic*. Boston: Harvard University Press.

Hopkins, R. (1988), 'Political Considerations in Subsidizing Food', in P. Pinstrup-Anderson (ed.), *Consumer-Oriented Food Subsidies: Costs, Benefits and Policy Options for Developing Countries*. Baltimore: Johns Hopkins.

Hossain, M. (1986), 'Credit for Alleviation of Rural Poverty: The Experience of Grameen Bank in Bangladesh', Research Report No. 65. International Food Policy Research Institute, Washington, DC.

Huppi, M., and Feder, G. (1989), 'The Role of Groups and Credit Cooperatives in Rural Lending', mimeo, Agriculture and Rural Development Department, World Bank, Washington, DC.

Hussain, A., and Liu A. (1989), 'Compendium of Literature on the Chinese Social Security System', Chinese Programme No. 3, Development Economics Research Programme, London School of Economics.

Jimenez, E., and Puffert, D. (1988), 'The Macroeconomics of Social Security in Brazil: Fiscal and Financial Considerations', mimeo, World Bank, Washington, DC.

Kanbur, R. (1988), 'The Principles of Targeting', mimeo, Department of Economics, University of Warwick.

Katz, L. F., and Meyer, B. D. (1990), 'The Impact of the Potential Duration of

Unemployment Benefits on the Duration of Unemployment', forthcoming in *Journal of Public Economics*, 41/1.

Kaufmann, D., and Lindauer, D. L. (1984), 'Income Transfers Within Extended Families to Meet Basic Needs: The Evidence from El Salvador', World Bank Staffing Paper No. 644, World Bank, Washington, DC.

King, R. (1977), *Land Reform*. London: C. Bell & Sons.

Knowles, J. C., and Anker, R. (1981), 'An Analysis of Income Transfers in a Developing Country', *Journal of Development Economics*, 8.

Kotlikoff, L. J. (1987), 'Social Security', in J. Eatwell, N. Milgate, and P. Newman (eds.), *The New Palgrave: A Dictionary of Economics*, iv. London: Macmillan.

Krueger, A. B., (1990), 'Incentive Effects of Workers Compensation Insurance', *Journal of Public Economics* (forthcoming).

Lewis, J. P. *et al.* (1988), *Strengthening the Poor: What Have We Learned?* Washington, DC: Transaction Books for ODA.

Lipton, M. (1988), 'The Poor and the Poorest: Some Interim Findings', World Bank Discussion Paper No. 25, World Bank, Washington DC.

Longhurst, R., Chambers, R., and Swift, J. (eds.) (1986), 'Seasonality and Poverty: Implications for Poverty and Research', *IDS Bulletin*, 17.

Lucas, R. E. B., and Stark, O. (1985), 'Motivations to Remit: Evidence from Botswana', *Journal of Political Economy*, 93.

Mackenzie, G. A. (1988), 'Social Security Issues in Developing Countries: The Latin American Experience', IMF Working Paper No. 21, Washington, DC.

Midgley, J. (1984), *Social Security, Inequality and the Third World*. Chichester: John Wiley & Sons.

Mirrlees, J. A. (1971), 'An Exploration of the Theory of Optimum Income Taxation', *Review of Economic Studies*, 38.

Moffitt, R. (1990), 'The Effect of the U.S. Welfare System on Marital Status', forthcoming in *Journal of Public Economics*, 41/1.

Murray, C. (1984), *Losing Ground: American Social Policy 1950–1980*. New York: Basic Books.

Newbery, D. M. G., and Stern, N. H. (eds.) (1987), *The Theory of Taxation for Developing Countries*. Oxford: Oxford University Press.

—— and Stiglitz, J. E. (1981), *The Theory of Commodity Price Stabilization*. Oxford: Oxford University Press.

Nichols, A., and Zekhauser, R. (1982), 'Targeting Transfers through Restrictions on Recipients', *American Economic Review*, 72.

Nugent, J. B. (1985), 'The Old Age Motive for Fertility', *Population and Development Review*, 11.

Parish, W., and Whyte, M. K. (1978), *Village and Family Life in Contemporary China*. Chicago: Chicago University Press.

Pinstrup-Andersen, P. (1988), *Food Studies in Developing Countries*. Baltimore: Johns Hopkins University Press.

—— (ed.) (forthcoming), *The Political Economy of Food and Nutrition*. Baltimore: Johns Hopkins University Press.

Powelson, J. P. and Stock, R. (1987), *The Peasant Betrayed: Agriculture and Land Reform in the Third World*. Boston: Oelgeschlager, Gunn, and Hain.

Puffert, D. J. (1988), 'Social Security Finance in Developing Countries', Policy Planning and Research Working Paper No. 36, World Bank, Washington DC.

Qureshi, M. L. (1985), 'Zakat and Ushr System for Relief and Rehabilitation of the Poor in Pakistan', in S. Mukhopapadhyay (ed.), *Case Studies on Poverty Programmes in Asia*. Kuala Lumpur: Asian and Pacific Development Centre.

Ram, N. (1986), 'An Independent Press and Anti-Hunger Strategies: The Indian Experience', paper presented at a Conference on Food Strategies held at the World Institute for Development Economics Research, Helsinki, July 1986; to be published in Drèze and Sen (1990).

Rao, C. H. H., Ray, S. K., and Subbarao, K. (1988), *Unstable Agriculture and Droughts: Implications for Policy*. New Delhi: Vikas.

Ravallion, M. (1988), 'Expected Poverty under Risk-induced Welfare Variability', *Economic Journal*, 98.

——(1989a), 'On the Coverage of Public Employment Schemes for Poverty Alleviation', forthcoming in *Journal of Development Economics*.

——(1989b), 'Constraints on Poverty Alleviation: Information, Incentives and Targeting', note for Poverty Research Group Meeting, World Bank, Washington, DC.

——and Dearden, L. (1988), 'Social security in a "Moral Economy": An Empirical Analysis for Java', *Review of Economics and Statistics*, 70.

——and Chao, K. (1988), 'Targeted Policies for Poverty Alleviation under Imperfect Information: Algorithms and Applications', mimeo, Australian National University.

Rosenzweig, M. (1988a), 'Labour Markets in Low-income Countries', in H. B. Chenery and T. N. Srinivasan, (eds.), *Handbook of Development Economics*, i. Amsterdam: North Holland.

——(1988b), 'Risk, Implicit Contracts and the Family in Rural Areas of Low-Income Countries', *Economic Journal*, 98.

——and Stark, O. (1989), 'Consumption Smoothing, Migration and Marriage: Evidence from Rural India', *Journal of Political Economy*, 97.

Runciman, W. G. (1966), *Relative Deprivation and Social Justice*. London: Routledge.

Runge, C. T. (1986), 'Common Property and Collective Action in Economic Development', *World Development*, 14.

Ryan, J., and Walker, T. (forthcoming), *Against the Odds: Village and Household Economies in India's Semi-Arid Tropics*. Baltimore: Johns Hopkins.

Sawhill, I. V. (1988), 'Poverty in the US: Why is It so Persistent?', *Journal of Economic Literature*, 26.

Schultz, T. P. (1988), 'Education Investments and Returns', in H. Chenery and T. N. Srinivasan (eds.), *Handbook of Development Economics*, i. Amsterdam: North Holland.

Sen, A. K. (1976), 'Poverty: An Ordinal Approach to Measurement', *Econometrica*, 44.

——(1983), 'Poor, Relatively Speaking', *Oxford Economic Papers*, 35.

——(1985), 'A Sociological Approach to the Measurement of Poverty: A Reply to Professor Townsend', *Oxford Economic Papers*, 37.

——(1987), *The Standard of Living*, Tanner Lectures with discussion by J. Muellbauer and others (ed. C. Hawthorn). Cambridge: Cambridge University Press.

——(1988), 'Africa and India: What Do We Have to Learn from Each Other?', in K. J. Arrow (ed.), *The Balance between Industry and Agriculture in Economic Development*, i, *Basic Issues*. London: Macmillan.

Sobhan, R. (1986), 'Politics of Hunger and Entitlements', paper presented at a Conference on Food Strategies held at the World Institute for Development Economics Research, Helsinki, July 1986; to be published in Drèze and Sen (1990).

Srinivasan, T. N., and Bardhan, P. K. (eds.) (1988), *Rural Poverty in South Asia*. New York: Columbia University Press.

Stern, N. H. (1984), 'Optimum Taxation and Tax Policy', IMF Staff Papers, 3/12.

Stiglitz, J., and Weiss, A. (1981), 'Credit Rationing in Markets with Imperfect Information', *American Economic Review*, 71.

Sugden, R. (1986), *The Economics of Rights, Co-operation and Welfare*. Oxford: Basil Blackwell.

Townsend, P. (1979), 'The Development of Research on Poverty', in Department of Health and Social Security, *Social Science Research: The Distribution and Measurement of Poverty*. London: HMSO.

——(1985), 'A Sociological Approach to the Measurement of Poverty: A Rejoinder to Professor Amartya Sen', *Oxford Economic Papers*, 37.

UNICEF (1989), *The State of the World's Children 1989*. Oxford: Oxford University Press.

United Nations (1987), *First Report on the World Nutrition Situation*, Administrative Committee on Coordination, Subcommittee on Nutrition, United Nations, Rome.

von Pishke, J. P., Adams, D. W., and Donald, G. (eds.) (1983), *Rural Financial Markets in Developing Countries*. Baltimore: Johns Hopkins.

Wade, R. (1988), *Village Republics*. Cambridge: Cambridge University Press.

Weisbrod, B. A. (1969), 'Collective Action and the Distribution of Income: A Conceptual Approach', in *The Analysis and Evaluation of Public Expenditures*, Joint Economic Committee, US Government Printing Office, Washington, DC.

——(1988), 'The Role of Government in the Provision of Social Services in Developing Countries', mimeo, World Bank, Washington, DC.

Winter, S. G. (1969), 'A Simple Remark on the Second Optimality Theorem of Welfare Economics', *Journal of Economic Theory*, 1.

World Bank (1986), *Poverty and Hunger: Issues and Options for Food Security in Developing Countries*. Washington, DC: World Bank.

——(1988a), *Social Indicators of Development 1988*. Washington, DC: World Bank.

——(1988b), *The World Bank's Support for the Alleviation of Poverty*. Washington, DC: World Bank.

3

Social Security in Developed Countries: Are There Lessons for Developing Countries?*

A. B. Atkinson and John Hills

1. INTRODUCTION

This book is concerned with the strategies open to developing countries to use public action to protect the living standards of the poor. The relevant strategies encompass a wide range of possible policy measures, including asset redistribution, food distribution, agrarian reform, and public works programmes. The focus of this chapter is on the measures that have emerged as components of the social-security systems of developed countries (these were referred to in the Preface to this book as 'formal' social-security measures). We shall consider the lessons that developing countries may or may not be able to draw from the experience of developed countries in devising social-security systems.

It is evident at the outset that such lessons are unlikely to concern concrete programmes or particular policy measures. It is certainly not suggested that the social-security systems of countries such as Britain or the United States offer a blueprint which should be adopted by countries whose circumstances are completely different. Rather, our intention is to examine the choices which developed countries have made and the constraints which have influenced their various choices. In particular, the description of the methods of analysis which have been developed to examine the forces which have acted in this process may be of some interest to those exploring analagous questions in developing countries.

In considering the experience of developed countries, one must bear in mind that the shaping of social-security systems has been influenced by a diversity of goals. In addition to the goal of protecting the living standards of the poor, social-security systems may have an important role in redistributing resources over the lifetime or within the family. They may also be directed at

* In preparing and revising this chapter the authors have benefited greatly from comments and suggestions made by Bill Andrews, Angus Deaton, Jean Drèze, Julian Le Grand, and Michael Lipton, as well as by other participants at the conference at which the paper on which it is based was presented. The research reported was undertaken as part of the Welfare State Programme at the Suntory Toyota International Centre for Economics and Related Disciplines at the London School of Economics. Our work has also benefited from research carried out as part of the Franco-British programme of the Economic and Social Research Council and the Centre National de la Recherche Scientifique, whose support, together with that of Suntory Limited for the Welfare State Programme, is gratefully acknowledged.

providing insurance against risks, such as sickness or disability, which lead to a fall in income but do not necessarily lead to poverty. Some writers have indeed suggested that the case for social security can be argued for reasons of efficiency as much as on distributional grounds:

The welfare state is much more than a safety net; it is justified not simply by any redistributive aims one may (or may not) have, but because it does things which private markets for technical reasons either would not do at all, or would do inefficiently. We need a welfare state of some sort for efficiency reasons (Barr 1987: 421).

It has therefore to be emphasized immediately that social-security systems in developed countries have neither been exclusively concerned with the protection of the poor, nor been seen as the only means to this end.

A related observation is that there is great diversity in the social-security provisions that are to be found even in countries of a similar level of development. This is illustrated by the three countries on which we focus in this chapter: Britain, France, and the United States. In Britain there is, for example, a universal child benefit but no income tax concessions for children; in France, the *allocation familiale* is only paid for the second and subsequent children, but the income tax, through the quotient system, offers tax advantages to families with children; in the United States there are no general cash benefits at all for children, but the income tax allows a deduction for children and for child care costs. In Britain the administration of social security is highly centralized; in France the *caisses* that administer benefits enjoy some limited degree of autonomy; in the United States important parts of the social-security system are operated by State governments with differences in benefit levels and conditions. These differences may simply reflect the historical path by which the systems have evolved; they may also reflect differences in objectives and constraints. In Section 2 of this chapter, we examine some of the factors which may explain the differences in the forms of social-security systems in different countries, paying particular attention to the constraints—economic, political, and administrative.

It is clearly not possible in the scope of this chapter to consider a wide range of social-security policies. We have therefore chosen to concentrate on a case-study of policies aimed at the support of children (Section 3). This serves to illustrate a number of key issues. While the first parts of the chapter concentrate on the situation in developed countries, in the final section we consider how far the methods and approaches adopted in the analysis of policy in those countries do indeed suggest wider lessons of relevance to developing countries.

2. SOCIAL SECURITY IN DEVELOPED COUNTRIES: OBJECTIVES AND CONSTRAINTS

2.1. *Form and Objectives*

Social security in developed countries typically combines three different elements—social assistance designed to relieve poverty, social insurance concerned with the provision of security and the spreading of income over the life cycle, and categorical transfers directed at redistribution between specific groups. The first category is typified in Britain by Income Support, which traces a direct line of descent from the Elizabethan Poor Law, in France by the *minimum vieillesse*, and in the US by welfare. The second category is illustrated in Britain by National Insurance pensions, unemployment benefit, and invalidity benefit, in France by a similar range of insurance benefits and in the US by OASDHI (Old-Age, Survivors, Disability, and Health Insurance). The third category is illustrated by Child Benefit and *Allocation familiale*, which, as we have noted, have no counterpart in the US.

These three elements contribute in varying degrees to different objectives. Social assistance usually has the objective of guaranteeing a minimum level of income and of meeting emergencies, either individual, such as family breakdown, or collective, such as the closure of most of a town's industry. The definition of the minimum level of income and of the conditions of entitlement poses substantial problems, as extensively documented in the literature on the measurement of poverty. Are we in fact concerned with income poverty, taking income as a general index of well-being, or with specific poverty, measured in terms of the consumption of particular goods, such as food? If we are concerned with income poverty, then we must consider the specification of the period over which resources and needs are to be assessed, which in turn depends on the scope for people to smooth out fluctuations in their income. We have also to define the unit which is taken as the target of public support—individual, family, or household. As Fiegehen and Lansley (1976) show, the numbers defined as being in poverty are sensitive to whether the family or the household is taken as the appropriate unit. If one allows for unequal distribution of income within the family, the numbers in poverty would be different again.

Social insurance too is seen as a means of combating income poverty. For Beveridge, the key to the abolition of want in post-war Britain lay in the expansion of social insurance to replace the deficient assistance scheme. Increasingly in recent years the poverty alleviation role of social insurance has come to be stressed. In the US in the 1970s the test question applied to social-security programmes came to be 'what does it do for the poor?', to use the title of Lampman's (1973) influential article in *Public Interest*. The 1985 White Paper in Britain on the *Reform of Social Security* described its objectives as being 'to maintain and develop state support for those in need' (Department of

Health and Social Security 1985: 2), without mentioning any wider role for the social-security system.

As we stressed at the outset, however, the combating of poverty is only one of several objectives. Indeed,

the French system of social security was never primarily conceived as a tool to fight poverty. Security, in terms of protection against the risks and hazards of life, was its first, paramount objective. Redistribution and equality were always supplementary considerations (Jallade 1988: 248).

Similarly, for Haveman, 'the primary economic gain from the welfare state is the universal *reduction in the uncertainty* faced by individuals' (1985: 449). The aims of social-insurance systems include insurance against loss of income through contingencies such as unemployment and sickness, and redistribution within the life cycle—for many ameliorating a fall in living standards at times of *relative* penury, rather than being permanently required to keep them out of poverty. State intervention in this form has been justified in terms of the failure of private insurance markets to provide adequate cover for the relevant risks as a result of adverse selection and moral hazard problems. Where insurance companies cannot identify the riskiness of individual customers, and there are problems of adverse selection, the private market for insurance is unlikely to be perfectly competitive. It is also possible that there is a 'markedly lower cost of administration in most forms of State Insurance' (Beveridge 1942: 286).

There are also wider principles of social solidarity underlying social insurance. As Ameline and Walker describe the position in France,

when statutory social insurance and family allowances were first introduced in the 1930s, their purpose was not to combat poverty but to establish a form of mutual support, *solidarité*, first between wage-earners, then between wage-earners' families and eventually among all categories of worker and family (1984: 193).

Although this concept has been of greater importance in continental Europe, it has also been influential in Britain: as Beveridge (1942) put it, 'men should stand together with their fellows'. Such an objective of solidarity cannot necessarily be met by economic measures such as the improvement of credit markets.

The aims of categorical transfers also go wider than the abolition of poverty. The origins of the French system of support for families with children lie in pronatalist concerns about *low* population growth (the exact reverse, of course, of the major concern in many developing countries). The extent to which such concerns are still paramount is disputed. For Kamerman and Kahn, the continuation of such policies despite their failure to arrest the declining birth rate indicates that income maintenance objectives have taken over:

Most French view individual fertility decisions as based upon far more complicated factors . . . than the availability of a cash benefit. . . . Thus, the French strongly support income maintenance policies designed to reduce the financial burden of families, especially those with very young children (1981: 21).

On the other hand, Baker argues that despite appearances the pronatalist element is still the most important: 'It is politically unacceptable to seek to increase births explicitly but desirable to make the lives of parents and children easier and more rewarding, with that hoped-for result' (1986: 423). Either way, it would be a mistake to assess the policy simply in terms of income maintenance.

2.2. Economic Constraints

The extent to which social-security programmes can meet their different objectives depends on the resources which can be mobilized by the government. The rise in taxation as a share of GDP with the level of development is a reflection not simply of the income elasticity of demand for public services, but also of the rise in taxable capacity with the monetization of an economy and increasing size of its formal sector.

Taxable capacity and the structure of social security are, of course, inter-related. The provision of social-security benefits may lead to a more effective and highly motivated labour-force, which increases production and hence increases the tax base. The existence of a State pension scheme may mean that people are no longer dependent on their children for support in old age and hence reduce the incentive to have children, with possible consequential beneficial effects on incomes per head. It is however the *negative* effects of social security on economic performance that have received most attention in the recent literature, particularly in the US. The disincentive aspects of social-security benefits have been emphasized, it being argued that they affect at the margin the decisions of individuals and firms. It is asserted that benefits distort an otherwise efficient allocation of resources, the point of reference being the standard competitive general equilibrium model. The particular areas of decision-making which have been investigated include the decision when to retire, the level of saving for retirement, whether to lay off workers, the hours of work supplied, whether to exit from unemployment and take a job, and whether to register as disabled.

Social-security benefits may therefore mean that people are induced to change their behaviour, for example retiring earlier than they would otherwise have chosen, and this may raise the cost of the programme. In an early article on the negative income tax, Diamond (1968) showed how the curve indicating the level of the feasible transfer lay below that estimated ignoring labour supply changes. Indeed it is argued by commentators such as Murray (1984) in *Losing Ground* that transfers to the poor have been counter-productive, in that more people are deterred from seeking self-help than are raised above the poverty line by the transfers. In the case of benefits in kind, it has been argued that households reduce their own purchases, or resell the goods, thus undermining any attempt to achieve specified consumption levels of particular goods.

The significance of behavioural responses for the design of social-security policy depends on the quantitative magnitude of the effects. We lack, however, firm, agreed empirical estimates in many cases. There has been a great deal of interesting empirical analysis, much of it involving imaginative use of data, particularly at the micro-economic level, and the development of econometric techniques which allow in sophisticated ways for the subtleties of the problem in hand. The results are, however, all too often conflicting, even when authors use the same kind of data, since findings appear often to be highly sensitive to the specification of the behavioural model, to the way in which taxes and benefits are introduced, to the treatment of unobserved variables, and to the choice of sample. For example, Atkinson (1987a: table 5.1) lists seven studies of the effect of pensions on retirement in the US using the same basic source (the Longitudinal Retirement History Survey), of which four conclude that pensions have a signficiant influence on retirement, but three conclude that the effect is either statistically insignificant or economically unimportant.

Moreover, the interpretation of the results is often open to question. For example, the samples studied are typically restricted to a subset of the population. This is illustrated by the US literature just cited on the effect of pensions on the date of retirement. If you are a white, married male in employment, then you stand a good chance of being included in the econometric analysis, but if you are black, or female, or self-employed, then your retirement decision is much less likely to have been modelled. This severely limits the extent to which the conclusions can be extrapolated to the population as a whole. A second example concerns the use of cross-section survey data, which has been the most active area of recent research. We observe differences in the behaviour of people with, say, different pension levels, but it is not clear what can be inferred from these cross-section differences about what would happen if pensions were to be increased for everyone. This depends on the general equilibrium of the economy, about which the empirical analysis may not be very informative.

It is for this kind of reason that, in an earlier review of the literature on the effects of income support on retirement decisions, on work-force participation by the disabled, on the behaviour of the unemployed, on family formation, and on retirement savings, one of us concluded, 'the great volume of empirical research in this field in the past decade has not led to robust or widely-accepted answers to the basic question as to how income support affects economic behaviour' (Atkinson 1987a: 880). None the less, it must be recognized that the belief on the part of governments that disincentives are important has been a significant element in the policy debate.

2.3. Political Constraints

As our concern here is with *public* action, the political constraints on the use of public resources are of key importance. In one direction, voter 'tax revolts' may put a cap on welfare programmes; in the other direction, civil unrest may compel action or, as in the case of Bismarck, action may be taken so as to forestall the development of radical political alternatives. The nature of a country's government and political structure conditions not only the aims of its social-security system (as discussed above), but also the resources available for it, the selection of which groups are assisted, and the numbers assisted. Indeed, the provision of social security at all is not an automatic consequence of economic growth, but reflects the political process.

The political acceptability of social-security programmes depends on the perceptions by the electorate of the benefits and costs. If, for example, universal schemes of social-insurance benefits are seen to be of general benefit, then there may be a rise in the acceptable share of tax in the economy. Conversely, if the public provision is seen to be inadequate, for instance where private insurance is necessary to cover medical costs, then this may lower the acceptability of taxation. The degree of acceptance may be influenced by the pattern of financing. The social-security 'contributions' which individuals make to finance social insurance may have little actuarial relationship with the likely benefits. Instead, they are in reality a hypothecated part of direct taxation. None the less, because they are generally conceived to be a payment for a clearly defined benefit, contributions (and the transfers they fund) may be significantly more acceptable than if general taxation was used. Here, as with other aspects of social security and its financing, perceptions of how the system works may be more important than its actual functioning.

The extent of redistribution via social security might be expected to vary with the degree of electoral support for socialist or radical parties, or with the strength of organized labour, but cross-national studies such as that by Heidenheimer *et al.* (1983) suggest that the relationship is complex. These authors note that

When a country must choose when to cross the line between public and private income distribution, the power of the political right probably is important in delaying, circumscribing, and otherwise restraining the vigor with which public policy goals are allowed to interfere with private arrangements (1983: 212).

However, they go on to point out that this conclusion may not hold if the political right seeks to defuse pressures for change by introducing 'defensive innovations'. More generally, the general level of support for social security is likely to reflect the prevailing political philosophy. Palmer, in his account of income security in the US under Reagan, refers to the widespread belief in the 'American dream' of individual opportunity, rejection of class-based politics and collectively orchestrated schemes of redistribution, suspicion of government power, and identification of personal freedom with private enterprise. These peculiarly American characteristics have conditioned public support for income security policies for decades. . . . Even during the extremely liberal 1960s, successful politicians generally eschewed collectivist visions of the public good (1987: 43–4).

Political factors may influence the form taken by social-security programmes. To the extent that the electorate are concerned with their own direct interests, they may be more likely to support programmes which are to the general benefit rather than those which are targeted towards small groups. Governments may be more willing to approve pension programmes where the costs fall on future generations not yet fully represented amongst the voters. In discussions of the relative merits of cash and in-kind transfers, it has been argued that the latter are more acceptable to electors, since their concern is more with the level of consumption of specific goods by low-income groups than it is with their general welfare. In the US it has been observed that food stamps are less unpopular with politicians and the general public than other forms of transfers, although by the same token some recipients have found them demeaning and stigmatizing (Wilson 1987: 57–8).

The role of interest groups is important. The 'middle class capture' thesis of Le Grand and Winter (1987) argues that in Britain under the Thatcher Conservative Government the programmes which have survived most successfully are those which have middle-class support, the middle classes being either beneficiaries or suppliers of services. Lynes has described the role played by different interest groups in shaping the evolution of pensions in France after the Second World War: 'national solidarity had not proved strong enough to overcome the numerous vested interests or to persuade the self-employed and higher-paid employees to throw in their lot with the manual workers' (1985: 25). In the US, food stamps are again an example, their expansion owing a great deal to the farming lobby (they are administered by the Department of Agriculture). According to MacDonald, the Food Stamp Act of 1964 was the result of a 'logrolling arrangement between backers of wheat and cotton price supports and proponents of food stamps' (1977: 7).

The form of the programmes which are enacted may reflect political preferences even where the motives are more disinterested. In the case of poverty alleviation, there may be differing weights on two different kinds of redistributional 'efficiency': horizontal efficiency in assisting all of the target group and vertical efficiency in assisting only the target group (Weisbrod 1969). If the 'target group' is taken as only the poor, systems based on universal contingency-based payments may perform badly by the second criterion. Child Benefit in Britain is received by all families with children and not just those below the poverty line. Means-tested systems may well perform badly by the first criterion. For instance, the official estimate of the percentage of those entitled to Family Income Supplement (now replaced by Family Credit) in Britain in 1984 who did in fact claim is 55 per cent, with only 65 per cent of the amount available being claimed (HM Treasury 1988: table 15.17). The failure to claim non-universal benefits may result not just from their usual greater complexity, but also from the effects of the stigma attached to claiming, itself a product of the public acceptability of transfers.

2.4. Administrative Constraints

The way in which social security is administered may have major implications for its effectiveness and for its cost. Success in channelling benefits to those for whom they are intended, both avoiding payment of benefit to those not entitled and avoiding non-payment of benefit to those who are entitled, depends on the identification of potential beneficiaries and the elicitation of the correct information. Errors of one kind—payments to the ineligible—may be reduced by a harsh system of administration, as has long been recognized. As Midgley says of the English Poor Law of the last century, 'by requiring the routine incarceration of the recipients of poor relief, the New Poor Law hoped to prevent fraud and to coerce the indigent to seek an honest living' (1984: 87). But the cost of imposing such ordeals is that fewer of those genuinely eligible can be induced to apply and more of those with rightful claims are rejected in error.

The administration of social security is likely to be constrained in terms of the measures which may be used. It is, for example, hard to imagine that it could be made compulsory for non-claimants to provide information to the benefit authorities in order to see if they are in fact eligible. Similarly, there are restrictions on the information which can be obtained from employers about their employees.

Administrative considerations are also likely to influence the form of social-security programmes. A key issue is the availability of information, particularly that collected from claimants. Direct measurement of the income of the poor as a way of identifying those to receive benefits is administratively difficult. The forms recently issued for claiming the new Family Credit in Britain are sixteen A4 pages long (compared with the one-page form for the universal Child Benefit). The administrative costs for the means-tested Supplementary Benefit (now Income Support) in Britain amounted to 11.3 per cent of spending on the benefit in 1985/6. This represented 45 per cent of the total administration costs of social security, for a benefit which represented only 18 per cent of total expenditure (HM Treasury 1988: tables 15.22, 15.23).

Targeting does not, however, have to take the form of means-testing. Regular life cycle contingencies like maternity, sickness, disability, unemployment, and old age can be used as more straightforward tests of the probability of being in need. The efficiency of contingency-based benefits as a way of targeting the poor (as opposed to the more general aim of reducing uncertainty for the population as a whole) depends on the extent to which those covered by the contingency are poor, and on the extent to which the poor fall into one or other of the contingencies chosen.

2.5. *Alternatives to Social Security: Family Support, Fiscal Welfare, and Occupational Welfare*

In most countries, social security has developed to supplement and to replace the support provided by family, local community, and charitable bodies. The extent and pattern of social-security provision is therefore likely to reflect the tradition and reality of support within the family and community, the strength and coverage of charities, and the level of development of collective organizations such as trades unions, friendly societies, and provident funds. The availability of these alternatives is related to the level of economic development—some positively (for example, the growth of trades unions with industrialization), others inversely (for example, the possible decline of family ties as geographical mobility increases).

Once again, the direction of causation runs both ways, and the level of public provision will itself affect the extent of family and community support; and this aspect of behavioural response must be taken into account. In the United States, for example, it has been argued that the ultimate beneficiaries from State pensions are not the retired but their children from whom the burden of support in old age has been lifted. In order to assess this argument, it is necessary not only to adopt a life-time view of redistribution, but also to consider redistribution between generations. The data required for such an analysis include transfers of income and capital (for example the effect of State pensions on the size of the estate left at death).

We have, however, to remember that social security is not the only form of provision that has grown up to replace family and community provision. Titmuss in his essay on 'The Social Division of Welfare' (1958) drew attention to the parallel systems of fiscal welfare and occupational welfare. Parallel to state pensions, for instance, are additional income tax deductions for the elderly (fiscal welfare) and occupational pensions paid by former employers (occupational welfare). In the case of fiscal welfare, it has been recognized by economists that tax expenditures serve a similar function to direct public spending on social security, but equally it has to be recognized that they are often viewed differently by politicians and taxpayers. Occupational welfare takes many different forms, depending on the nature of employment and of the contract between employers and employees, or their representatives such as trade unions.

In the case of all four systems of income support—social security, family or community support, fiscal welfare, and occupational welfare—we have to take account of the interactions between them. Are social-security benefits reduced on account of income received from employers, from friendly societies and so on? Does help from family reduce a person's State benefits? Are benefits subject to income tax? Is State welfare a residual scheme for those not covered by occupational provision? The answers to these questions are as likely to reflect the historical evolution of a particular society as the logic of economic or social planning.

3. SOCIAL SECURITY IN BRITAIN, FRANCE, AND THE US: A CASE-STUDY OF CHILD SUPPORT

3.1. *Social Security in Britain, France, and the US*

The social-security systems of Britain, France, and the US are in themselves illustrations of the way in which different traditions, objectives, and constraints lead to varied solutions to the problems of social security. What is more, they are embedded in an economic and social context that differs significantly between the countries, as is exemplified by the provision of health care, an issue that is often closely related and for which policy is often formulated in the same ministry.

In terms of the three types of social-security scheme identified in Section 2.1 (social assistance, social insurance, and categorical transfers), Britain has a means-tested system intended to guarantee a minimum income now known as Income Support (previously Supplementary Benefit and National Assistance) and descended from the reliefs offered under the New Poor Law of 1834 and before that the Poor Law of 1601. Social insurance, under the title of National Insurance, consolidated after the Beveridge Report of 1942, provides universal non-means-tested benefits like the retirement pension or Unemployment Benefit payable to those affected by certain contingencies and depending on their contribution records. The State pension consists of a basic flat-rate element and a more recent earnings-related scheme; the short-term benefits are essentially flat-rate. Despite Beveridge's original intention, a substantial proportion of those in receipt of National Insurance benefits depend on Income Support for supplementation, so that means-tested benefits play a major role. The system includes a categorical payment to those with children, Child Benefit, which depends on neither means nor contribution record. Occupational provision is widespread in the field of retirement pensions, where it is possible to 'contract out' of the state earnings-related scheme if covered by an occupational scheme, or since 1988 by a personal pension. Alongside the social-security system is the National Health Service, which provides free hospital care and general practitioner services, although prescriptions are subject to a charge.

The French system offers a contrast in a number of major respects, as has been described by Jallade:

[It owes] more to Bismarck than to Beveridge to the extent that the principle of universal, compulsory insurance is the rule and selective assistance the exception . . . universal benefits are much more important than means-tested benefits and the notion of minimum income to be reached by means of social benefits does not exist except in the case of old-age pensions . . . firm-based pension schemes are far less developed than their British counterparts (1988: 223).

Although social insurance is fragmented, and indeed labyrinthine, in its organization in France, it is of central importance and has its roots in rather different objectives from those in Britain. As far as the benefits available to those with children are concerned, pressure from the 'family movement' and concern about the consequences of slow population growth had by 1932 produced regulation of a high proportion of employers to provide additional wages for their own workers with children. It is from this that the system of wage-related payments into the *caisses d'allocations familiales* has evolved. The difference in evolution from the British system leaves a very different perception of the role of social security. The same is true of the relation with health care, where the provision is explicitly related to insurance coverage, there being compulsory health insurance, which reimburses a proportion of the expense, coupled with supplementary private insurance.

In the US, the oldest programme is the income-tested general assistance (welfare). This is administered by State and local governments and the entry of the federal government into the field is relatively recent: 'until 1933 the federal government paid no grants and organised no programmes for relief or insurance, except for its own employees' (Barr 1987: 24). This changed under Roosevelt with the Social Security Act of 1935, which introduced federal old-age insurance benefits financed by taxes on employees and employers. Originally these were intended to be calculated on an actuarial basis, but this was quickly abandoned. As time has gone by additional benefits have extended the range of social security to include survivors' benefits (1939) and disability (1956). The 1960s saw a major expansion under the War on Poverty of programmes directed at helping the poor. These were in large part income-tested, such as food stamps, subsidized housing, low-income scholarships, and Supplemental Security Income (converted from the earlier Old Age Assistance). In a number of cases there are federal grants for State income-tested programmes, including Aid to Families with Dependent Children (AFDC) for families with children, restricted in the majority of States to those with a single parent. The variation in programmes across States is a feature of the US which has no direct counterpart in Britain and France. Private provision for pensions is substantial, as in Britain. Health expenditures are, as in France, covered under social insurance, in that the 'H' was added to OASDHI in 1965 in the form of

Medicare, but this is limited to the aged and disabled. For those not covered, assistance may be provided in conjunction with income-tested programmes via Medicaid. There is also an income tax deduction for medical expenses.

Even for three countries with a relatively similar level of economic development, varying traditions and political objectives have led to rather different approaches to the problems of social security. These differences are illustrated in Table 3.1, which shows the spending on social security and health in the three countries, expressed as a proportion of national income. The first striking feature is the much greater relative extent of this spending in France, the proportion of GDP being nearly twice that in the UK and nearly three times that in the US. Since the figures are assembled from national sources, there may be differences in the definitions, but it is interesting to note that the International Labour Office (ILO) comparative enquiry (1985: table 1 and app. table) shows total social-security expenditure on ILO definitions in 1979/80 as being 12.2 per cent in the US, 16.7 per cent in Britain, and 25.5 per cent

Table 3.1. Public spending on social security and health[a]: France, UK, and USA

	France % of GDP 1983	UK % of GDP 1987/8	USA % of GNP 1984
Old age	11.0[b]	5.3[c]	3.6[d]
Unemployment	2.8	2.1[e]	0.4
Family	3.7	1.2	0.4[f]
Health	} 6.6	4.9	4.2[g]
Sickness and invalidity		0.8	} 1.9[h]
Disability and injury	2.3	0.6	
Other benefits including income-tested housing benefits and food programmes	1.6	1.0	0.9
Administration	1.6	0.6	–[i]
TOTAL	29.6	16.5	11.5

[a] Excludes pension payments to public employees, general spending on public housing, and provision of personal social services.
[b] Includes 'derived benefits'.
[c] Includes supplementary pensions.
[d] 'Social security' and SSI paid to aged.
[e] Includes supplementary allowances.
[f] AFDC only.
[g] Medicare, Medicaid, and other medical programmes.
[h] Includes OASDI and SSI except payments to aged.
[i] Included in figures above.

Sources: France: Jallade (1988: tables 1, 2). UK: HM Treasury (1988: tables 2.7, 12.1, 14.1, 15.1, 18.12). USA: US Department of Commerce (1987: tables 574, 578, 580).

in France (in 1980). Looking at the breakdown by 'risk', we can see that expenditure on old age accounts for a sizeable part of the difference. Despite the concern expressed in the US about the size of pension spending, it represents a much smaller fraction of GDP according to these figures. A second sizeable source of the difference is to be found in spending on family benefits. A striking similarity is the proportion of GDP allocated to public spending on health.

The pattern of spending by type of programme is shown in Table 3.2. Social insurance accounts for about half the total spending in France and the US, but a smaller fraction in the UK. This reflects in part the relative size of the National Health Service, but the smaller percentage of social insurance in Britain also reflects the greater weight of other cash benefits (such as child benefit). Among the non-social-insurance cash benefits, means-testing appears to play a larger role in the UK than in France, and an even larger role in the US, where there are no major categorical benefits unrelated to income.

Table 3.2. Breakdown of public spending on social security and health[a]: France, UK, and USA.

	Percentages of total spending		
	France 1983	UK 1987/8	USA 1984
Social insurance	53.7	38.4	50.4
Other non-means-tested	8.9	11.4	–
Means-tested	5.9	19.3	14.5
Health care	23.4	30.9	35.1
(of which means-tested)			(9.3)
TOTAL	100.0[b]	100.0	100.0

[a] Excluding administration for France and the UK.
[b] Including 8.1% not allocated above.

Sources: see Table 1.

We now turn to a more detailed examination of the systems of support for families with children. This case-study is not presented as 'typical'. It does not touch on the insurance aspects which are crucial for benefits such as those for sickness or unemployment; it is not of the same quantitative magnitude as the provision of old-age pensions. Nevertheless, it raises a number of issues relevant to developing as well as developed countries.

Child support in the three countries is summarized in Table 3.3, where we classify the programmes between the main headings of:

(1) universal cash transfers;
(2) tax expenditures;
(3) general means-tested cash transfers;
(4) income-tested cash transfers to families with children;
(5) means-tested benefits in kind.

This list is not intended to be exhaustive. We have not included occupational welfare nor other mechanisms, including subsidies to private suppliers of services, regulation of the private sector (for instance, minimum wages), or provision of public services (such as the National Health Service in Britain). It should also be noted that item (2) was not included in Tables 3.1. and 3.2, and is of some size, particularly in France and the US. It is not however likely to change the general ranking, which is that France has the most generous level, relative to GDP, of family support and the US the least generous.

3.2. Child Support in Britain

Universal payments to families with more than one child were one of the proposals in the Beveridge Report of 1942 and were implemented as family allowances from 1946. The rate of payment, originally set at some 4 per cent average adult male earnings for each child except the first, was lower than Beveridge had proposed (an age-related scale averaging more than 50 per cent higher). Subsequent upratings for inflation were infrequent, and by 1976–7 the real value of the allowance for taxpayers (taking account of taxation of the allowance and the 'clawback' of tax allowances) was only half the real value set in 1946 and even less important in relation to earnings (Child Benefits Now Campaign 1977). Meanwhile, additional child tax allowances had been given in respect of all children (including the first) for income tax purposes since 1909 (and before that between 1799 and 1806). These two systems were merged between 1977 and 1979 to give the current single system of Child Benefit. This is a flat-rate payment for each child, in 1988 equal to some 3 per cent of the average adult male earnings, paid usually to the mother (as had been the case with family allowances). Unlike its predecessor, Child Benefit is not taxable. The introduction of Child Benefit may be seen as the culmination of a long campaign which began with the 're-discovery' of family poverty in *The Poor and the Poorest* by Abel-Smith and Townsend (1965). This campaign was largely conducted by specialized pressure groups, such as the Child Poverty Action Group, but it was very much in the Fabian tradition, which sees the intensive use of statistical, case-study, and other evidence as a powerful force in influencing political opinion and achieving social reform.

With the replacement of child tax allowances by Child Benefit, there are no special tax concessions to those with children except that single parents are entitled to claim an additional tax allowance to give equivalence with the

Table 3.3. Child support in Britain, France, and the USA

	Britain	France	USA
Universal cash payments	Child Benefit	*Allocations familiales*	Additions to Unemployment Insurance payments in certain States
	One Parent, Benefit	*Allocation au jeune enfant, initiale*	
Tax expenditures	Additional personal allowance	*Quotient familial* base for income tax Deduction for child care	Extra tax exemption for each child Special tax schedule for 'heads of houshold' Earned income and child care tax credits
General-means-tested cash transfers	Income Support		
Income-tested cash transfers to families with children	Family Credit	*Complément familial*	Aid to Families with Dependent Children
		Allocation de rentrée scolaire	
		Allocation au jeune enfant maintenue	
		Allocation de parent isolé	
		Supplément de revenu familial	
Means-tested benefits in kind	Housing Benefit	*Allocation de logement*	Lower income housing assistance
	Free school meals/milk	*Aide personalisée au logement* (plus lower rate of *taxe d'habitation* and lower social housing rents)	Free/reduced-price school lunches Food stamps Women's, Infants', and Children's Supplemental Foods

treatment of single-earner couples. Single parents also receive a flat-rate benefit, One Parent Benefit, currently set at some 2 per cent of the average adult male earnings.

Social insurance benefits paid for short-term absence from work no longer include additions for those with children. On the other hand, there is a general system of means-tested minimum income provided through Income Support (known as Supplementary Benefit until April 1988). The 'applicable amount' allowances on which entitlement is calculated include age-related additions for dependent children and a premium for families with children. For a family with two children aged under 11 the total applicable amount is some 34 per cent of the average adult male earnings, which would rise to 38 per cent if the children were aged 11–15. The means-test is based on a 100 per cent rate of withdrawal of benefit from those with net income from other sources, including Child Benefit. The take-up for Supplementary Benefit in 1983 was estimated to be 76 per cent in terms of case-load and 89 per cent in terms of the amount available (HM Treasury 1988: table 15.17). Again there appears to be a major problem of horizontal inefficiency.

Families with children where one of the parents is in full-time employment (defined as more than twenty-four hours per week) are not entitled to claim Income Support, but can claim an alternative benefit, Family Credit (which in April 1988 replaced Family Income Supplement, originally established in 1971). This is means-tested with withdrawal at a rate of 70 per cent of net income after allowing for income tax and National Insurance Contributions. The amount payable and the income level up to which assistance is given rises with the number of children and their ages. The maximum entitlement for a family with two children aged under 11 is currently about 20 per cent of average adult male earnings and entitlement would be reduced to zero for this type of family at earnings of about 60 per cent of average adult male earnings. The corresponding figures for a four-child family (with two children aged less than 11 and two between 11 and 15) would be a maximum entitlement of some 30 per cent of average adult male earnings, reduced to zero at about 80 per cent of average adult male earnings.

Means-tested support in kind is provided on a general basis through Housing Benefit. This gives assistance with up to 100 per cent of rent and 80 per cent of rates (local property taxes) for those with incomes at or below their Income Support level, thus including those receiving Income Support. It is also means-tested, with a withdrawal rate of up to 85 per cent on net income (after tax and national insurance but including Child Benefit and Family Credit). There has been a succession of increases in the rate of withdrawal since 1983, when a taper of 28 per cent was applied to gross income (rate and rent rebates combined); the taper was increased to 38 per cent in 1984, 42 per cent in 1985, and 46 per cent in 1987. This increased withdrawal rate had the effect of substantially reducing the number in work with low enough incomes to be entitled, so that this provision in kind is now relatively unimportant for families with children where the head is in work.

Provision of subsidized or free school meals and free school milk date back to the 1944 Education Act and provision of meals back to legislation of 1906 and earlier philanthropic efforts (Barbor-Might 1988). Free school milk was originally a universal measure, but this was ended in 1971. Free school meals were always subject to a means-test (although throughout most of the post-war period meal prices were subsidized). From 1980 free school meals (and welfare milk for children of below school age) were restricted to those with parents either on Supplementary Benefit or Family Income Supplement. From April 1988 they have been further restricted to those receiving Income Support, so that there has been a continuing trend to reduce the importance of this provision in kind.

3.3. *Child Support in France*

In France, as in Britain, there is a tax-free child benefit, *Allocation familiale*, which is not subject to any contribution test nor to a means-test. The benefit differs, however, in that it varies with family size and with the age of children. No benefit is paid in France for the first child and the amount for the second child is less than for the third and subsequent children. For all except the elder child in a two-child family, there are age premia above 10 and 15. There is therefore a strong 'tilt' in France in favour of larger families and of older children. Whereas in 1987 the amount for a two-child family came out to be broadly similar in France and Britain (and the one-child family received no *Allocation familiale* in France), the payments for larger families were considerably larger in France (amounts compared at the ruling exchange rate—see Atkinson 1987b). The programme is funded from a 9 per cent payroll tax on earnings up to a relatively low ceiling (rather below average male earnings).

For higher income families, the income tax system offers significant benefits for those with children. The tax charged depends on the amount of taxable income of a family divided into separate parts according to the *Quotient familial*. This awards one part for each adult and half a part for each child (with a whole part for the third child). Thus a two-child family pays the same average income tax rate as a single person with three times the income. This provision only benefits those families which are paying income tax, or would otherwise have been paying tax and, despite some limits on the extent to which the quotient system can reduce tax payable, the system is clearly of greatest benefit to those with the highest incomes. Atkinson, Bourguignon, and Chiappori found that 'its effect in terms of net income appears to be strongly regressive' (1988: 372). There is in addition a deduction for child care costs for single parents, or couples where both work full-time, with a child aged under 5.

The favourable treatment of large families in France also applies to the income-tested benefits. The *Complément familial* is paid to families with at least three children aged 3 or over and provides a fixed payment if net income in the previous tax year is below a specified ceiling, and is reduced 1 f. for 1 f. if this ceiling is exceeded. The *Supplément de revenu familial* is paid to families with at least three children and whose net income in the previous year was below a specified ceiling. It brings income up to a specified level subject to a maximum. Other family benefits include the *Allocation au jeune enfant*, paid in pregnancy without an income-test and, subject to an income-test (the same as that for the *Complément familial*), to those with a child under 2, and the income-tested *Allocation de parent isolé*, paid to low-income single parents for a year or as long as there is a child aged under 3. Families with school-age children also receive an annual payment at the start of the school year, the *Allocation de rentrée scolaire*. This is a flat amount for each child (including the first) and the ceilings for receipt are somewhat lower than those applying to the *Complément familial*.

Means-tested assistance in France is in fact more important among families with children than for social security as a whole. The ceiling for the *Complément familial*, for example, is quite high—more than double average male earnings for a two-earner couple with three children—and this benefit is received by about half the total number of families in receipt of *Allocations familiales* (CERC 1988: annex IV). To the benefits described above must be added income-tested assistance with housing costs, which can be divided into two parts, the *Allocation de logement* and the *Aide personalisée au logement*. The former (divided in turn into two categories relating to families and other beneficiaries) depends on rent, family composition, and income (on a sliding scale). The latter is linked to the purchase of housing or renting of certain modernized dwellings. In addition, access to, and the rents of, social housing (*Habitations à loyer modéré* or HLMs) depend on family composition and income and the local tax charged (*tax d'habitation*) is reduced for larger families (Bradshaw and Piachaud 1980).

Whereas the British social-security system is controlled entirely by central government (even when local authorities are responsible for administration they now have minimal discretion over the benefits paid), the administration of equivalent benefits in France enjoys a degree of decentralization, being in the hands of quasi-autonomous local institutions. Child-related benefits are controlled by more than 100 local *caisses d'allocations familiales*. These have elected representatives in a majority on their controlling boards and, although the rates and entitlement rules for the main benefits are set centrally, they have control over *action sociale* spending programmes (about 10 per cent of their budgets) and over benefit administration (Simpson 1983). Participation in the administration of social security may on occasion retard reform, as in the case of pensions after the Second World War, but in general it may have led to a greater sense of identification and hence permitted France to maintain relatively high levels of benefit.

3.4. *Child Support in the United States*

Social insurance plays a major role in the US social-security system, but has little direct function as a means of child support. Only in the case of payments under unemployment insurance does the amount vary with the number of dependent children, and this provision applies only in a minority of states. Unlike Britain and France, there is no general categorical benefit for children and, interestingly, there seems to have been little public discussion of such a benefit.

By contrast, the income tax contains significant concessions for taxpayers with children. An additional exemption can be claimed for each child, equal to that for a single adult (just under $2000 in 1988). For a person paying a marginal rate of 15 per cent, this is worth $5.63 a week per child in 1988, for a person paying 28 per cent, it is worth $10.50 a week, or about 3 per cent of average production worker earnings. As with other exemptions, this is withdrawn from those on high incomes, but its effect would persist for incomes up to some $200,000 per year (married couples filing joint returns). The exemption again has no value to families that would not have been paying income tax anyway, and it may be noted that the 1986 Tax Reform Act reinstated the principle that those below the official poverty line should not be paying tax and by raising the exemptions and standard deduction (for those not itemizing deductions) this Act removed nearly 5 million people from the taxpaying population (Pechman 1987: 18). Secondly, heads of household (effectively single parents) benefit from a more favourable tax schedule than single people, with a larger standard deduction, a wider 15 per cent band, and a later threshold for the start of the exemption withdrawal. In each case the allowances and bands for single parents lie between those for single persons and those for couples filing joint returns. Thirdly, the earned income tax credit is open only to certain types of family, including couples with children and single parents. This provides a credit against tax on earnings limited to those with low incomes. Finally, a credit is given for child care expenses (unless there is a spouse at home). This is available whether the taxpayer itemizes deductions or not and is calculated as a percentage which falls with income (but, unlike the exemptions, is not phased out altogether from those on the highest incomes).

A principal policy concern in the US has been provision for the children of single-parent families, and the most important means-tested cash benefit for those with children is Aid to Families with Dependent Children (AFDC). As already noted, this is only available in general to single parents; only in twenty-three States (and the District of Columbia and Guam) is AFDC available where the principal wage-earner is present but unemployed. As a State-run programme, there are major variations across the US: 'Within . . . broad guidelines, the States may choose whom they will assist, how the assistance will be given and how much it will be. There is great variation among the States in their choice on these matters' (US Department of Health and Human Services 1986: 52). The calculation of the AFDC entitlement depends on the difference between a family's resources and the State's needs standard for that family type. The latter vary greatly, ranging in 1985 for a family of three children from $286 a month in Mississippi to $421 in Colorado and $474 in New York. States do not have to pay the full difference and can impose a limit on the amount paid. Average amounts paid vary widely: in December 1984 from $91 per month in Mississippi to $578 in Alaska, with a national average of $335 (figures from US Department of Health and Human Services 1986). Originally, the AFDC calculation involved a 100 per cent marginal tax rate of any earnings above a specified level; between 1969 and 1981, the marginal tax rate was reduced to two-thirds; in 1981 the disregard of a third of earnings was restricted to the first four months of receipt.

The emphasis on assistance to single parents, and the absence of any general support for families with children, has meant that the effects of AFDC on family break-up has been a major issue, even though the empirical evidence is open to debate. The role of AFDC has also to be seen in conjunction with that of the judicial system which determines liability to maintain by absent parents and there has been considerable discussion of the proposal for a system of unified child support insurance (Garfinkel 1985). The attempt to enforce payments of maintenance can be seen as a way in which the State tries to prevent the fall in income which otherwise creates the need for benefits. A further major issue in the recent evolution of AFDC has been that of 'workfare', the term covering a wide variety of schemes ranging from those mainly intended to ensure that claimants do not receive 'something for nothing' to those involving the provision of child care, good-quality training, and support in job-hunting (Burghes 1987).

Of equal importance in terms of spending are means-tested benefits in kind: food stamps, subsidized school lunches, and supplemental foods for women, infants, and children. The means-test for these programmes depends generally on income in relation to the State needs standard, although receipt of AFDC can act as a 'passport' (for instance to food stamps and medicaid). Entitlement to food stamps depends on a number of tests, including the requirement that income be below 130 per cent of the poverty line (even where entitlement is 'passported'). The average monthly value of food stamps was about $43 per person in 1984, with a total annual cost of over $10 billion. There is some degree of general subsidy for school lunches and they are available free, or at a reduced price, to those with incomes below certain levels. Finally, as well as general subsidies to public housing, means-tested assistance with housing costs is available through lower income housing assistance.

It is interesting that, while in both the US and Britain there has been an expansion of income-tested programmes, in Britain the role of cash assistance has increased and that of in-kind assistance has fallen; in the US the reverse is the case. Between 1976 and 1986 means-tested cash assistance to all households (not just those with children) fell in real terms in the US, whereas total means-tested assistance grew in real terms by about a quarter (Burtless 1986: 22).

3.5. Conclusions

As far as objectives are concerned, the elimination of poverty has received most attention in the US, where much of social policy in the past quarter-century stems from the War on Poverty. It is noteworthy that this has not led to any universal provision of child support. The trend has been in the direction of greater targeting and, in contrast to Britain, the greater use of income-testing has concentrated particularly on benefits in kind, like food stamps, with proposals for cash transfers such as a negative income tax, or Nixon's proposed Family Assistance Plan, not being enacted. In Britain the theme of targeting on the poor has been stressed more recently with the Conservative reforms and here has taken the form of greater emphasis on income-tested cash assistance. In France there are signs of greater emphasis on the poverty objective, as is evidenced by the pledge during the 1988 Presidential campaign to introduce a guaranteed minimum income, and the recent report from the Centre d'Etude des Revenus et des Coûts on *Protection sociale et pauvreté*. It is however striking that the country where poverty has been least discussed is that which provides the most generous cash support to families with children.

The explanation for this difference lies in part in the weight attached to other objectives, like the birth rate, but also in part in the way these programmes are perceived, with notions of solidarity and participation achieving a higher level of social support for these transfers. It is political considerations that have probably been as important as any economic factors in shaping the evolution of family policy in the three countries. The *caisses* in France provide a powerful lobby to protect the child benefits, and the benefit derived by families of all income levels ensures a wide basis of support. From a rather different direction, the farm lobby in the US has undoubtedly been influential in the extension of food stamps.

It is also the case that the shape of family support policy reflects administrative constraints resulting from decisions taken about other areas of policy. This is particularly true of fiscal provisions. The abolition of child tax allowances in Britain was a natural part of a process of moving towards the collection of income tax at source and towards simplification at the level of the individual taxpayer. The more complex French system is possible in a situation where income tax accounts for a smaller proportion of revenue.

This is not, however, to say that economic effects are unimportant. In particular, there has been considerable concern about the effect of the child support programmes in the three countries on the budget constraint faced by the individual family. For many low-income families, this is of considerable complexity. Receipt of one benefit can count as income in the assessment of entitlement to another benefit. Different income-tested benefits embody different withdrawal schedules and several have cut-off points set in relation to gross income while entitlements are calculated after allowing for various deductions. There is an overlap between social-security contributions and income tax, with the further complication in the US of the earned income tax credit. The total effect leads to the 'poverty trap' whereby families face overall marginal rates which are well above top income tax rates and may exceed 100 per cent (Lynes 1971; Lampman 1975). While the relationship between the different elements may be rationalized, as with the move to a net income basis for assessing benefits in Britain in 1988, it is not possible to avoid high marginal rates of tax without either reducing the benefit levels or extending the break-even points. At the same time, the French pattern of benefits may be seen as adopting the latter approach but increasing the targeting of benefits by greater use of categorization (for example via benefits confined to larger families).

4. ARE THERE LESSONS FOR DEVELOPING COUNTRIES?

4.1. *Two Answers*

The comparison of family support policies in Britain, France, and the US suggests that these countries could learn from each other's experience. Do the lessons, however, extend to developing countries? The answer to this question may appear to be self-evidently 'no'. The design of benefit withdrawal schedules is simply a matter of 'fine-tuning' compared with the problems faced by low-income countries. More generally, as we said at the outset, it does not make sense to regard the social programmes of Britain, France, and the US as a shop window from which a developing country can select the ingredients it prefers. Neither Beveridge nor Bismarck nor Roosevelt can provide a model for social security in developing countries. The level of development has an important influence both on the nature of the problem and on the instruments available for its solution, so that the experience of countries such as Britain, France, and the US is far removed from that of developing countries.

First of all, the problem is quite different in both scale and nature. If we ask whether it is possible to target benefits on the children of poor families, then the solutions are likely to be quite different if we are concerned with 60 per cent of the population rather than 10 per cent. Galbraith described in *The Affluent Society* (1958) how rising national output in the US had reduced poverty from the problem of a majority to that of a minority, and how this in turn meant that new policies had to be devised. By the same token, the policies which have emerged in countries such as the US are unlikely to be applicable in low-income countries. Where the focus of policy is famine relief and the avoidance of starvation, it is specific poverty in terms of food consumption that is of concern, rather than a generalized measure of well-being such as income, which is the principal target of social policy in developed countries. While income redistribution may be an effective means of famine prevention, the success or failure of policy is judged in terms of food adequacy rather than of the numbers with incomes above or below a particular level.

It is not just the level of development but also the structure of the economy that is different. Social insurance for example is predicated on the employment status (as is evidenced by the difficulties faced by many schemes in incorporating the self-employed or part-time workers), where individuals typically have an earnings and employment record and an arms-length relationship with their employer. This is not the case for many of those in the traditional or rural sectors of developing economies. As a result, the institutional assumption that social-security schemes can be introduced for the bulk of the population, while a reasonable goal of twentieth-century reformers in Western countries, has little applicability to developing countries. Midgley opens his survey of formal social-security systems in the Third World by saying that

although the development of social security in the Third World during the post-war years has been impressive, these schemes have brought few, if any, benefits to ordinary people. They cater primarily for those who are already privileged by having secure jobs and steady incomes and exclude those whose needs for social security are the greatest (1984: ix).

Systems paid for in part by taxation on the whole population which provide benefits for those in the formal sector—albeit at the bottom of the formal sector—will necessarily be regressive when that sector represents the top of the income distribution.

The policy instruments which need to be developed to protect vulnerable groups in developing countries are therefore different from those that have been found useful in developed countries. The shaping of social-security systems in developing countries needs to be responsive to their specific circumstances, relating *inter alia* to the nature of the contingencies to be covered (including, for example, crop failures and the threat of famine), informational constraints (such as those regarding the assessment of incomes), political influences (for example, the importance of 'urban bias'), and incentive problems (such as the interaction between state support and household formation).[1]

Systems for the targeting of aid, for instance, are unlikely to resemble the complex family assistance schemes which we have described in Britain and France. In the absence of reliable information about income, recourse has to be made to devices such as 'self-acting tests', categorical transfers based on

[1] For further discussion of these issues, with reference to specific regions of the world, see the case-studies included in the second part of this book.

correlates of income (such as landlessness or disability), or the involvement of village institutions in the implementation of social-security programmes. Self-acting tests based on the requirement to work have, for instance, been a major element of the relatively effective famine prevention systems of countries such as India and Botswana (see Chap. 10 below; also Drèze 1988). Self-acting tests have also been part of the experience of developed countries with social security, and there are common issues involved (such as the problem of 'take-up'). However, there may be a major difference between the efficiency of such tests as a way of distributing relief when the alternative is starvation, as opposed to the avoidance of less absolute poverty, which again limits the 'lessons' to be drawn from the developed country experience.

A second way of interpreting the question posed in the title of this section is to ask whether there are lessons to be learned, not from the actual policy choices, but from the methods of analysis applied to social-security policy in countries such as Britain, France, and the US? Again this may well be denied, the transfer of methods of analysis being seen as little more than intellectual imperialism. Indeed, much of the economic analysis in developed countries of the need for government intervention via social security takes as its starting point a model of a perfectly competitive general equilibrium which—whatever its applicability to countries such as Britain and the US—clearly cannot be transferred to most developing countries. Even if the limitations of the model are recognized, all too often it affects the way in which social security is viewed. By taking as a reference situation one where an efficient allocation is achieved, the case for intervention is put on the defensive. It can certainly be argued that a more appropriate starting point is a model that makes explicit the reasons why markets fail to clear, or are incomplete, or fail to exist altogether. The analysis of unemployment insurance, for instance, needs to consider the movement of labour between sectors in a dual economy (or triple economy, allowing for the urban informal sector) with rigidities, as well as the role of factors such as efficiency wages in the setting of pay. Similarly, the analysis of pension schemes has to take account of imperfect information, monopoly power, and the interlinking of transactions.

None the less, we believe that there are certain lessons to be drawn, as we argue below.

4.2. The Approach to Social Security Analysis

The first theme which has been stressed in our review of policies in Britain, France, and the US has been the need for the analysis to range outside the purely economic and in particular to seek to understand the political influences on the design of policy. The political economy of social security is of great importance. This may not perhaps require stress in the development context, where there has been greater awareness of the interdisciplinary contribution than in other branches of economics. But it is clear that the level and form of the programmes which can be sustained depends on the degree of political support. We have noted at several points the role played by interest groups and the 'middle-class capture' of the Welfare State. Two further elements may be noted here. The first is the role of participation in the administration of social security, which has historically played a greater role in France, and which may increase the acceptability of transfers. The second is the access to information and the accessibility of economic analysis. The 'Fabian' tradition in Britain has recognized the importance of statistical evidence not just in informing the public debate but also in campaigning on social issues. The Institute for Research on Poverty at Wisconsin has played a leading role in the public debate in the US. How far this is possible depends critically on access to basic data and on the support provided to empirical research.

A second major theme of the analysis of social security has been the need to view in entirety all measures which contribute to a particular objective. As Titmuss has stressed, fiscal and occupational welfare may be as important as explicit State welfare programmes, and may operate in conflicting directions. In the case of child support, a good example is provided by the income tax allowances for children in France and the US. In general the provision of a deduction for a child has a value to the family which increases with the marginal tax rate (the effect of the French quotient system is more complex), and in both countries the highest-income groups would benefit the most. In order to prevent this, a ceiling is placed on the net benefit in France and in the US the exemption is phased out altogether. But it remains the case that the tax provisions are of no benefit to those who would not be paying income tax anyway. In the context of a developing country, where the income tax paying population is likely to be a minority, the use of income tax deductions for children is likely to be highly regressive and in distributional terms may offset other direct measures of support for children. The application in several francophone African countries of the French quotient system is, for example, criticized by Goode as 'an example of the transplantation of an important income tax feature to an environment different from that in which it was conceived' and for which it seemed 'quite unsuitable' (1984: 107). In anglophone African countries too the existence of tax concessions for children owes its existence to the colonial past. Once established, however, such concessions are hard to remove, as witnessed by the recent rejection by the Zimbabwe government of that country's Tax Commission's modest recommendation that the number of children for whom income tax credits are given be gradually reduced from six to three (Commission of Inquiry into Taxation 1987).

The experience of developed countries suggests that the interactions between different programmes may have important effects. The superposition of different programmes has, for example, led to high cumulative marginal tax rates in a manner that was not always planned or desired. In the context of a low-income country the possibility of overlap in means-tested government programmes may appear less of a problem, but where different agencies are operating different targeted programmes (such as in health, education, and food relief) not dissimilar problems may arise.

A third major theme is the need to distinguish between the form and reality of social security. All too often economists have studied the social security manuals and taken for granted that the benefits actually paid correspond to what is intended in the legislation. In practice this is often not the case, as is well illustrated by the problem of take-up that we have discussed: for example, the fact that nearly half of the intended beneficiaries of the Family Income Supplement in Britain did not claim their entitlement.

The difference between form and reality is relevant when we come to examine a fourth theme, the effect of social security on the behaviour of households and firms. These behavioural reactions, and the resulting general equilibrium adjustments, are evidently important. The dimensions of household response studied in countries such as Britain, France, and the US are not necessarily those most relevant to developing countries, but they point to the kind of considerations which should be investigated. The study of divorce in the US may not be directly relevant, but analysis of the effect of social security on support by absent family members and other private transfers has a clear parallel. The potential importance of this problem has been recognized for a long time as can be seen, for instance, from the somewhat dramatic statement of the Famine Commission Report of 1880 in India:

Even where the legal right does not exist, the moral obligation of mutual assistance is scarcely less distinctly recognized (in rural India). . . . Any form of relief calculated to bring these rights into obscurity or desuetude, or to break down these habits by showing them to be superfluous, would be an incalculable misfortune (quoted in Drèze 1988: 24).

Similarly, the debate about benefits in cash versus benefits in kind which has taken place in developed countries may not have immediate relevance to low-income countries, but it raises relevant issues. The general equilibrium incidence of different types of provision (Foldes 1967) may, for example, help elucidate how the choice between providing food and providing cash in a famine depends on the food supply situation as well as the characteristics of the food market.

The reference to private transfers illustrates the last of the themes we would like to stress. It is evident that the extent of such transfers depends crucially on a person's family and local circumstances. In these there is great diversity, and the analysis of social security must take full account of such diversity. The experience in developed countries has shown that it may be quite misleading to base consideration of a policy change on a few hypothetical examples. The use of sample survey information to provide evidence about the impact of reforms on a representative sample of the population has been one of the significant advances in developed countries in recent years. At the same time, it is important to consider the choice of the unit of analysis. The typical sample survey in a developed country takes the household as the unit and considers a nationally drawn sample (possibly with some clustering to reduce survey costs). As such, the survey throws little light on the social context. The position of an unemployed couple with two children may be quite different depending on whether they have been long established in a village, surrounded by family members, or whether they are recent immigrants to a large city where they have no kin. The wider use of sample survey data in the analysis of policy reforms has therefore to be combined with information about local communities. Village studies can provide a rich source of such information (see, for instance, the study of Palanpur in Bliss and Stern 1982).

Seventy-five years ago, an Indian philanthropist provided funds for the Ratan Tata Foundation at the LSE for the study of poverty. Its officers, including R. H. Tawney, sought to provide answers to 'questions of poverty and destitution, their causes, prevention and relief, *whether at home or abroad*' (our italics). The main conclusion of this paper is that, while the answers at home are likely to be different from those abroad, the methods of analysis lying behind the answers may indeed be of value in both contexts.

References

Abel-Smith, B. and Townsend, P. (1965), *The Poor and the Poorest*. London: G. Bell.

Ameline, C. and Walker, R. (1984), 'France: Poverty and the Family', in R. Walker, R. Lawson, and P. Townsend (eds.), *Responses to Poverty: Lessons from Europe*. London: Heinemann Educational Books.

Atkinson, A. B. (1987a), 'Income Maintenance and Social Insurance', in A. J. Auerbach and M. Feldstein (eds.), *Handbook of Public Economics*, ii. Amsterdam, North-Holland.

——(1987b), 'Social Security Harmonisation in Europe: Evidence from Britain and France', in House of Lords, Select Committee on the European Communities, *Social Security in the European Community*. London: HMSO.

Atkinson, A. B., Bourguignon, F., and Chiappori, P. A. (1988), 'The French Tax Benefit System and a Comparison with the British System', in A. B. Atkinson and H. Sutherland (eds.), *Tax-Benefit Models*, STICERD Occasional Paper No. 10. London: London School of Economics.

Baker, J. (1986), 'Comparing National Priorities: Family and Population Policy in Britain and France', *Journal of Social Policy*, 15.

Barbor-Might, R. (1988), 'The Politics of Food', *Poverty*, No. 69. London: Child Poverty Action Group.

Barr, N. (1987), *The Economics of the Welfare State*. London: Weidenfeld & Nicolson.

Beveridge, W. H. (1942), *Social Insurance and Allied Services*, Cmd. 6404. London: HMSO.

Bliss, C. J. and Stern, N. H. (1982), *Palanpur: The Economy of an Indian Village*. Oxford: Clarendon Press.

Bradshaw, J., and Piachaud, D. (1980), *Child Support in the European Community*. London: Bedford Square Press.

Burghes, L. (1987), 'Does Workfare Work?', *Poverty*, No. 68. London: Child Poverty Action Group.

Burtless, G. (1986), 'Public Spending for the Poor: Trends, Prospects, and Economic Limits', in S. H. Danziger and D. H. Weinberg (eds.), *Fighting Poverty*. Cambridge, Mass.: Harvard University Press.

CERC (Centre d'Etude des Revenus et des Coûts) (1988), *Protection sociale et pauvreté*. Paris: La Documentation française.

Child Benefits Now Campaign (1977), *The Great Child Benefit Robbery*. London: Child Poverty Action Group.

Commission of Inquiry into Taxation (1987), *Report*. Harare: Government Printer.

Department of Health and Social Security (1985), *Reform of Social Security: Programme for Action*. Cmnd. 9691. London: HMSO.

Diamond, P. A. (1968), 'Negative Taxes and the Poverty Problem: A Review Article', *National Tax Journal*, 31.

Drèze, J. P. (1988), 'Famine Prevention in India', Discussion Paper No. 3, Development Economics Research Programme, London School of Economics; to be published in J. P. Drèze and A. K. Sen (eds.) (1990), *The Political Economy of Hunger*. Oxford: Oxford University Press.

Fiegehen, G., and Lansley, P. S. (1976), 'The Measurement of Poverty', *Journal of the Royal Statistical Society*, 139.

Foldes, L. (1967), 'Income Redistribution in Money and Kind', *Economica*, 34.

Galbraith, J. K. (1958), *The Affluent Society*. Boston: Houghton Mifflin.

Garfinkel, I. (1985), 'The Role of Child Support Insurance in Antipoverty Policy', *Annals of the American Academy of Political and Social Science*, 479.

Goode, R. (1984), *Government Finance in Developing Countries*. Washington, DC: The Brookings Institution.

Haveman, R. H. (1985), 'Does the Welfare State Increase Welfare? Reflections on Hidden Negatives and Observed Positives', *De Economist*, 133.

Heidenheimer, A. J., Heclo, H., and Adams, C. T. (1983), *Comparative Public Policy*. New York: St Martin's Press.

HM Treasury (1988), *The Government's Expenditure Plans 1988–89 to 1990–91*, ii, Cm. 288–II. London: HMSO.

International Labour Office (1985), *The Cost of Social Security*. Geneva: ILO.

Jallade, J.-P. (1988), 'Redistribution in the Welfare State: An Assessment of the French Performance', in J.-P. Jallade (ed.), *The Crisis of Redistribution in European Welfare States*. Stoke-on-Trent: Trentham Books.

Kamerman, S. B., and Kahn, A. J. (1981), *Child Care, Family Benefits and Working Parents*. New York: Columbia University Press.

Lampman, R. J. (1973), 'What Does it Do for the Poor? A New Test for National Policy', *Public Interest*, 34.

——(1975), 'Scaling Welfare Benefits to Income: An Idea That is Being Overworked', *Policy Analysis*, 1.

Le Grand, J., and Winter, D. (1987), 'The Middle Classes and the Defence of the British Welfare State', in R. E. Goodin and J. Le Grand (eds.), *Not Only the Poor*. London: Allen and Unwin.

Lynes, T. (1971), 'How to Pay Surtax While Living on the Breadline', Working Note 256, Centre for Environmental Studies, London.

——(1985), *Paying for Pensions: the French Experience*. London: Suntory Toyota International Centre for Economics and Related Disciplines.

MacDonald, M. (1977), *Food, Stamps and Income Maintenance*. New York: Academic Press.

Midgley, J. (1984), *Social Security, Inequality, and the Third World*. Chichester: John Wiley & Sons.

Murray, C. (1984), *Losing Ground: American Social Policy, 1950–1980*. New York: Basic Books.

Palmer, J. L. (1987), 'Income Security Policies in the United States: The Recent Record and Future Prospects', paper prepared for the International Atlantic Economic Conference, Munich, Apr.

Pechman, J. A. (1987), 'Tax reform: Theory and Practice', *Journal of Economic Perspectives*, 1.

Simpson, R. (1983), 'Cash and Care in France', *New Society*, 28 July.

Titmuss, R. M. (1958), *Essays on 'the Welfare State'*. London: Allen & Unwin.

US Department of Commerce (1987), *Statistical Abstract of the United States 1987*. Washington, DC: US Government Printing Office.

US Department of Health and Human Services (1986), *Social Security Bulletin January 1986*. Washington, DC: US Government Printing Office.

Weisbrod, B. A. (1969), 'Collective Action and the Distribution of Income: A Conceptual Approach', in Joint Economic Committee, *The Analysis and Evaluation of Public Expenditures, the PPB System*. Washington, DC: US Government Printing Office.

Wilson, D. (1987), 'The Welfare State in America', in R. Ford and M. Chakrabarti (eds.), *Welfare Abroad*. Edinburgh: Scottish Academic Press.

4

Traditional Systems of Social Security and Hunger Insurance: Past Achievements and Modern Challenges*

Jean-Philippe Platteau

This chapter is an attempt to assess broadly the performance of traditional systems of social security as they exist or have existed in Third World village societies. It does not aim at a full account of social-security institutions as they have been reported in the specialized literature (mainly, the anthropological writings). Rather, as a first step, the three following objectives will be pursued: (1) to identify the main characteristics of the institutions providing social security in the societies under concern; (2) to bring into light the basic principles which their functioning obeys; and (3) to identify the most important problems and limitations to which they are subject. These objectives will be achieved in the first two sections, adopting the Scott–Popkin controversy as a convenient point of departure for the whole discussion. In a second step, this chapter will provide a more detailed picture of apparently successful risk-pooling mechanisms as they have been found to prevail in several village societies. This will be done in Section 3. In a fourth section, the adequacy of traditional systems of social security will be evaluated in the light of modern challenges and present circumstances. Finally, a general conclusion will close the chapter.

1. THE SCOTT–POPKIN CONTROVERSY

The controversy between James Scott and Samuel Popkin which took place in the late 1970s is of direct relevance to our topic. Until then, the dominant approach to the study of Third World traditional (precolonial) village societies, especially among anthropologists and other social scientists, went basically unchallenged.[1] This approach, known today as the 'moral economy approach' (from the title of the well-known book published by Scott in 1976), is grounded

* I am grateful to all the persons who have offered me valuable comments on this chapter. I am especially indebted to Michael Lipton, Barbara Harriss, and Jean Drèze for their detailed reactions, as well as to Jean-Marie Baland, Pranab Bardhan, Frances Stewart, and Bina Agarwal for their useful punctual remarks.

[1] See Wolf (1955); Polanyi (1944, 1957, 1977); Service (1962, 1966); Dalton (1962, 1971); Belshaw (1965); Sahlins (1963, 1968, 1972); Migdal (1974); Scott (1972, 1976), among others.

upon the premiss that these societies are essentially geared to providing social and economic security for all their members. In an equally famous book published in 1979, Popkin strongly opposed the orthodox view and insisted that, on the contrary, social-security mechanisms are conspicuously absent in many precapitalist peasant communities. It is therefore useful to look a little more closely at the basic contentions of these two apparently irreconcilable views of traditional village institutions. This will provide a good starting point for the subsequent analysis and assessment of traditional social-security mechanisms.

1.1. *The Moral Economy Approach*

In the moral economy approach, precapitalist rural communities are viewed as societies in which social rights of minimum subsistence are secured to all members. The risk of hunger is insured against collectively and it is only under exceptionally adverse circumstances (like wars, epidemics, repeated crop failures) that traditional systems of social security may collapse and give way to social anarchy characterized by individual behaviour of the struggle-for-life type.[2] A particular person may lose his membership and, thereby, his traditional claims to guaranteed subsistence if he breaks some customary rules of the society to which he belongs. However, since villagers are keen to avoid subsistence crises in an environment fraught with serious uncertainties, and since it is always difficult to get accepted in other communities, open violation of customary laws is assumed to be rare.

According to this approach, social arrangements and economic institutions in traditional village societies have thus been especially designed to cope with the threat of hunger and other kinds of contingencies. It is in the light of this central objective that the high incidence of redistribution and reciprocity mechanisms (including patronage relations), to which anthropologists have given so much attention, must be accounted for. Market exchange is seen as a marginal form of transaction which is mostly confined to intertribal relations and to the exchange of goods with no special significance for physical or social survival. The idea here is that the functioning of the market could endanger the subsistence of individuals by reducing their food entitlements, and threaten the reproduction capacity of the group as a whole by promoting socio-economic differentiation and class polarization beyond the control of traditional power structures. As a consequence, market forces cannot be allowed a free play inside the community space.[3] In the words of Polanyi:

[2] For a particularly striking illustration of this possibility, see Turnbull (1984). See also Dirks (1980: 26–31).

[3] In the urban areas of ancient empires, food trade was also regulated because 'the authorities knew that as far as grain was concerned they might have a revolt on their hands among those who could not meet a free market price in times of scarcity' (Jones 1981: 87).

No community intent on protecting the fount of solidarity between its members can allow latent hostility to develop around a matter as vital to animal existence and, therefore, capable of arousing as tense anxieties as food. Hence the universal banning of transactions of a gainful nature in regard to food and foodstuffs in primitive and archaic society. The very widely spread ban on higgling-haggling over victuals automatically removes price-making markets from the realm of early institutions (1957: 255).

Within the community, a 'subsistence ethic' prevails to guarantee subsistence as a 'moral claim' or as a 'social right' to which every member is entitled. It finds its social expression 'in the patterns of social control and reciprocity that structure daily conduct' (Scott 1976: 32, 40). Notice that this 'subsistence ethic' is not tantamount to an egalitarian utopia: 'village egalitarianism in this sense is conservative not radical; it claims that all should have a place, a living, not that all should be equal' (ibid. 40).

As has already been pointed out, intervillage or intertribal relations are the privileged domain of market exchange transactions. What must be added here is that these market relations are not of the usual type postulated in the standard Walras–Arrow–Debreu general equilibrium framework. Called 'negative reciprocity' by Service (1966), they are akin to the concept of 'self-interest seeking with guile' elaborated by Williamson or to that of 'opportunistic behaviour' commonly used in transaction-cost economics. Typically, such behaviour is not restrained by any moral code of honesty or fairness: instead, agents are allowed to seek their personal advantage by using any kind of means at their disposal, including 'lying, stealing, and cheating' as well as more 'subtle forms of deceit' (Williamson 1985: 47). This explains why, in pre-capitalist societies, trade is usually equated to stealing and pure trading relations are authorized only with outsiders or foreigners (Pospisil 1958: 127; Bourdieu 1980; 196–7). However, when relations with outsiders involve the exchange of useful objects required for subsistence, or when they are needed to cope with temporary food shortages, 'the potential hostility which could break out into active aggression must be reduced, compensated for, and controlled' (Belshaw 1965: 14). This is sometimes achieved through complex procedures such as the 'ports of trade' characteristic of the early empires (Polanyi et al. 1957; Polanyi 1968); the kula system discovered by Malinowski (1920, 1921, 1922) in the Trobriand islands; the practice of 'silent trade' observed in some regions of Equatorial and West Africa (Sahlins 1968; Giri 1983: 22–3); or the settling of farmer clients in the oases and in the desert fringes among several African pastoralist societies (Colson 1979: 23–4; Torry 1979: 520; Fleuret 1986: 227).[4]

---

[4] In the 'ports of trade' system, commercial transactions are carried out in special trading centres under the aegis of representatives of policial entities. In the kula system, potential enemies involved in the trading relationships neutralize each other through a complex network of ceremonial gift-giving with strictly calculated reciprocity. In the 'silent trade' system, the trading agents never meet physically and the bargaining is effected through repeated journeys to and from an agreed place where each party proceeds in turn.

For our purpose, the following set of propositions can be drawn from the moral economy approach.

1. In precapitalist rural societies, villagers are constantly exposed to the threat of subsistence crises, which they have a compelling preoccupation to avert. As a result, such societies are largely organized around the problem of food contingencies and other subsistence hazards and they tend to act as guarantors of minimal subsistence for all their members.

2. In pursuance of this objective, traditional village societies aim at achieving a high degree of self-sufficiency in food and other essentials at the village level and even at the household level (unless there are strong scale economies like in the case of hunting).

3. To the extent that complete self-sufficiency cannot be achieved at the household level, or that household food supplies are subject to dangerous fluctuations, self-regulating markets are not considered as a reliable mechanism to ensure that food goes to the people who most need it. Other institutional arrangements (about which more will be said later) have been adopted that are supposedly more effective in providing food security to the local inhabitants. Such arrangements are backed by value systems and moral codes that emphasize the need for co-operation inside the community space.

4. If food exchanges within the community are insufficient to ensure adequate security for all the members, trade links are established with partners located outside the community space (as in the case of exchanges of grain against salt in West Africa). However, market forces are not allowed a free rein in that case either. Indeed, in so far as moral norms of good conduct for market behaviour cannot be shared among trading partners who belong to different communities (villages, clans, tribes, regions, and so on), and since securing access to food is of such paramount importance for survival, socio-political mechanisms are required to control the operation of market forces and ensure that exchange can actually take place in an orderly and predictable way.

1.2. *The Political Economy Approach*

The main point emphasized in the political economy approach advocated by Popkin (1979) is that traditional village institutions, arrangements, and norms 'have neither been motivated nor been effective to guarantee the subsistence needs of community members' (Hayami and Kikuchi 1981: 19). In the words of Popkin, 'insurance, welfare, and subsistence guarantees within precapitalist villages are limited' and 'the calculations of peasants driven by motives of survival in a risky environment led not to subsistence floors and extensive village-wide insurance schemes, but to procedures that generated and enforced inequality within the village' (Popkin 1979: 32–3). He further argues: 'It does not follow from individual risk minimization or security maximization that villages will function to minimize risk or maximize security for all.' Indeed, 'there are conflicts of interest, in addition to common interests, inherent within the village', and 'self-interest can lead also to coalitions organized to drive persons from the village or to deprive them of benefits' (ibid. 44).

In fact, Popkin starts from the observation that household-level strategies for avoiding risk or averting starvation—what is sometimes called 'self insurance' —are much more common than village- or community-level schemes designed for the sharing, pooling, and shifting of household risks. Thus, for instance, the household-level strategy of scattered fields 'is a clear example of conflict between individual and group rationality whereby each individual, following a safety-first strategy, ends up with less production than he would if the village as a whole could follow an aggregate safety-first strategy'. As a matter of fact, 'consolidated fields with higher average output and higher variance from year to year would be a better strategy for peasants to follow if the village could provide insurance for farmers to compensate for the increased variance of consolidated fields' (Popkin 1979: 49–50, 105). According to Popkin, this would be a clear case where 'the actions of individually rational peasants in both market and non-market situations do not aggregate to a "rational" village' (ibid. 31).

The fact that village-level strategies for risk avoidance are not adopted in spite of their higher efficiency is taken by Popkin as sufficient evidence that the moral economy assumptions about the behaviour of peasants are simply incorrect. More specifically, Popkin finds fault with the hypothesis that peasants are either altruistic actors or passive subjects willing to respect social norms of conduct and moral principles of reciprocity. On the contrary, he contends that peasants in precapitalist societies are egoist and hard-calculating agents intent on deriving maximum personal advantage from all actions in which they get involved. The opportunistic behaviour displayed by many villagers is bound to make collective action ineffective owing the the well-known free-rider problem; insurance or welfare schemes are among the collective goods which may thus be prevented from being produced (ibid. 24–5). As for social norms, they cannot be expected to mitigate the free-rider problem by instilling altruistic preoccupations into the people's internalized value systems, or by holding their most dangerous opportunistic tendencies in check. Indeed, norms are regarded by Popkin as malleable, continuously renegotiable, and shifting 'in accord with considerations of power and strategic interaction among individuals'. As a result, norms are often found to be inconsistent or conflictual so that they 'cannot directly and simply determine actions' (ibid. 22).

It is interesting to note that in his general approach to problems of collective action, Popkin is much more pessimistic than Mancur Olson. In actual fact, while Olson (1965, 1982) insists that co-operative strategies are much more likely to succeed in small than in large communities (since the costs of organizing such strategies, including the costs of detecting and policing free-riding, are comparatively low in the former), Popkin appears to believe that, as a matter of principle, co-operative endeavours are bound to fail *even in small* (*village*) *communities*.

2. TOWARDS A MORE BALANCED EVALUATION OF TRADITIONAL SOCIAL SECURITY SYSTEMS

2.1. *General Considerations*

There is little doubt that with the publication of *The Rational Peasant*, a gust of fresh wind entered into the mollycoddled world of anthropological ideas. Popkin's book forced a debate on rather moot questions and challenged the idealized view of traditional village societies which so many anthropologists are inclined to accept. In particular, he has strongly emphasized the point recently made again by Robert Wade that 'in the peasant context, even where all or most cultivators in a village could benefit from joint action, that action will by no means be automatically forthcoming' (Wade 1988: 188; see also Lipton 1985).

This being said, two basic criticisms can be levelled against the intellectual contribution of Popkin. First, the opposition he sees between his own ideas and those of the moral economists is sometimes overdone in view of the numerous qualifying statements that some of these writers have made. To give only one example, Migdal himself has amply commented on the limitations which 'mutual suspicion' among the villagers creates for collective action, including insurance schemes; in the same line, he has emphasized household-level strategies of risk coverage (Migdal 1974: 74–8). The overdrawing of the boundary between the moral economy and the political economy approaches also arises from Popkin's disregard of the obvious fact that selfish peasants can well adopt *apparently* altruistic behaviour (Posner 1981: 160; Hayami and Kikuchi 1981: 19; Booth and Sundrum 1985: 217). The problem with his approach in this respect is that he seems to overlook the fact that self-insurance is not the only way of coping with the risk of hunger for people who are irretrievably egoistic. As a matter of fact, selfishness does not preclude people from entering into relationships which can help all the parties concerned, or only the poorest among them, better to insure against that risk. This is particularly evident in the case of patron–client relationships as they have been analysed by Scott himself (1976: 35–44), and in the case of less hierarchical systems of insurance relations as will be shown at a later stage of this analysis.

Second, the view of traditional village societies which Popkin has put forward is no less partial and incomplete than the one advocated by the most radical proponents of the moral economy approach. For one thing, his judgement on the ability of these societies to elaborate village-wide insurance schemes or insurance substitutes is much too negative. It is certainly correct to insist that traditional systems of social security and hunger insurance were imperfect and lacking in some important respects. Yet, they were far from being simply absent and Colson (1979: 27) is probably close to the truth when she writes that they were 'moderately effective' in the sense that they worked reasonably well in situations of moderate hardship. For another thing, the explanation offered by Popkin to account for their alleged or real failures is not wholly satisfactory, essentially because he has concentrated too much on the self-interested motivation of villagers, taking the extreme view (inferred from the Prisoners' Dilemma) that rational people cannot achieve rational collective outcomes due to the insuperable difficulties of organization. By so doing, he has overlooked other, non-behavioural factors that are equally or even more important for understanding the conditions of collective action in the specific instance of insurance schemes.[5]

In Subsections 2.2. and 2.3. below, I will try to substantiate the two claims made in the second aforementioned criticism. This should allow us to assess properly the respective strengths and weaknesses of both the moral economy and the political economy approaches in regard to the issue analysed here.

2.2. Social Control over Essential Sources of Livelihood

2.2.1. *The Institutional Build-up of Traditional Village Societies*   In reviewing the central ideas of the moral economy approach, I have emphasized that, typically, market principles do not apply to intracommunity transactions in precapitalist village societies. As for intercommunity transactions, they are carried out under a system of trade which is either politically controlled (when the objects of exchange perform an important function for the physical or social survival of the trading partners' societies), or allowed to operate in the most unbridled way. In both cases, trade is akin to a state of war (either disguised or open). It is therefore no wonder that the two institutional pillars of the market system—the rule of contract and private property—are conspicuously absent in the societies under concern. This is a crucial fact to bear in mind in any attempt to understand and evaluate traditional systems of social security.

Private property means that a person has exclusive and alienable rights over the things that he or she owns. This requires that 'a sharp distinction be drawn between a thing and its owner' (Gregory 1982: 18), and that the rights of use and control over given resources or goods be precisely defined and allocated while being at the same time amenable to effective protection through judicial procedures. The rule of contract presupposes that relations can be established

---

[5] Incidentally, Popkin's characterization of insurance schemes as a collective good is not very helpful. As will be evident at a later stage of the analysis, problems of insurance are best analysed in terms of the economic theory of information.

between agents, that is between parties who are free and independent in the sense of being fully emancipated from all kinds of non-economic (social, ritual, religious, political) constraints. In the words of one economist, 'the identity of the parties to a transaction is treated as irrelevant' (Williamson 1985: 69). Moreover, the nature of the agreement must be carefully delimited and remedies must be narrowly prescribed, so that 'should the initial presentation fail to materialize because of nonperformance, the consequences are relatively predictable from the beginning and are not open-ended' (Macneil 1978, cited by Williamson). Legal rules, formal documents, and self-liquidating trans- actions are thus central characteristics of classical contractual relations (William- son 1985: 69). And the above institutional environment is congenial to the emergence and maintenance of anonymous, general, and abstract dependence relations that are typical of ideal market transactions or what Marx has called commodity exchange relations: indeed, 'commodity exchange is an exchange of alienable things between transactors who are in a state of reciprocal independence' (Gregory 1982: 12).

By contrast, traditional precapitalist societies are the domain of non- commodity (gift) exchange defined as 'an exchange of inalienable things between transactors who are in a state of reciprocal dependence'. 'Commodity exchange establishes a relationship between the objects exchanged, whereas gift exchange establishes a relationship between the subjects' (ibid. 12, 19). As sociologists like Mauss and Bourdieu have stressed, the gift economy is a debt economy: on the one hand, the gift creates a debt that has to be repaid at some future (determinate or indeterminate) time, and, on the other hand, through gift-giving the donor aims at establishing a durable personal relation- ship with the donee (Mauss 1925: 9–42; Bourdieu 1980: 167–231). In Section 3, it will be shown that gift exchange can be at least partly interpreted as an insurance mechanism through which transactors attempt to cover various kinds of contingencies. In the light of this interpretation, Gregory's observation that 'the aim of a transactor in such an economy is to acquire as many gift- debtors as he possibly can and not to maximize profit' (Gregory 1982: 19) can receive a straightforward explanation in terms of risk-spreading considerations.[6]

In precapitalist societies, considerations of status and fairness, as opposed to contract, played a dominant role. If considerations of status served the main purpose of maintaining social, political, and ritual stratification,[7] those based

---

[6] Gregory and Bourdieu have not adopted this line of enquiry since they have chosen to look at gift exchange as a means through which relations of domination and control are established. This is not necessarily contradictory with my own interpretation, in so far as a person who is well insured is in a good position to accumulate wealth and power in the long run.

[7] Thus, it has been noted that 'Indian legal procedure considered that contesting parties to a dispute were not discrete individuals but were connected to others by complex and multiple social, political, and ritual ties. It recognized the existence of socially, politically, and ritually unequal corporate lineages and castes, and understood cases of conflict as moments in ongoing relations among such groups' (Wolf 1982: 248).

on fairness fulfilled the important function of safeguarding the interests of the poor and the unlucky. As a matter of fact, in contrast to modern legal practice which insists on clear-cut decisions and rigid formal rules, considerations of fairness allowed for maximum flexibility and continuous negotiation in which all sorts of peculiar circumstances could be taken into account. They therefore provided an indispensable cushion in a world fraught with so many uncertainties and contingencies that no formal rule or contract could ever have specified all the relevant conditions. In such a world, as some writers have pointed out, rules other than general moral principles such as mutual help or the recognition of everyone's claim to continuous subsistence would be an ineffective means of policing, and would result in tremendous hardship for certain sections of the population. Only imprecision allows the unpredictable to be approached with appropriate flexibility (Scott 1976: chap. 2; Hayami and Kikuchi 1981: 16; Wolf 1982: 248; Wynne 1980: 41).

In this connection, it is worth pondering over the following description of legal practice in Aristotelian antiquity:

The obligation to keep one's promise or to abide by a contract (whether explicit or implicit) was only a moral rule and not a formal law. It remained subject to the general principle of justice and fairness. A magistrate was thus entitled to release a transactor from his duty to meet his obligations if he was of the opinion that the terms of the contract were unfair. His appreciation of the degree of fairness of a contract was not made by reference to a priori legal criteria; rather, it was based upon his own assessment of the situation in the light of all relevant concrete circumstances. A just distribution— of assets, honours, privileges, statuses—was then considered as the touchstone of social order and peace. The main function of the magistrate was . . . to restore a 'balanced' situation while taking into account peculiar circumstances and customary norms (Lepage 1985: 112–13, my translation).

It is difficult to accept Popkin's contention that in precapitalist societies social norms and values are malleable and continuously shifting, at least as a general statement about such societies. By definition, moral principles are general and liable to various kinds of interpretation;[8] but from this, as should be evident from the above analysis, it cannot be inferred that they are incapable of influencing or determining human actions. Clearly, Popkin's conception of precapitalist societies as 'amoral' human groups, devoid of any stable value system and completely abandoned to the free play of selfish motives, is no solid ground for analysing behaviour and social interaction among their members. It can only be useful to apprehend precapitalist societies which are in an advanced state of social disintegration due to slave raids, wars, epidemics, persistent famine conditions, or which are going through what Lipton (1985)

---

[8] If this were what Popkin meant by 'malleability', I would not find fault with his statement. However, this is clearly not the case since he precisely expressed the view that social norms cannot influence human actions owing to their volatility.

has called 'transition of trust' due to capitalist penetration, national integration, and other forms of transformation of societal control.

The absence of genuine rights of private property in productive assets is a well-known feature of traditional village societies. It means that no single owner can claim exclusive property in those assets nor use them at discretion in whatever way he likes (he does not have the rights of *usus*, *fructus*, and *abusus* typical of the Western concept of private property). In particular, he is not entitled to dispose of them (to transfer them, to donate them, and so on) by an act of will: assets are not freely alienable and, therefore, they may not be 'commoditized'. Note also that the non-exclusiveness of property rights typically manifests itself in the existence of various overlapping rights of use and control over the resources concerned. What needs to be stressed is that the foregoing characteristics hold true not only with respect to clan-based societies in which a communal (corporate) land-use system is in force but also with respect to more inegalitarian societies in which essential resources (like land and water) are concentrated in the hands of a small (feudal or quasi-feudal) élite. There is a saying among Kirghiz shepherds which illustrates perfectly the overlapping of the rights of use and control over the land in a strongly stratified society: 'God has given us the land of the Khan.' The statement is totally ambiguous because it recognizes at one and the same time that the land belongs to God (the ultimate owner in whom all property is vested according to Muslim belief), to the Khan (the lord), and to the common people.

The absence of exclusive and clear-cut, absolute and definite, private property rights in essential resources usually implies that customary rules and social control by the community play an important role in the allocation and use of these resources. An interesting explanation for this situation—especially when fields are widely scattered—is the need to overcome the complex problems created by pervasive production externalities, like those arising from the fact that croplands are transformed into pasture lands after the harvest (Dahlman 1980: 93–145; Hayami and Kikuchi 1981: 12–16; Wade 1988). In the present context, however, it is more relevant to concentrate on the social-security function which is performed by a mechanism designed to prevent the emergence of genuine private property rights and to restrict free land market transactions. First, in the case of tribal or clan-based village societies, such a mechanism allows for flexible adjustment in the allocation of rights of access to productive resources according to the subsistence needs of all the members. Thus, for example, a greater amount of land may be allotted to the households whose size has increased since the time lands were initially distributed within the village (and vice versa for households which have become smaller). Second, in the case of inegalitarian societies, the livelihood of the poor sections of the population is often protected by the very restrictions that have been imposed on the land use rights of the big landowning families. For instance, landowners are not entitled to evict the tenants working on their farm unless exceptional circumstances can be invoked before the customary authorities and complex procedures are followed to settle the issue.

2.2.2. Guaranteed Access to Productive Assets

In many traditional village societies, guaranteed access to vital resources (particularly land) for every resident household is the main method through which people are protected from the risk of hunger. This is especially evident in the case of tribal societies, where land is usually held under corporate tenure with the result that it is subject to strong communal regulation. The broad principle underlying this land tenure system is that each household head belonging to the group is entitled to be allocated a sufficient amount of land to support his family.[9] Moreover, the allottee has possession and use of the lands as long as they are being cultivated, and his heirs would normally be given the lands that were cultivated at the time of his death (unless the rights of access are subject to a periodic rotation). In a more general way, customary rules and institutional arrangements regulate all important rights and duties of landholdings such as possession, inheritance, transfer, mortgage, size of operation, access to water, woodland or pasture use, and tenancy (Cohen 1980: 353).

Possession of land and other productive assets in such societies is personal and statutory in the sense that access to a portion of the communal resources is mediated through membership in a social group. The relation is reciprocal: on the one hand, group membership is the basis of social rights (particularly, of the most important among them, the right to subsistence), but, on the other hand, maintaining access to a share of the corporate productive assets serves to validate membership in the group (Berry 1984: 91). Members not only include those who claim descent, actual or putative, from other members, but also strangers and migrants who have been accepted as members of, and reside with, the group (Noronha 1985: 182). Therefore, access to land and other vital resources is not necessarily predicated upon kinship or descent-based ties, but may also be grounded upon loyalty and patronage relations which are often associated with ascriptive forms of status or social identity (Smith 1959: chaps. 1, 3, 4; Berry 1984: 91; Meillassoux 1980: 62).

Popkin is basically correct when he points out that the stratum of residents named 'insiders' usually enjoy more rights and benefits than the stratum of 'outsiders' (Popkin 1979: 43). Clearly, tribal, clan-based, societies are much less egalitarian than they have often been depicted. But this is not a point of contention between Popkin and most moral economists. On the other hand, Popkin makes another valid point when he stresses that, with increasing pressure on the available land, coalitions may be organized by the 'insiders' to

---

[9] In stratified tribal societies, however, members belonging to the upper social strata (for instance, members who have a long period of residence in the village or can trace their ancestry back to the founders of the village) are entitled to parcels of greater size and higher fertility (Noronha 1985: 182).

drive the 'outsiders' away from the village or to confine them to marginal lands: as a result, 'the metaphor of corporate village as "collectivity" should be replaced by the metaphor of the corporate village as a "corpcration"' (ibid. 43–4, 46). In his extensive survey of land tenure systems in sub-Saharan Africa, Noronha (1985: 182–3) has also reached the conclusion that, as land availability diminishes, 'the circle of individuals who are entitled to access to land diminishes in two respects: membership is more narrowly defined in that increasingly, only those who can trace actual descent are entitled to land—the stranger being admitted more as a crop sharer or tenant or laborer without any right to land; and the type of land available for allocation to the newly-admitted member becomes increasingly marginal' (see also Smith 1959: 52–8).

Regarding the latter point, what deserves to be emphasized is that village societies undergoing the process of exclusion and 'corporatization' mentioned above have been profoundly transformed through processes of agricultural commercialization and rapid population growth in modern times. As a consequence, they have entered a phase of dynamic disequilibrium which caused a gradual erosion of their traditional mechanisms of social security or a restriction of the collective rights of subsistence to an increasingly small number of rural dwellers or migrants. Among the 'insiders', however, it would be wrong to assume that rapid population growth always promotes social and economic polarization. There are numerous instances in which scarce assets have been increasingly divided and subdivided to safeguard the customary rights of access of the 'insiders' (whether within or outside the framework of extended families). In many cases, also, teams working on jointly managed resources have agreed to incorporate new members and to share with them the income therefrom, even though their marginal productivity was negligible or perhaps even negative (due, for example, to overcrowding). A vivid illustration of such an income-sharing through work-spreading practice will be presented later.

Guaranteeing access to land (and other vital resources) may not be sufficient to provide for the minimum needs of households in all circumstances. Collective risks or specific risks may threaten from time to time the livelihood of either many or a few inhabitants. To face these uncertainties, villagers must adopt a range of coping strategies to reduce risks, to share and pool them, or to adjust to their consequences once they have materialized. These strategies of risk management may be carried out at the level of the household (in which case the term 'self-insurance' is appropriate), or within a wider social group (which always holds true for risk-pooling insurance mechanisms). At this juncture, it is especially worth noting that land allocation arrangements geared to securing minimum subsistence for all the resident households usually comprise an important mechanism of risk reduction through which peasants can counter a good deal of the hazards of their climate and environment. This mechanism consists of granting them access to a variety of lands of different quality, location, and soil characteristics among which production risks can be spread.

For example, in areas of the Sahel where flood-recession agriculture is the mainstay of livelihood, peasants have possession and use of different plots of land located at varying heights along the slope of the drainage basin of a river. The variance of yields can thus be reduced since there is a spatial spread of farm plots in response to variability in rainfall so as to ensure that at least some of them will always be flooded.[10] Another well-known example of spatial diversification of farm plots across heterogeneous agroclimates with non-perfectly correlated production risks is the traditional system of 'ecological floors' practised in the Andes and in the Himalayan region. Here, the scattering of agricultural fields takes into account altitudinal and latitudinal variations.[11] Note that dispersal of herds over a wide variety of pastures with different risk characteristics can be analysed in a way analogous to plot-scattering in agriculture (Colson 1979: 23; Torry 1987: 519).

It has been rightly emphasized that 'spatial diversification of farm plots is a closer substitute for crop insurance than other informal means of risk adjustment' (Walker and Jodha 1986: 25; see also Newbery 1989: 284–5). When it is viewed in conjunction with this possibility of holding a diversified portfolio of plots, communal control over the distribution and use of land assets therefore appears to be an effective mechanism of social security in traditional village societies. The security provided by this mechanism is, however, far from complete, particularly when village lands are more or less homogeneous. In these circumstances, other risk-coping devices are called for to cover the production uncertainties arising from weather and other vagaries (such as pest attacks).

Methods of self-insurance play an important role in this respect and they have actually received a lot of attention in the literature. They may pertain either to the production sphere or to the realm of household domestic management. To the former category belong such measures as crop diversification, intercropping, staggered planting, salvage crop planting, sequential decision-taking and adaptive flexibility in cropping patterns, diversification of seed varieties, selection of resistant, low-variance varieties, activity and livestock diversification, and so on.[12] As for the second category, it comprises all measures designed for the accumulation of assets that can be depleted in case of crop failure or food shortage. The assets so accumulated may be of very different kinds, running from durable consumption goods to stored foods through cash holdings and livestock.[13]

---

[10] In the normal situation, some plots will be over-flooded and others will remain beyond the reach of the rising level of water.

[11] See, in particular, the special issue of *Mountain Research and Development*, 5/1, 1985, and Mayer (1985).

[12] For a short survey of these risk reduction strategies, see Longhurst (1986). See also Corbett (1988), Chambers (1989), Drèze and Sen (1989), and the literature cited there.

[13] An interesting example of livestock accumulation as a hedge against critical emergencies (and as forced savings for future investment) is that of pig-raising in Mexico studied by Ralph Beals.

We have seen above that in agricultural tribal societies guaranteed access to land plots with varying risk and fertility characteristics together with self-insurance strategies normally allow all the member households to obtain a minimum income and to avert starvation over a full weather cycle. Likewise, in traditional village societies where the people's livelihood crucially depends upon the exploitation of a common property resource subject to significant production hazards, social arrangements must ensure that access to the resource enables all the households to have a maximum chance of earning their livelihood. As a matter of fact, this requires not only that the latter have equal or fair opportunities of access to the resource in question (pasturelands, rivers, forests, and so on), but also that the probabilities of reaping the produce therefrom are more or less equalized among them, at least to the extent necessary for safeguarding their possibilities of survival. Precapitalist village societies can be ingenious in devising subsistence-oriented systems of regulation of access to vital productive resources. A fascinating illustration of both imaginative and organizational capacities is provided by the system of rotating access to the sea in the traditional beachseine fishermen communities of southern Sri Lanka (Alexander 1980: 97–102, and 1982: chap. 7; Amarasinghe 1988, 1989). A similar sea tenure system has also been observed in Turkey (Berkes 1986).

2.3. An Illustration: Beachseining in Sri Lanka   Beachseining is one of the most common fishing techniques used in traditional maritime communities. The beachseine is a large bag-shaped net with coir wings of extensive length. Its name is derived from the fact that it is operated from the shore itself, though it always requires the help of a boat to be put out at sea (so that its two wings can be properly paid out). It is also important to note that, owing to the very size of the fishing gear, beachseining requires a large area of operation; moreover, the sea bottom must be sandy and free from rocks and other obstructions so that the net can be dragged smoothly. These constraints create a situation of scarce fishing grounds in the sense that all the existing nets cannot be laid out as often as their owners would like. In fact, the number of existing nets is typically higher than the maximum number of nets which can be used in a day. However, even if it were not so and each net could be worked once in a day, rules of procedure would still be needed to govern the rights of access to the fishery. Indeed, all the nets cannot be cast simultaneously, and expected fishing incomes are not independent of the timing of the fishing operations on a given day. For one thing, most of the big catches tend to occur in the early morning and, for another thing, fish caught in the morning bring higher prices (because fish brought late to the market cannot easily find willing buyers). The

Pig-raising is an accretionary type of savings since the pig has to be fed daily and his fattening makes his value increase gradually. According to the author, it is preferred to hoarding cash because it is a less liquid asset: having cash at hand would be too dangerous because it would induce people to spend it on consumption (Beals 1970: 237–8).

problem is further complicated by the fact that the probability distribution of the fish catches may differ significantly from one fishing spot to another.

To give every net equal chances not only in terms of access to the water but also in terms of access to catch and income opportunities, a rotating system has been devised, the rules of which enable the net owners to know when their turn is due. In the village of Gahavälla (Sri Lanka) studied by Alexander, the fishing area is divided into two stations: the harbour side (from which most big catches come) and the rock side. The net cycle begins on the harbour side and, after a net has had the dawn turn on that side, it is entitled to the dawn turn on the rock side on the next day. Subsequently, it may be used on the rock side each day once the net immediately following it in the sequence has been used. The sequence of net use over a period of five days, assuming that four nets can be used on each day on both fishing stations, is shown in Table 4.1.

Table 4.1. Sequence of net use in the village of Gahavälla

	Fishing Station							
	Harbour				Rock			
Day	Dawn		Night		Dawn		Night	
One	5	6	7	8	4	3	2	1
Two	6	7	8	9	5	4	3	2
Three	7	8	9	10	6	5	4	3
Four	8	9	10	11	7	6	5	4
Five	9	10	11	12	8	7	6	5

Source: Adapted from Alexander (1982: 145).

As can be seen from the table, twelve nets have been used at least once in a period of five days. Furthermore, nets 5–8 have been worked a maximum number of five times during this period; nets 4 and 9 have been used four times; nets 3 and 10 three times; nets 2 and 11 twice; and, finally, nets 1 and 12 only once. If the total number of nets is twelve, net 1 will reappear in the harbour site on the sixth day (where it will have the last turn) and in the rock site on the tenth day (where it will have the first turn). As for net 5, it will have a new dawn turn in the harbour site on the thirteenth day: a complete net cycle lasts twelve days. Over the full net cycle, each net will have been operated eight times (the total number of possible turns per day in all the existing fishing stations), that is for two out of three days on an average.[14] It is worth noting

[14] The intensity of use of each net is therefore equal to $(n.x/N)$, where N is the total number of nets; n is the number of fishing spots available; and x is the number of hauls per day which can be made in any fishing spot.

that for each net, the period of use is strictly continuous: in the above example, once its first turn has come, a net will be worked during eight days in succession and, thereafter, it will be left idle for four days.

Additional difficulties arise from the fact that there are significant inter-seasonal variations in fish catches. Thus, in southern Sri Lanka, a sizeable portion of yearly incomes from fishing are obtained during a flush season which lasts only one month, and the exact timing of which can never be known in advance (Alexander 1982: 147). These difficulties cannot be serious as long as the total number of nets does not exceed by too large a margin the total number of possible turns (or hauls) per day (in all fishing stations): this should be evident from the foregoing example. However, if the total number of beach-seines rises significantly due to population pressure, increasing entanglement with market forces and rising fish prices, or any other reason, as the period of net use is strictly continuous the annual returns of any beachseine will be governed mainly by its position in the net cycle: most incomes will accrue to the nets which happen to have many turns during the flush period.[15] This is exactly the situation which was observed in southern Sri Lanka from 1940 onwards: in Alexander's area of study, for example, only twenty-five of the ninety-nine nets received turns during the flush period in 1970–1 (Alexander 1980: 105–7, 1982: 147, 203–8).

Nevertheless, the problem must be viewed in its right perspective. Indeed, it is over a single year that the customary means of regulating access to the sea tend to make the distribution of the catch more and more unequal as the number of nets increases: over a longer period, returns should be expected to even out since the sequencing of net-laying rights ensures that fishermen do not get their turn in the same month each year and the flush period tends to appear in a given part of the year. Thus, Alexander writes: 'a particular net's turn is not tied to any point in the year, and over a four year period each net will be used in each month. As the fishermen are unable to predict the flush period with any great accuracy, each net has an equal chance of good catches each year' (Alexander 1982: 147). Yet, this clarification should not be taken to mean that the multiplication of nets does not eventually threaten the survival of the fishermen households. There is of course the problem that additional nets may have a zero marginal productivity, with the result that a growing fishing population will have to be content with a constant product.[16] But, even

[15] In the earlier example, if the number of nets is doubled (from 12 to 24), a net will be used only 1 out of 3 days and if it is quadrupled, it will be used 1 out of 6 days. In the latter case, the net will be idle during 40 days in succession after each 8-day period of use, thus implying that it *may* not be used once during the whole flush season (which lasts approximately one month).

[16] An interesting issue is the following: why did the growing fishing population choose to multiply the number of nets beyond any reasonable level instead of sharing employment in a number of nets corresponding roughly to the total number of possible turns per day? This would indeed have avoided a tremendous waste of capital. An answer to this puzzling question as well as a more elaborate treatment of the system discovered by Alexander is provided in Platteau and Baland (1989).

assuming this problem away, there remains the question as to how year-to-year fluctuations in income will be buffered by the fishermen households. Clearly, risk-pooling and intertemporal redistribution mechanisms become increasingly necessary to compensate for the partial failure of the traditional method of risk management.

Two last remarks are in order. First, even though the beachseine represents a heavy capital investment, all fishermen can normally have access to it: indeed, each net is traditionally divided into a number of shares which, like stock-market shares, refer to the enterprise as a whole, not to particular portions of the net. Moreover, if a fisherman is too poor to purchase a share, he may be invited by an incomplete team of shareholders to join a net as a partner, in which case he is given credit till the first bumper catch occurs. The system of share ownership is also highly flexible inasmuch as a share of a net may be held by more than one person, as when the property of a share has to be divided among several siblings on the death of a family head (ibid. 142–3, 149). These are all important aspects of the system since labour cannot be separated from capital ('ownership of a share carries the obligation to work the net when required' and there are normally as many workers as shareholders on a given net) and access to the water is preconditioned upon the ownership of a net share.[17] Easy access to capital therefore explains why the function of net shares as tickets of entry into the local fishery is compatible with the essential principle that membership in the village community (whether hereditary or acquired in a lifetime) involves a right of access to the community-controlled sea area.

Second, it is interesting to note that the rotating system of access to a natural resource has also been used in some traditional agricultural societies. Thus, in traditional village Ceylon, the customary practice was not for households to hold geographically diversified farm plots. Instead, it consisted of a radical form of communal land tenure which, according to Obeyesekere (1967), was based on the egalitarian ideology governing the concept of shares or 'pangu': 'One has shares in the "gama" [a communal land] as a whole, hence one must have access through a period of years to the total area of land, ensuring an equitable distribution of both fertile and infertile land among the respective shareholders' (quoted from Alexander 1982: 283). In Tamil Nadu, to take another example, there existed a land tenure system known as *mirasi* under which 'ownership tended to be not of specific parts of the village but of shares' and 'the parts of the village to which the shares corresponded were periodically reallocated in a sort of lottery'. The lottery was conducted during a ceremony called *Curray Edoo* during which the several portions of land comprising the village corporate tenure were written on tickets and the villagers drew the plots which they were entitled to use until the time of the next *Curray Edoo* (Haggis

[17] Up to recent times, there was no clear distinction between share-owners and wage labourers since many 'hired men' used to be 'the potential heirs of the share owner' (Alexander 1982: 151).

et al. 1986: 1446–7). What must be emphasized in the same way as has been done with respect to the use of the sea is the incompleteness of such arrangements from the standpoint of insurance: supplementary mechanisms of self- or collective insurance are therefore required to buffer the yearly income fluctuations which arise from shifting access to lands of varying quality.

2.2.4. Guaranteed Access to Work Opportunities   In strongly inegalitarian peasant communities (often called 'class-based' societies), social security cannot be ensured through guaranteeing direct access to or effective control of productive resources. Indeed, by the very definition of these societies, possession of the main means of production is concentrated in the hands of a small minority. In these circumstances, the livelihood of the members of the lower strata is often ensured by granting them access to the lands belonging to the higher strata. In the most common case (but surely not in all cases), decisions pertaining to the organization of production on the farm are left to the actual (or direct) cultivators of the soil and the latter's rights of access are secure as long as the customary obligations imposed on them by the landlords, the chieftains, or the overlords (payment of the rental, services in kind, and so on) are duly honoured. Still more effective social security is provided to the poor by the rich if these obligations are not rigidly fixed, but are adjustable downwards whenever abrupt output shortfalls threaten the survival of the land tillers (a possibility heavily emphasized by Scott). The widespread system of share-cropping is evidently a mode of rent payment which partially insures the cultivators against the risk of bad harvests—'partially' because the product net of rent may still fall below the subsistence threshold when the crop failure turns out to be particularly severe. Nevertheless, share-cropping arrangements can prevent extreme hardships for the tillers if (good) landlords offer special rebates or simply cancel off the payment of the share in times of great adversity (see, for example, Neale 1957: 226; Robertson 1987: 42, 189). Moreover, and contrary to what is often believed, the fixed rent system itself does not necessarily put all the risk of crop failures on the shoulders of the tenants. Indeed, it has been observed not infrequently that the rents thus fixed were subject to downward reduction according to crop conditions (see, for example, Ishikawa 1975: 463, Scott 1985: 185).

In other instances, hunger insurance for assetless households takes the form of guaranteed access to work opportunities in the village. A well-known illustration of an institutional arrangement based on this principle is the *bawon* system found in Java. Under this system:

rice harvesting is a community activity in which all or most community members can participate and receive a certain share of output. When the crop is ripe, a horde of harvesters enter the field and harvest the paddy using the *ani-ani* to cut the stalks at the neck of the panicles. The harvested stalks are bundled and brought to the farmer's house, where the harvesters receive a certain share (*bawon*) such as one sheaf out of eight. Typically, harvesting is open to anybody. By tradition, the farmer cannot limit the number of harvesters who participate (Hayami and Kikuchi 1981: 156).

The *bawon* system is thus a practice of work- and income-sharing that ensures food security for villagers with no or little control of agricultural resources. Note, however, that it falls short of offering them perfect hunger insurance since it uses a share system of labour payment. The risk of a crop failure is therefore shared between the landowner and the harvesters and there is good reason to believe that the latter are less able than the former to self-insure adequately against environmental hazards. Nowadays, interestingly, the *bawon* system is still in use even though its coverage is smaller than before and it increasingly takes on milder forms the evolution of which is often analogous to the 'corporatist' tendencies at work in tribal societies (see Section 2.2.2 above). A practice that has been frequently observed during the last decades is one in which harvesting is open only to people in the same village, and to outsiders only so long as the number of participants does not exceed a certain limit. A second system sets a limit to the total number of participants without restricting access to villagers. In a third system, participants are limited to those who received specific invitations from farmers (mainly relatives and neighbours); while in a fourth, still more exclusionary arrangement, known as *ceblokan*, eligible harvesters are only those who performed without pay such tasks as transplanting and weeding (ibid. 158–9; Kikuchi *et al.* 1984: 117–30; Hart 1986: 685–9). Clearly, the system of 'shared poverty' analysed by Geertz (1970) has limitations if only because the landholders do not allow the number of harvesters to rise above the point from which significant losses may occur due to labour overcrowding (marginal productivity of labourers then becomes negative) and to various moral hazard problems (Hayami and Kikuchi 1981: 157). On the other hand, dividing the economic pie into too tiny pieces under the pressure of rapid population growth may rapidly lead to a situation in which access to work can no longer prevent the labourers from sinking below the poverty line.

Mechanisms of output-sharing through work-spreading similar to the *bawon* system have been observed not only in agricultural communities outside Indonesia—as evidenced by the *hunusan* system in the coastal region of the Philippines—[18] but also in non-agricultural societies such as maritime fishermen communities. Thus, among beachseine fishermen communities of Africa and Asia, a common practice consists of permitting all fishermen from the same community who wish to participate to join in the hauling operations and thereby claim access to a portion of the catch (personal field observations).

---

[18] According to Hayami and Kikuchi (1981: 80): '*Hunusan* is a form of contract by which, when a farmer specifies a day of harvesting, anyone can participate in harvesting and threshing, and the harvesters receive a certain share of the output.'

This customary rule explains why the number of participants in these operations may greatly exceed the economic optimum. Furthermore, as the hauling is carried out from the shore, it is a rather simple task which can be performed by disadvantaged people (like old fishermen without any adult son or male adults who fear the open sea). Finally, when the catch is low, net owners usually forgo their capital share (but not their labour share) so that the entire catch is divided (in kind) among those who have participated in the fishing operations. This latter practice has also been often observed in the case of other fishing techniques than beachseining, when nets are used from boats at sea: thus, in Malaysia, Raymond Firth has noted that the distribution of fish catches may become 'definitely abnormal through special circumstances, such as a very small week's yield' (Firth 1966: 248). It is therefore evident that the risk-sharing mechanism underlying the share system of factor payment can be mitigated to the advantage of the labourers whenever their subsistence is at risk. This fact had already been pointed out earlier, in connection with agriculture (see above, this section).

Work being a traditional social right and duty in village societies (Bourdieu 1980: 198–9), it is only when no member of the household is fit for work that pure gifts are extended to the poor. In fishermen communities, for instance, children belonging to families in distress where there is no male adult bread-winner are usually entitled to take a few fish from every catch that is landed on the beach of their native village. In Sri Lanka, this customary practice is known as *Raula Kapanawa* (shaving the beard) (Amarasinghe 1988). In Senegal, the system is even more formalized since a certain share of the catch—known as the *ndawal* among the communities of *lebou* fishermen—must be handed over to the old and the poor persons in the (extended) family (Sow 1986: 12). In a more general way, the flexibility of the schemes of income distribution in the fishing sector often enables the capital owners to make allowances for special individual circumstances. Thus, according to Firth, a boat-owner or captain can give one man a bonus because of his old age or poverty, as a result of which he diminishes in effect either his own share or the shares of all the other crew workers. However, no objection is raised because this practice is 'admitted by his crew on grounds of equity' (Firth 1966: 257). In Senegal, an old custom consists of giving half-a-share (instead of a full share) of the catch to crew members who have been unable to go out fishing due to sickness (personal field observation).

Guaranteed access of poor households to productive resources or to work opportunities under share contracts of rent or labour payment does not constitute, as a matter of principle, a perfect way of protecting them against environmental and other uncertainties. However, it should be evident from the foregoing discussion that these arrangements often come close to an adequate, if not perfect, hunger insurance thanks to various mitigating devices whereby the richer, asset-owning households agree to shoulder a larger part of the risk of income fluctuations in times of adversity or environmental disaster.[19]

This being said, to the extent that the above arrangements do not guarantee the poorer households a fixed income capable of sustaining their livelihood in all circumstances, they must be distinguished from what Shigeru Ishikawa has termed the 'community principle of employment'. According to this principle, landlords feel a responsibility not only to supply work to all available labourers but also to ensure that their subsistence requirements can be met at a level set by prevailing social norms (Ishikawa 1975: 456). The most typical institutional arrangement evolved by precapitalist peasant societies to achieve this double objective is a highly personalized, multifaceted, and enduring employer-employee relationship known as the patron–client relationship.

Patronage relationships are usually understood as ties displaying the following characteristics: (1) they are highly asymmetrical; (2) they usually comprise, or are perceived as having, a strong element of affection which evokes the emotional tie between a father and his son; (3) they are comparatively stable (they typically apply for an indeterminate period of time) but it is only in a polar case that they are hereditary and that the clients are 'bonded labourers' or agrestic slaves; (4) they involve multiple facets of the actors concerned and imply a set of reciprocal obligations which stretch over a wide and loosely defined domain (see, for example, Pitt-Rivers 1954: 140; Wolf 1966: 17; Breman 1974: 16–23; Scott 1976: 167–92; Bardhan and Rudra 1978: 384; Bourdieu 1980: 226–9). The obligations incumbent upon the client consist essentially of being at the continuous disposal of his patron in order to help him in any circumstance for which the contribution of his labour is considered useful (participation in the cultivation of the patron's land, support of his political career through canvassing, involvement in showdown events, and so on). In return, the client receives an insurance against all hazards that may imperil his subsistence, meaning that he can expect from his patron any kind of protection or assistance that he may need to maintain his livelihood. Note that the haziness of the intervention domains of both the patron and the client can be explained in a way that has been suggested earlier in a more general context (see above, Section 2.2): in a world fraught with many uncertainties and contingencies, no precise rule or contract could ever provide for all the circumstances which can affect the economic position of the parties concerned.

An interesting illustration of the polar case of hereditary patron–client relationships is provided by the ancient *jajmani* system of India. It is as a customary arrangement of labour relations providing hunger insurance to the

---

[19] This is particularly obvious in the case of the mixed contracts commonly in use in traditional maritime fishing communities: here, before the catch proceeds are shared between the equipment owners and the crew workers according to some predetermined ratio, the latter are entitled to take a few fish for domestic consumption. If no surplus is left over after the fish for self-consumption has been removed, no sale takes place and the owners get nothing except their own handful of fish for home use (for more details, see Platteau and Nugent 1989).

dependent castes that this system deserves our attention in the context of the present analysis. In this perspective, the following features need to be thrown into relief (see Gough 1960/1: 86–9; Epstein 1967: 230–3):

1. Social organization is highly asymmetrical with the members of the higher castes (the *jajmans* or peasant masters) holding more power and being much better endowed with land resources than the members of the lower castes (the *kamans* or untouchables). Moreover, the latter's holdings are too small to ensure their livelihood, at least when adverse weather conditions prevail.

2. Labour relationships are established between two or more specific families of different castes in the same locality. These relationships are based on hereditary ties and are couched in kinship terms.

3. The peasant masters cannot use or dispose of their lands in whatever way they like and they may not, except under very special circumstances, abrogate their customary relationships with the labouring castes.

4. Reciprocal services and duties as well as the rewards associated with them are governed by customary rules. In particular, the rewards for the untouchables' labour services on the farms of the peasant masters are paid annually in the form of fixed quantities of farming produce. They are therefore independent of the actual amounts of effort applied and of the output resulting therefrom (the contract is not of the risk-sharing type).

5. The annual wages of the untouchable labourers are fixed in such a way as to assure them of a minimum subsistence income in bad harvests. In addition, the hereditary relationships which they maintain with *jajman* families provide them with 'benevolent' masters expected to look after them as fathers do their children.

If we go by the empirical results obtained by Scarlett Epstein in a village of the Mysore area, two further features can be added to the above list. First, in bad years the total product of the village is distributed more or less equally among all households because this is the only way to keep the families of the lower castes (as well, of course, as the higher castes) alive. Second, in good years economic differentiation tends to occur on a large scale and the consumption level of the peasant masters rises much above that of the untouchables (there is no accumulation of capital). This is so because the former have prior claim on the labour of the latter at a time when labour becomes scarce due to peak demand arising from bumper crop conditions (bumper crops require more weeding and more harvesting). Furthermore, as is evident from characteristic 4 above, the untouchables' annual wages are not adjusted upwards as a consequence of increasing tightness of local labour availabilities (Epstein 1967: 242–3). The untouchables are thereby assured of an adequate supply of food against the contingency of crop failure while the peasant masters are assured of a ready availability of labour when they most need it.

It is because of their weak bargaining position following from their vulnerability in bad years—which, in turn, can be traced back to poor land endowments—that the members of the dependent castes are unable to withstand the pressures exercised by the large landowners to obtain their labour services in good years. As a result, they cannot work on their own (small) farms as much as they would like, although they would probably be in a position to earn a decent living from their lands provided they could apply enough labour to them. In fact, the income forsaken by an untouchable in good years—since his wage is kept at the same level as prevails in bad years when labour is not in scarce supply and the productivity of labour efforts is definitely lower—can be interpreted as the sum of two components: a compensation for the fact that the wage he receives from his patron(s) in bad years probably exceeds his marginal productivity and the risk premium he is willing to pay in order to insure against the risk of starvation at times of weather hardship.[20]

Emerging from the above discussion is the picture that, in 'class-based' traditional village societies, assetless households derive whatever social security they enjoy from situations of labour scarcity. Scarcity of labour combined with an unequal distribution of productive assets give rise to mutually advantageous insurance contracts (such as patronage relations). This picture is not complete, however, in so far as control of scarce labour in these societies is a source not only of economic well-being but also of social prestige and political power. As a consequence, to provide for the subsistence of a large number of clients (hereditary servants, small tenants, and so on) may prove to be an effective strategy even though the retinue of rich families may appear to be oversized in purely economic terms. In a fascinating study of the 'agrarian origins of modern Japan' (1959), Thomas Smith has shown that in the early Tokugawa period (seventeenth century), large families could not easily get rid of their old patronage relations even when steadily increasing numbers pressed dangerously on the family's resources, thus reversing the situation of labour scarcity which initially gave rise to these relations. In the words of Smith (1959: 19—my italics), '*custom, pride, and public opinion* would not permit the large family with ample resources to solve these problems as poor families did: by merely eliminating surplus members, cutting them off summarily from the resources and protection of the group'. The solution adopted by large and rich families at the top of the village hierarchy usually consisted of giving (cultivation rights to) a small piece of land to conjugal groups from one of the outer circles of the extended family (hereditary servants, remote family branches, and so on) so as to enable them to make a (meagre) living. Such newly formed households (called *nago*) did not become fully autonomous overnight. If labour services

---

[20] Elsewhere (Platteau 1988), I have shown, however, that an attempt at formalizing the *jajmani* system as it has been described by Epstein brings into light a number of rather odd features. In particular, the system of equations thus obtained appears to be overdetermined and it is only through a special assumption that the model can be made to incorporate a true maximization procedure (on the part of the peasant caste).

continued to be periodically performed by them to the profit of the (extended) family headship, there was no relationship between the size of land allotments and amount of labour services (ibid. 24–8). On the other hand, the ancient master (called *oyakata*) remained the main source of hunger insurance for his *nago*:

he [the *oyakata*] helped *nago* survive the ever-recurring crop failures that were the marks of agricultural backwardness, and which hit everyone periodically but hit the weak most often and hardest. *Custom and self-interest, both*, obliged the *oyakata* to open his storehouse at such times, to provide his *nago* with food and seed until the next harvest *lest he be thought pitiless for thus driving them onto the highways* in search of sustenance and a more reliable protector. If that happened, it was usually because famine conditions prevailed and the *oyakata* was himself short of food (ibid. 27; my italics).

It would therefore be wrong to take a purely economicist view of the contractual arrangements between rich and poor families in ancient village societies, even class-based ones. In particular, labour services, 'far from being a means of payment for land . . . were clearly part of a far-reaching system of personal obligation'. Moreover, ritual acts expressing personal subordination were a common feature of these societies, in which they usually formed the basis of political power and social standing. In this connection, it is important to note that in Japan again, 'the participants themselves made no consistent distinction between ceremonial and labour services, often calling both by the same name. . . . This is not because people failed to observe that one had economic value and the other not, but because this difference though evident was insignificant in view of the fact that the two had the same social character' (ibid. 29–30).

2.3. *The Insurance Dilemma in Traditional Village Societies*

There are two well-known reasons why insurance (or quasi-insurance) schemes may be costly or may fail to emerge altogether: incentive problems and covariate risks (Rothschild and Stiglitz 1976; Binswanger 1986; Binswanger and Rosenzweig 1986; Newbery 1989). The first set of problems arise when economic agents are assumed to be opportunistic, an assumption clearly made by Popkin to account for the failure of most social security arrangements in precapitalist peasant societies. As for the second problem, Popkin has largely bypassed it. This is all the more curious as he has hinted at it in one long passage (Popkin 1979: 71–2). The fact that he did not push the argument further reflects his predilection for attributing failure to behavioural tendencies of the peasants: indeed, it was with respect to behavioural factors that he thought he could make his case against the moral economy approach.

Let us now look more carefully at each of the above issues in turn.

2.3.1. *Incentive Problems and the Solution of the Village Community*   Any kind of collective action—including social-security arrangements—is always under serious threat from incentive problems (Olson 1965, 1982). These problems actually arise when information is costly and asymmetrically distributed, and they usually take the form of moral hazard or adverse selection (Newbery and Stiglitz 1981: 165–6; Binswanger and Rosenzweig 1986: 507, 514–5; Newbery 1989: 278–9).[21] If the costs at which moral hazard and adverse selection can be controlled are high for the insurer, the premiums charged by him may exceed the amount people are willing to pay to get insured: in the circumstances, insurance fails to emerge.[22] Moreover, the more difficult it is to verify information on contingent claims or to monitor the actions of the insured agents, the greater the likelihood of a market failure.

In the specific context of traditional village societies, there are two factors which would tend to make insurance or quasi-insurance schemes apparently more difficult and more costly to operate. First, shortfalls of production from normal yields are frequent because, owing to the low level of technology development, production results are strongly exposed to climatic and environmental vagaries. As a result, the transaction costs of providing insurance (administrative and information costs) tend to be high. Second, almost by definition, traditional precapitalist societies are entities lacking elaborate record-keeping systems, formal laws and contracts, and judicial enforcement procedures. There is therefore a serious risk of incentive problems being altogether unmanageable: in so far as punitive procedures are weak or non-existent (there are no written contracts with enforceable clauses), free-riding would be an almost irresistible temptation that could undermine all kinds of collective action.

However, the above discussion should not be taken to mean that collective action is impossible or highly unlikely in traditional village societies, as Popkin has contended. Indeed, there is an almost absolute need for co-operation in many of these societies because there are not only many uncertainties to be insured against but also numerous production externalities to be internalized. And, as argued by Robert Wade, when the net benefits from collective action are large, co-operation is likely to emerge and to be sustained voluntarily—that is, without selective inducements or punishments bearing decisive weight and without the supply of local leadership being a constraint in initiating and

---

[21] In the economic theory of insurance, moral hazard arises 'when an agent who obtains insurance has an incentive to take less care to avoid the contingencies which give rise to claims'. As for adverse selection, it occurs 'when the insurance company cannot distinguish between agents who have differing probabilities of claims, and hence must offer all the same contract', with the result that the contract only appeals to (and adversely selects) those belonging to a comparatively high-risk category (Newbery 1989: 278). Both problems arise from 'asymmetric information' regarding the relevant personal characteristics of the agent seeking insurance.

[22] It is true that coinsurance clauses may also reduce the incentive problems. Yet, as they cause insurance to be incomplete, they also reduce the potential utility gain to the insured (Binswanger 1986: 78; Newbery 1989: 278).

sustaining co-operation endeavours (Wade 1988: 183–7, 205–10).[23] In fact, the traditional village community can be viewed as an ingenious solution to the incentive problems in the form of a tightly-knit, highly integrated society characterized by intense and multi-stranded interpersonal relationships. Thus, Hayami and Kikuchi (1981: 21) consider it to be a more efficient institution than the market in an economy dominated by pervasive interdependence in production activities and high information costs. And even Popkin is not far from holding this position (although he carefully avoids making it explicit) when he writes that 'peasant schemes generally tend to involve small groups' (1979: 48).

The reasons why small communities or social groups help reduce incentive problems are easy to understand. As a matter of fact, the cost of information collection and contract enforcement is reduced to manageable levels when it is common to many transactions and when a lot of information can be held in common due to restricted privacy (Hayami and Kikuchi 1981: 14; Wynne 1980: 48–9; Posner 1981: 146–8; Platteau 1986: 186–7; Platteau and Abraham 1987: 468–9). Historical ties and continued personalized relationships tend to allow further reductions of information costs because 'performances in past transactions comprise a reliable data set for prediction of future performance' (Hayami and Kikuchi 1981: 14). Moreover, given the interlinked nature of many transactions and the lack of alternative possibilities (other village communities being themselves tightly-knit social entities with entry barriers), the cost of free-riding or rule-breaking tends to be so high that even implicit contracts or tacit commitments can be considered as more or less self-enforcing.[24]

The importance of customary rules, moral principles, and community norms must also be viewed against the background of incentive problems since they constitute a powerful means of assuring each participant that co-operation will ensue and that the obligations created (to return a loan, to pay a risk premium, to contribute labour or income to a collective scheme, and so on) will be enforced. It is in this sense that moral systems or codes of conduct— including internalized community values emphasizing altruism and respect of the hierarchy—can be considered as a substitute for more coercive enforcement of law systems or for complex schemes of selective inducements and punishments (Collard 1978; Lipton 1985: 81; Platteau forthcoming; Wade 1988: 203). Many economists—including Popkin himself—are used to supposing that every human action is reducible to a voluntary act of personal choice. Wynne's reflection that this is hardly a satisfactory approach since

---

[23] Wade has rightly noted that, for Popkin, the temptations to free-ride with respect to leadership are typically so strong that insufficient leadership is normally available within peasant communities. As a result, leadership would have to come from outside the local community to make the villagers co-operate (Wade 1988: 207).

[24] It may be recalled in this context that the comparative ease of holding free-riding in check in small communities was one of the strong points made by Olson (1965, 1982).

villagers are always immersed in a universe of community norms (Wynne 1980: 45–7) is worth pondering, and represents a full departure from Popkin's superficial treatment of value systems (see above Section 2.2). According to Wynne, time- and resource-consuming activities like ceremonial rituals and myth-making were important activities in the course of which members of a given social group were appropriately socialized and identified with common systems of sympathy and belief. By helping to create reciprocal trust and an 'emotional cement' among them, these activities performed the function of 'our contemporary systems of taxation, book-keeping, business, law, and government' (Wynne 1980: 42–5). It is true that systems of values and beliefs can only be a partial substitute for institutional arrangements which give people the assurance that other participants will co-operate or will be punished if they do not comply with the rules. Some amount of coercion is always needed to back up agreements and to sustain collective action even when consensus has been sufficient to initiate it. In the words of Wade, 'the rules must be backed by a system of punishment, the existence of which helps to assure any one person that if he follows the rules he will not be suckered, and which at times of crisis can directly deter' (Wade 1988: 209). What needs to be stressed in the specific context of traditional village communities is that the cost of monitoring deviance and holding opportunism in check may not be too high because the sanctions usually take the form of social opprobrium or ostracism. As a matter of fact, due to their desire for social acceptance by a group and/or their fear of the material consequences of reputation loss, people are very concerned with social reputation and bounds within their community. As a result, 'reputation in a small agricultural community is not lightly exposed to attack' (ibid. 193). It is therefore the nature of the sanction system in these communities that helps explain why enforcement of promises and monitoring of rule-breaking are comparatively easy in spite of the fact that formal laws and judicial procedures are not available.

Even so, it would be wrong to assume that incentive problems were fully solved in precapitalist societies and that collective actions could always be undertaken at reasonable cost. Depending on historical circumstances, these societies achieved varying degrees of social cohesion and efficient leadership, and it is not hard to find evidence of societies affected by processes of social disintegration and unable to undertake group actions of any significance. In fact, even under normal circumstances, incentive problems can be kept under control only to a certain extent. The example of plot-scattering mentioned by Popkin (see above, Section 1.2) is perhaps a good illustration of the limits of collective action in many agricultural societies. Assume that in a given village land is of more or less uniform quality, yet, owing to the varying risk characteristics of different land locations, yields fluctuate significantly between farm plots. If there are economies of scale and if incentive problems could be handled at reasonable cost, it would then be a socially more efficient solution to allocate compact areas of land among the various household units rather than allowing them to scatter their fields so as to diversify their risks. But this would precisely require that, after production has taken place, income would be redistributed from peasants endowed with lands which performed rather well during the ending agricultural season to those in the opposite situation. And it is probably here, in the sphere of redistribution, that the society would have to incur considerable transaction costs to carry the scheme through.[25] However, in the case of insurance schemes, there is another cause of failure which can never be overlooked: it is to this cause that I shall now turn my attention.

2.3.2. Covariate Risks and the Insurance Dilemma

A fundamental theorem of the economic theory of risk and insurance is that the cost of an additional risk depends on its covariance with existing risks: the cost will be higher the stronger the degree of positive covariance, whilst negatively correlated risks will have the effect of reducing the total cost of risk-bearing. Consequently, there are potential gains from trade in risk when incomes or contingencies are uncorrelated while, if all agents face similar risks, risk cannot be reduced much by trading it between the participants (Newbery and Stiglitz 1981: 165; Newbery 1989: 270–2).[26] Typically, farmers living in an ecologically uniform area and carrying out activities which are similar from a risk point of view have little to gain by sharing or pooling their risks. In these circumstances, an insurance arrangement would degenerate to a centralized reserve scheme and each farmer could actually self-insure at the same cost; as self-insurance through holding reserves avoids all information and incentive problems, it is actually preferred by the peasants (Binswanger 1986: 78). Therefore, the prevalence of household over village granaries or food stores cannot be taken, as Popkin has done, as decisive evidence that peasants are too opportunistic to make insurance schemes viable. A technical reason alone—the high covariance of yields—accounts for the difficulty of providing insurance against collective risks, that is, risks which affect all the participants simultaneously.

As has been pointed out by several authors, access to credit may provide an important substitute for insurance where insurance is absent or costly (Binswanger 1986: 79; Platteau and Abraham 1987; Eswaran and Kotwal 1989).

---

[25] In a valuable study of the ancient English open field system of agriculture, Carl Dahlman has offered another, more positive, justification of the scattering of plots than the one given in the text: for him, the main advantage of plot scattering lies in the fact that it creates an incentive for the farmers 'to participate in the collective decision making and control necessary to regulate the use of the large grazing areas in both the commons and in the arable fields' (Dahlman 1980: 125).

[26] However, this need not be so if the participants have different degrees of risk aversion. Those with high risk aversion could dispose of risky assets to those with low risk aversion and purchase less risky, less profitable assets from them, with both sides obtaining consumer's surplus from the exchange transaction (I am indebted to M. Lipton for having drawn my attention to this point). Note, however, that trade in assets is only one of the ways in which people with different degrees of risk aversion can achieve mutual gains.

Thus, in situations involving uncertain income streams, consumption credit enables risk-pooling across time if people with good draws accept to lend to those with bad draws: in such a way, agents could stabilize their consumption streams without resorting to costly self-insurance methods like the hoarding of savings as a sort of contingency fund. Again, what needs to be stressed is that such an insurance substitute will not work if contingencies are correlated across the population. As a matter of fact, covariance of income risk leads to covariance of default risk: as a result, financial intermediaries would have to keep high reserve ratios (or require high collateral). Moreover, the incomes of both depositors and borrowers would also be correlated (Binswanger 1986: 79–80; Binswanger and Rosenzweig 1986: 516–17). Under the same conditions, co-operative credit schemes would fail for the same reason and only money-lenders lending out of equity funds (and able to reschedule loan repayments) would stay in business.

There is an obvious way of overcoming the problem of risk covariance: it consists of pooling risks over a wide geographical area so as to cover ecologically heterogeneous zones and economic activities which are complementary from a risk point of view. The difficulty with this solution is that it increases the incentive or information problems at the same time as it reduces the covariance problem: thus, the larger and geographically less concentrated the social group concerned in the insurance scheme, the lower the covariance of their incomes and contingencies is likely to be, but the more serious the moral hazard problem. The other side of this insurance dilemma is that while incentive problems tend to be less severe within restricted social groups where information asymmetries are comparatively small, such groups typically face a wide range of collective risks in so far as they live in localized areas with uniform ecological characteristics (Posner 1981: 156; Binswanger 1986: 78; Platteau and Abraham 1987: 468–9). Unfortunately, it cannot be taken for granted that a manageable trade-off always exists between the incentive and covariance problems: on a priori grounds, it is impossible to decide whether cost-effective insurance arrangements may be found that allow risk-pooling to take place in peasant societies. To put it in another way, one can never be sure that the costs imposed by the need to control moral hazard problems will be offset by the risk-pooling benefits, given covariate yields or incomes.

3. TRADITIONAL RISK-POOLING MECHANISMS AT WORK

3.1. The Case of Weather-Unrelated Specific Risks

There is a positive lesson to be learned from the above discussion: risk-pooling or mutual insurance arrangements have more chances to emerge and to be maintained successfully when there is a low covariance of risks within a highly integrated social group of limited size.[27] As pointed out by Posner (1981: 154–5), the family is the institution most likely to satisfy the latter requirement but, at the same time, it is often too small, even in its extended form, to create an adequate risk pool for insurance purposes and, therefore, to satisfy the former requirement. One anthropologist has however contended that the size of the domestic production and consumption unit in precapitalist agricultural societies is precisely determined in such a way as to insure it adequately against the risk of illness and accident among its productive members (Meillassoux, 1980: 69). Incidentally, it may also be noted with Meillassoux that vertically extended households (that is, households composed of nuclear units of successive generations) can provide insurance for covariate risks such as area-wide crop failures. This possibility arises when older individuals in such households have accumulated assets which can serve as insurance substitutes to younger household members (ibid.; Binswanger et al. 1989: 131; Newbery 1989: 287; Von Braun and Webb 1989: 526).

Be that as it may, what can be asserted with confidence is that members of these societies have frequently formed informal village associations—remaining within or stretching beyond the bounds of the extended family network—to insure themselves against contingencies uncorrelated across the group thus formed. This is hardly surprising in so far as a number of weather-unrelated risks can be considered as specific risks that do not affect all the village households simultaneously. Risk-pooling groups for such uncertainties can be either themselves specific or encompass a number of contingencies. Examples of the former are traditional burial societies or fire associations. Burial societies provide help for the organization of funerals whenever a member family suffers a bereavement: in this case, the occurrence of the event is certain but its timing is uncertain. As for fire associations, they are insurance schemes whereby every participant commits himself to help any victim in the group to extinguish a fire in his fields or in his farmstead and, if needed, to rebuild the house after the disaster. As with most insurance schemes, members of village fire associations are willing to pay a certain cost of moderate amount—since, given the high average frequency of fire occurrence, they are sure of having to contribute their labour from time to time to come to the rescue of unfortunate victims in the group—in order to avoid incurring an uncertain loss of considerable size (if their own property catches fire). Similar to fire insurance societies are sea rescue associations through which small-scale fishermen communities insure collectively against the risk of being lost at sea. As in the previous case, the insurance scheme is implemented in a completely informal and decentralized way. Each fisherman participating in the scheme agrees to come to the rescue

[27] Note, incidentally, that the latter aspect of this proposition has been emphasized by Popkin himself: 'There was, in fact, cooperation among small groups of peasants to stabilize production and provide insurance' (Popkin 1979: 96).

of a fellow fisherman who has not returned home on the scheduled time, and to bear all the expenses related to the rescue operation (labour time, fuel, and so on). This he does in the expectation that in the future he may also find himself in difficulty out at sea and in need of rescue by other fishing units.

Risk-pooling groups with wider risk coverage are also very common. They often take the form of co-operative labour-exchange pools. The commitment of every member is then to come to the rescue of any fellow member who has fallen into distress owing to an event considered to be a misfortune: illness or accident of the farmer or of other productive members in the family; death or illness of draught animals or of livestock; crop damage due to trampling of fields by wild animals; destruction of the house or the fields by a flood or a fire, and so on. The understanding is that labour (or any other kind of help) provided under the scheme does not give rise to any formal and immediate payment or return (except for some food and drink). This does not mean, however, that it is free since it is actually offered against the conditional promise of reciprocal help at a future indeterminate time. The promise is conditional because today's helpers will be entitled to claim reciprocity only if they themselves run into difficulties out of bad luck at some time in the future. Some insurance-like reciprocal arrangements have an even wider coverage, for example, the provision of minimal subsistence to widows. Thus, among the Siang Dyaks of central Borneo, 'If a woman is left with several small children and has no relatives upon whom she can call, she is usually assisted by the others in the village, through gifts of rice and wild pig or by help in the clearing of her field; at least until such time as the children have become old enough to help her' (Provinse 1955: 149). Again, those who bring assistance to unfortunate women are thereby assured that their own wife and children will be taken care of if they pass away and no close relatives remain alive in the village.

Contributions of the above kind can therefore be viewed as so many claims or lines of credit which are accumulated because they *might* always be mobilized in an emergency (see Belshaw 1965: 24). They are thus a close substitute or functional equivalent of our modern insurance policies. Furthermore, as with any insurance scheme, the *ex post* distribution of wealth is equalized since comparatively lucky community members extend more help than they receive while the opposite is true of unlucky members. And when 'bad luck' turns out to be an easy excuse for laziness or carelessness, the group reacts by refusing to extend any further help to the opportunist. For instance, we are told that, among the Siang Dyaks,

Occasionally help will be given unfortunate individuals by the other members of the village for which help no [immediate] repayment of any kind is expected by the donors; but such help is only tendered those whose misfortune has come through no misconduct on their own part and who are deserving of it . . . a man's shiftless ways quite soon spread to all the long houses. . . . No really deserving person who through sickness or other misfortune has come to difficulty will be permitted to suffer or starve among the

Siangs, but an undeserving person is seldom tolerated longer than is necessary to find out what he is (Provinse 1955: 147, 150).

As a matter of fact, it is precisely because informal insurance systems can be easily terminated if dissatisfaction arises, and also because being decentralized they do not involve the management of a common fund (which always turns out to be a highly complex and rioky affair in village societies), that peasants seem to have a predilection for them all over the world. It is noteworthy that the above kind of informal, risk-pooling, labour-exchange co-operative groups have been observed not only in Third World precapitalist societies but also in contemporary rural societies in the northern hemisphere (Bennett 1968: 291–3).

3.2. *The Case of Weather-Induced Specific Risks*

To my knowledge, the literature offers only a few instances of insurance schemes in which yield risks are pooled in the context of traditional societies. Nevertheless, these examples are very illuminating and cover most nature-related activities: hunting-gathering, stock-raising, agriculture, marine fishing. In all the cases examined, as could be expected, the covariance of yields is rather low while moral hazard problems are under reasonable control. More-over, as in the case of risk-pooling labour-exchange groups, the basic principle underlying these schemes is that of a collective disaster-avoidance strategy whereby the participants form a long-term 'partnership reservoir' which can be tapped in times of stress. Given the difficulties or costs of storing food (especially in moist climates where most foods get easily infested), the insurance-seeking agents make the following agreement: those who produce a harvest in excess of their consumption needs will give at least part of their surpluses to those who are short of food in exchange for the latter's commitment to reciprocate if their respective positions are ever reversed (Posner 1981: 153; Carter 1987; Kimbalt 1988; Coate and Ravaillon 1989).

This kind of arrangement is often referred to as 'generalized reciprocity' in the anthropological literature and it is assumed to operate in the social framework of kinship groups (Service 1966; Sahlins 1968; Orlove 1977). As a leading anthropologist has remarked: 'it is scarcity and not sufficiency that make people generous, since everybody is thereby insured against hunger', and 'in a community where everyone is likely to find himself in difficulties from time to time . . . he who is in need today receives help from him who may be in like need tomorrow' (Evans-Pritchard 1940: 85). In the following pages, some important cases of reciprocity arrangements will be investigated, with special emphasis on their insurance aspects.

3.2.1. *A Reinterpretation of the Potlatch System*   Observed among the Kwakiutl Indians of the north-west coast of America, the *potlatch* system has traditionally been viewed by anthropologists as a subtle way of forging or reinforcing alliances as well as achieving status and power through delayed and calibrated (though not necessarily balanced) gift exchanges conducted in the course of complex ceremonials (Boas 1920; Drucker 1955; Codere 1956, 1957; Belshaw 1965: 24–6). However, Piddocke has contended that the above characterization is only valid as an account of the modern *potlatch* as it has been influenced by direct contact with Western civilization and modified under the impact of new economic opportunities. In aboriginal times, by contrast, 'the *potlatch* had a very real pro-survival or subsistence function, serving to counter the effects of varying resource productivity by promoting exchanges of food from those groups enjoying a temporary surplus to those groups suffering a temporary deficit' (Piddocke 1965: 244). The analysis of Piddocke (ibid. 244–64) can be summarized in the following way.

1. The basic unit of Kwakiutl society was the *numaym* which had a social control over given fishing locations and hunting territories. Several *numayms* formed a tribe.

2. The *numayms* suffered from time to time from serious food scarcities which threatened their existence. These scarcities were primarily due to considerable year-to-year variations in their environmental conditions, which got reflected in the actual numbers of fish and game available for food.

3. Variations in resource productivities across different *numayms* were largely independent of each other, because the *numayms* operated in a variety of heterogeneous micro-environments associated with specific hunting grounds and fishing stations on rivers.

4. The *potlatch* exchange always took place between the *numayms* represented by their chiefs, and it ensured 'a continual movement of food from those groups enjoying a temporary abundance to those groups suffering privation' (ibid. 249). In fact, food was not the only item offered in the course of *potlatch* transactions: durable consumer or capital goods (mainly blankets, copper, and canoes) were also important objects of exchange. However, it has to be emphasized that durables could be converted into food outside the *potlatch* sphere proper.

5. The giving *numaym* obtained social prestige in return for (and in proportion to) the goods supplied to the receiving *numaym(s)*, thereby enhancing its rank position in the rivalrous competition for *numaym* leadership within the tribe or the region.

6. Since variations in the productivity of their resource base tended to be intermittent and short term, the direction of gift-giving was always liable to be reversed so that the long-term relative ranking of the *numayms* tended to remain more or less constant.

3.2.2. Insurance-motivated gift exchanges in Southern Africa The *hxaro* system practised by the Kung San hunter-gatherers of the Kalahari (north-west

Botswana, north-east Namibia, and south-east Angola) is based on a network of kinship ties (real or fictive blood kin) which spread the risk of drought-induced hunger over an area wide enough to avoid the covariance problem. This is possible because 'localized rainfall and biotic conditions in this semiarid territory vary resource productivity even within areas no larger than 50 square miles, checkering San country with pockets of dearth and sufficiency in relatively dry years' (Torry 1987: 325; see also Wiessner 1982: 65). Moreover, the Kung are a highly mobile people who can travel over a very large region of several thousand square kilometres (Cashdan 1985: 457). As we have seen above, the situation among the Kwakiutl Indians was different in this respect. Geographical mobility was much more restricted but, fortunately, environmental variations were considerable even within a comparatively small stretch of territory with the result that there was a low correlation of incomes between the various social groups.

The *hxaro* system can be described as a structured means of hunger insurance or, more precisely, as 'a social method of pooling risk through storage of social obligations': according to this practice, 'a person creates relationships of mutual reciprocity with others in the population and thereby spreads losses over a unit much larger and more varied than the local band' (Wiessner 1982: 65, 77).[28] Therefore, '*hxaro* partnerships are not economic contracts with set terms, but rather bonds of mutual help', the loose terms of which allow the coverage of a wide variety of needs and contingencies (ibid. 68). The insurance motivation of these relationships is evident from the fact that 'a person who has given assistance has no desire for an immediate and fixed return that would even the relationship and make it possible for it to be cancelled. Rather, the aim is to store the debt until the situation of have and have not is reversed' (ibid. 67).

Hxaro transactions obey a number of rules or procedures that can be inferred from Wiessner's careful empirical study of the Kung San (see also Torry 1987: 325–8). To begin with, there are two procedures to control problems of moral hazard. In the first place, *hxaro* relationships must be built up and maintained with great care using a well-established ceremonial. Thus, a person initiates a *hxaro* by giving a gift to a prospective partner, and the latter can express his willingness to enter the proposed relationship only by returning a gift of similar worth. However, it is only after a trial period of at least one year, during which several gifts of non-food items flow between the partners, that the relationship is eventually considered firm. Thereafter, gift exchanges which are both balanced and delayed (it would be an insult to return a gift immediately) must continually take place to inform the partners that the relationship is still intact, a practice that is all the more important the longer the distance between the

---

[28] Wiessner has observed that the storing of food is widespread among the Kung households. However, from the high incidence of *hxaro* relationships one can infer that self-insurance offers only an imperfect hedge against environmental hazards.

camps in which they live, if they live far apart. These continual flows of ceremonial gifts serve the important function of cementing strong bonds of friendship backed by a powerful ideology or moral code of generosity and equality. Note that, once a relationship is firm, a person is said to '*hai*' the partner in his heart, meaning literally to hold and figuratively to be responsible for that person: 'from then on, each partner can call on the other in times of need' (Wiessner 1982: 66–7).

In the second place, *hxaro* relationships are established among consanguineous relatives or persons who have been remembered over the years as kindred members: only the hearts of these people are considered to be known enough to do *hxaro* with them appropriately. Furthermore, conflicts are more easily amenable to a settlement when family ties exist between the contending partners. Indeed, 'if a quarrel does arise over *hxaro* between consanguines, the Kung feel that their common relatives will unite and try to resolve the conflict, while if one arose between affinal relatives, that each person's respective kin would side with their relative and a serious fight would arise between the two kindreds' (ibid. 66). In other words, choosing one's *hxaro* partners in the family network has the effect of reducing transaction costs and of keeping moral hazard problems within manageable limits. Yet, owing to long distances and asymmetrical information, transaction costs can never be negligible and 'considerable time is spent in trying to establish who has and who is in need' (ibid. 68). Wiessner has indeed observed that families tend to be discreet about the food they have gathered or could gather in the bush. Moreover, 'it is not unusual to hear a person with a full belly complain that he has not had anything to eat and is "dying of hunger"' (ibid.)

Another principle underlying *hxaro* relations is that the Kung San ought to hold a diversified portfolio of *hxaro* partners. In the specific context of the hunter-gatherers of the Kalahari, this strategy amounts to spreading one's partners geographically so that the risk of hunger is well distributed over the population of partners. As a matter of fact, individual *hxaro* networks cross many camps but partnership density and frequencies of exchange fall off with distance: approximately 70 per cent of the Kung's partners live within a radius of 50 km from their house, while the remaining 30 per cent reside in more distant areas between 50 and 200 km away. Furthermore, there are very few Kung who do not have at least one partner between 150 and 200 km away (ibid. 75, table 3.2 and 76). In times of hardship, a family begins by visiting its *hxaro* partners who live in adjacent areas; and it is only if their economic fortunes turn out to be affected by the same environmental failure that it will trek further afield to seek food help in more distant bands. The key role of *hxaro* is precisely to provide an individual with an alternative residence when he can no more make a living from the resources located in his own area of landrights. The rules of *hxaro* assistance have been described by Wiessner as follows:

Hxaro relationships with people in different areas allow individuals and their families to make extended visits to a partner's camp lasting from two weeks to two years. While living there, they will have access to the resources of the area and the partner will integrate them into the reciprocal relations within the camp. For the first few days the visitors will be supported, but after that they will be expected to hunt and gather their own living and share any surplus with their host and others as they would in their own camp (ibid. 60).

Third, the rules governing the *hxaro* system allow for a good deal of flexibility through indirect *hxaro* relationships. Indeed, *hxaro* networks extend the bond of a partnership in a given camp to the bandmates with whom the partner has reciprocal relations. Of course, the latter do not feel any direct obligation to the *hxaro* partner of their fellow camp resident (usually a close relative). Nevertheless, they are willing to include him in daily interactions of reciprocity within the camp when he comes to visit. And, conversely, they know his assistance may possibly be called on for their own benefit through the intermediary of his (direct) *hxaro* partner in the camp. In so far as adjacent areas of landrights within a particular camp are known for localized plant and animal foods, additional local contacts serve to open up access to a wider range of resources nearby and indirect *hxaro* relationships help further spread the risk of hunger for any individual (ibid. 62, 69–70, 76).

Finally, there is a good deal of stability in the *hxaro* system inasmuch as *hxaro* relationships tend to be reproduced from generation to generation when they have worked to the satisfaction of both parties: '*Hxaro* relationships are passed on in a family in a way which permits those who reciprocated well to be continued and those who did not to be quietly dropped and forgotten and still new ones added to meet changing needs' (ibid. 77). Note also that camp membership is rather stable with the result that 'when persons form relationships of reciprocity with other adults, they do so with a good idea of where and with whom their partners will be living' (ibid. 64).

To the extent that misfortune does not strike all equally and that the *hxaro* system works effectively as a risk-pooling mechanism, income is redistributed from the lucky to the unlucky households. This goes a long way towards explaining why the Kung San society has been able to maintain its strongly egalitarian pattern of wealth distribution (ibid. 67, 69).

Unlike the Kalahari Kung San, the Nata River Basarwa (Bushmen) inhabit a relatively well-watered area and today they depend primarily on cultivated crops and domestic livestock for their livelihood. However, like their desert-dwelling neighbours, they still rely to a considerable extent on reciprocal exchanges as a way of ensuring their long-term food security (Cashdan 1985: 454–74).

To understand the insurance function of reciprocity among the Basarwa, a number of their production conditions must be highlighted. First, it is important to bear in mind that most of them are rather poor people who do not own much livestock of their own, but receive cattle on credit from some wealthy owner (the so-called *mafisa* arrangement). In return for the labour expended on the livestock care, they are usually given a calf yearly and, moreover, they get the milk and the draft power of the 'loaned' animals. This last aspect is essential since cattle are indispensable to plough a field of reasonable size (ibid. 462; Schapera 1970: 115; Robertson 1987: 156–7). Second, the quantity of grain harvested per household depends crucially on the size of the area planted, while the latter is positively correlated with the number of years the field has been ploughed. This last fact results from the time-consuming nature of clearing and fencing tasks (Cashdan 1985: 466–7). Third, because the cattle owners frequently take their livestock away after a few years, the Basarwa are forced to move their compounds periodically to join the cattle post of a new employer (ibid. 468). Besides, as they do not have contracts of specified duration, they never know in advance when their next move will take place.

Unfortunately, Cashdan is rather obscure on certain important aspects of the role of reciprocity as a hunger insurance mechanism among the Basarwa (particularly with respect to its ability to buffer environmental variations). The following is an attempt to reconstruct the logic of the system from the information and data she provides.

As a result of their frequent changes of residence, the Basarwa face important periodic variations in food production even irrespective of weather and other environmental hazards. These variations are at least partly unpredictable, in so far as the Basarwa do not know the time when they will have to stop cultivating a comparatively large field in a given location to start with a small field in a new location. For the same reason (great mobility) and because of the high cost of food transportation, they do not engage in large-scale food storage to cope with the risk of having to move. At the same time, however, one must expect the variance of farm size, and consequently of farm productivity, to be large within a given location since the period of residence varies greatly across the different resident households. Therefore, the comparatively big farmers can share their surplus with the small ones who have recently settled in the area. Of course, the probability that the latter will face a food deficit is greater when rainfall is poor and drought sets in. Yet, even in conditions of collective environmental hardship, the sharing mechanism ought to be workable. Indeed, for one thing, their resource being larger, big farmers are likely to achieve more satisfactory (absolute) levels of agricultural output than small ones; and, for another thing, since bigger farmers have stayed longer in the area, they would presumably have stored some food surplus during the previous years which they can make available to those who did not have sufficient time to self-insure adequately.

Of course, for the system to be practicable, the bigger farmers must have an incentive to give their surplus to those in deficit. That this is precisely the case follows from the continuous movement of each household across the size-distribution of farms. In the words of Cashdan: 'because people who have stayed the longest at a location will change from year to year, the Basarwa households that plough the largest fields in any one year are not likely to remain forever in that category' (ibid. 468). As a consequence, the same household will not be always on the 'giving' side of the gift transactions, and the sharing of food surpluses can be grounded on the mutuality principle. It should be noted that this mutual insurance system can work satisfactorily only if the reciprocity network stretches across a wide range of locations within the Basarwa migration area (that is, along the Nata River). In this context of high mobility over rather long distances, ethnic identity serves the essential function of cementing ties among the migrant households so that incentive problems can be avoided or minimized.

To sum up, there are two important causes of variation in food production among the Basarwa: erratic rainfall patterns and frequent changes of residence arising from stock-raising activities. The solution adopted to cope with these risks is a combination of limited food storage and reciprocal sharing of food surpluses. Revealingly, the hoarding of food is much more important and reciprocal exchanges much less prevalent among other ethnic groups who happen to own moderately large herds and can therefore settle in a given location on a more or less permanent basis. In their case, owing to the high covariance of farm yields and the constancy of the size-distribution of farms, mutual insurance arrangements cannot be used as a means of coping with environmental hazards.

3.2.3. *Hunger Insurance through Reciprocal Credit in a Traditional Fishing Community*   The economic organization of traditional maritime communities is particularly interesting not only because fishermen are subject to considerable day-to-day fluctuations of their catches but also because the correlation of the outcomes of their fishing trips is notably low.[29] Thus, from an unpublished in-depth study of a small sample of households in a South Indian fishing village (the village of Poovar in South Kerala) I found that the coefficient of variation of daily catch values greatly exceeded unity in most cases (either on a monthly or on a yearly basis). On the other hand, the covariance of fishing incomes between various pairs of fishermen turned out to be slightly positive (up to a maximum value of 0.15), close to zero, or even negative (data pertaining to 1981–2).

The same study also reached the conclusion that the behaviour of Poovar fishermen is clearly motivated by their desire to stabilize food consumption in the face of highly uncertain income streams. Thus, the elasticities of current (daily) consumption expenditures with respect to income appear to be in the low range of 0.0004–0.008 (after correcting for autocorrelation through the

---

[29] The reasons accounting for these two phenomena have been spelt out in Platteau and Abraham (1987: 463–6).

Cochrane–Orcutt method). In actual fact, most of the (comparatively slight) day-to-day variations of recurrent consumption expenditures appear to be accountable in terms of seasonal movements of income and daily fluctuations of the price of necessities. As most of these fishermen live close to the margin of subsistence (Poovar is a poor village due to adverse ecological conditions), these price fluctuations tend to get translated into proportionate variations of nominal (recurring) consumption expenditures.

In order to buffer abrupt variations in their daily catches, the fishermen of Poovar resort to several devices or strategies: adjustment in the timing of non-recurrent (consumption or capital) expenditures which are not subject to strict timing constraints; movements in cash holdings; and changes in the house-hold's net indebtedness position through the use of consumption credit facilities. The former two strategies can be considered as self-insurance mechanisms. The latter really belongs to the category of mutual insurance arrangements and, as such, deserves our attention in the context of the present discussion.

What needs to be stressed first is that financial intermediaries specializing in day-to-day consumption credit are not likely to emerge in this situation and to develop the corresponding market. As a matter of fact, there are good grounds to believe that such agents would not be interested in transactions which are so frequent and involve such tiny sums that administrative costs per unit of money lent would be prohibitively high. In these circumstances, credit-givers have every chance to go bankrupt whether or not they choose to transfer the burden of their high operating expenses to their customers. This is obvious if they try to bear this burden themselves. On the other hand, if they pass it on to the borrowers, the latter would be asked to pay interest charges so high that they would probably prove unable to meet the financial obligations (payment of interests and amortization of the principal) they have willingly contracted: in the first instance, the demand side of the market does not exist, while in the second instance the supply side vanishes because the providers of credit cannot stay in business.

The fishermen of Poovar have, however, responded to these difficulties and overcome a potential market failure by evolving a decentralized system of consumption loans through which current receipts on the beach are regularly redistributed so as to provide a time-pattern of expenditures much more even than that of income. As was argued above, consumption credit can serve the role of partial insurance due to the intertemporal nature of risk-bearing provided that the uncertain income streams are uncorrelated across the population concerned. What is remarkable about the system of (subsistence) consumption credit in Poovar is that it really functions like a (partial) insurance market and thereby gives fishermen the advantage of maximum intertemporal flexibility in their consumption choices. In fact, this system bears close resemblance to the gift-exchange system of the anthropologists, since it is based on 'the ethical imperatives of reciprocal obligations' (Belshaw 1965: 11). Hence the name 'reciprocal credit' which has been given it elsewhere (Platteau and Abraham 1987: 467).

The insurance function of reciprocal credit is evident from certain specific aspects of the implicit contract between the lender and the borrower and from the particular role of the community or the larger social group. Thus, it is noteworthy that by accepting a reciprocal loan a fisherman implicitly recognizes that he will be concerned with the future economic fortune of his creditor. Such a commitment implies that in the case that the creditor falls into distress, the borrower will not only have to return his debt immediately, but also that he must be ready to come to the help of his benefactor even if he has already succeeded in paying back his initial loan. Conversely, if the debtor again finds himself on the brink of a subsistence crisis, the creditor is expected to come to his rescue irrespective of whether or not he has cleared his first debt. A link of solidarity is thereby forged between the two parties which arises from their mutual desire to insure themselves against the risk of a catch failure (ibid. 467–8).

It is clear from this account that there is typically no stipulated date for the repayment of reciprocal loans: the tacit rule is that the borrower will clear his debt as soon as he is in a position to do so. Moreover, the fact that reciprocal loans are given free of any formal interest does not mean that they carry no price: the price a borrower has to pay consists of a conditional promise to help his creditor should their economic fortunes be reversed in the future. In other words, 'the borrower does not end his relation with the lender by repaying his debt as would happen with standard (contractual) types of credit' (ibid. 470). Conversely, the interest forgone by the credit-giver can be interpreted as the functional equivalent of the risk premium he is willing to pay in order to insure himself against future (production) contingencies.

This system of reciprocal credit is clearly decentralized since lenders and borrowers enter into direct contact with each other without using the services of any specialized agent. A crucial feature of this mechanism is that the fishermen are well informed about their respective economic situations, as a result of which there is no important information gap that a financial inter-mediary could bridge. This characteristic follows from the fact that the fishermen involved in a given reciprocal credit network live and work very close to each other, all the more so if they have family ties, belong to the same crew, or co-operate in some way or other in the spheres of production and/or marketing (usually through their wives in the latter case). To the extent that incentive problems arise from costly and asymmetrical information, they are not likely to pose a major threat to the functioning of this mutual insurance scheme.

It would, however, be incorrect to assume that things work so well that no role is left for a monitoring or rule-enforcing structure, and that the market for reciprocal credit reduces itself to a number of dyadic relationships between pairs of fishermen who are willing to insure each other against the risk of falling below minimum earnings. There are, in fact, two essential functions which the community of Poovar—or, more exactly, any social group corresponding to a network of reciprocal credit relationships—performs to make the operation of the consumption credit market more effective. The first of these functions is to remedy situations where, owing to insufficient diversification of their financial claims, creditors are unable to obtain help from their debtors when they find themselves under stress. In such circumstances, the community may seek third parties ready to advance loans either to the embarrassed creditors or to the insolvent debtors so that they can clear their former debts.

A second useful function performed by the local community consists precisely of controlling the moral hazard problems that are still liable to arise either because, good though it may seem, information is not perfect, or because coercion turns out to be necessary to enforce some promises. Thus, for example, in the kind of problematic situations mentioned above, the community may first check whether the failing debtor is really unable to repay his debt to a creditor in distress and, if not, it will bring social pressure on him to meet his outstanding obligations (ibid. 468). The simple threat of social sanctions is usually sufficient to make the potential free-riders comply. Indeed, fishermen normally have grave fears of losing their social reputation, not only because they are eager to avoid being involved in conflicts with a high degree of public visibility, but also (and mainly) because harmful material consequences may follow from such loss in terms of employment or credit opportunities forgone. As a matter of fact, there is no doubt that owner-employers do not like to take on 'unreliable' workers in their crew, and that credit-givers are reluctant to advance money to persons who have been potential or actual defaulters in the past. Moreover, the fear of losing these opportunities is all the more effective as a check on opportunistic behaviour because debtors cannot easily run away from their native village (due to lack of alternative economic possibilities), with the consequence that any free-riding or violation of the implicit social code entails heavy social and economic costs (ibid. 468–9). Be that as it may, one can say that in Poovar as in the villages studied by Robert Wade, the problem appears to be 'less detection [of free-riding] than resolving conflicts between those seen to be cheating and those who see themselves as harmed by their cheating' (Wade 1988: 193).

Quantitative evidence shows that, in Poovar, reciprocal credit transactions play a major role in day-to-day adjustments to income fluctuations, especially among poorer fishermen. In other words, together with adjustments in the timing of non-recurrent expenditures (whenever this is possible) and, above all, with movements in cash holdings, reciprocal credit turns out to be an important way of stabilizing subsistence consumption throughout the year. Table 4.2 below provides a striking illustration of the crucial role which consumption credit can play in smoothing the impact of variations of fish

Table 4.2. Daily Movements in the total wealth position and in the financial assets owned by a crew member household of Poovar (October 1981)

Date	Variations in wealth (current savings) (1)	Variations in financial assets (2)	Amount of non-recurrent expenditures (3)
1	− 23.75	− 25	10
2	+ 4.25	+ 10	1
3	+ 7.75	+ 10	1
4[b]	− 20.25	− 20	0
5	− 19.75	− 20	0
6	− 1.0	0	0
7	+ 14.0	+ 10	2
8	− 8.75	− 10	0
9	− 16.50	− 10[a]	0
10	+ 5.0	+ 5[a]	1
11[b]	− 20.25	− 20	1
12	− 1.5	− 5	0
13	− 11.0	− 15	0
14	+ 2.0	0	0
15	− 11.5	− 10	0
16	− 9.0	− 10	0
17	+ 3.75	+ 5[a]	0
18[b]	− 17.0	− 20	0
19	− 16.5	− 10	0
20	+ 4.0	0	0
21	− 15.75	− 10	0
22	− 15.75	− 15	0
23	− 1.5	− 5[a]	0
24	+ 10.75	+ 15	1
25[b]	− 19.25	− 20	1
26	− 0.5	0	0
27	− 9.0	− 10	0
28	− 5.25	− 5	0
29	− 3.0	− 5[a]	2
30	− 3.5	0	0
31	− 8.75	− 10	0
MONTHLY TOTAL	Rs− 207.5	− 200	20

[a] This is the net outcome of simultaneous transactions running into opposite directions, typically a borrowal coupled with the repayment of a debt incurred in the past.
[b] Sundays.
Source: Adapted from original field data collected by Anita Abraham during the years 1980–81.

catches. It presents the daily variations in wealth (see column 1, obtained by subtracting all consumption expenditures from current income) and in financial assets (see column 2, obtained by adding loans given and debts repaid and subtracting loans recovered and debts contracted) for an assetless household of Poovar during the month of October 1981. In addition, the table displays the amounts of non-recurrent expenditures incurred on each day of the same month (note that these amounts have been subtracted from income in calculating the figures shown in the first column). Since the household concerned does not incur capital expenditures (it does not own capital assets), daily movements in cash holdings can be directly obtained from the table by subtracting column 2 from column 1. Finally, it is noticeable that all credit transactions have involved small amounts (varying from a minimum of Rs 5 to a maximum of Rs 25).

A number of interesting observations can be made on the basis of this empirical material. First, there is no systematic pattern by which non-recurrent expenditures are adjusted in accordance with income fluctuations: this results from the fact that not all of them have a flexible timing. Second, daily variations in financial assets are not only frequent but they always have the same sign as the daily wealth fluctuations: the household's net indebtedness position worsens when current expenditures exceed income (when the household dissaves) and it improves in the opposite case (when the household saves part of its income). Third, movements in cash holdings tend to occur when wealth variations are of comparatively low amounts: the household replenishes its cash holdings when it has a small surplus (saving) and depletes them when it has a small deficit (dissaving). Conversely, the household tends to give reciprocal loans or to return reciprocal debts when it has a sizeable enough surplus, while it tries to borrow in the reciprocal credit market or to recover past loans when it has a sizeable enough deficit. Fourth, over the whole month, the household's wealth variations have been translated into corresponding variations of its financial assets, which means that the level of its cash holdings has not varied significantly between the beginning and the end of the month. During the month under consideration, the household's net dissaving amounted to Rs 207.5, while its net indebtedness increased by Rs 200.

3.3. Concluding Comments on the Scott–Popkin Controversy

In the next section, an attempt will be made to assess the performance of traditional social-security systems and to highlight a number of dynamic issues related to them. In the process, the main points emerging from the above lengthy discussion will be summarized. Before embarking on this next step of the analysis, it is useful to make a few concluding comments on the Scott–Popkin controversy. Perhaps the most important conclusion in this respect is that both authors have somewhat gone astray by seeing the problem of the 'moral economy' as concerned only with the motivations of people in traditional village societies. Thus, Scott made the mistake of confusing social-security arrangements with altruistic behaviour or, at least, he seems to have read in such arrangements the prevalence of a pervasive 'subsistence ethics' in these societies. As for Popkin, he made the mistake of thinking that he had refuted Scott's thesis simply by arguing that people are basically selfish and that norms and values do not influence human behaviour. The fact of the matter is that the 'moral economy' of traditional rural communities can be largely interpreted as a 'social-security' economy in that people belonging to these communities are often eager to find collective methods to protect themselves against major contingencies and production hazards. In so far as these methods or mechanisms have proven to be workable, their success ought to be ascribed *both* to self-interested behaviour on the part of individuals and to ruling customs and norms that are designed to ensure their continuity and to control major incentive problems. On the other hand, the very fact that collective actions for social protection and hunger insurance happen to fail, or that some socially efficient solutions are not adopted, does not necessarily mean that selfish behaviour tends to ruin or block important attempts at better protecting people against major risks. Covariate risks and incomes seriously limit collective hunger insurance possibilities. Human institutions are determined by material constraints as well as by behavioural characteristics, which is not to say that the latter determinants should be downplayed.

4. TRADITIONAL SOCIAL-SECURITY SYSTEMS: PAST ACHIEVEMENTS AND MODERN CHALLENGES

Any inquiry into the concrete socio-economic organization of traditional (precapitalist) rural societies can only lead to more scientific humility, owing to the bewildering variety of the organizational forms encountered. The dangers of drawing general conclusions from a limited number of particular case-studies must always be borne in mind. In the present chapter, I have tried to reduce these dangers by considering a wide range of situations while striving to identify and assess traditional arrangements in the field of social security and hunger insurance. A number of important lessons appear to emerge from this analysis.

To start with, and given due consideration to their whole institutional build-up, traditional village communities can be portrayed as societies which are essentially geared to securing minimum subsistence for all their members. The variety of rules governing the people's right of access to food is large and the particular approaches to social protection adopted by a given society are partly determined by historical circumstances (including the history of class or caste relations) and partly by environmental factors (natural constraints, population density, characteristics of production risks, available technology, and so on). Two main types of social institutions aimed at the reduction of the risk of hunger can be distinguished. In the first place, there are all the collective rules and mechanisms that govern the distribution of available productive assets or work opportunities in such a way that every household in the community has a reliable guarantee of survival over the full weather cycle. At one extreme, one finds kin-based societies (for example, descent groups of a corporate kind such as the many African patrilineage systems) in which a relatively egalitarian access to natural resources is guaranteed to each member. And, at the other extreme, there are the strongly differentiated agrarian societies where members of the lower strata usually enjoy guaranteed access to employment on the lands of the rich. It is noteworthy that, in all cases, traditional social-security mechanisms entail major departures from private ownership and market exchange. In one way or another, social controls are always exercised over the access to, and the use of, key productive resources. Of course, this is mostly evident in the case of village communal resources which play a vital role in ensuring the livelihood of the weaker sections of the population.

The second important type of collective methods of risk management in peasant societies consists of reciprocity networks or gift-exchange arrangements through which villagers pool their risks in order to reduce the total cost they represent. These mutual insurance schemes can operate through the exchange of labour, grain, durables, or cash, and it is rather obvious that individuals need not be altruistic to participate in them (even though that could help reduce moral hazard problems). Reciprocity networks are a special kind of economic transaction in which, as anthropologists have untiredly emphasized, economic and social considerations are deeply intermingled. Interestingly, once gift exchange is interpreted as an insurance arrangement (at least in its form of 'generalized reciprocity'), this very characteristic appears to perform an essential function, namely that of tying the transactors together in such a way that they become mutually responsible for whatever misfortune may strike them.

Even though empirical evidence is scanty (but not altogether absent), the case can reasonably be made that, barring exceptionally unfavourable circumstances (such as repeated crop failures or crop diseases affecting entire communities), traditional methods for controlling the risk of falling into distress have usually enabled the people to counter natural and other hazards in a rather effective way. The well-established fact that people were very keen to avoid being expelled from their social group and that expulsion was viewed as the gravest possible sanction in any traditional village society suggests that the social protection it afforded its members was of utmost significance. This being said, it is also important to emphasize that traditional ways of coping with the risk of hunger were far from being perfect or complete social protection devices. Thus, one of their most glaring limitations arose from the fact that subsistence crises almost always had to be confronted within the narrow boundaries of a restricted local or regional economic space. There can be little quarrel with the claim that, thanks to the development of extended communication networks, efficient transportation means, and extensive redistribution mechanisms, the modern world is better equipped to prevent the kind of major collective disasters that traditional societies could hardly counter. In other words, at least with respect to such disasters, traditional arrangements were a second-best optimum given the absence of generalized food exchanges and the low level of development of the communication infrastructure.

There are other limitations to traditional practices of hunger insurance. Take the first type of institution mentioned above. A basic prerequisite for the effectiveness of asset-sharing or work-spreading mechanisms as hunger insurance devices is that productive resources or employment opportunities be sufficiently numerous in relation to the population. If population pressure becomes too severe, sharing methods may cease to guarantee the livelihood of most of the people. The main problem here is that, beyond a certain point, diminishing incomes resulting from population growth foster centrifugal tendencies even within rather egalitarian societies, and cause struggles over the distribution of productive resources and employment opportunities to intensify. Shifts in the institutions governing income and resource distribution may then occur which are likely to reduce the economic security of many individuals or social groups. Changes in property rights immediately come to mind. Indeed, it is a well-known fact that, under the impact of population growth (and increased commercialization of agriculture), markets tend to emerge to allocate the scarce goods or production factors available (Boserup 1965, 1981; Rosenzweig et al. 1988; Binswanger et al. 1989). In China, such a situation already arose by the middle of the eighteenth century, when reserves of suitable land started to run out, causing the gradual emergence of private rights in land. The state even encouraged reclamation of forest areas by granting legal ownership titles to cultivators once they had paid taxes on the land (Jones 1981: 216). In India, genuine property rights in the soil came much later, during the period of British rule. Yet, as recent historical research has tended to show, quasi-markets of land revenue-collecting rights developed during the Mughal period (such rights became inheritable, saleable, and leasable, possibly with prior approval of state or village authorities), sometimes several centuries before British rule came to be established (Habib 1963: 154–80; Fukuzawa 1982: 250–1; Kumar 1983: 210).[30] In most of Africa, however, the emergence of private property rights in land is a very recent phenomenon (Noronha 1985; Pingali et al. 1987; Platteau 1990 and forthcoming).

Social differentiation, polarization, and marginalization processes are the normal consequences of the above evolution (see, for example, Ishikawa 1975;

---

[30] For a summary of the findings of these studies, see Fuller (1988: 25–9).

Scott 1972, 1976, 1985; Hayami and Kikuchi 1981; Watts 1983, 1984). The gradual deprivation of 'outsiders' of their customary rights of access to village lands, and of tenants or share-croppers of their traditional land-use rights, are oft-quoted examples of such processes. Even the archetypical 'poverty-sharing' villages of Java do not escape this general tendency, as attested by the fact that exclusionary labour arrangements have multiplied since the late 1960s (Collier *et al.* 1974; White 1976, 1979; Hart 1986). In south Sri Lanka, the system of income-sharing through work-spreading that resulted from guaranteed rotating access to the sea collapsed during the 1950s in some villages and even before in other villages. As a matter of fact, the average share of each net in the total catch had become so small due to the overmultiplication of nets that 'ownership of a single share was insufficient to sustain life' (Alexander 1982: 206). A cumulative kind of involution resembling a 'tragedy of the commons' was initiated from then on, since to protect their income existing participants had to construct additional nets. This was with a view to preventing the number of their turns per unit of time and their chance of participating in the flush period from declining too much. Many fishermen who could not afford to finance new shares were forced to sell their existing shares to more affluent participants and to leave the fishery (ibid. chaps. 9, 10, 11). In one village, a social upheaval followed during which many small shareholders organized themselves to urge the government to limit the number of seines allowed to operate in their fishing zone (Amarasinghe 1989).

Population growth is not the only factor which may cause the erosion of traditional social-security mechanisms. As 'moral economists' and Marxist scholars have emphasized, market penetration and the gradual rise of a modern State system are equally powerful factors. In the above example of beachseining in south Sri Lanka, these factors have also been at work, especially since the Second World War when a dramatic increase in fish prices occurred which resulted from important developments in fish marketing and from growing integration of fisheries into the national economy. The new economic opportunities thus created attracted a class of wealthy capitalists and traders who usually belonged to the landed élite and had tight connections with the political establishment and strong positions in local state institutions (Amarasinghe 1988: 168–9). In a very short time, this élite gained control of most of the beachseine fisheries.

The problem is essentially that by opening up new and varied avenues for social and economic mobility, the growth of the market tends to encourage the overt expression of (perhaps latent) individualistic propensities among the people, to dissolve old co-operative ties and to disentangle the individuals' interests from those of the social group (Smith 1959: chaps. 10, 11, 12; Robertson 1987: 196–7). Deeper and deeper penetration of market values has the effect of loosening the web of traditional social relations: people become more and more free of group pressure to conform and less and less concerned about the well-being of the extended family or social group. Furthermore, the rise of a centralized modern State alongside the expansion of the domain of market forces tends to undermine old systems of authority. A 'transition of trust' problem arises both because community norms are weakened in response to market incentives that push personal advantage considerations to the foreground, and because locally based authority or consensus systems are gradually eroded by codified laws and new political structures (Lipton 1985).

Another difficulty with the first type of institution for social protection concerns inegalitarian societies. Indeed, one may justifiably wonder if the price paid by assetless households to guarantee their livelihood by entering into patronage relations is not too high. This question deserves serious pondering, especially so when the (feudal) landlord class appears to hold enormous power and privileges. Thus, Jones has noted that in India 'the caste system might be said to have provided job security and a form of insurance, but the price was high' (Jones 1981: 193). It is clear that social and economic inequality is particularly unbearable if the landlord, warlord, or bureaucratic classes are rapacious and oppress the peasantry without regard for its ability to make ends meet. Thus, in Mughal India: 'The peasants were left in destitution by taxes which were collected whatever the state of the harvest. They received no real help in the face of natural disasters, and these were frequent (there was for example a great run of famines between 1540 and 1670 when the empire was at peace)' (ibid.: 197; see also Popkin 1979 with reference to nineteenth-century Vietnam). Therefore, as underlined in a recent critique of the moral economy approach, 'the possibility that there were "immoral" societies introduces an important qualification into Scott's characterization of pre-colonial peasant life' (Haggis et al. 1986: 1450).[31]

Turning now to traditional risk-pooling mechanisms, one should note two fundamental limitations which are in fact typical of all insurance schemes: the incentive and the covariance problems. What needs special emphasis here is that in traditional societies lacking modern record-keeping systems and nation-wide law enforcement procedures, these two problems are interdependent, giving rise to an 'insurance dilemma': a reduction of the incentive problem is likely to make the covariance problem more intractable, and, vice versa, the incentive problem becomes harder to control when a wider geographical and social area is covered to diminish the correlation of risk across the various participant households. As a consequence, the scope for effective risk-pooling can, in many instances, be quite small.

Furthermore, incentive problems tend to become much more difficult to monitor when the prospects for shared values and trust or for an effective local

---

[31] Note that I have not dealt with the situation prevailing in the urban areas of precolonial empires or kingdoms. The contention that the right to subsistence 'certainly did not exist everywhere' (Haggis et al. 1986: 1449) is probably more valid for urban than for rural areas. A lot more research needs however to be done on this issue before any firm conclusion can be reached.

authority structure are undermined by the rise of a centralized modern State (colonial or post-colonial) and by the penetration of capitalism into the economic domain of the village (see above). If problems of societal control are serious during an inevitable transition phase, it is due to the fact that 'the new authority has not yet acquired the information, the power to reward or penalise, or the powers of moral suasion, permitting it to replace the old authority's lost powers' (Lipton 1985: 51). A void is thereby created which is likely to result in increased transaction costs of detection (of frauds), negotiation, and enforcement.

Finally, there exists an additional difficulty arising from the specific form of risk-pooling arrangements in these societies. Contrary to standard insurance schemes, reciprocity networks tend to discourage capital accumulation. As a matter of fact, while an insurance premium is fixed, and there is therefore no disincentive to accumulate, with a norm of 'sharing' and generalized reciprocity, 'the amount of the "premium" is directly related to one's ability to give, and individuals have less incentive to produce more than average' (Cashdan 1985: 456). In the words of Polly Wiessner: 'Limiting work effort over the long run can result in a lower-than-possible mean income in exchange for reaffirming a strong hold in social relations necessary for reducing the variance around the mean' (Wiessner 1982: 79). Thus, the limits on time which the Kung of the Kalahari desert put into the search for food is partially the result of their fear of being exploited in reciprocal relations whose terms are that the one who has gives to the one who needs. Conversely, spending time gathering more information about the economic position of partners and trying to collect food from them may be considered a better strategy than putting greater effort into hunting or growing food (ibid. 68, 78–9).

Disincentive effects resulting from specific forms of hunger insurance and social protection may not represent major problems in traditional village societies. Indeed, these societies obey a reproduction logic designed to ensure their continued subsistence as social groups, and not a logic of capital accumulation. In this context, individual accumulation of capital is normally kept under control by the society lest it lead to economic differentiation and thereby create tensions in the social and political fabric. In other words, there is great apprehension that accumulation of private productive assets may disturb the fragile social equilibrium upon which the group's collective subsistence crucially depends. Therefore, only certain forms and a certain extent of private (and, of course, collective) capital accumulation are allowed and these often serve the function of diversifying risks (such as the accumulation of cattle in many semi-arid countries, particularly for individuals belonging to the upper strata), or enhancing the group's social security (such as symbolic investments aimed at reinforcing co-operation ties among the members).

By contrast, in contemporary Third World countries confronted with the challenge of rapid economic growth (not only to absorb increasing numbers but also to raise the people's current standard of living), the disincentive effects of traditional risk-pooling arrangements on capital accumulation and technical change may be strongly felt and generate serious tensions among as well as within individuals. Thus, Wiessner points out that, having developed increasing interest in material possessions, 'many Kung are really torn between the desire to accumulate goods and the desire to remain within a secure system of mutual help' (ibid. 82; see also Ortiz 1967: 210–13).

The same kind of difficulties—formulated in terms of static or dynamic efficiency considerations—could actually be mentioned with regard to all traditional arrangements aimed at stabilizing access to key productive resources and at preventing the emergence of markets in order to insure community members against the risk of hunger. For example, David Newbery writes (1989: 286): 'If land were communally held and the harvest were divided among all those eligible, risks would be evenly shared but there would be little individual incentive to increase output and accumulate wealth.' Such conflicts between institutions that provide insurance benefits and those that encourage efficiency are in fact quite numerous. The question as to how property and use rights in vital resources (for example, land) can be specified and protected without involving too high a price in terms of lost opportunities for economic growth is probably one of the most difficult policy issues on the agenda of development economists. This is so because efficiency, equity, and insurance considerations need to be taken into account in a simultaneous way.

5. CONCLUSION

For policy purposes, four important conclusions emerge from the preceding analysis.

First, social-security systems did exist in numerous forms in precapitalist village societies. At the same time, they were far from being perfect hunger insurance mechanisms and, in many instances, they could probably be considered as second best optima given the many constraints confronting these societies: high weather-dependence of many income sources due to low technology development, shortages of roads and other communication means, high income and risk correlation across households, lack of record-keeping systems, and so on.

Second, many traditional village support systems entail high costs in terms of dynamic efficiency, because of their disincentive effects on work and investment efforts. If they were all to be maintained in the future, social security would be bought at the price of capital accumulation and economic growth.[32] This is true not only with respect to systems of rights of access and to

---

[32] In Europe, it was precisely with the advent of capitalism that the old values and institutions (like the Poor Laws in England) guaranteeing food security for everybody came under the strong

risk-pooling arrangements, but also with respect to law practices. Indeed, ancient laws were built on the notions of fairness and social status, and they took explicit account of personal situations and particular circumstances while defining responsibilities, interpreting agreements or commitments, and assigning liabilities. However, if highly flexible legal rules may be a good way of protecting the weaker sections of the population against serious contingencies, they are also liable to hinder economic growth. In actual fact, economic transactions are not likely to multiply, and division of labour is not likely to increase and to give rise to more or less continuous productivity gains, if business dealings appear too risky to willing transactors because of the lack of predictability of their consequences. As the history of advanced countries has taught us, explicit contracts, formal guarantees, and carefully delimited agreements which bind the parties without regard to their personal situations serve the function of minimizing the risks involved in many economic transactions (see, for example, North and Thomas 1973; North 1981).

Third, there has been a gradual erosion or weakening of many traditional systems of social security due to the joint impact of market penetration, population growth, and the rise of a modern State system. Nevertheless, contrary to what James Scott and other 'moral economists' have suggested, this is far from being a systematic or universal tendency. In a number of cases, such systems seem to have been strengthened or intensified. Thus, for example, when the labour market is tight, when productive operations must be done in a timely way (a constraint from which new agricultural technologies are not exempt) or require a large dose of husbandry skill (as in the case of farm animals or mechanical irrigation devices), employers tend to put a high premium on the ready availability and reliability of labour. Patronage may then be conceived of by the employers as a proper way to establish trust and to maintain stable relations with their workers. The latter may thereby get a guarantee of more or less continuous assistance in times of trouble through which the former aim at cementing labour-tying arrangements and securing long-term commitments of labour (Bardhan 1979, 1980, 1983; Bardhan and Rudra 1980; Platteau 1984; Binswanger and Rosenzweig 1984). The rise of industrial paternalism in nineteenth-century European factories could perhaps be interpreted along these lines. To take another example, the increased risk of being lost out at sea arising from the mechanization of fishing techniques has prompted the fishermen in many Third World countries to evolve or to strengthen informal, decentralized, mutual insurance schemes for sea rescue operations. Often, these schemes prove to be superior to more centralized

attacks of the heralders of the new '*laissez-faire*' order. Interestingly, incentive considerations were the main argument which the latter put forward: only poverty can incite (force) the lower classes to work and, according to Townsend (1786), hunger is actually the most effective pressure, because it is 'peaceful, silent and continuous' (quoted from Polanyi 1944: 113–14; see also Furniss 1930: 118).

mechanisms involving the management of a common fund by a rather bureau-cratized structure. That social-security mechanisms may still play an important role today is evidenced by the experience of Sub-Saharan Africa where powerful 'horizontal' solidarity networks allow many people to survive in a context of chronic economic crisis (Bayart 1989: 270; for Asia, and India in particular, see Das Gupta 1987)

Fourth, in the light of the above three points but with the foregoing qualifying statement in mind, one can agree with Gilbert that 'the continued usefulness of traditional systems as the *major* source of social protection' has become 'highly problematic' (Gilbert 1976: 365). One can think of a number of circumstances in which these systems need to be replaced by new social-security institutions. Such circumstances arise when traditional methods or arrangements have been largely undermined under the impact of new forces (see the preceding point); when they are rather ineffective in achieving their aims; when they are inadequate to cope with new types of insecurities emerging in the wake of development (such as those resulting from the use of new agricultural technologies which are embodied in costly inputs acquired through the market); or when they are not compatible with an acceptable measure of economic growth in the rural sector. What alternative social-security systems could be is a complex issue that clearly lies beyond the scope of the present analysis. While market forces and institutions may help in reducing the risk of hunger, particularly in so far as they increase self-reliance by diversifying sources of income and supply as well as market outlets,[33] they also open the way for new sources of vulnerability. The need for carefully thought public policy measures, discussed at length in other contributions to this book, is an inescapable aspect of the challenge of social security in the modern world.

---

[33] For a useful distinction between the concepts of self-sufficiency and self-reliance, see Streeten (1987: 39–40).

References

Alexander, P. (1980), 'Sea Tenure in Southern Sri Lanka', in *Maritime Adaptations: Essays on Contemporary Fishing Communities* (ed. A. Spoehr). University of Pittsburgh Press, 91–111.

—— (1982), *Sri Lankan Fishermen: Rural Capitalism and Peasant Society*. Canberra: Australian National University Press.

Amarasinghe, O. (1988), 'The Impact of Market Penetration, Technological Change, and State Intervention on Production Relations in Maritime Fishermen Communities: A Case Study of South Sri Lanka'. Ph.D. thesis, Faculté des Sciences Economiques et Sociales, Namur.

—— (1989), 'Technical Change, Transformation of Risks and Patronage Relations in a Fishing Community of South Sri Lanka', *Development and Change*, 20/4.

Bardhan, P. (1979), 'Wages and Unemployment in a Poor Agrarian Economy: A Theoretical and Empirical Analysis', *Journal of Political Economy*, 87/3.

—— (1980), 'Interlocking Factor Markets and Agrarian Development: A Review of Issues', *Oxford Economic Papers*, 32/1.

—— (1983), 'Labor-Tying in a Poor Agrarian Economy: A Theoretical and Empirical Analysis', *Quarterly Journal of Economics*, 98/3.

—— and Rudra, A. (1978), 'Interlinkage of Land, Labour and Credit Relations: An Analysis of Village Survey Data in East India', *Economic and Political Weekly*, 13/6–7.

—— —— (1980), 'Types of Labour Attachment in Agriculture: Results of a Survey in West Bengal', *Economic and Political Weekly*, 15/35.

Bayart, J. F. (1989), *L'Etat en Afrique—La politique du ventre*. Paris: Fayard.

Beals, R. L. (1970), 'Gifting, Reciprocity, Savings, and Credit in Peasant Oaxaca', *Southwestern Journal of Anthropology*, 26.

Belshaw, C. (1965), *Traditional Exchange and Modern Markets*. Englewood Cliffs, NJ: Prentice-Hall.

Bennett, J. W. (1968), 'Reciprocal Economic Exchanges Among North American Agricultural Operators', *Southwestern Journal of Anthropology*, 24.

Berkes, F. (1986), 'Local Level Management and the Commons Problem', *Marine Policy*, 10.

Berry, S. (1984), 'The Food Crisis and Agrarian Change in Africa: A Review Essay', *African Studies Review*, 27/2.

Binswanger, H. P. (1986), 'Risk Aversion, Collateral Requirements, and the Markets for Credit and Insurance in Rural Areas', in P. Hazell, C. Pomareda, and A. Valdès, (eds.), *Crop Insurance for Agricultural Development: Issues and Experiences*. Baltimore and London: Johns Hopkins University Press.

—— McIntire, J., and Udry, C. (1989), 'Production Relations in Semi-arid African Agriculture', in *The Economic Theory of Agrarian Institutions* (ed. P. Bardhan). Oxford: Clarendon Press.

—— and Rosenzweig, M. (1984), 'Contractual Arrangements, Employment, and Wages in Rural Labor Markets: A Critical Review', in H. P. Binswanger and M. Rosenzweig, *Contractual Arrangements, Employment, and Wages in Rural Labor Markets in Asia*. New Haven, Conn., and London: Yale University Press.

———— (1986), 'Behavioural and Material Determinants of Production Relations in Agriculture', *Journal of Development Studies*, 22/3.

Boas, F. (1920), 'The Social Organization of the Kwakiutl', *American Anthropologist*, 22.

Booth, A. and Sundrum, R. M. (1985), *Labour Absorption in Agriculture*. Oxford, New York, and Melbourne: Oxford University Press.

Boserup, E. (1965), *The Conditions of Agricultural Growth: The Economics of Agrarian Change under Population Pressure*. London: George Allen & Unwin.

———— (1981), *Population and Technology*. Oxford: Basil Blackwell.

Bourdieu, P. (1980), *Le Sens pratique*. Paris: Éditions de Minuit.

Breman, J. (1974), *Patronage and Exploitation: Changing Agrarian Relations in South Gujarat*. Berkeley: University of California Press.

Carter, M. (1987), 'Risk Sharing and Incentives in the Decollectivization of Agriculture', *Oxford Economic Papers*, 39/3.

Cashdan, E. (1985), 'Coping with Risk: Reciprocity Among the Basarwa of Northern Botswana', *Man*, 20/3.

Chambers, R. (ed.) (1989), *Vulnerability: How the Poor Cope?* IDS Bulletin, Special Issue, 20/2.

Coate, S. and Ravallion, M. (1989), 'Reciprocity without Commitment: Characterization and Performance of Non-cooperative Risk-Sharing', mimeo.

Codere, H. S. (1956), 'The Amicable Side of Kwakiutl Life: The Potlatch and the Play-Potlatch', *American Anthropologist*, 58.

———— (1957), 'Kwakiutl Society: Rank Without Class', *American Anthropologist*, 59.

Cohen, J. (1980), 'Land Tenure and Rural Development in Africa', in R. H. Bates and M. F. Lofchie, (eds.), *Agricultural Development in Africa: Issues of Public Policy*. New York: Praeger.

Collard, D. (1978), *Altruism and Economy*. Oxford: Martin Robertson.

Collier, W. L., Soentoro, G., Wiradi, and Makali, (1974), 'Agricultural Technology and Institutional Change in Java', *Food Research Institute Studies*, 13/2.

Colson, E. (1979), 'In Good Years and in Bad: Food Strategies of Self-Reliant Societies', *Journal of Anthropological Research*, 35/1.

Corbett, J. (1988), 'Famine and Household Coping Strategies', *World Development*, 16/9.

Dahlman, C. (1980), *The Open Field System and Beyond: A Property Rights Analysis of an Economic Institution*. Cambridge: Cambridge University Press.

Dalton, G. (1962), 'Traditional Production in Primitive African Economies', *Quarterly Journal of Economics*, 76/3.

———— (1971), *Economic Anthropology and Development: Essays on Tribal and Peasant Economies*. New York: Basic Books.

Das Gupta, M. (1987), 'Informal Security Mechanisms and Population Retention in Rural India', *Economic Development and Cultural Change*, 36/1, 101–20.

Dirks, R. (1980), 'Social Responses during Severe Food Shortages and Famine', *Current Anthropology*, 21/1.

Drèze, J. P., and Sen, A. K. (1989), *Hunger and Public Action*. Oxford: Clarendon Press.

Drucker, P. (1955), *Indians of the Northwest Coast*. New York: McGraw-Hill.

Epstein, T. S. (1967), 'Productive Efficiency and Customary Systems of Rewards in

Rural South India', in R. Firth (ed.), *Themes in Economic Anthropology*. London: Tavistock Publications.

Eswaran, M., and Kotwal, A. (1989), 'Credit as Insurance in Agrarian Economies', *Journal of Development Economics*, 31/1.

Evans-Pritchard, E. E. (1940), *The Nuer: A Description of the Modes of Livelihood and Political Institutions of a Nilotic People*. Oxford: Clarendon Press.

Firth, R. (1966), *Malay Fishermen: Their Peasant Economy*. London: Routledge & Kegan Paul.

Fleuret, A. (1986), 'Indigenous Responses to Drought in sub-Saharan Africa', *Disasters*, Mar.

Fukuzawa, H. (1982), 'Agrarian Relations and Land Revenue: The Medieval Deccan and Maharashtra', in *Cambridge Economic History of India*, i. Cambridge: Cambridge University Press.

Fuller, C. J. (1988), 'Misconceiving the Grain Heap: A Critique of the Concept of the Indian Jajmani System', mimeo, London School of Economics.

Furniss, E. (1930), *The Position of the Laborer in a System of Nationalism*. Boston: Houghton Mifflin Co.

Geertz, C. (1970), *Agricultural Involution: The Process of Ecological Change in Indonesia*. Berkeley and Los Angeles: University of California Press.

Gilbert, N. (1976), 'Alternative Forms of Social Protection for Developing Countries', *Social Service Review*, Sept.

Giri, J. (1983), *Le Sahel demain*. Paris: Karthala.

Gough, K. (1960/1), 'The Hindu Jajmani System', *Economic Development and Cultural Change*, 9, pt. 1.

Gregory, C. A. (1982), *Gifts and Commodities*. London and New York: Academic Press.

Griffin, K. (1974), *The Political Economy of Agrarian Change*. London: Macmillan.

Habib, I. (1963), *The Agrarian System of Mughal India (1556–1707)*. Bombay: Asia Publishing House.

Haggis, J., Jarrett, S., Taylor, D., and Mayer, P. (1986), 'By the Teeth: A Critical Examination of James Scott's *The Moral Economy of the Peasant*', *World Development*, 14/12.

Hart, G. (1986), 'Exclusionary Labour Arrangements: Interpreting Evidence on Employment Trends in Rural Java', *Journal of Development Studies*, 22/4.

Hayami, Y., and Kikuchi, M. (1981), *Asian Village Economy at the Crossroads: An Economic Approach to Institutional Change*. Tokyo: University of Tokyo Press.

Ishikawa, S. (1975), 'Peasant Families and the Agrarian Community in the Process of Economic Development', in *Agriculture in Development Theory* (ed. L. Reynolds). New Haven, Conn., and London: Yale University Press.

Jones, E. L. (1981), *The European Miracle: Environments, Economies and Geopolitics in the History of Europe and Asia*. Cambridge: Cambridge University Press.

Kikuchi, M., Hafid, A., and Hayami, Y. (1984), 'Changes in Rice Harvesting Contracts and Wages in Java', in H. P. Binswanger and M. R. Rosenzweig, (eds.), *Contractual Arrangements, Employment, and Wages in Rural Labor Markets in Asia*. New Haven, Conn., and London: Yale University Press.

Kimball, M. (1988), 'Farmers' Cooperatives as Behavior Toward Risk', *American Economic Review*, 78/1.

Kumar, D. (1983), 'Agrarian Relations: South India', in *Cambridge Economic History of India*, ii. Cambridge: Cambridge University Press.

Lepage, H. (1985), *Pourquoi la propriété?* Paris: Hachette.

Lipton, M. (1985), 'The Prisoners' Dilemma and Coase's Theorem: A Case for Democracy in Less Developed Countries?' in R. C. O. Matthews (ed.), *Economy and Democracy*. London: Macmillan.

Longhurst, R. (1986), 'Household Food Strategies in Response to Seasonality and Famine', *IDS Bulletin*, 17/3.

Macneil, I. R. (1978), 'Contracts: Adjustments of Long-Term Economic Relations Under Classical, Neoclassical, and Relational Contract Law', *Northwestern University Law Review*, 72.

Malinowski, B. (1920), 'Kula: Circulating Exchange of Valuables in the Archipelagoes of Eastern New Guinea', *Man*, July.

—— (1921), 'The Primitive Economics of the Trobriand Islanders', *Economic Journal*, 31/1.

—— (1922), *Argonauts of the Western Pacific*. London: Routledge & Kegan Paul.

Mauss, M. (1925), *The Gift*. London: Routledge & Kegan Paul.

Mayer, E. (1985), 'Production Zones', in S. Masuda, I. Shimada, and C. Morris, (eds.), *Andean Ecology and Civilization*, Tokyo: University of Tokyo Press.

Meillassoux, C. (1980), *Femmes, greniers et capitaux*. Paris: François Maspéro.

Migdal, J. (1974), *Peasants, Politics, and Revolution*. Princeton, NJ.: Princeton University Press.

Neale, W. C. (1957), 'Reciprocity and Redistribution in the Indian Village: Sequel to Some Notable Discussions', in Polanyi *et al.* (1957).

Newbery, D. (1989), 'Agricultural Institutions for Insurance and Stabilization', in P. Bardhan (ed.), *The Economic Theory of Agrarian Institutions*. Oxford: Clarendon Press.

—— and Stiglitz, J. (1981), *The Theory of Commodity Price Stabilization: A Study in the Economics of Risk*. Oxford: Oxford University Press.

Noronha, R. (1985), 'A Review of the Literature on Land Tenure Systems in sub-Saharan Africa', Research Unit of the Agriculture and Rural Development Department, World Bank Report ARU 43, Washington, DC.

North, D. C. (1981), *Structure and Change in Economic History*. New York and London: W. W. Norton and Co.

—— and Thomas, R. P. (1973), *The Rise of the Western World: A New Economic History*. Cambridge: Cambridge University Press.

Obeyesekere, G. (1967), *Land Tenure in Village Ceylon*. London: Cambridge University Press.

Olson, M. (1965), *The Logic of Collective Action*. Cambridge, Mass.: Harvard University Press.

—— (1982), *The Rise and Decline of Nations*. New Haven, Conn., and London: Yale University Press.

Orlove, B. (1977), 'Inequality Among Peasants: The Forms and Uses of Reciprocal Exchange in Andean Peru', in R. Halperin and J. Dow, *Peasant Livelihood: Studies in Economic Anthropology and Cultural Ecology*. New York: St Martin's Press.

Ortiz, S. (1967), 'The Structure of Decision-making among Indians of Colombia', in R. Firth (ed.), *Themes in Economic Anthropology*. London: Tavistock Publications.

Piddocke, S. (1965), 'The Potlatch System of the Southern Kwakiutl: A New Perspective', *Southwestern Journal of Anthropology*, 21.

Pingali, P., Bigot, Y., and Binswanger, H. (1987), *Agricultural Mechanization and the Evolution of Farming Systems in Sub-Saharan Africa*. Baltimore: Johns Hopkins University Press.

Pitt-Rivers, J. (1954), *The People of the Sierra*. London: Weidenfeld & Nicolson.

Platteau, J. P. (1984), 'The Drive Towards Mechanization of Small-Scale Fisheries in Kerala: A Study of the Transformation Process of Traditional Village Societies', *Development and Change*, 15/1.

——(1986), 'La fonction euphémisante et mystificatrice de l'aide', in X. Dijon and J. Burton, (eds.), *Dis-moi qui tu aides. . . .* Namur: Presses Universitaires de Namur.

——(1988), 'A Two-season Model of Hunger Insurance through Patronage: The Jajmani System Put to the Test', *Cahiers de la Faculté des Sciences Economiques et Sociales*, Facultés Universitaires of Namur.

——(1990), 'The Food Crisis in Africa: A Comparative Structural Analysis', in J. Drèze and A. K. Sen (eds.), *The Political Economy of Hunger*. Oxford: Oxford University Press.

——(forthcoming), *Land Reform and Structural Adjustment in Sub-Saharan Africa: Controversies and Guidelines*, Rome: FAO.

——and Abraham, A. (1987), 'An Inquiry into Quasi-Credit Contracts: The Role of Reciprocal Credit and Interlinked Deals in Small-Scale Fishing Communities', *Journal of Development Studies*, 23/4.

——and Baland, J. M. (1989), 'Income-Sharing through Work-Spreading Arrangements: An Economic Analysis with Special Reference to Small-Scale Fisheries', *Cahiers de la Faculté des Sciences Economiques et Sociales*, Facultés Universitaires of Namur.

——and Nugent, J. B. (1989), 'Contractual Relationships and their Rationale in Marine Fishing', *Cahiers de la Faculté des Sciences Economiques et Sociales*, Facultés Universitaires of Namur.

Polanyi, K. (1944), *The Great Transformation*. New York: Holt, Rinehart, & Winston.

——(1957), 'The Economy as Instituted Process', in Polanyi *et al.* (1957).

——(1968), 'Ports of Trade in Early Societies', in G. Dalton (ed.), *Primitive, Archaic and Modern Economies*. New York: Doubleday.

——(1977), *The Livelihood of Man*. New York and London: Academic Press.

——Arensberg, C. W., and Pearson, H. W. (eds.), (1957), *Trade and Market in the Early Empires*. New York: Free Press; London: Collier-Macmillan.

Popkin, S. L. (1979), *The Rational Peasant: The Political Economy of Rural Society in Vietnam*. Berkeley and Los Angeles: University of California Press.

Posner, C. (1981), *The Economics of Justice*. Cambridge, Mass., and London: Harvard University Press.

Pospisil, L. (1958), *Kapauka Papuans and their Law*, Yale University Publications in Anthropology, No. 54. New Haven, Conn.: Yale University Press.

Provinse, J. H. (1955), 'Cooperative Ricefield Cultivation Among the Siang Dyaks of Central Borneo', in E. A. Hoebel (ed.), *Readings in Anthropology*. New York: McGraw-Hill.

Robertson, A. F. (1987), *The Dynamics of Productive Relationships: African Share Contracts in Comparative Perspective*. Cambridge: Cambridge University Press.

Rosenzweig, M. R., Binswanger, H. P., and McIntire, J. (1988), 'From Land Abundance to Land Scarcity: The Effects of Population Growth on Production Relations in Agrarian Economies', in R. D. Lee *et al.*, (eds.), *Population, Food, and Rural Development*. Oxford: Clarendon Press.

Rothschild, M. and Stiglitz, J. E. (1976), 'Equilibrium in Competitive Insurance Markets: An Essay on the Economics of Imperfect Information', *Quarterly Journal of Economics*, 90/4.

Sahlins, M. (1963), 'On the Sociology of Primitive Exchange', in *The Relevance of Models for Social Anthropology* (ed. M. Banton). London: Tavistock Publications.

——(1968), *Tribesmen*. Englewood Cliffs, NJ: Prentice-Hall.

——(1972), *Stone Age Economics*. Chicago: Aldine.

Schapera, I. (1970), *Tribal Innovators: Tswana Chiefs and Social Change, 1795–1940*. London: Athlone Press.

Scott, J. (1972), 'The Erosion of Patron–Client Bonds and Social Change in Rural Southeast Asia', *Journal of Asian Studies*, 32/1.

——(1976), *The Moral Economy of the Peasant*. New Haven and London: Yale University Press.

——(1985), *Weapons of the Weak: Everyday Forms of Peasant Resistance*. New Haven and London: Yale University Press.

Service, E. R. (1962), *Primitive Social Organization: An Evolutionary Perspective*. New York: Random House.

——(1966), *The Hunters*. Englewood Cliffs, NJ: Prentice-Hall.

Smith, T. C. (1959), *The Agrarian Origins of Modern Japan*. Stanford: Stanford University Press.

Sow, F. (1986), 'L'Économie du poisson sur la petite côte (Sénégal): Le Rôle des femmes', *Études Scientifiques*, (Université de Dakar), Mars.

Streeten, P. (1987), *What Price Food?* London: Macmillan Press.

Torry, W. I. (1979), 'Anthropological Studies in Hazardous Environments: Past Trends and New Horizons', *Current Anthropology*, 20/3.

——(1987), 'Evolution of Food Rationing Systems with Reference to African Group Farms in the Context of Drought', in M. H. Glantz (ed.), *Drought and Hunger in Africa*. Cambridge: Cambridge University Press.

Townsend, W. (1786), *Dissertation on the Poor Laws*.

Turnbull, C. (1984), *The Mountain People*. London: Triad/Paladin Books.

Von Braun, J., and Webb, P. J. R. (1989), 'The Impact of New Crop Technology on the Agricultural Division of Labor in a West African Setting', *Economic Development and Cultural Change*, 37/3, 513–34.

Wade, R. (1988), *Village Republics: Economic Conditions for Collective Action in South India*. Cambridge: Cambridge University Press.

Walker, T. S. and Jodha, N. S. (1986), 'How Small Farm Households Adapt to Risk?', in P. Hazell, C. Pomareda, and A. Valdés, (eds.), *Crop Insurance for Agricultural Development: Issues and Experiences*. Baltimore and London: Johns Hopkins University Press.

Watts, M. (1983), *Silent Violence*. Berkeley: University of California Press.

——(1984), 'The Demise of the Moral Economy', in E. Scott (ed.), *Life Before the Drought*. Boston: Allen & Unwin.

White, B. (1976), 'Population, Involution and Employment in Rural Java', *Development and Change*, 7/3.

White, B. (1979), 'Political Aspects of Poverty, Income Distribution and their Measurement: Some Examples from Rural Java', *Development and Change*, 10/1.

Wiessner, P. (1982), 'Risk, Reciprocity and Social Influences on !Kung San Economics', in E. Leacock and R. B. Lee (eds.), *Politics and History in Band Societies*. Cambridge: Cambridge University Press.

Williamson, O. (1985), *The Economic Institutions of Capitalism*. New York: The Free Press.

Wolf, E. R. (1955), 'Types of Latin American Peasantry', *American Anthropology*, 57.

——(1966), 'Kinship, Friendship, and Patron–Client Relations', in *The Social Anthropology of Complex Societies* (ed. M. Banton). New York: Frederick A. Praeger.

——(1982), *Europe and the People Without History*. Berkeley: University of California Press.

Wynne, E. (1980), *Social Security: A Reciprocity System Under Pressure*. Boulder, Colo.: Westview Press.

5

Social Security and the Family:
Coping with Seasonality and Calamity in Rural India

Bina Agarwal

INTRODUCTION

How do poor agricultural families seek to cope with the problem of food insecurity associated with seasonal troughs in the agricultural production cycle? How do they cope with calamities such as drought and famine? How effective are the mechanisms they adopt? Does the burden of this coping fall equally on all family members or are some more equal than others?

Answers to questions such as these could be seen as necessary inputs in the designing of public policy, or other forms of external interventions for social security, on at least two counts:

1. To ensure that such interventions complement and strengthen rather than substitute for people's own efforts in dealing with contingencies; that they are appropriate to actual and not assumed needs, and that people are seen as actors in the process of change rather than as passive recipients of aid and relief.

2. To address explicitly any intrafamily inequalities in the impact of contingencies. Rooted implicitly (and sometimes explicitly) in public policies and programmes are certain assumptions about the family, the responsibility of its members towards each other's well-being and welfare, and their capability and willingness to fulfil that responsibility. For instance, government programmes that direct resources or employment mainly at men assume implicitly that the associated benefits will be shared equitably with the women and children. Since the effectiveness of these and similar interventions can depend crucially on the validity of such assumptions regarding family behaviour and intrafamily relations, clearly we need to know much more about how the family in fact operates as a unit, especially under contingencies, and how certain interventions will affect particular members. Also, assumptions made about the family in times of normality may not hold equally under severe crisis situations as in a drought or famine.

Drawing upon existing studies, this chapter addresses some of these questions, focusing on the issue of social security essentially in terms of food security. In specific terms, in Section 1, a conceptual framework for understanding intrafamily relations is discussed and certain analytical propositions on the ways in which seasonality and calamity might impinge on these relations are put forward. Sections 2 and 3 examine the nature and effectiveness of the mechanisms adopted by poor agricultural families (namely, those of agricultural labourers and small cultivators) to provide food security for their members, against seasonality and calamity; the ways in which family coping mechanisms in the two contexts might differ; and intrahousehold inequalities (if any) in the burden of coping. Section 4 analyses how the family itself may begin to disintegrate in an extreme calamity such as famine, using the Bengal famine of 1943 as a case-study. The concluding Section 5 highlights some aspects of appropriate external interventions.

The issue of food security has been considered here in the narrow sense of ensuring maintenance of food consumption levels in the context of specific circumstances and contingencies rather than in the wider sense of ensuring adequate food intake for all. (This last would imply raising consumption levels substantially above existing ones for a large part of the population, and would impinge on the entire domain of development policy and anti-poverty programmes.) Broadly, a household is seen as effectively coping with seasonality and calamity where it is able to go through such periods without irreversible damage to the productive capacity of its members, or to its net assets position. The terms household and family have been used here interchangeably to connote commensal units.

The focus of this chapter will be on India, although supportive material from other South Asian countries will also be brought to bear on these issues. In general, material on family coping mechanisms in this region is rather limited, and even more so on intrahousehold aspects of coping. India's ecological and social diversity again cautions against easy generalizations where the evidence is typically region-specific. This chapter therefore essentially attempts to provide pointers, and to raise some issues for debate and further research.

1. THE FAMILY, SEASONALITY, AND CALAMITY

In examining the relationship between seasonality, calamity and the family, Sen's (1983) conceptualization of family relations as embodying both co-operative and conflicting elements, and his entitlement approach to famine and starvation (Sen 1981), prove useful starting points. Sen conceptualizes the family as a unit in which various household arrangements (who does what and gets what goods and services) are fixed on the basis of the implicit bargaining strength of its members. He argues that there are many co-operative outcomes possible—beneficial to all parties compared with non-cooperation—but the different parties have strictly conflicting interests in the choice among the set of efficient co-operative arrangements. Which co-operative solution emerges depends on the relative bargaining power of the different family members. A member's bargaining power, in turn, may depend on various parameters, especially the strength of the person's 'fall-back position'[1] if co-operation should fail, and on feelings of love, affection, concern, and so on. In other words, it could depend on both the economic and extra-economic (including 'moral') factors.

Further, Sen in his entitlement approach argues that a person's ability to command food depends in particular on his/her ownership endowments (of land, labour, and so on) and exchange entitlement mapping (although he notes that entitlements may also operate through various forms of non-market processes). In the present context, the approach could usefully be extended to cover especially two types of entitlements which neither fall within the purview of ownership nor are specifically exchange entitlements, namely, those stemming from (1) traditional rights to communal resources (such as village commons, forests, and so on), and (2) external social-support systems (such as those of patronage, kinship, friendship) embodying relationships between social groups or persons in which considerations other than the mere economic take precedence, that is, they fall under the rubric of what some authors have termed the 'moral economy'. These typically relate to non-market exchanges, but do not altogether preclude market exchanges such as those existing between shopkeepers and favoured customers who get privileged treatment in access to goods, or goods on credit (Scott 1976; Greenough 1982).

Taking these as analytical starting points one could propose that:

1. A person's 'fall-back position' (and associated bargaining strength within the family, *vis-à-vis*, say, food) would depend, among other things, on his/her ownership endowments, exchange entitlements, and external (social and communal) support systems (for example, patronage, kinship, friendship, and rights to communal resources).[2] In other words, factors which impinge on a person's command over food in general would also impinge on intrafamily co-operative conflicts over food. And inequalities among family members in their ownership endowments, exchange entitlements and access to external support systems would place some members in a weaker bargaining position relative to others. Gender could be one such basis of inequality, age another.

2. Crises of seasonality and calamity can negatively affect ownership endowments and exchange entitlements as well as the strength of external support systems for both sexes, but in so far as men and women are affected unequally it would alter their relative intrafamily bargaining strengths as well. A crisis which leads to a total collapse of or even a large decline in the wife's fall-back position (as could happen for instance during a famine) while that of the husband sustains (in relative terms) could weaken her bargaining power even to a point where non-cooperation is found more beneficial by the man than

---

[1] In his more recent writings, Sen (1987) substitutes this term by the term 'break-down position'. I prefer to retain 'fall-back position'.

[2] It could depend too on State and non-traditional support systems. These will, however, be discussed specifically in Section 4 below.

cooperation, creating a tendency towards the disintegration of families, and the abandonment of spouses. The same could apply to children and the aged. Whether or not an actual breakdown occurs would be subject of course to other considerations as well, such as 'moral' ones, and to the ties of love and affection which hold a family together.

An examination of the evidence on household coping mechanisms during seasonality and calamity would help throw light on how the relative strength of intra-household fall-back positions impinge on and are affected by such contingencies, and how the 'co-operative conflicts' resolve themselves in the two contexts. Also we might ask: are responses to a calamity qualitatively and/ or quantitatively different from those to seasonality? The differences may stem both from the relative predictability of the one contingency as against the other, and from the relative intensity of shortfalls experienced in the two contexts. Given their periodicity, seasonal fluctuations can be anticipated, giving households greater scope for undertaking protective measures, although, in actuality, not all households may be in a position to protect themselves effectively.

Drawing upon a diversity of cross-disciplinary evidence, the next two sections will focus on the family's mechanisms for coping with seasonality and with calamity respectively. In this process the nature and extent of differences in the mechanisms adopted in the two contexts, as well as in the relative contributions of and burdens borne by male and female members of the family, will be examined.

2. COPING WITH SEASONALITY

Seasonal variations in climate and crop cycles are associated, among other things, with variations in employment, wages, and food prices, which in turn can have repercussions on a poor agricultural household's immediate as well as long-term command over food. Agricultural employment in India fluctuates seasonally both in terms of labour-force participation rates and the number of days of work available during particular months, as revealed in national-level surveys[3] as well as region-specific studies;[4] and it is associated with high levels of involuntary unemployment among those dependent substantially or mainly on agricultural wage labour for a livelihood: for all-India, the Rural Labour Enquiry (RLE) of 1974–5 recorded 124 days of not working during the year due to want of work for female agricultural labourers and 76 for male (see Table 5.1 for a breakdown by State).[5] The length and frequency of seasonal

[3] e.g. National Sample Survey (NSS), 1977–8, conducted by the Government of India.

[4] See Lipton's (1983a) review piece; also Patel et al. (1975) and Chinnappa and Silva (1977).

[5] Also see Jodha's (1986) estimates of involuntary unemployment based on village-level data collected at the International Crop Research Institute for Semi-Arid Tropics (ICRISAT, Hyderabad) relating to four districts in three states.

Table 5.1. Employment, unemployment and annual real earnings from agricultural wage work of women and men of agricultural labour households, (1974–1975)

Region/State	Average annual full days of:				Annual real[a] earnings per person		Ratio of male to female earnings
	employment		not working due to want				
	F	M	F	M	F	M	
North-Western							
Haryana	131	203	88	88	213.3	406.8	1.91
Punjab	170	233	111	64	239.5	618.1	2.58
Rajasthan	163	239	97	49	150.2	310.7	2.07
Uttar Pradesh	124	200	114	57	133.2	277.4	2.08
Western and Central							
Gujarat	160	206	111	67	168.0	278.1	1.66
Maharashtra	180	221	90	57	114.3	241.2	2.11
Madhya Pradesh	125	198	141	70	114.1	162.9	1.43
Eastern							
Bihar	114	186	155	90	119.7	229.5	1.92
Orissa	111	164	158	92	73.1	155.7	2.13
West Bengal	147	210	166	88	167.1	294.3	1.76
Southern							
Andhra Pradesh	138	193	103	61	104.8	198.2	1.89
Karnataka	175	204	81	58	134.2	246.4	1.84
Kerala	108	138	162	126	159.4	286.5	1.80
Tamil Nadu	118	148	142	98	93.4	183.9	1.97
All India	138	193	124	76	121.9	243.3	2.00

[a] Money earnings have been deflated by the Agricultural Consumer Price Index with 1964–5 as the base.

Sources: GOI (1981: 140, 143, 206, 212; 1979: 102, 103, 162).

peaks and slacks as well as the average level of employment show considerable and complex interregional differences—varying by cropping patterns, the intensity of cropping, and the availability of irrigation.[6] However, while intensification of crop rotations and expansion of irrigation may significantly increase labour requirements and alter the patterns of seasonality, fluctuations persist in greater or lesser degree, and certain months may still usually be

[6] See the analysis in Ghodake *et al.* (1978) for six villages in Maharashtra and Andhra Pradesh; Dasgupta *et al.* (1977) for a review of village studies across India; and Clay (1981) for a comparison of four districts in Bangladesh.

identifiable as chronically lean periods over fairly wide geographic areas.[7] Seasonal fluctuations in wages (linked to task specificity of labour use as well) are typically lower than those in employment,[8] but seasonal variability in wage earnings (dependent both on days of employment and on wages) is still likely to be substantial.[9] This especially affects the purchasing power of those dependent on casual labour, in full or in part, for a livelihood (the less productive among whom may even be weeded out during slack periods).[10] For households living on the margin of subsistence, these troughs in income (in cash or in kind) can constitute crisis situations. At the same time, as noted, seasonal fluctuations can be anticipated by rural households which can seek to devise various means of coping with them.

Existing literature which in one way or another throws light on the mechanisms adopted by a household for coping with seasonal shortages points to a range and variety of methods, which broadly fall into five categories:

(1) diversifying sources of income, including seasonal migration;
(2) drawing upon communal resources—village common lands and forests;
(3) drawing upon social relationships—patronage, kinship, friendship—and informal credit networks;
(4) drawing upon household stores (of food, fuel, and so on) and adjusting current consumption patterns;
(5) drawing upon assets.

These are not mutually exclusive and are typically adopted in combination. Consider each in turn.

2.1. *Diversifying Sources of Income*

Diversification of income sources—seeking employment where available, growing a range of crops including mixed cropping where the household has some land, keeping a variety of livestock (cows, buffaloes, goats, pigs, sheep) and poultry, and trading are common ways of dealing with seasonality and more generally with the subsistence risk that traditional farming systems entail.[11] Some village studies list over ten different earning activities undertaken during the year by poor agricultural households.[12]

[7] Clay (1981) notes, for instance, that across four geographically dispersed districts of Bangladesh, Sept./Oct. continues to be the slackest period, with little increase in employment in this period despite technological change.

[8] See Drèze and Mukerjee (1987) for a useful review of and discussion on the reasons for this lower variability.

[9] See especially Hossain's (1987) six-village study of poor households in Bangladesh, which gives a breakdown of earnings by seasons among landless and land-poor households. Also see Lipton's (1983a) review.

[10] Rudra (1982) notes this for West Bengal, and Drèze and Mukherjee (1987) for Uttar Pradesh.

[11] See e.g. Caldwell *et al.* (1986); Chen (1988); Jodha (1979); Majumdar (1978).

[12] See e.g. Majumdar's (1978) study of tribals in Meghalaya, and Hossain's (1987) study in Bangladesh.

Seasonal migration could be seen as a form of spatial diversification, made possible by interregional variations in peaks and slacks, and is usually especially high from unirrigated semi-arid areas to more prosperous irrigated ones.[13] While national-level surveys (National Sample Survey, Census) do not throw much light on the scale of seasonal migration in India (since this is not separated out from other forms of migration), they do indicate that among agricultural labourers (who are affected most by seasonal troughs) the migrants are typically individual males moving from rural to rural areas, and more commonly within the district than across districts and states (Bardhan 1977). Region-specific studies reveal a variety of migration patterns: by distances covered, such as circulatory migration within a limited region (as noted by Breman 1979a, 1985, in South Gujarat) and long-distance movements as from Bihar to Punjab; by the periods of absence—some go for a single agricultural operation, others for an entire season, yet others for much of the year (see Chen 1988, for Gujarat); by form, that is whether as individuals or in groups; and so on. Those migrating with capital assets, such as bullock or camel carts that can be used to transport produce, can command higher rates. It is noteworthy though that while seasonal migration clearly helps in mitigating region-specific stresses it can also depress wages in the areas to which the migrants go, and generate considerable hostility from local workers (Breman 1985).

While individual migration of younger males appears to be the most common pattern,[14] individual women also migrate seasonally, especially among tribal communities (Bardhan 1977;[15] Banerjee 1988), as do entire families hired in groups through contractors (Breman 1979a, 1985), or through money-lenders seeking to ensure that their loans are repaid (Banerjee 1988). Caste groups may be formed as well, with young men and women of a single caste constituting work teams under the overall charge of a male member (Chen 1988), or, somewhat more commonly, women alone comprising work teams (Breman 1985). The nature of the labour process may itself dictate group migration: in Gujarat, the labour hired seasonally for sugarcane harvesting, for instance, has to work in teams—the male cutter followed by a helper (usually a wife, sister, or daughter) to clean the stalks of leaves, followed, in turn, by a child to bind the cleaned stalks together (Breman 1979a).[16] Whole families are

[13] About the migrants from the arid parts of West Maharashtra to South Gujarat, Breman (1979a) notes that the limited employment opportunities and overall poverty cause labour to migrate out for a large part of the year, and particularly 'in times of serious and substantial drought—as occurs once every three to four years on average—the supply is virtually inexhaustible'.
[14] Connell et al. (1976: 39) in their survey of migration patterns as revealed by village studies note: 'Almost everywhere, migration concentrates extremely heavily on villagers aged 15–30.'
[15] Bardhan (1977: A–45) notes: 'The phenomenon of tribal and scheduled caste women in paddy areas migrating in the busy season to take up agricultural work like transplantation in prosperous villages seems not to be an isolated one but rather of some general validity.'
[16] Similarly, Mencher and Saradamoni (1982) observed in some Thanjavur villages that harvesting operations are customarily done by teams of two—a man and a woman. This seriously

also more likely to migrate among the landless than among the cultivators who tend to retain some members to take care of the farm (Salva 1973). Bardhan's (1977) review indicates that migration over longer distances (interstate relative to intrastate, and interdistrict relative to intradistrict), and from villages to towns, features more of male individuals and less of entire families or female individuals.

Essentially, coping with seasonal variation in employment opportunities and diversifying income sources requires close family co-operation. The labour of women and children is a specially critical input both in terms of earnings from wage employment and in enabling families to explore additional earning sources. Livestock and poultry, for instance, are typically looked after by women and children (see Mitra 1985; Banerjee 1988; George 1988), and individual male out-migration again requires them to assume additional responsibilities (see Desai 1982; Jetly 1987).

Typically too, agricultural labour women: (1) face much greater seasonal fluctuations in employment and earnings than men due to the greater task specificity of their work,[17] are noted to have sharper peaks and longer slacks than men in the irrigated rice regions of South India (Harriss 1977), and have a lesser chance of finding employment in the slack seasons;[18] (2) are much more dependent on wage labour than men,[19] have lower average days of annual employment (and more days of involuntary unemployment), and lower daily wages (often even for the same tasks), which makes for considerable gender differences in annual real earnings (Table 5.1);[20] (3) within agricultural wage work, are usually only employed as casual labour, typically men alone being hired on long-term contracts, possibly because they substitute for family men in ploughing, night operations, and market transactions—work in which women are socially disadvantaged or (as in the case of ploughing) socially excluded; (4) are much less likely to have meal provisions built into their

disadvantages female-headed households, especially if they do not have a brother or son to team up with them.

[17] See Agarwal (1984) who gives the operation-wise use of labour by gender in three Indian States.

[18] Ryan and Ghodake (1980). Also, in a sample study of 432 West Bengal villages in 1972–3, women of agricultural labour households showed the greatest percentages of slack-season decline in both average wage-rate and average duration of work: 'A female labourer's weekly wage earnings dropped . . . during the slack quarter to 20% of the (levels) during the busiest quarter. In the case of a male labourer, they dropped to 67% . . .' (quoted in Lipton 1983a: 85).

[19] By the NSS 'usual status' criterion, in 1983, of the rural women workers of over 5 years of age, 35% were employed as casual labour on a daily or piece-rate basis; 62% were self-employed (in family enterprises) in agricultural and rural non-agricultural work, and 3% in regular employment (waged or salaried) especially in domestic service. In contrast, of the male workers, 29% were casual agricultural labourers, 61% self-employed, and 10% in regular employment.

[20] In the table, based on the Rural Labour Enquiry of 1973–4, the annual earnings from agricultural wage work of women agricultural labourers are less than half of the men in five states, and close to half in the rest.

contracts;[21] (5) have more limited information on jobs due to lower literacy levels, and lesser access to mass media and to the market place;[22] (6) have lower job mobility due to their primary and often sole responsibility for child care, the ideology of female seclusion, and their vulnerability to class/caste-related sexual abuse. Indeed given purdah ideology and the social defining of gender roles, there are clear limitations to women's control over their own labour power and ability to exchange it as they please, limiting their overall exchange entitlements.

Nevertheless their contribution to household earnings is substantial, as evidenced by studies from across the country.[23] In particular, Mencher's (1987) detailed quantitative evidence for landless and near landless agricultural labour households in twenty sample villages in Tamil Nadu and Kerala brings out several important features. She finds (taking a weighted average for each village) that (see Table 5.2): (1) although the wife's earnings from agricultural wage work were typically half or one-third of the husband's, in absolute terms her contribution from her earnings towards household maintenance was greater than his in six of the twenty sample villages, equal to or close to equal in five others, and substantial in the rest; (2) the wives typically contributed 90–100 per cent of their earnings and the men rarely gave over 60–70 per cent of theirs, keeping the rest for personal use;[24] (3) the minimum contributed by all household females was greater than by all household males in thirteen of the twenty villages.

To the extent that male and female labour peaks in wage employment and other tasks do not entirely coincide (given the sex-typing of certain agricultural tasks), one might ask to what extent there is a seasonal switching of responsibil-

[21] A Karnataka-related study of rural labour found that 70% of male labour contracts and only 20% of female labour contracts had meal provisions (Ryan and Wallace 1985: 24).

[22] The notion of 'territorial purdah' (prevailing in much of northwest India)—the effective segregation of village space by gender whereby there are clearly identifiable spaces which essentially constitute male areas, such as the *bazaar* (market-place), that women are expected to avoid—strongly disadvantages them in their search for employment and in managing land independently. Although seniority, age, whether she is a daughter or daughter-in-law, her class/caste all affect a woman's freedom of movement, so that older women with grown-up sons, village daughters, and women of poor and low caste families enjoy greater liberty, even they are supposed to avoid spaces of predominantly male presence (see especially Sharma 1980; also personal observation). These restrictions are even greater in countries such as Bangladesh and Pakistan.

[23] See Gulati (1978) for Kerala; Mencher and Saradamoni (1982) and Mencher (1987) for Kerala, Tamil Nadu, and West Bengal; and Dasgupta and Maiti (1987) for Himachal Pradesh, Madhya Pradesh, Uttar Pradesh, Maharashtra, and Assam. The last study finds that in terms of wage earnings alone women's contribution ranged from 20% of household annual earnings in Assam to 26% in Himachal Pradesh.

[24] Other micro-studies, which have looked at male and female expenditure patterns within poor households with earners of both sexes, provide additional evidence to the effect that while female earnings typically go towards the family's basic needs of food, fuel, etc., a not insignificant part of male earnings goes towards tobacco and liquor (see Gulati 1978; Mies, *et al.* 1983; Sharma 1980; Mencher and Saradamoni 1982). A study for rural Punjab also showed that an agricultural labour household with a heavy drinker on average spent 40 per cent less on food per capita and less on clothing than a 'non-drinker' household (Dass, quoted in Harriss 1986).

Table 5.2. Relative contributions by males and females to household maintenance, Rs per year

State/village	Wife			Husband			Proportion of wife's to husband's		All females		All males		Ratio males to all females
									Max.	Min.	Max.	Min.	
	E	C	C/E	E	C	C/E	E	C	C	C	C	C	C
Kerala													
Cannanore 1	1,138	962	0.85	1,954	1,249	0.64	0.58	0.77	1,924	500	2,935	211	1 : 0.79
Palghat 1	–	854	–	–	645	–	–	1.31	1,394	361	2,799	113	1 : 1.29
Palghat 2	1,065	990	0.93	2,039	1,406	0.69	0.52	0.70	1,606	104	3,029	115	1 : 0.62
Malappuram 1	435	421	0.97	1,219	1,020	0.84	0.36	0.41	1,333	101	3,517	45	1 : 0.25
Trichur 1	–	467	–	–	377	–	–	1.24	1,585	313	790	56	1 : 1.20
Trichur 2	786	688	0.88	1,787	1,294	0.72	0.44	0.53	1,323	309	2,824	380	1 : 0.56
Alleppey 1	752	691	0.92	748	569	0.76	1.01	1.21	1,181	14	1,072	49	1 : 1.30
Alleppey 2	530	438	0.83	743	541	0.73	0.71	0.81	600	211	970	137	1 : 0.77
Trivandrum 1	1,027	938	0.91	2,214	943	0.43	0.46	0.99	1,371	370	1,518	544	1 : 0.97
Trivandrum 2	1,420	1,209	0.85	2,235	1,141	0.51	0.64	1.06	1,797	480	2,165	317	1 : 1.16
Tamil Nadu													
Chingleput 1	–	301	–	–	155	–	–	1.94	1,223	140	614	27	1 : 1.20
Chingleput 2	–	265	–	–	216	–	–	1.23	368	100	540	36	1 : 0.86
South Arcot 1	699	693	0.99	1,449	1,226	0.85	0.48	0.57	1,040	164	1,885	225	1 : 0.52
South Arcot 2	587	566	0.96	935	667	0.71	0.63	0.85	907	61	1,330	41	1 : 0.71
Thanjavur 1	–	468	–	–	490	–	–	0.96	816	801	616	127	1 : 1.20
Thanjavur 2	759	756	1.00	1,247	901	0.72	0.61	0.84	1,510	80	1,544	263	1 : 0.80
Tirunelveli 1	1,173	1,099	0.94	1,653	1,478	0.91	0.71	0.74	1,997	428	4,651	289	1 : 0.63
Madurai 1	564	556	0.99	1,240	938	0.76	0.45	0.59	1,072	184	1,716	135	1 : 0.60
Kanya Kumari 1	–	369	–	–	365	–	–	1.01	577	204	1,463	174	1 : 0.85
Kanya Kumari 2	599	570	0.95	1,297	808	0.62	0.46	0.71	891	156	1,681	399	1 : 0.61

Notes: Districts within each State are listed from north to south. The dash indicates a village where data on earnings were not collected. E = earnings; C = contributions.

Source: Mencher (1987).

Table 5.3. Daily time utilization of women by season (in hours)

Name of village and State	Season	House-hold work	Cooking and food processing	Personal work	Recreation and social activities	Animal husbandry	Agricultural work	Non-agricultural work	Cottage craft	Fuel search	Collection of forest produce	Market-ing	Total time
N. Suriyan (Himachal Pradesh)	Rainy	1.96	2.46	0.25	0.18	1.62	2.62	0.81	1.06	0.12	–	–	11.08
	Winter	3.25	3.85	0.50	0.15	3.55	0.25	1.05	1.05	0.25	–	0.15	14.05
	Summer	4.00	3.30	0.40	0.75	1.00	–	0.78	0.05	0.08	–	–	10.36
Sehar (Madya Pradesh)	Rainy	2.15	4.10	1.15	1.25	1.05	3.15	–	–	1.30	1.00	–	15.15
	Winter	3.75	4.98	1.15	1.01	0.50	1.45	–	0.10	2.05	–	–	14.99
	Summer	1.75	5.43	1.30	1.30	0.45	0.30	–	3.07	2.00	1.00	–	16.60
Malari (Uttar Pradesh)	Rainy	1.44	3.85	0.56	0.19	1.12	5.61	–	–	0.56	–	0.06	13.39
	Winter	3.01	4.45	0.63	0.12	2.37	1.37	–	–	0.75	–	–	12.70
	Summer	3.65	4.41	0.76	0.08	2.51	1.85	0.17	–	0.77	–	–	14.20
Deokhop (Maharashtra)	Rainy	2.25	3.00	0.81	0.37	–	2.50	–	–	1.75	0.25	0.93	11.86
	Winter	2.60	2.85	0.75	0.30	0.50	0.95	0.90	–	3.85	–	–	12.70
	Summer	1.41	1.66	1.00	–	–	–	6.16	–	2.83	–	0.16	13.22
Rajapara (Assam)	Rainy	3.29	3.90	1.10	–	0.55	5.21	–	–	0.17	–	0.07	14.29
	Winter	2.37	3.75	1.12	–	0.50	6.00	–	1.25	–	–	–	14.99
	Summer	2.91	4.41	1.52	–	2.05	2.33	–	0.33	–	–	0.16	13.71

Note: Sample consisted of two women observed in each village in each season, 1983–4.

Source: Dasgupta and Maiti (1987: 42).

ities within the family, especially for child care and domestic work, as found, for instance, by White (1976) among Javanese agricultural labourers. He noted that in the interests of maximizing household incomes, during periods of the year when women's labour was in highest demand, men remained at home to cook and babysit, and when both parents were out earning, children herded the family livestock, cut fodder, and even undertook domestic work and child care. In the Indian context there is little systematic information to indicate whether traditionally gender-typed tasks are switched between the sexes to adjust for differential seasonal labour demand, but data on women's time allocation to various tasks by seasons relating to five States (Table 5.3) does not suggest such shifts.[25] Rather there appears to be a combination of a rise in women's work burden and a squeezing of domestic work and child care during periods of high activity—agricultural or non-agricultural. On average too, time-allocation studies indicate that women in poor rural households typically work longer hours than men when all activities including domestic work are taken into account.[26]

2.2. Drawing upon Communal Resources

Access to village common property resources (CPRs) and state forests plays a critical role in enabling poor rural households to obtain essential items for daily use, to diversify income sources, and to increase the viability and stability of traditional farming systems by allowing a more integrated and diversified production strategy involving crops, trees, livestock, and so on. Communal resources serve as a source of various types of food, medicinal herbs, fuel, fodder, water, manure, silt, small timber, fibre, house-building with handicraft material, resin, gum, spices, and so on for personal use and sale, especially for the landless and land-poor. A study of the food habits of tribals in Madhya Pradesh lists 165 trees, shrubs, and climbers that they use as food in various forms (Tiwari, quoted in Randhawa 1980); and an other in Kerala lists eighty different forest items used as medicine (KFRI 1980).

Jodha's (1986) study covering semi-arid regions in seven States of India shows that while all rural households use CPRs in some degree, for the poor (identified by him as the landless and those with less than 2 ha of dry-land equivalent) they account for as much as 20 per cent or more of total income in seven out of the twelve districts examined on this count, and 9–13 per cent in the remaining, while providing 1–4 per cent only of the incomes of non-poor households (Table 5.4). In six of the twelve districts the average income per year from CPRs for poor households exceeded Rs 700 even without counting

[25] See Dasgupta and Maiti (1987) who also note that a man rarely cooks except if the wife is seriously ill and in the absence of a daughter to substitute for her.

[26] Ryan and Ghodake (1980) find this in all six villages of Andhra Pradesh and Maharashtra in which they gathered time allocation data by gender. Also see Sen (1988) for Madhya Pradesh, and Agarwal (1984) for a review of other studies.

Table 5.4. Average annual household income from CPRs in study villages of selected districts[a]

| Districts[b] | Per household annual average income (Rs) | | | | | | | |
| | Poor households[c] | | | | Other households[d] | | | |
	Number of households	Value of CPR products collected	CPR share in livestock income	Total value[e]	Number of households	Value of CPR products	CPR share in livestock income collected	Total value[e]
Mahbubnagar	15	382	152	534 (17)	10	109	62	171 (1)
Mehsana	26	421	309	730 (16)	24	88	74	162 (1)
Sabarkantha	35	432	336	818 (21)	19	111	97	208 (1)
Mysore	26	534	115	649 (20)	11	112	58	170 (3)
Mandsaur	23	400	285	685 (18)	18	113	190	303 (1)
Raisen	37	568	212	780 (26)	15	283	185	468 (4)
Akola	16	342	105	447 (9)	9	85	49	134 (1)
Aurangabad	22	405	179	584 (13)	21	110	53	163 (1)
Sholapur	17	443	198	641 (20)	9	143	92	235 (2)
Jalore	24	447	262	709 (21)	27	170	217	387 (2)
Nagaur	32	473	358	831 (23)	25	143	295	438 (3)
Dharmapuri	30	530	208	738 (22)	11	112	54	164 (2)

[a] Based on field work during 1982–5. CPRs are common property land resources in which all village members have rights, such as village forests, community pastures, uncultivable and barren land, and so on.
[b] Number of villages covered was one each in Mahbubnagar, Akola, and Sholapur, and two each in other districts.
[c] Includes landless households and those owning less than 2 ha. dryland equivalent.
[d] Larger farmer households.
[e] Figures in brackets give percentage of CPR income to total household income.

Source: Jodha (1986).

their contribution towards the productivity of private property resources, such as owned land. The dependence of the poor on CPRs is especially high for fodder and for firewood which constitutes the single most important source of cooking fuel in rural India, providing 67–69 per cent of the domestic energy in the hills and desert areas of the north (NCAER 1981). In semi-arid regions, CPRs supply 91–100 per cent of firewood, 66–84 per cent of all domestic fuel, and 69–89 per cent of the grazing needs of the landless and land-poor (Jodha 1986); and some 8–9 per cent of total dietary requirements in many of these villages (Ryan *et al*. 1984). Even in the green revolution belt of Delhi and Uttar Pradesh, in two villages studied by Dasgupta (1987), agricultural labourers derived some 17 per cent and 24 per cent of income from free collection, including collection both from CPRs and other people's fields; and for most poor households items collected free formed the bulk of dietary supplements to cereals bought or earned in kind through wage work.

Forests serve a similar function, especially for tribal populations—providing a basis for swidden cultivation, and a source of minor forest produce (MFP). Nearly 5 million persons (half of them in the north-east and the rest in central and eastern India) are assessed to be involved in shifting cultivation, covering an area of about 0.7 million ha (Srivastava 1977). In addition, MFP accounts for an estimated 13.6 to 38 per cent (varying by region) of total tribal income in Madhya Pradesh (a state containing in absolute numbers the largest concentration of tribals in the country), 10 to 55 per cent in Andhra Pradesh, and 35 per cent in parts of Gujarat (GOI 1982). In Orissa, 13 per cent of the forest population is estimated to subsist exclusively on MFP and for another 39 per cent it is an important source of secondary income (CSE 1985–6: 91). Roughly, some 30 million people in the country are estimated to depend on MFP for a livelihood (Kulkarni 1983). An indication of some of the diverse forest-based activities undertaken by tribal families for survival is provided by Table 5.5 which also highlights the criticality of intra-family co-operation towards this end.

Seasonality impinges on this overall dependence in two ways: first, the degree of dependence on communal resources gets intensified during slack seasons; second, the availability of products from village commons and forests is itself subject to seasonal variations (see Banerjee 1988; Jodha 1986; Dasgupta 1987; Briscoe 1979). To the extent that periods of slack in crop production do not entirely coincide with lean periods of CPR and forest output, this helps sustain the poor when there is a trough in agricultural employment. Among tribals in central India, during normal pre-harvest seasonal shortages, gathered food provides 12 per cent of energy intakes compared with 2 per cent in the post-harvest period (Pingle 1975). For tribals in Bihar, forests are noted to be the only means of survival in the lean seasons, when the undergrowth of trees is picked for edible herbs, mushrooms, tubers, and so on. Wild millets, edible leaves, and fruits are found to be crucial sources of food for the poorest in the lean periods in some north Indian villages (Dasgupta 1987). Irrigation tanks and river beds provide land for cultivation during the off-season. A recent study of six villages in semi-arid parts of South India (Ryan *et al.* 1984) also questions the universal validity of Chambers's (1981) argument that nutritional distress is the most severe in the rainy season by pointing out that in many areas this is the time when wild leafy vegetables are most readily available. Again, Jodha's (1986) estimation of employment provided by CPRs based on village-level surveys in 5 semi-arid districts of four States in 1982–3 indicates that for the poor (1) CPRs provided exclusive employment for an estimated 43–49 days per household or 18–31 days per adult worker during the year, that is marginally more than the days worked on their own farms, in addition to part-time employment when CPR-based activity was undertaken casually while doing other jobs; (2) in most districts CPRs were the only source of employment for 23–30 per cent of the total days for which the adults of poor households would otherwise have been involuntarily unemployed; (3) in some areas the total employment provided by CPRs was higher than that created by various anti-poverty government programmes.[27]

It is therefore during the periods when food or income are available through neither source, that poor households would be most vulnerable. Unfortunately, there is virtually no quantitative cross-matching by season of the employment and income generated via crop production with that generated via CPRs or forests, to identify such periods. A broad descriptive calendar of activities among the tribals of Orissa indicates that June to August is the leanest period when new crops are being sown, old stocks of grain have been depleted, and little food is available from the forest (see Table 5.6). Banerjee (1988) in the context of tribals in West Bengal similarly identifies July as the leanest month when there is a slack both in the crop calendar and in the availability of MFP, so that families have to resort to seasonal migration.

It is necessary to note, though, that the rights to CPRs are not unrestrictedly granted to all comers. Typically they are extended to members of the village community by birth or marriage (Dasgupta 1987) and have been described by some scholars as part of the 'moral' claim of village members upon the village community (Scott 1976). Rights to forest produce are today also severely restricted by forest laws and a good deal of gathering of MFP is done illegally and under constant threat of harassment from forest guards (see Fernandes and Menon 1988; CSE 1985–6; Agarwal 1986a).

Typically it is women and children who play a primary role in the collection of CPR and forest produce (see Dasgupta 1987; Agarwal 1986a; Brara 1987),

[27] Unfortunately Jodha does not provide an assessment of the relative productivity of or earnings from the different sources of employment. Also where a greater number of days spent in CPR collection reflects lower productivity (e.g. with deforestation women spend longer hours collecting the same quantum of firewood), the 'days of CPR employment' could be a misleading indicator in cross-time as well as cross-regional comparisons. However it is still useful as an indicator of some productive use of time as opposed to no employment at all.

Table 5.5. Division of family labour in a Garo village, Meghalaya

Activity	Males	Females	Children
Home-based	(1) Making of basketry material (2) Construction of house and bringing materials for the same (3) Repairing of the house (4) Fishing (5) Hunting (6) Propitiation for small ailments (7) Decanting rice beer for guests (8) Looking after domestic animals (9) Threshing paddy (10) Husking paddy and other grains	(1) Cooking (2) Bringing firewood (3) Fetching water (4) Preparing beer (5) Looking after small children (6) Accompanying husband when he goes to fish (7) Going to jungles in search of vegetables, mushrooms, crabs, snails, etc. (8) Digging up of wild roots and tubers in times of scarcity	(1) Looking after infants during absence of parents (2) Helping the mother to look after domestic animals (3) Helping the mother in fetching water (4) Helping the mother in washing cooking utensils
Shifting cultivation	(1) Clearing of jungles (2) Burning of plots	(1) Planting and sowing (2) Weeding	(1) Scaring away small animals and birds in day time

(3) Construction of the field house	(3) Transporting household articles to field houses and back to village	(2) Looking after small children when the parents are busy
(4) Making roads to the plots	(4) Harvesting	
(5) Transporting household articles to field houses and back to village	(5) Transportation of crops to the granary	
(6) Keeping watch over the field at night		
(7) Helping in harvesting		
(8) Transportation of crops from field to the granary		
Market-related		
(1) Working as wage labourer	(1) Selling of vegetables	(1) Working for daily wages
(2) Selling of cash crops	(2) Selling of firewood in the town	(2) Selling of vegetables etc.
(3) Selling of fuel wood	(3) Preparation of rice beer for selling	(3) Selling of fodder
(4) Selling of beef etc.	(4) Selling of milk, fowl, pigs, etc.	
	(5) Selling of rice beer/distilled liquor in the town	

Source: Majumdar (1978: 88–89).

Table 5.6. Seasonal activities in three tribal villages in Orissa

Month	Settled cultivation			Shifting cultivation			MFP collected		
	V1	V2	V3	V1	V2	V3	V1	V2	V3
January	Harvesting winter crops	Harvesting winter crops, sowing late varieties of millet and paddy	Harvesting winter crops	Nil	Harvesting late crops	Harvesting late crops	Siali leaves, datun[a]	Siali leaves, datun,[a] broomsticks	Not much collected
February	Nil	Sowing horsegram if rain; planting vegetables chilli, etc.	Nil	Nil	Nil	Harvesting late varieties and preparation for storage	Mahua, amla, behada, harada	Tamarind	Mahua
March	Nil	Some vegetable harvesting	Nil	Nil	Burning plot for bogodo	Clearing and burning plot	Mahua, mango, kendu fruit	Raw mango, jackfruit, processing of tamarind for storage (de-seeding and salting)	Mahua
April	Nil	Clearing of plot	Nil	Nil	Burning and clearing plot or digging	Digging	Kendu leaves and fruit, mango, mahua, char, jackfruit	Jackfruit, ripe mango	Siali fruit, kendu, tamarind

May	Preparation of field; manuring	Preparation of plot	Preparation of field; ploughing	Clearing and burning; softening mud	Sowing cereal	Sowing cereal	Kendu seeds and leaves, char	Mango, jackfruit, cashew	Mango, jackfruit, kusumo, tulo, mahua seeds
June	Ploughing and sowing	Sowing cereals; rice and mandia	Guarding of plot	Planting cereal in the latter half	Weeding	Weeding	Not much collected, kanda roots, shoots, and tubers	Mango, jackfruit	Mango processing (drying), jamun
July	Sowing, transplanting, ploughing again to soften mud; weeding	Sowing and transplanting vegetables; cultivation on dry land	Sowing	Sowing continued	Sowing pulses	Sowing pulses	Same as June	Not much	Not much, some bamboo shoots, etc.
August	Same as July	Transplanting, weeding, clearing	Weeding and clearing	Same as July	Weeding, clearing	Harvesting early varieties and vegetables	Same as June	Same as July	Same as July
September	Harvesting early varieties	Weeding, planting more cereals, harvesting mandia in the plains	Clearing bunds, sowing ragi	Harvesting early vegetables	Weeding, planting	Harvesting, guarding	Same as June	Sitaphal, Siali leaves[a]	Not much,

Month	Settled Cultivation			Shifting Cultivation			MFP collected		
	V1	V2	V3	V1	V2	V3	V1	V2	V3
October	Harvesting, bunding, planting	Late planting of pulses, first mandia harvesting	Watering guarding	Harvesting, making bundles	Late planting, mandia harvesting, vegetable growing: pumpkin, bottle-gourd, etc.	Nil	Sitaphal, bamboo, kendu	Sitaphal, Siali leaves[a]	Same as Sept.
November	Harvesting paddy, mandia	Harvesting ragi	Harvesting paddy	Harvesting paddy, mandia	Harvesting makka, ragi, chana, etc.	Nil	Same as Oct.	Siali leaves[a]	Not much only honey
December	Same as Nov.	Late planting, harvesting other crops	Harvesting ragi, mustard	Same as Nov.	Same as Nov.	Nil	Same as Oct.	Same as Nov.	Salap (for liquor)

[a] Siali leaves and datun are available throughout the year but are collected mainly in lean months like January when no other minor forest produce is available.

Note: V1 = Bhawanipatna; V2 = Kerandimals; V3 = Mohana. These are the villages studied.

Source: Fernandes and Menon (1987: 64).

except in some tribal and scheduled caste communities dependent solely or mainly on forests, where men may be found to contribute substantially as well (Fernandes and Menon 1987). Women are also noted to have a more detailed knowledge of cultivated and wild crop varieties than men, among some tribes;[28] and more generally it has been argued that poor peasant and tribal women as the main foragers and gatherers have a specially detailed reserve knowledge of edible forest produce that can help tide over prolonged shortages.[29] Of particular note too are the many examples of divergence between male and female priorities in CPR and forest development—with men typically favouring commercial varieties and women opting for trees and plants that fulfil the subsistence needs of food, fuel, and fodder.[30] Essentially, CPRs and forests provide women, children, and even the aged with an independent source of subsistence, unmediated by dependency relationships on young male adults. Indeed the significance of CPRs and forests as food security systems for the poor needs particular underlining.

In this context, the rapid decline in and degradation of forest and CPR area would be a cause of particular concern. Area under forests, for instance, declined from 55.5 million hectares in 1972–5 to 46.4 million in 1981–2—an annual fall of 1.3 million hectares.[31] Again Jodha's (1986) analysis for twenty-one semi-arid districts in seven states reveals that over the past three decades the area under CPRs has declined from 15–42 per cent (varying by region) in 1950–2 to 9–28 per cent in 1982–4; in other words, a decline ranging from 26 per cent to as much as 58 per cent in some regions (Table 5.7). In addition, the productivity of CPRs has been falling rapidly (Jodha 1985a), manifesting itself in shortening periods of assured supplies of fuel, food, fodder, and timber, a deterioration in the botanical composition of vegetation, the silting of water sources, and so on.

The decline in CPRs is attributed by Jodha partly to population growth and to the physical submersion of land under large irrigation projects, but mainly to land privatization, as a result of three causes: illegal encroachments by larger farmers made legal over time; government distribution of CPRs to individuals under various schemes officially intended to benefit the poor, such as the land reform programme implemented in the 1950s and the twenty-point programme in the 1970s; and the auctioning of parts of CPRs by the government to private contractors for commercial exploitation. In practice, much of this privatization favoured the larger farmers: in six of the nineteen districts surveyed, the poor received between 0.8 and 1.6 hectares per household, and the larger farmers 1.5 to 4.9 hectares per household (Table 5.8). In the Jodhpur district of

[28] See e.g. Burling (1963) on the Garos of the north-east.
[29] See e.g. Boulding (1976); also Shiva (1988).
[30] See Brara's (1987) village study in Rajasthan, and Agarwal (1986a) for several examples from the Chipko movement for forest protection and regeneration in the hills of Uttar Pradesh.
[31] Figures provided by the National Remote Sensing Agency, Government of India.

Table 5.7. Extent and decline of CPR land in study villages of selected districts

State and District	Number of villages	Area of CRP land (ha)	CPRs as % of total village area		% decline in CPR area since 1950–2
			1982–4	1950–2	
Andhra Pradesh					
Anantapur	2	221	15	24	36
Mahbubnagar	5	408	9	16	43
Medak	3	198	11	20	45
Gujarat					
Banaskantha	5	167	9	19	49
Mehsana	5	224	11	17	37
Sabarkantha	5	198	12	22	46
Karnataka					
Bidar	3	297	12	20	41
Dharwad	3	242	10	18	44
Gulbarga	3	291	9	15	43
Mysore	3	335	18	27	32
Madhya Pradesh					
Mandsaur	4	327	22	34	34
Raisen	6	770	23	42	47
Vidisha	4	338	28	38	32
Maharashtra					
Akola	5	192	11	19	42
Aurangabad	4	304	15	21	30
Sholapur	4	422	19	25	26
Rajasthan					
Jalore	5	639	18	29	37
Jodhpur	3	591	16	38	58
Nagaur	3	619	15	41	63
Tamil Nadu					
Coimbatore	4	187	9	17	47
Dharmapuri	3	225	12	26	52

Note: Based on village-level records and field work during 1982–5.
Source: Jodha (1986).

Rajasthan, 62 per cent of the privatized commons went to farmers already owning 10–15 hectares or more, and included 90 per cent of the good-quality land—while the landless got only 13 per cent, much of it of poor quality (Jodha 1983). Hence the collective loss of the poor was not made up by the private gain of a few of them.

2.3. *Drawing upon Social Relationships and Informal Credit Systems*

2.3.1. *Patronage*   Patron–client relationships as forms of traditional social-security systems for poor rural households have been widely commented on.[32] For instance, the *jajmani* system in northern India, and variations therein all over the subcontinent, of labour and service relations between upper-caste landlord-patrons and their clients—including share-croppers, agricultural labourers, household servants, and the service castes (priests, artisans, barbers, scavengers, and so on)—traditionally involved a set of reciprocal (though asymmetrical)[33] obligations between patrons and clients. On the side of the clients was the obligation to provide labour, rent, or services (as the case may be). On the side of the patron was the obligation to provide a fixed payment in grain, annually or semi-annually (although the amounts differed across regions),[34] and to honour a variety of rights (which varied by the type of client and the region). These rights might include gifts of food on ceremonial and festive occasions, a site for a house, the collection of weeds and leaves from standing crops, asking for old clothing from time to time, gleaning the fields for grains after a harvest, free dung, and in general a right to assistance such as interest-free loans during periods of dire need. These obligations between patrons and clients, often defined in moral and ritual terms, assured (among other things) a stable labour supply for the dominant cultivator castes, by tying the client to the patron and thus limiting his mobility, and provided the client some guarantee of a minimum subsistence. The privileges of collection and so on could be seen as providing clients with access to the private property resources of patrons supplementing their access to CPRs, for fulfilling seasonal needs.

Agriculture-related patron–client relationships were essentially those between landowners and men who worked as permanent farm servants or share-croppers (although their wives and children could also be called in to provide domestic help). While Wiser's (1936) contention that the *jajmani* relationships were essentially harmonious and symmetrical is disputable, since various forms of exploitation and coercion of the clients were in fact to be found in the system,[35] there is general agreement that the system did provide some security

---

[32] See Wiser (1936); Lewis (1958); Epstein (1967); Vatuk (1981); Commander (1983); Breman (1985); Dasgupta (1987); Torry (1987). See also Chap. 4 above.

[33] With the possible exception of priests who constituted a somewhat distinct category. Commander (1983: 295), for instance, observes: 'The purohit is thus donated grain in an act of symbolic obeisance, while, on the contrary, the bulk of kamins are given grain in return for labour . . .'

[34] Vatuk's (1981) survey of literature on the *jajmani* system indicates that such fixed payments did not bear a direct relationship to the actual amount of work done per year, which was variable. The nature of tasks to be completed were, however, clearly specified. Also see Commander (1983) on interregional differences in payments.

[35] Wiser (1936), who was the first to conceptualize and describe the *jajmani* relationship as an interrelated system, observes: 'Each serves the others. Each in turn is master. Each in turn is servant' (p. xxiii). However others have questioned this apparent symmetry on the basis both of

Table 5.8. Distribution of privatized CPRs in study villages of selected districts[a]

State, district, (Number of villages)	Total land given (ha)	Total households (No.)	% of land to		% of recipients among		Hectares per per household		Hectares per household			
			Poor	Others	Poor	Others	Poor	Others	Poor		Others	
									Before[b]	After[b]	Before[b]	After
Andhra Pradesh												
Mahbubnagar (3)	418	343	50	50	76	24	0.8	2.6	0.3	0.9	3.0	5.1
Medak (3)	75	58	51	49	59	41	1.1	1.5	1.0	2.2	3.1	4.6
Gujarat												
Banaskantha (3)	75	29	18	82	38	62	1.3	3.4	0.8	2.0	5.4	8.8
Mahsana (2)	85	63	20	80	36	64	0.7	1.7	1.0	1.7	8.0	9.8
Sabarkantha (3)	127	74	23	77	55	45	0.9	2.8	0.5	1.1	7.0	9.8
Karnataka												
Bidar (3)	89	55	39	61	64	36	1.0	2.8	1.0	2.0	6.4	9.2
Gulbarga (3)	112	50	43	57	60	40	1.6	3.2	0.8	2.4	4.5	7.7
Mysore (3)	161	98	44	56	67	33	1.2	2.9	0.9	1.9	4.1	11.6

Madhya Pradesh												
Mandsaur (2)	120	55	45	55	75	25	1.3	4.7	1.2	2.5	7.7	12.4
Raisen (4)	115	72	42	58	68	32	1.0	2.9	1.3	2.2	6.2	9.0
Vidisha (4)	123	77	38	62	48	52	1.3	1.9	1.3	2.5	4.9	6.8
Maharashtra												
Akola (3)	101	100	39	61	58	42	0.7	1.5	1.0	1.6	3.1	4.6
Aurangabad (2)	83	55	30	70	42	58	1.1	1.8	1.1	2.2	6.4	8.3
Sholapur (3)	132	72	42	58	53	47	1.5	2.3	0.7	2.2	3.4	5.6
Rajasthan												
Jalore (2)	83	27	14	86	37	63	1.4	4.9	0.3	1.7	7.2	12.5
Jodhpur (2)	405	318	24	76	35	65	0.9	1.5	0.4	1.3	2.3	3.8
Nagaur (3)	147	81	21	79	41	59	1.2	3.1	1.3	2.5	2.4	5.2
Tamil Nadu												
Coimbatore (4)	206	145	50	50	75	25	1.1	2.9	0.8	2.5	3.8	5.8
Dharmapuri (3)	241	127	49	51	55	45	0.9	2.1	1.0	1.9	4.6	7.5

[a] Based on field work during 1982–5.   [b] Before and after receiving CPR land.

Source: Jodha (1986).

Table 5.9. Decline in patron-client relationships in Rajasthan

Indicators	% households during	
	1963–6	1982–4
Households with one or more members working as attached/semi-attached labour	37	7
Households residing on patron's land/yard	31	0
Households resorting to off-season borrowing of food-grain from patrons	77	26
Households taking seed loans from patrons	34	9
Households marketing farm produce only through patrons	86	23
Households taking loans from others besides patrons	13	47

Note: Data relates to 35 households whose per capita annual income (at 1964–6 prices) declined during 1982–4 compared to 1964–6.
Source: Jodha (1985*b*: 12).

against seasonal troughs and the guarantee of a bare subsistence minimum to poor agricultural households during 'normal' years, even though it is clear that it did not sustain under acute crisis and generalized shortages as during a drought or famine (of which more later).[36]

However, much of the literature also indicates an erosion of these relationships over time, although not their disappearance, attributable to several factors impinging on both demand and supply. On the demand side there has been an increase in the possibility of hiring in cheaper labour seasonally from outside without involving patron obligations (Breman 1985); the competition from factory products which has affected the demand for items made locally by the service castes; the possibilities of making a profit by selling the goods earlier distributed free to clients with improved transportation and storage facilities, and so on (Dasgupta 1987).[37] On the supply side, clients are noted to

Wiser's own ethnography and of other empirical evidence (see esp. the discussion in Commander 1983). Breman (1985), for instance, notes that the permanent farm servants (*halis*) in south Gujarat got from the master 'everything necessary for a bare living' but at the same time 'they were at their master's beck and call not only during the day but in the evening as house servants and if necessary at night as well'.

[36] Epstein's (1967) contention that the system worked well even during years of bad harvests in that the landlords, in order to keep lower castes alive, reduced their own consumption and shared available grain with clients, so that consumption between all village households tended towards equality in such situations, has, however, been disputed on both methodological and empirical grounds (see esp. Chap. 4 above; also Torry 1987).

[37] In the two north Indian villages studied by Dasgupta, it is now found profitable to sell milk and transport it out, substantially reducing the supply of buttermilk earlier transported free to needy villagers. Also dung is now increasingly valuable to owners as manure and fuel, and the

opt out of such a relationship where more secure or profitable alternatives (especially urban jobs) can be obtained (Chen 1988). Table 5.9 which traces patron–client support available to thirty-five families in Rajasthan in 1963–4 and again in 1982–4, reveals a decline in all forms of support: for instance, the percentage of households resorting to off-season borrowing of foodgrains from patrons declined from 77 to 26 over the two decades. Among the halis of South Gujarat, Breman (1985) argues that this decline is associated with a slide from poverty to pauperization.

2.3.2. *Kinship and Friendship*   Social relationships with kin, and with villagers outside the kin network, can serve as a means of support in various ways (although the information available on this is essentially descriptive). For instance, women draw upon other women for borrowing small amounts of food stuffs, fuel, fodder, and so on (Maclachlan 1983; Jetly 1987; Chen 1988); similarly, 'helper' relationships among men, with friends, neighbours, and local kin, can provide for reciprocal labour, a sharing of irrigation water, and the loaning and renting of agricultural implements, draft animals, and machinery, thus enabling the enhancement of small farm productivity (as noted by Montgomery 1977 in Tamil Nadu). Also, group help for peak operations and various labour exchange arrangements have been characteristic of tribal communities (Kar 1982; Majumdar 1978). Traditional support systems exist too along caste lines, and often it is easier for the poor to draw upon help from the richer peasants of their own caste than from outside it (Caldwell *et al.* 1986).

Women typically play a significant role in the cultivation of social relationships—especially through marriage alliances that they are frequently instrumental in arranging, and through complex reciprocal gift-giving systems (Maclachlan 1983; Vatuk 1981; Sharma 1980). At the same time, they are often less able to seek the help of their natal kin than men. Patrilocality, which greatly facilitates male ability to call upon the support of consanguinous kin, can at the same time restrict women's ability to do so—the degree of such restriction depending on the physical and social distance between the natal and marital homes.[38] Especially in north-west India, marriages into villages at substantial distances from the woman's natal village and home, taboos against marrying close kin, limited social contact between parental and marital

village council has ruled that dung belongs solely to the cattle owners and cannot be collected free. Also see Commander (1983) for additional evidence on this decline.

[38] Post-marital residence is found to be patrilocal among virtually all caste and class groups in India, the exceptions being a few matrilineal tribes of the north-east and some communities (such as the Nayars) in the south-west, which traditionally practised matrilocality, although even these have been shifting to patrilocality over the past few decades (Agarwal 1988). Of course patrilocality need not in itself necessitate women's leaving their parental village, if village endogamy is allowed and practised, as it is in many parts of India—here the constraints on women seeking natal kin support would be less severe, as discussed further on.

families, discouragement of extended stays by married daughters in their natal home, and the considerable formality that marks their relationship with their natal kin after marriage, may all prevent women from seeking their support in times of crisis.[39] These factors impinge with less severity where village endogamy and cross-cousin marriages are allowed, and social contact between the two sets of in-laws is more frequently possible, as, for instance, in the south and north-east of India, or in Muslim communities there and elsewhere.[40] Here instances of women seeking frequent help from parents when in need are not uncommon (see Caldwell *et al.* 1986 for Karnataka, and Nath 1979 for Bangladesh, where women are observed to increase the frequency of their visits to their parental homes during the 'hungry season').

Existing, rather fragmentary evidence (from India and neighbouring countries) suggests, however, that among the poor, even such social-support systems as existed are getting increasingly eroded. In one Bangladesh village study only 54 per cent of all widows were found to have the security of being integrated members of their sons' households (Cain *et al.* 1979). Jansen (1986) likewise found several cases in the Bangladesh village he surveyed of old parents, widowers, and widows complaining that they had been abandoned by sons. In the Indian context, the erosion of family support, and support from kin and friends, has been documented especially in the context of tribal communities, traditionally characterized by team work in agriculture and mutual labour-exchange and community support arrangements. With growing land privatization, monetization of production, and class differentiation, there has been a general decline in such arrangements. Fernandes and Menon (1987: 115) give a graphic description of this in relation to the tribals in Orissa:

the earlier sense of sharing has disappeared. This has affected women's condition more than of men, since they are responsible for the day to day running of the household. . . . Earlier they could rely on their neighbours in times of need. Today this has been replaced with a sense of alienation and helplessness . . . The trend is to leave each family to its own fate.

They note too that community support is no longer forthcoming for women if they want to separate from their husbands due to ill-treatment, or for widows neglected or exploited by relatives, where such support was customary, earlier. The overall neglect of widows by kin is also noted by Drèze (1988a). However,

---

[39] During fieldwork in Kithoor village (Rajasthan) I found that most of the twenty-odd agricultural labour women with whom I raised this issue said that they preferred to borrow from the money-lender even at usurious rates or from other villagers, rather than from their natal kin for fear of 'spoiling the relationship' if they defaulted. Jetly (1987) found this as well in her study of the impact of male migration on rural females in central and eastern Uttar Pradesh. She notes that women avoided borrowing from relatives 'since this brings loss of prestige', and a neighbour or friends were more commonly approached for small sums.

[40] For a review and discussion of these cross-regional variations in marriage patterns based on village studies see Agarwal (1988).

much more systematic research is needed on the decline of family support systems, especially with marital breakdown and old age.

2.3.3. *Other Informal Credit Systems* While there is considerable literature on interlinked credit-labour systems, much of it does not distinguish between traditional patronage (which also provided informal credit) and emerging new forms of dependency linkages associated with the development of capitalist farming in agriculture (Bhalla 1977; Breman 1985). Yet such a distinction appears warranted in that the new relations are found to contain most of the exploitative features of the old without the guaranteed subsistence that patronage was said to have provided (Breman 1985; Banerjee 1988). What is clear is that consumption credit from landlords and traders, whether extended within interlinked credit-labour systems (Bardhan and Rudra 1981),[41] or independent of such linkages (Bliss and Stern 1982), continue to be critical in tiding over seasonality, although such borrowings at usurious rates of interest may lead to long-term bondage (Mundle 1979). Outside the context of tied relationships, however, such loans may not be forthcoming readily for poor households. Binswanger and Rosenzweig (1986) note on the basis of ICRISAT (International Crop Research Institute for the Semi-Arid Tropics) data for South India that the probability of getting credit from money-lenders depends critically on wealth endowments. Landless households often get short shrift from money-lenders, and small farmers are granted crop loans usually in kind, to be repaid also usually in kind, with a 25 to 50 per cent interest over the crop cycle, that is, at annual interest rates of 75 to 100 per cent.

2.4. *Drawing upon Household Stores and Adjusting Current Consumption*

Drawing upon stored items—grain, animal products, dung cakes, dried berries, grasses, and so on—many of them built up by women and children, is another way of coping with seasonal fluctuations.[42] Although there appears to be little quantitative evidence for India to indicate the extent of this depletion by households (most surveys on this count are confined to the effects of drought and famine), data from Bangladesh (Table 5.10) clearly show the seasonal depletion in average cereal stock associated with troughs in agricultural wage employment and peaks in grain prices, especially during the lean months from August to October.

However, stock depletion and other measures adopted do not prove adequate for all times of the year, and the hungry season—true to its description—

---

[41] Such linkages could also restrict the labourer's freedom to migrate seasonally.

[42] For instance, women in poor rural households in West Bengal and Bangladesh are known to put aside a handful of rice (*mustischaal*) when cooking the day's main meal. This then becomes a store for use in lean seasons (see e.g. Siddiqui 1984).

Table 5.10. Seasonal variations in prices, wages, and cereal stocks in Matlab Thana, Bangladesh

Month	Wholesale price of medium rice (taka/mound) 1976–7	Agricultural labour wage (taka/day) 1977–8	Average household cereal stocks (mounds) 1976–7
March	116	10.0	2.1
April	111	8.0	2.9
May	122	7.5	5.1
June	118	7.5	3.1
July	123	6.0	2.8
August	123	–	2.1
September	123	–	1.0
October	125	6.0	0.7
November	105	7.5	3.2
December	111	7.5	5.3
January	113	7.0	2.8
February	118	n.i.	1.1

Notes: Data relate to 205 households in Matlab Thana. The dash indicates extremely limited agricultural work opportunities. n.i. = no information given in the original table

Source: Chaudhury *et al.* (1981: 55)

typically calls for consumption adjustments by the poor in one or more of the following ways:

1. change in the content of the diet such as shifting to coarse grains, drawing on wild vegetables, berries, and so on from the village commons and forests, with some tribal groups in West Bengal reportedly even consuming bats during the lean season (Banerjee 1988);

2. reduction of total intake: missing meals, reducing the number of meals cooked per day, stretching available food supplies by, say, eating rice gruel instead of boiled rice every day, and so on (Mitra 1988);

3. adjusting intra-household distribution of available food. A part of this adjustment reflects perceptions about needs, especially arising out of differential activity levels, but a part also appears to reflect a gender bias. Fernandes and Menon (1987) note, for instance, that among the tribals of Orissa, during months of low food availability, children get first preference, then men, and finally women. During the month when ploughing has to be done food is allocated in favour of men, and women either borrow from neighbours or go hungry. There is no mention, however, of any reverse adjustments by the men when women have a heavy load of work, as during the rice transplanting season. Also, working adults are favoured over non-working elders (typically old women). Fernandes and Menon emphasize that observed gender inequalities

are recent: 'In the traditional tribal society they used to eat together. Today the woman has to starve quite often. Because of food shortages, she gives all that is available to the man and keeps nothing for herself.' Caldwell *et al.* (1986) similarly find that women in rural Karnataka deny themselves food during seasonal shortages.

In general, the extent and causes of gender biases in food allocation within the household have been the subject of considerable discussion in recent literature, and are still being debated.[43] However, there is a broad agreement that while anti-female biases may not exist as a universal feature across India, there is undeniable discrimination in food allocation against females in certain regions, such as the north-west of India, and in certain social groupings, especially the poor (including the poor in parts of South India).[44] Also Sen's (1981) and Kynch and Maguire's (1988) work suggests that gender differentials among children tend to increase during crisis. And Behrman (1986), on the basis of a modelling exercise using data on child nutrition for South India, concludes that 'parents display male preference, at least during the lean season, particularly in lower caste households' and that 'the nutritionally most vulnerable—especially females—may be at considerable risk when food is scarcest'.

Further, in so far as there is a closer positive link between children's nutritional status and the mother's wage employment than the father's, among agricultural labour households (as found, for instance, in Kerala by Kumar 1978 and Gulati 1978), seasonal slacks in female employment may deprive the children as well. Kumar observes (1978: 43, 46) that 'when mothers are not in the labour force, an increase in (the household's) wage income shows absolutely no incremental effect on child nutrition', but 'for those mothers who are in the labour force, it is their own wages that primarily account for the positive wage income effect in child nutrition'.[45] And while the greater length of the mother's employment (and therefore presumably less time devoted to child care), especially during peak periods, was negatively related to child nutrition, this did not outweigh the positive income effect of the mother's earnings.[46]

[43] See e.g. Sen (1981); Sen and Sengupta (1983); Harriss (1986); Lipton (1983*b*); Behrman (1986); Agarwal (1986*a*, 1989); Bardhan (1983); Rosenzweig and Schultz (1982); Drèze and Sen 1989.   [44] See especially Harriss's (1986) review of ICRISAT data.

[45] The likely reason for this (as already noted in n. 24 above) is that in such households women's earnings in much greater proportion than men's tend to go towards fulfilling basic needs. Also, Kumar notes: 'since women do the shopping for food and preparation of family meals, it is possible that their participation in the generation of income gives them better control over its allocation and they might more equitably distribute assets among family members'.

[46] Leslie (1988) arrives at broadly similar conclusions on the basis of a fairly comprehensive review of existing studies for Third World countries on the relationship between women's work, child nutrition, and infant feeding practices. While noting the methodological problems that confound clear-cut answers she observes that: (1) there is surprisingly little evidence of a negative effect of women's work on either breast-feeding or child nutritional status; (2) few studies measured women's income but most of those that did found a more positive effect of the mother's income than household income on child nutritional status.

The net effect of maternal wage incomes was thus positive during both peak and slack seasons, although more so in the latter. Gulati (1978) again found that in agricultural labour households, daughters, in particular, were left much worse off than sons on the mother's non-working days, although she does not give details of seasonal fluctuations and whether this would be so at all times of the year.

All this suggests that periods or days of lowest food consumption during the year need not coincide for all household members, but may vary by age and gender, and be conditional upon the combined effects of several factors, including the woman's employment and earnings, actual activity levels, as well as perceptions about needs. For the household on an average too, not all slack periods, and not all parts of given slack periods, need be periods of hunger. Usually there is a lagged effect as earnings in periods of peak labour demand help tide over the initial part of the following slack. The worst time is usually noted to be the start of a busy season after an extended slack when stored items have been depleted and the agricultural peak calls for additional energy inputs.[47]

Where variations in energy requirements do not match with food availability and intake levels, these may be reflected in seasonal changes in bodyweights as found in several African studies,[48] as well as in Asia: a Bangladesh study of mothers noted that fluctuations were highest for the landless among whom stocks were entirely depleted during the critical lean month of October, while landowning families had sufficient stocks to maintain adequate family consumption throughout the year (Chaudhury et al. 1981). However the extent of these fluctuations could vary by region, age, and gender. A six-village ICRISAT study for Andhra Pradesh and Maharashtra found no significant differences in the weights of adults by seasons (Ryan et al. 1984) but a village study in Uttar Pradesh did find such changes, the seasonal loss of weight among women being greater than among men (Kynch and Maguire 1988).

Where seasonal changes in intake are not observed to affect bodyweight it could mean either that food intakes are being adjusted to activity levels, and/ or, as is being argued by some, that individuals are able to 'adapt' over certain ranges of reduced intakes, by increasing the efficiency of energy utilization, without any change in bodyweight. On the issue of efficiency—which has provoked considerable discussion—Osmani (1987), in an excellent unravelling of the various threads in the debate and a careful examination of the available evidence, notes that: 'There is . . . some evidence to show that phenotypic adaptation of a kind may take place in the efficiency of energy utilisation, but it

[47] Hossain (1987: 90) from his six-village survey in Bangladesh notes: 'the lowest point in per capita foodgrain consumption for households . . . is neither the summer trough nor the fall or spring slack time, but rather the winter busy season. Reserves are usually not sufficient to permit inhabitants to break out of the long hungry slump, beginning during the rainy season and continuing unabated into winter.' (Also refer to Table 5.11.)

[48] Quoted in Longhurst and Payne (1981).

seems almost always to be accompanied by alteration of bodyweight', and further that 'what is relevant is "pure" adaptation. *But the existing evidence does not indicate that such adaptation is possible*' (1987: 41; emphasis mine).

It has of course also been suggested that a seasonal decline in bodyweight need not impair functioning efficiency, since the body evolves effective storage mechanisms for various essential nutrients that are able to smooth out seasonal peaks and troughs in supply (Longhurst and Payne 1981). But this would still leave at least certain sections of the population at risk: the very poor, and among them typically pregnant and lactating women and pre-school age children, are found to be especially vulnerable to bodyweight changes and seasonal malnutrition.[49] Childbirth, breast-feeding and weaning practices, and morbidity, also show a seasonal pattern, especially among agricultural workers, the burden of which falls mainly on women and children.[50]

Finally, social consumption such as celebrations of marriages and festivals reflect seasonal adaptations as well, often clustering around post-harvest periods.

2.5. *Drawing upon Assets*

As noted earlier, to judge the effectiveness of a household's coping mechanisms we would need to know whether or not at the end of the year the household has suffered a reduction in the productive capacity of its family members or in its assets, especially (but not only) productive assets such as land and draught animals. On nutrition, as noted, available evidence is limited and provides no clear direction. Unfortunately, there also appears to be little quantitative information on seasonal changes in a household's asset position in the Indian context. However, the detailed Bangladesh study by Hossain (1987) is indicative. It examines, among other things, seasonality in the distribution of employment, earnings, expenditure, borrowings, and the sale of assets in net terms, and observes noteworthy seasonal variations (see Table 5.11). Consumption expenditure exceeds earnings in virtually every season, though the deficits are especially high in the July–August slack. Deficits are made up by net borrowings, mostly from relatives (30 per cent), merchants (21 per cent), and moneylenders (11 per cent); the sale of assets (though it is not indicated what type of assets are sold, to which family members the sold assets belong, and whether any are mortgaged); and the transfer of receipts of various kinds (from friends, relatives, neighbours, political leaders, and so on).

---

[49] See e.g. Chambers *et al.* (1981*b*); Rajgopalan *et al.* (1981); Ryan *et al.* (1984); Brown *et al.* (1982).

[50] For instance the peaking of births before the main transplanting season noted in Tamil Nadu negatively affected breastfed infants (Rajgopalan *et al.* 1981). Of course in so far as smaller sized persons have lower BMR needs, women on average being of smaller build than men may *ceteris paribus* need less food to survive in a situation of nutritional constraint (Osmani 1987). But clearly much depends on the extent of nutritional reduction.

Table 5.11. Seasonal distribution of employment, earnings, and expenditure in six villages, Bangladesh

Season (weeks)	Corresponding date	Income-earning work (Takas)	Earnings (Takas)	Transfer receipts (Takas)	Net assets sale (Takas)	Net borrowing (Takas)	Value food consumed (Takas)	Food-grain consumption (Seers[a])	Total consumption expenditure (Takas)
Slack (1–5)	1 July–4 Aug. 1984	58.15	133.70	15.07	2.97	32.52	98.51	15.09	176.86
Busy (6–10)	5 Aug.–8 Sept. 1984	65.44	179.72	25.89	16.49	30.06	106.50	15.69	193.91
Slack (11–20)	9 Sept.–17 Nov. 1984	55.92	155.85	22.09	3.05	35.93	104.04	14.50	177.74
Busy (21–31)	18 Nov. 1985–2 Feb. 1985	64.75	160.18	21.63	-5.24	29.45	103.01	14.49	175.93
Slack (32–40)	3 Feb.–6 Apr. 1985	64.60	168.09	16.37	-5.49	17.49	99.76	14.77	170.44
Busy (41–50)	7 Apr.–15 June 1985	68.12	239.22	16.89	0.19	-1.56	100.62	16.01	184.96
Slack (51–52)	16 June–29 June 1985	57.51	192.48	24.76	-1.37	12.04	102.51	17.60	220.16
Average for year (1–52)	1 July 1984–29 June 1985	62.83	176.36	19.80	0.41	22.40	102.08	15.13	180.59

[a] 1 seer = 900 grams.

Source: Hossain (1987: 148).

The overall deficits suggest the operation of what Chambers (1981a) has termed 'poverty ratchets' where seasonal troughs may leave poor households worse off each year in relation to the previous year, to the extent that they are unable to replenish the assets or repay the loans incurred by year's end, as opposed to what he terms the operation of 'screws' which create pressures in certain seasons but from which the household can recover in other seasons.

In broad overview therefore, our examination of the mechanisms adopted by the poor agricultural family for coping with seasonality indicates the following:

1. The inputs of all family members are critical in tiding over the troughs, although the burden of coping in terms of work and consumption adjustments appears to fall disproportionately on women (see summary below):[51]

Coping mechanism	Relative gender contributions (W=women M=men)
Seasonal migration	W < M
Keeping livestock, and other forms of income diversification	W > M
Drawing on communal resources	W > M
Drawing on social relationships:	
patronage	W < M
husband's kin	W < M
wife's kin	W > M
neighbours/friends	W = M
Adjusting work loads	W > M
Drawing on household stores	W > M
Consumption adjustments	W > M
Drawing on assets	Unclear

2. CPRs, income diversification strategies, and seasonal migration possibilities are significant for cushioning seasonal distress, and need strengthening. In contrast, traditional patron and kin support and informal credit systems provide limited help, are not always dependable, and (especially the former two) are eroding over time.

3. The effect of seasonability on poor households is likely to vary between households—especially cross-regionally—causing some to suffer temporary hardships and others to face a downward slide with each sharp trough. The latter households are more likely to be those with least assets, belonging to low

---

[51] This should be taken only as a very rough assessment.

castes/tribes, and located in semi-arid regions. However, much more systematic research is needed on this in the Indian context (and in fact the overall South Asian context) by region, community (tribal/non-tribal, scheduled caste and other, and so on), gender and age, both on coping mechanisms and on the effectiveness of these mechanisms, before more generalizations are possible.[52]

3. COPING WITH CALAMITY: DROUGHT AND FAMINE

The literature on drought and famine (as discussed in detail below) indicates that disasters and severe food crisis situations bring few radical departures in coping mechanisms from those noted under seasonality, but they accentuate the degree of dependence on the same. In so doing they also bring out the critical limitations of these arrangements in providing subsistence security and crisis relief under calamity. Mechanisms of coping may then shift to measures of desperation as the family itself begins to disintegrate, vagrancy and destitution grow, and conflicts over food may even take the form of looting and violence. Indeed seasonality, drought, and famine may be seen as three points in a continuum, representing increasingly severe threats to the food security of the family. This section considers strategies and experiences of coping during drought and famine.

3.1. *Communal Resources: Intensified Use and Conflicts*

Dependence on communal resources which are already strained in their ability to cushion seasonal fluctuations increases significantly during severe food shortage situations. All studies of drought and famine without exception note shifts to 'famine' foods not consumed normally and many of which could be toxic.[53] The Indian Famine Commission of 1880 lists a vast number of berries, grasses, and roots consumed in such contexts, identifying those that are toxic. In addition, dependence on CPRs for fuel, fodder, and water, increases. In Reddy's (1988) Andhra Pradesh village study, in the pre-drought years an estimated 25–30 per cent of the incomes of landless households and 15–20 per cent of the income of the whole village came from CPRs; during the 1983–7

---

[52] There appears to have been much more research on these aspects in the African context. See, for instance, various articles in IDS Bulletin (1986) and Food and Nutrition (1985).

[53] During the Bihar drought of 1966–7, children were found eating the skin of toddy palms, jungle berries, edible roots, mushrooms, and even these were not available in plenty (Gangrade and Dhadda 1973). In Andhra Pradesh during the drought years of 1983–7, women collected a cactus creeper to be mixed with lentils, wild fruit, vegetables, leaves, and so on (Reddy 1988); rats, and grains stored by rats, were eaten during the Karnataka drought of 1965 (Maclachlan 1983); ground nettles are reported to have been consumed in the 1987–8 drought in Rajasthan; snails plus a variety of food otherwise considered inedible during the 1943 Bengal famine (Greenough 1982); and wild arum, plantain saplings, leaves, and rice husk during the Bangladesh famine of 1974 (Currey 1978; Rahaman 1981).

drought period, 33–45 per cent of the income of the landless (for six families the percentage was 60) and 30–35 per cent of the village income came from CPRs.

At the same time, both the availability of CPR products and access to them for the poor declines, and conflicts over access intensify. Reddy (1988) notes that during the drought period, farmers blocked off rivulets flowing through their land to get a larger share of the water, and also to create pools for raising the water table of their private irrigation wells; people were denied access to neem trees located on private land to which earlier there was open access; and the poor were no longer allowed to collect tree leaves essential for roofing. In Gujarat during the 1987–8 drought, some of the fights among graziers over access to village grass patches ended in physical violence (Chen 1987). In this context, the *panchayat* (village council) is usually found to favour the better-off.[54]

3.2. *Patrons, Kin, Friends, and Informal Credit Systems: Decreasing Reliability*

Patron–client relationships, already weak, are found virtually to snap during periods of severe food stress, especially during a generalized food shortage, say caused by a drought. This decline in patronage can take several forms:

(1) reduction of payments for traditional services (usually enforced through the panchayat), or a failure to meet obligations altogether, in some cases leading to a break in the relationship (Lewis 1958; Reddy 1988; Jodha 1978);

(2) denial of access to free gifts (Reddy 1988);

(3) denial of loans—the very poor being considered bad risks (Caldwell *et al.* 1986; Reddy 1988; Rao 1974; Borkar and Nadkarni 1975; Singh 1975).

Greenough (1982) identifies a hierarchy of patron–client relationships—noting that some ties snap more easily and earlier than others. For instance, during the Bengal famine of 1943, the more 'fixed' clients—attached to the family for generations, providing caste-linked ritual and other services—held on the longest; and those essentially market-linked, such as between shopkeepers and favoured customers, were the first to snap; semi-market relationships as with share-croppers came in-between.

However, the failure of patrons to meet their obligations to clients is attributed by many authors to their inability to do so in a period of overall

---

[54] During the Andhra Pradesh drought, claims of the landless to dead tamarind trees from the community orchard were rejected by the *panchayat* secretary who chose to sell them to his followers at a nominal price (Reddy 1988). Again, denial of rights to collect free dung and the imposition of fines on those who persist is enforced by the *panchayat* on behalf of cattle owners in villages in the north (Lewis 1958; Dasgupta 1987).

shortages. Reddy (1988) notes that in 1984, the second year of the drought in his Andhra village, most of the landowning families 'lost their capacity to meet the obligations of their clients in matters of annual payments in relation to services'. Epstein (1967: 24) argues that the *jajmani* system only broke down 'during extended periods of crisis . . . in extremely bad harvests, when the total produce was not sufficiently large to provide subsistence to all members of the society'. Greenough (1982) observes likewise that: 'In my view, the really difficult period of famine begins when the rural patrons exhaust their resources and are no longer able to succour their dependents.' The assumption here is that the failure of patrons to keep obligations is dictated by adverse circumstances shared by all sections of the population, including the better-off, even if not in equal degree, and, by inference, once these circumstances improve the relationships will be restored. However, the collapse of patronage in calamities, even in the absence of a serious generalized food shortage, as noted in the Bengal famine of 1943 when there was in fact large-scale speculative holding back of food-grains by surplus cultivators and organized traders (Sen 1981), reflects more than an 'inability' on the part of patrons to fulfil their obligations —it indicates, as noted in Section 2, also a long-term irreversible erosion in these relationships.

At the same time, Prindle's (1979) description of a village community's response in Nepal during the drought of 1971 indicates that where the local population can exert group pressure, even a generalized shortage can be more equitably shared. He describes how the combined pressure of the less well-off brahmins and bhujels (the latter being hereditary ploughmen for the richer brahmins) succeeded in (1) preventing surplus farmers from selling their grain outside the village at a profit and making it available instead to villagers on interest-free credit; (2) preventing wealthy brahmins from reducing their daily wages for agricultural work; (3) persuading the wealthiest and most influential brahmin village patron to secure a loan of Rs 15,000 from shopkeepers in the market centre in the nearby town and re-lend it to almost every villager, thus enabling the villagers to buy grains at lower rates than those prevailing later when the drought worsened; (4) getting this patron to secure government credit assistance for them, as well as obtain cloth on credit from cloth merchants in the town and provide the cloth to the villagers on credit; and (5) getting the rich to maintain the system of sponsoring festival feasts at which poorer brahmins and bhujels were fed. In this co-operative pressure, the fact that many of the brahmins were also poor, appears to have helped create a tie of solidarity between them and the bhujels; at the same time the poorer brahmins could draw upon their caste connections to persuade the wealthy brahmins to cede to the demands that benefited not only them but also the bhujels. Here group pressure did not merely help to maintain traditional patron–client obligations but also to extend them, and so distribute the burden of food shortages more equitably. The significance of such group solidarity and pressure clearly has a lesson to offer in drought management (of which more later).

Typically, however, as with patron–client relationships, friends and relations provide only limited support during severe food shortages (especially those caught up in a similar crisis). In the initial phases, relatives located in non-drought-affected regions or urban areas, and the better-off friends and neighbours may help out. In particular, several South Asian studies mention the family's ability to take help from the wife's parental home. In Nepal every family in the village studied by Prindle (1979) visited the wife's kin at least once to secure loans during the 1971 drought. Caldwell et al. (1986) found that 43 per cent of the families they studied in nine Karnataka villages received such help. However, for reasons spelt out in the previous section, this kind of support is unlikely to be regionally widespread in India. Also the amounts of loans given are typically small and form only a limited percentage of total borrowings by needy families—the rest being obtained from money-lenders and institutional sources (ostensibly for production but often redirected to consumption). In near-famine conditions the limited help from friends and relatives can virtually dry up: in the Bihar drought of 1966–7, 88.8 per cent of those surveyed in Palamau district said that they could not or did not help their neighbours (Singh 1975). Small borrowings of food items and cash, possible during seasonal troughs, are also no longer possible. Experiences of African famines point to a gradual shrinkage of the food-sharing arrangements common among women in normal times, the cessation of hospitality in terms of sharing food with visitors, and various other manifestations of atypical social behaviour (Vaughan 1987).

Demand for consumption credit from various sources other than friends, relations, and patrons also increases sharply during calamity. Again, while the better-off can get loans from the government agencies, the poor are usually forced to depend on money-lenders or to disinvest.[55] During the 1983 drought in Karnataka those who got least loans were either the upper-caste landlords and merchants or the harijan agricultural labourers—the former because they did not need credit, the latter because they could not get it. This bias was especially apparent in loans from banks and co-operatives (Caldwell et al. 1986). A similar pattern was observed by Borkar and Nadkarni (1975) in their study of two villages during the Maharashtra drought of 1970–3.

---

[55] See e.g. Jodha (1978) who makes a strong plea for extending consumption credit to the poor as a drought relief measure. Also see Gaiha (1988) who, on the basis of all India panel data, compares the situation of the chronically poor in areas that faced three years of adverse weather conditions between 1968 and 1970, and finds that borrowings among this category of households increased sharply as a result, with 42% in 1970, relative to 19% in 1968, disinvesting.

3.3. Work and Demographic Adjustments

3.3.1. Short-Term Work Shifts
Both long- and short-term work adjustments by families have been noted as a result of calamity. In the short term, changes in work patterns include:

(1) increased time spent in searching, foraging, gleaning, and the processing of food; in looking for fodder, fuel, and water; and in the more careful grazing of cattle—typically women's and children's time getting so extended (Jodha 1975; Caldwell *et al.* 1986; Chen 1988);

(2) shifts in traditional caste and gender divisions of labour: for instance, people from the Reddy caste were found selling vegetables during the 1971–3 drought in Medak district, Andhra Pradesh—a task that they considered below their status in normal years (Rao 1974); and women not belonging to the shoemaker caste were found taking up shoemaking during the 1966–7 Bihar drought (Singh 1975). This flexibility can prove crucial for survival: in the Nepal drought of 1971, the bhujels who willingly took up whatever work was going survived the drought better than the brahmins who held on more rigidly to caste status norms and many of whom were finally forced to emigrate (Prindle 1979);

(3) migration in various forms: Jodha (1975) describes the typical patterns in Rajasthan following the drought of 1963–4.[56] However, his emphasis that migration is undertaken only as a last resort after adjustments in current consumption, depletion of household stocks, and the mortgage or sale of assets has been undertaken, appears surprising given that seasonal migration is common in Rajasthan—clearly what changes is the scale on which migration takes place. Also, reports from Western India (quoted in McAlpin 1983) suggest that in the nineteenth-century famines, migration took the form of aimless wandering, but in the twentieth century a few men were typically sent out from each village to scout for work as soon as the failure of early rains made harvest losses inevitable. Accounts of recent famines, however, do not suggest such community co-operation.

3.3.2. Long-Term Work and Demographic Shifts
While short-term adjustments of work during crisis are noted in several studies, few have examined long-term adjustments resulting from an experience of severe or recurrent crisis. Among these few are Jodha's (1975) study of fifteen poor, upper-caste families in Rajasthan, and Caldwell *et al.*'s (1986) and Maclachlan's (1983) studies in

[56] This includes migration to irrigated areas along with bullocks to work as share-croppers, or to commercial centres with bullocks and camel carts for transporting goods; gangs of youths moving to irrigated or non-drought-affected areas in the peak seasons; and cross-state migration with animals in search of greener pastures—the last being most important in West Rajasthan.

Karnataka. In Rajasthan, due to recurrent droughts in the 1930s, the families studied permanently adopted the work patterns and life-styles of the lower castes—essentially a situation of downward economic and social mobility for survival. The Karnataka examples, however, indicate greater success in adaptation. Caldwell *et al.* (1986) note that the farming families in the nine villages they studied were extremely conscious of the need to diversify future income streams as risk insurance against seasonality and drought, and sought to do this by some members systematically seeking non-farm employment, investing in the children's education as an entry into urban employment, and looking for sons-in-law with urban jobs.

Maclachlan (1983), by contrast, documents the case of a farming community that built up drought resistance through farm-based diversification itself. He compares the experience of the village during the severe drought of 1965 when no deaths occurred as a result, with that of 1876–7 when a large number died in the area, and asks the question: why didn't they starve in the 1960s? His answer: agricultural intensification, especially the cultivation of gardens made possible by deploying substantial amounts of family labour, first to dig a large number of open surface wells and then to tend the fields and gardens. The long-term strategy included the building up of large joint families with a careful selection of brides from poorer hard-working families, especially first daughters (presumably used to managing a number of siblings), a preference for cross-cousin marriages, and a strong ideological emphasis on the joint family as the ideal and most productive family form. The ideological under-pinnings of efficient labour deployment were provided by the concept of *dharma* (duty) used to order a certain sexual division of labour and norms of behaviour.

On testing the relative productivities of households with more than one adult male (loosely classified by him as 'joint' families)[57] and others, Maclachlan found that the former did indeed have higher yields per acre and per capita than those with only one male adult (Table 5.12). Joint family households were favoured by landlords when seeking tenants, derived economies in the division of farm tasks, and had higher savings, a more intensive use of equipment, the advantages of interactive decision-making, and the advice of the elders. Although the number of women is not found to affect agricultural productivity much, households with more than one woman had distinct advantages in terms of diversification, with livestock, dairy, and sericulture being looked after

[57] Maclachlan's descriptions suggest that when he speaks of 'joint' families, he has more than one married son living with the parents in mind, but he does not explicitly state this. Other scholars examining household structures in India have used more precise classifications (e.g. Kolenda 1987; Caldwell *et al.* 1984; Hill 1980). While there appears to be agreement among them that commensal units consisting of a conjugal couple and unmarried children constitute 'nuclear' families, and those with two married siblings living with or without the parents are 'joint' families, the classification of those with only one married child living with the parents differs. Such families are classified by Kolenda as 'joint' but by Caldwell *et al.* as 'stem'. Shah (1973) also provides a useful review and discussion on the subject.

Table 5.12. Economic performance of sixteen households with the poorest ratio of land to household size

Type of household	Yield/acre	Per capita income	Sample family labour used/acre	Distribution of labour (%)			
	(Rs)	(Rs)	(hr)	Family lands	*Kuli*	Tenant	Others
One man (N=7)	119.0	160.9	132.8	43.1	52.6	1.9	2.3
More than one man (N=9)	283.8	355.1	192.6	37.6	35.8	25.2	4.2

Source: Maclachlan (1983: 147).

mainly by them. Less time was also needed by women for domestic work, since work-sharing was possible.

However, the factors which keep families joint are clearly weaker than those pulling them apart; and Kolenda's (1987) complex and detailed classification of household structures on the basis of existing studies from across India suggests that the typical family in India is nuclear, not joint (as defined in note 71). This is corroborated by more region-specific studies.[58] And while there appears to be no clear-cut evidence of a decline over time in the incidence of joint families,[59] there is found to be a noteworthy variation in this incidence by region (for instance, joint families are more common in the north-west than in central India), and by economic class (jointness is more prevalent amongst the rich than the poor), although less so by caste.[60] Kolenda (1987), who finds a

[58] Detailed case-studies in Karnataka by Caldwell *et al.* (1984) in 9 villages and Hill (1980) in 6 villages also indicate that nuclear families are in the majority. Caldwell *et al.* found that 7% of the households were 'joint' and 27% were 'stem', while Hill found that 10% were 'joint'. However, both the studies note that several times the number observed to be living in joint families at any one point in time would have lived in such families at some point in their lives—typically during the first few years of marriage. A 'developmental cycle' pattern is thus noted to exist, and one which appears to have persisted over several generations in the past.

[59] Kolenda's (1987) cross-country review suggests some slight tendency towards a decline in jointness in parts of India; while Caldwell *et al.* (1984) argue that their Karnataka evidence shows no apparent change. However their conclusion does not entirely tie up with some of their observations which suggest a possible decline. They note, for instance (see especially pp. 223–4), that the proportion of younger couples leaving to seek work elsewhere (which is one of the causes of joint family partition) 'has been rising constantly' and further that 'certainly, the case studies of the causes of partition appeared to show that conditions that were tolerated without partition only a generation ago are much less likely to be tolerated now'.

[60] See Kolenda (1987) on the regional patterning of family structures as well as on cross-class and cross-caste variations. On class differences also see Caldwell *et al.* (1984) and Hill (1980) both of whom find a systematically lower incidence of jointness among the poorer households in the Karnataka villages. Caldwell *et al.* find a systematic decline in jointness with a fall in land-holding size. Also landed households tend to have larger houses, capable of accommodating larger families.

lesser tendency towards jointness among the untouchable castes relative to the 'twice born', argues that among high-caste groups social opinion still discourages break-ups as long as the parents are alive (ownership of unpartitioned land by the father also serves to postpone the split), but among the untouchable castes, sons do not consider the obligation to their parents binding. Be that as it may, in so far as low-caste households are also often poor, even economically they would be in a less favourable position to fulfil such obligations.

Unfortunately, Maclachlan focuses almost entirely on the largely selfsufficient cultivating households and gives us little idea of how agricultural labour households survived the drought, what strategies they followed, whether they gained from the agricultural intensification undertaken by the farmers, and what their relationship with the cultivating households was during their drought. For instance, did the farmers help sustain the labourers?

Nevertheless, there are lessons to be learnt from Maclachlan's study: small irrigation works and agricultural intensification as ways of countering drought conditions; joint cultivation for increasing agricultural productivity and labouruse efficiency; and work-sharing arrangements within the household for greater income diversification and for increasing the efficiency of domestic labour. The question is: what institutional arrangements can re-create cooperative labour deployment networks successfully, outside the context of the family?

3.4. Consumption Adjustments: Growing Hunger

Apart from increased dependence on a variety of 'famine foods' noted earlier, drought conditions or the onset of famine lead to shifts in the types of foods eaten—for instance, from fine to coarse grains such as from rice and dal to ragi and jowar (sometimes even that used normally as cattle feed) (Caldwell et al. 1986; Reddy 1988). As scarcity worsens there is also likely to be a decline in the consumption of protective foods such as milk, meat, fruits, vegetables, and so on;[61] the stretching of food to make it last longer; a reduction in the quantity eaten by cooking fewer meals a day, or going hungry for several days.[62] In severe shortages yams and roots may be eaten to kill the appetite—the tribals of Gujarat use a bitter root called *kand* for this purpose (Rangaswami 1985). Most studies record a fall in consumption per capita during drought years.[63] In

However, neither Caldwell et al. nor Hill find variations in family structures by caste although they provide no satisfactory explanation of why this should be so, given the usually noted correlation between caste and economic situation.

[61] Jodha (1978) on comparing drought and post-drought years in Rajasthan and Gujarat found a decline in protective food consumption by 28% to 48% (varying by region) and a decline in per capita grain intake by between 11% and 23%.

[62] Reddy (1988); Currey (1978) on Bangladesh.

[63] For a quantification of declines in consumption during droughts see Jodha (1975, 1978); also see Chowdhury and Bapat (1975) for Rajasthan and Gujarat; Desai et al. (1979) for Gujarat.

addition, there is a decline in expenditure on clothing, children's education, socio-religious ceremonies, a postponement of marriages, and so on.[64] The passage from severe drought to famine is a progressive worsening in consumption as entitlements to food collapse.

There are, however, noteworthy gender differences in food-sharing—essentially an accentuation of gender differences noted in normal times, especially but not only in northern India. In Caldwell et al.'s (1986) study of the 1983 Karnataka drought, male heads of households were asked who bore the greatest burden of food shortages—43 per cent reported that all shared equally from the cutbacks; 35 per cent said adults (but none said 'men') and 22 per cent identified mostly women, children, and the old. (Possibly the same questions addressed to the women would have made the gender bias more explicit.) On morbidity, 60 per cent of the families reporting illness identified only women, children, and the aged; 22 per cent listed adults and 17 per cent mentioned a broad division by age and sex. Campbell and Trechter (1982), who explicitly examined differences in gender responses to varying degrees of food shortages in North Cameroon, found that under severe shortage situations, while women's actions commonly included going hungry for the whole day, men's more typically included migration.

3.5. Depleting Assets

Jodha (1975) observes in a much commented-on debate with Morris (1974, 1975) that the primary concern of rural families when faced with extreme food shortages is not the protection of current consumption but protection of productive assets—which are disposed of as a last resort, since their loss is likely to affect the household's long-term prospects of recovery from the crisis. He argues, on the basis of his data on the Rajasthan drought of 1963–4, that, to begin with, households reduce their consumpiton and deplete stocks of fodder, fuel-wood, grain, animal products, dung-cakes, and so on, which have been stored for the lean period. Subsequently household goods such as ropes, cots, utensils, and jewellery—the non-productive assets—are disposed of (also see Table 5.13). Some small livestock may also be sold. It is noteworthy that unlike the price of livestock which plummets during drought (Jodha 1978), that of jewellery may show little decline (Borkar and Nadkarni 1975). Finally, draught animals and land are disposed of—the former being sold outright, the latter first mortgaged where possible. The disposal of productive assets thus becomes a barometer of the degree of distress and is typically associated with famine conditions.

According to the Mahalanobis et al. (1946) estimates, during the Bengal famine of 1943, between April 1943 and April 1944, one-fourth of all families

---

[64] See e.g. Jodha (1978); Singh (1975); Caldwell, et al. (1986).

Table 5.13. Monthwise foodgrain consumption, depletion of inventories and assets, and outmigration in Jodhpur district (Rajasthan), 1963–1964 (drought year) and 1964–1965 (post-drought year)

| | % of households consuming | | | | | |
| | 300–450 g/day | | 451–600 g/day | | 601–750 g/day | |
	D	PD	D	PD	D	PD
October 1963	7.7	–	21.2	67.3	71.1	32.7
November 1963	21.3	–	25.0	73.0	53.8	27.0
December 1963	34.6	1.9	38.5	69.2	26.9	28.9
January 1964	48.1	5.7	34.6	74.9	17.3	19.4
February 1964	57.7	3.8	35.5	76.8	5.8	20.4
March 1964	60.5	5.7	32.7	78.7	5.8	15.4
April 1964	69.2	7.6	25.0	78.7	5.8	13.9

| | % of households who | | | |
	Sold inventories	Sold assets	Mortgaged assets	Outmigrated
October 1963	22.9	–	0.7	–
November 1963	40.9	1.4	–	–
December 1963	55.0	–	2.8	–
January 1964	50.1	–	5.6	–
February 1964	52.2	2.1	14.5	1.4
March 1964	35.3	0.7	26.4	4.2
April 1964	36.7	4.2	22.2	21.5
TOTAL	100.0[a]	8.4	68.8	27.5

Notes: D = drought year; PD = post drought year. Data for consumption relate to a sample of 52 farming households in one village. Data for activities relate to a sample of 144 farming households.
[a] Some households took some steps more than once.
Source: Jodha (1975: 1613, 1615).

(numbering nearly 1.6 million) owning paddy land before the famine had either sold it in full or in part, or mortgaged it. Sales in full were highest among those with less than two acres: these, constituting 6.1 per cent of all families, thus lost their main source of livelihood. Those buying the land were largely based outside the village, many of them urban dwellers. Thirteen per cent of plough cattle was also lost (due to sales or deaths) and only 25 per cent of it could be replaced later. Losses during droughts which do not escalate into famines are usually less severe but there is also found to be a considerable variation in their extent in different drought contexts. In the Bihar drought bordering on famine in 1966–7, for instance, of the total value of property lost in Palamau district, the sale and mortgage of land accounted for 24 per cent, of cattle 50 per cent, and of jewellery and household utensils 25 per cent. During other droughts, however, the losses recorded, especially of land, were less severe.[65] Both droughts and famines, however, typically leave in their wake considerable increases in inequalities in asset distribution.[66]

Once mortgaged or sold the chances of these assets being redeemed in full in the post-calamity period are often slim, especially for the small farmers and landless agricultural labourers. Jodha's (1978) comparision of the asset position of farmers in the pre-drought, drought, and post-drought years in three states shows only a partial recovery in productive assets, and a further depletion in non-productive assets in virtually all cases in the post-drought years (Table 5.14), suggesting lagged effects of the calamity.

Table 5.14. Indices of asset position[a] in drought and post-drought years relative to pre-drought years (pre-drought year = 100)

Farm size group/year	Jodhpur (Rajasthan) 1963–64[b]		Barmer (Rajasthan) 1969–70[b]		Banas Kantha (Gujarat) 1969–70[b]		Aurangabad (Maharashtra) 1972–73[b]		Sholapur (Maharashtra) 1972–73[b]	
	P	NP	P	NP	P	NP	P	NP	P	NP
Small Farms										
Drought year	63	72	82	98	59	81	74	50	69	50
Post-drought year	73	68	95	99	79	73	NA	NA	60	29
Large Farms										
Drought year	75	89	40	46	87	97	79	62	95	88
Post-drought year	83	91	42	47	93	97	NA	NA	88	108
All Households										
Drought year	63	69	66	79	84	85	77	87	84	69
Post-drought year	83	64	76	77	97	85	NA	NA	78	66

[a] All assets are valued at 1972–3 prices.
[b] Drought years.
Notes: P = productive assets, which include livestock, farm implements, machinery, etc., but exclude land. NP = non-productive assets, which include jewellery, financial assets and consumer durables. NA = Not available.

Source: Jodha (1978: A-39).

Also, detailed case-studies collected by him of seven families in Rajasthan hit by successive droughts over twenty-five years, although inadequate for generalization, are illustrative of the process of impoverishment that can set in: the land possessed by these families decreased from forty-three acres to less than five acres per family over this period. Similarly, an investigation of land transfers in three drought-prone districts in Rajasthan over ten years showed

[65] See Caldwell *et al.* (1986) on the Karnataka drought of 1983; Borkar and Nadkarni (1975) on the Maharashtra drought on 1970–3; and Jodha (1978) on droughts in 5 districts of Rajasthan, Gujarat, and Maharashtra at various points in time.
[66] See e.g. Oughton (1982) on the Maharashtra drought of 1970–3; Mahalanobis *et al.* (1946) and Ghose (1979) on the Bengal famine of 1943; Alamgir (1980) on the Bangladesh famine of 1974.

that 85 per cent of all land disposed of was due to drought-induced mortgages. The absence of any significant land transfers during the Maharashtra drought of 1970–3 is thus seen as one of the important indicators of the success of government relief programmes (Drèze 1988b).

However, in this literature on asset disposal during drought and famine two aspects need specific comment: first the loss of certain types of assets has gone virtually unrecorded— one such is trees. Chen (1987) who monitored the 1987–8 drought in Gujarat found that in one village where virtually no trees were cut in the pre-drought year, some 150 trees were cut and sold in 1986 when the monsoon rains failed, and an additional 300 or more were cut in the second year of the drought—most of them being slow-growing species such as mango and neem. Reddy (1988) likewise notes that between 1983–7 almost 2,000 trees were cut and sold in the village he surveyed.

Second, in the noted sequencing of asset sales, what appears to have been missed in the literature is that the assets which are the first casualty—namely, household utensils and jewellery[67]—also happen to be those typically owned and controlled by women. Underlying the sales is of course an economic rationality, especially in the case of jewellery, in that in addition to the importance of holding on to productive assets such as land and cattle, jewellery is a much more liquid asset than land, and unlike cattle less prone to price plummeting.[68] Jewellery (and gold and silver in general) clearly serves as a store of value for crisis situations. However, such sales have a special significance when we note that usually these are the only assets possessed by women.

For instance, while there is no comprehensive data on land ownership by gender, several factors would support the view that few rural women own agricultural land or homestead plots.[69] First, legally, even under post-independence laws, among all communities in India (except essentially those in the matrilineal south-west which is governed by different laws), women have highly unequal rights to agricultural land. Second, customarily too, barring a few matrilineal groups in the south-west and north-east, and exceptional circumstances elsewhere (for example, of daughters in son-less families) women in most communities had virtually no recognized inheritance rights in land, and even less the right to control or alienate it. Usufructory rights were somewhat more common, but basically confined to tribal communities; and, over time, these too have been systematically eroded, especially with the privatization of communal land typically registered in male names. Third, while legislation today allows women in most communities to own, use, and dispose of land (though not on an equal basis with men), practices such as

[67] Jodha (1975); Singh (1975); Borkar and Nadkarni (1975); Greenough (1982); Currey (1978).

[68] Borkar and Nadkarni (1975) found that during the Maharashtra drought in 1972–3 the price of jewellery did not register any fall while that of livestock registered a steep decline. A sharp decline in livestock prices is common in such contexts as sellers begin to flood the market.

[69] See Agarwal's (1988) review both of the legal position and of customary practices among 145 communities across India, based on village studies.

patrilocal post-marital residence, village exogamy, female seclusion and restriction of movement, in many parts of India prevent women from claiming
their legal share. Especially in northern India, as a result, women typically give
up their claims in favour of brothers, and widows face considerable hostility in
their assertion of claims. What applies to agricultural land applies equally to
other immovable property, including homestead plots.

For assets other than land such as livestock it is difficult to establish
individual ownership within the household, except in the context of cattle
distribution under the government's Integrated Rural Development Programme
(IRDP) for poverty alleviation, where the person receiving the cattle loan is the
registered owner, and in customary practices among some communities where
animals are gifted to the daughter on marriage (Mitra 1985; Miller 1981).
While livestock is typically looked after by women and children, this does not
imply rights of disposal.

A woman's assets, then, would consist at best of some small animals,[70] and
items obtained as gifts during marriage, such as jewellery and utensils, and
even these may not always be under her control.[71] Once these are disposed of,
even if the household is able to protect its productive assets during the
calamity, women would be left with nothing to fall back on if abandoned or if
there is a drought recurrence, since in the cycle of mortgage–indebtedness–
sale, jewellery once sold is unlikely to be easily redeemed. Most households are
often unable to make up even for cattle losses: as noted in Table 5.14, on small
farms, the indices of productive assets rose in the post-drought year (although
not up to the pre-drought level) while those for non-productive assets,
including jewellery, typically fell further. This leaves women especially vulnerable during a severe calamity such as famine, when families may themselves
begin to fragment and disintegrate.

4. THE DISINTEGRATING FAMILY

Famines in a sense represent the extreme end of the spectrum in terms of food
crisis. They also pose in the most stark terms the economic and moral dilemmas
relating to intrahousehold food sharing, and provide a mirror to intrafamily
relations that few other contexts can. The Bengal famine of 1943 serves as a
specially poignant case-study in this respect.

A variety of evidence points to some of the specific disadvantages suffered by
women and children of poor households during the famine. To begin with,
Mahalanobis *et al.*'s (1946) estimates of persons made destitute in rural Bengal,

---

[70] In Africa, small livestock are typically owned by women, and again are among the first
casualties during famines (Watts 1983).

[71] In some communities a portion of the dowry is customarily taken away by the in-laws (see
e.g. Madan 1975; Miller 1981; Minturn and Hitchcock 1966).

revealed a predominance of young and middle-aged females: in January 1943, 55 per cent of all destitutes and 66 per cent of destitutes in the 15–50 age-group were females; women of this age-group also constituted the largest number of new additions to destitutes between January 1943 and May 1944 (and amounted to twice the number of new male destitutes of this age group). Children (of both sexes) in the 5–15 age category were the next largest in number. Occupationally, in absolute terms the largest number of destitutes were agricultural labourers, and in terms of the percentage affected in a given occupation, the worst hit were those dependent on fishing, transport, agricultural labour, paddy-husking, and craft, in that order (Tables 5.15 and 5.16).

Second, Greenough's construction (based on the Bengal Famine Committee's records) of the social profile of those who came to State relief centres during the most intense months of the famine, and were able to pay cash for food as compared to those who were absolutely destitute, is revealing (although the categories are overlapping). The cash-paying chief recipients of relief tended to be male adults; Hindus of the trading, cultivating, and high Sudra castes; and heads of households averaging 3.6 persons and willing to go some distance to seek out relief goods being sold at a discount. In comparison, those dependent entirely on gratuitous relief tended to be females (mostly adults) 84 per cent of whom got gratis aid compared with 43 per cent of the male destitutes (see Table 5.17); Muslims and Hindus of lower, fishing, and untouchable castes; widows and married persons often with absent spouses; heads of households averaging less than 2.5 persons; those in need principally due to a loss of income, and those able to secure relief only at their place of residence.[72]

Third, consider the famine mortality figures in Table 5.18. The general pattern appears to be one of relative female advantage: for most age groups and for all ages taken together, survey-based estimates of the absolute number of deaths during the period from January to December 1943, as well as the absolute and proportionate increases in mortality rates due to famine ('excess mortality') were greater for males than females. But the exceptions to this general pattern, especially the age-grouping 20–40, are noteworthy in the context of the present discussion. For this age-grouping the estimated absolute number of famine deaths during the critical year of 1943 as well as the absolute increase in mortality rates were greater for women than men, though the proportionate increase showed gender parity. Men of this age-grouping showed the least excess mortality (in absolute terms) of all age groups of either sex. The greater mortality disadvantage in absolute terms suffered by women relative to men in the 20–40 age-grouping is particularly noteworthy as this is despite the reduction in child-birth and child-bearing associated risk due to famine-induced reduction in birth rates. Also the bulk of women in this age-grouping

[72] Famine relief in general was much delayed and, when it came, was grossly inadequate (Greenough 1982: 127–38; GOI's Famine Enquiry Commission Report on Bengal 1945: 96–102).

Table 5.15. Estimated number of destitute persons in rural Bengal by age and sex (100,000s)

Age group (yrs.)	Estimated number of destitute persons						Estimated number of new destitute persons between Jan. 1943 and May 1944		
	Jan. 1943			May 1944					
	Male	Female	Total	Male	Female	Total	Male	Female	Total
0–5	0.27	0.31	0.58	0.60	0.50	1.10	0.33	0.19	0.52
5–15	1.61	1.06	2.67	2.19	1.68	3.87	0.58	0.62	1.20
15–50	0.98	1.95	2.93	1.43	2.92	4.35	0.45	0.97	1.42
Over 50	0.50	0.77	1.27	0.59	0.85	1.44	0.09	0.08	0.17
TOTAL	3.36	4.09	7.45	4.81	5.95	10.76	1.45	1.86	3.31

Source: Mahalanobis et al. (1946).

Table 5.16. Estimated number of destitute persons in May 1944 in rural Bengal (100,000s)

Family occupation	Infants	Children	Men	Women	Old persons	Total	% destitute persons in total population in that occupation
Agriculture	0.10	0.36	0.14	0.22	0.08	0.90	0.75
Agriculture and labour	0.13	0.15	0.05	0.09	0.07	0.49	0.82
Agricultural labour	0.21	0.70	0.27	0.58	0.23	1.99	3.02
Non-cultivating owner	0.03	0.11	0.05	0.06	0.02	0.27	0.98
All agriculture	0.47	1.32	0.51	0.95	0.40	3.65	1.30
Fishing	0.07	0.15	0.09	0.12	0.02	0.45	7.75
Craft	0.03	0.23	0.10	0.15	0.05	0.56	2.70
Husking paddy	0.01	0.01	–	0.04	–	0.06	2.73
Transport	0.01	0.03	0.02	0.02	–	0.08	7.06
Trade	0.02	0.18	0.05	0.12	0.03	0.40	1.31
Profession and service	0.04	0.17	0.08	0.11	0.04	0.44	1.30
Non-agricultural labour	0.01	0.05	0.03	0.02	–	0.11	2.00
Other occupations	0.02	0.04	0.02	0.02	0.04	0.14	1.83
Living on charity	0.42	1.69	0.53	1.37	0.86	4.87	73.86
TOTAL	1.10	3.87	1.43	2.92	1.44	10.76	3.39

Source: Estimated from Chattopadhyaya and Mukerjee (1946: 18).

Table 5.17. Heads of households receiving relief[a] from the Bengal Relief Committee between October 1943 and June 1946[b]

Sex of chief recipients	Cash-paying recipients		Gratis recipients		Both	
	No.	%	No.	%	No.	% cash-paying
Male	965	84.4	726	44.1	1 691	(57.1)
Female	178	15.6	922	55.9	1 100	(16.2)
TOTAL	1 143	100.0	1 648	100.0	2 791	(41.0)

[a] Mostly food but also clothing and medicine.
[b] About 87% of these received relief between Oct. 1943 and June 1946.
Source: Greenough (1982: 190).

would be within marital relationships, that is women who may normally be expected to have the support of husbands (of which more later).

Fourth, a survey of 2,537 destitutes living on the pavements of Calcutta in September 1943 quoted by Greenough showed that 52.7 per cent of them were female, and among the married destitutes (excluding those widowed or divorced) 63.6 per cent were female. The pavement-dwellers had earlier belonged to 820 families; half of these had recently broken up, 70 per cent as a result of husbands and wives separating. The women, on being asked why they had left the village for Calcutta, said that their husbands had been unable to maintain them and had either deserted them or asked them to go elsewhere in search of food (Greenough does not say how many gave this answer).

In addition, Greenough provides anecdotal evidence on women being abandoned by husbands, and being forced into begging or prostitution; and quotes several reports of parents selling their children into bondage and especially their girl children (even in the ages 2–13) into prostitution. The observation of the Nari Seva Sangha, a private women's service society set up in 1944 for sheltering abandoned women during the famine, is again telling: 'Women were being thrown out into the streets and multitudes of them were being forced into a life of shame in a country which has always boasted about its purity and modesty' (quoted in Greenough 1982: 225).

On the basis of such evidence Greenough argues that there was a striking fragmentation or disintegration of families during the famine, and further that this familial disintegration 'did not occur randomly but seems to have been the result of the intentional exclusion of the less valued family members (women and children) from domestic subsistence', by a decision to this effect on the part of the male head of the household (which he sees as parallel to the decision of the village patron to withhold support towards clients). He notes that the

Bengali family is not only a social but also a moral unit where the male head—the *korta*—controls all family members and their corporate interests; he is the *annadata*—the provider of sustenance for the family—and during the Bengal famine he increasingly favoured adults over children and males over females. However, Greenough argues that 'decisions as to who will eat and who must starve are not taken suddenly or arbitrarily in the heat of the famine but draw upon an existing cultural arrangement that assigns a value to family members according to their roles'. It is a decision in keeping with the powerful existing ideal of family continuity, equated with the continuity of the patriline through the adult male, whose survival thus counts over that of women and children:

If the separated 'master' survives a crisis, he is enabled to marry again despite the death or violation of his spouse, and he may then engender children who can be expected to maintain the lineage under more prosperous conditions (Greenough 1982: 224).

In other words, no contradiction is seen here between the male self-interest and the preservation of the moral order in the Bengal context.

The evidence on familial disintegration and the abandonment of women and children presented by Greenough (and as can also be gleaned from the surveys of destitutes mentioned earlier), while largely indirect (and from which the scale of this disintegration cannot be assessed), is nevertheless sufficiently indicative that this was not an isolated phenomenon, and could even have been fairly widespread.[73] This is also a phenomenon which has been noted, although mainly in passing, in accounts of other famines. Alamgir (1980: 135) observes of the 1974 Bangladesh famine: 'Besides, there were many cases of desertion. In Rangpur, special homes for deserted children were set up. In Dacca, there were many women who were deserted by their husbands among the inmates of vagrant homes.' And in her reconstruction of the 1949 famine in Malawi, Vaughan (1987: 123) notes: 'Women stress how frequently they were abandoned by men, how harrowing it was to be left responsible for their suffering and dying children.'[74]

What needs closer examination and some discussion, however, is Greenough's explanation of what underlay the male decision to abandon. Appadurai (1984: 485) offers an alternative explanation to Greenough's, suggesting that the abandonment of women and children could be seen as

an effort to maximise the life-chances of each and every member of the family in circumstances where co-residence was clearly not feasible. Thus the sale of children might be seen as an effort to construct a better set of life-chances than those of the existing family structure.

[73] A fair number of widows who had earlier been supported by relatives are also noted to have been turned out (Chattopadhyay and Mukerjee 1946: 15).

[74] Gangrade and Dhadda (1973) also mention cases of abandonment of women, but especially of children and the aged, during the 1966–7 Bihar drought. Also Dirks (1980: 30) in his cross-country review of the social responses to famine, notes: 'Both sale and abandonment of children have been recorded in a wide variety of cultural settings.'

Table 5.18. 1943 Bengal famine mortality by age and sex

Age group (years)	No. of persons in sample survey who died over Jan.–Dec. 1943		Death rates in sample survey %		Death rates 1931 census calculations %		Increase in death rates attributable to 1943 famine (excess mortality)				Gender differences in excess mortality rates	
							In absolute terms (%)		In proportionate terms		In absolute terms (F–M)	In proportionate terms
	M	F	M	F	M	F	M	F	M	F		
(1)[a]	(2)[b]	(3)[b]	(4)[b]	(5)[b]	(6)[c]	(7)[c]	(8)[d]	(9)[e]	(10)[f]	(11)[g]	(12)[h]	(13)[i]

Age	(2)	(3)	(4)	(5)	(6)	(7)	(8)[d]	(9)[e]	(10)[f]	(11)[g]	(12)[h]	(13)[i]
1–5	189	168	8.43	7.99	5.9	5.2	2.53	2.79	0.43	0.54	+0.26	+0.11
5–10	366	330	6.00	6.57	1.6	1.4	4.40	5.17	2.75	3.69	+0.77	+0.94
10–15	195	137	4.92	3.95	1.0	1.2	3.92	2.75	3.92	2.29	−1.17	−1.63
15–20	146	148	4.20	3.89	1.2	1.7	3.00	2.19	2.50	1.29	−0.81	−1.21
20–30	190	287	3.21	4.49	1.8	2.5	1.41	1.99	0.78	0.80	+0.58	+0.02
30–40	223	226	4.94	5.58	3.0	3.4	1.94	2.18	0.65	0.64	+0.24	−0.01
40–50	282	191	8.77	6.77	4.2	4.3	4.57	2.47	1.09	0.57	−2.10	−0.52
50–60	277	169	14.08	10.78	5.5	5.0	8.58	5.78	1.56	1.16	−2.80	−0.40
over 60	225	122	17.10	12.66	9.8	9.1	7.30	3.56	0.74	0.39	−3.74	−0.35
All ages	2 093	1 778	6.40	5.89	3.1	3.2	4.18	3.21	1.35	1.12	−0.97	−0.23

[a] Infants under 1 year excluded.
[b] Mahalanobis et al. (1946) sample survey.
[c] Taken as the 'normal' period rates.
[d] Col. 4 less col. 6.
[e] Col. 5 less col. 7.
[f] Col. 8 divided by col. 6.
[g] Col. 9 divided by col. 7.
[h] Col. 9 less col. 8.
[i] Col. 11 less col. 10.

Source: Greenough (1982: 311); some taken directly, in other cases computed.

However, Appadurai's explanation is difficult to uphold in a context where female chastity is held in very high regard (indeed loss of female life may be considered preferable to loss of chastity in many communities in India, including Bengal),[75] and where the husband would know that the abandoned spouse would most likely fall easy prey to sexual exploitation. In fact, the women were doubly victimized, since even if they managed to physically survive, they were unlikely to be accepted back as wives by the husbands or their families; and in the aftermath of the famine, they filled the shelters opened to accommodate them. Similarly, the sale of girl children into prostitution could hardly be seen as a step taken by parents to improve their life chances.

An alternative way of viewing this process of family break-up and female victimization would be in terms of shifts in the relative male/female entitlements and fall-back positions—and so in their relative bargaining strengths within the family, along the lines discussed in Section 1 of this chapter. What Greenough vividly describes is a process of family disintegration during a calamity when the normal rules governing the sharing of resources and arrangements of reciprocity are beginning to shred. The rules that he emphasizes, however, are those stemming from a culture-specific moral code that ultimately favours male survival over female.

Without denying the persuasiveness of the moral explanation, it seems to me that the decision by the man to abandon the wife and children occurs at a point when the wife's entitlements have collapsed completely while those of the husband are weakened but not entirely gone. It is a telling point that 57 per cent of the males compared to only 16 per cent of the female recipients of relief in the earlier mentioned survey were able to pay cash for the food received, and also that the least excess mortality (in absolute terms) occurred among men of 20–40 years of age.[76] Also, one of the traditional (and few) fall-back occupations of women in Bengal—paddy-husking—clearly did not sustain beyond a point. Paddy-huskers ranked among the first four categories of those hardest hit by the famine; and the large number of new entrants to this occupation (noted by Sen 1981: 72) during the worst phase of the famine would not only be a symptom of the growing marginalization of women in other occupations but would also have depressed earnings in this occupation further.[77] Again, it is noteworthy that in the three illustrative accounts of abandoned women presented by Greenough, one is of a woman of 18 found wandering in Calcutta

---

[75] The concept of *pativrata* popularized by the Puranic writers implied absolute fidelity to the husband and demanded that the wife always remain chaste and pure. The Dharmashastras stressed this as the guiding principle of a woman's life (Kapadia 1966).

[76] As noted, this is also part of the age-group within which the number of female destitutes was substantially higher than male destitutes in the Mahalanobis *et al.* (1946) survey.

[77] It is of note that during the 1943 Bengal famine, there was a virtual absence of government famine relief works, which are known typically to attract more women than men, and which would have provided an alternative source of earnings.

whose husband pushed her out and 'decided to stay on the (one acre of) land to look after his coming betel-vine' (1982: 218); in the second, the husband divorced and abandoned the wife saying he was going 'to join the army'; and in the third, the husband left and was not heard of subsequently. In general, Greenough notes: 'If there were still limited resources in the village and little likelihood of obtaining subsistence outside the village, the husband would stay behind. Alternatively, if a source of food or work was offered outside the village, and local resources had been exhausted, the husband would migrate, leaving the wife and children behind' (ibid).

All this appears to suggest that the men's fall-back position was stronger than of the women on at least two counts: first, their greater mobility and ability to migrate over longer distances for a job without the fear of sexual exploitation that women faced, and second, the possibility of left-over assets, while women's jewellery, and so on, had already been disposed of.[78] In other words, the women would have been left with virtually no bargaining strength within the family at a much earlier stage in the process of famine impoverishment.[79] Within the bargaining view of the family, at this point non-cooperation by the husband would make sense in the interests of his individual physical survival, and do him no harm in terms of his social survival (he could marry again), whether or not this was in keeping with the moral order. If he additionally had an ideological (moral) justification that self-preservation was in keeping with the preservation of the moral order, it would merely have eased the decision.

Essentially, Greenough's view of the family (and one which Appadurai implicitly accepts) comes close to what Sen (1987) has described as the 'despotic' family in which the male family head takes all decisions and others just obey (indeed 'acquiesce even as victims')—although Greenough sees the male head as essentially a benevolent despot, guided by moral considerations. What I am suggesting here is that the victimization process could fit in equally with the co-operative-conflict (bargaining) view of the family.

The point, however, is that what view we take of the family—the despotic one or the co-operative-conflict one—could point to basically different policy

---

[78] Greenough (1982: 197) notes: 'One of the first signs of economic distress in rural Bengal was the sale of women's jewellery and ornaments.' As distress continued, household utensils followed, and cooking implements, brass pots, tin roofs all found their way to the market. In 1943, in Contai town, sales of utensils and jewellery were noted to be 'brisk'. Only subsequently were cattle and land sold. Currey (1978) documents a similar sale of household utensils during the Bangladesh famine of 1974.

[79] In this context, Vaughan's (1987: 124) observation on the experience of women (married uxorilocally) during the Malawi famine of 1949–50 is also striking: 'it was the men who had the external social and economic linkages—both with other ecological zones and with the labour economy. These external linkages became more and more crucial as the famine increased in severity. The scarcer the food the smaller became the units of consumption. *Beyond a certain point the advantages of co-residence with kin ceased to be apparent* and women were increasingly dependent on husbands (if they had any) or on themselves' (emphasis mine).

conclusions. Under the former, one could, for instance, make a case for strengthening the economic position of the benevolent male head of household to enable him better to support his wife and children (the passive recipients of his bounty or rejection). Under the latter view where women are seen as active (if disadvantaged) agents in the arrangements of reciprocity within the family, one would make a case for strengthening their fall-back positions and bargaining power within the family. That this view of the family may be the more accurate is suggested not the least by the experiences of some of the non-governmental initiatives (discussed in the next section of this chapter), where the enhancement of poor women's earnings opportunities, such as by cheap credit, has made a noteworthy difference to their position within the family.

5. ON POLICY AND EXTERNAL INTERVENTIONS

Our examination of a poor agricultural household's coping mechanisms during periods of food shortages associated with seasonality and calamity, reveals several aspects which have a bearing on policy.

Firstly, seasonality reveals a face of the family which is essentially one of (unequal) co-operation; famine mirrors one of disintegration. In both contexts, the burden of coping falls disproportionately on female members within poor households—in terms of consumption adjustments, asset depletion, work burden, and, in extreme contexts, destitution and abandonment. Seen within the framework of families as arenas of co-operative conflicts, this unequal burden may be traced (among other things) to women's weaker bargaining strength within the family.

Secondly, common property resources and forests play a critical role in cushioning the effect of seasonality and, although to a lesser extent, also of drought-related food troughs for poor households, especially for the more vulnerable members within such households whose ownership endowments are few and entitlement position relatively weak.

Thirdly, a poor agricultural household's long-term capacity to survive the trough can depend crucially on whether it is able to pass through such periods without any permanent depletion in its assets, especially (but not only) in terms of livestock and land.

Following from this, policies that stem the ongoing depletion and erosion of village commons and forests and indeed help expand this communal base; alternative credit and employment systems which protect the household from having to reduce consumption, or mortgage or sell assets, including those owned by women; and any measures (in addition to those above) which strengthen women's fall-back position by enhancing their entitlements base, would contribute to strengthening the coping mechanisms of poor households.

The question then is: what would or could be the intervening forms and agencies for doing this? In much of the existing literature on seasonality or calamity there is a strong emphasis on direct State intervention especially in the form of public works, and relatively little on interventionist forms that do not directly depend on the State.

State success in preventing the Maharashtra drought of 1970–3 from escalating into a large-scale famine, and in significantly containing the extent of productive asset depletion, nutritional distress, and excess mortality through the provision of guaranteed employment on a massive scale through public works, appears to have been particularly influential in pointing policy in this direction. There are clearly significant lessons to be learnt about drought and famine management from the Maharashtra example (as brought out by Drèze's (1988b) excellent and insightful review paper). Not the least is the fact that the State was able to protect entitlements to food not only of the most vulnerable households but also of the more vulnerable sections within the household, such as women, by providing them with direct (and not male-mediated) entitlements in the form of guaranteed employment. It is noteworthy that in recent years women have constituted at least 40 per cent according to official figures (and over 50 per cent according to field studies) of the labour force in the Maharashtra Employment Guarantee Scheme (EGS) (Dandekar 1983).

At the same time, in the context of the present discussion, several factors would caution against dependence on the State alone for providing food security in contingencies. First, although the government has been able to deal fairly effectively with the threat of large-scale famine since independence, and in situations verging on famine (for example, due to successive droughts) there may perhaps be few alternatives to substantial State interventions in the form of public works (as Drèze 1988b argues), the record of the Indian government in dealing with less acute situations has been poor.[80] Even in the implementation of the EGS in Maharashtra there are shortcomings, and it has not been possible to absorb all those who seek work through it even in normal times;[81] while outside Maharashtra attempts at guaranteeing employment have had even less success: in Tamil Nadu they have been found to be largely ineffective (Guhan 1981).

Second, there are contradictions in State policies themselves. For instance, those relating to CPRs, forests, and environmental protection in general are noted to have systematically weakened the ability of the poor themselves to cope with food crisis situations.[82]

---

[80] See e.g. various articles on drought management in the *Economic and Political Weekly*, especially over the years 1987–1988.

[81] See especially Deshpande (1982) for a critique of EGS functioning in the *adivasi* (tribal) parts of Thane district in Maharashtra. See also Chap. 7 below.

[82] For a critique of these policies see especially discussions in CSE (1985–6); Agarwal (1986a); Shiva (1988); and various articles over the past 5 years in the *Economic and Political Weekly*.

Third, the degree to which the State responds to the demands of the vulnerable sections would depend not least on the degree to which these sections can make their demands heard—be it for minimum wage implementation, relief works, or for a guaranteed subsistence throughout the year. Sen (1984), for instance, lays particular stress on the role of a vigilant press and diverse political parties in giving voice to those affected by situations bordering on famine. At the same time, he notes the limitations of these agencies in dealing with regular and endemic malnutrition. It is in giving the poor a voice that the role of grass-roots social action groups in which the poor are direct participants is likely to have particular relevance (in complementing if not substituting for the role played by some of the political parties).[83] The issue here is one not only of being entitled, but of being able effectively to enforce those entitlements.

To elaborate, consider the concepts of 'enfranchisement' and 'empowerment' in relation to that of entitlement. Sen's entitlement approach 'concentrates on the ability of people to command food through the legal means available in the society, including the use of production possibilities, trade opportunities, entitlements vis-à-vis the State, and other methods of acquiring food' (Sen 1981: 45). However, access to what a person may legitimately or legally be entitled to is often mediated by political economy considerations. In seeking to incorporate these considerations, Appadurai (1984) introduces the notion of enfranchisement, which he defines as 'the degree to which an individual or group can legitimately participate in decisions of a given society about entitlements'. He suggests that command over food during famine, for instance, would depend not only on entitlements but also on enfranchisement:

In the patterns of victimisation during the Bengal famine of 1943–44 we see those who are enfranchised—the controlling classes, the male heads of households in general—deciding to withhold the entitlement rights of dependents, women and children. Entitlement without enfranchisement, the fate of rural clients, women, children, slaves and household pets in many societies, is not a safe condition when famine sets in.

He argues that over the last century the rural poor in South Asia have traded a situation in which they were entitled (to receive help from village patrons, for instance) without being enfranchised, for one in which they are partly enfranchised (through the spread of universal franchise and mobilization of the poor by political parties) without being securely entitled.

One might, however, argue that the mere participation in the process of decision-making about entitlement (that is, enfranchisement), is not yet sufficient to guarantee entitlement. Here adding the concept of empowerment could take us a step further. This term has been used variously in recent years by several social action groups in India, and in the present context may be

---

[83] It is necessary to distinguish between different political parties in this respect—especially in terms of the extent to which they incorporate the concerns of the poor in their political agendas.

defined as the ability of an individual or group legitimately to ensure that decisions relating to entitlement are taken in its favour (be it within the family, or of the family *vis-à-vis* the community or the State).

The Nepalese example may be recalled here of the effectiveness of group pressure from the poorer families in the village in getting credit and grain, and in maintaining wage rates and many of the traditional elements of patron–client support through a severe drought. However, it is the experience of grass-roots organizing in South Asia which has significant lessons to offer on this count. Group organizing has been one of the crucial means of empowering the vulnerable sections—the poor, the low caste, the women—not only the better to enforce their legal entitlements within the community and family, but also to expand the scope of these legal entitlements through agitating for changes in the laws themselves.[84]

A review of the nature, experience, and effectiveness of these groups— which vary considerably in their issue-focus, organizational form, and political outlook—is not attempted here; but for illustrative purposes some features of selected groups providing credit to the rural poor are worth highlighting, especially since credit has received a considerable emphasis in State policies on poverty alleviation, but very little success in reaching the poorest,[85] and is seen to play an important role in the family's coping mechanisms.

One such initiative is that of the Grameen Bank of Bangladesh launched as an experiment by an individual in 1976 and, after its proven success, institutionalized by the Bangladesh government in 1983 as a specialized credit agency for the rural poor.[86] Today it has 250 branches in five districts, and a membership of 200,000 in 3,700 villages. Among its noteworthy features are the following: first, its clientele is essentially class-homogenous—it caters exclusively to the landless and those owning 0.5 acres or less of land. Second, it follows a group approach to loan disbursement: borrowers must form groups of five persons each, each group selecting its own chairperson and secretary and holding weekly meetings. While loans are given to individuals there is an implicit group pressure and responsibility for repayment.[87] Third, the loans are given without collateral, for any viable income-earning activity of an individual's choice, as well as for joint enterprises such as leasing in land for joint cultivation, investment in shallow tube-wells, and so on. Fourth, it recognizes the especially vulnerable position of women within the family, and

---

[84] See especially Dhagamvar (1987), and various issues of the *Lawyers' Collective* (Bombay).

[85] See especially the recent literature criticizing the government's IRDP programme, including Copestake (1987), Hirway (1985), Rao and Erappa (1987), Drèze (1988a), and Chap. 7 below.

[86] For details see especially Siddiqui (1984), Chandler (1986), and Hossain (1988).

[87] In contrast, the government's IRDP loan subsidy scheme for the rural poor in India targets at individual families (GOI 1987). If the husband defaults, the wife is refused a loan. However, as a subscheme of the IRDP, a pilot project DWCRA (Development of Women and Children in the Rural Areas) has been initiated in 1983 in 50 districts to try out the group approach for loan disbursement to women.

seeks to draw them in as members—the credit operation for women being entirely independent of the transactions with male borrowers and needing no mediation by husbands or male relatives. Fifth, the concept of empowerment by collective activity and solidarity is emphasized in meetings and in special training programmes. Sixth, repayment is made easy by enabling loans to be repaid in weekly instalments at a meeting in the village itself to which the bank worker comes for this purpose. This is especially helpful to women borrowers in a purdah society. Seventh, built into the system are various social-security schemes such as a group savings fund set up primarily to advance consumption loans; an emergency insurance fund against default, accident, and deaths; and various other schemes such as for house-loans, and so on. Eighth, to ensure that bank ownership stays with the members, each member has compulsorily to buy shares in the bank.

Since its inception there have been several evaluations of the Grameen Bank[88] which indicate first of all that the credit indeed reaches the target group, spill-overs being minimal.[89] Second, the loan recovery rate is about 97–99 per cent. Third, per-capita income per borrowing household has increased significantly.[90] Fourth, the borrowing households have been able to build up some capital assets and also improve their consumption. Fifth, the bank has improved the bargaining power of the families *vis-à-vis* the landlords, enabling them to raise their wages.[91] Sixth, women have been significant gainers: by recent figures they constitute 70 per cent of the borrowers, receive 55 per cent of the cumulative disbursement, and are considered by the Bank to be better credit risks (their repayment record is better), with a higher sense of social responsibility and making a more productive use of the loan than the men (women divert a smaller percentage of the loan to consumption). It is also noteworthy that most of the female borrowers manage the loans themselves (despite pressure from husbands),[92] in general presenting a very different face from Greenough's 'acquiescing victims'. As a result of the investments, their incomes have increased multifold, especially since most of them were un-employed prior to taking the loans.[93] Their standing within the family is also noted to have improved:

[88] Ahmed (1985); Hossain (1984, 1988); Siddiqui (1984); R. Rahman (1986); A. Rahman (1986); Chandler (1986).

[89] In 1984, 86% of the borrowers were the landless, only 5.6% were found to be owning more than the specified 0.5 acres, and 1.7% had over 1 acre.

[90] By one estimate the increase was on average 32% over 2 years (1980–2) after taking the loan, during which period the per-capita income of Bangladesh increased only by 2.6% (Hossain 1984).

[91] In some areas the increases are estimated to be as high as 25% (Yunus 1982).

[92] By R. Rahman's (1986) evaluation of the scheme in 5 villages, of the female borrowers, 77.4% kept 75% of the loans under their own management, and only 12% surrendered the entire loan sum to the male head of household.

[93] The average income of female borrowers (who invest mainly in milch cattle, paddy-processing, beef-fattening, and oil-pressing), in R. Rahman's (1986) evaluation, was 5,140 Taka (constituting 33% of the household income) while that of a non-borrowing housewife in the target

its membership and access to institutional credit also means an access to some fixed assets and it endows those women with a special status within the family. Other family members become more conscious about the comfort and well being of the loanee women (Rahman 1986).

Another study found a significant reduction in verbal and physical abuse and threats of divorce by husbands since their wives joined the Bank (Ahmed 1985). Problems of replicability, of expanding the Bank's geographic coverage without reducing efficiency in functioning, and of sustaining noted income increases over time, of course, remain.

An equally important example, in the Indian context, is that of SEWA (the Self Employed Women's Association, started in 1972 in Ahmedabad city and since spread to several other cities and the rural areas of Gujarat), which focuses on the economic livelihood needs of poor women, through credit and other means.[94] First of all, for providing credit it has set up its own co-operative bank mainly drawing on member deposits. Loans are advanced not only for production purposes without collateral but also for consumption needs, and for redeeming any assets such as jewellery or land that women may have had to mortgage to the money-lender. Large consumption loans are also given against jewellery as collateral. A fixed savings deposit scheme protects their savings from pressures for withdrawal from family members. Second, the association functions as a union for women in various trades, each trade organized into a group composed of anything up to 100 or more members, with group leaders elected from among them. Third, also like the Grameen Bank, SEWA operates a variety of social-security schemes including a group-based insurance fund, widowhood insurance, life insurance, maternal protection, and so on. Fourth, specifically in the rural areas, in order to reduce the burden of seasonal unemployment among women agricultural labourers (employment is available only for three months during the year in the area) and to increase their bargaining power *vis-à-vis* the employers, diversification of incomes is being promoted by reviving traditional crafts such as weaving, pottery, and so on, through craft co-operatives (and training), and through dairy co-operatives —a link being forged for this purpose with the National Dairy Development Board and the IRDP programme of the government. Like the Grameen Bank, SEWA too appears to have been successful in raising incomes (although there are no studies quantifying the exact income benefits), strengthening women's position within the family, raising consciousness about the advantages of group solidarity, and, for the rural women agricultural workers, raising agricultural wages by strengthening their bargaining power *vis-à-vis* the employers.

group of the project village was 92 Taka. Twenty-two per cent of the female borrowers contributed 50% or more of the family income, and some 30% earned 6,000 Taka per year, sufficient (according to Rahman) to maintain two persons above the officially specified poverty line.

[94] Description based on Sebstad (1982) and conversations with Ela Bhatt (who initiated SEWA).

The Working Women's Forum in South India,[95] which has much in common with SEWA, again caters exclusively for poor women, loans being given to groups, with the additional feature that while the loans are in individual names there is group liability,[96] and the elected group leader has to personally guarantee repayment.

Group-financed insurance schemes against food troughs are in fact a feature of several social-action initiatives. For instance, the Bhoomi Sena Movement of tribals in Maharashtra, as part of its struggle for higher wages, minimum wage implementation, and access to land, set up a grain bank on the basis of crops threshed collectively and stored for the next season, as an insurance against seasonal fluctuations and harvest failures. In addition, a fund was set up to provide loans to small farmers for bullocks, seed, and consumption needs (Silva et al. 1979).

All these are also potentially effective substitutes for the declining traditional arrangements based on feudal patronage and exploitation; and, where group ventures are undertaken, they offer the potential advantages and economies of labour deployment and team work that joint families are noted to have in the Maclachlan example. A more detailed review and evaluation of such initiatives from the point of view of social security for the poor, and a comparison with existing State attempts at providing similar services, are clearly needed. Equally useful would be a systematic review of the effectiveness of initiatives that have sought to provide direct relief against seasonality[97] and droughts;[98] as well as of those which are explicitly agitational in nature, and which would include many groups and regional movements fighting for the enforcement of minimum wages, for a right to the land they have been tilling for generations, for the protection of forests and the environment, and working against intra-family inequalities and violence.[99]

Here it would suffice to note that underlying these and many like ventures (be they those providing services such as credit, or those with more explicitly political overtones) is a recognition that the effective implementation of existing State laws, programmes, and even relief measures, can be contingent

[95] See especially Noponen (1987); and Kalpagam (1987).

[96] A pilot project launched under the Small Farmer's Development Programme in Nepal followed a similar procedure of individual loans and group liability with considerable success (PIDT 1982).

[97] See Marum (1981) for an evaluation of several food-for-work programmes for women, initiated by non-governmental organizations in Bangladesh to deal with seasonal troughs in employment.

[98] Several such initiatives sprung up during the 1987–8 drought in various parts of India for fodder distribution, well digging, etc.

[99] For a brief review of the women-related initiatives see Agarwal (1989); on ecology movements see Shiva (1988); for an overview of these and other movements and initiatives see Sethi (1987); also various articles in the *Lokayan Bulletin* (Delhi) over the past two years.

on group initiative and pressure from below; and that the group needs to be economically and often also socially (by caste, gender) homogeneous.[100]

It is difficult to say whether these ventures, by providing women with an alternative to the family for survival and so improving their fall-back position, will in the long run weaken the family as a unit or strengthen it. But either way, they offer the possibility of more egalitarian intrafamily gender relations.

---

[100] Social and economic homogeneity is typically found to be important in ensuring the successful functioning of such initiatives. See Dixon-Mueller (1979); PIDT (1982); and Wade (1987) whose examples of successful collective action by villagers for regulating the use of common property resources are of special interest in the present context.

References

Agarwal, B. (1984), 'Rural Women and the HYV Rice Technology', *Economic and Political Weekly*, 31 Mar.

——(1986*a*), *Cold Hearths and Barren Slopes: The Wood fuel Crisis in the Third World*. Delhi: Allied Publishers; London: Zed Books, Maryland: Riverdale Press.

——(1986*b*), 'Women, Poverty and Agricultural Growth in India', *Journal of Peasant Studies*, 13.

——(1988), 'Who Sows? Who Reaps? Women and Land Rights in India', *Journal of Peasant Studies*, 15.

——(1989), 'Rural Women, Poverty and Natural Resources: Sustenance, Sustainability and Struggle for Change', *Economic and Political Weekly*, 28 Oct.

Ahmed, M. (1985), *Status, Perception, Awareness and Marital Adjustment of Rural Women: The Role of Grameen Bank*. Dhaka: Grameen Bank Publication.

Alamgir, M. (1980), *Famine in South Asia: Political Economy of Mass Starvation*. Cambridge, Mass: Oelgeschlager and Hain Publishers.

Appadurai, A. (1984), 'How Moral is South Asia's Economy? A Review Article', *Journal of Asian Studies*, 43.

Banerjee, N. (1988), 'Women's Work and Family Strategies: A Case Study from Bankura, West Bengal', mimeo, Centre for Women's Development Studies, New Delhi.

Bardhan, K. (1977), 'Rural Employment, Wages and Labour Markets in India: A Survey of Research', *Economic and Political Weekly*, 25 June, 2 July, 9 July.

Bardhan, P. (1983), 'On Life and Death Questions: Poverty and Child Mortality' in P. Bardhan, *Land, Labour and Rural Poverty: Essays in Development Economics*. Delhi: Oxford University Press.

——and Rudra, A. (1981), 'Terms and Conditions of Labour Contracts: Results of a Survey in West Bengal, 1979', *Oxford Bulletin of Economics and Statistics*, 43.

Behrman, J. R. (1986), 'Intrahousehold Allocation of Nutrients in Rural India: Are Boys Favoured? Do Parents Exhibit Inequality Aversion?' mimeo, Center for Analysis of Developing Economies, University of Pennsylvania.

Bhalla, S. (1977), 'New Relations of Production in Haryana Agriculture', *Economic and Political Weekly*, Review of Agriculture, 27 Mar.

Binswanger, H. P., and Rosenzweig, M. R. (1986), 'Credit Markets, Wealth and Endowments in Rural South India', paper presented at the VIIIth World Congress of the International Economic Association, New Delhi, 1–5 Dec.

Bliss, C., and Stern, N. (1982), *Palanpur: The Economy of an Indian Village*. Oxford: Oxford University Press.

Borkar, V. V., and Nadkarni, V. (1975), *Impact of Drought on Rural Life*. Bombay: Popular Prakashan.

Boulding, E. (1976), *The Underside of History: A View of Women Through Time*. Boulder, Colo.: Westview.

Brara, R. (1987), 'Shifting Sands: A Study of Rights in Common Pastures', mimeo, Institute of Development Studies, Jaipur.

Breman, J. (1979*a*), 'Seasonal Migration and Cooperative Capitalism: The Crushing of Cane and Labour by the Sugar Factories of Bardoli, South Gujarat', paper presented at the ADC-ICRISAT Conference on Adjustment Mechanisms of Rural Labour Markets in Developing Areas, ICRISAT, Hyderabad, 22–4 Aug.

——(1979b), *Patronage and Exploitation: Changing Agrarian Relations in South Gujarat.* Delhi: Manohar Publications.

——(1985), *Of Peasants, Migrants and Paupers: Rural Labour Circulation and Capitalist Production in West India.* Delhi: Oxford University Press.

Briscoe, J. (1979), 'Energy Use and Social Structure in a Bangladesh Village', *Population and Development Review*, 5.

Brown, K., Black, R. E., and Becker, S. (1982), 'Seasonal Changes in Nutritional Status and the Prevalence of Malnutrition in a Longitudinal Study of Young Children in Rural Bangladesh', *Abstract in American Journal of Clinical Nutrition*, 36.

Burling, R. (1963), *Rengsanggri: Family and Kinship in a Garo Village.* Philadelphia: University of Pennsylvania Press.

Cain, M. T., Khanam, S. R., and Nahar, S. (1979), 'Class, Patriarchy and the Structure of Women's Work in Rural Bangladesh', Working Paper No. 4, Center for Population Studies, The Population Council, New York.

Caldwell, J. C., Reddy, P. H. and Caldwell, P. (1984), 'The Determinants of Family Structure in Rural South India', *Journal of Marriage and the Family*, Feb.

——(1986), 'Periodic High Risk as a Cause of Fertility Decline in a Changing Rural Environment: Survival Strategies in the 1980–1983 South Indian Drought', *Economic Development and Cultural Change*, 34.

Campbell, D. J., and Trechter, D. D. (1982), 'Strategies for Coping with Food Consumption Shortage in the Mandara Mountains Region of North Cameroon', *Social Science and Medicine*, 16.

Chambers, R. (1981), 'Introduction', in Chambers *et al.* (1981a).

——Longhurst, R., and Pacey, A. (eds.) (1981a), *Seasonal Dimensions of Rural Poverty.* London: Frances Pinter.

——(1981b), 'Seasonality in Rural Experience', in Chambers *et al.* (1981a).

Chandler, A. F. D. (1986), *Participation as Process: What We Can Learn from Grameen Bank, Bangladesh.* Oslo: NORAD.

Chattopadhyaya, K. P., and Mukherjee, R. K. (1946), *A Plan for Rehabilitation.* Calcutta: Statistical Publishing House.

Chaudhury, A., Huffman, S. L., and Chen, L. C. (1981), 'Agriculture and Nutrition in Matlab Thana, Bangladesh', in Chambers *et al.* (1981a).

Chen, M. (1987), 'Update on Drought Situation in Devdholera Village', mimeo, Harvard Institute for International Development, Harvard University.

——(1988), 'Women and Household Livelihood Systems', mimeo, Harvard Institute for International Development, Harvard University.

Chinnappa, B. N., and Silva, W. P. T. (1977), 'Impact of the Cultivation of High-Yielding Varieties of Paddy on Employment', in B. H. Farmer (ed.), *Green Revolution?* (London: Macmillan).

Chowdhury, K. M., and Bapat, M. T. (1975), 'A Study of Impact of Famine and Relief Measures in Gujarat and Rajasthan', Research Study No. 44, Agro-Economic Research Centre, Sardar Patel University, Ahmedabad.

Clay, E. (1981), 'Seasonal Patterns of Agricultural Employment in Bangladesh', in Chambers *et al.* (1981a).

Commander, S. (1983), 'The Jajmani System in North India: An Examination of its Logic and Status Across Two Centuries', *Modern Asian Studies*, 17.

Connell, J., and Lipton, M. (1977), *Assessing Village Labour Situations in Developing Countries*. Delhi: Oxford University Press.

——Dasgupta, B., Laishley, R., and Lipton, M. (1976), *Migration from Rural Areas: The Evidence from Village Studies*. Delhi: Oxford University Press.

Copestake, J. (1987), 'Loans for Livelihood? Government Sponsored Credit Schemes in India: Proposals for Reform', mimeo, Department of Agricultural Economics and Management, University of Reading.

CSE (Centre for Science and Environment) (1985–6), *The State of India's Environment: A Citizen's Report*. Delhi: Centre for Science and Environment.

Currey, B. (1978), 'Famine Symposium Report: The Famine Syndrome, Its Definition for Relief and Rehabilitation in Bangladesh', *Ecology of Food and Nutrition*, 7.

Dandekar, K. (1983), *Employment Guarantee Scheme: An Employment Opportunity for Women*. Pune: Orient Longman.

Dasgupta, B., Laishley, R., Lucas, H., and Mitchell, B. (1977), *Village Society and Labour Use*. Delhi: Oxford University Press.

Dasgupta, M. (1987), 'Informal Security Mechanisms and Population Retention in Rural India', *Economic Development and Cultural Change*, July.

Dasgupta, S., and Maiti, A. K. (1987), 'The Rural Energy Crisis, Poverty and Women's Roles in Five Indian Villages', Technical Co-operation Report, World Employment Programme, International Labour Organization, Geneva.

Desai, G. M., Singh, G., and Sah, D. C. (1979), 'Impact of Scarcity of Farm Economy and Significance of Relief Operations', CMA Monograph No. 84, Indian Institute of Management, Ahmedabad.

Desai, R. X. (1982), 'Migrant Labour and Women: The Case of Ratnagiri', World Employment Programme Research Working Paper No. WEP 10/WP28, International Labour Organization, Geneva.

Deshpande, V. (1982), *Employment Guarantee Scheme: Impact on Poverty and Bondage among Tribals*. Pune: Tilak Maharashtra Vidyapeeth.

Dhagamvar, V. (1987), 'The Disadvantaged and the Law', paper presented at a Workshop on Poverty in India, Queen Elizabeth House, Oxford, Oct.

Dirks, R. (1980), 'Social Responses during Severe Food Shortages and Famine', *Current Anthropology*, 21.

Dixon-Mueller, R. (1979), *Rural Women at Work: Strategies for Development in South Asia*. Baltimore: Johns Hopkins University Press.

Drèze, J. (1988a), 'Social Insecurity in India: A Case Study', paper presented at STICERD/WIDER Workshop on Social Security in Developing Countries, London School of Economics, July 1988.

——(1988b), 'Famine Prevention in India', Discussion Paper No. 3, Development Economics Research Programme, London School of Economics; to be published in J. P. Drèze and A. K. Sen (eds.) (1990), *The Political Economy of Hunger*. Oxford: Oxford University Press.

——and Mukherjee, A. (1987), 'Labour Contracts in Rural India: Theories and Evidence', Discussion Paper No. 7, Development Economics Research Programme, London School of Economics.

——and Sen, A. (1989), *Hunger and Public Action*. Oxford: Clarendon Press.

Epstein, S. (1967), 'Productive Efficiency and Customary Systems of Rewards in Rural South India', in R. Firth (ed.), *Themes in Economic Anthropology*. London: Tavistock Publications.

Fernandes, W., and Menon, G. (1987), *Tribal Women and Forest Economy: Deforestation, Exploitation and Status Change*. Delhi: Indian Social Institute.

——— (1988), *Forests, Environment and Tribal Economy: Deforestation, Exploitation and Status Change*. Delhi: Indian Social Institute.

Food and Nutrition (1985), 'Special Issue on Minor Crops, Seasonality, Women's Activities: Three Crucial Issues in Rural Food Production and Consumption', 11/2.

Gaiha, R. (1988), 'Are the Chronically Poor also the Poorest in Rural India', mimeo, Faculty of Management Studies, University of Delhi.

Gangrade, K. D. and Dhadda, S. (1973), *Challenge and Responses: A Study of Famines in India*. Delhi: Rachana Publications.

George, S. (1988), 'The Female of the Species: Women and Dairying in India', paper presented at a Workshop on Women in Agriculture, Centre for Development Studies, Trivandrum, 15–17 Feb.

Ghodake, R. D., Ryan, J. G., and Sarin, R. (1978), 'Human Labour Use in Existing and Prospective Technologies of the Semi-Arid Tropics of Peninsular India', Progress Report, Economics Program-1, ICRISAT, Hyderabad.

Ghose, A. K. (1979), 'Short-term Changes in Income Distribution in Poor Agrarian Economies: A Study of Famines with Reference to the Indian Sub-Continent', World Employment Programme Research Working Paper, WEP 10-6/WP28.

GOI (Government of India) (1945), *Famine Enquiry Commission Report on Bengal*. Delhi: Government of India Press.

—— (1979), 'Rural Labour Enquiry 1974–1975, Final Report on Wages and Earnings of Rural Labour Households', Chandigarh: Labour Bureau, Ministry of Labour.

—— (1981), 'Rural Labour Enquiry 1974–75, Final Report on Employment and Unemployment of Rural Labour Households', Chandigarh: Labour Bureau, Ministry of Labour.

—— (1982), *Report of Committee on Forests and Tribals in India*. Ministry of Home Affairs.

—— (1987), *Integrated Rural Development Programme and Allied Programme of Training of Rural Youth for Self-Employment (TRYSEM) and Development of Women and Children in Rural Areas (DWCRA): A Manual*. Delhi: Dept. of Rural Development, Ministry of Agriculture, Government of India.

Greenough, P. R. (1982), *Prosperity and Misery in Modern Bengal: The Famine of 1943–1944*. Oxford: Oxford University Press.

Guhan, S. (1981), 'Social Security: Lessons and Possibilities from the Tamil Nadu Experience', Madras Institute of Development Studies Bulletin, 11.

Gulati, L. (1978), 'Profile of a Female Agricultural Labourer', *Economic and Political Weekly*, Review of Agriculture, 25 Mar.

Harriss, B. (1986), 'The Intra-Family Distribution of Hunger in South Asia', paper presented at a Conference on Food Strategies held at WIDER, Helsinki, July 1986; to be published in J. P. Drèze and A. K. Sen (eds.) (1990), *The Political Economy of Hunger*. Oxford: Clarendon.

Harriss, J. (1977), 'Implications of Changes in Agriculture for Social Relations at the

Village Level: The Case of Randam', in B. H. Farmer (ed.), *Green Revolution?* London: Macmillan.

Hill, P. (1980), 'Joint Families in Rural Karnataka, India', *Modern Asian Studies*, 14.

Hirway, I. (1985), 'Garibi Hatao: Can IRDP Do It? A Discussion', *Economic and Political Weekly*, 30 Mar.

Hossain, M. (1984), 'Credit for the Rural Poor: The Experience of Grameen Bank in Bangladesh', mimeo, Bangladesh Institute of Development Studies.

——(1987), *The Assault that Failed: A Profile of Absolute Poverty in Six Villages of Bangladesh*. Geneva: UNRISD.

——(1988), 'Credit for Alleviation of Poverty: The Grameen Bank of Bangladesh', Research Report No. 65, International Food Policy Research Institute, Washington, DC.

IDS Bulletin (1986), 'Seasonality and Poverty', 17/3.

Jansen, E. G. (1986), *Rural Bangladesh: Competition for Scarce Resources*. Oslo: Norwegian University Press.

Jetly, S. (1987), 'Impact of Male Migration on Rural Females', *Economic and Political Weekly*, 22/44.

Jodha, N. S. (1975), 'Famine and Famine Policies: Some Empirical Evidence', *Economic and Political Weekly*, 10/41.

——(1978), 'Effectiveness of Farmer's Adjustment to Risk', *Economic and Political Weekly*, 13/25.

——(1979), 'Intercropping in Traditional Farming Systems', Progress Report 3, Economics Programme, ICRISAT.

——(1981), 'Role of Credit in Farmers' Adjustment Against Risk in Arid and Semi-Arid Tropical Areas of India', *Economic and Political Weekly*, 15/42–3.

——(1983), 'Market Forces and Erosion of Common Property Resources', paper presented at the International Workshop on Agricultural Markets in the Semi-Arid Tropics, ICRISAT, Andhra Pradesh, October.

——(1985a), 'Population Growth and the Decline of Common Property Resources in Rajasthan', *Population and Development Review*, 11.

——(1985b), 'Social Research on Rural Change: Some Gaps', paper presented at the Conference on Rural Economic Change in South Asia: Differences in Approach and in Results between Large Scale Surveys and Intensive Micro-Studies, Bangalore, 5–8 Aug.

——(1986), 'Common Property Resources and Rural Poor', *Economic and Political Weekly*, 5 July.

Kalpagam, U. (1987), 'Working Women's Forum: A Concept and an Experiment in Mobilisation in the Third World', Offprint 6, Madras Institute of Development Studies.

Kapadia, K. M. (1966), *Marriage and Family in India*. London: Oxford University Press.

Kar, P. C. (1982), *The Garos in Transition*. New Delhi: Cosmo Publications.

KFRI (Kerala Forest Research Institute) (1980), *Studies on the Changing Pattern of Man-Forest Interactions and Its Implications for Ecology and Management*. Trivandrum: Kerala Forest Research Institute.

Kolenda, P. (1987), *Regional Differences in Family Structures in India*. Jaipur: Rawat Publications.

Kulkarni, S. W. (1974), *Survey of Famine Affected Sinnar Taluka*. Poona: Gokhale Institute of Politics and Economics.

Kulkarni, S. (1983), 'Towards a Social Forestry Policy', *Economic and Political Weekly*, 6 Feb.

Kumar, B. G. (1987), 'Poverty and Public Policy: Government Intervention and Levels of Living in Kerala, India', unpublished Ph.D. thesis, University of Oxford.

Kumar, G., and Stewart, F. (1987), 'Tackling Malnutrition: What Can Targeted Nutritional Interventions Achieve?', paper presented at a Workshop on Poverty in India, Queen Elizabeth House, Oxford, Oct.

Kumar, S. K. (1978), 'Role of the Household Economy in Child Nutrition at Low Incomes', Occasional Paper No. 95, Dept. of Agricultural Economics, Cornell University.

Kynch, J., and Maguire, M. (1988), 'Wasted Cultivators and Stunted Girls: Variations in Nutritional Status in a North Indian Village', mimeo, Institute of Economics and Statistics, Oxford.

Leslie, J. (1988), 'Women's Work and Child Nutrition in the Third World', *World Development*, 16.

Lewis, O. (1958), *Village Life in Northern India: Studies in a Delhi Village*. Urbana: University of Illinois Press.

Lipton, M. (1983a), 'Labour and Poverty', World Bank Staff Working Paper No. 616, The World Bank, Washington, DC.

——(1983b), 'Poverty, Undernutrition and Hunger', World Bank Staff Working Paper No. 597, The World Bank, Washington, DC.

Longhurst, R., and Payne, P. (1981), 'Seasonal Aspects of Nutrition', in Chambers *et al.* (1981a).

McAlpin, M. (1983), *Subject to Famine: Food Crisis and Economic Change in Western India, 1860–1920*. Princeton, NJ: Princeton University Press.

Maclachlan, M. D. (1983), *Why They Did Not Starve: Biocultural Adaptation in a South Indian Village*. Philadelphia: Institute for the Study of Human Issues.

Madan, T. N. (1975), 'Structural Implications of Marriage in North India: Wife-givers and Wife-takers Among the Pandits of Kashmir', *Contributions to Indian Sociology*, 9.

Mahalanobis, P. C., Mukherjee, R., and Ghosh, A. (1946), *A Sample Survey of After-Effects of the Bengal Famine of 1943*. Calcutta: Statistical Publishing Society.

Majumdar, D. N. (1978), *Culture Change in Two Garo Villages*. Calcutta: Anthropological Survey of India.

Marum, E. M. (1981), *Women at Work in Bangladesh*. Dhaka: BRAC.

Mencher, J. (1987), 'Women's Work and Poverty: Women's Contribution to Household Maintenance in Two Regions of South India', in D. Dwyer and J. Bruce (eds.), *A Home Divided: Women and Income Control in the Third World*. Stanford: Stanford University Press.

—— and Saradamoni, K. (1982), 'Muddy Feet and Dirty Hands: Rice Production and Female Agricultural Labour', *Economic and Political Weekly*, Review of Agriculture, 25 Dec.

Mies, M. (1983), 'Landless Women Organise: A Case Study of an Organisation in Rural Andhra', *Manushi*, 3.

Miller, B. (1981), *The Endangered Sex: Neglect of Female Children in Rural North India*. Ithaca, NY: Cornell University Press.

Minturn, L., and Hitchcock, I. T. T. (1966), *Rajputs of Khalapur*. New York: John Wiley & Sons.

Mitra, M. (1985), 'Women and Work in the Livestock Economy: An Introduction', in *Women in Dairying: A Set of Case Studies and Recommendations*. Delhi: Ford Foundation.

——(1988), 'Women's Work and Household Survival Strategies: A Case Study of Santal Women's Lives and Work', draft, Centre for Women's Development Studies, Delhi.

Montgomery, E. (1977), 'Social Structuring of Nutrition in Southern India', in L. Green (ed.), *Malnutrition, Behaviour and Social Organisation*. New York: Academic Press.

Morris, D. M. (1974), 'What is a Famine?' *Economic and Political Weekly*, 2 Nov.

——(1975), 'Needed: A New Famine Policy', *Economic and Political Weekly*, 10/5–7.

Mundle, S. (1979), *Backwardness and Bondage: Agrarian Relations in a South Bihar District*. Delhi: Indian Institute of Public Administration.

Nath, J. (1979), 'The Role of Women in Rural Bangladesh: A Study of Nantupur Village', in *Women for Women: Situation of Women in Bangladesh*. Dhaka: BRAC.

NCAER (National Council of Applied Economic Research) (1981), *Report on Rural Energy Consumption in Northern India*, Environment Research Committee. Delhi: National Council of Applied Economic Research.

Noponen, H. (1987), 'Organising Petty Traders and Home-Based Producers: A Case Study of Women's Forum, India', in A. M. Singh and A. Kelles-Vittamen (eds.), *Invisible Hands*. Delhi: Sage.

Osmani, S. R. (1987), 'Controversies in Nutrition and their Implications for the Economics of Food', Working Paper No. 16, WIDER; to be published in J. P. Drèze and A. K. Sen (eds.) (1990), *The Political Economy of Hunger*. Oxford: Clarendon.

Oughton, L. (1982), 'The Maharashtra Droughts of 1970–73: An Analysis of Scarcity', *Oxford Bulletin of Economics and Statistics*, 44.

Patel, V., Indu, R., and Patel, V. P. (1975), 'Employment in Rural Gujarat: A Study of Four Villages in Anand Taluka, 1970–1971', Agricultural Economics Research Centre, Sardar Patel University, Vallabh Vidyanagar.

Patil, S. (1978), 'Famine Conditions in Maharashtra: A Survey of Sakri Taluka', *Economic and Political Weekly*, 28 July.

PIDT (People's Institute for Development and Training) (1982), *Towards Participation: Case Studies of Small Farmers Development Programme Nepal*. New Delhi: People's Institute for Development and Training.

Pingle, V. (1975), 'Some Studies of Two Tribal Groups of Central India. Part 2: Importance of Foods Consumed in Two Different Seasons', *Plant Food for Man*, 1.

Prindle, P. H. (1979), 'Peasant Society and Famines: A Nepalese Example', *Ethnology*, 1.

Rahman, A. (1986), 'Impact of Grameen Bank Intervention on the Rural Power Structure', Working Paper No. 2, Grameen Bank Evaluation Project, Bangladesh Institute of Development Studies, Dhaka.

Rahaman, M. M. (1981), 'The Causes and Effects of Famine on the Rural Population, A Report from Bangladesh', in J. R. K. Robson, (ed.), *Famine: Its Causes, Effects and Management*. New York: Gordon & Breach.

Rahman, R. I. (1986), 'Impact of Grameen Bank on the Situation of Poor Rural Women', Working Paper No. 1, Grameen Bank Evaluation Project, Bangladesh Institute of Development Studies, Dacca.

Rajgopalan, S., Kymal, P. H., and Pu-ai, P. (1981), 'Births, Work and Nutrition in Tamil Nadu, India', in R. Chambers *et al.* (1981*a*).

Randhawa, M. S. (1980), *A History of Agriculture in India*. Delhi: Indian Council of Agricultural Research.

Rangaswami, A. (1985), 'Women's Roles and Strategies during Food Crisis and Famines', International Workshop on Women's Roles in Food Self-sufficiency and Food Strategies, 14–19 Jan., ORSTOM, Paris.

Rao, N. V. K. (1974), 'Impact of Drought on the Social System of a Telengana Village', *Eastern Anthropologist*, 27.

Rao, V. M., and Erappa, S. (1987), 'IRDP and Rural Diversification: A Study in Karnataka', *Economic and Political Weekly*, Dec.

Reddy, G. P. (1988), 'Drought and Famine: The Story of a Village in a Semi-arid Region of Andhra Pradesh', paper presented at a Workshop on Afro-Asian Studies on Social Systems and Food Crisis, India International Centre, 26–9 Mar.

Rosenzweig, M. R. and Schultz, T. P. (1982), 'Market Opportunities, Genetic Endowment and Intrafamily Resource Distribution: Child Survival in Rural India', Center paper No. 323, Economic Growth Center, Yale University.

Rudra, A. (1982), 'Extra-Economic Constraints on Agricultural Labour: Results of An Intensive Survey of Some Villages Near Shantiniketan, West Bengal', Asian Employment Programme Working Paper, ARTEP, ILO, Bangkok.

Ryan, J. G., and Ghodake, R. D. (1980), 'Labour Market Behaviour in Rural Villages in South India: Effects of Season, Sex and Socio-economic Status', Progress Report, Economic Programme 14, ICRISAT.

——Bidinger, P. D., Rao, N. P., and Pushmpamma, P. (1984), 'The Determinants of Individual Diets and Nutritional Status in Six Villages of Southern India', Research Bulletin No. 7, ICRISAT, Hyderabad.

——and Wallace, T. D. (1985), 'Determinants of Labour Market Wages, Participation and Supply in Rural South India', Progress Report 73, Economics Group, Resource Management Program, ICRISAT, Hyderabad.

Salva, C. (1973), 'Some Aspects of Out-Migration from Gujarat', Ph.D. thesis, Bombay University.

Scott, J. C. (1976), *The Moral Economy of the Peasant: Rebellion and Subsistence in Southeast Asia*. New Haven, Conn.: Yale University Press.

Sebstad, J. (1982), 'Struggle and Development Among Self-Employed Women: A Report on the Self-Employed Women's Association, Ahmedabad', Report submitted to USAID, Washington, DC.

Sen, A. K. (1981), *Poverty and Famines: An Essay on Entitlement and Deprivation*. Delhi: Oxford University Press.

——(1982), 'Food Battles: Conflicts in the Access to Food', Coromandel Lecture No. 1, New Delhi, 13 Dec.

——(1983), 'Economics and the Family', *Asian Development Review*, 1.

——(1984), *Resources, Values and Development*. Delhi: Oxford University Press.

——(1987), 'Gender and Cooperative Conflicts', mimeo, Department of Economics, Harvard University.

Sen, A. K., and Sengupta, S. (1983), 'Malnutrition of Rural Children and the Sex Bias', *Economic and Political Weekly*, 19, Annual Number.

Sen, I. (1988), 'Class and Gender in Work Time Allocation', *Economic and Political Weekly*, 13 Aug.

Sethi, H. (1987), 'Refocusing Praxis', Report of the UNU/UNDP Interaction Programme of Senior Activists/Researchers in South Asia, held in collaboration with PIDA, Sri Lanka, and SETU, Lokayan, Delhi.

Shah, A. B. (1973), *The Household Dimension of the Family in India*. Delhi: Orient Longman.

Sharma, U. (1980), *Women, Work and Property in North-West India*. London: Tavistock Publications.

Shiva, V. (1988), *Staying Alive: Women, Ecology and Survival in India*. Delhi: Kali for Women.

Siddiqui, K. (1984), *An Evaluation of the Grameen Bank*. Dhaka: Grameen Bank Publication.

Singh, K. S. (1975), *The Indian Famine 1967: A Study in Crisis and Change*. Delhi: People's Publishing House.

Silva, G. V. S., Mehta, N., Rahman, M. A., and Wignaraja, P. (1979), 'Bhoomi Sena: A Struggle for People's Power', *Development Dialogue*, 2.

Srivastava, R. (1977), 'Shifting Cultivation in India', *Man in India*, 57.

Torry, W. I. (1987), 'Evolution of Food Rationing Systems with Reference to African Group Farms in the Context of Drought', in M. H. Glantz (ed.), *Drought and Hunger in Africa*. Cambridge: Cambridge University Press.

Vatuk, S. (1981), 'Sharing, Giving and Exchanging of Foods in South Asian Societies', mimeo, final draft, University of Illinois at Chicago Circle.

Vaughan, M. (1987), *The Story of an African Famine: Gender and Famine in Twentieth Century Malawi*. Cambridge: Cambridge University Press.

Wade, R. (1987), 'The Management of Common Property Resources: Finding a Cooperative Solution', *Research Observer*, 2.

Watts, M. (1983), *Silent Violence: Food, Famine and Peasantry in Northern Nigeria*. Berkeley: California University Press.

White, B. (1976), 'Population, Involution and Employment in Rural Java', in G. E. Hansen (ed.), *Agricultural Development in Indonesia*. Ithaca, NY: Cornell University Press.

Wiser, W. H. (1936), *The Hindu Jajmani System*. Lucknow: Lucknow Publishing House.

Yunus, M. (1982), 'Experience in Organising Grass-Root Initiatives and Mobilising People's Participation: The Case of Grameen Bank Project', paper presented at SID World Conference, Baltimore.

PART II
Case-Studies

6

Social Security in China:
A Historical Perspective*

Ehtisham Ahmad and Athar Hussain

1. OVERVIEW

We take social security to cover various social mechanisms for preventing contingencies such as interruption of earnings, sickness, and crop failures, or alleviating their effects, and for protecting vulnerable social groups such as the elderly and the chronically poor. These social mechanisms need not take the form of special programmes, but instead may be embedded in the economic organization or social relations. This is of special importance in the case of developing economies, because unlike developed economies they often lack comprehensive social-security programmes, and may not be able to afford them in the foreseeable future. Thus the effects of the organization of the economy on the incidence and alleviation of deprivation assumes a central importance in the discussion of social security in developing economies.

When analysing the Chinese social-security system, it is important to bear in mind that the Chinese economy has undergone a series of revolutionary transformations since 1949. The development of social-security programmes has been intertwined with changes in the pattern of ownership and State control of the economy. In China, the pervasive State control of industry and fundamental changes in the land tenure have made it possible for measures for preventing and alleviating deprivation to be built into the fabric of the economy to a degree that simply would not be feasible in an evolutionary framework. Thus, apart from discussing social-security programmes to cater for contingencies and particular categories of persons, we devote considerable space to the features of the rural and the urban economy which have a direct bearing on social security.

We begin in Section 1.1 with a schematic historical background relevant for the present purposes, and then go on to present an overview of social security. The details of the social-security programmes and the relevant features of the

* The paper on which this chapter is based arose out of the programme of research funded by the Overseas Development Administration of the UK government, the Ford Foundation, and the Bradley Foundation. We are grateful to Anthony Atkinson, Meghnad Desai, Jean Drèze, John Hills, and Nicholas Stern for comments and suggestions, and owe special thanks to Hong Liu for research assistance. Athar Hussain would also like to thank the British Academy for a personal research grant during the initial stages of his work on the Chinese social-security system.

economy are discussed in Section 2 with reference to rural areas, and in Section 3 with reference to urban areas. We end in Section 4 with a conclusion.

1.1. *Historical Background*

Schematically, Chinese economic history since 1949 may be divided into three phases marked by the following events:

Period	Main features
1949–57	Consolidation of social and political control; formation of a planned economy; land reforms; industrialization on the Soviet model.
1958–78	1958–60: the Great Leap Forward, involving rural collectivization, infrastructural works and rural industrialization; 1958–62: the great famine; 1966–76: the Cultural Revolutionary Period with its emphasis on equality and the collective economy.
1978–	Reversion to family farming; removal of restrictions on household enterprise; granting of financial and operational autonomy to industrial enterprises; promotion of mixed ownership; shift away from egalitarianism; erosion of some collective welfare arrangements.

The economic reforms since 1978 have spanned the rural and urban economies, and the most far-reaching of the transformations have been the shift to family farming and the disbanding of collective agriculture that had been the central feature of the Chinese economy since 1958. Agricultural land remains under collective ownership but has been leased out to households under what is termed the 'Responsibility System'. In contrast to agricultural reforms, the industrial or urban reforms started later and have been comparatively modest as yet. As in East European economies, their central feature has been the granting of financial and operational autonomy to State-owned enterprises. But unlike them, China has gone further towards adopting the principle of diversified ownership, allowing State, collective (co-operative), private, and foreign-owned enterprises to proliferate side by side. Freed of many of the stifling restrictions, household economic activities have flourished. A notable feature of industrial development in recent years is the exceptionally fast growth of rural industry, owned collectively by rural townships and villages. Thus in many areas the collective economy still remains strong, with the difference that it is now anchored in industry rather than in agriculture.

The economic reforms have had a dramatic effect on incomes and consumption. During the nine years of reforms (1978–87), per capita income more than doubled (ZTN 1988: 799). The increase in per capita consumption expenditure during this period, which is a more accurate index of improvement in the living standard, has been even more striking: it exceeded the total increase over the previous twenty-five years from 1952 to 1977 (ZTN 1988: 801). However, the increase in incomes and consumption has been unevenly spread among different regions and occupational groups. The rural areas along the densely populated coastal rim in the east and in the vicinity of large cities have experienced a higher increase than the rest. And in urban areas, there have been significant changes in relative incomes. The incomes of those engaged in the production of goods and services for sale and of the self-employed have risen faster than the incomes of groups engaged in providing non-marketed goods and services such as education, health, and public administration. Lately with the acceleration in the rate of inflation from 1987, a substantial proportion of the urban population has not merely fallen behind in the race for personal betterment, but suffered a decrease in real incomes. With the unfolding of the economic reforms, regional disparities in rural areas, which had always been substantial, and an increase in income inequality in urban areas, which used to be very low, have come to the fore as major social issues in the Chinese economy.

Turning to a brief history of social security in China, in the 1950s the government formally guaranteed to its citizens provisions for basic needs. And it has reiterated the commitment in successive constitutions. More important, preventing deprivation has been a permanent concern of policy, notwithstanding the changes in leadership and abrupt shifts in the organization of the economy. Generally speaking, this concern has taken two forms: first, building protective measures in land tenure and employment practices, and, second, instituting social-security programmes to cater for specific contingencies and for the protection of vulnerable groups. Preventing rural households from falling into destitution has been a continuous strand running through the transformations in the rural economy from the land reforms, which began in the 1940s, to the shift to household farming from 1979. Similarly, the prevention of mass unemployment in urban areas has remained a permanent preoccupation of the government. The assumption of State control of industry in the 1950s went together with the introduction of an ambitious system of labour insurance, covering health care and old-age pensions, for the employees of the government and State-owned enterprises. Since then the coverage of labour insurance has widened with the increase in employment in the State-owned sector and the government (on the history of labour insurance, see Hussain and Liu 1989: sec. 6).

With the nationalization of trade in 1953, the government assumed an obligation to provide rations of staple items at low prices in urban areas, and to redistribute grain from surplus to deficit areas in the countryside. Both these still hold true. The 1950s saw the enunciation of the health charter, which gave primacy to preventive over curative health care, and the development of government-financed or supported hospitals and health centres. In the field of primary health care, the most important event was the spread of health insurance to over three-quarters of the rural population following Mao's instruction to put stress on rural areas (Mao 1974: 232–3). Equally significant has been an almost total dismantling of the collective rural health insurance systems set up during the 1960s and the 1970s in the wake of the decollectivization of the rural economy. However, a large part of the urban labour-force and their dependents still benefit from partly or fully paid health care through labour insurance.

In comparison with other developing economies, China has been notably successful in reducing the threat of starvation and destitution to its citizens (World Bank 1985: 16–19). This success, however, is not unblemished. As the Chinese authorities themselves admit, the natural calamities of 1959–61, combined with the upheavals of the Great Leap Forward, condemned tens of millions to an early death. The estimates of excess deaths vary from ten to thirty million (see Coale 1984; Ashton et al. 1984; Peng 1987; see also the population figures in the Statistical Year Books). Liu Shaoqi, who was an object of popular wrath during the Cultural Revolution, remarked that the Great Leap claimed more lives than the building of the Great Wall. Pockets of transitory or permanent poverty have always existed in China, particularly in rural areas, and do so even now despite a massive increase in farm output and rural incomes since 1978. Only a few years ago Deng Xiaoping candidly admitted that around 100 million people or about 10 per cent of the population still did not have enough to eat and wear (Beijing Review, 5, Jan. 1985).

China is a low-income economy, yet in terms of welfare indicators it is akin to low or high 'middle-income' economies. The per capita intakes of principal nutrients in China markedly exceed those common in low-income economies, attaining the levels common in middle-income economies. The crude death rate, except for a sharp peak during the famine years of 1959–61, declined steadily from 20 per 1,000 in 1949 to 6.3 in 1978. It has since then risen due mainly to an increase in the percentage of the elderly in the population (see Hussain and Stern 1988). Life expectancy rose from 40 years in 1953 to 68 years in 1981. Adjusting for the underrecording of deaths, the figure for the 1980s is around 65 (SYB 1986: 91; Banister 1987: 116). Among low-income countries only Sri Lanka matches the Chinese level (see WDR 1989). According to a UN estimate, China's achievement in increasing life expectancy at birth since 1949 is matched by a few small countries such as Taiwan, Chile, and Sri Lanka (see UN 1984: 126–45; Banister and Preston 1981; and World Bank 1985: 174–5). This achievement is all the more impressive because a sustained gain in life expectancy is more difficult to achieve in a large heterogeneous country such as

China than in a small country such as Sri Lanka. The high life expectancy is corroborated by the cause-pattern of mortality: diseases related to old age rank high and infectious and parasitic diseases, which are the hallmarks of poverty, rank low—again a pattern which is similar to that of middle-income economies (World Bank 1984: 13). Thus in its income class, China is an 'outlier' in terms , of the average level of nutrition, life expectancy at birth, and the cause pattern of mortality. This raises the central question: why has China been more successful than many other developing economies?

The steady gain in life expectancy coupled with low birth rates since the early 1970s has hastened China's transition to the 'tertiary demographic' phase of low birth and life expectancy. This has brought in its train a rising percentage of the elderly in the population—a trend expected to gather pace in the coming decades. In 1986, there were around 57.5 million individuals over 64 (5.43 per cent of the population), and their numbers are expected to rise by 64 per cent to 94.5 million (around 8 per cent of the population) in the year 2000, soaring to over 200 million by 2030 (World Bank 1985: 138–9). The ageing of the population has been quicker in China than in European countries or even in Japan (see Hussain and Liu 1989: sec. 4.7). As a result, China faces a 'premature' problem of supporting the elderly similar in magnitude to that in middle-income countries. As we shall see, how to provide for a relatively high percentage of the elderly, when per capita income is still low, is a central problem of social security in China.

1.2. The Social-Security System

The important point about the Chinese social-security system is that it operates in an economy which has built into it the following two features:

(1) all rural households have had access to agricultural land, either individually or collectively;
(2) recruitment and employment practices have been geared to maintaining a high rate of employment in urban areas.

Since the extension of the land reforms to the whole of mainland China in the early 1950s, all rural families have had guaranteed access to agricultural land either individually or collectively, enabling them to earn a living by deploying their labour. Details are discussed in Section 2 on rural areas. Turning to urban areas, most of the employed labour-force in China has been in government departments, and in State-owned and collective (co-operative) industry. Labour recruitment, especially in government departments and State-owned enterprises has been geared to providing employment to new entrants to the permanent urban labour-force. Life-long employment, which still remains a prevalent norm in China, has helped to keep unemployment in check by ruling out spells in between jobs. Broadly speaking, the urban population has benefited from, as it were, a comprehensive employment guarantee. This guarantee has in recent years begun to erode at the edges. Formally, the government no longer promises jobs to all new entrants to the labour force with urban registration (*hukou*). More important, the massive influx of rural inhabitants has swelled the ranks of urban residents without urban registration, who are outside the umbrella of employment guarantee altogether. Nevertheless, as we elaborate later in Section 3, a large majority of the urban labour-force still benefits from some form of guaranteed employment.

The guaranteed access to land in rural areas and the employment guarantee in urban areas have together provided the Chinese population with a degree of economic security which is rare in developing economies. Although they are not components of the social-security system, they have had a strong bearing on it. They limit the numbers in need of assistance and reduce the contingencies for which social-security programmes have to cater. They have had two striking effects that mark out China from other developing economies. The first is the absence of landless poor, though not of poor with land. The second is the absence of large visible unemployment, though not of 'disguised unemployment' in China's urban areas. However, this has begun to change rapidly with the increase in immigrant workers from the countryside, who are exposed to a much greater risk of unemployment than permanent urban residents and are not covered by urban social-security programmes. Notwithstanding this change, the map of poverty for China still looks very different from those for other developing economies. Urban destitution and squalor is much less visible, and extreme poverty is still a predominantly rural phenomenon, confined mostly to remote and sparsely populated areas. Arguably, there may be less poverty in China, but whatever is there is often not immediately visible.

In China, greater economic security goes in tandem with a web of controls on personal conduct. The guaranteed access to land in rural areas and the employment guarantee have rested on stringent restrictions on population migration. The control on migration from the countryside to cities has served to keep in check the urban labour-force and thus the numbers benefiting from the employment guarantee. The guaranteed access to land has not been unqualified, but has taken the form of the permanent residents of a village having access to the village land. Normally, 'outsiders' have had no right of access, but until recently their numbers have been very small because of the low rate of population migration within the countryside. The point which needs emphasizing is that the two guarantees have been premissed upon a very limited migration of the population. Their coverage has begun to erode, as the loosening of controls on movement swell the numbers of 'temporary' residents who are outside the umbrella of the two guarantees.

In China changes in the place of residence have been rationed through a system of household registration (*hukou*), which we discuss further in Section

3. In particular, rural inhabitants are not allowed to settle permanently in cities without permission, which for a big city may be especially hard to obtain. Since the 1950s, successive Chinese leaderships have sought to encourage the development of industry in rural areas, and thereby accomplish the usual historical process of the shifting of labour from farming to other activities without a large-scale migration from urban to rural areas. 'Leave the land but not the countryside' (*Li tu bu li xiang*), as the slogan goes. Until the early 1980s, household registration in combination with restrictions on travel and a diverse array of administrative controls did succeed in keeping the proportion of urban population remarkably low. Thus, as compared to other economies, China has exhibited an anomalous combination of a high share of industrial output in national income and a low proportion of the urban population in the total (for a discussion see Perkins 1986: pt. 2). With the unfolding of the economic reforms, whilst household registration remains as an instrument for controlling migration, many of the other economic impediments to migration have withered away. And the government has come to accept the inevitability of an increase in urbanization with economic development, and has considerably relaxed the issue of urban registration for small or medium-size towns, but not for large cities such as Beijing, Shanghai, and Guangzhou. Increasingly, rural inhabitants are leaving not only the land but also the countryside for urban areas, including large cities—*li tu ye li xiang*. The result is a massive increase in that proportion of the population of large cities who are not recognized as permanent urban residents, presenting the government with huge problems of social control and deprivation.

The Chinese population is marked by two forms of division which bear upon the social-security system. The first is the distinction between rural and urban residents, which has existed since the 1950s. And the second, applying to the urban population, is the distinction between permanent residents—namely, those with registration for the locality—and temporary residents. This distinction is assuming greater importance with the increase in population migration. Urban registration confers a privileged economic status, providing the holder with possibilities for a comparatively higher living standard. Rural inhabitants have guaranteed access to land, but, as economic opportunities vary widely with the locality, this does not rule out poverty. In some areas it may mean no more than a precarious existence between poverty and distress. Many of China's large cities, in particular Guangzhou, are flooded with large numbers of itinerants who have no permanent abode and no regular source of income. Recent years have also seen a significant increase in migration within the countryside. Migration poses a special problem for a social-security system which still remains premissed on the assumption that the population will be immobile and has no special provisions for migrants either in cities or in the countryside.

China has a complex collection of disparate programmes that may be grouped under the general rubric of social-security system. Social-security cover provided to citizens varies according to place of residence and employment status, which are closely related. Most of these social-security programmes date from the 1950s, but have undergone transformations with the twists and turns of government policies. And they are surrounded by a formidable array of social and economic imperatives for self-sustenance. Principal among these have been participation in labour up to physical capacity, and obligation to provide assistance to kin in need, especially to parents in old age. Means-tested public assistance has been seen and projected as the safety net of last resort. Notwithstanding a permanent concern with basic needs on the part of successive Chinese leaderships, the discussion of social security from a comprehensive perspective is relatively recent, dating only from the period of economic reforms since 1978. We provide an analytical account of the system in terms of the agencies responsible for social security and then turn to the social-security programmes.

1.2.1. *Main Agencies*   Generally speaking, the responsibility for social-security programmes is diffuse, divided between five agencies: the family, the government, work units (*danwei*), collective (or communal) organizations in rural areas, and 'mass organizations'. Collective rural organizations date back to the collectivization of agriculture in the 1950s and still survive following the shift from collective to household farming, albeit radically transformed in status and functioning. They perform governmental functions, yet are not regarded as part of the formal governmental apparatus. Mass organizations include *inter alia* the 'All China Federation of Trades Unions', the 'Women's Association', and neighbourhood organizations, which are concerned with the welfare of their respective constituencies. The last, specifically Chinese institutions, are urban organizations covering residential neighbourhoods. They perform a variety of social-welfare and policing functions, and are supervised by the Ministry of Civil Affairs.

Three features characterize the institutional structure of the Chinese social-security system. First, the public social-security system, which excludes family support, is tiered. The first tier consists of rural collective organizations, work units (*danwei*), and neighbourhood organizations. These grass-roots bodies are the proximate sources of funds and organize and disburse assistance. The second tier consists of the government agencies which supervise the organizations in the first tier, and provide them with funds when they are unable to meet their obligations or cope with certain contingencies. The second feature of the structure is that it is 'cellular'. The organization and the financing of the various social-security programmes are divided among the large number of units in the first tier—in the main, among work units (*danwei*) in urban areas and among collective organizations in rural areas. Thus relative to other developing economies China has a surfeit of agencies concerned with social welfare. The cellular structure goes together with a wide variation in the levels and methods of provision. This is especially pronounced in the case of rural social-security programmes, but also holds for urban programmes as well. Within the government itself, responsibility is split between the provincial governments and various ministries of the central government. The third significant feature of the Chinese social-security system is the important role played by collective institutions and mass organizations in the provision of social security, especially in rural areas. We would suggest that China's relative success in developing rural social-security programmes is due in large measure not to the government but to collective organizations.

As in other developing economies, family and kin support remains a significant source of protection against destitution for the population at large. All the same, what is special about China is that the government has sought to incorporate family and kinship support as a basic component of social-security arrangements. The obligation of children to support their old parents is written into the constitution, which the 1980 Family Law has prudently extended to include grandparents as well. Authorities take pains to make sure that discretionary public support does not displace but merely supplements family support. Local government and collective institutions, especially in rural areas, police the discharge of filial obligations. Reliance on social relief, especially what is termed *wubao*, is projected as a shaming last resort, branding both the recipients and their immediate and extended families with social stigma (see Wolf 1985: 196, 199, 248). The family is, and is likely to remain for the foreseeable future, the mainstay of old-age support in rural areas. Generally speaking, urban residents get old-age pensions and rural residents rely on sons for old-age support.

The family may not, however, continue to be as important a source of old-age support as it has been, especially in rural areas. Notwithstanding the long tradition of filial piety in China, a variety of factors point to a gradual diminution in the role of the family. The support of the elderly by their children, although not conditional on, has rested on multi-generational households. An increasing number of the young prefer nuclear households, and the shortage of housing in urban areas and the household registration system limit the formation of multi-generational households. Added to these, the demographic changes in the offing will increase the burden of old-age support on families. With an increase in life expectancy, at a mature age in particular, each succeeding generation of the elderly will have to be supported for a longer period than the preceding one. Further, the one-child policy promoted by the government does not fit in with heavy reliance on support of the elderly by their families, which the government also encourages. As most rural couples do not have old-age pension but only social relief—or *wubao*—to look forward to, they have an incentive to produce more than one child in order to make sure that they have at least one male offspring. Conversely, if the one-child policy does succeed, which it has in urban areas, then the ensuing change may simply make it impossible for many families to support their elderly (see Hussain and Liu 1989: introduction).

1.2.2. Social-Security Programmes   In China there are four programmes which fit in with the conventional definition of a social-security system:

(1) labour insurance (*laodong baoxian*);
(2) occupational and communal provisions—often termed in China social welfare (*shehui fuli*), a term which we use subsequently;
(3) social relief (*shehui jiuji*) and disaster relief (*ziran zaihai jiuji*);
(4) public provisions for health care.

We provide an outline of these programmes in this section, leaving details for the later sections. Labour insurance extends only to the employed labour-force, excluding the peasants altogether, because they are regarded as self-employed. Moreover, it covers only a percentage of the formally employed labour-force, consisting of government employees and employees of State-owned enterprises and larger collective enterprises. The employees of smaller collective enterprises in urban areas and of rural township and village enter-prises are outside the umbrella of labour insurance. In recent years, the percentage of the labour-force covered by labour insurance has remained fairly steady around 23 per cent (ZSTZ 1987: 111). Promising disability and old-age pensions, maternity and sickness benefits, and subsidized health care, labour insurance is akin to schemes in Welfare States, except that unemployment benefit has not been its main component. For unemployment has been regarded as a problem to be solved by job creation. However, the government has finally come to recognize that job creation may lead to disguised unemploy-ment with a heavy cost to the economy. It now accepts that at least some unemployment is inevitable in a socialist market economy, and has created an unemployment insurance scheme. However, the scheme is, as we shall see in Section 3, still severely restricted in scope. As almost all organizations under the umbrella of labour insurance are in urban areas, and a large percentage of the urban labour-force is employed in such organizations, labour insurance is broadly synonymous with urban-cum-industrial social security. This is, how-ever, subject to the important qualification that the percentage of the urban labour-force outside the umbrella of labour insurance has been increasing in recent years. This includes a proportion of the urban labour-force and the growing numbers of rural immigrant workers in cities. The rapidly increasing labour-force of rural industry is excluded from labour insurance altogether. Unless checked, this trend would turn labour insurance into a selective scheme, applying only to a proportion of the employed labour-force. Details of labour insurance are discussed in Section 3.

What is descriptively termed here 'occupational and communal welfare provisions'—social welfare (*shehui fuli*) in China—covers a wide range, including inflation, hardship and bereavement allowances, social facilities such as kindergartens, educational and recreational facilities, and institutions for orphans, the mentally ill, and the disabled. In sum, it is a miscellaneous category covering diverse income-maintenance provisions and social facilities at the work unit or in residential areas, villages included. In urban areas, it supplements labour insurance, with which it is often grouped together.

Social relief (*shehui jiuji*) covers for the most part assistance to the rural poor, including to the elderly without relatives to depend on, and is termed '5 Guarantees' (*wubao*). Broadly, social relief is synonymous with rural-cum-agricultural social security. Unlike labour insurance, it does not cover contingencies as a matter of right, it is discretionary. The eligibility for social relief is highly restrictive: not only should the recipient be non-self-subsistent, but also have no relatives to depend on. In organization, it varies between private charity and public philanthropy. Unlike labour insurance, it lacks an underlay of laws and regulations specifying entitlements. Further details of social relief are discussed in Section 2 on rural areas. Disaster relief (*ziran zaihai jiuji*) is of special importance for rural areas, as around 70 per cent of the population lives in rural areas, and over 60 per cent of the labour-force is still employed in agriculture. Vast and varied as China is, natural disasters are recurrent contingencies in rural areas.

Public provision for health care is not unified, it consists of two main components. The first is government provision in the form of a network of hospitals and preventive health services. And the second is the coverage of health care costs through health insurance, predominantly through labour insurance. Until the shift to the Responsibility System, there used to be an extensive rural health insurance system, but that has all but disappeared. Health care costs of those who are neither covered by health insurance nor able to pay for themselves are covered as part of social welfare (*shehui fuli*) and social relief (*shehui jiuji*). Because health care is a large topic in need of a separate treatment, we confine the discussion to the selective features of health care in rural areas (see Section 2).

Besides these four arrangements, which would normally be grouped under the social-security system, we would also include the pricing and trading policies of the government. These have an important bearing on personal real incomes in both rural and urban areas. Price controls and the rationing of necessities play an important part in income maintenance in many developing economies, but their importance is all the greater in the Chinese economy because of the pervasive State control of prices and trading. Notwithstanding the reduction in government control of the economy since 1978, the control of prices and trading by national and local government is still more extensive in China than in most developing economies. Government agencies remain the largest purchasers of agricultural commodities, and a ration of grain and cooking oil at low prices is provided to all permanent, but not to temporary urban residents. Added to that, municipal governments in urban areas often provide low-price rations of 'non-staples' such as vegetables and meat. The cash income of farmers depends crucially on the purchase prices paid by the government, and the real incomes of urban consumers depend heavily on government-determined price and on the rationing of consumer goods. We discuss the expenditure on price subsidies further in this section.

1.2.3. *Social-Security Expenditure (SSE)*   The economic importance of social security is usually expressed in terms of the total expenditure on social-security programmes and its ratio to national income. The time series on the total expenditure are available only for the period since 1979 (Table 6.1), and do not include government expenditure on health, because in the government accounts it is grouped together with culture, education, and science in one category.

Table 6.1. Social security expenditure (SSE): 1979–1985

Year	SSE as % of national income	Labour insurance as % of SSE	Social relief as % of SSE	Social welfare as % of SSE
1979	4.8	45 —	12 —	43 —
1980	5.0	52 (32)[a]	9 (−20)	39 (4)
1981	5.1	55 (15)	9 (9)	36 (2)
1982	5.2	57 (16)	8 (1)	35 (7)
1983	5.5	58 (18)	7 (6)	35 (18)
1984	5.3	59 (18)	7 (10)	34 (12)
1985	5.5	60 (29)	6 (11)	34 (27)

[a] Figures in parentheses represent percentage growth rate at current prices.
Source: ZSTZ (1987: 123).

As a percentage of national income, the expenditure on social security is comparatively high in China, and has risen since 1979, with the start of the economic reforms. The increase of 0.7 percentage points over 6 years to 1985, as shown by Table 6.1, is due to the dramatic rise in expenditure on labour insurance at 21 per cent a year, 60 per cent higher than the exceptionally rapid rate of growth of 13 per cent per year in national income at current prices—9 per cent per annum at constant prices. As may be seen from Table 6.2, the other two components of social-security expenditure, social welfare and social relief, grew more slowly than national income. The steep rise in labour insurance expenditure is not due to an increase in the proportion of the labour-force covered by labour insurance, which in recent years has remained constant at around 23 per cent. In fact, as we point out in Section 3, the proportion of the employed labour-force covered by labour insurance has in

Table 6.2. Average annual rates of growth: 1979–1985 (%)[a]

National income	Total social-security expenditure	Labour insurance	Social relief	Social welfare	Price level
13	15.5	21	2	11	4

[a] All rates of growth refer to magnitude in current prices.
Source: ZSTZ (1987: 123); the inflation figure is from ZTN (1988: 778).

fact declined. Rather the increase in expenditure is largely the result of an increase in the number of the retired entitled to pensions. The wide variation in annual growth rates of labour insurance expenditure reflects the fact that the number of pensioners increased by highly uneven steps. In particular, the massive growth rate of 32 per cent in 1980 was caused by the bunched retirement of large numbers who should have retired earlier but did not do so because of the Cultural Revolution.

In contrast to labour insurance, expenditure on social relief in nominal terms increased relatively little over the period. As may be seen from Table 6.1, the expenditure fell sharply in 1980 with the start of the rural reforms. The decrease came immediately after a massive rise in the procurement prices of agriculture commodities in 1979, leading to large increase in rural incomes (TPS 1987: 115). Moreover, the annual expenditure on social relief during the three years between 1980 and 1983 remained lower than it had been in 1979, and began to rise only from 1984. In fact, taking into account that the rate of inflation averaged 4 per cent per annum, expenditure on social relief fell in real terms. The main reason for the low rate of increase of 2 per cent in social-relief expenditure in nominal terms over the six years to 1985 is simply that social relief is subject to a stringent means test, and is only meant to alleviate extreme poverty. Prima facie, the sharp increase in rural incomes after 1979 may have reduced the number qualifying for relief.

In sum, social-security expenditure has risen sharply since 1979, with an increasing proportion of it going to labour insurance. The change is adverse from the point of view of equity, as labour insurance covers barely a quarter of the labour-force. Further, the fact that the percentage of the labour-force with labour insurance cover has remained constant over the six years to 1985 despite a steep increase in expenditure makes it doubtful that the percentage would rise in the near future. We discuss this in Section 3. The general implication is that for financial reasons, at least, the Chinese social-security system is likely to remain segmented, with a comprehensive labour insurance for a small proportion of the labour-force, almost all in urban areas, and a stringently means-tested social relief for the rest.

1.2.4. *Financing of Social Security and Price Subsidies*   The rapid growth in social-security expenditure, especially labour insurance expenditure, raises the question of how it is financed. Generally speaking, all but a small percentage of social-security expenditure is financed from current revenues of work units and rural collective organizations. As we shall see in Section 3, this is now a major source of problems facing the labour insurance system. As yet personal contributions do not play an important part in the financing of social security. A proportion of the employees of collective enterprises and the employees of State-owned enterprises recruited since 1986, termed 'contract employees', contribute towards their labour insurance, but they still constitute a small proportion of the employed labour-force. Thus an overwhelming proportion of social security benefits are non-contributory. Given the mounting cost of labour insurance and the increase in personal incomes, the argument for personal contributions towards labour insurance is strong. This would not only help to diversify the sources of finance, but may make it feasible to extend labour insurance cover to a larger percentage of the formally employed labour-force. Apart from a limited introduction of personal contributions on the part of contract employees, there is as yet no plan to tap personal contributions as a source of finance for labour insurance. Rather the policy seems to be to encourage the growth of private or contributory group insurance for employees outside the umbrella labour insurance, which adds to the segmentation of the social-security system.

Schematically, the three main social-security programmes are financed as follows:

Labour insurance	Work units (*danwei*) and the government;
Social welfare	Work units, collective organizations and the government;
Social relief	Collective organizations and the government.

To get an idea of the relative importance of different sources of social-security expenditure we look at the government's share in total expenditure over the period 1979–85 (Table 6.3). Two features stand out in this table. First, looking at the composition of government expenditure as a whole, the share going to social security is remarkably small. In fact, since 1952 the share has usually been below 2 per cent (see ZTN 1988: 758). Second, the government share in total expenditure on social security, which was relatively low to start with, has fallen rapidly to just over half of its original proportion. Over the period from 1979–1985, whilst total social-security expenditure in nominal terms rose by an average of almost 16 per cent per year, government expenditure on social security, also in nominal terms, increased at a comparatively low average rate of 6 per cent per year, although government expenditure in general rose by an annual average of 9 per cent. Thus not only is most of social-security expenditure

Table 6.3. Government expenditure on social security[a]

	1979	1980	1981	1982	1983	1984	1985
Government expenditure as % of total spent on social security	14.0	11.0	11.0	10.0	9.0	8.0	8.0
Government expenditure on social security as % of total government expenditure	1.7	1.7		1.9	1.8	1.7	1.7

[a] All figures refer to nominal magnitudes.
Source: ZSTZ (1987: 123); ZTN (1988: 747, 761).

in China financed by work units and rural collectives; but also their share in the total has been increasing.

At first sight both these features seem unusual, because a high and increasing expenditure on social security relative to national income usually goes hand in hand with a high and increasing proportion of government expenditure devoted to social security. The main reason for the anomaly is that what would elsewhere be financed by general or social-security taxes is in China financed largely from the current revenue of a vast number of work units. Prior to the reforms, the difference between government and non-government financing was purely nominal, as the budgets of enterprises were not separated from the government budget. But now that they are, the difference matters, and the requirement that each enterprise is responsible for financing the labour insurance of its employees on an individual basis has important implications for maintaining labour insurance cover. For the labour insurance liabilities of an enterprise bear no particular relation to its financial capacity to meet those liabilities. This is a source of problems for labour insurance, which we discuss in Section 3. The current system of financing social security in China is highly decentralized, even in comparison to systems functioning under a federal government. Thus the stylized fact that decentralized financing of social security goes in tandem with variations in the level of provisions holds with even greater force in the Chinese context. We discuss specific examples of variations in Sections 2 and 3 with respect to rural and urban social-security programmes.

If government expenditure on social-security programmes is low, price subsidies from the government budget are exceptionally high, as shown by Table 6.4. These figures underestimate price subsidies because they do not include municipal government subsidies on 'non-staples' such as meat, vegetables, sugar, and eggs. The fact that a high proportion of total subsidies goes

Table 6.4. Price subsidies by central government

| | | Composition of subsidies (%) | | |
Year	Subsidies as % of government expenditure	Consumer goods	Agricultural inputs	Imported goods
1978	8	58	25	17
1979	14	75	12	13
1980	20	74	8	18
1981	29	66	7	27
1982	28	75	7	18
1983	26	79	4	17
1984	24	87	2	11
1985	16	92	2	6
1986	11	95	2	3

Source: ZTN (1988: 763).

to 'consumer goods' is due to the procurement prices of agricultural goods being typically higher than the sale price. Chief among these are grain and cooking oil which are supplied at subsidized prices to all permanent residents of urban areas and some rural residents. Therefore a substantial part of subsidies on consumer goods is tied to the rationing of consumer goods in urban areas. Most of the subsidy on agricultural inputs goes on fertilizers, although this has been reduced along with the increase in the procurement prices of agricultural goods. The subsidy on imported goods arises out of the fact that domestic prices of grain, fertilizers, sugar, and agricultural chemicals have been lower than border prices at the official rate of exchange. Generally speaking, most price subsidies are directed towards urban inhabitants. The main problem with these subsidies is, however, not their urban bias, but that such a large proportion of government expenditure is devoted to a non-targeted programme.

In the next two sections we discuss social security in rural areas and urban areas respectively. In China the distinction between rural and urban is administrative, and in many instances at variance with an economic classification. Some of the areas classified as rural are better regarded as urban from the point of view of population density and of the relative importance of non-agricultural income. This is especially true of the regions where rural industry has grown rapidly in recent years. The arbitrariness of the category may be seen from the fact that following an administrative reclassification, the percentage of the rural population as a proportion of the total decreased from 77 per cent in 1983 to 68 per cent in 1984 (ZTN 1988: 97). Nevertheless, the distinction remains important in any discussion of social security in China because residential status plays a central role in the organization of the social-security system.

2. SOCIAL SECURITY IN RURAL AREAS

Earlier we pointed out that the rural social-security programmes operate in an environment where all rural families have guaranteed access to land. So we shall begin by looking briefly at the institutional transformations in rural areas since 1949, and then turn to other issues in the following order:

(1) agricultural pricing and trading policies of the government;
(2) social relief (*shehui jiuji*) and disaster relief (*ziran zaihai jiuji*);
(3) health provisions.

The rural social-security system consists of the programmes under headings 2 and 3. Whilst social relief includes various income maintenance programmes, disaster relief and health provisions cover specific contingencies. Agricultural pricing and trading are included because of the important role they have played in determining real personal incomes and alleviating nutritional contingencies. Although China has been comparatively successful in preventing and alleviating deprivation in rural areas, the rural social-security system is, as we shall see, strikingly sparse. Social relief is contingent on stringent means-testing, which is often concerned more with preventing the non-deserving from claiming relief than with ensuring a comprehensive coverage of all those in need. Although social-security programmes in rural areas are by no means significant, on their own they do not seem weighty enough to account for China's success in preventing deprivation in rural areas. Thus we would suggest that the success is due in large measure to the organization of the rural economy.

2.1. *Transformations in the Rural Economy*

Since 1949, the rural economy has undergone three fundamental transformations: first, land reform, which began before 1949; second, formation of rural co-operatives and then rural communes from 1956; and third reversion to family farming from 1979. For our purpose, the land reform has been the most fundamental of the transformations in that it laid the foundations of the income-generating mechanism in farming and rural areas generally. The shift back to family farming since 1979 has reversed collective farming but not the essential feature of the land reform: guaranteeing all rural households access to land. In fact, land is now more 'equally' distributed than it was on the eve of collectivization in the mid-1950s. We take a brief look at the three transformations in turn.

Given that 89.4 per cent of the Chinese population in 1949 was rural, the land reform left a strong imprint on income distribution (SYB 1983: 104). A fundamental aim of the reform was to provide each rural household with at least enough land and the wherewithal to meet basic needs; and its most important feature was the redistribution of land to the poor peasants. To assess the exact impact of the land reform one has to turn to the specific form it took. First, given that the reform was in effect a war waged by poor peasants against landlords and rich peasants, the possibilities of evading the transfer of land were non-existent. Second, the range of beneficiaries was wide, encompassing 'middle' as well as poor peasants. Third, the reform concerned not only land but also agricultural implements. Yet there were severe limits to what could be achieved by these measures. Improvements in the standard of living of the poor were limited by land-to-labour ratios and the level of agricultural technology. As in other East Asian economies, the ratio of cultivable land to rural population in China was, at the time of the land reforms in the early 1950s, exceptionally low by international standards. Since then the ratio has steadily decreased due to the increase in the agricultural labour-force. But the rate of growth of agricultural productivity in China seems to have been higher than in most other developing economies (see Hussain 1989). Besides, as elsewhere, land reform in China took the form of local redistribution of land, usually within the boundaries of the village (for a discussion of the geographical scope of land redistribution see Schurman 1971: chap. 7). As it did not involve a redistribution of rural population, the land-to-population ratio at village level set the upper limit on minimum landholding. Although the land reform did lead to a more equitable distribution of land within a village, it could not address the problem of poverty on any broader scale. In particular, it left untouched the important problem of regional poverty, which has always existed in rural China, but has become more striking because of the rapid but uneven increase in rural incomes since 1978.

Land reform had a profound and still persisting effect on the characteristic attributes of needy households in rural China. It eliminated landlessness as a cause of destitution. Herein lies a crucial difference between the attributes of the rural poor in China and those in most other developing economies, where rural poverty and landlessness often go together. There have been, since the land reform, landless households in rural China, and their numbers have grown rapidly in recent years with the economic reforms. But 'specialized households', as they are termed now, are not poor; on the contrary, they are landless by choice and are more likely to be among the more prosperous households.

Broadly speaking, poverty in rural China is associated with two groups of factors. The first consists of natural circumstances such as poor soil, inhospitable climate, and geographical isolation. These are the main attributes of poor regions, or causes of a low average income over a whole area. The second arises from lack of sufficient labour power due to age, death, and a large number of children, and it is causes such as these which determine whether any one household will be poorer than the rest in the area.

The land reform dovetailed into the formation of co-operatives and shortly after into full-scale collectivization of rural economic activities. In retrospect, the co-operatives were no more than a preliminary stage of the rural commune. The history of collectivization is turbulent, and the flux of institutional changes is too complex for a short account. We confine ourselves to a minimal sketch of the rural commune and its effects relevant for the present purpose.

The rural commune combined local government and the organization of economic activities encompassing not only farming but also infrastructural investment and rural industry. Collectivization of land went in tandem with restrictions on household economic activities and on migration, tethering rural inhabitants to their place of birth. The leadership saw collectivization as an organizational device by which to mobilize surplus rural labour for investment in the infrastructure and to transfer labour from farming to non-farming activities without geographical migration. The low mobility of the population, which has characterized the Chinese economy until recently and on which the Chinese social-security system is still premissed, could in large measure be attributed to rural collectivization. In geographical terms rural collectivization covered a much wider area than land redistribution in that it bound together a large number of villages—'big in size and collective in operation' (*yida ergong*), as described by a common slogan. To convey an idea of its scale, after 1962 the rural commune, for the most part, consisted of three tiers: the production team (around 30 households), the production brigade (around 250 households), and the commune (around 3,000 households) (see SYB 1981: 134). Treating the production brigade as equivalent to a natural village, the rural commune encompassed around twelve villages, on average. This is no more than a very rough estimate because the size of villages varies widely.

Broadly speaking, collectivization was marked by two features: first, the centralized allocation of labour and, second, the collective disposal of income. Households were left with little discretion over the deployment of their own labour. In effect, the collectivization of land also implied a collectivization of rural labour. The distinguishing feature of centralized deployment of labour was the heavy allocation of labour for infrastructural investment. Aside from a relatively small income from heavily constrained private activities, all income accrued initially to the collective. This gave the collective power to decide upon the disposal of income in cash and kind, which was done according partly to need and partly to work (see Parish and Whyte 1978: chap. 5; Croll 1982; Perkins and Yusuf 1984: chap. 5; Endicott 1988: 123–6). Remuneration for labour and income maintenance were intertwined; the relative weight assigned to each varied across units. Distribution according to needs reduced the risk of loss of income to a household from the diminution of its labour force. To use an adage common in China, rural collectivization provided each rural family with an iron rice bowl—the bowl symbolizes provision and iron the fact that the level of provision remains unaffected by everyday knocks and bumps, or, in other words, variations in labour performed by a household.

The adverse effect of collectivization on incentives has been emphasized in the literature, but it should also be borne in mind that the iron rice bowl provided a guaranteed income not only to shirkers but also to households lacking sufficient labour due to sickness, old age, and deaths. Under collectivization, the financing of social security, rural health insurance, and infrastructural work posed no special problem. Local cadres decided upon the uses of income and the deployment of resources with or without the consent of households. However, coercion was not the sole prop of the system. Collective cultivation did engender a spirit of solidarity conducive to social security through local co-operation, albeit not to the same degree everywhere. Besides, the fact that income accrued to the collective in the first instance had a special significance in terms of insurance: that is, any diminution of income or damage to assets due to natural factors was automatically borne by all and not just a few households. By its very nature collectivization involved a pooling of risks; and as with most insurance systems, it went together with adverse effects on incentives.

A major aim behind the formation of the rural commune was to mobilize labour for infrastructural work during slack seasons. During the period of collective agriculture, there was a massive investment of resources and labour in infrastructure. Heroism rather than economic calculations guided much of this, and in terms of consumption forgone and return on investment, the economic propriety of many of the schemes undertaken is open to question. We would, however, single out the massive investment in hydraulic construction as having a special significance for income maintenance in rural areas. At the end of the era of collective farming 45 per cent of the cultivable area in China was irrigated—an exceptionally high figure for a large and diverse country (see World Bank 1983: ii. 23–4). Much of this hydraulic construction was undertaken during collectivization, involving a massive mobilization of labour, and bears the hallmarks of bursts of heroic but ill-planned effort. Notwithstanding this, the high proportion of irrigated area prima facie did help both to increase and to stabilize yields.

Collective agriculture is now heavily discredited in China, and the speed with which it was displaced by family farming suggests that many of its features were strongly resented by the rural population. Assessed from the vantage point of what has happened in the rural economy since decollectivization, there is little doubt that the collective rural economy stunted incentives, misallocated resources, and held back personal incomes by putting household economic activities in a strait-jacket of collectivism. Yet it is also true that the shift to family farming has adversely affected communal social-security arrangements and the investment in and maintenance of the infrastructure, particularly irrigation systems. We turn now to the reversion to family farming.

Since 1979, the collectively owned land and productive assets of the production team have been parcelled out to households under the Responsibility System, and most of the restrictions on non-farming activities by rural households have been lifted. The pattern of distribution of land varies geographically, and so too do the terms on which the land has been parcelled out. Predominantly, the land has been assigned to households in proportion to their size. Notwithstanding regional variations, implicit in the distribution of cultivable land there remains a concern to provide each household with the means to make a living. The living which households are able to make depends crucially on the locality. Since the land is still *de jure* collectively owned, there exists a possibility of changing the distribution of land to take account of any movement of population from agricultural to non-agricultural activities, and of demographic changes. (For examples of readjustments in the distribution of land, see AYB 1986: 40–1.) Households in receipt of collectively owned land have to pay land tax, local accumulation and welfare tax, and are obliged to sell to the government a portion of the produce. Taxes and the procurement quota obligation are divided pro rata to the land area. In effect, households are subject to a lump-sum tax. However, things are neither as orderly nor as uniform as this sparse description might suggest. The shift to family farming has cut the ground from underneath the local government in rural areas, which was intertwined with collective organization of economic activities. Generally speaking, the reorganization of local government has lagged behind economic changes. As a result, there are problems in collecting accumulation and welfare taxes and in organizing public activities, at least in some rural areas. Under the Responsibility System diversity in the countryside is much greater than it was under collectivism.

Turning to its effects on social security, the Responsibility System has undone many of the features associated with collectivization. Granting each household the power to dispose of any income generated from the plot allocated to it does not necessarily accord with notions of distribution according to needs, which is now limited by the size of the local welfare tax. This is intentional, since the aim has been to 'smash the iron rice bowl'. *Ipso facto*, the household has to bear the risk of any loss in income or assets due to a diminution of its labour-force, and to damage from natural factors. The general point is that the Responsibility System has increased incentives, but it has also increased the risks to be borne individually by rural households. The financing of social-security programmes can no longer be decided by an administrative fiat; it depends on the willingness of households to contribute, and on the welfare tax the rural administration manages finally to collect. The parcelling out of land and restoring to households the power to allocate their own labour have unravelled the arrangements built around the collective deployment of income and resources. In particular, the rural health insurance system has, in most areas, been replaced with 'payment according to treatment'. This means that in case of illness a household not only faces the risk of loss of income but also of larger expenditure. The Responsibility System has also decreased the ability of rural collectives to mobilize labour for infrastructual works. In fact, the government has explicitly forbidden the use of labour and resources without adequate compensation (for a case-study see Zweig 1989: chap. 7). The irrigated area declined steadily from 1978 to 1985, though since then the government has succeeded in partially reversing the trend (see ZTN 1988: 233). From the point of view of social security, the displacement of the collective economy by the household economy has to be coupled with a growth in either tax-financed social insurance or private insurance to cover the extra risks created by this displacement, but that has yet to happen.

When assessing the impact of the Responsibility System on rural social security, one should bear in mind that rural incomes have risen at a record pace since the introduction of the system. Between 1978 and 1987, rural income per capita at current prices grew by 13 per cent annually (ZTN 1988: 799). Given that the rate of inflation over the period has averaged around 6 per cent per annum, the rate of growth of real incomes still comes to a high 7 per cent. By doing away with restrictions on private activities, the economic reforms have provided rural households with wider and more varied opportunities for earning an income. Such opportunities, however, vary greatly with the locality. Added to that, the economic reforms have given a fillip to rural industry. Employment in rural industry (township and village industry) occasionally brings with it occupational benefits such as old-age pensions and subsidized medical care, though not on the same scale as in urban areas. And, since most of that industry is collectively owned, a portion of its profits is used for subsidizing agriculture and financing rural social welfare. Rural industry's contribution to rural welfare in nominal terms has been growing at 10 per cent per year over the ten years 1978–87 (see YRSES 1986: 168; ZTN 1988: 287). However, rural industry is very unevenly distributed. For example, in 1987 around 60 per cent of the total national profits from rural industry accrued to only six out of twenty-nine provinces, containing 28 per cent of the total rural population (ZTN 1988: 289; SYB 1987: 69). All these provinces are along the eastern seaboard of the country.

2.2. Pricing and Trading Policies of the Government

Although land tenure is the most important determinant of personal incomes in rural areas, trading arrangements have had a significant bearing on rural incomes. A part of the agricultural produce is sold to the government, voluntarily or not. In addition, farmers purchase agricultural inputs such as fertilizers, manufactured consumer goods, and also, in the case of a shortfall, staples such as grain. As government agencies have been by far the most important buyers of agricultural produce and the sellers of inputs to farmers, the pricing and trading policies of the government have had an important effect on the cash income of farmers. These policies have frequently been used for income maintenance in rural areas. The welfare impact of the pricing and trading policies of the government on rural areas is a large subject. Here we concentrate on two issues: first, the role of the State marketing network in alleviating nutritional contingencies in rural areas, and, second, the implications of the pricing policy for agricultural commodities as far as personal incomes are concerned.

We analyse the first issue in terms of how much grain is purchased from rural areas and the geographical pattern of sale of the purchased grain. On average, the government has purchased around a quarter of grain output, and resold around a third of its purchases back to rural areas—termed 'return sales' (*fan xiao*). Both these proportions have gone up since 1978, reflecting an increase in specialization in cropping patterns (see TPS 1987: 57). Until 1978, under the regime of 'taking grain as the key link' each rural locality, except a few permitted to specialize in cash crops, was expected to devote enough of the cultivated area to grain to ensure self-sufficiency. With the relaxation, but not the disappearance, of the regime, there has been an increase in specialization, hence the increase in the proportion of return sales in recent years. The time series of return sales make it clear that the State marketing network has not been used merely to siphon grain from rural to urban areas. It has also performed the important function of redistributing grain within rural areas. During the period of 'taking grain as the key link', prima facie, an overwhelming proportion of grain resold in rural areas was designed to alleviate nutritional contingency. Although the grain-rationing system does not apply to rural areas, there has been in operation a system of guaranteed grain. All rural inhabitants are supposed to have at least a certain amount of grain for their own consumption. The minimum level, which has varied historically and regionally, is taken into account in setting procurement quotas. Villages (or production teams or brigades) falling short of the minimum level are supplied with grain from the State marketing network to make up the shortfall. The terms of supply are determined by a means test. Poor areas or areas struck with natural disasters are supplied with grain either free or on loan (for details see Hussain and Feuchtwang 1988: 64–70). The provision of grain is the most important component of social relief (*shehui jiuji*) in rural areas. In general outline, the system has not changed during the period of reforms, except that with the increase in personal incomes in rural areas, the government is less willing to supply grain on concessional terms.

Turning to government pricing policy, since 1978 there has been a substantial increase in procurement prices for agricultural produce. Specifically, in the nine years between 1978 and 1986, the index of purchase prices of agricultural commodities rose by 77 per cent, which exceeds the total increase in the twenty-six years between 1952 and 1977 (TPS 1987: 115). In addition, the government has allowed farmers to sell any output above the procurement quota in private markets, where prices are higher than the procurement prices. The emergence of free markets means that the government cannot set both the purchase price and the procurement target, as it did earlier. The increase in procurement prices has been an important source of the increase in personal income in rural areas since 1978. However, the effect of procurement prices on the cash incomes of the farmers is complicated by changes in the prices farmers pay for their input. In recent years the government has been cutting subsidies on agricultural inputs (see Table 6.3 above; for a discussion see Sicular 1988). The net effect of government pricing policy on the distribution of incomes in rural areas remains an issue for research.

2.3. Rural Social Security

For the purposes of discussion here we divide social-security arrangements in the countryside into two functional categories:

(1) measures to maintain income and promote the development of poor regions;

(2) public provisions for health, including co-operative rural insurance.

2.3.1. *Income Maintenance and Income Promotion*   This category covers three programmes: first, social relief (*shehui jiuji*), including *wubao*; second, disaster relief (*ziran zaihai jiuji*); and third, development assistance to poor regions. For reasons of space, we restrict ourselves to the first two, whose main purpose is to provide a safety net to stop the rural population from slipping into the depths of deprivation. Social relief is means-tested, and not meant to eliminate poverty in the sense of bringing everyone up to an adequate level. Thus, as we shall see, many who are officially recognized to be poor may not receive any assistance. Social relief is for the most part financed by the government. Rural collectives usually finance only that part of social relief which is provided to *wubao* households (explained below); and some also have special programmes to help poor households in their locality. Such programmes vary greatly between localities, and depend crucially on the initiative of the local leadership. It is these local programmes which have been affected by the recent changes in the rural economy—adversely in some cases, and favourably in others. However, social relief provided by the government seems to be better organized in the post-reform than in the pre-reform period. Before going into the details of the scheme, we turn first to disaster relief.

In contrast to social relief, which is targeted towards the very poor, disaster relief is a much larger programme providing cover to the whole of the rural population against severe damage from natural causes. To give an idea of the relative sizes of the two programmes, in the four years 1983–7 between 70 and 80 per cent of the total expenditure on social relief and disaster relief has been devoted to disaster relief (see NTN 1986: 296; NTN 1987: 274). Around a half of disaster relief is provided to households in the form of living allowances consisting mainly of grain. Thus a significant part of the resale of grain to the countryside (*fanxiao*) consists of grain provided to households in disaster-affected areas. The eligibility for disaster relief has traditionally been assessed in terms of the shortfall in grain per capita from a minimum level. The usual practice has been to provide relief to all households in eligible areas regardless of means. In recent years, the government has tried to shift the emphasis of the programme from assistance after the incidence of disaster towards the prevention of damage from disaster, and there have been increasing criticisms of the 'grain test' to assess the extent of damage and eligibility for relief. The rural reforms have rendered the 'grain standard' increasingly obsolete. The cropping pattern has shifted away from grain, and an increasing proportion of income is derived from non-farming activities which are less affected by natural disasters. There is a gradual, but still not a complete, switch from the 'grain standard' to the 'monetary standard' based on money income from all activities (for further discussion see Hussain and Liu 1989: introduction and sec. 3).

What is the extent of protection provided to the rural population against natural disasters, which are among the main risks it faces? When assessing the extent of protection one needs to take into account not merely disaster relief provided by the government, which covers only severe damage, but also self-protection by rural communities. For rural inhabitants are expected to bear at least a part of the damage from natural disasters. As pointed out earlier, collective cultivation involved a pooling of risks from crop loss. With the parcelling out of land under the Responsibility System each household has to bear the risk of damage to crops on its land plot individually, which increases the risk of loss of income facing households. Thus from the point of view of social security against natural hazards, the growth of the household economy should be coupled with the growth of insurance, either private or social, to cover the extra risk, but this has yet to happen on a significant scale.

Returning to social relief, this covers assistance to two types of households, as distinguished in the Chinese literature: 5-Guarantees households (*wubao hu*) and poor households (*pinkun hu* or *kunnan hu*). *Wubao*, which is a term dating from the 1950s, refers to the guarantee of food, health care, shelter, clothing, and funeral costs for all citizens, hence the term 5 Guarantees. However, over time the term has come to designate a special category of households or persons unable to earn a living and lacking relatives to depend on. Thus, as we shall see, the recipients of *wubao* relief are predominantly the elderly without family support. Although narrowly focused on people without support and available to a relatively small number of people, *wubao* has a special significance in that it is linked to the tradition of looking after parents in old age. *Wubao* is seen as an obligation of rural collectives. In recent years, this obligation has been cited in birth control propaganda to demonstrate that couples without sons need not fear for support in old age, as the collective will be there ready to look after them. In contrast, poor households (*pinkun hu*) constitute a wider category, and although distributed over the whole countryside, they are much more prevalent in underdeveloped areas, often with poor soil and an inhospitable climate.

Table 6.5. The recipients of social relief

Year	No. of recipients[a]	% of rural population	% of poor assisted[b]	% of the poor in rural population[c]
1978	30.2	4.0	n.a.	n.a.
1980	46.4	6.0	54.3	11.0
1983	35.0	4.5	56.2	8.0
1984	38.0	5.4	46.9	11.5
1985	38.0	5.8	39.4	14.7
1986	40.0	6.4	39.0	16.4
1987	37.0	6.4	n.a.	n.a.

[a] The figures for the recipients are in million, those for 1978–84 are from YRSES (1986: 259, and 264); the rest are from ZTN (1988).
[b] As provided in NTN (1986: 294), the figure for 1986 is from NTN (1987: 272).
[c] As implied by the percentage of the poor who are assisted.

The details of social relief for recent years are given in Table 6.5. The figures in column 1 refer to the recipients of relief, predominantly in kind; they do not include the recipients of assistance in the form of employment or production subsidies. For a low-income country, the percentage of the rural population receiving assistance seems to be strikingly small, and, more important, so too is the percentage of the poor in the rural population. As shown by column 3, only a fraction of those officially recognized as poor receive social relief, and this fraction has been falling since 1983 for reasons explained below. Yet the percentage of the recipients of social relief in the rural population has been rising due to the decrease in the rural population. The percentage of the poor, including both the recipients and the non-recipients, in the rural population, as shown by column 4, is an indirect estimate derived from the percentage of the rural poor receiving social relief. Considering the rapid and widespread rise in personal incomes over this period, there is no plausible explanation for this apparent rise in poverty other than a better identification of the poor due to a greater sensitivity to rural poverty on the part of the government. This brings home the point that the existing figures for the rural poor in China have to be treated with great caution because to our knowledge there is as yet no systematic attempt at estimation.

The decrease in the percentage of the recognized poor receiving social relief shown by column 3, we would suggest, does not represent an erosion of social security, but a steady shift from consumption subsidies to production subsidies and public works programmes. The recipients of the former are counted under social relief but the latter are not. In recent years, there has been a proliferation of employment provision schemes in rural areas. The numbers of such schemes increased from 20,000 in 1980 to 50,000 in 1986 (NTN 1986: 294; NTN 1987: 252). Such schemes have been commonly used in developing economies such as India to alleviate deprivation in rural areas. But until recently China has not used public works schemes for this purpose. This may seem surprising because China has long been famous for massive mobilizations of rural labour for infrastructural works. The reason for this apprent paradox lies in the method of mobilization of labour and resources for capital projects during the era of collectivism.

During the period of collective cultivation, the labour and resources used for infrastructural projects were frequently not remunerated at all. This resembled the traditional Chinese practice of requiring rural communities to supply labour and resources for the construction and maintenance of monuments and economic infrastructure. On occasions when labour and resources were paid for, more often than not the remuneration came from collective rather than government funds. Infrastructural works were seen and commended by the leadership as attempts by rural communities to lift themselves from poverty through their own efforts. They were not used by the government for making income transfers to poor areas. For raising current consumption in deprived areas, the government tended to use the State marketing system to supply grain and agricultural inputs on concessional terms. There has been an important change in the government policy towards infrastructural works in rural areas. One of the first acts of the reform leadership in China was to ban unrewarded exactions of labour and resources by rural collectives (for a case-study see Zweig 1989: chap. 7). This, together with the change in the ideological climate, has cut the ground from underneath revolutionary mobilizations of labour for collective ends. A result of this is the neglect of irrigation works to which we referred earlier. Now that the deployment of labour has been devolved from collectives to households, relieving rural poverty by providing employment on government-funded public works schemes is gaining in favour.

Broadly speaking, there has been an important difference between the methods for relieving rural poverty in China and in India. The Chinese government with its tight control of trade in agricultural produce and inputs, and with its relatively underdeveloped public finance system has tended to rely more on assistance through commerce than on assistance from the government budget. In contrast, the Indian government with its more developed public finance system and its looser hold over trade in agricultural produce and inputs has tended to rely more on budgetary assistance than on assistance through commerce. This contrast still holds but not as starkly as it did in the pre-reform period. As the system of public finance still remains comparatively under-developed, the Chinese government is naturally disposed towards using trade as a policy instrument for a wide variety of purposes.

Turning to the details of *wubao* relief, Table 6.6 presents the available figures. As indicated earlier, the recipients of *wubao* relief are predominantly the elderly without relatives to depend on. For example, in 1985–6, they constituted on average 83 per cent of the recipients; the rest were orphans and the disabled (NTN 1987: 266). In effect, *wubao* is a support scheme for indigent elderly in rural areas. What proportion of the elderly in rural areas receive *wubao*? Taking the 1982 population census figure for over-65s in the countryside and assuming that 83 per cent of the recipients of *wubao* relief are elderly people, the estimate for 1982 comes to just over 3 per cent. The proportion for recent years would be lower because, whilst the numbers of over-65s has increased, the number of recipients has since 1982 remained nearly constant. This percentage may seem derisory by the norms of a Welfare State, but it is exceptional for a developing economy. In most developing economies, public provisions for the indigent elderly in rural areas simply do not exist. Turning to column 2, there has been a sharp decrease in the percentage of *wubao* elderly supported by collective institutions. According to circumstantial evidence, this represents a centralization of *wubao* relief away from villages, which are collective institutions, to townships, the lowest tier of the government in rural areas (for case-studies see Hussain and Liu 1989: sec. 3).

Table 6.6. Recipients of *Wubao* relief

Year	Persons in millions	% supported by collectives
1978	3.0	85
1980	2.9	86
1981	2.9	90
1982	3.0	90
1983	3.0	96
1984	3.0	91
1985	3.0	74
1986	3.0	75

Sources: STZ (1987: 120); NTN (1987: 266); the figures are rounded.

The essential feature of the *wubao* system is that it is local, founded upon solidarity in rural communities. The levels and methods of provision have not been uniform. They have varied greatly both in time and space, as do the criteria of eligibility for assistance. *Wubao* relief, although grounded in the constitution, lacks a detailed legal and regulatory framework specifying the sources of funds, the range of coverage, the rights of recipients, and the obligations of collectives. In terms of organization, it ranges between charitable assistance, which carries a social stigma, and a formal social-security programme with codified details of provision. *Wubao* relief is predominantly non-residential: the recipients live on their own or with relatives. However, an increasing proportion of them are accommodated in 'Houses of Respect' (*jinglao yuan*), and they receive a higher level of support than those living at home. Some of the richer areas have gone a step further and have introduced old-age pensions for farmers. As yet such schemes are restricted to a few prosperous rural areas (for case-studies see Hussain and Liu 1989: introduction and sec. 1).

In recent years *wubao* relief has come under strain from two sources. Prior to the reforms, it was organized at the level of the village (production team) and was intertwined with collective cultivation. There is evidence that, following the introduction of the Responsibility System, it has been neglected or in some rural areas has broken down completely (for examples see World Bank 1985: 30, 92–3, and 165; Bernstein 1985; Hussain and Liu 1989: sec. 3). There is a trend towards the township government taking over the responsibility for *wubao* relief, which in future may become a norm for the whole of the countryside and provide the basis for a formalization of the system.

The second source of strain arises from the changing age structure of the population and the birth control policy. As pointed out earlier, the percentage of the elderly in the population has been increasing. Added to that, the percentage of the elderly is higher in the rural than in the urban areas (Hussain and Liu 1989: sec. 4.2). The discrepancy between rural and urban areas is likely to increase with additional migration from the countryside, which occurs mostly among the young. This raises a doubt whether the *wubao* system, informally organized as it is, will be able to cope with the mounting burden implied by demographic trends. *Wubao* support is used to persuade couples to forgo children. Yet, as presently organized, it does not have much power of persuasion. On the contrary, it provides an incentive to breach the one-child policy. For it is strictly restricted to the elderly without children or near relatives to depend on. In most areas, *wubao* is designed more to prevent the 'non-deserving' elderly from claiming relief than to ensure that all the 'deserving' elderly in fact get relief. For example, the property of *wubao* recipients is inherited by the collective not by their relatives. Rural authorities take measures to prevent families from transferring the burden of supporting their elderly to the collective. And *wubao* is intended as no more than a safety net against destitution. For couples of child-bearing age, *wubao* is an inferior alternative to having a son who would support them in old age. The general point is that a scheme which is expressly designed for the elderly without relatives cannot appeal to couples who have the option of depending on their children in old age. This is increasingly realized in China, and concern to decrease rural birth rates is the main source of pressure for an improvement in public support for the elderly in rural areas.

2.3.2. Public Provision for Health in Rural Areas Aside from the land reform, which guaranteed access to land to the whole of the rural population, the extension of health care to a vast majority of the rural population has been a major achievement of the Chinese economy in the field of social security. Here we confine ourselves to two aspects, which have been distinguishing marks of health provision in rural China. The first is the emphasis on public hygiene and preventive care and the second is the provision of primary medical care at the grass-roots level in the 1960s and 1970s.

Historically, the promotion of public hygiene and preventive health care has relied heavily on mass campaigns. The biggest of these was the 'Great Patriotic Health Campaign' of the 1950s which was aimed against four pests: flies, mosquitoes, rats, and (mistakenly) sparrows. Since then there have been many other campaigns directed against opium addiction, a legacy of colonialism, and specific diseases such as smallpox, venereal diseases, typhus, plague, and schistosomiasis, a severe debilitating disease spread by snails which was once endemic in the Yangtze basin (for details of campaigns see a personal account in Horn 1971). Such health campaigns involved promoting hygiene, eliminating disease 'vectors', and mass screening to identify and treat the afflicted. They relied on elementary medical precepts and owed their effectiveness to the mobilization of the population on an epic scale. Thanks to them, within two decades (1950–70), China managed to reduce drastically, if not to eliminate, the incidence of common parasitic and infectious diseases. A testimony of their success is provided by the massive national mortality survey of 1973–5, which revealed that the cause pattern of mortality in China was closer to that of middle-income than of low-income economies, where parasitic and infectious diseases rank high among the causes of death (on the details of the mortality survey, see Banister 1987: 96–8). In form, health campaigns were similar to campaigns in other fields such as those for investment in infrastructure or politics, all involving a massive mobilization of the population through a mixture of propaganda and coercion, which the collective rural economy facilitated. From an economic point of view, their main feature was their very low financial cost, because in most cases labour was not remunerated at all, or, on the few occasions when it was, rates were very low.

The decollectivization of the rural economy has, as it were, weakened the social immune system (for an account see Endicott 1988: chap. 12). For example, schistosomiasis, which had been eradicated by the 1970s, has now reappeared, and the percentage of inoculated infants decreased in the 1980s. Health campaigns have continued, but they have neither the same appeal nor the same effect as they did in the pre-reform period. The economics of campaigns has changed radically. With the shift to household economy, the opportunity cost of labour to rural households has increased; neither are they willing nor can they be easily coerced into performing free or low-paid labour for wider social ends, as they did before. The basic problem is that campaigns can no longer be sustained by propaganda alone, they require an adequate remuneration of labour for their success. The maintenance of preventive health care and public hygiene in rural areas requires a system of public finance which has been slow to develop. The government has taken a few steps to arrest the decline in preventive health care. For example, alarmed by the evidence of rise in infant mortality (for a discussion see Hussain and Stern 1988), the government in conjunction with UNICEF has now embarked on a national plan to achieve inoculation of at least 90 per cent of infants by 1991.

A major achievement of the period of the Cultural Revolution (1966–76) was the extension of primary medical care to villages. This involved dispatching medical personnel from cities and county towns to villages, the establishment of village health stations, training a huge number of paramedics—'barefoot doctors' and part-time medical personnel—and developing co-operative health insurance in villages. The policy was a success because it addressed the two issues central to the provision of primary medical care in rural areas of developing economies. The first is how to train medical personnel in sufficient numbers and, more important, to deploy them in the countryside. The second is how to finance medical care. The barefoot doctors, who became famous throughout the world, were the main medical personnel at village level. They were rural residents who had received an elementary medical training which was short, focused on a few tasks, and did not presuppose a high level of education. They worked part or full time aided by medical workers whom they trained. They dispensed basic primary health care and referred patients with severe illnesses to commune and county hospitals. Notwithstanding their name they did wear shoes, especially when performing medical tasks. The use of paramedics for primary health care is not peculiar to China; earlier the Soviet Union too relied on paramedics (known as *feldshers*) for the same purpose. China's main achievement was to train a very large number within a very short period of time. For example, in 1979 there were around two barefoot doctors per 1,000 inhabitants. This had its negative side too, in that their level of training was highly variable, and many of them were entrusted with tasks well beyond their competence (see Chen 1989: pt. 2). Further, barefoot doctors could not be the permanent mainstay of primary health care in rural areas. For their training, elementary and narrowly focused as it was, ran the risk of being made obsolete by successes in improving public hygiene and eliminating parasitic and infectious diseases.

Starting from 1965 there was a concerted attempt to develop co-operative health insurance in the countryside. On the eve of decollectivization in 1979, around 80 per cent of production brigades (the middle tier of the commune, now termed villages), or about 85 per cent of the rural population had some form of health insurance system—an unparalleled achievement for a large developing economy (see World Bank 1984). Brigade members paid an annual fee in return for the reimbursement of out-patients and hospital costs, including medicines. The extent of coverage varied widely. Contributions from brigade members only covered a part of the costs, villages (production teams and production brigades) paid the rest from collective funds. The co-operative health insurance system was founded on collective agriculture, and together with barefoot doctors it came to be closely identified with the discredited period of the Cultural Revolution. Thus it seems that the leadership made no attempt to retain the system as land was parcelled out to households. As a result, in 1985 the rural health insurance system survived in a mere 5 per cent of brigades or villages as compared to 80 per cent in 1979 (Shao 1988). The rural health insurance system did suffer from some major defects, but its almost total disappearance is due in large measure to wilful neglect by the leadership.

The Responsibility System has had a debilitating effect on the rural health care system. Not only has health insurance been replaced with payment according to treatment, including the inoculation of children, but there has also been a massive decrease in medical personnel in rural areas (for details see Hussain and Stern 1988). The government has decontrolled drug production without developing an effective system to monitor quality (see Chen 1989: pt. 2). Many village health stations are left unattended because of lack of personnel. The main reason for the decline in the number of personnel is financial. Subsidies for health care from collective funds have decreased, and the government tried to keep medical fees under a tight control, while rural incomes were rising. As a result, many barefoot doctors and other part-time medical personnel have found it more profitable to engage in non-medical pursuits.

Nevertheless, there have been some attempts to develop an alternative health care system for rural areas. Following Deng Xiaoping's advice that barefoot doctors should start wearing straw sandals, if not leather shoes, a proportion of them have acquired further medical training and been upgraded to the status of 'rural doctors' who work full time. In fact, the term 'barefoot doctors' is no longer used. Further, the Ministry of Public Health has introduced pilot rural insurance schemes in a number of villages (for details, see Shao 1988). However, the cost per head of these schemes is much higher than that of previous schemes. While such schemes may be applicable to richer rural areas, their introduction in poorer areas would depend crucially on subsidies from the government. Given the pressure on the government to keep its expenditure on a tight rein, comprehensive health insurance in poorer areas is a distant possibility. But one may well witness a rapid spread of health insurance in richer areas.

3. SOCIAL SECURITY IN URBAN AREAS

The urban counterpart of access to land for rural households is an employment guarantee for residents with urban registration. As in the previous section, we first outline the environment in which urban social-security programmes operate. For the present purposes, the two most important components of the environment are:

(1) entitlements, employment and earnings;
(2) household registration and rationing of consumer goods.

The urban social-security system consists largely of what is usually termed 'occupational welfare'. That is, most urban residents receive their social-security benefits and a wide range of social provisions through their work units (*danwei*), and not from a social-security agency. In fact, work units have a pervasive influence on every aspect of their employees' lives. There is also a residual social-security system built around the residential neighbourhood to cater for those cases which are not covered by occupational welfare. As we shall see, unlike in rural areas, the urban social-security system is fairly elaborate.

3.1. *Entitlements, Employment and Earnings*

The formally employed labour force, most of which is in urban areas, is heavily segmented by differing entitlements to social security. These vary with employee status and the status of the work unit (*danwei*), which makes the distribution of social-security provisions in urban areas heavily dependent on the employment pattern. As we shall see, the reforms have had a profound effect on this pattern. By status, employees may be divided into permanent (*guding*), contract (*laodong hetongzhi*), and temporary (*linshi*) workers, each with a different entitlement to labour insurance. The permanent and contract employees together form the regular labour-force of work units. Such or similar divisions have existed since the 1950s but have assumed greater significance in the wake of the reforms. Beside employees, there are also the self-employed, who existed in large numbers up to 1955 and became almost extinct during the Cultural Revolution period. They have proliferated since 1978 and accounted for 4 per cent of the non-agricultural labour force in 1987 (ZTN 1988: 153). Their growth, which is expected to continue apace, is of special significance for urban social security, as the self-employed are outside the ambit of occupational welfare altogether.

Work units (*danwei*) are officially classified into 'owned by the people'—the State sector—collective enterprises, and the rest—private and foreign enterprises. The first two constitute what may be termed 'the socialized sector', which has since the early 1950s accounted for almost all of the employed labour-force. Despite the encouragement given to private and foreign enterprises in recent years, they accounted for only 0.5 per cent of the employed labour-force in 1987 (ZTN 1988, p. 153). The term 'socialized sector' denotes no more than the absence of private ownership; its employees do not all have the same entitlement to labour insurance. Whilst all employees of the State sector are covered by labour insurance, either partially or fully, only two-thirds of the employees of collective enterprises are. Furthermore, the employees of collective enterprises often contribute towards their labour insurance, but a vast majority of employees of the State sector still do not.

As compared to the employees of collective enterprises, State employees have more secure jobs and higher pay on average, 28 per cent higher in 1987 (ZTN 1988: 194, 198). The higher-tier collective enterprises tend to emulate State-owned enterprises. Collective enterprises are graded into two categories according to the tier of the subprovincial government supervising them. The first consists of those supervised by the county or supra-county tiers of the government, and the second of the rest. The lower-tier includes the collective enterprises run by urban neighbourhoods and rural townships and villages. Generally speaking, the State sector is heavily regulated and is comparatively uniform in matters of pay and labour insurance. In contrast, the collective sector is highly diverse.

To avoid going into lengthy detail, we focus mainly on the State-sector employees, who at the end of 1988 constituted around 73 per cent of the formally employed labour-force (ZTYB Dec. 1988: 5). In 1978 this figure was around 79 per cent (ZLGTZ 1987: 15). Such employees are nearly all in urban areas, as rural industry is collectively rather than State-owned. For the present purposes, the State-sector employees may be divided into the following two broad categories, relating to the extent of labour insurance coverage:

	% of State-sector labour-force
Fully Covered	
Permanent Employees	78
Contract Employees	8
Not Fully Covered	
Temporary workers	14

Contract employees are recently introduced replacements for permanent employees, and the two together constitute the regular labour-force of work units.

Permanent employees, who are all in the State sector, also constitute a majority of the formally employed labour-force, around 57 per cent at the end of 1988 (ZTYB 1988: 5). Until recently, they had the right to a job in their work unit for life, which frequently was taken to mean the right to occupy the same job for life. They amounted, therefore, to a fixed factor of production, as it was rare for permanent employees to change their work unit. Permanent employment for the regular labour-force has had a special significance for social security in that it restricted the incidence of unemployment to what has usually been a small minority of the urban labour force, consisting of temporary employees and new entrants, and now contract workers as well. The labour market reforms of recent years have sought to reduce the security enjoyed by permanent employees, and to encourage greater labour mobility between jobs and work units. Permanent employees may now be dismissed for persistent indiscipline and be made redundant in the event of bankruptcy, which is not possible but still rare. They no longer have the right to remain in the same job and can be redeployed in a variety of ways. They can be laid off, but only with pay. They still have a privileged status as compared to other categories of employees in that they have the right to income, if no longer to a job. In as yet infrequent cases of dismissal or redundancy due to bankruptcy, they are entitled to unemployment benefit, which, aside from contract workers, is not available to the rest of the urban labour-force. This includes temporary employees of the State sector and almost all of the collective-sector employees. And, unlike other categories of employees, they do not contribute towards their labour insurance. In principle, this is taken into account in determining their pay. The 1986 Labour Regulation put an almost total end to permanent employment by providing for all new recruits to be on fixed-term but renewable contracts. As intended, this will lead to a steady decrease in the numbers of permanent employees, as those reaching retirement will not be replaced. But it will also increase the ratio of retired to still working permanent employees. This, as we shall see, is likely to pose a special problem for the financing of pensions for permanent employees in the future.

Contract employees, or 'labour contract system employees' (*laodong hetongzhi gong*) as they are termed, have increased rapidly in numbers since the 1986 Labour Regulation. The government's intention is that in future the regular labour-force of enterprises will consist entirely on contract employees. Employment on contract in various forms has existed since the 1950s, but until 1986 this covered only the residual category of temporary workers (for details, see Walder 1986: chap. 2; White 1987). Unlike permanent employees, contract employees contribute towards their labour insurance, in particular old-age pensions. The change-over from permanent to contract employment is meant to promote efficiency by allowing workers greater freedom to switch jobs on the one hand, and by enabling enterprises to adjust their regular labour force on the other. However, the change-over is also likely to create new problems for social security. First of all, it introduces the possibility of recurrent large-scale unemployment arising out of spells between successive jobs, which in the past applied only to temporary workers. Second, since, as elsewhere, unemployment spells in between jobs are likely to vary with the age, sex, and qualifications of the unemployed, contract employment may lead to long-term unemployment among certain categories of urban workers such as the middle-aged, the unskilled, and women. The full consequences of contract employment will take some time to surface, because contract employees still constitute a small percentage of the regular labour-force, and the system has not been in operation long enough for many of even the initial set of contracts to expire.

Temporary employees form a residual category, including both workers with urban registration, and also growing numbers of rural immigrants with only temporary urban registration. Although temporary employment is a transitory state for both, they do not face the same range of future possibilities. For workers with urban registration, temporary employment may lead on to a regular job, preferably contract employment in the State sector. But for immigrant workers, temporary employment leads either to another temporary employment, perhaps only after a spell of unemployment, or forced return to the countryside. They have a limited prospect of graduating to regular employment, because they stand a very small chance of obtaining urban registration. Almost all immigrant workers are in unskilled and manual jobs; many are employed on building sites. Being temporary urban residents, they are not entitled to low-price rations of grain and cooking oil. They may be housed by their work units, often in makeshift single accommodation on building sites. Temporary workers in the State sector are usually better protected than temporary workers in the collective sector, in that they benefit from some of the labour insurance provisions. But they are not entitled to old-age and disability pensions.

As well as rural immigrants in temporary jobs, Chinese cities also attract from the countryside a large number of itinerant casual labourers, petty traders, female domestic servants, and people in search of a better life. They constitute a marginal population, completely outside the umbrella of urban social security. They are covered neither by occupational social welfare nor by programmes organized around urban neighbourhoods, which are restricted to permanent residents. The so-called floating population, including all types of rural immigrants, has grown rapidly in recent years and is already sizeable. For example, it is estimated that in 1985 as much as 12 per cent of Beijing's population consisted of residents without urban registration (JPRS 1986: 48–52). More recent figures for Beijing would be higher, and higher again for Guangzhou. A rough guess is that the nation-wide floating population may be as much as 50 million, which is around 9 per cent of the total urban population. The rapid growth in their numbers is creating a social and economic rift in China's urban areas which is far deeper and more extensive than any existing in the pre-reform period. This rift is not temporary, because it is founded upon the system of household registration, which is likely to stay in force for the foreseeable future. And the economic factors responsible for immigration into urban areas are likely to remain strong.

China has had a complex system of administrative assignment to jobs, which has been more extensive than those in East European economies. In the 1950s when it was introduced, the system covered only the State sector, but was extended to the collective sector during the period of the Cultural Revolution. The job assignment system does much more than bring together prospective employees and work units. It is as much concerned with employment creation as it is with matchmaking. Built into the system there has been an obligation on the part of the government (labour bureaux) to provide jobs to university graduates and new entrants to the permanent urban labour-force. The reforms have cut down on this obligation, but as yet only marginally. In the past, job assignment by labour bureaux imposed considerable restrictions on both prospective employees and work units. Employees were not free to choose their occupation or work unit. And work units had to accept candidates channelled to them by labour bureaux, even if they were unqualified for the job and redundant to their requirements. Work units were not allowed by bypass labour bureaux by recruiting employees directly, except in special cases and within limits. In effect, it was the labour bureaux rather than the work units which made recruitment decisions. Administrative assignment to jobs also helped to keep in check unlicensed immigrants from rural areas, as they were not entitled to job assignment and had very limited possibilities of being hired directly by work units.

As part of the economic reforms, the government has been seeking to transform recruitment and employment practices. One aim is to relieve the pressure on the State sector to create jobs by encouraging the growth of employment in collective enterprises, and the proliferation of private businesses. Although formally the government no longer guarantees employment to new entrants to the labour-force with urban registration and to university graduates, they are still covered de facto by an employment guarantee. What has changed, however, is that they now stand a lower chance of getting a regular job in the State sector than they did before the reforms. However, the creation of jobs so as to keep in check unemployment among the urban labour-force still remains a central aim. Recent years have witnessed the proliferation of so-called 'labour service companies'. These are established by a diverse variety of work units, including labour bureaux, State-owned enterprises, and government organizations. They are, in effect, job creation schemes. But the jobs they provide are usually not on a par with regular jobs: the pay is lower and there is little or no labour insurance cover. Thus employment creation through labour service companies is a cheaper alternative to creating regular employment in work units, because it saves on both pay and labour insurance benefits. Added to that, investment per extra worker is low in such companies.

A long-term aim of the labour reforms is completely to replace administrative assignment with direct recruitment by employers. Work units are now allowed a much wider leeway in direct recruitment, which has weakened the previous controls on hiring rural immigrants. Direct recruitment does give both job-seekers and work units a greater freedom of choice, but it also removes the employment guarantee which goes with administrative assignment. As channels of direct recruitment are still very underdeveloped, administrative assignment to jobs is likely to remain important for a long time to come (for a discussion of labour reforms see Feng and Zhao 1984).

Backed by stringent restrictions on immigration from rural areas, employ-ment and recruitment policies have succeeded in keeping urban unemployment rates exceptionally low by international standards. For example in the decade 1978–87 (inclusive), the unemployment rate among the labour-force with urban registration averaged around 3 per cent; and the average over the last five years of the decade was even lower at 2 per cent (ZTN 1988: 175). However, China has gone through periods of comparatively serious urban unemploy-ment, for example in the early 1950s, in the late 1950s to the early 1960s following the collapse of the Great Leap, and, recently, in the years from 1979 to the early 1980s when youths sent to the countryside during the Cultural Revolution returned. Recently recorded levels of urban unemployment would be much higher if urban residents without registration were included in the figures. Notwithstanding these qualifications, an exceptionally low rate of urban unemployment by international standards still remains a distinguishing feature of the Chinese economy. This may change in the future. The un-employment rate would rise steeply if the government were to press ahead with labour reforms designed to reduce feather-bedding in State-owned enterprises. And, as we pointed out earlier, contract employment may in time lead to a higher unemployment rate.

The absence of sizeable urban unemployment is, however, not without serious negative features. The low rate of manifest unemployment goes together with a high rate of disguised unemployment, or 'in-house unemploy-ment' (neibu diaye) as it is aptly termed in China. According to the Minister of Labour, there may be as many as 20 million surplus workers in State-owned enterprises, which is equal to a fifth of their labour-force in 1987 (Beijing Review, 19–25 Dec. 1988, p. 18). The figure is likely to be no more than a rough guess, but it does convey the magnitude of the problem. Feather-bedding has had an adverse effect not merely on labour productivity but also, we would argue, on total factor productivity. For the existence of surplus labour goes together with an organization of production in which an efficient utilization of factors does not figure as a central consideration. How to reduce feather-bedding without causing a social upheaval is one of the most difficult problems facing the economic reforms in China. The problem cannot be solved quickly without a significant increase in at least temporary unemployment. The urban social-security system is not equipped, either financially or organizationally, to cope with a sizeable number of unemployed. In the past, it never had to face such a problem, and, as we discuss later, the newly introduced unemployment insurance scheme is designed to cater for only a limited category of the unemployed.

Historically, the government has sought to keep the task of providing jobs to urban residents within manageable limits by imposing stringent restrictions on the growth of the labour-force with urban registration, though, interestingly, not by reducing labour participation. Prior to the reforms, rural–urban migration was exceptionally low, and urban registration was strictly rationed. The former no longer holds, but the latter still does. And the government periodically pared the urban labour-force by dispatching immigrants back to the countryside (*fang xia*), as in the late 1950s and the early 1960s, or by sending the educated youth to the countryside, as during the period of the Cultural Revolution. The latter move, however, was dictated more by ideology than by a manpower policy. Reducing urban unemployment by repatriating rural immigrants depends crucially on the ability of the government to force rural communities to absorb the rusticated labour-force. This was relatively easy during the period of collective agriculture, but now it is more difficult. Added to that, the mechanisms for ensuring that repatriated people do not drift back to cities are now much weaker.

Yet the government has not attempted to contain the problem of urban unemployment by reducing labour participation. The reason is that work has not been regarded simply as a source of income, but also as a source of virtue. Much of the ideological education and social control of adults in China is based around the work unit. A host of measures has served to keep labour participation high. For example, facilitated by maternity benefits under labour insurance and the widespread provision of child care facilities by work units, female participation is exceptionally high in urban areas. However, attitudes towards female participation have begun to change. For the reasons discussed later, many enterprises now exert pressure on women workers to withdraw from the labour market. Moreover, there are increasing reports of discrimination against women in labour recruitment. The leadership, however, still remains committed to maintaining a high rate of female participation.

Turning to labour compensation, it may be argued that the urban labour-force has had implicitly to trade high employment for low pay and administrative assignment to a job, which has left little room for occupational choice. Low wage rates have also served to sustain a high rate of female participation by making it difficult to subsist on one income alone. In the past, wage rates were governed by the national wage scale, which varied little across work units, and was independent of the financial performance of enterprises. Income inequality in urban areas was exceptionally low. As the economic reforms have unfolded, there has been an increase in bonuses and other forms of earnings linked to the financial performance of enterprises. Higher profits mean higher bonuses. Conversely, as we point out later, losses may reduce pay and erode labour insurance cover. Added to that, the reforms have also driven a wide wedge between the earnings of different occupational groups; in particular, the earnings of workers producing marketed goods and services have risen faster than those of people producing non-marketed goods and services such as medical care and education. A common refrain has been that a barber earns more than a surgeon, and a waiter more than a university professor (Liu 1989). The proliferation of labour service companies adds yet another dimension to differences in income by occupation.

3.2. Household Registration and Rationing of Consumer Goods

Household registration (hukou), which is compulsory for all households, is not merely a source of data but also a means for controlling citizens. Whilst rural registration is simply a matter of record, urban registration is a privilege which is either inherited or acquired under certain restrictive conditions. Given this asymmetry, household registration can be used for rewarding and punishing citizens, indeed it has been and still is. Acquiring hukou in a small town is relatively easy, but very difficult in cities such as Beijing, Shanghai, or Tianjin. 'Temporary residents' are required to have a temporary household registration, but the requirement is increasingly violated. Household registration booklets (hukou bu) contain full details of the family and the history of births, deaths, and marriage. In effect, they contain all the information needed to target social-welfare payments according to family size and income. However, household registration has been used less for social welfare and more to control population migration. The way in which it is implemented has an important influence on household formation. For a spouse is not automatically entitled to reside in the same place as the other, nor parents in the same place as grown-up children.

In the pre-reform period, household registration, in conjunction with other restrictions, did succeed in keeping migration exceptionally low. But in recent years, the host of restraints which in the past kept the numbers of temporary visitors to cities low have either disappeared altogether or lost their rigour. Travel is no longer restricted. With the shift to the Responsibility System, leaving the land has become a matter for individual choice rather than for official discretion. In addition, the economic attraction of migrating to cities has increased. The urban construction boom has increased the demand for manual labourers. The removal of controls on private trading, self-employment, and direct recruitment by enterprises has provided rural immigrants with much wider opportunities for earning a living. With the opening of private markets in grain and other necessities, household registration is no longer needed for their purchase. In sum, population movement in China is increasingly governed by the usual economic forces. Since urban registration is still strictly rationed, the result has been a massive increase in the numbers of people who live in urban areas but are not recognized as permanent urban residents. Thus household registration, as well as restricting migration to large cities, is also creating a marginal population with uncertain residence status and a precarious economic position.

Apart from opening doors to jobs with higher pay and in most cases with labour insurance cover, urban registration also confers entitlement to obtain rations of selected necessities at low prices. A central feature of the rationing of consumer goods in China is that it is targeted according to residential status and age, but not according to income or other economic characteristics. The rationing of consumer goods in China has lasted longer and has been more comprehensive than in any other economy in the world. Since the early 1950s when it began, the range of rationed goods has varied in time and place. The two decades spanning the Great Leap and the Cultural Revolution (1958–78) saw the extension of rationing to all but a few goods. Since 1978, most commodities have been de-rationed, leaving only the three main staples of grain, cooking oil, and cotton cloth, which are rationed nationally. In addition to these, there may be local rationing of such goods as meat and eggs. Further, the government has allowed the emergence of free markets in rationed commodities (for details of rationing of consumer goods see Tian 1989).

With the reforms, the financial burden on the government of maintaining rationing has mounted, as we pointed out in Section 1. This has put pressure on the government to raise the sale price of rationed goods on the one hand, and to restrict the issue of urban registration on the other. In smaller towns, the government has increasingly resorted to granting urban registration with the condition that the holder should not be entitled to low-price rations, thus introducing yet another status distinction in the urban population (see Fei Xiaotong et al. 1989: 199–200). In fact, were it not for the probability of resistance from households with urban registration, the government would like to do away with rationing altogether. Initially at the start of the reforms, consumers welcomed the removal of rationing because it meant the lifting of quantitative restrictions on purchases. But with the emergence of parallel markets in rationed commodities, consumers are free to buy more than the ration at higher market prices. The ration coupons simply entitle the holder to receive price subsidies, determined by the size of the ration and the price difference. Further, ration coupons have a cash value because they can be sold, a practice which, although illegal, seems to be widespread. As a result, households with urban registration have a vested interest in the continuation of rationing.

How valuable has the rationing of consumer goods been as an income maintenance measure? Historically speaking, the introduction of rationing was motivated by the desire to ensure a just distribution of daily necessities. Theoretically, rationing of consumer goods is justified when the government lacks the means to control household incomes or transfer income, and when households differ widely (Weitzman 1977). Neither of these two conditions applied strictly to the pre-reform economy. Salaries and wages were controlled by the government, the degree of inequality in urban areas was low, and the household registration system provided possibilities for targeting assistance. Thus the continuation of rationing beyond the periods of emergency such as the early 1950s and the period of the Great Famine in 1959–62, lacked a coherent rationale in terms of social welfare. Rationing of consumer goods was a natural extension of government monopoly control of trade and prices, and motivated by a profound distrust of markets. Paradoxically, some of the arguments for rationing have gained in validity since the reforms. The government has much less control over incomes than before, and income inequalities in urban areas have considerably widened. But the traditional practice of targeting rations by residential status and age rather than by economic characteristics is becoming increasingly anomalous. The association between residential status and economic characteristics has become much looser. The increase in the numbers of urban residents without urban registration means that a substantial section of the low-income group in urban areas is excluded from low-price rations. In fact, household registration which is used to target rations by residential status can also be used to target rations by the economic characteristics of households.

3.3. *Urban Social Security*

The urban social-security system is largely anchored in the work units (*danwei*). Modelled on the army, *danwei* do not just perform a particular activity, but also take care of all aspects of their employees' lives. For example, a large majority of urban residents live in housing provided by their work units, and the rest in municipal housing. Private housing is still extremely rare in urban areas. Scarce consumer goods are often distributed through work units. Retired workers receive their pensions and health care from their former work units, which, in most cases, continue to house them. Work units often provide employment for children of their employees, though this is not as important as it used to be (on the tutelary role of work units see Walder 1986; Henderson and Cohen 1984). Generally speaking, Chinese work units perform social-welfare functions which in other economies would be performed by the government. Preliminary attempts at enterprise reform have highlighted the need to change urban social security, making it increasingly apparent that any radical reform at enterprise level is not possible without an overhaul of the occupational-welfare system, covering labour insurance and diverse range of benefits provided by work units.

The main benefits provided by labour insurance are, for the most part, grounded in the laws and regulations of the 1950s, when the system was introduced. Schematically, they are (for details see Wong and Macquarrie 1986: sec. 2.4)

health care and paid sick leave;
disability and retirement pensions;
maternity leave and benefit;
unemployment insurance (introduced only recently).

In addition to labour insurance, occupational benefits also include *inter alia* a diverse variety of cash allowances, such as those to compensate for inflation and for transport. In addition, work units provide various benefits in kind, such as child care facilities and subsidized meals (for a case-study see Wong 1989). By far the most important benefit in kind is heavily subsidized housing, which does not figure in social-welfare expenditure. Thus the total income of urban workers, including benefits in kind, far exceeds their salaries or wages. Moreover, as occupational benefits vary widely with employee status and work unit, total income inequality is prima facie much higher than wage and salary inequality.

For a developing economy, labour insurance in China provides generous benefits and covers a substantial percentage of the labour-force. For example, between 1978 and 1985, on average around 23 per cent of the total labour-force and around 91 per cent of the employed labour-force were covered by labour insurance (calculated from ZSTZ 1987: 111; and ZTN 1988: 153). After the 1950s, the percentage of the insured labour force increased with the expansion of employment in government departments and State-owned enterprises. However, the percentage has remained almost constant since 1978, because of the policy to shift the employment patterns away from the State sector. Although labour insurance regulations apply only to the State sector, the higher-tier collective enterprises in urban areas have tended to follow State-owned enterprises in adopting such measures, fairly closely in the pre-reform period but less so in recent years. For example, the percentage of the labour-force in collective enterprises covered by labour insurance fell slightly from 70 per cent in 1978 to 68 per cent in 1985 (calculated from ZSTZ 1987: 111; and ZTN 1988: 153).

By the norms of developing economies, the coverage of labour insurance in China is indeed impressive, but the question remains whether it is likely to extend to the whole of the employed labour-force, including that in rural industry, in the foreseeable future. This question is of some significance because the percentage of the employed labour-force covered by labour insurance fell from 94 per cent in 1978 to 88 per cent in 1985. The reason for this reduction is the change in the distribution of the labour-force away from the State sector, where the coverage is total, to collective enterprises, where the coverage is less total and has fallen slightly. The shift in employment away from the State sector seems set to continue. This by itself would lead to a decrease in the coverage. Besides, future enterprise reforms are likely to transform the status of a large number of State-owned enterprises. In fact, this has already happened with the leasing out of small State-owned enterprises to managers. As we point out later, such enterprises have cut down on benefits. In sum, the developments in the offing seem to indicate a steady decrease rather than an increase in the percentage of the employed labour force covered by labour insurance. This impression is reinforced by the problems besetting labour insurance.

The fundamental problem with labour insurance is that its method of financing is *ad hoc*, and not commensurate with the long-term liabilities entailed by the labour-force presently covered by labour insurance. During the period from 1978 to 1985, whilst expenditure on labour insurance rose steeply (see Table 6.2 above), the percentage of the employed labour-force covered by labour insurance fell by 6 percentage points. Added to that, the ratio of expenditure on occupational welfare (labour insurance and other occupational provisions) as a proportion of the wage bill has risen from 14 per cent in 1978 to 27 per cent in 1987 (ZTN 1988: 203). At the time when the system was introduced, labour insurance was financed by joint contributions from employees and employers, and provision was made for future pension liabilities. With the beginning of the Cultural Revolution in 1966, employee contributions were abolished, the funding of pensions ceased, and so too, it seems, did any forward planning of labour insurance expenditure. Since then, all labour insurance expenditure, including pensions, has been financed on an *ad hoc* basis out of the current revenue of work units. This did not pose any problem until 1977, as the proportion of the total wage bill spent on occupational welfare remained almost constant between 1966 and 1977 (ZLGTZ 1987: 189). But *ad hoc* financing has not been able to cope well with the sharp and unforeseen increase in expenditure on occupational welfare witnessed since 1978.

This sharp rise is due partly to the massive increase in expenditure on old-age pensions, which alone accounted for nearly half of the total increase between 1978 and 1985. And the proportion of total expenditure devoted to pensions rose from 24 per cent to 42 per cent (ZLGTZ 1987: 191). The reasons for the increase lie partly in the legacy of the Cultural Revolution and partly in the demographic trend towards a higher percentage of elderly people in the population as a whole. During the period of the Cultural Revolution retirement due to old age was suspended. Employees kept on working past retirement age unless physically incapacitated. The post-Mao leadership inherited a large backlog of employees past retirement age. It not only reinstated retirement, but also provided generous incentives for early retirement. This was done do make place for the returning youths who had been sent to the countryside during the Cultural Revolution, and also to clear the ranks of party cadres and government officials. It is this move that accounts for the sharp jump in the ratio of the retired to the employed between 1978 and 1983, as shown in Table 6.7.

Table 6.7. Numbers of retired people as % of employed

Year	%
1978	3.3
1979	6.0
1980	7.8
1981	8.7
1982	9.9
1983	11.2
1984	12.3
1985	13.2

Source: ZSTZ (1987: 114).

However, the increase in the percentage of the retired is not due to the legacy of the Cultural Revolution alone. It is also a result of increasing numbers of elderly people in the population, a trend which is expected to continue apace and even accelerate. For a low-income economy, China has an unusually large proportion of the aged in the population. The process of ageing has been faster in China than in most other economies because of the rapid decrease in fertility from the beginning of the 1970s and the rise in life expectancy. The rise in the percentage of the elderly in the population has not been evenly spread but highly skewed towards recent years. The rising trend seems to date from the latter half of the 1970s, which has presented the social-security system in the 1980s with a problem which it was ill equipped to handle after the upheavals of the Cultural Revolution. The financing of pensions, which is a topical subject in China, concerns two distinct issues. The first is a highly uneven distribution of the percentage of the retired to the employed across enterprises and provinces, and the second is the increasing percentage of elderly in the population. The first poses a problem only because the financing of pensions is, as we shall see, highly decentralized.

Turning now to problems posed by the economic reforms, the industrial reforms have sought to grant financial and operational autonomy to State enterprises, and have re-established the principle of the autonomy of collective enterprises. Many small and medium State-owned enterprises have been leased out to managers. China has around half a million enterprises, most of them dating from the pre-reform period. By and large, they were not created on the basis of financial viability, immediate or distant. Granting them financial autonomy immediately raises the issue of survival for many of these enterprises. This poses a problem for labour insurance, which each enterprise is supposed to finance for its employees. Until the onset of the industrial reforms, the decentralized financing of social security was of nominal significance because enterprise budgets were not completely separated from the government budget. The separation of enterprise from government budgets, as sought by industrial reforms, converts nominal into effective liabilities. This brings in its train the possibility that some enterprises may not be able to maintain labour insurance cover for their employees. In fact, the rapid increase in the number of retired from 1979 onwards coincided with the onset of industrial reforms, and soon made it apparent that many of the now financially independent enterprises could not meet their pension liabilities.

Following the industrial reforms, the labour insurance system has to take account of the consequences of the risk that some enterprises may be insolvent. The risk of insolvency is all the greater in the Chinese economy because its enterprise population has not been 'naturally selected' for financial viability. The basic dilemma of enterprise reforms in China is that strict adherence to financial autonomy erodes the coverage of labour insurance, which, in principle, is meant to be independent of the place of employment. Conversely, efforts to maintain labour insurance cover through grants from the government seriously compromise the main aim of reforms. The government has tried to deal with this dilemma through a series of compromise principles. Loss-making enterprises, except in extreme cases, are not allowed to go bankrupt, though there is now a bankruptcy law.

What is needed is a disengagement of the coverage of labour insurance from the financial performance of particular enterprises. In the main this would involve a centralized funding of labour insurance, covering a group of enterprises. Such funding would insulate the coverage of labour insurance from sporadic financial insolvency. The extent of insulation would depend upon how heterogeneous the financial prospects of enterprises in the group are. The Chinese government has already taken some steps towards centralized funding by encouraging the piecemeal pooling of pension liabilities. The pooling schemes are local and predominantly organized by city governments. Under these schemes, participating enterprises contribute a percentage of their payroll to a pool which pays the pension of their retired employees. The percentage of the payroll paid into the pool and the proportion of pensions the pool pays out vary between schemes but not within schemes. In some cases, the pool pays out only a percentage of retirement pensions. Whilst in most areas the pooling schemes cover only the State-owned enterprises, some cities have also introduced separate schemes for collective enterprises. Although 2,000 cities and counties have introduced pooling schemes, there is as yet no national framework for them. Neither is there any arrangement for pooling other items of labour insurance such as health care costs and maternity benefits.

The pooling schemes do no more than redistribute the current financial burden of pensions, and even that only among a relatively small number of enterprises usually in one city. As the ratio of the retired to the labour-force in the State sector varies widely across provinces, prima facie the burden is very unevenly distributed among the schemes (see ZSTZ 1987: 115). More important, the schemes do not address the problem of redistributing the financial burden of pensions over time raised by the increasing percentage of the elderly in the population, which is expected to continue well into the next century. The government has taken a small step in that direction by reintroducing the funding of pensions by joint employee and employer contributions. But this covers contract employees alone, the new recruits in the State sector from 1986. It does not address the pressing problem of redistributing the rising burden of pensions in the immediate future. The reason is that for several decades to come pensioners will be drawn from the ranks not of contract but of permanent employees, whose pensions have not been funded.

By opting for a separate funding of the pensions of contract workers, the government has forgone the promising possibility of financing the pensions of permanent employees from the contributions of the rising numbers of contract employees. Given that no new permanent employees are to be recruited, the ratio of the retired to still working permanent employees will keep on rising. Further, as contract employment applies only to new recruits, for the next twenty to thirty years almost all those reaching the age of retirement will be permanent employees, whose pensions have not been funded. As a result, funding the pensions of contract workers would do nothing to solve the proximate problem of the increasing burden of old-age pensions over the next 20 to 30 years. This would be possible if the pensions of both permanent and contract workers were financed from the same fund. The general point is that pooling the pension liabilities and contributions of various segments of the labour-force in such a way as to include all age-groups makes it possible to redistribute the immediate burden of pensions, which separate financing of pensions for each segment fails to do. Extending this point, it may be argued that as the formally employed labour-force is rapidly rising, and most of the new entrants are relatively young, China could easily solve the problem of financing old-age pensions in the immediate future by instituting a contributory pension scheme covering the whole of the employed labour-force. But the Chinese government seems more disposed towards maintaining labour market segmentation and instituting a separate scheme for each segment.

The problem with labour insurance does not consist merely of financing what the pre-reform laws provided for. As in agriculture, reforms in industry have created new contingencies that labour insurance needs to take into account. The most important of such contingencies are, first, unemployment, and, second, a decline in income due either to poor performance by particular enterprises or to inflation. Unemployment, which was once assumed to be a problem particular to capitalist economies, is being recognized as a recurrent contingency. The economic reforms have created four potential sources of large-scale urban unemployment; as yet only one of them has led to significant unemployment. This is the system of employing large numbers of rural immigrants on short-term contracts or as casual labourers. The curb on investment imposed in the autumn of 1988 triggered large-scale redundancies among rural immigrants. Contrary to government expectations, those who had been laid off did not return immediately to the countryside, creating a massive social and economic problem in large cities, particularly Guangzhou. On the contrary, even while rural immigrants were being laid off, Guangzhou continued to attract large-scale migration from the country. The problem was accentuated by the fact that, being regarded as temporary residents, the migrants were not covered by urban social-security programmes. This episode brings home the general point that the massive influx of rural immigrants creates problems of unemployment and destitution in urban areas. It is no longer feasible for the government to make these problems disappear by dispatching the unemployed and the destitute back to the countryside, as it did in the past.

Among the remaining three potential sources of unemployment, the first is contract employment, which has built into it the possibility of spells of unemployment in between jobs. This may in future lead to significant unemployment, as the percentage of contract workers in the urban labour-force becomes large. The second is the possibility of loss-making enterprises, including the State-owned ones, going bankrupt. As pointed out earlier, bankruptcies among loss-making enterprises are still rare. The third is disguised unemployment in enterprises, which the government wants to reduce in order to further technical efficiency. But, as we point out below, until now enterprises have been expected to tackle the problem of disguised unemployment without large-scale redundancies. In 1986 the government set up a limited unemployment insurance scheme financed by a payroll levy on enterprises (see Hussain and Liu 1989: sec. 5.1). The scheme is designed specifically to reduce resistance to the replacement of permanent employment with contract employment and to bankruptcies. It is restricted to the employees of State enterprises only and promises relatively generous compensation, including *inter alia* a cash income related to basic wage in employment, health care costs, an allowance for dependents on death, and funeral expenses.

Until now, the scheme seems to have played little role in reducing feather-bedding. Enterprises use a variety of methods to redeploy their surplus labour. They may retrain workers in order to redeploy them internally, or pay part wages to their redundant workers while they look for a job outside the enterprise. Another common method is the establishment by individual enterprises of auxiliary or 'labour service' companies to create jobs for their surplus labourers. These auxiliary companies may engage in activities far removed from the parent enterprise's main line of activity. Thus, many enterprises have their own separate unemployment insurance schemes and labour placement and employment creation agencies—hence the common term 'in-house unemployment' (neibu daiye). The widespread reliance on internal redeployment is due mainly to the fact that the unemployment insurance scheme set up by the government does not cover redundant labourers in viable enterprises. As a scheme to reduce feather-bedding, internal re-deployment is bound to be uneven in its effectiveness, because the opportunities available to an enterprise to redeploy its labour internally may not be com-mensurate with the amount of surplus labour it has. The government wants to encourage the reduction of surplus labour through external redeployment across enterprises; and it recognizes that this would involve redundancies and dismissals at a rate much higher than at present. The main question is, if that were to happen, would the unemployment insurance fund still be capable of providing the same generous coverage to all the unemployed as is provided for in the law? As indicated earlier, a rough estimate is that up to 20 per cent of the labour-force in State-owned enterprises may be redundant. And the un-employment scheme is financed by only a 1 per cent levy on the payroll.

Apart from unemployment, the other contingency which has arisen in the wake of the reforms is a decline in income due to poor financial performance by particular enterprises and to inflation. As we have already mentioned, by way of incentive the reforms have introduced a link between financial performance and industrial earnings. Such an incentive scheme has implications for social welfare because it opens up the possibility of earnings falling below the sustenance level. Prima facie, this is likely to be the case for a significant section of the industrial labour-force, because there are, and will continue to be for some time, large numbers of loss-making enterprises which are regarded as not yet ripe for bankruptcy. There is some evidence that employees of such enterprises suffer a substantial decrease in wages and occupational benefits (Hussain and Liu 1989: sec. 2.17). This points to an anomaly: whilst the employees of bankrupt enterprises are provided with adequate income and benefits on a par with labour insurance, there is no mechanism to ensure the same for the employees of loss-making enterprises. The general point is that, prior to the reforms, the indepedence of wages and occupational benefits from the financial performance of their work units amounted to an income guarantee, which has been partially invalidated by the industrial reforms. For social security, this raises the important issue of the extent to which employees ought to bear the risk of a loss of income and occupational benefits which is due to poor financial performance on the part of their enterprises.

Urban residents are increasingly exposed to the risk of a decline in real income due to inflation, which did not exist in the pre-reform period. During the reform decade (1978–88), the inflation rate averaged 6 per cent per year and accelerated sharply to over 20 per cent in 1988. As a result, as much as 35 per cent of the urban population experienced a reduction in real income in 1988 (*Beijing Review*, 6–12 Mar. 1989, Documents). The Chinese economy still lacks regular procedures for reducing the adverse impact of inflation on social welfare. The official price indices are generally regarded as unreliable. Incomes, allowances, and pensions are periodically adjusted to take account of inflation, but they are not tied to any particular index of inflation. The group most at risk from the effects of inflation is pensioners. A survey conducted in 1987 revealed that as many as 20 per cent of retired workers in large cities had incomes below subsistence level (Hussain and Liu 1989: sec. 2.12). China has yet to introduce a regular uprating of pensions in line with inflation.

We turn to two particular cases to illustrate the problems arising out of the situation in which the industrial reforms have been introduced without corresponding changes in the labour insurance system. The first concerns leased-out enterprises, and the second maternity benefits in enterprises with a large percentage of female workers. A large number of small and medium State-owned enterprises have been leased out to management. Although formally such enterprises are expected to maintain labour insurance cover for their employees, many of them do not, skimping on paid sick and maternity leave, and injury and disability compensation. Similarly, enterprises with a large percentage of women employees increasingly default on maternity leave and on the benefits normally provided in labour insurance (for details, see Hussain and Liu 1989: sec. 2). Both these raise general issues of incentives and monitoring in respect to labour insurance. Prior to the reforms, enterprises, being financially dependent on the government, had no economic incentive to reduce labour insurance cover. But after the reforms, enterprises, concerned as they are meant to be with the pursuit of profit, have a strong financial incentive to cut down on those items of labour insurance which they finance individually. These include all but old-age pensions, for example, sickness and maternity leave and benefit. The decentralized financing of maternity benefits creates widespread anomalies because the percentage of women workers varies widely with enterprises and industries, and a reduction in the percentage of women workers may therefore appear attractive to certain enterprises. This may explain the increasing reports of discrimination against women referred to earlier.

The problem, however, is not that all enterprises have cut down upon the coverage of labour insurance. The industrial reforms have led to a divergence in the goals pursued by individual enterprises. Whilst some have switched over to the pursuit of profit, as intended by the reforms, many still remain occupied with enhancing the income and welfare of their employees. Profit-seekers try to shed their welfare obligations, expecting the government to take on the burden—termed in China 'shifting the burden to a maid' (*baomu diti*). In welfare-oriented enterprises, managers and workers form a coalition, and use financial and operational autonomy to further their own parochial interest. This happened under the traditional system too, but it was heavily constrained. Both these pose problems. Profit-seeking reduces the coverage of labour insurance; and whilst welfare-oriented enterprises do not undermine the labour insurance system, they nullify the central aim of enterprise reform.

A reform of the labour insurance system, which is generally considered to be urgently needed, has to keep in view the origins of the system and the general implications of the economic reforms. In the main the present labour insurance system dates from the 1950s and was designed for State enterprises and government agencies. This is evident from the fact that most of the laws and regulations governing labour insurance apply only to the State sector. At the time of the inception of the system the assumption was that in time all enterprises would evolve into State-owned enterprises, thereby extending the coverage of labour insurance. The process of evolution was accelerated during the two decades from 1958 to 1978. The government took over a large proportion of non-State enterprises, and those which had not been taken over behaved like State-owned enterprises. In the wake of these reforms, the perspective on the evolution of enterprises has undergone a fundamental change. It is now generally accepted that the Chinese economy will retain diverse forms of ownership; State, collective, foreign, and private, indefinitely into the future. Further, State ownership itself is likely to undergo a fundamental change.

The close link between the labour insurance system and State ownership is becoming increasingly anachronistic. This would suggest that the labour insurance system should cover the whole of the employed labour-force. Such a move would be desirable on the grounds not only of equity but also of efficiency, because the segmentation of the labour-force by differing entitlement to labour insurance is a massive hinderance to labour mobility between different categories of enterprises. But this cannot be done without a fundamental reassessment of the levels of benefits provided by labour insurance. The benefits are generous for a developing economy, especially for a low-income economy such as China. This is due to the fact that benefits stipulated by laws and regulations have been governed more by ideals than by financial feasibility. The problem of financing is not particular to old-age pensions. Although less pressing, similar problems exist with respect to maternity benefits and subsidized health care.

4. CONCLUSION

We return to the question raised in Section 1 together with a supplementary question: why has China been comparatively successful in preventing deprivation, and will it be able to sustain that success in future? It should be noted that China's comparative success is neither unblemished nor unqualified. Apart from the famine of 1959–61, there have been local shortages of grain occasionally verging on famine. The threat of natural disasters leading to local starvation is still not completely ruled out. Pockets of poverty have existed in China and still do. The post-Mao leadership has been candid in admitting that there is still a sizeable problem of poverty in rural areas. Nevertheless, we still lack a systematic account of the patterns of poverty. There is need for further research, particularly into the patterns of rural poverty and into rural immigrants in cities. The usual assumption has been that poor households are largely confined to poor areas. This may be broadly correct, but there has been little work on the incidence of poverty in relatively prosperous areas. At various points in this chapter we have emphasized the problems posed by the growing number of rural immigrants in urban areas. Apart from impressions, there is very little material on either the size of the immigrant population or their economic and social conditions.

Taking a broad historical view, we would attribute China's comparative success to the joint effect of the following three sets of factors:

(1) capacity to mobilize the population for collective ends;
(2) providing rural households with access to land, and maintaining a high rate of employment in urban areas;
(3) social security programmes.

They are, however, not all on a par. The second set of factors has been far more important than the other two for reasons indicated below. More important, some of these factors no longer apply or, are not as effective as before.

We have included campaigns involving the mobilization of the population because China's achievements in certain areas such as improvements in public hygiene and preventive health care cannot be explained without these. As instruments of change, campaigns have some severe limitations. By their nature they are transitory, they may help to launch initiatives but cannot sustain them. Whatever may be their pros and cons, the point is that the ability of the leadership to mobilize the population for collective ends has diminished, and is likely to diminish even further.

Providing all rural households with access to land either collectively or individually, and guaranteeing some form of employment to all urban residents with urban registration—the two guarantees as we termed them—have provided the Chinese population with a degree of economic security which is rare in developing countries. The two guarantees, by eliminating landlessness and keeping down unemployment, have heavily reduced the population in need of assistance, leaving only those people who are unable to work and lack family ties to be cared for through social-security programmes. Broadly speaking because of the two guarantees, the Chinese social-security system has had a relatively light burden to carry. However, the effectiveness of the two guarantees in reducing the incidence of deprivation has depended crucially on keeping the numbers of urban residents without urban registration to a minimum, and on virtually banishing unemployment in urban areas. Before the reforms both these conditions held true, but increasingly less so after the reforms.

As we have pointed out, there has in recent years been a massive influx of rural immigrants into cities. Although resident and working in urban areas, they are officially classified as rural residents. A vast majority of them are in temporary employment which may be terminated at short notice. The rest are either self-employed, in casual employment, or unemployed. They do not benefit from any employment guarantee, as they are expected to return to the countryside. In the pre-reform period, the government simply repatriated rural immigrants when they were no longer needed. But repatriation is no longer a straightforward option. Rural immigrants are much larger in numbers, around 50 million according to a common guess. And there is now a problem of enforcing repatriation orders.

Unemployment is no longer a purely urban phenomenon, but now constitutes a problem in rural areas as well. In the wake of the reforms, there has been a massive shift of the labour-force within rural areas from farming to other activities. In particular, recent years have witnessed an explosive growth in rural industry—the township and village enterprises. This shift has a particular significance for the incidence of unemployment in rural areas, because whilst self-employment is almost a universal norm in farming, formal employment is prevalent in the non-farming sector. The sectoral shift in the rural labour-force creates a potential problem of unemployment, in that the employed can be laid off. In fact, this has already happened. The curb on investment in township and village industries imposed since autumn 1988 has led to redundancies on a large scale.

The general implication is that an employment guarantee extended only to the labour-force with urban registration is increasingly insufficient to maintain a low rate of unemployment in the economy as a whole. And the provision of land to the agricultural labour-force is no longer adequate to ensure that the means of earning a living are given to the whole of the rural labour-force, which also includes the workers in the non-farm sector. In fact, households which opt out of farming altogether, termed 'specialized households', surrender their claim to agricultural land. It is not easy for them to revert to farming when they cannot make a living out of their non-farming activities. China needs extensive employment schemes in rural areas and also special provision for rural immigrants in cities if it is to maintain the level of economic security its citizens have enjoyed in the past.

In addition, the traditional method of keeping unemployment in check by creating jobs in State or collective enterprises has paid a heavy price in terms of efficiency, as is illustrated by the estimate that as much as 20 per cent of the labour-force in the State sector may be unemployed in disguise. The drive for efficiency and the traditional method of creating employment are increasingly in conflict. The implications of the economic reforms for unemployment have been hidden by spectacular rates of growth in national income, ranging between 10 and 14 per cent over the last five years (ZTN 1988: 53). The acceleration in the rate of inflation since 1988, which has continued into 1989, suggests that such rates of growth are unsustainable. A slow-down, which the government is aiming for, would lead to a massive increase in unemployment. Even though there is an unemployment insurance scheme, the Chinese social-security system is neither organizationally nor financially capable of handling unemployment on a large scale.

Turning to social-security programmes, we have seen that these are fairly sparse in rural areas, but elaborate in urban areas, particularly for those who are employed in the State sector. Rural social-security programmes were to a considerable degree intertwined with the collective economy; and the end of collective farming has cut the ground from underneath many of them. Rural social-security programmes require a new financial foundation, which takes account of the fact that increasingly income from economic activities accrues to households and not to collectives. There is also a need for a legal framework to meet social-welfare obligations, which can no longer be left entirely to bene-volence and the spirit of solidarity in villages.

The comparatively elaborate social-security system in urban areas has come under strain due to enterprise reform and also to the increasing numbers of the retired. The system suffers from two main problems: first, it largely takes the form of 'occupational welfare' based on work units; and, second, labour insurance, which is the main component of the system, does not cover the whole of the employed labour-force. Not only is the proportion of the employed labour-force with no labour insurance cover increasing in urban areas, but also labour insurance does not apply at all to the rapidly growing labour-force in township and village enterprises. The rural labourers are regarded as self-employed, as it were, even when employed. Unless the labour insurance system is overhauled, it may in time be reduced to a selective scheme applying only to a part of the urban labour-force.

A pervasive feature of the Chinese economy is the segmentation of the labour-force by differing entitlements to social security. In the main, the seg-mentation runs along two lines which overlap partially. The first is the distinction between the rural and the urban labour-forces, which is based on household registration and not on the current place of residence. The second, which applies to the urban labour-force, consists in the distinction between regular employees, including permanent and contract workers who are all in the State sector, and non-regular employees, including temporary workers and workers in the collective sector. These distinctions have become increasingly anomalous with the economic reforms. We have seen that there are now large numbers of rural immigrants who live and work in urban areas. They are excluded to a great extent from urban social-security programmes, since for administrative purposes they are regarded as rural residents. In principle, labour insurance does not extend to rural areas because rural inhabitants are regarded as self-employed. Yet there is now in rural areas a large employed labour-force. In urban areas, labour insurance laws and regulations, strictly speaking, apply only to the State-sector employees, even though the policy of the government is to shift employment away from the State sector. By default, if not by design, the government is seeking to reduce the percentage of the employed labour-force which is covered by labour insurance.

The Chinese social-security system still remains tied to pre-reform distinctions even though the changes brought about by the reforms are rendering them obsolete. In particular, the assumption that 'rural' corresponds to 'self-employed' and 'urban' to 'employed', which underlies labour insurance, is increasingly at variance with the actual pattern. The general tenor of reforms is to reduce security of employment or income where it conflicts with efficiency. This is illustrated by the attempt to replace permanent employment with 'terminable' employment. Further, the reforms have given rise to phenomena which increase the risk of deprivation, such as immigration from rural areas on a large scale. Apart from the problems posed by the economic reforms, the Chinese social-security system also needs to take account of the growing percentage of the elderly in the population. The implication is that the system has to shoulder a heavier burden of alleviating deprivation than it did in the past, if the population is to enjoy a reasonable degree of economic security. But, as we have pointed out, this would require a fairly major overhaul of the present system.

References

Ashton, B., Hill, K., Piazza, A., and Zeitz, R. (1984), 'Famine in China: 1958–61', *Population and Development Review*, 4.

AYB 1986 (*China Agricultural Yearbook 1986*) (1987), Beijing: Agricultural Publishing House.

Banister, J. (1987), *China's Changing Population*. Stanford: Stanford University Press.

—— and Preston, S. H. (1981), 'Mortality in China', *Population and Development Review*, 1.

Bernstein, T. (1985), 'Reforming Chinese Agriculture', *China Business Review*, Mar./Apr.

Chen, C. C. (1989), *Medicine in Rural China*. Berkeley: University of California Press.

Coale, A. J. (1984), *Rapid Population Change in China: 1952–82*, Report No 27, National Research Council Committee on Population and Demography, Washington DC: National Academy Press.

Croll, E. (1982), *The Family Rice Bowl*. London: Zed Press.

Dixon, J. (1981), *The Chinese Welfare System*. New York: Praeger.

Endicott, S. (1988), *Red Earth: Revolution in a Sichuan Village*. London: I. B. Tauris.

Fei X (HS) (Fei and Others) (1989), *Small Towns in China*. Beijing: New World Press.

Feng L. and Zhao L. (1984), 'Urban Employment and Wages', in Yu Guangyuan (ed.), *China's Socialist Modernization*. Beijing: Foreign Languages Press.

Feuchtwang, S. (1987), 'Changes in the System of Basic Social Security in the Countryside Since 1979', in A. Saith (ed.), *The Re-Emergence of the Chinese Peasantry: Aspects of Rural Decollectivization*. London: Croom Helm.

Harding, H. (1987), *China's Second Revolution*. Washington DC: The Brookings Institution.

Henderson, G., and Cohen, M. S. (1984), *The Chinese Hospital: A Socialist Work Unit*. New Haven, Conn.: Yale University Press.

Hinton, W. (1966), *Fanshen: A Documentary of Revolution in a Chinese Village*. New York: Monthly Review Press.

Horn, J. S. (1971), *Away With All Pests: An English Surgeon in People's China*. New York: Monthly Review Press.

Hussain, A. (1989), 'Science and Technology in the Chinese Countryside', in M. Goldman and F. Simon (eds.), *Science and Technology in Post-Mao China*. Cambridge, Mass.: Harvard University Press.

—— and Feuchtwang, S. (1988), 'The People's Livelihood and the Incidence of Poverty', in S. Feuchtwang *et al.* (eds.), *Transforming China's Economy in the Eighties*, i. London: Zed Press.

—— and Stern, N. (1988), 'On the Recent Increase in Death Rates in China', *China Programme, Research Working Papers*, No. 12, STICERD, London School of Economics.

—— and Liu H. (1989), 'Compendium of Literature on the Chinese Social Security System', *China Programme, Research Working Papers*, No 3, STICERD, London School of Economics. (This work contains an annotated bibliography of the Chinese literature on social security.)

JPRS (*Joint Publication Research Service*) (1986). 'Beijing's Floating Population During Economic Reforms', CEA-86-107, 6 Oct., Washington DC.

Liu G. (1989). 'A Sweet and Sour Decade', *Beijing Review*, 2–8 Jan.

Mao Z. (1974), 'Directive on Public Health', in S. Schram (ed.), *Mao Tse-Tung Unrehearsed: Talks and Letters*. London: Penguin Books.

NTN (*Nongcun Tongji Nianjian*) (Agricultural Year Book), (1986, 1987), Beijing: Zhongguo Tongji Chubanshe.

Parish, W. L., and Whyte, M. K. (1978), *Village and Family in Contemporary China*. Chicago: University of Chicago Press.

Peng X. (1987), 'Demographic Consequence of the Great Leap Forward in China's Provinces', *Population and Development Review*, 4.

——(1989), 'Major Determinants of China's Fertility Transition', *China Quarterly*, 117.

Perkins, D. (1986), *China: Asia's Next Economic Giant*. Seattle: University of Washington Press.

——and Yusuf, S. (1984), *Rural Development in China*. Baltimore: Johns Hopkins University Press.

——(1988), 'Reforming China's Economic Structure', *Journal of Economic Literature*, 2.

——and Yusuf, S. (1984), *Rural Development in China*. Baltimore: Johns Hopkins University Press.

Schurman, F. (1971), *Ideology and Organization in Communist China*. Berkeley: University of California Press.

Shao Y. (1988), *Health Care in China*. London: Office of Health Economics.

Sicular, T. (1988), 'Plan and Market in China's Agricultural Commerce', *Journal of Political Economy*, 2.

SYB (*Statistical Year Book of China*) (1981, 1983, 1986, 1987), Beijing: State Statistical Bureau.

Tian J. (1989), 'Consumer Goods Rationing in China', mimeo, *China Programme Research Reports*, STICERD, London School of Economics.

TPS (*China Trade and Price Statistics in 1987*) (1987), Beijing: State Statistical Bureau.

UN (1984), *Mortality and Health Policy*. New York: UN.

Vermeer, E. B. (1979), 'Social Welfare Provisions and the Limits of Inequality in Contemporary China', *Asian Survey*, 9.

——(1982), 'Income Differentials in Rural China', *China Quarterly*, 89.

Walder, A. G. (1986), *Communist Neo-Traditionalism: Work and Authority in Chinese Industry*. Berkeley: University of California Press.

WDR (*World Development Report*) (1989), Oxford: Oxford University Press.

Weitzman, M. L. (1977), 'Is the Price System or Rationing More Effective in Getting a Commodity to Those Who Need It Most', *Bell Journal of Economics*, 8.

White, G. (1987), 'The Politics of Economic Reform: Introduction of the Labour Contract System', *China Quarterly*, 111.

Whyte, M. K., and Parish, W. L. (1984), *Urban Life in Contemporary China*. Chicago: University of Chicago Press.

Wolf, M. (1985), *Revolution Postponed: Women in Contemporary China*. Stanford: Stanford University Press.

Wong, L., and Macquarrie, L. (1986), *China's Welfare System: A View From Guangzhou.* Hongkong: Hongkong Polytechnic.

Wong, T. T. (1989), 'The Salary Structure, Allowances and Benefits of Shanghai Electronics Factory', *China Quarterly*, 117.

World Bank (1983), *Socialist Economic Development*, i and ii. Washington DC: World Bank.

——(1984), *China: The Health Sector.* Washington DC: World Bank.

——(1985), *China: Long-Term Development Issues and Options.* Washington DC: World Bank.

Yang, C. K. (1959), *The Chinese Family in the Communist Revolution.* Cambridge, Mass.: MIT Press.

YRSES 1986 (*Yearbook of Rural Social and Economic Statistics 1986*), Beijing: State Statistical Bureau.

ZLTGTZ 1987 (*Zhongguo Laodong Gongzi Tongji Ziliao: 1949–1985*), Beijing: Zhongguo Tongji Chubanshe.

ZSTZ (*Zhongguo Shehui Tongji Ziliao*) (1987), Beijing: Zhongguo Tongji Chubanshe.

ZTN (*Zhongguo Tongji Nianjian 1988*) (1988), Beijing: Zhongguo Tongji Chubanshe.

ZTYB (*Zhongguo Tongji Yuebao, 12, 1988*) (Dec. 1988), Beijing: Guojia Tongji Ju.

Zweig, D. (1989), *Agrarian Radicalism in China: 1968–1981.* Cambridge, Mass.: Harvard University Press.

7

Social Security in South Asia*

S. R. Osmani

1. INTRODUCTION

Social security in the Western sense occupies a marginal place in the social and economic policies of the South Asian countries. The reasons for this are not far to seek. In the first place, there is the question of scale. If income support of the kind given through the Western social-security system were to be given to over half the population rather than to 10 to 15 per cent of it as in the West, it would require an incomparably higher level of fiscal commitment in relation to resources. Secondly, given the structure of these economies, some of the conventional social-security measures may not even be operationally feasible. For example, where the labour-force is still predominantly self-employed and where unemployment is manifest mainly in the form of underemployment, it is not easy to devise a scheme of unemployment benefit; and where the proneness to falling sick is endemic due to poor food and hygiene, the idea of a sickness insurance scheme may turn out to be an actuarial disaster.

There is no doubt, however, that the millions of poor in South Asia need social security of some sort. If is often pointed out that one particularly venomous instance of insecurity, namely famine, has been largely conquered in South Asia in recent times—the sole exception being the Bangladesh famine of 1974. There is none the less an enormous problem of endemic insecurity that still remains. The problem is not merely that a vast number of people continue to live below some norm of poverty line; more disturbingly, many of those who live on the edge of subsistence are in constant danger of falling further into a state of destitution. While the eradication of poverty may have to be a long-term goal, depending as much on overall growth as on direct action targeted to the poor, there is certainly an immediate need for a safety net for those who do not even have the security of hanging on to a subsistence level of living.

What is not so clear, however, is which kinds of security measures are best suited for this purpose.[1] It is perhaps wise to consider an inclusive set of policies to begin with, gradually discarding those which are found wanting on

* The author is deeply grateful to V. K. Ramachandran, J. P. Drèze, P. K. Bardhan, and C. Fonseka for incisive comments on an earlier draft. The responsibility for the views and any errors is of course the author's alone.

[1] For a useful discussion of the conceptual issues related to the nature of social-security policies appropriate for developing countries, see Chap. 1 above.

closer scrutiny. Keeping in mind the nature of South Asian economies and the experience of various anti-poverty programmes pursued in this region, we present below a tentative classification as a starting point. One may think of three broad categories: (1) policies relating to land: these include land reforms (both ownership and tenancy reforms), assistance for small and marginal farmers, crop insurance, and so on; (2) policies relating to employment: these may include creating opportunities for either self-employment or employment through co-operatives in non-agricultural activities, providing wage employment through public works, and reserving employment for members of the disadvantaged groups in salaried employment; and (3) direct public provision: this may include both income support of various kinds as well as public provision of basic needs such as food, housing, health, and so on.

All these measures have been tried to varying extents in different parts of South Asia. We cannot, however, attempt a comprehensive evaluation of all of them within the space of a single chapter. Instead we pick out a few of them for close scrutiny and classify them under the following four headings: security through control over land, security through self-employment, security through wage employment, and security through public provision of basic needs.[2] The objective is to analyse the experience in these areas so as to learn something about the possibilities and limitations of offering social security through these channels. Furthermore, instead of covering the South Asian region as a whole, we shall look at only three countries, namely India, Bangladesh, and Sri Lanka.

2. SECURITY THROUGH CONTROL OVER LAND

In the predominantly agrarian economies of South Asia, security of livelihood for a majority of people clearly depends on control over land and its produce. This naturally accords a position of pre-eminence to the policies relating to land control in any discussion of social security in this region. Three types of policies are going to be discussed in this context, namely, ceiling-cum-redistribution policy, tenancy reform, and the alienation of State-owned land.

The ceiling-cum-redistribution policy is by far the most radical in nature, and also the one that has been least successful in practice. Attempts have been made in all three countries to acquire the excess of land beyond a certain ceiling from large landowners and distribute it to the land-poor people.

By the mid-1980s about 1.5 per cent of the cultivated land in India had been acquired under ceiling laws passed in the 1950s, and less than 80 per cent of it

---

[2] Drèze (1988) contains an in-depth case-study of the actual operation of some of these policies in an Indian village. On the feasibility and desirability of other forms of social security, such as old-age pension, survivor benefits, insurance against occupational hazards, etc., again in the Indian context, see the important contributions of GOI (1984) and Guhan (1988).

was actually distributed.[3] In the process, nearly 3.4 million persons received on an average a little over 1.3 acres of land. This has no doubt enhanced the security of livelihood for the beneficiary families, especially since more than half of the beneficiaries belong to the scheduled castes and scheduled tribes who are among the most disadvantaged social groups in India (Bandyopadhyay 1986). However, since the amount of land available for distribution was itself so small, the total number of beneficiaries amounts to a minuscule proportion of land-poor households. The record of Bangladesh is even more dismal. The excess of land over the stipulated ceiling would have amounted to no more than 1 per cent of the cultivated land even if the ceiling were strictly enforced. In the event, only 15 per cent of the potential surplus has been acquired and out of the acquired land no more than a quarter has been distributed (Siddiqui 1979).

Sri Lanka's achievement appears far more remarkable at first sight—as much as 20 per cent of cultivated land was promptly acquired following the legislations of 1972 and 1975. But the landless and small peasants gained very little; only 12 per cent of the land acquired, which amounts to 2.4 per cent of cultivated land, accrued to the peasantry (Wickramasekara 1985a). The reason for this dissonance between acquisition and redistribution lies in the special nature of land reform enacted in Sri Lanka. The reform was aimed mainly at the plantation sector: 60 per cent of the area planted with tea, 30 per cent of the area planted with rubber and 10 per cent of the area planted with coconut in the plantation sector was taken over by the State, but only just over 1 per cent of paddy land was acquired in the process. A conscious decision was also taken at the time not to distribute plantation land to the peasant sector on the ground of economies of scale. Whatever the merit of this decision, there was clearly an element of irony in this. For since the very early days of the nationalist movement in Sri Lanka, political agitation against the plantation sector has been conducted in the name of the peasantry, especially the peasants of the Kandyan highlands where the plantation estates were mostly situated.[4] Perhaps in deference to history, a small amount of estate land was distributed to the Kandyan peasants; but the bulk of it came under State-run corporations which did little to enhance the control of the land-poor over the fruits of the land. Initially an attempt was made to combine peasant control with economies of scale by transferring a part of the acquired land to farmers' collectives, but the collectivist institutions were abolished by the government which came to power in 1977.

The general picture all over the region is, thus, one of negligible impact as a

[3] Out of a total operated area of 163 million hectares (according to the Agricultural Census of 1980/1), only 2.97 million hectares were declared surplus, 2.36 million were taken possession of, and 1.82 million distributed by the mid-1980s (Bandyopadhyay 1986: A-50).

[4] The Kandyan peasants have had a long-standing grievance that plantation agriculture has endangered their livelihood by encroaching on their land. There is, however, a good deal of controversy on the degree to which such encroachment did in fact occur. An interesting account of this controversy is given by Moore (1985).

result of redistributive land reform. The proximate reason for this failure lies in the stipulation of an exceedingly high ceiling—so high in Bangladesh (33 acres) and Sri Lanka (25 acres for paddy land) that the proportion of land above these limits is too miniscule even to appear as a separate category in any official statistics on the distribution of land. Even the meagre amount of land that should have been legally available could not be fully acquired as the landowners made use of various legal loopholes to keep possession of their land.

Political imperatives have no doubt played a paramount role in leaving the land of large landowners (outside the plantation sector) virtually untouched in all three countries.[5] It is therefore of some interest to note what has happened in two isolated pockets in the region, namely the states of West Bengal and Kerala in India, where the polity has been dominated for a considerable stretch of time by parties with avowedly radical intents.[6] Although constrained by the Constitution of India, the State governments were not entirely powerless to implement radical land reforms if they intended to do so, because considerable autonomy was given to the States in matters relating to land reform. As we shall see, both States did in fact take advantage of this autonomy to push through tenancy reforms which were much more radical than anything attempted elsewhere in South Asia; but when it came to redistribution of land through ceiling legislations, both failed like the rest. The ceiling was fixed at 20 acres in Kerala and 25 acres in West Bengal, which yielded a surplus of less than 2.5 per cent of the cultivated land in Kerala (Raj and Tharakan 1981: 17) and just over 1 per cent in West Bengal (computed from the figures given in Bandyopadhyaya et al. 1985: 14).

Ceiling legislations have thus achieved very little in any part of South Asia. It has been claimed, however, that considerably more progress has been made, at least in some parts of the region, in enhancing the security of a certain class of peasants, namely, the tenant-cultivators who lease in land from others. The terms and conditions of lease contracts are known to be highly unfavourable to the tenants; under share-cropping—the most predominant form of tenancy all over South Asia—the tenants usually supply most of the input and retain only half the produce. Moreover, there is no security of even the meagre livelihood eked out in the process as the landlords can evict tenants at any time at their will. The tenants also tend to belong mostly in the smaller landholding groups. Consequently, along with landless labourers, share-croppers are found to be the most deprived section in rural South Asia.

There is much uncertainty about the precise number of the share-croppers in this region, but even the rough estimates are adequate to reveal the

[5] On the political economy of land reform in this region, see, *inter alia*, Joshi (1975) on India, Siddiqui (1979) on Bangladesh, and Peiris (1978), Samaraweera (1981) and Moore (1985) on Sri Lanka.

[6] The Communist Party of India (Marxist) has been controlling the State government of West Bengal since 1977. Two major Communist parties have dominated the polity of Kerala for most of the period since 1956, although often in coalition with more conservative elements.

enormous extent of this practice. Official estimates based on agricultural censuses show that tenants (including owner-cum-tenants) constituted some 35 to 40 per cent of all farmers in Bangladesh in the late 1970s and 53 per cent in Sri Lanka in the early 1960s. In India the extent of tenancy varies widely across the States; we shall consider here only the States of West Bengal and Kerala where tenancy reforms are claimed to have had the most pronounced effect. Tenants (including owner-cum-tenants) constituted 40 per cent of all farmers in West Bengal according to the National Sample Survey of 1971/2, and 52 per cent of all farmers in Kerala according to the Land Reform Survey of 1966/7.[7] Noting that micro-level surveys reveal that official statistics almost invariably underestimate the extent of tenancy, we may describe the overall picture as one where something like half of the farmers in South Asia cultivate some amount of rented land. Any improvement that can be brought about in the terms of their contracts can thus have a potentially significant effect on the security of livelihood for a large segment of the rural population, provided the same changes do not undermine their access to land.

The issue of tenancy, however, never received any prominence in the political movements of pre-independence Sri Lanka. It began to be discussed more seriously after independence in 1948, but even then the prevailing view did not seem to consider share-cropping to be a particularly exploitative institution. In fact, the majority of social scientists tended to regard it either as a mutually beneficial contract between parties who are socially equal in the village hierarchy but who differ in their relative endowments of land and labour, or a benevolent gesture on the part of the well-off families to help out their less fortunate friends and relatives.[8] In so far as the institution was criticized at all, it was mainly because of a presumed disincentive effect on agricultural production. This effect was never quite documented, but the theoretical arguments closely resembled the familiar Marshallian argument about the inefficiency of share-cropping.

It was, however, an entirely different kind of reasoning that eventually led to the first serious attempt at tenancy reform in Sri Lanka. The Marxist Minister for Agriculture, Philip Gunawardena, who was instrumental in attempting this reform through the Paddy Lands Act in 1958, was of the view that peasant production in general, including both tenant and owner cultivation, suffered from the diseconomies of small scale and was hence a drag on production. His long-term objective was therefore to replace peasant production by collective farming; but as a first step he felt it necessary to liberate the tenants from the clutches of 'feudal' landlords so that a community of equal peasants could

[7] The estimates of tenancy quoted in this paragraph are taken from BBS (1985) for Bangladesh, Hameed et al. (1977) for Sri Lanka, Bandyopadhyay et al. (1985) for West Bengal, and Raj and Tharakan (1981) for Kerala.
[8] See Peiris (1976) for a discussion of the studies which expounded this view as well as of the few that contested it.

eventually make the transition to a collective form of agriculture. With this end in view, sweeping provisions were made for enhancing tenants' control over land. Evictions were prohibited except under special circumstances, hereditary rights of cultivation were conferred on tenants, and the traditional 50 per cent share of the landlord was reduced to 25 per cent or a fixed amount per acre (allowing for regional variation) whichever was less. More importantly, Cultivation Committees were to be formed in each village, *excluding the landlords*, initially to ensure that the tenants' rights were established and eventually to pave the way for collective agriculture. These Committees were also supposed to provide credit and other input facilities for the tenants so that they would not have to turn to the rural élite for help.[9]

In the event, not even the immediate goal was achieved, not to speak of the distant one. Under intense political pressure, the minister was forced to resign, landlords had to be allowed to join the Cultivation Committees, and conditions were relaxed under which the landlords could resume cultivation. As a result, a spate of evictions was noted throughout the 1960s and the rental share remained virtually unchanged in most parts of the country. Significantly, the only region where the rental share showed some improvement was the Hambantota district, which has long been a centre of radical politics and where, unlike in other parts of Sri Lanka, absentee landlordism was the order of the day. It has been rightly argued that improvement was possible in this region only because of the special circumstance in which the landlords, being absent, were unable to control the Cultivation Committees (Peiris 1976).

In terms of political preconditions for tenancy reform, the situation in pre-independence Bengal (comprising both Bangladesh and West Bengal) was vastly different from that of Sri Lanka. Share-cropping was widely seen here as an exploitative institution. In fact the grievances of share-croppers were made a central pillar of political agitation by the peasant leaders of Marxist persuasion, which led to the famous Tebhaga movement of 1946/7. The movement sought to improve tenurial security and to ensure a two-thirds shared instead of the traditional half in favour of the share-cropper. A Bill was also introduced by the government of Bengal in early 1947 recognizing these demands. But then came independence, and the issue of share-croppers has been shelved ever since in the territory now comprising Bangladesh. A Tenancy Act was indeed passed in the early 1950s, but it was aimed solely at giving relief to the owners of land from the exploitation of rent-receiving intermediaries. As every student of Indian history knows, these intermediaries were the zamindars who were empowered by the colonial government to collect land revenue from the peasants in return for the obligation of handing over a fixed sum to the government. As protégés of the colonial rulers, this class of intermediaries was an immediate target of nationalist attack. With the advent of independence, it

---

[9] For a fuller account of these measures and their effect, see, *inter alia*, Sanderatne (1972), Peiris (1976), Herring (1981), and Moore (1985).

was politically both expedient and feasible to isolate them and dispossess them of their rent-receiving rights. This obviously eliminated a long-standing source of exploitation of the peasantry, but only to the benefit of those who had legal title to the land, regardless of whether they cultivated or not. The share-croppers found no relief, as they could not claim ownership rights on leased-in land. Not until 1983 did a Lands Reform Committee deal with this issue for the first time and recommend more security and a higher share of the share-croppers, but the recommendations still remain only on paper.

While inheriting the same history, West Bengal, however, took a different course. The rent-receiving rights of zamindars were promptly taken away, as in Bangladesh, but the rights of share-croppers were also recognized at the same time. They were not given ownership rights, but eviction was made legally difficult and their share was raised to 60 per cent in the 1950s and then to 75 per cent in the early 1970s.[10] Similar laws were enacted also in many other States of India, but everywhere in the 1950s and 1960s they not only failed to improve the tenants' control over land, but in fact made their condition worse by prompting large-scale eviction as in Sri Lanka.[11]

Lack of 'political will' and 'bureaucratic lethargy' have often been blamed for this reverse. But it is being increasingly recognized that the root of failure lay in a basic flaw in the very conception of these reforms. It was assumed by the reformers that the mere existence of a law would encourage tenants to confront landlords with their legitimate rights. This assumption was, however, based on a profound misunderstanding of the socio-economic relationship between the share-croppers and the landlords. When we speak of this relationship as an unfavourable one for the share-croppers, this is mainly in relation to an alternative social scenario where the land would be owned by the share-croppers themselves. But given the existing ownership rights and the acute land-hunger on the part of the landless and marginal peasants, those who are able to lease in land have reasons to consider themselves privileged compared to their peers. The purely economic contract is enmeshed in a complex web of socio-cultural relationship in which the landlords often provide 'subsistence insurance' and other material support to their tenants in return for their acquiescence in the prevailing social hierarchy. In a situation where the majority live a precarious existence owing to adverse man–land ratios, few opportunities of alternative employment, and the vagaries of weather, and where the provision of State-sponsored social security is all but non-existent, a high value is naturally attached to the 'subsistence insurance' mediated through traditional owner–tenant relationships.

The reforms called upon the tenants to strike at the roots of these relationships;

---

[10] For a comprehensive account of the history of tenancy reform in West Bengal, see Dasgupta (1984).

[11] This failure has been noted not only by numerous independent observers but also by an official report on the impact of tenancy reform in India (GOI 1959).

any attempt to alter the prevailing hiearchy of rights in their favour was bound to do so. But since any such attempt would also put their 'subsistence insurance' in jeopardy, the tenants can only be expected to rise against the landlords if they can be assured of an alternative source of security. Two conditions must be fulfilled for this to be possible. First, the tenants must feel assured that their action against the landlords will not boomerang by prompting eviction. The mere existence of law is not enough; the tenants must have countervailing political power at the local level to neutralize the pre-existing superior power of the landlords. Secondly, mere security against eviction will also not be enough; this will only give them access to land. They will also need access to new sources of consumption loan, working-capital loan, distress relief, and other elements of subsistence insurance which will no longer be forthcoming from the traditional channel.

It was precisely the non-fulfilment of these two conditions that led to the universal failure of tenancy reform in India. Interestingly, it was also precisely these two conditions that Philip Gunawardena had sought to fulfil through the institution of Cultivation Committees in Sri Lanka. But he failed because the ruling coalition, in which his breakaway Marxist party was only a minor partner, did not share his commitment. As a result, the Cultivation Committees could not find either the political power or the financial resources to carry out their task.[12] This perspective also helps to explain how the present Left Front government of West Bengal has achieved a measure of success, albeit a limited one.

The strategy of the Left Front was to fulfil the first condition (namely, the creation of countervailing political power) by a process of what Kohli (1987) has described as the separation of political from social power at the local level. Since no attempt was made to alter the existing pattern of ownership rights, it was expected that the landlords would continue to maintain their superior social power. But it was hoped that if political power was effectively wrested from them at the local level, the tenants would be assured of protection against eviction (that is, the first condition would be met) and would hence begin to assert their rights. However, since the tenants, left to themselves, could hardly be expected to bring about the required separation of power, it was also felt necessary that an external power must act as the catalyst. With this end in view, the dormant *gram panchayats* (village councils) were first revitalized—not by openly excluding the landlords as Gunawardena had intended to do, but by popular election along party lines. Since the Left Front parties, especially the Communist Party of India (Marxist), enjoyed majority popular support in the countryside, it was hoped that their members and sympathizers would be able to dominate the *panchayats*. And so they did, which paved the way for the next step.

[12] An authoritative account of the problems faced by the Cultivation Committees can be found in Weerawardena (1975).

It was realized that since share-cropping was seldom carried out under written contract, it would not be possible to prevent pre-emptive or punitive eviction unless there was documentary evidence of who was share-cropping whose land. This led to the campaign of what has come to be known as the *Operation Barga*,[13] during the course of which the share-croppers were asked to register themselves in public meetings. There was nothing novel about the idea of registration as such; it had been in the statute books for a long time without achieving its intended objectives in any part of India. What was novel, however, was the existence of countervailing power at the local level through the presence of politicized *panchayats* and party activists who exercised political power for the benefit of tenants. Consequently, registration was a huge success. The exact measure of this success is in some dispute, as the exact number of share-croppers is itself unknown. However, even by conservative estimates, anywhere between 65 and 85 per cent of the share-croppers have been registered[14]—an achievement unparalleled in other parts of South Asia.

It is now time to ask to what extent all this has helped to improve the security and level of livelihood of share-croppers in West Bengal. Registration and the continued presence of countervailing power at the local level have presumably gone a long way towards improving the security of their tenure. But security in itself is not much of a gain. It is evidently a gain in comparison with the immediate past when evictions had become common. But these evictions were themselves a consequence of attempted reforms that backfired. One must therefore compare the present situation with the status quo ante, when traditional landlord–tenant relationships existed in full force. Eviction as such was not a problem at that time, at any rate not for the whole class of potential tenants as opposed to an individual.[15] The problem was in the use that was made of the threat of eviction—to keep the rent high, for example. Presumably, as the threat of eviction was removed, the tenants would then be able to press for a higher share, especially since the law provided for it and countervailing power existed at the local level to enforce the law. Such an outcome would indeed constitute a genuine gain from tenancy reform. But the available evidence does not suggest that this has happened to any significant extent. In the largest survey that has so far been conducted on the consequences of tenurial reform in West Bengal, Bandyopadhyay *et al.* (1985) found that only 20 per cent of the registered share-croppers were able to pay the legally stipulated share; in fact, as much as 71 per cent of the share-croppers

---

[13] *Barga* is the local name for the system of share-cropping.

[14] According to official records, nearly 1.3 million share-croppers were registered by the mid-1980s (Bandyopadhyay 1986: A-50). As against this, estimates of the total number of share-croppers in West Bengal vary between 1.5 million (according to peasant leaders) and 2.0 million (an early official estimate). See Bandyopadhyaya *et al.* (1985) for a discussion of these estimates.

[15] If eviction took place at that time, it would usually mean replacing one tenant by another rather than taking back the land for cultivation by hired or family labour. Eviction of the latter kind is much more of a modern phenomenon.

continued to pay the traditional share of half the produce. In a survey of four villages, Westergaard (1986) observed that the tenants' share had improved in only one village, but even there the share was less than the legal minimum. A contrasting result is presented by Kohli (1987) who found, again in a small survey, that the proportion of tenants paying the legal rent had increased sharply from 13 per cent to 66 per cent. It is, however, significant to note two very interesting features of his findings: first, 80 per cent of the landlords in his sample were absentee landlords and secondly, as Kohli himself presents the puzzle, although the Communist Party activists were particularly strong in one of his survey areas (in the Burdwan district), the tenants' share failed to improve in that region.

The implication of all these findings can be summed up as follows. In spite of the fulfilment of the condition of countervailing power, tenants are in general reluctant to break up the traditional landlord–tenant relationship by demanding a higher share, except in the case of absentee landlordism where this relationship did not in any case exist to begin with.[16] The clue to this apparent paradox lies partly in the fact that there is no guarantee of continued rule by the Communist Party for an indefinite future. The tenants are naturally apprehensive of the consequences that might befall them once the parties more favourably disposed to the landlords return to power. But partly the explanation also lies in the non-fulfilment of the second condition of a successful tenancy reform, namely, the assurance of an alternative source of material support. The reformers were not altogether unaware of this potential pitfall. In fact, the provision of credit and input facilities for the registered share-croppers was made, at least on paper, an integral part of the reform programme. But all the existing surveys show that the amount and timing of credit was not enough to make the tenants' traditional dependence on landlords economically redundant. Whether adequate resources can be found for this purpose and whether institutional methods can be devised to channel these resources to the right person at the right time in the right amount are difficult questions that cannot be fully answered at present. What is clear, however, is the lesson that tenancy reform is by its very nature caught in a trap. It seeks to improve the security of tenants by freeing them from the clutches of the landlords, but the tenants will refuse to remove themselves from those clutches unless there is prior provision for adequate social security.

It can be argued, and it has been argued forcefully in the context of the West Bengal debate,[17] that the solution of this problem lies in the abolition of tenancy altogether by according full ownership rights to tenants. The pre-

---

[16] The importance of absentee landlordism in shaping the success of tenancy reform is borne out both by Kohli's sample and the experience of the Hambantota district in Sri Lanka. It is only fair to mention, though, that Kohli himself does not draw this link; instead he interprets his findings as pointing to the success of *Operation Barga* as such.

[17] For a sampling of this debate, see Khasnabis (1981), Rudra (1981), Bose (1981), and Dasgupta (1984), among many others.

sumption is that once the tenants are able to claim the entire produce of the land, their economic condition will improve sufficiently to eliminate the material basis of their dependence on the landed élite. Spurred by this incentive they would then be willing to take advantage of the existing counter-vailing power to break the traditional relationship in a way they are unwilling to do while the only alternative is to remain as tenants deprived of traditional patronage. As for the political feasibility of this approach, it is pointed out that the government of Kerala has been able to abolish tenancy through the same political party that rules in West Bengal and under the same constraints imposed by the Constitution of India. If Kerala can, why cannot West Bengal?

This apparently persuasive argument has one rather serious flaw. It ignores the fact that the agrarian structure of Kerala which had emerged over the colonial period gave its tenancy reform an entirely different political and economic content from that which would be entailed by a comparable pro-gramme in a State like West Bengal.[18] Due to complex historical reasons which we cannot go into here, tenancy had become, by the end of British rule, a widespread phenomenon only in the north-central region of Kerala comprising Malabar and Cochin.[19] Nearly two-thirds of all tenants were to be found in this area, whereas 80 per cent of the owner-cultivators were in the south, in Travancore. Tenancy reform therefore essentially affected only the northern part of Kerala.

Several factors contributed to the political feasibility of this reform. First, the landlords in the north were relatively few in number, possessing a vast amount of land; some 80 per cent of all leased-out land came from holdings of 25 acres of more. Secondly, while these landlords did not enjoy full ownership rights on the land in the pre-British era (they only had a superior claim in a hierarchy of customary rights), they were accorded full ownership by the colonial regime and thus became identified as its protégés. Thirdly, unlike the rich landowners in the south, they were themselves never involved in the management of cultivation, and were thus regarded as parasitic landlords. In all these respects—namely, being relatively few in number, being identified as colonial protégés, and being seen as parasitic landlords—the landed aristocracy of Malabar was no different from the zamindars of Bengal. Consequently, the abolition of tenancy in Kerala was of the same order of political feasibility as the abolition of zamindari in Bengal.[20] Furthermore, just as the abolition of

[18] The final chapter of Bandyopadhyay et al. (1985) is one of the few analyses which have actually highlighted this contrast.

[19] See Varghese (1970) for a detailed account and Raj and Tharakan (1981) for a brief but lucid exposition of this history. All the statistics quoted in this paragraph and the next are taken from the latter source.

[20] The Keralite problem would have been of an altogether different order of feasibility if the politically powerful landowners of Travancore (southern Kerala) had had to be antagonized. Initially, such an antagonism did in fact arise. But it was kept under control by legally allowing the smaller owners to retain their land. This largely took care of the problem, since the prevalence of tenancy was in any case rather small in Travancore.

zamindari left the underlying production structure basically untouched (in so far as it failed to tilt the balance in favour of the small peasantry), so in Kerala the abolition of tenancy did very little to alter the vast inequalities in the distribution of landholdings (see Raj and Tharakan 1981). It would thus appear that both the political and the economic implications of the abolition of tenancy in Kerala were essentially similar to those of the successful abolition of zamindari in Bengal and elsewhere.[21]

The abolition of tenancy in Bengal, however, would have come up against a political problem of an entirely different order of magnitude. It would have had to confront not just a handful of absentee overlords (as in Kerala), but a large number of owners many of whom were small and actively engaged in cultivation. In Kerala the small landlords (possessing no more than 5 acres of land) were exempted from dispossession, and yet most of the land under tenancy went to the tiller. But a similar exemption in West Bengal would leave out nearly 80 per cent of all landlords and as much as 50 per cent of all leased-in land.[22] A meaningful 'land to the tiller' policy cannot leave out this group, nor can the Communist Party alienate such a huge repository of local power as long as it sticks to the electoral path. It would of course be a different matter if the 'revolutionary' path were to be chosen, but that can only be a goal for a distant future.

One cannot, therefore, avoid the conclusion that the immediate political limit of tenancy reform in a State like West Bengal is not much above what has been achieved so far. But this also means that tenancy reforms by themselves cannot expect to achieve a great deal by way of improving the material conditions of living of the share-croppers. As we have concluded in the light of West Bengal's experience, prior provision of social security is a prerequisite for this purpose.

In addition to ceiling legislation and tenancy reform, a third method of enhancing the land-poor's control over land consists in the alienation of State-owned land. To some extent this has happened in all three countries of South Asia, but its scope has been very small in both India and Bangladesh. Historically the process of clearing and possessing wasteland was left to private initiative in these two countries. Consequently the State came to control very little of potentially alienable land. But in Sri Lanka land policy has evolved differently, under the impetus of the colonial policy of promoting plantation agriculture. Under the Waste Lands Ordinance of 1840, the State took control of all land except that for which pre-existing private ownership could be clearly demonstrated. In the process, nearly 40 per cent of the total land area of the

---

[21] Raj and Tharakan (1981) have themselves drawn a similar parallel between the post-colonial abolition of tenancy in Kerala and the pre-colonial tenurial reforms in Travancore under the aegis of the princely states of the region.

[22] These figures are based on National Sample Survey data for 1971/2 quoted in Bandyopadhyay et al. (1985: table 2.5).

country came under direct State control. Initially, the colonial government used this land to promote plantation agriculture; but there was a decisive shift in policy in the first quarter of the present century. By the 1920s population growth had created a serious problem of landlessness and land-hunger among the peasantry; at the same time food production was stagnating at a level that was increasingly inadequate to feed the growing population. As the nationalist movement made the cause of peasantry a rallying cry at this stage, and as the Donoughmore Constitution of 1931 devolved considerable power to national politicians, the land alienation policy shifted decisively in favour of the peasantry. The Land Development Ordinance of 1935 set the stage for the pattern that has been evolving up to the present (see Samaraweera 1981 and Moore 1985).

Most of the alienation has taken place under two major schemes, namely the Dry Land Colonization Scheme and the Village Expansion Scheme. The first involved clearing land and developing irrigation in vast tracts of the sparsely populated dry zone, and the second promoted the creation of new habitats around the existing villages, especially in the densely populated wet zone. Several features of these schemes are worth mentioning. First, the land was given exclusively, and virtually free of cost, to landless or extremely land-poor households. Secondly, the cost of clearing and developing land was borne entirely by the State. In the case of colonization schemes, the State also had to provide health and education facilities in order to attract residents of the wet zone into the malaria-infested wastelands of the dry zone. As a result, the beneficiaries not only got access to fully developed land complete with irrigation facilities, many of them also received the benefit of welfare services specially designed for them. Although the problem of landlessness was by no means eliminated in the process, a significant proportion of the land-poor population clearly gained a security they did not enjoy before. It has been estimated that nearly a quarter of all households in Sri Lanka now possess land granted under the Village Expansion Scheme with an average allotment of 1.3 acres per household (Moore 1985: 42). The Dry Zone Scheme has catered to rather fewer households—roughly 4 to 5 per cent of all households in the country up to 1980 (computed from figures quoted in Wickramasekera 1985*b*). Since then, the amibitious Mahaweli Accelerated Programme has aimed at more than doubling the number of beneficiaries within less than a decade.

Over the years, many shortcomings of these settlement schemes have been pointed out. For instance, it has been noted that the land alienated under the Village Expansion Scheme was often of inferior quality (Moore 1985); social anthropologists have often pointed out the lack of social cohesion among the uprooted households and the resulting absence of traditional redistributive and mutual insurance mechanisms that provided some degree of social security in the old villages (Moore and Perera 1978); others have noted renewed landlessness and concealed tenancy under onerous terms in dry-zone colonies

(Wickramasekara 1985*b*); yet others have pointed out that the value of agricultural output yielded by the newly developed land has not been commensurate with the cost of development (Wimaladharma 1982).

All these problems are genuine enough. But on balance, it must still be concluded that the land alienation policy pursued since 1935 has entitled over 30 per cent of households in Sri Lanka to a level of land-based security that would be a matter of envy to the land-poor population of India and Bangladesh. It is revealing to contrast the Sri Lankan experience with the most recent historical phase of reclamation of wasteland in Bengal, which occurred during the British rule. This reclamation took place in the north-western and south-eastern parts of Bengal through the private initiative of wealthy individuals; and it is precisely in these regions that the agrarian structure is the most inequitable, the tenurial condition most oppressive, and the problem of landlessness most acute.[23] Unfortunately, history has foreclosed the possibility of replicating the Sri Lankan experience in most parts of India and Bangladesh where very little reclamable wasteland is currently available.

But the Sri Lankan potential is not yet exhausted. Cultivated land still accounts for just over 30 per cent of all land area in the country. Although much of the rest will have to remain under perennial forest, particularly in the central highlands, enormous possibilities still remain in the potentially cultivable dry zone. This zone accounts for 70 per cent of total land but only 30 per cent of cultivated land. However, two serious impediments stand in the way. First, given the huge cost of development, trying to achieve too much too soon may place an unbearable burden on budgetary resources, as the ongoing Mahaweli Accelerated Programme has amply demonstrated. A second, and perhaps more serious, problem is the current ethnic conflict between the Tamils and the Sinhalese, since the Tamils tend to regard dry zone colonization as Sinhalese encroachment on traditional Tamil territory. These problems cast grave doubt on the possibility of enhancing land-based security in the future for the still significant land-poor population of Sri Lanka.

3. SECURITY THROUGH SELF-EMPLOYMENT

One possible alternative to land-based security is to enable the land-poor to engage in those self-employed activities which are not crucially dependent on land. These so-called non-farm activities occupy a significant position in the occupational structure of South Asia, accounting for 34 per cent of the rural labour-force in Bangladesh, 46 per cent in Sri Lanka, and 19 per cent in

---

[23] For a fascinating discussion of the relationship between the reclamation process and agrarian structure in different regions of Bengal, see Bose (1986).

India.[24] There are also indications that the share of the work-force engaged in this sector is rising over time. The question is to what extent the livelihoood of the land-poor population can be secured through participation in this sector. As it is, a considerable number of them are already engaged in these activities. For instance, sample surveys in Bangladesh have shown that of all the gainful activities (both primary and secondary) pursued by the workers owning no more than 0.5 acres of land, more than 50 per cent belong to the non-farm sector; in contrast, agricultural labour accounts for only a third of the total (Hossain 1986: 126). This does not, however, indicate the extent of their self-employment in these activities since many of them are actually employed as wage labour. Moreover, even among the self-employed category, the members of the land-poor group are usually engaged in less productive lines of activity compared to those who are better endowed with land and other resources (Hossain 1984a; Muqtada and Alam 1983). Presumably, the imperfections in the rural credit market prevent many of the land-poor households from obtaining the resources required for engaging in remunerative activities. The provision of resources through credit and/or subsidy is therefore an essential prerequisite for ensuring security through self-employment.

Over the years a variety of programmes have been tried in order to address this problem throughout the region, the most outstanding among them being the Grameen (Rural) Bank in Bangladesh and the Integrated Rural Development Programme (IRDP) in India. They both took off around 1979–80 with essentially the same objective, but were conceived in a somewhat different manner. There is also a difference in scale. While Grameen Bank covers only about 3 to 4 per cent of all villages in the country, with the hope of extending countrywide at some unspecified time in the future, the IRDP was launched with a countrywide coverage almost from the beginning. Thus the Grameen Bank is still only a model while IRDP is already a full-blown programme. There is, finally, a notable difference in the evaluation of their performance. The Grameen Bank has been widely acclaimed as a huge success, while most of the evaluations of IRDP range from mixed to derisory. It will be instructive to see to what extent their relative performance is related to differences in approach or to the difference in scale, and what lessons they together provide on the possibility of ensuring security through self-employment.

Let us first take a brief look at their relative performances. The Grameen Bank defines all those households who own no more than 0.5 acres of land as its target group. Independent evaluations show that singular success has been achieved in confining the benefits to the genuine target group: only 5 per cent of the beneficiaries owned land above the specified limit, while 52 per cent

---

[24] These figures are quoted from Islam (1987: table 1.1). They refer to the situation prevailing in 1984/5 in Bangladesh (Labour Force Survey) and in 1981 in India and Sri Lanka (Population Censuses).

owned no land at all.[25] The average pre-intervention income of the recipients of loans (in 1980) was half the national average, which indicates that most of them would belong to the bottom 40 per cent of the income scale. Considering that anywhere between 60 and 80 per cent of the rural population were below the poverty line around that time, the beneficiaries must be considered to constitute the poorest segment of the rural population. There is also clear evidence that the operations of the Grameen Bank have provided new employment opportunities to previously unemployed rural women; the rate of female participation in the labour-force rose from 5 per cent to 25 per cent within the households receiving loans in a period of two years. Women also figured prominently in the overall operations of the Bank—by 1984 nearly 54 per cent of the beneficiaries were females, receiving 42 per cent of all loans.

According to rough estimates based on a sample survey, the per capita real income of aided households increased (net of interest payments) by 32 per cent over a period of two and a half years (starting from 1980), while at the national level per capita income rose by only 2.6 per cent. To what extent this picture is distorted by the well-known difficulties of collecting accurate income data is not clear, but the rates of return estimated for various investment activities give an independent indication that the income gain must have been substantial. In most of the trading activities and a few of the manufacturing activities for which loans were utilized, the return on family labour (after meeting all costs and repaying the loans with interest) was found to be marginally higher than the prevailing agricultural wage rate. On the other hand, in the majority of manufacturing activities as well as in cattle and poultry raising, the return on labour was lower than the agricultural wage rate. However, it is important to note that almost all of these low-return activities are dominated by females, whose scope for employment in agriculture or elsewhere in rural Bangladesh is negligible. Consequently, even though the return is rather low, nearly all of it represents a net addition to family income. As for male-dominated activities, not only is the return on labour (per man-day) higher than the agricultural wage in most cases, the duration of employment is also much longer. All this is not to suggest, however, that the recipients of loans have been able to secure a livelihood above any acceptable norm of poverty line. With 1.5 earners and 3.5 dependants per loan on the average, they could not possibly do so, even with year-round employment, at a level of earning that is below or only slightly above the prevailing agricultural wage rate.

One other aspect of the Grameen Bank's performance that has been widely commented upon is its success in terms of a purely banking criterion. The recipients are charged an effective interest rate of 18 per cent which is above the

---

[25] All the statistics quoted in this paragraph and the following two are taken from Hossain (1984b, 1988)—both these reports are based on the most comprehensive evaluation of the Grameen Bank done so far. For further details, see Siddiqui (1985) and the references cited therein.

general rate of interest (between 12 and 15 per cent), and are required to repay the loan in weekly instalments over a year. Despite these stringent conditions, the proportion of overdue loans after two years of loan disbursement was found to be less than 1 per cent, and only 4 per cent of the recipients had not fully repaid the loan by the time it was due. It is thus clear that the Grameen Bank has succeeded in giving income support to the poor without degenerating into the kind of dole-giving institution that so many other poverty-alleviation programmes have tended to become.

In comparison with these achievements of the Grameen Bank, the performance of IRDP appears decidedly poor. One point should, however, be clarified before highlighting the contrasts. The goal of IRDP was pitched at a much more ambitious level than that of the Grameen Bank, and consequently the former is likely to suffer in any comparison between aims and achievement. While the Grameen Bank had the modest goal of providing a more secure source of income for a few assetless people without necessarily eliminating their poverty in the immediate future, IRDP was aimed at lifting the beneficiary households above the poverty line with a one-shot intervention. The Sixth Five Year Plan (1980–5) set the target that over a period of five years as much as 30 per cent of the officially designated poor population would be assisted and lifted out of poverty, starting from the poorest group and moving gradually upwards.

Some of the evaluation studies have indeed claimed a rather spectacular rate of progression above the poverty line; for example, nearly half of the beneficiaries are supposed to have made the transition, according to NABARD (1984) and PEO (1985). But these estimates suffer from some elementary methodological problems, such as comparing current income with a base-line poverty level and estimating net income without adjusting for loan repayment. After some rough adjustments on these counts, Rath (1985) has estimated that not more than 10 per cent of the beneficiaries (or 3 per cent of the base-line poor population) could have made the transition to the status of non-poor over the Sixth Five Year Plan period. Based on a much more systematic countrywide survey for the year 1985–6, Kurian (1987) finds that less than 5 per cent of the beneficiaries may have crossed the poverty line. And even that was possible only because in many cases the assistance went to people just below the poverty line rather than to the poorest, in violation of the declared bottom-up procedure. It was, in fact, demonstrated by Sundaram and Tendulkar (1985) that given the level of assistance and even accepting the highly optimistic capital–output ratio assumed by the Plan, none would be able to cross the poverty line if all the assistance went to the bottom half of the poor population. There was thus a manifest contradiction between the level of assistance and the proclaimed bottom-up procedure on the one hand and the target of transition beyond the poverty line on the other. Consequently, IRDP made itself a sitting duck to be merrily shot down by its numerous critics.

Deservedly so, one might say, in view of the contradictions built into the programme. But it is still necessary to evaluate to what extent IRDP did in fact ensure a more secure livelihood for the poor, even if it meant that they continued to live below the official poverty line. The first issue is the degree of success in reaching the target group. In order to capture the poorest group, the eligibility criterion was fixed at a level of income that was some 23 per cent below the official poverty line. After reviewing four major evaluations done during the 1980–5 period, Bagchee (1987) has estimated that about 15 to 20 per cent of the beneficiaries were above the cut-off point to begin with.[26] The survey of 1985–6 has also revealed a leakage of some 20 per cent (Kurian 1987). This is a fairly commendable achievement compared with the experience of earlier target-group-oriented programmes, especially if one notes that many of the 'ineligible' households would actually have had an income below the official poverty line although above the eligibility criterion.

There is, however, some doubt as to whether the bottom-up procedure has been strictly followed. For example, the results of the countryside survey conducted in 1985–6 show that nearly 60 per cent of the beneficiaries belonged to the top half of the poor population (Kurian 1987: table 1). For the state of Karnataka during the same period, Rao and Erappa (1987) have shown that landless households constituted less than half of all beneficiaries. In none of these cases is there reason to believe that the potential beneficiaries in the poorest segment were exhausted before the less poor households were catered to. In this respect, there is some similarity with the experience of the Grameen Bank. Although, as we have noted, as much as 95 per cent of the Grameen Bank beneficiaries belong to the target group, the programme has not succeeded in catering to the need of agricultural labourers who (along with share-croppers) are recognized to be the most deprived group in rural Bangladesh. As Ahmad and Hossain (1985) have pointed out, this group constituted only one-tenth of those receiving loans although they formed one-third of the target group. We shall comment later on the significance of this phenomenon common to both the Grameen Bank and IRDP.

To continue with IRDP's performance, we next look at its impact on the beneficiary households' ability to sustain a higher flow of income. The findings in this respect are much less clear-cut, mainly because of the well-known difficulties in estimating income and, to an even greater extent, in finding a suitable reference point for comparison. By analysing the data from a country-wide evaluation for 1985–6 Kurian (1987) has estimated that, over a period of two years, 84 per cent of the assisted households enjoyed some positive increment in family income and as many as 38 per cent did so to the tune of more than 50 per cent. This is taken by Kurian as an indication that IRDP has

[26] There was a good deal of interstate variation in this respect. In Gujarat, for example, the figure was as high as 47%.

succeeded in giving a significantly higher level of living to a large group of households.

But his conclusion cannot be taken seriously because of certain definitional problems, quite apart from the problems of eliciting information on past income through the recall method. In the first place, the amount of loan repayment is not netted out of gross income when estimating the post-assistance income of the beneficiary families.[27] Secondly, it is not clear whether the income data for the two periods have been converted into constant prices. Without access to basic data, it is not possible to correct Kurian's estimates for the factors mentioned above. However, one can see how a very different picture emerges if some rough corrections are made on his data concerning income generated by the IRDP assets (Kurian 1987: table 11). Some 24 per cent of the assets are found to have generated no income at all. Another 26 per cent of the assets generated an income of up to Rs 1,000, but this income is in current prices and does not exclude loan repayment. Taking the standard loan specifications of the IRDP, namely, an average loan of Rs 2,000 per family, a repayment period of 3 years, and an interest rate of 10 per cent per annum, and assuming 10 per cent inflation over the two-year period, it is easy to see that, after loan repayment and price adjustment, an asset yielding an income of up to Rs 1,000 would add nothing or little to a family's real disposable income. Thus a total of 50 per cent of the assets can be said to have made no or negligible contribution to net disposable income.

As for the remaining 50 per cent of the assets, the evidence of positive contribution must be tempered by the fact that once a family engages on an occupation based on the newly acquired assets, its income from other sources tends to fall because of diversion of labour. Working on the same set of data as used by Kurian, but focusing on the state of Uttar Pradesh alone, Rao and Rangaswamy (1988) have found that the fall of income from other sources was about 20 per cent of the pre-assistance income of an average family. The opportunity cost from the point of view of the family is thus seen to be quite substantial; consequently, many of the assets which did make a positive contribution to disposable income, even after adjustment for loan repay-ment, may not turn out to do so after this opportunity cost is also accounted for. In the absence of more detailed information, we cannot be sure exactly what picture emerges at the end, but the least one can infer from the preceding

---

[27] Kurian does not mention this, but Rao and Rangaswamy (1988) do while analysing the same set of data for Uttar Pradesh. The latter authors also defend this procedure on the ground that 'since the concept of net income followed is the same in respect of IRDP as well as other sources (both in the pre- and post-assistance periods), per cent *changes* in such incomes may approximate to *changes* in disposable income' (p. A-71). This argument is tenable only if the pre-assistance income did in fact include a loan repayment component of comparable magnitude. Since this is highly unlikely to have been the case for most beneficiaries, the methodology followed by these authors is bound to give an inflated picture of the change in disposable income.

arguments is that more than half the assets failed to add to the beneficiaries' net disposable incomes, properly defined.

Rao and Rangaswamy (1988), in their study of Uttar Pradesh, have corrected their estimates of income for the opportunity cost mentioned above, but not for loan repayment, and it is not clear whether they have made any corrections for price increase. According to their estimates, an average beneficiary enjoyed a net increment of 32 per cent of pre-assistance income over a period of two years. In absolute terms, the increment comes to Rs 1078 (computed from ibid. table 12). On the other hand, the annual burden of loan repayment can be seen to be somewhat higher than this figure, if one applies the three-year repayment period and 10 per cent annual interest on the average loan size (reported to be Rs 2,797, ibid. table 10). Thus the net contribution to disposable income once again turns out to be negligible at best for the average beneficiary.

One major problem with all these studies is that they take a static view of income gain, whereas the crucial issue in the evaluation of IRDP must be whether the beneficiaries can sustain a higher flow of income in the long term after paying all dues and replacing the old assets when they become obsolete. Such long-term effects on income mobility have been rarely explored. One partial effort was made by Subbarao (1985) who calculated an income mobility matrix from the data collected by IFMR (1984) on five districts in southern India. He compared the assisted households with a carefully chosen control group and showed that the upward mobility of the poorest among the assisted households was decidedly superior to that of the poorest non-beneficiary households. His estimates of the proportions of upwardly mobile households is not of much use, since, as rightly pointed out by Swaminathan (1988), he did not adjust the nominal incomes for price increase. But his comparison between beneficiaries and non-beneficiaries is not vitiated by this flaw.

There is, however, a more serious problem with Subbarao's findings. As once again pointed out by Swaminathan (1988), the mobility he looks at relates to a time gap of only fifteen months, which is too short a period to judge whether the beneficiaries would be able to maintain a higher level of consumption over the long term. They may not be able to keep the assets after some time, or they may find their extra income insufficient to enable them to set aside the money required for replacing the old assets. Swaminathan's (1988) own micro-level survey of two villages in Tamil Nadu was addressed precisely to this question of the long-term asset position of the assisted households. She found, after six years since the initiation of IRDP, that the upward mobility of the assisted households in terms of assets was no better than that of the sample of unassisted households.[28]

---

[28] Although the mobility studied by Swaminathan refers to a time gap of eight years (from 1977 to 1985), there was no serious problem of recall lapse as the recall method was not used to collect

Clearly, more studies of this type are needed to form a clear picture of how far the IRDP has succeeded in improving the long-term economic viability of beneficiary households. But the evidence and arguments presented above do not inspire much optimism. The same large-scale survey from which Kurian (1987) draws a mildly optimistic picture, also shows that 29 per cent of the assets were 'not intact' only two years after the receipt of assistance; and as much as 24 per cent of the assets were found to yield no income at all either because the assets were disposed of, or had perished, or had never been procured in the first place. Piecing together a number of earlier surveys both large and small, Rath (1985) found that the proportion of beneficiaries whose assets ceased to exist after two to three years varied between 20 and 50 per cent.

Even in the cases where the assets contined to exist, the correctly measured contribution to disposable income, as we have noted, was often rather low. The most talked-about example of low return is that of milch cattle, which have come to bear the rather sarcastic appellation of the 'IRDP cow'. In the early years of IRDP, as much as 60 to 80 per cent of the assets consisted of cattle; even in 1985–6 the share of cattle in all assets was 37 per cent (Kurian 1987). There are innumerable accounts, albeit of an informal nature, of how the milch cattle have yielded a pitifully low rate of return either because most of them were of inferior breed, or because fodder and veterinary care were utterly inadequate, or simply because they died of disease or drought. While the problem with milch cattle was especially acute, the other assets were not particularly productive either. Those who framed the Sixth Plan had expected that the IRDP investment would yield an average incremental capital–ouptut ratio of 1.5 : 1. In the event this ratio was achieved only in the case of 26 per cent of the assets, and the overall ratio was close to 3 : 1 (Kurian 1987). On top of this, one must also take note of the numerous accounts of how the prospective beneficiaries had to incur a substantial initial cost by way of paying the intermediaries (and sometimes the bank officials too) and searching for a suitable assets. According to the National Committee on the Development of Backward Areas, these expenditures often amounted to 50 to 70 per cent of the subsidy component (GOI 1981: 24). Taking all these factors into account— namely, 20 to 50 per cent cases of vanishing assets, low yield of existing assets, and high initial cost—one cannot but be sceptical about IRDP's success in ensuring a sustained flow of a perceptibly higher level of income.

What about the future? Can the programme be reconstituted so as to offer a genuinely secure source of higher income for resource-poor households? In order to answer this question, one must first identify the sources of IRDP's weakness. At one level, it can be argued that much of the problem lies in disregarding the basic economics of a massive self-employment programme. If assets are to become a viable basis of self-employment, at least three kinds of

past data—a set of households surveyed in 1977 in connection with a different study were resurveyed in 1985, and the data from the two surveys compared.

'matching' must be ensured. First, the structure of assets must be such that the resulting structure of output corresponds to the existing or prospective pattern of demand for that output. Secondly, the structure and quantum of assets to be acquired by the households must be matched with the existing or potential supply of assets. Finally, there has to be a matching between the type of asset (as well as the size of investment) and the pre-existing resources (land, labour, and entrepreneurial capacity) of a household. If a mismatch occurs in any of these respects, the yield of investment is bound to suffer. There are enough indications to believe that IRDP suffered from mismatches of all three kinds.

Excessive concentration on milch cattle is a clear example of the neglect of the demand side. Working with the IFMR data, Subbarao (1985) noticed that the only district (out of five) where milch cattle had yielded a satisfactory rate of return was that blessed with a number of milk-chilling plants. The demand generated by these plants, as well as other infrastructural facilities associated with them, obviously helped in maintaining a high level of return. In other districts, there were simply too many heads of cattle in relation to demand.[29] Similarly, Kurian (1987) narrates the case of dozens of sewing machines being supplied to different women in a single village; and stories like this can be multiplied. The neglect of the supply side is equally glaring. As Rath (1985) notes, something like 5 million cattle were purchased by the IRDP households during the Sixth Plan period, without there being any arrangement for producing that many high-breed cattle. As a result, not only did the beneficiaries have to purchase inferior cattle, but sometimes even the required number of cattle were not available. As a result, the price of cattle went up, which often induced the purchasing households to sell off the cattle to other households. In this way, the same animal moved from household to household satisfying aggregate demand in the absence of matching supply (Kurian 1987). With more than a tinge of sarcasm, V. M. Dandekar has for this reason described the 'IRDP cow' as 'circulating capital' (quoted in Kurian 1987: A-175).

Similar failures have been noted in respect of matching IRDP assets to household resources. Kurian (1987), for example, mentions that cases were reported where hundreds of animals were distributed in drought-affected areas although the purchasers did not have the grazing facilities to feed the animals. At a more general level, Rath (1985) has argued that the poorest of the households who have traditionally sold nothing but raw labour may simply not have the entrepreneurial ability to engage in viable self-employed activities. A degree of support for this contention is provided by our earlier observation that agricultural labourers were mostly left out by both IRDP and the Grameen Bank.[30] It is, however, difficult to agree with Rath when he goes on to argue

---

[29] The fact that IRDP usually performed better in areas with developed infrastructures has also been noted by Rao and Erappa (1987) and Rao and Rangaswamy (1988), among others.

[30] It is also interesting to note that most of the beneficiaries of the Grammeen Bank scheme engage in those activities where their households have already had some entrepreneurial experience. It

that the whole idea of promoting self-employment should be de-emphasized and that the expansion of wage employment through public works should constitute the principle direct intervention programme. The notion that the poorest households do not as a rule possess entrepreneurial ability cannot simply be true; for a large number of them are traditionally engaged in various self-employed activities such as cottage industries, petty business, and services; moreover, it has been noted from the IRDP experience that the poorest households who participate in the programme do no necessarily fare worse compared to the less poor ones (Rao and Rangaswamy 1988). However, the essential point that the chosen activity must correspond to the entrepreneurial ability and other resources of the household still remains valid.

The observed mismatch in IRDP has generally been attributed to two factors. The first relates to the absence of a comprehensive local development plan, without which matchings of the various kinds described above could scarcely be ensured. Plans are required for the purpose of both assessing and augmenting the supply of assets on the one hand and demand for their products on the other. This will make it possible to endow the prospective beneficiaries with assets that are both available in required specification and viable enough in terms of the demand for their products. Initially, this is precisely what the programme was supposed to have ensured; hence the name Integrated Rural Development Programme. In actual practice, however, planning for the creation of supply and demand was never integrated in the programme. There was some rough attempt to carry out an assessment of existing supply and demand, but that too was thoroughly inadequate. The second factor relates to the imperative of fulfilling a numerical target within a specified time limit. A severely understaffed local administrative machinery was burdened with the tasks of identifying the eligible beneficiaries, motivating them to participate in the programme, preparing suitable investment projects for individual households, and often identifying and procuring the assets for them. Under pressure of meeting the target, they frequently took the easy option of pushing through whatever assets were readily available, disregarding the need to match described above.

One might pause to ponder at this stage why is it necessary to ensure the required matchings through planned intervention—why cannot one simply transfer some financial resources to the poor households and leave the task of matching to the market process? In this context, it is instructive to contrast the experience of IRDP with that of Grameen Bank. As opposed to the bureaucratic-interventionist approach of IRDP, the Grameen Bank of Bangladesh has adopted what may, with some liberty, be described as the *laissez-faire* approach. It is true that Bank officials do apply a strict eligibility criterion, motivate the prospective beneficiaries to participate in the programme, and subject them to

is no coincidence that some 40 per cent of the loan is taken for trading activities and some 30 per cent of the beneficiaries had trading as their prior occupation (Hossain 1984b: 125, 29).

strict discipline; but there is no attempt to determine the structure of activities either in the aggregate or for individual households. The whole underlying philosophy of the Grameen Bank is that most local people have a pretty shrewd idea of what opportunities are potentially available and they also know which of these they are capable of handling; all they need is the access to credit in order to take those opportunities.

It will be wrong, however, to describe it as an entirely hands-off approach, because the Bank does employ a highly imaginative method of indirectly pressurizing the beneficiaries to be particularly careful in the choice and execution of their projects. This is done by enforcing a rigorous discipline of loan repayment. There are a number of components of this strategy. First, the beneficiaries are required to form a group of five people. Although the loan is given to an individual and he or she alone is responsible for repayment, a kind of group pressure is brought to bear upon the recipients by the stipulation that default by one member of the group will make the rest of the members ineligible for loan. Secondly, the repayments are to be made in weekly instalments in local meetings which all beneficiaries in a particular locality are required to attend. This again acts as group pressure. All this is motivated by the basic premiss that if the repayment discipline can be rigorously enforced, the recipients will be careful in seeking out truly viable projects. Thus the combination of people's personal knowledge of local opportunities and the Bank's insistence on the discipline of repayment is considered to be an adequate guarantee of securing the productive use of credit. Apparently, this strategy has worked remarkably well.

Does the *laissez-faire* approach operated by the Grameen Bank, then, offer a viable strategy for self-employment programmes? We believe there are reasons to be sceptical about it. A very important consideration here is the question of scale. As mentioned before, the Grameen Bank has so far covered only 3 to 4 per cent of the villages in the country; even in the limited area of its operation only half of the target group has been covered (Hossain 1984b). While operating at such a low scale, it may not be so essential to worry about supply and demand. The modest purpose at this level is to enable a few of the poor to take advantage of the opportunities that are somehow being created within the economy. In this sense the Grameen Bank does little more than marginally augment the 'trickle-down' process. But if a massive self-employment pro-gramme of the IRDP type is to be launched, it will not do to disregard the need for integrating credit-giving within a broader framework for planned expansion. There are already indications of this even in the limited scale of the Grameen Bank's operation. A couple of Hossain's (1984b) findings are worthy of note in this context. First, the rate of return from repeat loans is generally lower than that of the original loan and secondly, the relatively large-size loans are seldom fully invested. This indicates the presence of limits to the expansion of self-employment within the existing configuration of supply and demand.

The need for genuinely integrated rural development cannot, therefore, be denied. One might argue, however, that while macro-matching is ensured through an integrated plan, micro-matching between household and assets may still be left to the individual, as in the Grameen Bank approach. Some degree of individual autonomy is certainly desirable, but its limits should also be recognized. The Grameen Bank may be right in assuming that even the poorest households may have a shrewd idea of what opportunities are available, provided that the local economy is only slowly evolving. But that assumption may no longer hold if massive interventions are to be made at the local level to alter the macro-configurations of supply and demand. The resulting uncertainty about the new economic environment may be difficult to handle even for the well-off entrepreneurs, but at least they can be expected to take their losses along with their profits; in any case their subsistence will not be threatened in the event of a loss. But even a single loss-making venture by a poor household may ruin the slender basis of subsistence it may have had by saddling it with a net liability of loan repayment. That would be the cruelest outcome of a programme whose ostensible purpose is to enhance the security of poor households.

It is therefore clear that a successful programme of security through self-employment will require detailed planning at the local level with regard to all three kinds of matching discussed earlier. It should also be clear that just any kind of integrated rural development programme will not do, for one may have integrated development which caters to the needs of the better-off section. One therefore comes back to the question of countervailing power at the local level for safeguarding the interest of the poor. This question has not been systematically explored in the various evaluations of IRDP that have been carried out in India. But some indication of its importance may be seen in the findings of Rao and Erappa (1987) and Thimmaiah (1988) for Karnataka, and Sharma and Gianchandani (1988) for Rajasthan. They all noted that the opportunities opened up by IRDP were seized more effectively by middle-level households than by the bottom-placed agricultural labourers. It is also interesting to note that by several accounts the performance of IRDP has been somewhat better in West Bengal where the rule of the Communist Party of India (Marxist) has created a countervailing power, however partially.[31] A survey conducted by the Programme Evaluation Organisation of the Planning Commission of India showed that the proportion of beneficiaries drawn from the poorest group is the highest in West Bengal (along with Tamil Nadu) among all Indian states (Bandyopadhyay 1985: 112). The subsequent country-wide survey of 1985–6 showed that West Bengal was also among the best performers in terms of utilization of resources: while the assets ceased to yield income after two years of loan disbursement in 24 per cent of the cases at the

---

[31] See discussion in the preceding section.

national level, this happened in West Bengal in only 7 per cent of the cases (Kurian 1987).[32] Finally, the same survey also showed that while the incremental capital–output ratio was 3 : 1 at the national level, West Bengal achieved the ratio of 1.5 : 1 in 70 per cent of the cases—the best performance among all States.

These illustrations are meant to be indicative rather than conclusive. But they do lend credence to the a priori proposition that the presence of countervailing power at the local level is a precondition for an effective programme of social security through self-employment of the poor.[33]

4.   SECURITY THROUGH WAGE EMPLOYMENT

A large proportion of the rural labour-force in South Asia depends on wage labour as their principal means of livelihood. The proportion of principally wage-dependent persons (including landless agricultural labourers, marginal farmers, and households engaged in non-cultivating labour) is at least one-third of the rural labour-force in India and well over half in Bangladesh. They are also among the poorest of all households. In Bangladesh as much as 90 per cent of such households are counted as poor, while in India a reasonable estimate would be around 60 per cent.[34] This massive poverty is due partly to low wages and partly to lack of secure employment throughout the year. Recognizing that the amount of employment generated through the normal process of development is thoroughly inadequate to meet the challenge, both countries have launched huge programmes of employment generation, largely through public works. It is worthwhile to see to what extent these programmes have been or can be useful in providing security to the poor people.

The major programme in Bangladesh goes under the name of Food For Work (FFW). It came into existence in 1975 and by now it is the most important of all employment-generating programmes. Its distinctive feature, compared with earlier programmes, is the payment of wages in kind, mainly wheat that is obtained as food aid from the Western world.[35]

Like most other programmes of its kind elsewhere in the developing countries, FFW is not free from the usual allegations of leakage and the misuse of funds; one study has estimated that the underpayment of labourers may have amounted to about 30 per cent of total allocation (BIDS-IFPRI 1983). Yet the benefits derived by the employed workers were not inconsequential. Some

[32] Only Gujarat, an infrastructurally developed state, and Tripura, another CPI (M)-dominated state, did any better.

[33] For more on this point see Bandyopadhyay (1988).

[34] See Rahman and Haque (1988: table 17), on Bangladesh; and Sundaram and Tendulkar (1985: tables 3–7), on India.

[35] In 1982–3, the amount of wheat distributed under FFW accounted for 42 per cent of all food aid and 21 per cent of total food imports (Ahmad and Hossain 1985: 77).

of the positive features noted by a comprehensive survey (Osmani and Chowdhury 1983) may be summarized as follows: first, there is no doubt that the benefit of employment went mostly to the poorest segment of rural population. Nearly 70 per cent of the employees belonged to what is called the functionally landless category, that is, those who own less than half an acre of cultivated land. Since they constitute about half of the rural population, it is evident that this group has found more than proportionate representation in total employment. Secondly, the net income gain of participating households amounted to roughly 10 per cent of their annual wage income or 7–8 per cent of total household income. Thirdly, the consumption of food (especially foodgrains) improved significantly for those who were more or less regularly involved in the FFW projects.

While noting these positive aspects, it must also be admitted that in terms of its aggregate impact the achievement does not amount to much. An illustrative calculation can give the picture. According to the Labour Force Survey of 1983/4, the total rural labour-force of that year was 24.3 million. It has been observed from various scattered sources of evidence that the extent of under-employment in rural Bangladesh varies from 31 to 40 per cent (Islam 1986). Taking the conservative estimate of 30 per cent, the extent of underemployment in 1983/4 was the full-time equivalent of 7.3 million people unemployed. Against this background, FFW created 101 million man-days in that year, which comes to about 0.34 million man-years (taking a standard man-year to consist of 300 days). This means that FFW was able to eliminate just under 5 per cent of underemployment among the rural labour force in 1983–4.

This is a rather modest achievement, clearly inadequate in relation to need. The question therefore arises: can the scale of operations be expanded to provide complete security of employment? One constraint can be noted immediately. Our illustrative calculation shows that the scale of operation will have to be expanded at least twentyfold in order to provide complete security. Considering that the amount of wheat distributed under FFW constituted roughly 20 per cent of total food imports in recent years, such an expansion would involve a sixfold increase in the quantum of food import from its present level—clearly an unfeasible proposition. There may be other constraints also. For instance, will it be possible to find an adequate number of public-works schemes which are the same time both labour-intensive and sufficiently productive? This question takes us to a much wider range of issues which have relevance not just for Bangladesh but for the rest of the region as well. We shall return to it after taking a brief stock of India's experience with similar programmes.

After experimenting with various forms of employment generation schemes in the 1960s and the 1970s, India too decided to adopt Food For Work as the major programme in 1977. There was, however, a major difference from Bangladesh. Instead of depending on food aid, India supplied the required food-grain from its own rapidly accumulating stock. Indeed, one of the motivations behind shifting from a system of cash payment to a system of partial payment in food was to dispose of this huge stock, which was something of an embarrassment for a country where anywhere between one-third to one-half of the population were reported to be suffering from endemic hunger. In any case the existence of this stock implies that India is in a much better position to expand the programme compared with Bangladesh, provided that other constraints do not become binding.

As it happens, a severe constraint seems already to have emerged as far as the food-grain component of the programme is concerned. This is indicated by the sharp fall in this component after the FFW was merged into a new expanded programme called the National Rural Employment Programme (NREP) at the start of the Sixth Plan (1980–5). In 1980/1 an average of 3.2 kg of food-grain was utilized per person per day, but the average for the next four years was only 0.5 kg, although the official stipulation was that at least 1 kg of food-grain should be given as part of the wage. Difficulties in public distribution and workers' preference for coarse cereal over the finer cereals (wheat and rice) which are distributed by the programme have been suggested as the main reasons for this phenomenon.[36]

This did not, however, hinder the progress of the programme as a whole, since the shortfall in grain payment was made up by cash. What the planners were worried about was the possibility that the benefit might not be going mostly to the neediest group, namely, the landless population. Consequently, in 1983, a new scheme called the Rural Landless Employement Guarantee Programme (RLEGP) was initiated alongside NREP, with the specific objective of guaranteeing up to 100 days of employment to at least one member of every landless household in the country. These two programmes were merged in 1988 and are together expected to create 490 million man-days in a year during the Seventh Plan period (1985–90).

How significant are these efforts in relation to need? Once again an illustrative calculation will help. Assuming that the Seventh Plan target is met, and taking a standard man-year to consist of 300 days, a total of 1.6 million full-time jobs will have been created in 1986. Exactly what this means in terms of removing unemployment is not certain, as no estimate of unemployment is available for the recent period. However, we can get a rough picture by projecting past estimates. It was noted in the Sixth Plan document that in 1980 some 15.4 million job-seekers in rural India remained unemployed on a typical day, that is to say, total unemployment was the equivalent of 15.4 million full-time jobs. Even if we make the optimistic assumption that total employment has grown since then at the same rate as the labour-force, this will mean that the absolute size of the unemployed labour-force has grown at that rate too. On that basis,

---

[36] See the discussion on NREP in the Seventh Five Year Plan, GOI (1985: ii. 58–9).

just as about 9 per cent of unemployment would have been removed by the two programmes in 1986.

This is indeed some achievement, and decidedly better than that of Bangladesh, but still clearly inadequate in relation to need. In order to eliminate unemployment completely through NREP and RLEGP, the scale of operation will have to be expanded at least tenfold. Considering that the Seventh Plan allocates 2.1 per cent of total outlay on these two programmes, such an expansion would imply an allocation of as much as a quarter of total Plan expenditure.

This shows the financial implications of ensuring social security through guaranteed employment. It is worth noting in this context that the concept of guaranteed employment is enshrined in the Indian Constitution where the right to work is given the status of a (non-justiciable) directive principle. However, it was only with the introduction of RLEGP in 1983 that the concept of guarantee was explicitly recognized for the first time in a national-level programme. Even then the recognition was incomplete. First, only one rather than all the working members of each landless household was to have guaranteed employment. Secondly, the guarantee was given only in the form of a ceiling rather than as a floor of minimum employment, namely 'up to 100 days per year'. This means that the authorities can claim to have honoured the guarantee even by offering just a single day's employment. In one of the few evaluations of RLEGP done so far, the authors did in fact find that only 5 per cent of the participants received more than 100 days of employment in Punjab (Singh and De, n.d.).

Much more serious commitment to the concept of the guarantee is evident in the State of Maharashtra. The State government had been implementing an Employment Guarantee Scheme (EGS) from its own finances long before RLEGP came into being at the national level. Several other States have also been trying to emulate Maharashtra with schemes of their own. But it is the Maharashtra scheme that has come to be acclaimed as a resounding success. For that reason, it is worthwhile to look into it in some detail.

Although EGS was formally sanctioned only in 1978/9, it had in fact been in operation since the late 1960s. Starting at a low level of activity it began to pick up from 1975, and it has now become the most important social-welfare programme in the State (consuming nearly 10 per cent of the State budget in 1979/80). In its present form, the scheme guarantees that every adult who wants a job in rural areas will be given one, provided he/she is willing to do unskilled manual work on a piece-rate basis. In order to ensure that only truly needy persons will come forward to take up the guarantee, a mechanism of self-selection has been built into the programme in a number of ways. First, no choice of work is given—only unskilled manual work is made available. Secondly, the wage rate is kept below the ongoing agricultural wage; the piece rate is fixed in such a way that with average effort the daily wage would equal the minimum of all statutory minimum wage rates obtaining in different parts of the State. In practice, the process of self-selection is further reinforced by the widespread prevalence of underpayment.[37] Thirdly, although the official instruction is that work is to be provided preferably within a radius of 5 km from a worker's residence, in practice the guarantee operates at the block level, which may sometimes require a person to travel a long distance for a few days of temporary work (Bagchee 1984).

On the whole the self-selection mechanism has worked reasonably well, but not with complete success. An evaluation done in 1977/8 found that 45 per cent of the workers came from landless households and 42 per cent belonged to the deprived social groups of the scheduled castes and the scheduled tribes (Dandekar and Sathe 1980). However, according to the same survey, 42 per cent of the workers came from cultivating households owning up to 5 acres of land. While some of them, especially the so-called marginal farmers owning less than 2.5 acres (of mostly unirrigated land), belonged to the neediest group, not all of them did. It has been observed that small, and sometimes not-so-small, farmers participate to a considerable extent in the EGS during the lean season when many of them would otherwise remain idle. This explains the finding of an official evaluation that, as a proportion of those needing work, the small and medium farmers have secured more employment than the landless group (PEO 1980b).

This is perhaps an unavoidable consequence of offering an open-ended guarantee to everyone regardless of economic status. Perhaps there would not be much wrong with this if it did not happen at the expense of the neediest group. It is, therefore, important to see how far the EGS has succeeded in meeting the employment gap of landless workers and marginal farmers. In sheer absolute size, the employment created under the EGS certainly exceeds by a wide margin anything that has so far been achieved elsewhere in India (or for that matter other parts of South Asia). In 1977/8, for example, an average participant was found to have received 160 days of employment under the EGS (Dandekar and Sathe 1980). By comparison, FFW provided just 44 days of employment per participant all over India (PEO 1980a) and NREP provided 51 and 55 days in Gujarat and Karnataka respectively (ILO 1984). Also, the EGS contributed two-thirds of the annual income of participants (Dandekar and Sathe 1980), while the corresponding contribution of NREP in Gujarat and Karnataka was found to be one-fifth (ILO 1984).

Despite such impressive figures, there remains some doubt as to the achievement of the EGS in relation to need. Dandekar and Sathe (1980) have claimed that in 1977/8 the EGS eliminated as much as 75 per cent of unemployment among the 'weaker sections', defined as the set comprising landless labourers and the bottom 10 per cent among cultivators. This estimate

[37] One observer encountered rates as low as 10 per cent of the minimum, though 33 to 50 per cent was more common (Herring and Edwards 1983: 590).

appears to be highly inflated in view of the doubtful procedures they have employed.[38] They assume, for instance, that all employment went to the weaker sections whereas their own survey shows that only 45 per cent of the workers came from the landless group. Of course we do not know how many came from the bottom 10 per cent of the cultivators, only that 42 per cent came from households owning no more than 5 acres. Given this information, it is in fact impossible to deduce how much of the EGS employment went to the weaker sections, and by how much their unemployment was reduced.

As an alternative, we offer an estimate for a subset of the 'weaker sections', consisting only of landless labourers. We know from Dandekar and Sathe (1980) that 45 per cent of the EGS workers were landless labourers, but not how much of total employment went to them. It is, however, possible to estimate an upper limit from the finding that an average worker found employment for 160 days in the EGS but hardly anyone exceeded 180 days. If we assume (liberally) that all the landless workers had reached the maximum limit of 180 days, then their share in total employment was 50 per cent (45 × 180/160). Thus the upper limit of the landless labourers' EGS-employment, out of a total of 117.3 million man-days in 1977/8, turns out to be 58.6 million man-days.

Next, we require an estimate of the level of unemployment that would have prevailed among the landless in the absence of the EGS. For this purpose we use the data from the 1974/5 Rural Labour Enquiry, as the EGS was still operating on a modest scale in that year. Unfortunately no data is available separately for the landless labourers; so we must take the rate of unemployment prevailing among the primarily labour-selling households instead. Assuming a standard man-year to consist of 300 days, the extent of unemployment turns out to be 86 days per worker (average of male and female). From the data presented by Dandekar and Sathe (1980), it appears that in 1977/8 there were about 3.1 million landless workers in the whole of rural Maharashtra.[39] This gives a total unemployment figure among the landless labourers of about 266 million man-days. Recalling that a maximum of 58.6 million days of employment came their way by courtesy of the EGS, it would thus appear that the scheme was able to eliminate no more than 22 per cent of unemployment among this group in 1977/8, and that under a host of liberal assumptions. The size of the EGS has of course expanded since then; for example, the volume of employment generated in 1979/81 was 60 per cent higher than that in 1977/8 (Herring and Edwards 1983). But since the landless population has also expanded at the same time (albeit at a slower rate), the total impact could hardly amount to more than a third of unemployment among landless labourers.

[38] For a detailed critique of Dandekar and Sathe's methodology, see Tilve and Pitre (1980).
[39] There were reportedly 5.95 million households of landless labourers, with a worker ratio of 0.52 per household (Dandekar and Sathe 1980: 710).

Illustrative as they are, the preceding calculations show that perhaps too much has been made of the guarantee aspect of the Maharashtra scheme. What is not in question, though, is its relatively superior performance compared with similar schemes elsewhere in South Asia. This, combined with the fact that the scheme is still expanding, invites the question: does not the Maharashtra experience indicate that it is possible to achieve much more by way of providing security through employment than has been the experience so far in the rest of the region? In order to form a perspective on this matter, it is first necessary to take cognizance of a special feature of the Maharashtra scheme.

As mentioned before, the EGS was initiated as a fully State-financed project without any financial support from the central government. Half of the finance was raised by means of special taxes legislated for this purpose and the other half came from the general revenues of the State government. It is highly instructive to look at the range of these special taxes. The bulk of the revenue was extracted from the urban sector, particularly from the city of Bombay. Taxes on agriculture were originally supposed to contribute roughly one-fifth of the total EGS revenue. In the event their share turned out to be a maximum of 3 per cent during the period between 1975/6 and 1978/9, while as much as 60 to 70 per cent was collected from the city of Bombay alone (Herring and Edwards 1983: 585). As opposed to this urban orientation of finance and almost total exemption of the rural sector from the sharing of cost, the distribution of benefit was disproportionately in favour of the richer farmers. It is true that the workers also benefited during the course of specific projects but the lasting benefits went to farmers in the form of assets that were created under the EGS. It is of course a commonplace that asset creation through rural works generally benefits the landed people more; but this commonplace assumes a particular poignancy in rural Maharashtra because of the nature of assets created by the EGS. While earth-roads and other non-durable assets usually dominate the portfolio of assets in a typical rural works programme, a predominant share in Maharashtra was taken up by irrigation works of various kinds. As an official evaluation of the EGS showed, these irrigation works and other agriculture-related land development works yielded remarkable benefits to the farmers, specially the middle and large farmers (PEO 1980b).

This contrast in the distribution of costs and benefits of the EGS is not unrelated to the fact that the State politics of Maharashtra are known to be strongly dominated by the richer landowners (MHJ 1980; Herring and Edwards 1983). Of course, they were assisted in this matter by the presence of a very rich urban sector. Maharashtra is one of the wealthiest States in India in terms of per capita income but one of the poorest in terms of rural income, which means that almost all of its enormous wealth originates from the prosperous urban sector. In a spectacular reversal of the 'urban bias' hypothesis, the politically powerful rural élite of Maharashtra has succeeded in extracting surplus wealth from the urban sector, combined it with the raw labour of a marginalized rural population, and created assets for the benefit of their own land.[40]

The secret of Maharashtra thus lies in forming a triangle between a dominant rural élite, a materially prosperous urban sector which for some reason was willing to foot the bill, and a poor but abundantly available rural labour-force. The third corner of this triangle can be safely assumed to exist all over South Asia, but one cannot be too certain about the first two. This is what sets the limit to the possibility of emulating Maharashtra in the rest of the region.

There are, of course, other limits too. If an employment programme is to be something more than a pure relief operation, it must create assets that are not only productive but are also capable of creating long-term employment, ideally leading to a stage where special programmes for employment generation will no longer be needed. Experience shows that well-executed projects for irrigation and flood control can have a significant effect on both crop production and long-term employment (BIDS-IFPRI 1985). The FFW in Bangladesh is indeed slanted heavily in favour of such agriculture-related activities, but there is some doubt as to how well they are executed (Asaduzzaman and Huddleston 1983). The situation is somewhat different in India, where the preponderance of 'roads that are washed away' have been a source of constant criticism (Basu 1981; Bandyopadhyay 1985).

The transitory nature of the benefit accruing from employment programmes and the dependency they allegedly tend to generate among workers on continuous support from public works, have led some scholars to argue that the creation of self-employment through IRDP-type programmes is a superior mode of supporting the poor (see, for example, Dantwala 1985). In contrast, others, such as Rath (1985) and Dandekar (1986), have argued that wage employment is the only feasible means of supporting the poor since the majority of them do not possess the entrepreneurial skill needed for doing well in IRDP-type programmes. The controversy that has ensued over 'wage employment versus self-employment' does seem to be rather sterile, however. We have noted in the preceding section that a blanket denial of the entre-preneurial acumen of the poor is hard to sustain; many of them can and do make a regular living out of self-employed activities. On the other hand, it is also true that many may not want to take the risks and troubles of independent occupations, and may much prefer to seek their livelihood in the labour market. There is no reason why both types of employment cannot be generated in a complementary fashion for furthering the security of livelihood of the poor. This will, however, require truly integrated local-level planning of the kind discussed in the preceding section. Without such planning, neither mode of supporting the poor will have a sustained effect—the programmes for self-employment will fail to be productive enough to raise permanently the asset

[40] Herring and Edwards (1983) provide an interesting analysis of the political economy of the Maharashtra EGS along these lines.

base of the poor, and the programmes for wage-employment will fail to create
the assets required for raising the long-term employment-generating capacity
of the economy. Whether the countries of South Asia have the ability to
undertake such poverty-focused local-level planning on an extensive scale is a
moot question. What is clear, however, is the inference that in the absence of
such ability the programmes of employment promotion will fail to provide
lasting security to the poor. Some temporary relief will indeed be provided
and, if operated on a modest scale, even lasting security can be ensured for a
small segment of the poor, but not generalized long-term security for the bulk
of the poor. In that event, other methods of providing social security will have
to be seriously contemplated.

5. SECURITY THROUGH PUBLIC PROVISION OF BASIC NEEDS

If the goal of social security is to ensure guaranteed access to a certain minimal
standard of living, and the standard of living is itself defined in terms of
functionings and capabilities (Sen 1985), then the policies and programmes
discussed in the preceding sections are best described as indirect means of
achieving that goal. They are supposed to provide the resources with which the
beneficiaries will hopefully acquire the inputs—such as food, clothing, housing,
health care, education, and so on—which will in turn create the desired ways
of functioning, such as living a healthy active life. An alternative, and
potentially complementary, approach is to make those inputs more easily
accessible to the people so that more of them can be acquired with given
resources. When public policy takes this latter, more direct approach we may
describe it as social security through public provision of basic needs. The
attribute of directness, however, does not necessarily confer upon it the
attribute of superiority. But the empirical evidence in South Asia does make a
strong case for emphasizing the direct approach. The experience of Sri Lanka
and the Indian state of Kerala has already attracted widespread attention in this
regard. Before looking at their record of public provision, we may take a
glimpse of their achievement from the comparative picture laid out in Table
7.1.

By all the indicators of quality of life presented in Table 7.1, Sri Lanka and
Kerala are clearly ahead of the rest of South Asia. Their lead can be appreciated
even better by noting how long ago they had achieved the levels that Bangladesh
and India (as a whole) are enjoying only now. The levels of infant mortality, the
death rate, and life expectancy obtaining in India today were reached by Sri
Lanka in the late 1940s and the corresponding level of literacy was achieved as
early as the second decade of this century (Rasaputra 1986: app. tables 8, 9).
Similarly the current all-India levels of mortality and life expectancy were
already achieved in Kerala in the early 1960s, while literacy was achieved even

Table 7.1. Comparative quality of life in Bangladesh, all-India, Kerala, and Sri Lanka

Indicator	Bangladesh 1985	India 1984/85	Kerala 1980/81[b]	Sri Lanka[a]
Infant mortality rate (per 1,000)	112	106	37	30
Crude death rate (per 100)	12	12	7	6.5
Life expectancy	55	56.5	66[c]	69
Literacy %[d]	29	36	70	87
Per capita income (US $)	150	270	225	380

[a] Reference period varies as follows: 1981 for IMR, 1984 for CDR, 1980 for life expectancy, 1981 for literacy, and 1985 for per capita income.
[b] Except for per capita income for which the reference period is 1985, and see (d), below.
[c] Refers to rural Kerala for the period 1976–80.
[d] References period is 1981 in all cases. The reference population varies as follows: adults of 15 years of age and over in Bangladesh, all people over 10 years of age in Sri Lanka, and all people of 5 years and above in India and Kerala.

Sources: For Bangladesh data on IMR, death rate, life expectancy, and literacy are from World Bank (1988: statistical appendix, tables 1.3, 1.7). Indian data on IMR, death rate, and life expectancy are from GOI (1985: vol. 2, table, 2.11). Literacy rate is from Vaidyanathan (1987: table 1). IMR and literacy data for Kerala are from Vaidyanathan (1987: table 1); death rate and life expectancy are from Kumar (1987: tables 2, 4). Sri Lankan data on IMR, death rate, life expectancy, and literacy are from Rasaputra (1986: app. tables 8, 9). Data on per capita income of India, Bangladesh, and Sri Lanka are from Bhatia (1988: table 2). The estimate for Kerala was derived from the figure for India by applying the ratio between the per capita State domestic product of Kerala and the per capita NNP of India for 1984/5 as given in Agarwal *et al.* (1987: 39).

earlier.[41] Differences in the levels of per capita income cannot explain all this. It is true that Sri Lanka enjoys a higher per capita income than the rest of the region, but not high enough to explain the difference in quality of life.[42] The dissonance between per capita income and quality of life is manifest even more starkly in the case of Kerala.

As for other possible explanations, our preceding discussion shows that neither land reforms nor the employment-generating programmes could possibly hold the clue. In Sri Lanka, as we have seen, land reforms have had a negligible impact on the poor, and programmes for the generation of employment were not even tried there on the same scale as has been attempted elsewhere in the

[41] The information on literacy, death rate, and life expectancy is from Kumar (1987: tables 1.2 and 4), and on infant mortality from Jose (1984: 124).
[42] Per capita income would have to be as high as in the developed countries to achieve the Sri Lankan level of quality of life on the strength of income alone (Isenman 1980; Sen 1981).

region. Kerala has of course experienced a more effective land reform, but the resulting distribution of land is not any more equitable than that of India as a whole. In fact, in absolute terms the rural poor of Kerala control a much smaller size of land per capita because of the extreme density of population.[43] Nor is there any evidence that Kerala did spectacularly better in respect of the employment-generating programmes; in any case these are of fairly recent origin while Kerala's lead dates back long into the past.

It is in respect of public provision of basic needs that Sri Lanka and Kerala stand out with striking distinction. Both tried to ensure for every citizen a guaranteed access to three basic amenities—food, health care, and education. It will be instructive to see how their approach differed in this area from the rest of the region.

The history of public distribution of food-grain in South Asia dates back to the crisis years of the Second World War. The elaborate network of rationing set up during the war was retained afterwards, but since then it has evolved differently in the three countries. In Sri Lanka it was further consolidated and extended so as to cover the entire population; in Bangladesh too it was steadily consolidated but its principal focus remained on the urban population; in India it alternated between periods of consolidation and abandonment (or weakening), but focusing always on the urban sector whenever it was in force (except in Kerala, as we shall see).

The rural segment of the rationing system in Bangladesh has all along been a residual claimant on available food-grain. The priority claim was vested in the urban dwellers, especially those engaged in the formal sector. Even so, rural rationing accounted for about 55 per cent of total distribution in the 1960s. Since then its share has progressively come down, standing at less than 20 per cent in the 1980s (MOF 1986). As a result, the system is now capable of catering to only a small fraction of eligible rural households; and even those receive only a meagre ration. To illustrate, a sample survey conducted in the mid-1980s found that the contribution of subsidized ration amounted to only 2 per cent of total income for an average recipient household (MOF 1986).

The official justification for the scaling down of rural rationing has rested partly on the ground that one other component of the distribution system, namely Food for Work, has been making an increasing contribution to food-grain availability in the rural areas. There are at least two problems with this justification. First, even after allowing for the food-grain distributed under Food for Work, only about 6 to 8 per cent of the rural population was estimated to have been covered by public distribution in the second half of the 1970s (MOF 1986: table 7.3). Secondly, an argument based on total availability

---

[43] This is partly offset by the fact that per acre productivity (value) of land in Kerala is also one of the highest in India. None the less, rural poverty is one of the most acute here. See Vaidyanathan (1987) for more on these regional comparisons.

cannot be enough to justify the withdrawal of guaranteed food security for the vulnerable population. While it is true, as we have seen, that FFW not only increases availability but also distributes the benefit mostly to the landless and land-poor population, it cannot ensure security for such households as are handicapped by the absence of required labour power. Moreover, the nature of FFW activities is such that they can be undertaken primarily in the dry season, leaving out a protracted slack period in agriculture during the rainy season. The substitution of rural rationing by FFW cannot adequately take care of the problem of food security in the latter period.

Even in the favoured urban sector, the scope of security given to the neediest people has shrunk in recent years. Since the early 1970s, new ration cards have not been issued in the urban areas except under special circumstances. This has left out of the security net the vast number of rural immigrants who flocked into the urban areas, particularly the capital city, in the immediate post-1971 period. As a result, the proportion of urban residents covered by subsidized rationing has come down drastically from near 100 per cent to just around 50 per cent in the 1980s (MOF 1986: table 7.3). That the left-out segment consists primarily of the poorer group is indicated by a recent finding that the average household income of urban ration-receivers is higher than the average income of all urban households (MOF 1986).

All this has happened as a result of a basic shift that has occurred in the whole underlying philosophy of the public distribution system. Instead of offering targeted security to individual households, the aim now is to ensure a generalized security in times of crisis by stabilizing prices through open market interventions. In this aim some notable success has indeed been achieved. First in 1979 and again in 1984, the capability of the public distribution system to intervene vigorously in the open market helped contain speculative price hikes of the kind that wreaked havoc in the famine of 1974, despite the fact that the potential scarcity was greater in the later two years.[44] This story of success however needs to be qualified in two important respects. First, the country has not yet acquired the ability permanently to sustain a level of buffer stock that would guarantee similar success in the future. In both 1979 and 1984 the crisis was averted by taking recourse to huge imports—financed in one instance by unusual generosity on the part of the international aid community, and by the bounty of an unexpected trade surplus in another (Osmani, 1990). Secondly, even if the task of crisis management is adequately performed, there remains the question of that huge number of vulnerable households who do not have the security of a minimum consumption of food in normal times. The public distribution system of Bangladesh was never adequate to face up to this task; today it is utterly irrelevant for this purpose.

---

[44] This issue has been discussed in some detail in Osmani (1990).

A shift in policy similar to that of Bangladesh is also evident in India, especially since the dawn of the so-called Green Revolution era (around 1967/8). In the earlier phase, the aim of public food distribution, as in Bangladesh, was to offer targeted security to the urban population. Its potential role as a mechanism for price stabilization, and thus as a purveyor of generalized security, first received official recognition during the drought years of 1965/6 and 1966/7. Since then '. . . its role has undergone a basic change: from an agency for distributing rations to the target groups under the scheme of statutory and non-statutory rationing, it has now become an instrument of agricultural price support and price stabilization policies of the Government' (Bhatia 1983: 69). In contrast to Bangladesh, however, India has built up a huge buffer stock from its own production, which gives her a more secure basis for managing crisis. This ability was tested most severely in 1979/80 when the production of food-grains fell by 18 per cent from the previous year's level, and in the ensuing three years when production stagnated at the level of the mid-1970s. That this protracted crisis was averted without a serious price hike is largely attributable to the existence of the buffer stock.[45]

While recognizing this success in assuring some degree of generalized security in times of crisis, one must also point out that, as in Bangladesh, the public distribution system in India is incapable of offering targeted security to those who need such security even in normal times. In the case of India, moreover, this failure assumes an added irony. The buffer stock has arisen in the first place because the development strategy pursued in India has failed to engender enough effective demand among the majority of its people while production was being pushed up by the Green Revolution, and the government was obliged to take up the slack in fulfilling its commitment to agricultural price support.[46] It would thus appear that India has acquired the ability to offer generalized security in times of crisis by neglecting the lack of security that remains endemic for a large section of the people.

A striking contrast is presented by the Indian state of Kerala. Its distribution system covers almost the entire population (97 per cent) at a level of per capita off-take that is by far the highest among all the Indian states. In 1977, for example, the per capita off-take in Kerala (61 kg per annum) was more than double that of all the states except two (Jammu and Kashmir with 47 kg and West Bengal with 40 kg). Furthermore, the rural-to-urban ratio of per capita off-take was almost 100 per cent in Kerala, whereas in other states the ratio varied between 2 and 22 per cent. As a result, the rural per capita off-take

---

[45] The key role was played not by the distribution of food as such but by the very existence of the stock which dissuaded speculative hoarding. For more on this, see Bhatia (1983). See also Drèze and Sen (1989: chap. 8), on the primacy of price stabilization over income generation through the Indian Public Foodgrain Distribution System.

[46] Many analysts of the Indian economy have made this point. See Dandekar (1986) for a forceful recent exposition of the argument.

in Kerala stood at 61 kg as against a range of 0.8 to 15.5 kg in other states.[47]

The sheer scale and spread of public distribution in Kerala means that the rationed food-grains figure prominently in household consumption. A survey conducted in two villages in 1977 showed that the rice purchased from ration shops accounted for two-thirds of all the rice consumed by the poorest 40 per cent of households (George 1979: 32).

An even more ambitious programme of subsidized food distribution was in force in Sri Lanka until recently. The coverage was, as in Kerala, near universal. Food-grain was distributed through the rationing system—in varying combinations of totally free or heavily subsidized amounts at different times. The principle of universal coverage was abandoned in 1978 when the richer 50 per cent of the population became ineligible for subsidized rationing. In 1979, the system of rationing was itself abolished and replaced by a food stamp scheme, targeted once again at the bottom half of the population. These stamps were redeemable in exchange for food-grain (and a few other essential commodities) sold in designated outlets at unsubsidized prices. Initially, the change-over from rationing to food stamp did not make much difference to the bottom quintile of the population in terms of the subsidy received.[48] But since the value of stamps was kept fixed in nominal terms, their real value became quickly eroded in the face of rapid inflation; by 1981/2, the real value had nearly halved (Edirisinghe 1987: 18).

During the period of subsidized rationing the amount of rationed food-grains figured prominently, as in Kerala, in the total consumption of Sri Lankan households. In 1969/70, for example, it was estimated from a nation-wide survey of household expenditure that rationed rice amounted to 18 per cent of the calories consumed by all households, and to 21 per cent in the case of the bottom quintile (Gavan and Chandrasekera 1979). A similar survey in 1978/9 showed that the value of the ration subsidy was the equivalent of 18 per cent of total expenditure of all households, and 25 per cent of total expenditure of the bottom quintile (Edirisinghe 1987).

An example of how well the rationing system was able to protect the poor is provided by the experience of 1973/4 when rice distribution through rationing was reduced by 20 per cent. Production was above average and total calorie availability was only slightly below the trend level, and yet in 1974 the mortality rate increased from 7.7 to 8.9 (Isenman 1980). It is also significant that the incidence of increased mortality was most pronounced among the estate workers who depended on the rationing system much more heavily than

[47] De Janvry and Subbarao (1986: table 1.5). It is worth noting in this context that there is some difficulty in comparing rural Kerala with the rural sector of the other states as the rural–urban distinction is not as clear-cut in Kerala as in the rest of India.
[48] The value of food stamps at the time of inception was only 3 per cent less than the ration subsidy received by the bottom quintile, though for all the recipients taken together it was 17 per cent less; Edirisinghe (1987: table 5).

the rest of the population. It will perhaps be wrong to attribute the entire increase in mortality to reduced rationing, because during the same period there was also a sharp increase in the price of wheat, which the estate workers tend to consume in large amounts (Gavan and Chandrasekera 1979). Nevertheless the fact that increased mortality was also found among the rest of the population, who consume very little wheat, does point to the presence of a rationing effect as well. Further evidence can be gleaned from the changes in nutritional status that have reportedly occurred after the subsidy was halved within three years of the introduction of food stamps in 1979. The incidence of wasting among children in the age-group of 6 to 60 months has gone up from 8.4 per cent in 1975/6 to 13.8 per cent in 1980–2 (Sahn 1987: 814).

Despite such evidence, there must be some doubt about how far the spectacular indices of mortality and life expectancy achieved by Kerala and Sri Lanka are due to the security provided by subsidized food-grain. This is best appreciated by noting the extent of the contribution made by the subsidy in the total consumption of calories. We have seen earlier that the value of subsidy as a proportion of total income is remarkably high in both Kerala and Sri Lanka. But the value of the subsidy as such, or the calorie-equivalent of that subsidy, does not indicate the amount of calories contributed by the subsidy. The contribution would depend on the marginal propensity to consume calories out of the additional income coming by way of subsidy, plus any possible substitution effect. It would appear from the (admittedly crude) estimates made by George (1979: 37) that the net contribution of the subsidy was about 18 per cent of rice consumption among the bottom 40 per cent of the households. Since rice accounts for about 40 per cent of calories in an average Keralite diet, the net contribution of subsidy amounts to a maximum of 7 to 8 per cent of total calories.[49] A similar figure—6 per cent for the bottom quintile of households—seems to emerge from the estimates for Sri Lanka (1969/70) made by Gavan and Chandrasekera (1979: 41).[50]

Even considering the margin of error that is likely to be associated with these estimates, it will perhaps be fair to conclude that the net contribution of the subsidy to the total intake of calories was nothing spectacular. It is difficult to see how a contribution of this magnitude could explain the phenomenal progress made with respect to mortality and life expectancy. This impression is further reinforced by looking at the actual levels of calorie intake enjoyed by the poorer groups. The overall per capita intake in Sri Lanka, estimated at 2,010 Kcal per day in 1978/9, is somewhat lower than in India; but even more

---

[49] This is probably an overestimate because the share of rice is lower and the share of tapioca higher in the diet of the poorer groups compared to an average Keralite diet.

[50] It should be noted though that 1969/70 was a year of exceptionally good harvest which enabled even the poorer groups to consumer more calories compared to a normal year. Consequently, the percentage contribution of subsidy to total calorie intake in a normal year would be higher than is suggested by this figure.

importantly, the average intake for the bottom half of the population is only 1,607 Kcal (Anand and Harris 1987: 6a), a figure that is way below any reasonable standard of requirement. In Kerala, the situation is even more precarious according to the official estimates of the National Sample Survey; even the average intake of the total population appears to be some 20 per cent below the national average. There are disputations about these official figures which, according to some studies, do not take sufficient note of the varieties of non-cereal sources from which the Keralites get their calories.[51] But even the findings of smaller surveys which have tried to capture the variety in diet do not alter the basic conclusion that the poor in Kerala do not consume more calories than the poor in the rest of India. One such study, looking at some of the South Indian States, found that a poor Keralite adult consumes less calories (1,751) than his or her counterpart in the neighbouring states of Andhra Pradesh (1,847), Karnataka (1,902), and Tamil Nadu (2,019).[52]

The preceding discussion is not meant to deny the importance of public food-grain distribution in Kerala and Sri Lanka but to put its role in perspective. As the Sri Lankan experience in 1973/4 and again in 1980–2 shows, it has clearly made a difference to the nutritional achievement of the population. However, the extraordinary improvement made in mortality and life expectancy must be attributed largely to other factors.

The most obvious candidate in this respect is the singular effort made by both Kerala and Sri Lanka in the field of public provision of health care and education. Public action in these fields has a long history in both these regions, dating back far into the colonial era.[53] In interpreting this history, however, there has sometimes been a tendency to emphasize certain fortuitous circumstances and a concurrent tendency to de-emphasize the role of public provisioning as such. For example, in explaining the reduction in mortality in Sri Lanka, Bhalla (1988b) has made much of the malaria eradication programme that was undertaken in 1946 with the help of the newly available DDT. It is true that this programme had a most dramatic result—the crude death rate fell from 20 to 14 and infant mortality fell from 141 to 101 in a single year—a phenomenon rightly described by the World Health Organization as an unparalleled achievement in world demography (Gunatilleke 1984). Nevertheless, it would be wrong to ascribe Sri Lankan health achievement primarily to this programme. The most careful assessment of the programme made to date shows that it can explain only about 20 to 25 per cent of the improvement in the death rate

[51] For example, the National Sample Surveys suggest that per capita calorie intake in Kerala was as low as 1,620 Kcal in 1961/2 and 1,618 in 1971/2 (as against the all-India average of 2,445 and 2,263 respectively). But an alternative estimate from the food balance sheets give an average figure of 2,339 Kcal in Kerala for the period between 1961/2 and 1970/1 (CDS 1975).

[52] Quoted from Gwatkin (1979), p. 254. See also Mencher (1980) and Kumar (1987) for further evidence from micro-data.

[53] For detailed accounts of this history, see Alailima (1985) for Sri Lanka and CDS (1975) for Kerala.

between 1936–45 and 1956–60 (Gray 1974). In fact throughout the period from 1920 up to the present, one can notice a secular improvement in all the health indicators, fortified of course by the structural break of 1946. Furthermore, the tempo of improvement has been more or less maintained in the post-independence (which is also the post-malaria) period. For instance, infant mortality dropped at the annual compound rate of 2.7 per cent between 1920 and 1950, and at the rate of 2.8 per cent between 1950 and 1982. Similarly, the rates of improvement in life expectancy (measured as the reduction in shortfall from a ceiling of 80 years) for the corresponding periods were 2.6 per cent and 2.3 per cent respectively (see Rasaputra 1986: app. table 9).

The case of Kerala is even more clear-cut. It did undertake a malaria eradication programme in the 1950s, but that was part of an all-India campaign and cannot as such explain the difference in the health performance between Kerala and the rest of India. In fact both Sri Lanka and Kerala have achieved what they have, not by a one-off campaign to conquer malaria, but by sustained efforts to provide either free or heavily subsidized health services to their entire populations. Some basic statistics would be illuminating. In the mid-1980s, Sri Lanka had one hospital bed for every 350 persons as against a ratio of one to 1,200 persons in India. More importantly, Sri Lanka has always paid special attention to maternal health care, which has contributed significantly to the reduction of infant mortality. In the mid-1970s, for instance, Sri Lanka had one maternity centre for every 400 expectant mothers as against one for every 3,200 in India; as a result, nearly 98 per cent of Sri Lanka mothers received pre-natal care as against 10 to 15 per cent in India (Gwatkin 1979). Similarly, a comparison with the all-India performance shows Kerala in a distinctly impressive light. For example, in 1977, there were 1,975 hospital beds per million of population in Kerala as against 791 in India as a whole (Jose 1984). More importantly, the health facilities were spread widely across the State instead of being concentrated in the urban areas, as is usually the case in the rest of India as well as other developing countries. As a result, some 80 per cent of Kerala's population are treated in hospitals every year compared with 40 to 50 per cent in the other States of India (CDS 1975).

It is important to recognize, however, that it is not merely the physical volume of facilities that has made the difference. In fact there are States in India which out-perform Kerala in terms of indices such as per capita expenditure on health, the number of persons per hospital bed, and even rural medical facilities per person, and yet have inferior indices of health compared to Kerala.[54] What has made the difference is the efficiency with which medical facilities have been used. There are two aspects to this efficiency. First, in both Kerala and Sri Lanka, at least as much attention has been paid to preventive health care as to curative service, and this proved to be a highly cost-effective

---

[54] These regional contrasts are brought out sharply by Panikar (1979) and Nag (1985).

method of reducing mortality. Secondly, a highly health-conscious population made sure that the existing facilities were effectively utilized.[55]

The degree of awareness about health was itself the result of a long history of public provision of education. That the spread of education, apart from being a good thing in itself, was also instrumental in bringing about an efficient health care system in both Sri Lanka and Kerala has been noted by many commentators. The Sri Lankan scholars, for example, never tire of pointing out how politicians had to move towards strengthening the welfarist State in response to the felt need of an educated electorate after the Donoughmore Constitution had granted universal adult franchise in 1931.[56] In Kerala, an added force came from the high degree of politicization created among the masses by the active presence of communist parties at the grass-roots level. Mencher (1980), for example, has noted from her field experience how the educated and politicized people of rural Kerala make sure that the existing health centres are fully geared to their service, while similar health centres in the neighbouring State of Tamil Nadu remain inactive or underutilized.[57]

6. CONCLUSION

The problem of poverty in South Asia is both massive and acute. The task of providing the security of a minimal standard of living cannot, therefore, be an easy one. This sobering thought recurs time and again in our review of the programmes and policies that have been pursued in this part of the world. The only encouraging note comes from the experience of some parts of the region where a good deal more has been achieved compared with the rest. Correspondingly, some of the policies seem to hold a much greater promise than others. It was indeed the major aim of this chapter to evaluate the relative possibilities and limitations of alternative courses of action so as to identify the more promising ones.

This task cannot by any means be said to have been completed. For each of the policies we have considered, there is need for a much more thorough probing of its political, financial, and organizational implications. Besides, there are a good number of alternatives which we have not considered at all. Nevertheless, it may be useful to lay out some of the tentative conclusions that emerge from this preliminary analysis.

As expected, the most difficult policies to implement are those that try to provide security through control over land. This could hardly be otherwise in a

---

[55] See Panikar (1979) for an elaboration of these arguments.

[56] An example is Wickremeratne (1977).

[57] See also Panikar (1979) on the role of education in Kerala. For a wide-ranging analysis of the role of education, health care, and food distribution in enhancing the quality of life in Kerala, Sri Lanka, and several other regions of the world, see Caldwell (1986).

political system which is based on the primacy of private ownership rights. But even where a more favourable political condition prevails, as in West Bengal, nothing substantial has been achieved. The share-croppers may have gained a more assured security of tenure, but in the majority of cases their rental share has not improved. Consequently, the security of a better standard of living still remains an unattained goal. We have in fact argued that tenancy reform is not likely to achieve this goal until there is prior provision of social security through other public actions.

Among these other actions, the most popular in current official thinking is the set of programmes whose aim is to create employment—either self-employment in non-crop activities or wage employment in public works. There is no doubt that these programmes have an immediate appeal. Those who receive credit and/or subsidy for self-employed activities, or get wage employment in the slack season certainly receive a temporary benefit. What is crucially missing from these programmes, however, is the ability to provide a basis for a sustained increase in the standard of living. This deficiency is in principle remediable, but this will require a fundamental change in the orientation of these programmes. Instead of being seen purely as a support programme for the poor, the employment-generating schemes must be conceived as an integral part of the development process itself. In order that employment can generate a sustained flow of a higher level of income, it is first necessary to create viable employment opportunities. This in turn requires integrated planning of available resources—both human and material. Obviously, the distinction between social-security programmes and development planning tends to get blurred in the process. But this is inevitable in a situation where security is sought to be provided through income generation, encompassing the majority of the population rather than a few.

The alternative option of providing security through public provision of basic needs has enjoyed much less popularity at the official level. The exceptions are Sri Lanka and the Indian State of Kerala; and both have been outstandingly successful in improving the quality of lives of their people. Their poverty has not been conquered. In fact, in both Sri Lanka and Kerala people are desperately poor. But a long history of public provision of such basic needs as food, health, and education has given them the basic security of avoiding premature mortality due to disease and malnutrition. We have argued that much more significantly than the provision of food, it is the provision of basic health care and education that has played the crucial role. A similar course of action is also likely to prove the most promising way of providing social security to the rest of the region.

But can such a programme be financed by the poor countries of this region without sacrificing long-term growth? This question assumes a particular significance in view of an ongoing debate on whether Sri Lanka has jeopardized her long-run prospects of growth by choosing to become excessively 'welfarist', that is, by ignoring her development needs in the pursuit of 'basic needs'. This is not the occasion to enter this lively debate;[58] we shall only make a couple of simple observations. First, as the experience of Kerala shows, the success of a health care programme may depend more on how efficiently the facilities are utilized than on the amount of money spent. Secondly, even granting that additional resources will have to be allocated to the welfare programmes, it is not clear why this should be seen as a dent in the resources for growth. 'Welfare' and 'development' (meaning growth) are not the only heads of expenditure in a typical government budget. It is significant that while spending heavily on welfare programmes, Sri Lanka kept its defence spending at a surprisingly low level of around 2 per cent of total government expenditure (in the 1970s), compared with India's 10 to 15 per cent. Obviously, 'growth' need not always be the opportunity cost of social-welfare programmes.

[58] See, among others, Sen (1981, 1988), Bhalla (1988a, b), Bhalla and Glewwe (1987), and Anand and Kanbur (1990).

References

Agarwal, A. N., Verma, H. O., and Gupta, R. C. (1987), *India: Economic Information Yearbook 1987–1988*, 2nd edn. New Delhi: National Publishing House.

Ahmad, Q. K., and Hossain, M. (1985), 'An Evaluation of Selected Policies and Programmes for the Alleviation of Rural Poverty in Bangladesh', in R. Islam (ed.), *Strategies for Alleviating Poverty in Rural Asia*. Dhaka: BIDS; and Bangkok: ILO-ARTEP.

Alailima, P. (1985), 'Evaluation of Government Policies and Expenditure on Social Welfare in Sri Lanka During the 20th Century', mimeo, Ministry of Finance and Planning, Colombo.

Anand, S., and Harris, C. (1987), 'Changes in Nutrition in Sri Lanka, 1978/79–1981/82', mimeo, World Institute for Development Economics Research, Helsinki.

—— and Kanbur, R. (1990), 'Public Policy and Basic Needs Provision: Intervention and Achievement in Sri Lanka', mimeo, to be published in J. P. Drèze, and A. K. Sen (eds.), *The Political Economy of Hunger*. Oxford University Press.

Asaduzzaman, M., and Huddleston, B. (1983), 'An Evaluation of Management of Food for Work Programme', *Bangladesh Development Studies*, 11/1 and 2.

Bagchee, S. (1984), 'Employment Guarantee Scheme in Maharashtra', *Economic and Political Weekly*, 19/37.

—— (1987), 'Poverty Alleviation Programmes in the Seventh Plan: An Evaluation', *Economic and Political Weekly*, 22/4.

Bandyopadhyay, D. (1985), 'An Evaluation of Policies and Programmes for the Alleviation of Rural Poverty in India', in R. Islam (ed.), *Strategies for Alleviating Poverty in Rural Asia*. Dhaka: BIDS; Bangkok: ILO-ARTEP.

—— (1986), 'Land Reforms in India: An Analysis', *Economic and Political Weekly*, Review of Agriculture, 21/25–6.

—— (1988), 'Direct Intervention Programmes for Poverty Alleviation: An Appraisal', *Economic and Political Weekly*, Review of Agriculture, 23/26.

Bandyopadhyaya, N. *et al.* (1985), *Evaluation of Land Reform Measures in West Bengal, A Report*. Bangkok: ILO-ARTEP.

Basu, K. (1981), 'Food for Work Programmes: Beyond Roads that Get Washed Away', *Economic and Political Weekly*, 16/1.

BBS (1985), *Statistical Yearbook of Bangladesh 1984/85*. Dhaka: Bangladesh Bureau of Statistics.

Bhalla, S. S. (1988a), 'Is Sri Lanka an Exception? A Comparative Study of Living Standards', in T. N. Srinivasan and P. K. Bardhan (eds.), *Rural Poverty in South Asia*. New York: Columbia University Press.

—— (1988b), 'Sri Lanka's Achievements: Fact and Fancy', in T. N. Srinivasan and P. K. Bardhan (eds.), *Rural Poverty in South Asia*. New York: Columbia University Press.

—— and Glewwe, P. (1987), 'Growth and Equity in Developing Countries: A Re-interpretation of Sri Lankan Experience', *World Bank Economic Review*, 1.

Bhatia, B. M. (1983), *A Study In India's Food Policy*. Kuala Lumpur: Asian and Pacific Development Centre.

Bhatia, V. G. (1988), 'Asian and Pacific Developing Economies: Performance and Issues', *Asian Development Review*, 6.

BIDS-IFPRI (1983), *Characteristics and Short-run Effects of the WFP-aided Food for Work Programme in Bangladesh*. Dhaka: Bangladesh Institute of Development Studies; Washington DC: International Food Policy Research Institute.

—— (1985), *Development Impact of the Food-for-Work Program in Bangladesh, Final Report, Summary*. Dhaka: Bangladesh Institute of Development Studies; Washington DC: International Food Policy Research Institute.

Bose, B. (1981), 'Agrarian Programme of Left Front Government in West Bengal', *Economic and Political Weekly*, 16/50.

Bose, S. (1986), *Agrarian Bengal: Economy, Social Structure and Politics 1919–1947*. Cambridge: Cambridge University Press.

Caldwell, J. C. (1986), 'Routes to Low Mortality in Poor Countries', *Population and Development Review*, 12.

CDS (Centre for Development Studies) (1975), *Poverty, Unemployment and Development Policy: A Case Study of Selected Issues with Special Reference to Kerala*. New York: United Nations.

Dandekar, K. and Sathe, M. (1980), 'Employment Guarantee Scheme and Food for Work Programme', *Economic and Political Weekly*, 15/15.

Dandekar, V. M. (1986), 'Agriculture, Employment and Poverty', *Economic and Political Weekly*, 21/38–9.

Dantawala, M. L. (1985), ' "Garibi Hatao": Strategy Options', *Economic and Political Weekly*, 20/11.

Dasgupta, B. (1984), 'Sharecropping in West Bengal: From Independence to Operation Barga', *Economic and Political Weekly*, Review of Agriculture, 19/26.

de Janvry, A., and Subbarao, K. (1986), *Agricultural Price Policy and Income Distribution in India*. New Delhi: Oxford University Press.

Drèze, J. P. (1988), 'Social Insecurity in India', paper presented at the STICERD/WIDER workshop on Social Security in Developing Countries held at the London School of Economics, July 1988.

—— and Sen, A. K. (1989), *Hunger and Public Action*. Oxford: Clarendon Press.

Edirisinghe, N. (1987), 'The Food Stamp Scheme in Sri Lanka: Costs, Benefits and Options for Modifications', Research Report 58, International Food Policy Research Institute, Washington, DC.

Gavan, J. D., and Chandrasekera, I. S. (1979), 'The Impact of Public Foodgrain Distribution on Food Consumption and Welfare in Sri Lanka', Research Report 13, International Food Policy Research Institute, Washington, DC.

George, P. S. (1979), 'Public Distribution of Foodgrain in Kerala: Income Distribution Implications and Effectiveness', Research Report 7, International Food Policy Research Institute, Washington, DC.

GOI (Government of India) (1959), 'Report of the Committee on Tenancy Reform', in *Reports of the Committees of the Panel on Land Reforms*. New Delhi: Planning Commission, Government of India.

—— (1981), *National Committee on the Development of Backward Areas: Report on General Issues*. New Delhi: Planning Commission, Government of India.

—— (1984), 'Against Undeserved Want: Report of the Working Group on Social

Security', mimeo, Economic Administration Reforms Commission, Government of India, New Delhi.

—— (1985), *The Seventh Five Year Plan 1985–1990*. New Delhi: Planning Commission, Government of India.

Gray, R. H. (1974), 'The Decline of Mortality in Ceylon and the Demographic Effects of Malaria Control', *Population Studies*, 28.

Guhan, S. (1988). 'Social Security in India: Looking One Step Ahead', *Bulletin of the Madras Development Seminar Series*, 18.

Gunatilleke, G. (ed.), (1984), 'Intersectoral Linkages and Health Development: Case Studies in India (Kerala State), Jamaica, Norway, Sri Lanka and Thailand', WHO Offset Publication No. 83, World Health Organization, Geneva.

Gwatkin, D. R. (1979), 'Food Policy, Nutrition Planning and Survival: The Cases of Kerala and Sri Lanka', *Food Policy*, 4.

Hameed, N. D. A., et al. (1977), *Rice Revolution in Sri Lanka*. Geneva: United Nations Research Institute for Social Development.

Herring, R. J. (1981), 'Embedded Production Relations and Rationality of Tenant Quiescence in Tenure Reform', *Journal of Peasant Studies*, 8.

—— and Edwards, R. M. (1983), 'Guaranteeing Employment to the Rural Poor: Social Functions and Class Interests in the Employment Guarantee Scheme in Western India', *World Development*, 11.

Hossain, M. (1984a), 'Productivity and Profitability in Bangladesh Rural Industries', *Bangladesh Development Studies*, 12.

—— (1984b), *Credit for the Rural Poor: The Grameen Bank of Bangladesh*, Research Monograph No. 4, Bangladesh Institute of Development Studies, Dhaka.

—— (1986), 'Employment Generation Through Cottage Industries: Potentials and Constraints', in R. Islam and M. Muqtada (eds.), *Bangladesh: Selected Issues in Employment and Development*. New Delhi: ILO-ARTEP.

—— (1988), 'Credit for Alleviation of Rural Poverty: The Grameen Bank in Bangladesh', Research Report 65, International Food Policy Research Institute, Washington, DC.

IFMR (1984), 'An Economic Assessment of Poverty Eradication and Rural Employment Programmes and Their Prospects', mimeo, Institute for Financial Management and Research, Madras.

ILO (1984), 'Summary Results of the Socio-economic Survey on Sample Projects of the National Employment Programme', mimeo, Employment and Development Department, International Labour Organization, Geneva.

Isenman, P. (1980), 'Basic Needs: The Case of Sri Lanka', *World Development*, 8.

Islam, R. (1986), 'Rural Unemployment and Underemployment: A Review', in R. Islam and M. Muqtada (eds.), *Bangladesh: Selected Issues in Employment and Development*. New Delhi: ILO-ARTEP.

—— (1987), 'Rural Industrialisation and Employment in Asia: Issues and Evidence', in R. Islam (ed.), *Rural Industrialisation and Employment in Asia*. New Delhi: ILO-ARTEP.

Jose, A. V. (1984), 'Poverty and Inequality: The Case of Kerala', in A. R. Khan and E. Lee (eds.), *Poverty in Rural Asia*. Bangkok: ILO-ARTEP.

Joshi, P. C. (1975), *Land Reforms in India: Trends and Perspectives*. Bombay: Allied Publishers.

Khasnabis, R. (1981), 'Operation Barga: Limits to Social Democratic Reformism', *Economic and Political Weekly*, Review of Agriculture, 16/25–6.

Kohli, A. (1987), *The State and Poverty in India*. Cambridge: Cambridge University Press.

Kumar, G. (1987), 'Well-being, Deprivations and Basic Needs: A Perspective on the Development Experience in Kerala', mimeo, Balliol College, Oxford.

Kurian, N. J. (1987), 'IRDP: How Relevant Is It?', *Economic and Political Weekly*, 22/52.

Mencher, J. P. (1980), 'Lessons and Non-Lessons of Kerala: Agricultural Labourers and Poverty', *Economic and Political Weekly*, Special Number, 15/41–3.

MHJ (1980), 'Who Pays For and Who Gains From EGS?', *Economic and Political Weekly*, 17/31.

MOF (1986), 'The Existing System of Public Foodgrain Distribution in Bangladesh and Proposal for Restructuring', Draft Report, preparerd by Beacon Consultants for the Ministry of Food, Government of Bangladesh, Dhaka.

Moore, M. (1985), *The State and Peasant Politics in Sri Lanka*. Cambridge: Cambridge University Press.

—— and Perera, U. L. J. (1978), 'Land Policy and Village Expansion in Sri Lanka', *Marga*, 5.

Muqtada, M., and Alam, M. M. (1983), *Hired Labour and Rural Labour Market in Bangladesh*. Bangkok: ILO-ARTEP.

NABARD (1984), 'Study of Implementation of Integrated Rural Development Programme', mimeo, National Bank for Agricultural and Rural Development, Bombay.

Nag, M. (1985), 'The Impact of Social and Economic Development on Mortality: Comparative Study of Kerala and West Bengal', in S. B. Halstead, J. A. Walsh, and K. S. Warren (eds.), *Good Health at Low Cost*. New York: Rockefeller Foundation.

Osmani, S. R. (1990), 'The Food Problems of Bangladesh', to be published in J. P. Drèze and A. K. Sen (eds.), *The Political Economy of Hunger*. Oxford: Oxford University Press.

—— and Chowdhury, O. H. (1983), 'Short Run Impacts of Food for Work Programme in Bangladesh', *Bangladesh Development Studies*, 11.

Panikar, P. G. K. (1979), 'Resources Not the Constraint on Health Improvement: A Case Study of Kerala', *Economic and Political Weekly*, 14/44.

Peiris, G. H. (1976), 'Share Tenancy and Tenurial Reform in Sri Lanka', *Ceylon Journal of Historical and Social Studies*, NS 6/1.

—— (1978), 'Land Reform and Agrarian Change in Sri Lanka', *Modern Asian Studies*, 12.

PEO (1980a), 'A Quick Evaluation Study of the Food for Work Programme: An Interim Report', Programme Evaluation Organization, Planning Commission, Government of India, New Delhi.

—— (1980b), 'Joint Evaluation Report on Employment Guarantee Scheme of Maharashtra', Programme Evaluation Organization, Planning Commission, Government of India, New Delhi.

—— (1985), 'Evaluation Report on Integrated Development Programme', Programme Evaluation Organization, Planning Commission, Government of India, New Delhi.

Rahman, A., and Haque, T. (1988), 'Poverty and Inequality in Bangladesh in the

Eighties: An Analysis of Some Recent Evidence', mimeo, Bangladesh Institute of Development Studies, Dhaka.

Raj, K. N., and Tharakan, M. (1981), 'Agrarian Reform in Kerala and Its Impact on the Rural Economy: A Preliminary Assessment', Working Paper WEP 10–6/WP49, Rural Employment Policy Research Branch, World Employment Programme, International Labour Organization, Geneva.

Rao, C. H. H., and Rangaswamy, P. (1988), 'Efficiency of Investments in IRDP: A Study of Uttar Pradesh', *Economic and Political Weekly*, Review of Agriculture, 23/26.

Rao, V. M., and Erappa, S. (1987), 'IRDP and Rural Diversification: A Study in Karnataka', *Economic and Political Weekly*, 22/52.

Rasaputra, W. (1986), 'Public Policy: An Assessment of the Sri Lankan Experience', mimeo, World Institute for Development Economics Research, Helsinki.

Rath, N. (1985), ' "Garibi Hatao": Can IRDP Do It?', *Economic and Political Weekly*, 20/6.

Rudra, À. (1981), 'One Step Forward, Two Steps Backward', *Economic and Political Weekly*, Review of Agriculture, 16/25–6.

Sahn, D. (1987), 'Changes in Living Standards of the Poor in Sri Lanka During a Period of Macroeconomic Restructuring', *World Development*, 15.

Samaraweera, V. (1981), 'Land, Labour, Capital and Sectional Interests in the National Politics of Sri Lanka', *Modern Asian Studies*, 15.

Sanderatne, N. (1972), 'Tenancy in Ceylon's Paddy Lands: The 1958 Reforms', *South Asian Review*, 15.

Sen, A. K. (1981), 'Public Action and the Quality of Life in Developing Countries', *Oxford Bulletin of Economics and Statistics*, 13.

—— (1985), *The Standard of Living*. Cambridge: Cambridge University Press.

—— (1988), 'Sri Lanka's Achievements: How and When', in T. N. Srinivasan and P. K. Bardhan (eds.), *Rural Poverty in South Asia*. New York: Columbia University Press.

Sharma, R., and Gianchandani, D. (1988), 'IRDP and Rural Diversification', *Economic and Political Weekly*, 23/19.

Siddiqui, K. (1979), 'The Political Economy of Land Reform in Bangladesh', *Journal of Social Studies*, 6.

—— (1985), 'An Evaluation of Grameen Bank Operations', in S. Mukhopadhyay (ed.), *Case Studies on Poverty Programmes in Asia*. Kuala Lumpur: Asian and Pacific Development Centre.

Singh, S. and De, N. (n.d.), 'A Study of Rural Landless Employment Programme in Punjab', mimeo, Punjab State Institute of Public Administration, Chandigarh.

Subbarao, K. (1985), 'Regional Variation in Impact of Anti-Poverty Programmes: A Review of Evidence', *Economic and Political Weekly*, 20/43.

Sundaram, K. and Tendulkar, S. D. (1985), 'Anti-Poverty Programmes in India: An Appraisal', in S. Mukhopadhyay, (ed.), *The Poor in Asia: Productivity-Raising Programmes and Strategies*. Kuala Lumpur: Asian and Pacific Development Centre.

Swaminathan, M. (1988), 'Inequality and Economic Mobility: An Analysis of Panel Data from a South Indian Village', Oxford University D.Phil thesis.

Thimmaiah, G. (1988), 'Concurrent Evaluation of IRDP', *Economic and Political Weekly*, 23/7.

Tilve, S. and Pitre, V. (1980), 'Employment Guarantee Scheme and Food For Work: A Comment', *Economic and Political Weekly*, 15/47.

Vaidyanathan, A. (1987), 'Poverty and Economy: The Regional Dimension', paper presented at a conference on Poverty in India held at the University of Oxford.

Varghese, T. (1970), *Agrarian Change and Economic Consequences: Land Tenures in Kerala 1850–1960*. Bombay: Allied Publishers.

Weerawardena, I. K. (1975), 'Lessons of an Experiment: The Paddy Lands Act of 1958', Evaluation Studies No. 3, Department of Rural Institutions and Productivity Laws, Colombo.

Westergaard, K. (1986), 'People's Participation, Local Government and Rural Development: The Case of West Bengal, India', Research Report No. 8, Centre for Development Research, Copenhagen.

Wickremeratne, L. A. (1977), 'The Economy in 1948', in K. H. de Silva (ed.), *Sri Lanka: A Survey*. Honolulu: University Press of Hawaii.

Wickramasekara, P. (1985a), 'Strategies and Programmes for Raising the Productivity of the Rural Poor in Sri Lanka', in S. Mukhopadhyay (ed.), *The Poor in Asia: Productivity-Raising Programmes and Strategies*. Kuala Lumpur: Asian and Pacific Development Centre.

—— (1985b), 'The Role of Land Settlement Programmes in Raising the Productivity of the Poor: A Sri Lankan Case Study', in S. Mukhopadhyay (ed.), *Case Studies on Poverty Programmes in Asia*. Kuala Lumpur: Asian and Pacific Development Centre.

Wimaladharma, K. P. (1982), 'Land Settlement Experiences in Sri Lanka', mimeo. Colombo.

World Bank (1988), 'Bangladesh: Adjustment in the Eighties and Short-Term Prospects', Report No. 7105-BD, Washington, DC.

8

Social Security in Latin America and the Caribbean: A Comparative Assessment

Carmelo Mesa-Lago

1. INTRODUCTION

The term 'social security' is used in this chapter in its 'formal' sense, which, following the traditional ILO (International Labour Organization) concept, covers several programmes such as: social insurances (old-age, disability, and survivor pensions; non-occupational sickness and maternity care, and corresponding monetary benefits; occupational accident and disease care, and monetary benefits; unemployment compensation); family allowances; social or public assistance (such as pensions for low-income persons not eligible for social insurance benefits, food stamps, and so on); national health systems or public health programmes; provident funds. Even in this conventional sense, social security is much broader than social insurance since the latter is only a part of the former. In addition, there are differences between the two terms concerning historical inception, administration, population coverage, financing, and benefits.

Social insurance, introduced by Chancellor Bismarck of Germany in the 1880s, derives from the employment relationship and has the following features: (1) separate programmes for different social risks (especially occupational risks, pensions, and health care); (2) coverage of the employed, salaried labour-force, especially urban workers; (3) wage contributions made by the insured, the employer, and the State; (4) benefits which tend to be directly related to the contributions; and (5) full or partial capitalization methods of financing (thereafter we call this the 'Bismarckian model').

Social security, which began with Sir William Beveridge's report at the beginning of the 1940s, reflects a series of new principles that promote (1) the unification, under one single administrative or co-ordinating agency, of the diverse programmes of social insurance, along with social assistance, health care (integrating preventive and curative medicine), employment programmes, and family allowances (principle of unity); (2) the standardization of legal conditions for entitlement and the elimination of unjustifiable inequalities among the insured (principle of equality); (3) total coverage of the population, regardless of employment status (principle of universality) and for all social risks (principle of completeness); (4) financing by means of taxation, the provision of minimum but sufficient benefits—not related to contributions—

and the progressive redistribution of income (principle of solidarity); and (5) the use of the pure assessment financing method.

This chapter broadly covers all thirty-four countries of Latin America and the Caribbean (LAC). Traditionally, Latin America includes the twenty countries which reached independence from Spain and Portugal in the nineteenth century, plus Haiti. The non-Latin Caribbean embraces fourteen countries, which in the second half of the twentieth century became independent from Great Britain, France, and the Netherlands. More data are provided here on Latin America than on the Caribbean, although systematic information is also given on Bahamas, Barbados, and Jamaica. Technically speaking the majority of LAC countries either have compulsory social insurance programmes or are between the social-insurance stage and the more advanced stage of social security. Only a few countries have systems with characteristics more typical of social security than of social insurance. The transition between the two stages is often blocked by structural barriers which only a few countries have been able to overcome (see Section 4.4).

This chapter does not deal with programmes included under the broader definition of social security used elsewhere in this book, such as famine prevention, agrarian reform, education, employment promotion, and so on. A major reason for this exclusion is that the 'formal' concept is typical of the LAC countries, most of which rank as middle-income economies according to the World Bank classification.[1] The majority of these countries is urban, its labour-force is mostly salaried and it is rich in natural resources. A comparison among world regions (a total of 113 countries) using 1980 data on health conditions (such as crude and infant mortality rates and life expectancy) shows that after the industrialized countries (and developing European countries), the highest average health standards are found in the LAC region, considerably better than the averages for African and Asian regions.[2]

The LAC region led the rest of the Third World in the introduction of social-security programmes. A comparative study of the dates of enactment of legislation establishing social-insurance pensions and sickness-maternity programmes among 114 countries shows that the industrialized (and European developing) countries were the first to introduce such programmes, followed by LAC: by 1950, sixteen LAC countries had enacted laws on both programmes compared with only three African countries on pensions and two countries on sickness-maternity, and two Asian countries on pensions and four on sickness-maternity.[3]

---

[1] Out of 21 LAC countries included in the tables of *World Development Report 1987*, all, except Haiti, are in the middle-income category and, within it, 7 countries rank in the upper middle-income group.

[2] Based on data from *UN Demographic Yearbook, 1980 to 1985*. For instance infant mortality means (rates per 1,000) were: LAC 66.4, Asia and Middle East 80.7, and Africa 121.1; female life expectancy means (years) were: LAC 63.8, Asia and Middle East 57.5, and Africa 46.6.

[3] Based on data from US Social Security Administration (1985).

In most LAC countries there remain large pockets of poor who are not covered by social security of any kind, and the question is whether the formal system can succeed in protecting them. In the least developed countries of the region (for example, Haiti, Honduras), socio-economic conditions and the magnitude of poverty may be more similar to those of most African and Asian countries. In these countries the broader concept of social security might be more suitable because social insurance has been able to cover a tiny percentage of the population only. This chapter, however, concentrates on formal social security and its associated issues.

2. THE HISTORICAL EVOLUTION OF SOCIAL INSURANCE/SECURITY IN LAC

This section discusses the forces (pressure groups, the State) behind the inception and development of social security in LAC, and identifies three stages and groups of countries in that historical evolution.[4] Each of the three stages of historical inception (to be summarized below), and each of the three groups of countries, roughly corresponds with one of three types of systems distinguished by their degree of social insurance/security development: (1) the 'pioneer' countries, which currently either have a social-security system or are very close to it; (2) the 'intermediate' countries, which are at different stages in the transition from social insurance to social security (a few have been able to go beyond the traditional Bismarckian model of social insurance); and (3) the 'late-comer' countries, in which we distinguish between the Latin American subgroup (with Bismarckian social insurance) and the non-Latin Caribbean subgroup (rapidly moving towards social security).

2.1. Pioneer Countries

In a small group of pioneer countries, which were the most developed (Chile, Uruguay, Argentina, Cuba, Brazil), the social-insurance system emerged at an early stage (during the 1920s), but it did so in a gradual and piecemeal fashion, giving rise to a multiplicity of managing institutions which protected different occupational groups through independent subsystems with their own legislation, administration, financing, and benefits. The State made a financial contribution by introducing specific taxes or through direct budgetary support. Gradually, subsystems were created which incorporated broader occupational groups or labour sectors as well as their dependants, but generally with more scanty benefits and more stringent entitlement conditions. The subsystems made their appearance approximately as follows: first among the armed forces, civil

---

[4] For a detailed analysis of these topics, see Mesa-Lago (1978).

servants, and teachers; then among blue- and white-collar workers in transport, energy, banking, communications, and other public utilities (the so-called 'labour aristocracy'); much later among the mass of urban workers (frequently separated into two large groups: white- and blue-collar); and finally among agricultural and self-employed workers, small farmers and petty entrepreneurs, and domestic servants.

This type of evolution resulted in a stratified social-insurance system, since it acquired a pyramidal structure, with relatively small groups of persons protected by privileged subsystems at the apex and centre and the majority of the population with subsystems providing less protection at the base. There were significant and usually unjustified differences between the subsystems, and the overall system lacked co-ordination. The stratified system had negative effects: legal confusion, administrative complexity, high operating costs, difficulty in establishing a single register and effective control of evasion, obstacles to combining length of service and contributions accredited in various institutions, significant inequalities (for example, in benefits available, entitlement conditions, financing, and so on).

Considerable debate has been going on for more than a decade now about the role of the two main driving forces of social insurance evolution in LAC: pressure groups and the State. The power base of the occupational groups described above lies either in their military strength, their administration of the government, the scarcity of their skills in the labour market, or their union organization. They bring pressure to bear on the State—sometimes in conjunction with political parties—in order to obtain social-insurance concessions. Studies of various countries in the region show that, in general, the more powerful the pressure groups are, the greater the extent to which they enjoy earlier and more comprehensive coverage, more generous benefits, and more advantageous means of financing. The State may not be a mere passive receiver of pressures from groups. It may also exercise its own initiative by using social security as the instrument to co-opt, neutralize, and control those groups in order to maintain some sort of social order.[5] That form of development in which the role of the pressure groups has been preponderant is typical of populist and democratic-pluralist political systems, such as those in Chile and Uruguay during the first seven decades of the twentieth century. Development in which the State plays a preponderant role is more typical of political systems with authoritarian and corporatist inclinations alongside populist features, such as those in Brazil under Getulio Vargas and Argentina under Juan Perón. In practice, both forces (pressure groups and the State) have worked hand in hand in both types of political systems and it is sometimes difficult to determine which was predominant.

[5] A major exponent of the theory that the State is the key force in the evolution of social security is James Malloy (1979). On the role of political leaders and the bureaucracy as major factors, see Rosenberg (1980).

As economic development, urbanization, unionization, and political mobilization processes advanced in the pioneer countries, the groups which lacked protection gained enough power to secure coverage within already existing or new subsystems. In some countries, they were even able to acquire some benefits that had been reserved for the old systems, thereby achieving some extension of privileges to the masses (what I have called 'massification of privilege'). The costs of universalizing coverage, and of providing generous benefits and liberal entitlement conditions, became excessive and provoked first actuarial and then financial imbalances in many subsystems. (An actuarial imbalance, in funded systems, occurs when the reserves plus the projected revenue are insufficient to meet the projected expenditures within a given period of time, say, twenty years; a financial imbalance, in any system, occurs when current expenditures in one given year are higher than revenues, thus resulting in a deficit.)

Social-insurance reform, promoted by national and international technical studies, advocated the unification and uniformity of the subsystems and the elimination of costly privileges. But the recipient groups were so powerful that the State was compelled to postpone reforms, sometimes for decades. The political changes that occurred in these countries during the 1960s, 1970s, and 1980s reinforced State power *vis-à-vis* the pressure groups (which in many cases were disbanded or had their power significantly reduced) and facilitated the process of reforming social security.[6]

· In some countries (Cuba, Brazil), virtually the entire system was unified. In others (Argentina, Uruguay) a central integrating or co-ordinating agency was formed which combined different organizations under a uniform system. Finally in one country (Chile) some measures were taken to make the old system uniform and eliminate most privileges, but above all a new system was created, strongly influenced by private insurance and favouring individuality and multiplicity.

2.2. *Intermediate Countries*

The second stage in the evolution of social insurance took place in countries whose main systems were established after the 1940s and were influenced by the new trends inspired by the International Labour Organization and the Beveridge Report, which sought to avoid the problems created in the pioneer countries. At the time, some of the countries in question were relatively developed (Mexico), but most of them had a low level of industrialization and in almost all of them the rural sector predominated over the urban sector. In these countries, a general managing agency was established which was responsible eventually for covering the entire population, although at the start the system was limited to the capital and the main cities.

[6] See Borzutsky (1985).

In the more developed countries of this second group, before the establishment of the general managing agency there had been a number of social-insurance institutions which protected the most powerful pressure groups: the armed forces, civil servants, teachers, and energy and railroad workers (Colombia, Costa Rica, Mexico, Paraguay, Peru, Venezuela). Furthermore, in some countries (Mexico, Costa Rica) a number of exceptions were made after the general managing agency was created, to establish separate subsystems for certain groups (almost always in the public sector). However, these groups were usually small and (except for the armed forces and civil servants) represented only a small percentage as compared to coverage under the general managing agency.

In any event, although there is a certain degree of stratification in all these countries, it has never approached the level it reached in the pioneer group. Because social insurance was introduced later in this second group, and also because of its relative unity and uniformity and its lower coverage of risk and population, these systems generally did not face the administrative and financial problems of the first group and therefore no radical changes were needed. Even so, the countries heading this group (those with the highest coverage, growing maturity of the pension programme, and high costs) are now beginning to face the financial problems typical of the first group.

Costa Rica is a special case within this group, because its system was introduced in the 1940s, but it achieved virtually universal coverage at the end of the 1970s, and its costs became similar to those of the countries in the first group even though its pension programme has still not fully matured.

2.3. Late-Comer Countries

Lastly, we can identify a third group of countries, the so called 'late comers', which also have relatively unified social-insurance systems but to a greater degree than those of the second group. Within this group there are two different subgroups. First there are the least developed countries of the region: Central America (except for Costa Rica and Panama) and the Latin American Caribbean (except for Cuba). In this subgroup, social insurance did not generally appear until the 1950s and 1960s, and the general managing agency covers virtually all the persons insured (although the armed forces and sometimes civil servants have separate subsystems); population coverage is very low and sometimes limited to the capital city and the most heavily populated cities. These countries are not usually faced with short- and medium-term financial difficulties, and their main problem is to extend coverage to the population at large.

The other subgroup consists of the non-Latin countries in the Caribbean which achieved independence in the 1960s and 1970s. In the former British colonies, a national health system was usually introduced prior to independence, but social insurance programmes were created after independence. In spite of their newness these programmes reached universal coverage about the 1980s. As in the first subgroup, these programmes are highly unified and relatively solvent financially.

Although in general the unification process has advanced in the Latin American region, there still remain systems where this process has not been completed or where stratification remains. Furthermore, the integration of the health institutions (social insurance, the ministry of health, and so on) and their policies is urgently needed in the majority of countries.

3. TRENDS AND TYPOLOGY OF THE LEVELS OF SOCIAL INSURANCE/ SECURITY DEVELOPMENT IN LAC

In 1983–4 a comparative study was made of social security among the twenty countries of Latin America (Mesa-Lago 1985*b*) and the major findings are summarized in Table 8.1. Three sets of countries are identified, following the scheme outlined in the preceding section, and based on eleven variables with data from 1980. The fourteen Caribbean countries were not included because they have a different historical evolution and social security model, and also because of a lack of sufficient data on all of them. Notice that the ranking is not a measure of performance of the systems (that is, it does not necessarily reflect their quality) but indicates their level of social security development; furthermore it provides a picture of overall trends in the region.[7]

3.1. *Trends*

Generally, the higher a country is ranked in Table 8.1: (1) the older the pensions programme (column 1); (2) the higher the percentage of the total population and the economically active population covered (columns 2 and 3); (3) the higher the contribution as a percentage of payroll (column 4); (4) the higher the social-security expenditure as a percentage of GDP and government expenditure (columns 5 and 6); (5) the higher the proportion of social-security expenditure devoted to pensions (column 7); (6) the greater the financial imbalance (column 8); (7) the higher the ratio of pensioners to contributors (column 9); (8) the higher the percentage of the population who are aged 65 and over (column 10); and (9) the higher the life expectancy at birth (column 11). An exercise of multiple correlation among the variables produced positive correlation coefficients between one another, suggesting that social security has developed in such a way that progress in one variable tends to be accompanied by progress in the others.

[7] See Mesa-Lago (1985*b*, 1986).

3.2. Types or Groups

Data from the previous section and from Table 8.1 allow us to describe the typical patterns of the systems in the three groups.

3.2.1. Pioneer Group The typical features of the social-security systems of countries in the pioneer group (which are roughly in the first stage of evolution described in Section 2.1) are as follows: the first pension programmes were set up in the 1920s; social security covers more than 60 per cent of both the total population and the economically active population and it becomes practically universal when assistance for the very poor is included; the total contribution rate exceeds 26 per cent of earnings; social-security expenditure comes close to or exceeds a tenth of the gross domestic product (GDP) and a third of the national budget; about half of the expenditure is on pensions, due to the age of the scheme, the maturity of the pensions programme, and very high life expectancy; the pensioner/contributor ratio is very high, rising to as much as 0.6, which means that one pensioner is financed by less than two contributors (this is because coverage has reached a maximum level and the growth rate of the population is low). The system was or is stratified, and its present impact on savings may be negative (the financial technique of the scheme is pure assessment or 'pay-as-you-go'), but it is probably neutral or slightly progressive in its distributive effects (especially progressive in the health programmes). The system faces a serious actuarial and financial disequilibrium with an in-built tendency to get worse in the future, giving rise to pressure for an overall reform.

3.2.2. Intermediate Group The typical features of the social-security systems of countries in the intermediate group (roughly in the second stage of evolution) are as follows: the first pension programmes were introduced in the 1930s or 1940s; the system covers between 18 and 52 per cent of the population; the total contribution rate is around 20 per cent of earnings; social-security expenditure is about 3 per cent of the GDP and between 14 and 23 per cent of the national budget; most of this expenditure goes to health programmes, as the countries concerned are in a period of demographic transition and have a high-dependency ratio, whilst only between 20 and 40 per cent is spent on pensions, owing to the relative immaturity of the pension scheme and to lower life expectancy; the pensioner/contributor ratio varies between 0.5 and 0.15 for the above reasons, and because of the scope for extending coverage and high population growth. The system is only relatively unified, as there exist some subsystems independent of the general scheme; its impact on distribution is probably slightly regressive, but its effect on savings may be moderately positive; the system produces an accounting surplus, and for its pension programme it uses the financial technique of scaled premium or assessment of

Table 8.1. Ranking of Latin American countries grouped according to the degree of development of social security, 1980

Group/countries	Initial pensions law[a]	Population Covered[b]		Statutory contribution rate[c]	Social-security expenditure as percentage of[d]			Surplus (or deficit) as % of income[e]	Ratio: pensioners/contributors[f]	Population aged 65 and over	Life expectancy at birth (years)
		Total	Economically active		GDP	National budget	Pensions				
	(1)	(2)	(3)	(4)	(5)	(6)	(7)	(8)	(9)	(10)	(11)
PIONEER GROUP											
Uruguay[g]	6	69	81	33	11	39	79	(60)	0.65	10.4	70
Argentina	6	79	69	46	10	38	55	(13)	0.32	8.2	69
Chile	6	67	62	29	11	32	53	17	0.46	5.5	68
Cuba[g]	6	100	93	10	9	13	44	(46)	0.21	7.3	73
Brazil	6	96	96	26	5	38	45	(7)	0.18	4.0	64
Costa Rica	4	78	68	27	9	36	21	0	0.06	3.6	71
Typical range[h]	6	67–100	62–96	26–46	9–11	32–39	44–79	0–(60)	0.18–0.65	4.0–10.4	68–73
INTERMEDIATE GROUP											
Panama	4	50	46	21	7	23	34	(11)	0.12	4.4	70
Mexico	4	53	42	18	3	18	21	17	0.08	3.6	64
Peru	5	17	37	21	3	15	35	12	0.09	3.6	58
Colombia[i]	4	12	22	20	4	20	20	(8)	0.05	3.5	62
Bolivia	3	25	18	25	3	14	40	8	0.33	3.2	51

Ecuador	5	8	23	21	3	10	48	36	0.15	3.5	60
Paraguay	4	18	14	20	2	22	31	15	0.07	3.4	64
Venezuela	2	45	50	14	3	15	33	26	0.06	2.8	66
Typical range[h]	3–5	12–53	18–50	18–25	3–7	14–23	20–40	26–(11)	0.05–0.15	3.2–4.4	60–70
LATE-COMER GROUP											
Dominican Republic	4	8	14	14	2	16	21	4	—	2.9	60
Guatemala[i]	2	14	33	20	2	14	14	3	0.06	2.9	58
El Salvador	3	6	12	12	2	12	18	23	0.08	3.4	62
Nicaragua	3	9	19	16	2	13	16	34	0.08	2.4	55
Honduras[j]	3	7	13	14	3	12	7	19	0.02	2.7	57
Haiti	2	1	2	12	1	—	10	15	—	3.5	51
Typical Range[h]	2–3	1–9	2–19	12–16	1–2	12–16	7–18	3–34	0.02–0.08	2.4–3.4	51–60

[a] Number of decades prior to the 1980s when the first pension law was enacted.
[b] Percentage of the total population covered by the sickness programme and of the economically active population covered by the pensions programme.
[c] Total statutory percentage of payroll to be contributed by the insured person, the employer and the State.
[d] Social-security expenditure includes total health expenditures.
[e] Deficit of surplus resulting from the subtraction of total social security expenditure from total income, expressed as a percentage of income.
[f] Dependency ratio: number of pensioners divided by the number of contributors.
[g] For Cuba and Uruguay, some figures are from 1981, the rest being for 1980.
[h] Calculated by extracting not more than one extreme or outlying variable.
[i] 1979.
[j] 1982.

Source: Mesa-Lago (1985b: 274–5).

constituent capitals. The system is generally in actuarial imbalance and faces the prospect of financial deficit in the short or medium term.

3.2.3 Late-comer Group   The typical features of the social-security systems of countries in the late-comer group (roughly in the third stage of evolution) are the following: the first pension programmes were set up in the 1950s or 1960s; the coverage of the population is very limited, being less than 10 per cent of the total population and 19 per cent of the economically active population, and is concentrated in the capital and the largest cities; the contribution from earnings is low, between 12 and 16 per cent; social-security expenditure amounts only to 2 per cent of the GDP and not more than 18 per cent of the national budget; some 80 per cent of this goes to health programmes, because of the high population growth rate, and less than 20 per cent to pensions, as the pensions programme is new and life expectancy is very low; the pensioner/ contributor ratio is extremely low, between 0.02 and 0.08, for the foregoing reasons, and there is substantial scope for extending coverage and also a very high population growth rate (nevertheless, the ratio is increasing because of the freeze on the extent of coverage of the population). The system is basically unified (except for the armed forces) and tends to have a regressive impact on distribution, but may have a positive effect on savings; it functions with a substantial surplus and the financial technique for pensions is that of the scaled- or general-level premium. At least in the short and medium term, it does not face financial imbalance, but it needs to increase population coverage.

3.2.4. Countries Difficult to Classify   A few of the Latin American countries do not fit perfectly into one single group; rather their variables are split into two groups although with the majority in one. For instance, most of Costa Rica's variables come within the range of the pioneer group, except for three that belong to the intermediate group: the newness of the pension law (and hence, the low percentage of expenditures that goes to pensions and low ratio of pensioners to contributors) and the youthfulness of its population. The rapid acceleration in coverage of population and risks in the 1960s and 1970s catapulted Costa Rica from the intermediate to the pioneer group.

Although the non-Latin Caribbean countries were excluded from the comparison, a recent study on three of them (Bahamas, Barbados, and Jamaica) indicates some similarities with the Costa Rican system: recent enactment of the pension law, universal population coverage, low ratio of pensioners to contributors, relatively young populations, and high life expectancy. On the other hand, because these Caribbean systems are even newer and their benefits are usually less generous than those of Costa Rica, the former are different: their contribution rates and costs are lower, and most of them have substantial financial surpluses.[8]

[8] See Mesa-Lago (1988).

An important question is whether, if the present trend of social security does not change, the Latin American countries in the intermediate group and possibly in the late-comer group may face problems similar to those today afflicting the countries in the pioneer group. A satisfactory answer to this question would have required a detailed analysis of all the countries concerned. As this was impossible, the study mentioned earlier (Mesa-Lago, 1985b) thoroughly analysed four countries at various levels of the pioneer group (Uruguay, Chile, Cuba, and Costa Rica) and two countries in the upper part of the intermediate group (Mexico and Peru). These case-studies suggest that the question may well have a positive answer but, to reach a more reliable conclusion, it is obvious that more case-studies of Latin American countries in the intermediate and late-comer groups are needed. Furthermore the application of this model to the non-Latin Caribbean countries could help to answer that crucial question.

4. COVERAGE OF RISKS AND POPULATION

4.1. Coverage of Risks

The coverage of risks by social insurance in LAC has evolved gradually (as can be seen from Table 8.2). With one or two exceptions, coverage invariably depends on employment. The first risk to be covered was that of occupational accidents and diseases, based on the theory of employer liability. The second risk was that of non-occupational sickness and maternity, but like the previous category this was related to employment; thus maternity care was provided

Table 8.2. Number of countries in Latin America and the Caribbean providing social insurance and family allowance legal coverage of various risks: 1922–1985

Programmes	1922	1932	1942	1952	1962	1972	1982	1985
Social Insurances								
Occupational accidents and diseases	12	18	23	27	27	29	30	30
Sickness and maternity[a]	0	1	7	13	17	24	29	30
Old-age, disability, and survivors	0	2	8	14	17	31	34	34
Unemployment	0	0	0	2	4	5	6	6
Family allowances	0	0	0	1	5	6	7	7

[a] In practically all the non-Latin Caribbean, social-insurance sickness-maternity programmes only award cash benefits, while health care is provided by public-health programmes.

Sources: Based on US Social Security Administration (1985).

only for female salaried employees and workers (the coverage was later extended to maternity of wives or common-law wives of workers, and sickness coverage to some of their dependants). In the non-Latin Caribbean, however, social insurance does not administer a sickness-maternity programme but this is provided under a national health system or public health programme. In Latin America, old-age disability and survivor pensions were established about the same time as sickness-maternity insurance. In the non-Latin Caribbean, pension and other cash benefit programmes were introduced much later. By the mid 1980s all LAC countries (with the exception of Haiti and a few non-Latin Caribbean countries) had these three programmes in operation though they covered the whole population only in a minority of countries.

The last programmes to come into being were family allowances and unemployment benefits, which exist only in a few countries: family allowances in Argentina, Bolivia, Brazil, Chile, Colombia, Costa Rica (this is not a true family allowance programme), and Uruguay; and unemployment benefits in Argentina, Barbados, Brazil, Chile, Ecuador, and Uruguay. In general, the extension of risk coverage has been much faster than that of population coverage. This is due to the fact that priority has been given to vertical extension (risks covered) rather than horizontal extension (population protected): quite often a minority of the population is covered against all risks, but the majority is not protected against any risk at all.

4.2. Legal and Statistical Coverage of the Population

When referring to coverage of the population, one has to distinguish between the legal or statutory and the statistical coverage. The former is what is prescribed by law, but not always in effect; the second comes from estimates of the population protected, which are closer to reality but not always trustworthy. In Latin America generally the social-insurance sickness-maternity programme is the one that has the broadest statutory coverage; in half the countries it covers the entire employed labour force (in some cases, only those employed by others) and in the other half it covers only some employees, usually those in the public sector and in industry, mining, commerce, and financial services. However, in Cuba all residents are covered by the legislation, whilst in Costa Rica and Chile the whole population is covered except those with high incomes who are not working. On the other hand, in the remaining Central American countries and in Haiti the statutory coverage is normally limited to the capital and the larger cities. Only in eight countries does the law protect self-employed persons (compulsorily only in two), but in almost all the countries it covers the dependants of insured persons (normally the wife or common-law wife and children) and pensioners.

In practically all the non-Latin Caribbean every resident has the legal right to public health care. Social insurance provides pensions for all salaried employees and wage-earners in all countries, as well as sickness-maternity cash benefits for the same group in all but four countries; the self-employed are compulsorily covered in both programmes in only four countries.

In summary, under the statutory coverage, in most countries those insured are urban wage-earners and their closest dependants, whilst self-employed persons, agricultural workers, and those in domestic service, as well as the unemployed, and their dependants are not covered by social insurance, in addition, in a quarter of the Latin American countries (the least-developed ones) the coverage is limited to the capital and the larger cities.

Statistical estimates of coverage in LAC are affected by multiple deficiencies, which I have described elsewhere. Usually figures on coverage of the economically active population (EAP), or the active insured, are more precise than those of the total population because the latter includes the insured's dependants who are often estimated in a very rough manner. Table 8.3 provides data on coverage of both the EAP and the total population under the social-insurance sickness-maternity programme including both health care and monetary benefits; for the non-Latin Caribbean only the latter benefits are reported since social insurance does not provide the former; however in most of these countries public health care is reportedly available for practically all the population. Coverage under the national health system or the ministry of public health is not reported in Table 8.3 except for Cuba's total population and this is the statutory coverage. Coverage of the EAP by the social-insurance pension programme is very similar to that presented in Table 8.3 for the sickness-maternity programme.

According to the Table 8.3, in Latin America, coverage of the EAP expanded very rapidly between 1960 and 1980 (or 1985) in five countries: about four times in Brazil and Venezuela, and three times in Costa Rica, Mexico, and Panama. Although there is no accurate estimate for Cuba at the end of the 1950s (figures in Table 8.3 refer to sickness-maternity coverage of the EAP), scattered information indicates that health care coverage increased five- to sixfold in that period. Coverage in the Southern Cone was close to universal by the mid 1980s, although the 1960–85 data suggest a decline in coverage in the case of Chile and Uruguay—in the latter probably due to statistical problems—and a significant increase in Argentina. In the three reported countries from the non-Latin Caribbean, universal coverage was reached in a very short period. But in the remaining nine Latin American countries, in spite of some advances, in 1980–5 social insurance covered about one-third or less of the EAP (except in Peru in which coverage has been below 40 per cent but stagnant). In general, coverage is higher in the most developed countries, and in those with the oldest social-insurance programmes.

In the penultimate line of Table 8.3 an estimate is made of overall coverage in Latin America in 1980, which is put at 61 per cent for both the EAP and the total population. There is no doubt that in this respect the region is ahead of

Table 8.3. Total and economically active population covered by social insurance in Latin America and the Caribbean: 1960, 1970, 1980, and 1985 (%).

Countries	Economically active population				Total population	
	1960	1970	1980	1985	1980	1985
Argentina	55.2[a]	68.0[a]	69.1[a]	79.1[b]	78.9	74.3[b]
Bahamas	n.a.	n.a.	85.3	85.9	n.a.	n.a.
Barbados	n.a.	75.3	79.8	96.9	n.a.	n.a.
Bolivia	8.8[c]	9.0	18.5	n.a.	25.4	n.a.
Brazil	23.1	27.0	87.0	n.a.	96.3	n.a.
Chile	70.8	75.6	61.2	70.0	67.3	n.a.
Colombia	8.0	22.2	30.4	30.2	15.2	16.0
Costa Rica	25.3	38.4	68.3	n.a.	81.5[d]	84.6[d]
Cuba	62.6[e]	88.7[f]	93.0[f,g]	n.a.	100.0[f]	n.a.
Dominican Republic	n.a.	8.9	n.a.	11.3	n.a.	5.9
Ecuador	11.0	15.8[h]	21.3	23.4[i]	9.4	11.1[i]
El Salvador	4.4	8.4	11.6	n.a.	6.2	n.a.
Guatemala	20.6	27.0	33.1	26.8	14.2	12.9
Honduras	3.7	4.2	14.4	12.8[b]	7.3	10.3[b]
Jamaica	n.a.	58.8	80.9	93.2	n.a.	n.a.
Mexico	15.6	28.1	42.0	41.7[i]	53.4	59.7[i]
Nicaragua	5.9	14.8	18.9	31.5	9.1	37.5
Panama	20.6	33.4	52.3	56.4[b]	49.9	58.1[b]
Paraguay	8.0	10.7	14.0	n.a.	18.2	n.a.
Peru	24.8[c]	35.6[h]	37.4	38.0	16.6	18.6
Uruguay	109.0[j]	95.4[a]	81.2[a]	72.4[a i]	68.5	67.0[i]
Venezuela	11.9	24.4	49.8	54.3	45.2	49.9[i]
Latin America	n.a.	n.a.	61.2	n.a.	61.2	n.a.
Excluding Brazil	n.a.	n.a.	42.7	n.a.	42.7	n.a.

[a] Coverage in pensions.
[b] Figures for 1984.
[c] Figures for 1961.
[d] Includes coverage of the dispossessed (indigents).
[e] Figure for 1958.
[f] Estimate based on legal coverage and population census.
[g] Figure for 1981.
[h] Figures for 1969.
[i] Figures for 1983.
[j] More than 100% due to multiple coverage.

Source: Mesa-Lago (1987, 1989).

most developing countries and that a group of Latin American countries have reached levels of coverage similar to those of the developed world. Thus in the pioneer countries, and in one or two of the intermediate group, the coverage has been extended rapidly and, if we take into account the protection of the poor (called 'indigent') by welfare programmes for health care and pensions, it has become almost universal. But in most of the countries of Latin America social-insurance coverage is very low and there are structural barriers in the way of its extension. A more detailed analysis of Table 8.3 shows that the total coverage of the region is strongly influenced by the very high cover in Brazil, a country which contains more than half of all the insured in Latin America. When Brazil is excluded from the calculations (see the last line of Table 8.3), coverage in Latin America drops to less than 43 per cent of the EAP and the total population; what is more, in about half the countries the coverage is less than one-third and in seven countries it is less than 25 per cent.

4.3. Inequalities in Coverage of the Population

Alongside the problem of low overall coverage, most Latin American countries suffer from inequality in the degree of coverage among different occupational groups, economic sectors, and geographical areas. The coverage tends to be positively correlated with income, the degree of labour skills, and the power of pressure groups.

Surveys carried out in seven countries—Argentina, Costa Rica, Cuba, Chile, Mexico, Peru, and Uruguay—show that the historical appearance of coverage of various occupational groups was largely determined by the power of pressure groups, with a gap of almost 200 years between the first and the last groups covered by pensions: those in the armed forces and civil service began to be covered between the beginning of the nineteenth century and the beginning of the twentieth; teachers between 1880 and 1930; the police between 1890 and the 1940s; the labour aristocracy (public utilities, banks, merchant marine) between 1910 and 1940s; the great mass of the urban labour force (white- and blue-collar workers) between 1920 and the 1940s; agricultural workers between 1930 and the 1950s; domestic servants between 1930 and the 1970s; and the self-employed between 1930 and the 1970s. One has to take account of the fact that in the majority of these countries all groups are covered, although there exist substantial differences in the degree of coverage, in spite of the measures taken in most of them to make it more universal, unified, and uniform. The differences mentioned are much more noteworthy in the countries with low coverage, inasmuch as the majority of the population is excluded from the social-insurance system. A recent analysis for Brazil also shows a positive correlation between coverage on the one hand, and skill and income on the other, with the lowest coverage being found among the unemployed, unskilled workers (especially those in agriculture and self-employment), and the lowest income group.[9]

Information from six countries (Colombia, Costa Rica, Chile, Ecuador, Mexico, and Peru) on the degree of coverage of the EAP in 1979–84, by economic branch, indicates that the highest level of coverage is to be found in the electricity, gas, and water industries (65 to 100 per cent), manufacturing (40 to 90 per cent), and transport and communications (32 to 71 per cent); whilst the lowest is in agriculture (4 to 59 per cent), with the highest percentages being in Costa Rica and Chile (countries where coverage is almost universal). Finally, information from ten countries (Argentina, Colombia, Costa Rica, Chile, Ecuador, Guatemala, Mexico, Panama, Peru, and Uruguay) on differences in the degree of geographical coverage in 1979–84 shows that the States or provinces or departments which are most highly developed (industrialized, unionized, urbanized, having the highest percentage of wage-earners and the highest per capita incomes) are covered to a substantially higher degree than the States, provinces, or departments which are least developed (agricultural, little unionized, rural, with a high proportion of self-employed persons and lowest per capita incomes). Coverage in a particular geographical region varies between 6 and 100 per cent in Argentina, 3 and 25 per cent in Colombia, 54 and 100 per cent in Costa Rica, 39 and 95 per cent in Chile, 3 and 20 per cent in Ecuador, 0.2 and 33 per cent in Guatemala, 17 and 100 per cent in Mexico, 11 and 75 per cent in Panama, 3 and 27 per cent in Peru, and 17 and 69 per cent in Uruguay (Mesa-Lago 1989). With one exception, the province or State or department where the capital is located is the one with the highest coverage.

Those below the poverty line in Latin America are not normally protected by social insurance. The poor are either unemployed or underemployed, are seasonal or temporary workers, or are employed by a relative without pay and therefore not on a permanent full-time basis. They may also be employed, but in occupations not covered in the majority of countries, such as agriculture (especially small farmers, share-croppers, and so on), handicrafts, domestic service, and self-emloyment. PREALC (Regional Employment Programme for Latin America and the Caribbean) has estimated that, in 1980, 33 per cent of the population in Latin America was below the poverty line and that the proportion increased to 39 per cent in 1985. According to Table 8.3, in 1980, 39 per cent of the total population of Latin America was not covered by social insurance and we have seen that, due to the economic crisis, coverage had not increased significantly by 1985. It is not possible to ascertain that the percentage of the population under the poverty line exactly corresponds with the percentage of the population not covered by social insurance. However, analysis of the characteristics of the insured (their income, occupation, and geographical

---

[9] See Mesa-Lago (1978: 265–6), and Isuani (1985: 96–7).

location) allows us to conclude that the poor are generally not covered by social insurance, and only have access to public health and social assistance, services usually underfinanced and insufficient. The LAC countries with the highest degree of social insurance coverages are also those that have the lowest proportion of poor, but even in the most advanced countries the percentage of the population uncovered is greater than the percentage of those below the poverty line.[10]

In summary, the most needy groups appear to be deprived of social-insurance protection in the great majority of the countries; the key question is whether it is feasible to extend coverage to include these groups.

4.4 The Limits of the Bismarckian Model

A number of experts have pointed out that the Bismarckian model of social insurance has not been able to operate satisfactorily in most of the countries in Latin America in spite of the major changes made to the original model. This is due to the fact that in the developed countries of Europe, most of the labour-force consists of wage-earning urban workers, whilst in at least one-third of Latin American countries the mass of the labour force is composed of agricultural workers, the self-employed, and unremunerated family members.[11]
The revised Bismarckian model finances social insurance through contributions from the worker and employer based on the worker's wage; but in many Latin American countries self-employed persons cannot afford the employer's contribution; and agricultural workers have low incomes, are scattered, and are frequently migrant, often changing employer.

The first section of Table 8.4 shows that in the most developed countries of the region, wage-earners comprise from 63 to 94 per cent of the labour-force (Argentina, Barbados, Brazil, Chile, Costa Rica, Cuba, Panama, Trinidad and Tobago, Uruguay, and Venezuela) and less than a third of the labour-force works on its own account or as unpaid members of the family. This explains why the Bismarckian social-insurance model has been able to function and extend its coverage in these countries. On the other hand, in the least developed countries (such as Bolivia, Guatemala, Haiti, Honduras, Paraguay, and Peru) from 48 to 70 per cent of the labour force is self-employed or working unpaid for a member of the same family (and a similar proportion are engaged in agriculture). These countries are precisely those which have the lowest social-insurance coverage and it is obvious that the Bismarckian model makes extension of coverage in them very difficult if one goes beyond the limits of the wage-earning labour-force.

[10] See 'Poverty and the Social Debt', *PREALC Newsletter*, No. 17 (July 1988), pp. 1–2; and Mesa-Lago (1983).
[11] See Arroba (1979) and Isuani (1985).

Table 8.4. Percentage distribution of labour-force in Latin America and the Caribbean, between 1980 and 1983

| Countries | By Occupational Category[a] | | | By sector | | | |
| | | | | Urban | | Rural | |
	Wage-earners	Self-employed	Unpaid families	Formal	Informal	Modern	Traditional
Argentina	71.2	25.1	3.2	65.0	19.4	8.8	6.3
Barbados	78.2	9.8	0.8	n.a.	n.a.	n.a.	n.a.
Bolivia	38.2	48.9	9.2	17.9	23.2	5.2	50.9
Brazil	65.3	27.0	5.1	45.2	16.9	9.8	27.6
Chile	66.7	25.3	3.6	54.1	20.1	14.0	8.8
Colombia	53.5		42.5	42.6	22.3	15.8	18.7
Costa Rica	75.2	19.6	3.9	52.9	12.4	19.6	14.8
Cuba	94.1	5.7	0.2	n.a.	n.a.	n.a.	n.a.
Dominican Rep.	51.3	36.5	3.3	n.a.	n.a.	n.a.	n.a.
Ecuador	47.6	37.3	5.8	22.7	25.4	13.7	37.9
El Salvador	59.2	28.2	10.9	28.6	18.9	22.3	30.1
Guatemala	46.9	42.2	6.7	26.7	17.8	22.3	33.1
Haiti	16.6	59.4	10.4	n.a.	n.a.	n.a.	n.a.
Honduras	45.4	33.3	14.6	n.a.	n.a.	n.a.	n.a.
Jamaica	54.5	41.1	4.4	n.a.	n.a.	n.a.	n.a.
Mexico	_[b]	_[b]	_[b]	39.5	22.0	19.2	18.4
Panama	63.3	23.2	3.6	45.3	20.9	9.1	24.6
Paraguay	36.7	41.2	11.6	n.a.	n.a.	n.a.	n.a.
Peru	45.1	49.1	5.8	35.0	23.8	8.0	32.0
Trinidad & Tobago	80.1	14.6	3.5	n.a.	n.a.	n.a.	n.a.
Uruguay	69.4	23.8	2.0	63.3	19.0	9.5	8.0
Venezuela	64.1	26.5	3.1	62.6	16.4	4.4	15.1

[a] Excludes a small percentage of non-classified workers. The years do not correspond to 1980–3 in Bolivia (1976), Honduras (1977), and Uruguay (1975). No data were available for Bahamas and Jamaica.
[b] The results of the 1980 census are unreliable and give a very high percentage (22%) of non-classified workers.

Sources: The first distribution is based on ILO, *Yearbook of Labour Statistics, 1980 to 1985* except Cuba, which is taken from Oficina Nacional del Censo (1984). The second distribution is from PREALC (1981).

The second section of Table 8.4 shows the distribution of the labour-force between sectors, using the ILO PREALC method. When the percentage of the EAP in the formal urban sector is compared with the percentage of the EAP covered by social insurance, one notes in most of the countries a very marked degree of correspondence between them. A few countries have been able to extend coverage somewhat beyond the formal urban sector, because they have: (1) social-assistance programmes that provide reduced benefits to the dis-possessed not entitled to social-insurance benefits (for example, Costa Rica and Chile for pensions and sickness-maternity; Bahamas, Barbados, Cuba, Jamaica, and Uruguay for pensions); (2) national health systems that cover the whole population (for example, most of the non-Latin Caribbean, Cuba); (3) relatively modern and unionized rural sectors entitled to social insurance/ security (for example, Argentina, Costa Rica, Chile, Cuba, Uruguay, and part of the non-Latin Caribbean); and/or (4) special social-insurance programmes (mainly health care) for the poor in large, traditional rural sectors (for example, Brazil, Mexico; see descriptions below). In Colombia and Venezuela, the number covered by social insurance is substantially less than the number in the formal urban sector, indicating that these countries—particularly the latter, which has relatively abundant resources—could make a greater effort to extend coverage, even within the narrow limits of the Bismarckian model. In only two countries (Brazil and Uruguay) does social-insurance coverage exceed the sum of the formal urban and modern rural sectors, which indicates the obstacles that lie in the way of extending coverage to the informal urban and traditional rural sectors. In these two sectors we find self-employed persons and those working without pay for a member of their family, who are typically underemployed and with low incomes, which means that it is difficult for them to finance their own coverage.

Two important models of extension of coverage to the rural sector are those of Brazil and Mexico. FUNRURAL, established in Brazil in the early 1970s, rapidly extended primary health care coverage to the rural sector and small towns, through a network of rural posts, ambulatories, and small hospitals, financed by taxes paid by urban employers and large agricultural producers. COPLAMAR was created in Mexico in 1976 and, through an agreement signed in 1979 with the social-insurance institute (IMSS), expanded health care coverage in the early 1980s to some 13 million people. The infrastructure consists of a network of rural posts and small hospitals, built by IMSS, plus the tertiary-level hospitals of the ministry of health; 60 per cent of the programme is financed by the federal government and 40 per cent by IMSS, while the insured peasants contribute communal work. Unfortunately, these two pro- grammes have been negatively affected by the economic crisis of the 1980s and, in Mexico, part of the IMSS–COPLAMAR facilities and population have been transferred to the ministry of health (see Mesa-Lago 1989).

Recent team research has been conducted at the University of Pittsburgh on determinants of social-insurance (pension) coverage of the EAP in all Latin American countries. Several independent variables were tested and the regression showed that the per cent of the salaried (or wage-earners) labour-force (EAP) explained 0.622 of coverage. A dummy variable 'political commitment' was introduced, whose value was one when State initiative was present (for example, through law and direct state action on social security) and zero when it was absent. The best fit was obtained when the salaried labour force and political commitment were regressed jointly, and they explained 0.793 of coverage. In this study, salaried labour-force was used as a surrogate of pressure groups, whilst political commitment as representative of State initiative; these two independent variables were seen as mutually reinforcing rather than exclusionary.[12] This study confirms, therefore, that social-insurance coverage is mainly determined by the proportion of the labour-force which is salaried. But it also suggests that such a boundary can be overcome by political will in countries with abundant resources (as in Brazil and Mexico). Unfortunately the current economic crisis has apparently arrested or reversed such advances.

4.5. *How to Reach the Goal of Universal Coverage*

The possibilities of rapid extension of social-security cover seem remote for many LAC countries. Between 1950 and 1980 (years of rapid economic expansion in the region), the formal urban sector grew by more than 14 per cent in the region, but the modern rural sector was reduced by almost 10 per cent. The growth of the formal sector was insufficient to absorb the increase in the supply of labour and in participation rates, together with the intense rural–urban migration and the previously existing levels of underemployment. Capital-intensive methods of production did not help in the absorption of manpower. In the same period, the traditional and informal sectors in the region were reduced by 4 per cent (the traditional sector dropped by almost 10 per cent but the informal sector increased by almost 6 per cent). To reduce the traditional and informal sectors by a third by the year 2000, it was calculated that an annual growth in GDP of 7.5 per cent would be needed. And yet the economic crisis of the 1980s has actually resulted in a negative growth rate in the region (a cumulative variation of −5.5 per cent in 1980–7). Employment in the formal sector declined by 6 per cent in 1980–5, while employment in the informal sector increased by 5 per cent and the rate of unemployment rose by 1 per cent.[13] According to Table 8.3, coverage of the EAP by social insurance declined in some countries in 1980–5, probably as a result of the economic crisis.

However, the discussion above should not lead to the conclusion that there is no solution to the problem of coverage. We have mentioned the significant role of political commitment in coverage expansion and have seen that in a good number of countries in the region, coverage has been rapidly expanded in the last twenty-five years thus overcoming, partly or totally, the barriers of the Bismarckian model, as, for example, in Argentina, Brazil, Chile, Cuba, Costa Rica, Mexico, Uruguay, and most of the non-Latin Caribbean. And yet, practically all these countries are among the most developed in LAC and efforts made in less developed countries to expand coverage to the rural low-

---

[12] See Cruz-Saco *et al.* (1987).
[13] See PREALC (1981: 35–54), ECLAC (1987: 16), IADB (1988: 117–34), and Tokman (1986: 535).

income areas (for example, in Ecuador and Peru) have not achieved significant success.

A specialist has suggested, as a remedy designed to break the barrier, the inclusion of social insurance in an integrated development policy which should include a change-over to labour-intensive methods of production which promote full employment and the satisfaction of basic needs.[14] But this approach has been criticized for being unrealistic and not taking into account the heterogeneous nature of the countries in the region and their differing degrees of industrialization, agricultural modernization, and demographic development, or of other development priorities. According to this criticism, universality is possible only in the most advanced countries (Argentina, Uruguay, Chile, Cuba) and perhaps in the near future in countries at an intermediate level of development (Costa Rica, Panama) but not in the others (Leon 1985). Still the suggested integrated development policy, with different priorities, might be more appropriate to the means and needs of the least developed countries to expand coverage even if only by providing of selected, minimal benefits. In any event there is an obvious need to replace the Bismarckian model of social insurance by a new social-security model, which would imply substantial reforms in financing and benefits.

5. FINANCING SOCIAL INSURANCE/SECURITY

5.1. *Sources of Finance*

The financing of social insurance in LAC is dependent mainly on contributions based on the earnings (mostly salaries and wages) of insured persons. The law lays down the percentages of contribution payable by the insured person, the employer and, sometimes, by the government (on a tripartite basis as well as in its capacity as an employer). The State also contributes to financing through special taxes or by covering all or part of the deficit in the system, or by granting other subsidies. In the few countries where self-employed persons are covered, they have to pay a contribution based on an estimated income equivalent, at the total rate paid by employees and their employers. Pensioners often have to pay a contribution from their pensions. Another source of financing is the investment income of the reserve funds, mainly of pensions.

As shown in the first section of Table 8.5, by 1985 in fourteen of the twenty-four LAC countries shown, the percentage contribution demanded of the insured is less than a third of the total contribution; in nine other countries, the insured's percentage varies, between a third and a half of the total; only in

---

[14] Isuani (1985: 99–101). a similar position concerning all basic needs is taken by COPLAMAR in *Macroeconomia de las Necesdades Esenciales en Mexico: Situacion Actual y Perspectivas al Ano 2000* (Mexico, Siglo XXI, 1983), pp. 105–10.

Table 8.5. Financing of Social Insurance/Security in Latin America and the Caribbean by Source:1980 and 1985

Countries	Legal contributions for social insurance: % of salary (1985)			% distribution of social-security revenue (1980)				
	Insured[a]	Employer	State	Insured	Employer	State & tax[b]	Investment	Others
Argentina	14.0	28.0[e]	7.8–10.6[c]	38.4	49.4	10.2	2.0	0.0
Bahamas	1.7–3.4	5.4–7.1	–[c]	n.a.	n.a.	n.a.	n.a.	n.a.
Barbados	4.6–5.5	4.9–6.0	–[c]	22.7	28.8	31.0	17.5	0.0
Bolivia	3.5	20.0	1.5	28.7	53.6	6.2	7.9	3.6
Brazil	8.5–10.0	17.1–19.2	–[c]	36.9[d]	53.9	5.0	0.1	3.6
Chile old	24.6–26.5	0.85	–c	20.5	38.3[g]	34.2	2.0	5.0
new	19.6	0.85	0–0					
Colombia	3.8–5.5	14.0–24.0	–[c]	16.0	49.8	16.2	6.4	11.6
Costa Rica	8.0	22.7	1.5	27.6	45.9	20.4	5.2	0.9
Cuba	0.0	10.0	–[c]	n.a.	n.a.	n.a.	n.a.	n.a.
Dominican Rep.	2.5	9.5	2.5	n.a.	n.a.	n.a.	n.a.	n.a.
Ecuador	9.4	9.8	–[c]	37.0	43.0	0.1	19.9	0.0
El Salvador	3.2–3.5	7.6–8.2	0.5[c]	23.4	63.0	0.9	11.8	0.9

Guatemala	4.5	10.0	—c	31.6	53.1	8.2	6.9	0.2
Haiti	2.0–6.0	4.0–12.0	—c	n.a.	n.a.	n.a.	n.a.	n.a.
Honduras	3.5	7.0	3.5	n.a.	n.a.	n.a.	n.a.	n.a.
Jamaica	2.5f	2.5f	—c	17.2	20.7	36.8	25.1	0.2
Mexico	3.8	12.4	1.9	24.0d	50.3	19.7	2.5	3.5
Nicaragua	4.0	11.0	0.5c	21.2	58.0	16.2	2.5	2.1
Panama	7.2	12.4	0.0	28.6	45.1	4.3	9.6	12.4
Paraguay	9.5	16.5	1.5	n.a.	n.a.	n.a.	n.a.	n.a.
Peru	6.0	16.0	0.0	n.a.	n.a.	n.a.	n.a.	n.a.
Trinidad and Tobago	2.8	5.6e	—c	18.2	36.0	26.9	18.9	0.0
Uruguay	12.0–19.0	19.0–24.0	—c	25.1	34.0	38.3	1.5	1.1
Venezuela	4.0	7.0–9.0	1.5	26.8	53.5	6.8	12.7	0.2

[a] Salaried or wage-earner; the self-employed have to pay a much higher percentage.
[b] Includes financing of public health care in countries with national health system.
[c] Budgetary contributions, deficit coverage, taxes, and other subsidies.
[d] Distribution in 1974.
[e] Excludes contribution for occupational risks.
[f] In addition there is a flat contribution.
[g] Since 1981 the employer does not contribute.

Sources: Legal contributions based on US Social Security Administration (1985). Percentage distribution from ILO (1985).

Chile is the insured's percentage greater than half the total percentage. In fourteen of the countries, the insured's contribution is subject to a maximum or ceiling on wages. The percentage contribution payable by the State is usually small, less than a tenth of the total contribution, but this does not take into account the other sums provided by the State. By law, however, the principal source of financing for social insurance/security is the employer's contribution, which represents more than two-thirds of the total in fourteen countries and more than two-fifths in seven others (but in Chile only a fifth).

The second section of Table 8.5 gives the most recent statistics (for 1980) available for seventeen countries, covering the distribution of social-security revenue by source. Although the trend is towards an increase in the insured person's contribution, the statistics confirm what has already been said, although the government contribution appears to be much higher than would be indicated by simply taking the legal percentage (because in most countries, the State contribution is through budgetary allocations or taxes rather than as a percentage contribution based on salaries). In almost every country, the insured person contributes less than a third of total revenue; in three slightly more than a third, but in eight less than a quarter. In thirteen countries, 60 per cent or more of the revenue is contributed by the employer plus the State, and in five countries two-thirds or more. The income from investments is less than a tenth of the total, with six exceptions; but in six countries it does not exceed 5 per cent. All this suggests—on the basis of legislated contribution rates and without taking into account the question of incidence—that the insured do not meet the main cost of their social security and that the situation is more inequitable in those countries which have very low coverage; thus, in Colombia, the coverage of the population in 1980 was 16 per cent, the insured contributed 16 per cent of the revenue, whilst the employer and the State together contributed two-thirds, which suggests a regressive effect in the distribution of the financial burden. To confirm this point, one would need to analyse the incidence of social-security contributions, questioning the assumption of a 'right' generated by the insured persons' payments and the argued need for close correspondence between the 'premium' (contribution) and the 'reward' (benefit). These assumptions have justified discrimination in treatment as between the users of social insurance and public assistance, and have increased the barrier standing in the way of extending social-security coverage in those countries which have a small employed labour-force. If one questions these assumptions, one opens the way to replacing financing based on salary-related contributions by financing through another type of tax (for example, on income) which could make universal coverage easier and correct other possible negative economic effects of the current type of financing upon employment and/or distribution.

In only a few countries are there transfers from the national budget (or from urban employers) to cover the rural sector. In Mexico, the state contributes directly to the operation of the health programme for marginal rural groups (COPLAMAR). In Brazil, the programme of social assistance for health care and pensions which covers the rural sector (wage-earners, self-employed, those working unpaid for a member of their family) is financed by taxes on both the payroll of urban enterprises and the value of agricultural production. In Costa Rica, the State contributes to the health and pensions assistance programme for the very poor (rural and urban) who are not covered by insurance.

5.2 Financial Equilibrium

In a number of countries of Latin America, the financial stability of social insurance is delicately balanced. The pioneer countries, which have the oldest and most highly developed systems, are those facing the largest disequilibrium. These countries have increasing expenditure due to (1) the universal extension of coverage; (2) quite liberal legislation on benefits; (3) a capital-intensive system of curative medicine; (4) pension schemes which have matured; (5) an increasing number of pensioners who are living longer than was envisaged both in the original legislation and in older actuarial estimates, thus receiving their pensions and health benefits for longer periods; and (6) adjustments to pensions and other benefits in line with the cost of living. Social-security revenues in the pioneer countries are becoming proportionately lower for the following reasons: (1) coverage cannot be extended any further (and if it were, it would be to bring in lower-income groups, which would worsen the disequilibrium); (2) the number of active contributors is dropping progressively in comparison with the growing number of beneficiaries; (3) there is a high level of employer's evasion and delay, particularly in the countries which have high and sustained inflation (where delaying payment means a reduction in the real contribution); (4) the State—under pressure to meet multiple and urgent demands—fails to comply with its financial obligations, thus leading to the accumulation of very large debts; (5) the contribution burden of social security is very heavy and it is very difficult, politically and economically, to increase either social-security contributions or taxes; (6) the yield on pension funds has turned out to be very low, and even negative in the high-inflation countries; and (7) transfers (or 'loans') from pension funds to cover deficits in health programmes are difficult to reimburse in practice, which has contributed to the de-capitalization of the funds at a time when it is necessary to use the accumulated technical reserves to meet the current pension payments. As Table 8.1 shows, four of the pioneer countries had financial deficits in 1980, and obviously their actuarial disequilibria were even larger.

As indicated in Table 8.1, most of the Latin American countries in the intermediate group (including Mexico and Peru), and all the countries in the late-comer group, had a financial surplus in social security in 1980. Nevertheless, Panama had a deficit, and an analysis of the situation in Mexico and Peru indicates that in 1983–4 there was already either a financial deficit or an immediate threat of one and the situation was worse as regards the actuarial balance of the pension scheme in these two countries. An analysis of the case of Ecuador carried out in 1984 also indicated that there were reasons for fearing financial disequlibrium in the short term and a serious actuarial deficit. A study of Colombia conducted in 1986 showed a financial surplus for the entire system but an actuarial disequilibrium in the pension funds.[15] Therefore, the situation of the intermediate group is very mixed, and is less favourable today than it appeared in 1980.

Probably most of the countries in the late-comer group are in the most solvent position (because of relatively new pension programmes, young populations, and low life expectancy); their problem is how to extend coverage beyond a tenth of the total population and a fifth of the economically active population. Nevertheless, their social-insurance systems basically follow the model of the pioneer countries, with the shortcomings described, so that probably they will eventually face similar problems. These countries, however, have more time to change the current model for one which can extend coverage on a more solid financial base. The social-insurance systems in the three non-Latin Caribbean countries also had a substantial surplus at least until 1986, although their situation is not as good with regard to actuarial equilibrium. These countries come close to universal coverage but their pension programmes are very new and health care is not covered by social insurance (Mesa-Lago 1987: 493–5).

The severe economic crisis which has hit the region since the beginning of the present decade has aggravated the financial situation of social security in the pioneer countries but, in addition, it has had repercussions in other countries. The increase in unemployment and the enlargement of the informal sector, the reduction in real wages, and the collapse of firms have led to a drop in social insurance revenue; the pressure of external debt and other urgent domestic needs has obliged many governments to reduce or postpone their contributions even further (in Costa Rica, Ecuador, and Peru, State debt has reached at some points alarming proportions); further, galloping inflation has accentuated the existing tendency to evade and delay payment and has contributed to lower real yields of investment. In addition, in those countries where coverage is almost univeral, many older insured persons (contributors) who have now retired are receiving health care as poor persons (while health costs remain at the same level) or have taken early retirement, and extremely high inflation has made it essential to adjust pensions to some extent in order to avoid their losing all their real value.

---

[15] Mesa-Lago (1985b: chaps. 5, 6), and De Geyndt and Mesa-Lago (1987).

5.3 *The Financial Techniques of the Schemes*

Because of financial disequilibrium, the region—following a universal trend—has been experimenting with a gradual change in the technical method of financing, abandoning full funding and replacing it by other intermediate systems of partial funding and, in some cases, adopting the pure assessment (pay-as-you-go) method. There are three basic financial techniques; the function of all of them is to balance the income and expenditure of the scheme, but over different periods which range from infinity down to one year: the longer the period of equilibrium, the greater the reserves needed.[16] The programmes covering short-term risks (sickness-maternity, family allowances, unemployment) generally use the simple 'pay-as-you-go' system, under which the period of equilibrium is one year and the reserve is simply to meeting contingencies and statistical variations; in many countries, however, this reserve is insufficient to meet the expenditure. Initially, almost all the pension schemes in Latin America adopted the method of full funding or general level premium. This method aims to maintain equilibrium for an indefinite period (or at least for several decades) by a fixed premium which is calculated actuarially on the basis of estimates of future liabilities (which take into account demographic, economic, and other variables). But this method requires that the benefits are not increased without an immediate adjustment in revenue, that the planned revenue be received in full and on time, that the reserve fund be administered efficiently, and that periodic actuarial valuations be carried out. In practice, political pressures, the lack of administrative control, inflation and rising life expectancy lead to a situation where these requirements cannot be met, thus forcing abandonment of this method of funding. Some countries then adopted the method of funding with a scaled premium and only partial reserves, in which the equilibrium is maintained for shorter periods (for example, a decade), with a premium being established at a fixed rate for each period, but normally being increased in successive periods. This method defers the costs, so that there is a redistribution between generations. It depends absolutely on frequent actuarial valuations and adjustment of the premium for each period in the light of these. But legal inflexibility (in some countries, the contribution is fixed by law) and political opposition, resulting from trade-union and employer pressures, are major obstacles in the way of making such adjustments. In practice, some countries fixed only the initial premium and did not specify the duration of the periods to be covered, they failed to carry out the actuarial valuations, and they did not adjust the premiums. The scaled average premium was in some cases replaced *de facto* or *de jure* by the method of pay-as-you-go. But this method, which is based on very short periods, requires even more flexibility in increasing income more frequently which, naturally, is more

---

[16] See Thullen (1985), and ISSA (1979).

difficult to achieve. A recent survey in this area carried out by the Inter-American Development Bank (IADB) concludes as follows:

The persistence of deficits is the [situation] generally faced by the social security programmes in Latin America financed by the simple pay-as-you-go method, as confirmed in the annual reports and balance sheets of the administering institutions, as well as by numerous studies both national and international; and this is also confirmed by the results of the survey in the countries in our sample.[17]

Among the pioneer countries, Argentina, Chile (in the old system which still applies to a third of the insured persons), Uruguay, Cuba, and Brazil use pay-as-you-go methods either officially or in practice, with resulting deficits. Once they are no longer able to replace one method of financing by another which postpones the financial costs arising from the system, a number of these countries have to face a serious financial imbalance, aggravated even further by the over-all economic crisis in the region. The country in the worst situation is Uruguay, which in 1983 had a demographic burden ratio of 0.8, in other words, approximately one active insured had to finance one passive person (in contrast, the actuarial calculations of the United States project that, at the beginning of the twenty-first century, the ratio will be two active persons financing one non-working person). If these countries were unable to achieve financial and actuarial balance when the demographic burden ratio was much lower, they will be less able to do so in the future when the ratio will be much higher. To cope with this situation it is necessary to carry out a general reform of the social-security system and some of the countries in the region have already introduced reforms based on widely differing models.

6. BENEFITS, OTHER EXPENDITURE, AND TOTAL COSTS

6.1. *Benefits and their Inequalities*

Most of the expenditure of social security (from 76 to 97 per cent) is on benefits. Information from the ILO on the distribution of expenditure by programme indicates that the pioneer countries spend a greater proportion on pensions (and family allowances), whilst the countries where social insurance appeared at a late stage spend the largest proportion on the sickness-maternity programme. In 1980, in most of the Latin American countries, more than half the expenditure of social security was on health, and in five countries the proportion was as high as two-thirds. This is partly the result of the demographic changes and the fact that the pension schemes are now maturing. In the non-Latin Caribbean, the percentage spent on pensions is relatively small because of the newness of this programme. Until 1977, public health appeared

[17] Arroba *et al.* (1980: 49). See also (p. 202) the comparison of the technical financing methods of 7 countries, which supports the analysis of this section.

to have the highest percentage of social-security expenditures in these countries, but thereafter data on public health expenditures were deleted in the ILO series. In Bahamas and Barbados, public assistance is paid by social insurance and, since 1978 (because of the deletion of public health expenditures in the ILO series) welfare appears to have the highest percentage of social-security expenditures (ILO 1980, 1985).

The pioneer countries tend to cover all the social risks and to provide a greater number of benefits and more liberal ones. Argentina, Brazil, Chile, and Uruguay are the only countries which cover all risks, including unemployment and family allowances (Cuba does not include these last two schemes). A study of five countries (Argentina, Chile, Mexico, Peru, and Uruguay) based on information from the beginning of the 1970s demonstrated that the older the social-security system, the greater the number of benefits provided. The old systems have granted exceptional and costly benefits such as the long-service or seniority pension (which entitles the insured to retire at any age after a certain number of years at work, thus allowing some people to retire at the age of 45) and the old-age pension with relatively low retirement ages (because they were established by law at a time when the life expectancy was considerably less than now). In these countries, entitlement conditions for health benefits also tend to be more generous: for example, no qualifying period is required, or it is limited to a few weeks' contributions; a sickness and/or maternity allowance is paid at the same rate as the wage (or very close to it) and sometimes additional benefits are offered such as orthodontics and contact lenses. In these countries, too, there are many so-called 'social benefits' such as housing plans, personal and mortgage loans, purchasing facilities, and other recreational, sporting, and cultural services for insured persons and their dependants.

The stratification of social security typical of the pioneer countries (at least until they introduced procedures to unify and standardize their systems) led to considerable inequalities in the benefits because the most powerful groups received more and better benefits than the least powerful. In the study of five countries already mentioned, the legal differences between the occupational groups covered were measured on the basis of six criteria: entitlement conditions; base salary used to compute benefits; amount of benefit; pension cost-of-living adjustment; possibility of obtaining several pensions or combining one pension with a paid job; and time required to process and receive the benefit. The study also compared the availability of health services (hospital beds and doctors per insured person) and their quality for the various groups. The occupational groups were ranked on the following order, from most to least privileged: (1) armed forces, (2) civil servants, (3) the 'labour aristocracy', (4) private white-collar employees, and (5) blue-collar workers.

In the Latin American countries where social security appeared late, the principal inequality in benefits is the result of the lower level of coverage: a minority of the population is covered by a number of different benefits—

vertical extension—whilst the majority who are not covered can use only the public health and social-assistance services, which generally receive a small proportion of the available resources. The non-Latin Caribbean countries appear to have much less inequality in benefits because they have universal coverage combined with unified programmes; however civil servants usually enjoy better pensions than the rest of the insured.[18]

6.2. *Administrative Costs*

The administrative costs of social security are much higher in LAC than in the developed countries of North America, Europe, and Asia where they vary between 2 and 3 per cent of total expenditure. According to the first column of Table 8.6, in 1980 the LAC percentages ranged as follows: from 4 to 6.9 per cent in Argentina, Barbados, Panama, and Costa Rica; from 7 to 10.9 per cent in Chile, Uruguay, and Jamaica; from 11 to 14.9 per cent in Peru, Nicaragua, Guatemala, Brazil, Colombia, Trinidad and Tobago, El Salvador, and Venezuela; and from 15 to 27 per cent in Ecuador, Bolivia, Mexico, and Dominican Republic. With very few exceptions the administrative percentages increased from 1977 to 1980. In those countries where social insurance was introduced recently (as in the non-Latin Caribbean) the high percentage of administrative expenditures is partly explained by the need of minimum personnel, equipment, and physical plant to operate the system, combined with low initial benefit expenditures (particularly on pensions); as the latter increase the proportional cost of operation is gradually reduced.

Personnel takes the bulk of expenditures within administrative costs and its importance in each LAC country is measured in the second column of Table 8.6 by the number of employees per 1,000 insured. The enormous social insurance bureaucracy in the Dominican Republic, El Salvador, Ecuador and Mexico largely explains the high administrative costs in these four countries. The ratios of Jamaica and Barbados are much lower than that of Bahamas (all three are 'late-comers'), explaining the highest administrative costs in the latter.

6.3. *The Growing Cost of Social Security*

The cost of social security in LAC is growing. According to ILO data comparable for fifteen Latin American countries, social-security expenditures as a percentage of GDP increased between 1965 and 1977 in ten countries and declined in five. The highest percentages for the region in 1977 were equal to that in Japan and approximated that of the United States; in 1971 Chile reached 17.2 per cent, only surpassed by some developed European countries.

---

[18] See Mesa-Lago (1978, 1987).

Table 8.6. Indicators of administrative efficiency of social insurance in Latin America and the Caribbean between 1980 and 1985

Countries[a]	% of administrative expenses over total expenditures (1980)	Employees per 1,000 insured (1980–6)
Argentina	4.4	n.a.
Bahamas	21.8[b]	3.8[b]
Barbados	5.0[b]	2.4[c]
Bolivia	19.3	6.7[d]
Brazil	12.1[e]	n.a.
Chile	7.5	n.a.
Colombia	12.4	7.4[b]
Costa Rica	6.9	10.5[b]
Dominican Republic	27.0[c]	20.5[b]
Ecuador	17.4[d]	13.2[d]
El Salvador	14.0	13.5[f]
Guatemala	11.7	7.1[f]
Jamaica	10.4[b]	0.6[c]
Mexico	19.5[g]	7.5–10.4[h]
Nicaragua	11.6	4.5[d]
Panama	5.4	11.7[i]
Peru	11.5[j]	8.1[i]
Trinidad and Tobago	13.6	n.a.
Uruguay	7.7	n.a.
Venezuela	14.0	4.1[f]

[a] No data are available for Cuba, Haiti, Honduras, and Paraguay.
[b] Figures for 1985.
[c] Figures for 1986.
[d] Figures for 1982.
[e] Figure for 1977.
[f] Figures for 1980.
[g] Figure for 1983, in major institution only (IMSS).
[h] Figures for 1982, in two major institutions.
[i] Figures for 1984.
[j] Figure for 1981, excludes personnel expenditure.

Source: Mesa-Lago (1989: table 21).

ILO data for 1980 are available for only twelve Latin American countries and indicate a declining trend: increases in the percentages of three countries, stagnation in one, and decreases in eight (see Table 8.7). I have argued elsewhere that methodological changes in the ILO series may be responsible

Table 8.7. Social-security expenditures as a percentage of GDP in Latin America (ILO Series): 1965, 1977, 1980

Countries	Social-security expenditures as % of GDP		
	1965	1977	1980
Argentina	3.2	7.3[a]	9.4
Bolivia	3.6[b]	3.1[c]	2.7
Brazil	4.3	6.2	–
Chile[d]	12.2	10.1	10.6
Colombia	1.1	3.7	2.8
Costa Rica	2.3	5.8	7.0
Ecuador	2.9	3.0[e]	3.0
El Salvador	2.2	2.9	1.6
Guatemala	2.0	1.6	1.2
Haiti	–	0.8	–
Mexico	2.6	3.4[e]	–
Nicaragua	2.1	2.3	–
Panama	6.0	7.9	6.2
Peru	2.9	–	–
Dominican Republic	2.7[f]	2.5	2.0
Uruguay	14.5[g]	10.3	8.0
Venezuela	3.1	4.1	1.3

[a] Figure for 1975.
[b] Figure for 1961.
[c] Figure for 1976.
[d] In 1971 the percentage reached the record level of 17.2.
[e] Figure for 1977.
[f] Figure for 1970.
[g] Figure for 1969.
Sources: ILO (1978, 1981, 1985).

for the apparent decline, and I have estimated higher percentages for 1980 than those of the ILO for several countries (see Table 8.1).[19]

Table 8.7 does not reproduce ILO data for Barbados, Jamaica, Guyana, and Trinidad and Tobago on social-security expenditures as a percentage of GDP. The reason is that, since 1978, medical-care expenditures of public health (which by 1977 took at least two-thirds of total social-security expenditures) were deleted from the ILO series. As a result, the percentage of social-security expenditures over GDP declined by about 60 per cent in 1978 *vis-à-vis* 1977 in most of those countries. In 1980 the ILO figures for Barbados and Jamaica were respectively 2.3 and 1.4 per cent but, adding public health expenditures

[19] See ILO (1981, 1985) and Mesa-Lago (1986).

(as officially reported by those countries to ILO), the proportions rose to 5.5 and 4 per cent indicating an increasing trend in 1965–80 rather than a decline.[20]

The Latin American pioneer countries, which have the oldest programmes, broadest coverage, and most liberal benefits, have the highest percentages of social insurance/security expenditures to GDP. Conversely the 'late-comer' countries of Latin America, which have the newest programmes, smallest coverage, and usually less liberal benefits, have the lowest percentages. According to Table 8.1, the percentages of social-security expenditures over GDP in 1980 ranged: in the pioneer group from 9 to 11 per cent (except Brazil with 5 per cent); in the intermediate group from 2 to 4 per cent (except Panama with 7 per cent); and in the late-comer group from 1 to 2 per cent (except Honduras with 3 per cent). The non-Latin Caribbean countries have broad coverage (as in the countries of the pioneer group) but their programmes are the newest in the region (newer than in most of the countries of the late-comer group). Based on the ILO series (which underestimate costs) these Caribbean countries could be placed within the late-comer group. And yet my adjusted figures for Barbados and Jamaica place these two countries at the top of the intermediate group, close to the percentage of Brazil.

6.4. *The Cost of Reaching Universal Coverage*

The cost of extending social-insurance coverage to all the population in Latin America with the current Bismarckian model would not be economically viable in many countries (even if they were able to overcome structural barriers). Table 8.8 shows how social-insurance expenditures over GDP would increase if coverage were granted to the whole population with the current model.[21] The estimates in the third column of Table 8.8 were roughly obtained by extrapolating the expenditures for a 100 per cent coverage assuming that such expenditures would increase proportionally with coverage.

While linear extrapolation of current costs and coverage may be useful to establish broad orders of magnitude for the costs of universal coverage in the concerned countries, this may not be an accurate portrayal for a number of reasons. First, it is difficult to establish the effects of joint provisions, such as health care and pensions, as opposed to either of these in isolation. Intercountry comparisons are also difficult since different countries have varying coverage for various programmes. Further, there are two factors which might increase costs of universal provision beyond that implied by linear extrapolation: (i) the

---

[20] Based on ILO (1981, 1985) and Mesa-Lago (1988).

[21] I use social-insurance expenditure in Table 8.8 rather than all social-security expenditures as in Table 8.1, because the former are more statistically precise and better correspond with the social-insurance-covered population, thus excluding the population protected by public-health programmes. The difficulties of statistical estimation of coverage, mentioned earlier, must of course be borne in mind in interpreting the data presented in Table 8.8 for specific countries.

Table 8.8. Social-insurance expenditure as a percentage of GDP, in 1980, and extrapolated on the base of universal coverage, in Latin America and the Caribbean

Countries	% social-insurance expenditures/GDP (1980)[a]	% of total population covered (1980)[a]	Extrapolation of % of social-insurance expenditures over GDP when 100% of population is covered
Argentina	11.9	78.9	15.1
Bahamas	0.7	85.3[b]	0.8
Barbados	1.0	79.8[b]	1.2
Bolivia	2.9	25.4	11.4
Brazil	5.2	96.3	5.4
Chile	11.0	67.3	16.3
Colombia	2.8	15.2	18.4
Costa Rica	7.5	81.5	9.2
Cuba	8.6	100.0[c]	8.6
Dominican Rep.	0.7	5.9[d]	11.9
Ecuador	3.7	9.4	39.4
El Salvador	1.3	6.2	21.0
Guatemala	1.6	14.2	11.3
Honduras	0.9	7.3	12.3
Jamaica	0.4	80.9[b]	0.5
Mexico	2.9	53.4	5.4
Nicaragua	2.3	9.1	25.3
Panama	6.1	49.9	12.2
Paraguay	1.2	18.2	6.6
Peru	2.6	16.6	15.7
Uruguay	8.1	68.5	11.8
Venezuela	1.3	45.2	2.9

[a] Data for Argentina, Colombia, Costa Rica, Dominican Republic, and Ecuador have been updated and are not always the same as in Table 8.1.

[b] Economically active population covered by monetary benefits, the total population is legally covered on health care by public health.

[c] Legal coverage.

[d] Figure for 1985.

Sources: Same as Table 8.3.

non-covered population is poor and has a lower health status than the covered population, thus it probably suffers from a higher incidence of sickness and cannot afford private medicine, and hence it might use social-insurance/security services more; and (ii) administrative costs to cover the informal and rural sectors might be higher than for the covered formal sector because of difficulties in detecting, controlling, and collecting from the former. On the other hand, the non-covered population probably has a lower life expectancy than the covered population and hence pension costs of the former could be lower. Finally, in the less developed countries where current coverage is low, most social-insurance expenditures go to sickness-maternity care rather than pensions, hence the net outcome might be higher costs than the simple extrapolation of Table 8.8 suggests.

In spite of these limitations of the exercise, it clearly emerges from Table 8.8 that extension of formal coverage in the region (particularly in the less developed countries) cannot be attained with the present levels of benefit and the current administrative structure, as the financial burden is likely to be excessive (as has happened in some of the 'pioneer' countries). Obviously one cannot simultaneously have universality, an excessively generous package of benefits, and very high administrative costs. As we have already said in the sections on coverage and financing, the area of benefits also calls for an overall reform, which must be integrated with the other two aspects of the problem.

7. CONCLUSIONS

This chapter makes it clear that the Bismarckian model of social insurance is not suitable for most of Latin America, particularly for the less developed countries. A few countries in that region, the most developed, have been able to achieve universal coverage (or are close to that goal), but at a very high economic cost and in most cases without significantly correcting inequalities in coverage, financing, and benefits. The social-insurance systems of these countries have faced (or currently suffer) serious financial and actuarial disequilibria and the State is no longer capable of subsidizing the deficit, particularly under the current economic crisis.

This situation has prompted reforms of the Bismarckian model. The two most radical reforms have been full statization in Cuba (but without solving the problem of escalating costs) and partial but increasing privatization in Chile (developing a new solvent system but with an enormous increase in the cost of the old system). More moderate reforms have been introduced in Brazil and Costa Rica by extending coverage to rural, urban marginal, and/or the indigent population either with equal treatment of the insured or with a dual system of benefits. Minor reforms applied in Argentina and Uruguay have not been able to correct the previous situation and these two countries are urgently searching for solutions.

The non-Latin Caribbean countries are the latest late-comers in the region but some of them have been able to extend rapidly coverage to almost all of the population. Because of the newness of their pension programmes (and in some cases a more efficient investment of their funds, as in Bahamas) and the establishment of health care outside social insurance, these systems are among the most solvent of the region at least for the time being.

Latin American countries at an intermediate level of development of their social-security systems cover less than half of their population and appear to be in better financial shape. A few of these countries were able to extend population coverage rapidly in the 1970s (for example, Panama, Mexico, Venezuela) by covering part of the rural sector, or partly integrating health services, or aided by the oil boom. The crisis of the 1980s seems to have paralysed or slowed down these advances and some of these countries have begun to experience the disequilibria typical of the most developed countries in Latin America.

The least developed countries typically cover less than one-fifth of their populations and, at least until 1980, enjoyed financial stability. But the extension of coverage is limited by both structural barriers and the economic crisis; furthermore the latter has contributed to a deterioration in the financial situation of some of these systems. Finally, if these countries continue in the same path as the pioneer ones they probably will face the same fate.

The prolonged economic crisis of the current decade has precipitated a latent crisis of social security. Revenues have often declined due to an increase in unemployment, informal employment, employers' evasion, and the State debt, as well as a decrease in real yields of investment and real wages. Real pensions have declined and health services have deteriorated in many countries. At least the crisis has prompted some countries to introduce reforms to curtail unnecessary expenses and excessively generous benefits, and to improve efficiency in administrative and health services. The crisis has also alerted international financial organizations to the crucial economic importance of social security (moving them to include the latter in technical missions and studies) and promoted collaboration among some of them, for example, between the ILO and WHO.

In spite of all these changes, the most crucial dilemma of social security in Latin America and the Caribbean remains unsolved: how to achieve universal coverage with a financially viable and socially equitable system.[22]

---

[22] See the final sections on policies in Mesa-Lago (1985b, 1989).

References

Arroba, G. (1979), 'The Financing of Social Security in Latin America', in ISSA (1979).

—— Moles, R., et al. (1980), *El Impuesto al Valor Agregado en el Financiamiento de la Seguridad Social y el Proceso de Integración Latinoamericano*, i. Washington, DC: IADB/INTAL.

Borzutzky, S. (1985), 'Politics and Social Security Reform', in Mesa-Lago (1985a).

Cruz-Saco, M. A., Mesa-Lago, C., and Zamalloa, L. (1987), 'Determinants of Social Insurance/Security Costs and Coverage: An International Comparison with a Focus on Latin America', mimeo, Department of Economics, University of Pittsburgh.

De Geyndt, W., and Mesa-Lago, C. (1987), *Colombia: Social Security Review*. Washington, DC: World Bank.

ECLAC (Economic Commission for Latin America and the Caribbean) (1987), *Preliminary Overview of the Latin American Economy 1987*. Santiago: ECLAC.

IADB (Inter-American Development Bank) (1988), *Economic and Social Progress in Latin America: 1987 Report*. Washington DC: IADB.

ILO (International Labour Office) (1978), *The Cost of Social Security 1972–1974*. Geneva: ILO.

—— (1981), *The Cost of Social Security 1975–1977*. Geneva: ILO.

—— (1985), *The Cost of Social Security 1978–1980*. Geneva: ILO.

ISSA (International Social Security Association) (1979), *Methods of Financing Social Security: Their Economic and Social Effects*, Studies and Research No. 15, ISSA, Geneva.

Isuani, E. A. (1985), 'Social Security and Public Assistance' in Mesa-Lago (1985a).

León, F. (1985), 'Comment', in Mesa-Lago (1985a).

Malloy, J. (1979), *The Politics of Social Security in Brazil*. Pittsburgh: University of Pittsburgh Press.

Mesa-Lago, C. (1978), *Social Security in Latin America: Pressure Groups, Stratification and Inequality*. Pittsburgh: University of Pittsburgh Press.

—— (1983), 'Social Security and Extreme Poverty in Latin America', *Journal of Development Economics*, 12.

—— (1984), 'Social Security in Ecuador', mimeo, World Bank, Washington, DC.

—— (ed.), (1985a), *The Crisis of Social Security and Health Care: Latin American Experiences and Lessons*, Latin American Monograph and Document Series No. 9, Center for Latin American Studies, University of Pittsburgh.

—— (1985b), *El Desarrollo de la Seguridad Social en América Latina*, Estudios e Informes de la CEPAL, No. 43, Santiago.

—— (1986), 'Comparative Study of the Development of Social Security in Latin America', *International Society Security Review*, 39.

—— (1987), 'Social Security in Bahamas, Barbados and Jamaica: A Report for the ILO', mimeo, ILO, Geneva.

—— (1988), 'Social Insurance: The Experience of Three Countries in the English-Speaking Caribbean', *International Labour Review*, 127.

—— (1989), 'Financiamiento de la Atención de la Salud en América Latina y el Caribe con Focalización en el Seguro Social', mimeo, Economic Development Institute, World Bank, Washington, DC.

Oficina Nacional del Censo (1984), *Censo de Población y Viviendas 1981, República de Cuba*, xvi. Havana.

PREALC (1981), *Dinámica del Subempleo en América Latina*, Estudios e Informes de la CEPAL, No. 10, Santiago.

Rosenberg, M. (1980), *Las Luchas por el Seguro Social en Costa Rica*. San José: Editorial Costa Rica.

Thullen, P. (1985), 'Social Security Financing: Principles, Current Issues and Trends', in Mesa-Lago (1985a).

Tokman, V. (1986), 'Adjustment and Employment in Latin America', *International Labour Review*, 125.

US Social Security Administration (1985), *Social Security Programs throughout the World 1985*. Washington, DC: GPO.

9

Social Security in Sub-Saharan Africa: Reflections on Policy Challenges*

Joachim von Braun

1. INTRODUCTION

Exceptionally high insecurity of livelihood continues to plague the great majority of sub-Saharan Africa's population. In contrast with Asia and Latin America, famines have continued to exist in Africa during the 1980s. Food shortage, health, and sanitation constraints pose risks to livelihood for a large share of the rural and urban population. Low levels of income, lack of physical and social infrastructure, and limited administrative capacities, including the human capital required for them, inhibit implementation of social-security systems that protect effectively against falling into absolute poverty, disability, or sickness.

1.1. *Arguments for 'Social Security with Growth'*

It seems straightforward to start with the premiss that social security in sub-Saharan Africa can only be achieved as a consequence of, and after, economic growth. At least two reasons, however, argue against a 'growth *before* social security perspective'. First, economic growth in sub-Saharan Africa must, to a large extent, result from agricultural growth, with an increase in labour productivity. Increased labour productivity in agriculture is inseparable from improved production technology (capital) and nutritional well-being and health (Kumar 1987). The need for nutritional and health improvement argues for 'social security *with* growth'. Secondly, Africa must achieve a swift 'demographic transition' from its present regime of high mortality and fertility rates (with a high rate of population growth) to a regime of considerably lower mortality and fertility rates (with slower population growth). Improved social security is likely to make a substantial contribution to this objective by (1) reducing mortality rates; (2) reducing the number of births needed in a family to ensure a given number of surviving children; and (3) reducing the demand for surviving children. Some of these effects may, of course, require relatively long adjustment periods.

* Helpful comments by Jean Drèze, Ehtisham Ahmad, and Michael Lipton on earlier drafts are gratefully acknowledged. Graciela Wiegand-Jahn provided valuable research assistance for this chapter.

1.2. *The Challenge to Combine State-Based and Community-Based Systems*

In Africa, social security is increasingly thought of in terms of pension funds, medical insurance, and disability insurance schemes. Substantial elements of social-security systems of the European type exist in most African countries, though they are mainly limited to the formal employment sector (Mouton 1975). Most of these schemes evolved in the 1960s and 1970s. International agencies played an important role in setting them up.[1]

The formal elements of social-security provision may form important building blocks of social-security systems in the long run, but for a considerable time to come, social-security policy in sub-Saharan Africa will have to concentrate on the basic needs of food and health. Food security policy and health and sanitation policy are, therefore, cornerstones for social-security policy. This chapter deals with these in a broad social-security agenda.

Existing formal social-security systems in Africa tend to be urban-biased and to serve the privileged rather than the poor (Mouton 1975). Broader approaches to social security, however, have a part to play in development and actually do already play a significant role. Yet, in most instances they are, at this stage, not State-based, but rather community- and family-based systems. A broad perspective is needed, not only for instruments and types of interventions for social security, but also for institutional and organizational modes of social-security provision. We shall therefore be addressing the roles of State-based social-security systems and community-based systems, viewing family-based systems as a subset of the latter, and examine interaction between the two.

1.3. *Choice of Development Strategy and Demand for Social Security*

In the process of modernizing and diversifying the economy, optimal structures and sizes of insurance systems will change. Community-based systems may lose some of their advantages and new functions for State-based social security will emerge.[2] To identify and design appropriate systems for the appropriate phases of economic development in the very heterogeneous regional, cultural, and geographical settings of sub-Saharan Africa is a challenge for the decades ahead.

One of the critical policy questions for a long-term strategy is the identification of appropriate roles for State action versus community-based social-security systems. These roles will change in the development process and the nature of

---

[1] A record of this process, and of the important role that International Labour Organization played in it, can be found in ISSA (1985) and earlier volumes of similar conferences.

[2] An example of this is the account by Duncan Clarke (1977) for Rhodesia (Zimbabwe). The respective roles of community-based and State-based security systems are discussed in Torry (1987), and in Chap. 4.

change will depend to a great extent upon the development strategy. An urban-biased, industrialization-promoting strategy will create a rapidly expanding role for State action in the field of formal social security. An agricultural-based development strategy expands rural employment and can generate the resources for rural community-based social-security systems.[3] A strategic issue remains to combine these community-based systems creatively with State-based systems in the long run, when scale economies and structures of demand for social security change in favour of the latter.

Given the severity of resource constraints in Africa, it is important to establish the economic costs and benefits of alternative systems (community-based and State-based) and system mixes. Only if the costs of alternative systems providing specified social-security benefits are known can a cost-effective perspective for social-security policy be established. Very little is known about the costs and social returns of State-based social-security systems in developing countries, and even less about community-based systems. The latter also change quite rapidly in the course of economic development. Community-based social-security systems in Africa need to be seen as an asset on which improved social security may be built in the long term. The stock of institutional capital needs to be evaluated in the appropriate regional and temporal context in order to make creative use of it in changing social, cultural, and economic development.

This chapter does not provide a comprehensive description or account of the scale and nature of the lack of social security in sub-Saharan Africa. Its objective is rather to raise some fundamental issues related to current structures of and long-term strategies for social security in the region, particularly the changing roles of State action and community support in social security provision. For this task, lessons will be drawn from the contrasting developments of social-security policy in different countries at the aggregate level (Section 2) and from contrasting micro-level insights into the strengths and weaknesses of community-based social-security provision in a specific land-rich setting in West Africa as against a land-scarce setting in Central Africa (Section 3).

2. STATE-BASED SOCIAL-SECURITY PROVISION

Taking a broad definition, the sub-Saharan African countries spent about 10.7 per cent of central government budgets on social security in the mid 1980s.[4] This puts sub-Saharan Africa at the average of low-income economies as

---

[3] On the employment effects of choice of development strategy, see Mellor (1976).

[4] Including spending for health, housing amenities, social insurance, and welfare. Based on a narrower definition, Mouton (1975) estimates that State-based social-security schemes in Africa represented about 1–2% of GDP and about 5% of State budgets in the 1970s.

Table 9.1. Government spending on social security and services in sub-Saharan Africa
in comparison with other groups of countries, 1985

	Government spending on social security as % of government budget
Sub-Saharan Africa	10.7
Low-income economies	10.9
Lower middle-income economies	13.6
Upper middle-income economies	23.6
Industrial market economies	46.9

Sources: World Bank (1987, 1988).

defined by World Bank classifications (Table 9.1). As can be seen from the
table, the relative share of public spending on social security tends to increase
drastically only when economies reach the upper middle-income level where
spending reaches about a quarter of government expenditures. Very limited
information exists on what share of these expenditures actually reaches the
absolute poor.

2.1. *Growth and Public Spending on Social Security*

A strong relationship between income (GNP per capita) and State-level social-
security expenditure, however, also exists among the African countries. In
fact, this relationship appears to be exponential: dollars spent on social security
increase more than proportionately with dollars of per capita GNP (Fig. 1).
This impression is further supported by a regression exercise which suggests
an exponential growth of State social-security expenditures in association with
economic growth (Table 9.2, column 1). The regression results suggest that
GNP growth (in US$ equivalents) from $300 to $600 per capita may increase
public spending on social security by $16 from $4 to $20 per capita,
and a further $300 increase fromn $600 to $900 per capita may expand
social-security spending by an incremental $25 per capita per annum. The
responsiveness of social-security expenditure to GNP is even greater in non-
African developing countries. On the basis of the parameter estimates from the
non-African developing countries, an increase of GNP per capita from $300 to
$600 meant an increment of social-security expenditures by $25 and from $600
to $900, by $35 (based on Table 9.2, column 2).

Hardly any developing country has failed to combine growth with a massive
expansion of public-sector spending on social security. It is very unlikely that

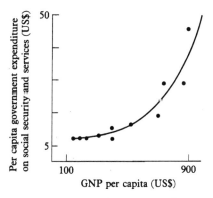

Fig. 9.1. GNP per capita and public expenditure on social security and services in sub-Saharan Africa, 1985.

Source: As Table 9.1.

Table 9.2 Regression analysis of the relationships between GNP per capita and public expenditure on social security, 1985–1986[a]

Exogenous Variables	Africa[b]	Other developing countries[c]
GNP per capita	0.1339	0.1597
	(4.34)	(3.27)
ln GNP per capita	−35.057	−31.638
	(−2.74)	(−0.894)
Constant	163.446	135.681
R^2	0.822	0.656
F	28.8	45.3
Degrees of freedom	10	22

[a] Dependent variable is US$ per capita of central government expenditure on social security. For definition, see Table 9.1.
[b] Selection of countries for this analysis was dictated by constraints of data availability. For sub-Saharan Africa, it includes Botswana, Burkina Faso, Cameroon, Côte d'Ivoire, Ghana, Kenya, Lesotho, Liberia, Malawi, Sierra Leone, Tanzania, Togo, Zimbabwe.
[c] The 'other developing countries' sample includes Egypt, Turkey, Morocco, Tunisia, Jordan, Republic of Korea, Papua New Guinea, India, Bangladesh, Nepal, Burma, Pakistan, Sri Lanka, Indonesia, Philippines, Thailand, Haiti, Bolivia, Dominican Republic, Paraguay, Ecuador, Costa Rica, Uruguay, Brazil, El Salvador, Mexico.

this will be different in sub-Saharan Africa. The policy question is then less one of levels of social-security expenditures in the long run, but rather one of setting priorities within social-security spending in the process of economic development, especially at low levels of per capita income. Priorities can, of course, range over a large number of issues, but increasing life expectancy at birth will certainly rank high in any circumstances. Decreased rates of infant mortality, as a key determinant of life expectancy, are closely related to economic growth and the expansion of social-security expenditures in developing countries in general (Fig. 9.2.i). A few outliers exist and are widely recognized, such as in Sri Lanka, China, and the state of Kerala in India. They suggest that at low-income levels, a clear-cut trade-off does not necessarily exist between social security and economic growth, and that sustained public action in the context of low national income can reduce mortality quite rapidly and sustainably.[5] Such outliers hardly exist in sub-Saharan Africa (Fig. 2.ii). Nevertheless, the general association between economic growth, social-security expenditures, and reduced infant mortality is also evident in sub-Saharan Africa.

A few lessons can be drawn from this broad-based comparison of social-security spending across developing countries and in Africa.

(1) Revitalized growth in sub-Saharan Africa will lead to a rapid expansion of State-based social-security systems; strategies for guiding this expansion are needed.

(2) Given the low base of economic wealth in sub-Saharan Africa, an extraordinarily rapid growth process would be required to achieve the desired rapid improvement in social security in the foreseeable future along standard patterns of growth in the developing world.

(3) The critical policy issue remains to direct the expansion of social-security spending towards the truly needy, namely, the food and health insecure.

Public action has to get ahead of economic growth for social security. Learning from the outliers of Asia and emulating their social-security achievements in the African context by utilizing the stock of community-based institutions (rather than 'copying' the Asian and Latin American outliers' experiences) appears to be of critical relevance.

2.2. *Food Security and Famine Prevention as Basic Elements of Social Security*

With the given resource constraints, public action for social security in sub-Saharan Africa can have only a limited set of priorities, including primarily the improvement of nutrition and health. Public action to improve on food security—that is, the ability of all people in a country actually to acquire sufficient food for an active and healthy living—is at the core of social-security

---

[5] For further discussion of the experiences of China, Kerala and Sri Lanka, see Chaps. 7 and 6 respectively, above.

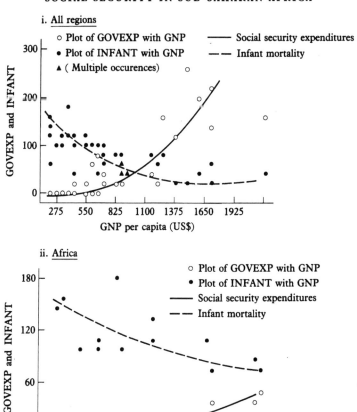

Fig. 9.2.   State social-security expenditures in developing countries, income level, and infant mortality, 1985–1986.

Notes: The vertical axes represent government expenditure per capita on social security (GOVEXP) in US$ and infant mortality in deaths per 1,000 born (INFANT).

policy. The relevance of food security within a broad social-security pro-gramme increases with poverty. It also increases in environments with extremely deficient infrastructures, such as Sudan, or with excessive policy failures, such as Ethiopia in the 1980s. Investment in rural infrastructure and policy reform for the stimulation of agricultural growth are a high priority for social security in these settings.

Unlike in some Asian and many Latin American environments, the relationships between domestic food production, regional and local food availability, and household-level food security remain close in the famine-prone countries of sub-Saharan Africa.[6] This suggests a different set of priorities under these circumstances—priorities related to increased levels and reduced instability of domestic food production, and priorities related to infrastructure for improved market integration (not only food market integration but integration of labour and capital markets as well). Furthermore, famine mortality in Africa is closely associated with health and sanitation constraints and with the limitations of related delivery systems, which again arise partly from deficiencies in infrastructure.

Employment generation is a key requirement for the expansion of access to food for famine prevention. The lack of availability of food in famine-prone areas has often resulted in drastic price increases, which limit the impact of income transfer-related programmes that do not provide for a simultaneous expansion of food availability. This problem—short-term explosive food price inflation—is highlighted by dramatically deteriorating domestic terms of trade between livestock and staple foods, or between cash crops and staple foods, during famines, sometimes amplified by policies disrupting domestic trading. These large changes in terms of trade in domestic markets undermine the purchasing power of those who depend on net purchases of food for their survival. For example in Kordofan (Sudan), the cereal–livestock terms of trade increased from 1 : 1 to 1 : 8 during the 1984/5 famine in disfavour of livestock.[7] This change, which meant a sharp reduction of purchasing power for some groups (especially pastoralists), contributed to an instantaneous translation of food shortage into increased prevalence of severe malnutrition among pre-school children (Fig. 9.3).

Clearly, social security in its basic sense continues to relate closely to prices and their stability. Price instability, in this environment of deficient infrastructure, is largely a result of production instability. Along with employment and income transfer programmes, the food production and supply side of famine prevention requires particular emphasis in the African context of thin and fragile markets. Decentralized (self-targeting) public works are so far limited in sub-Saharan Africa, but some positive examples[8] suggest that this may be more due to lack of programme and policy focus and weak local

[6] On famines in Asia, see Sen (1981); Drèze (1988); Drèze and Sen (1989), and the large body of literature cited there. Famine records and analyses in Africa are much less comprehensive; for some studies, see Watts (1983); Hay et al. (1986); Glantz (1987); Vaughan (1987); Downing et al. (forthcoming); von Braun and Teklu (1988); Webb and von Braun (1989); Curtis et al. (1988).

[7] Other indicators relating to food shortage and purchasing power for the same year were a deterioration of the terms of trade between food crops and cash crops (groundnuts) from 1 : 1 to 1 : 4, and a much deteriorated rural wage rate (in terms of food prices); see von Braun and Teklu (1988).

[8] See Drèze (1988) on Botswana and Cape Verde.

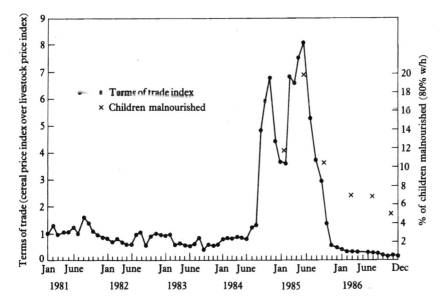

Fig. 9.3.   Seasonal cereals-livestock terms of trade (sorghum to cattle) and child
malnutrition in Kordofan, Sudan, January 1981–December 1986.
Notes: Malnourished children are below 80% of weight for height of reference
population, using World Health Organization standards.
Sources: Republic of Sudan, Ministry of Agriculture; Republic of Sudan, Ministry of
Health (Nutrition Division): OXFAM, UNICEF (computing from unpublished data).

institutions than genuine inappropriateness of the instrument. The need to
generate infrastructure is certainly huge in rural Africa and this should offer
potentials for employment-intensive programmes which will produce long-
term income flows beyond the short-term employment effect of public works.
The high degree of interregional labour mobility and the low extent of
customary constraints on the participation of the female labour-force in rural
Africa suggest that there exists a high level of latent demand for employment—
with favourable effects by gender—in such schemes during the off-season and
during times of production shortfalls.
      Improved technology in agriculture increases production and makes agri-
culture less shock-prone. Improved infrastructure enhances trading and permits
gain from specialization. These two—technology and infrastructure—and a
conducive foreign trade policy contribute to basic social security by reducing
the impacts of production fluctuations. Currently basic social security
is impaired by the far-reaching effects of production shocks. Given the close
relationships between the agricultural production and livelihood of the poor
in Africa—partly mediated via price, wage and, employment effects (as

exemplified in the Sudan case)—it is in the agricultural policy area that a number of sub-Saharan African countries can most rapidly contribute to social security with growth (Mellor *et al.* 1987).

3. COMMUNITY-BASED SOCIAL-SECURITY PROVISION

Sub-Saharan Africa is poor in state institutions, but rich in community institutions for social-security provision. These are not confined only to rural areas but reach out into peri-urban and urban areas as well, partly by maintained urban–rural linkages (Mitchell 1987). The nature and causes of poverty in sub-Saharan Africa are extremely heterogeneous and do not lend themselves to any simplistic categorization.[9] The structural poor of pre-colonial Africa were mainly those lacking access to labour to exploit land—both their own labour (when they were disabled, or old or young) and the labour of others (when they were bereft of family or other support) (Iliffe 1987). Structural poverty resulting from land scarcity appeared only slowly in Africa.

3.1. *Contrasting a Land-Rich and a Land-Scarce Setting*

Today, emerging land scarcity in generally still land-rich Africa is becoming an important concern in any long-term outlook for rural social security based on community support systems. Contrasting a land-rich with an extremely land-scarce rural environment in sub-Saharan Africa may therefore suggest some lessons. We hasten, however, to say that extrapolations from cross-sectional comparisons which largely neglect historical processes, location, and differences in culture are quite limited.

In the more land-rich parts of rural Africa (for instance parts of semi-arid West Africa), access to labour and technology which will increase labour productivity are dominating factors for poverty alleviation. In the land-poor environments (for instance, in the extreme cases of the Central African highlands), poverty is closely related to shortage of land and absence of yield-increasing technology.

Actions by the poor to achieve greater security in land-rich environments frequently entail the formation of large households or kinship relationships across communities, which permits the exploitation of scale economies and the pooling of labour and risk (Binswanger and McIntire 1988). In land-scarce environments, the diversification of income sources appears to be the prevalent strategy coping with the risks of specialization. Extended family-based social-security systems are less prevalent. It is probably in these environments that state involvement in social security is currently in greatest (latent) demand.

---

[9] For an excellent review, see Iliffe (1987), particularly chap. 10.

More generally, this will be more and more so in the long run as land scarcity increases.

In the following, two distant points on the continuum between land-rich and land-scarce rural environments in sub-Saharan Africa will be contrasted to highlight different issues for the different environments in terms of emerging need for social security action. The two environments are in West Africa (The Gambia) and Central Africa (Rwanda). The latter is the most densely populated area in sub-Saharan Africa (man–land ratio of 10.1 persons per hectare of farm land), while the former is still to be considered a land-surplus area—sparsely populated not only in terms of population per square kilometre but also in terms of carrying capacity. The non-agricultural income share in Rwanda is already more than 50 per cent whereas it is about 20 per cent in the Gambian study area. Information for this comparison is based on detailed household-level survey work in both areas in the mid-1980s.[10]

In both study areas, the social-security challenges are indicated by high levels of infant mortality, a small but rapidly growing percentage of old people, high levels of morbidity, child malnutrition, and the hunger problem visible in chronic calorie deficiencies (Table 9.3).

Table 9.3. Rwanda and The Gambia: Comparisons of selected social-insecurity indicators

	The Gambia	Rwanda
Infant mortality (per 1000 live births)[a]	160	116
Population over 60 (% of total)	5	3
Malnutrition among children (%)[b]	27	28
Morbidity (women, sick previous month, %)[c]	62	52
Calorie-deficient households (%)[d]	18	41

[a] Rwanda: 1986, from *World Development Report*, table 33, p. 286. The Gambia: Government Medical and Health Department, *Annual Report*, 1982.
[b] Percentage of children 6–60 months below 80% of weight for age standard.
[c] Computed from International Food Policy Research Institute (IFPRI) surveys; The Gambia dry season percentage for women's morbidity 50.8; the table shows wet season information for The Gambia and mid-year for Rwanda.
[d] Percentage of households below 80% of calorie requirements.

Food insecurity is a combined chronic and transitory problem in both settings. In the West African study environment, seasonality continuously affects the poorest quartile in terms of per capita income in the wet season, but not the rest of the rural poor. Calorie deficiency and workload result in

[10] Field research is based on the IFPRI studies in The Gambia and Rwanda on the effects of commercialization and technological change in traditional agriculture. See von Braun *et al.* (1989); and von Braun *et al.* (1990).

symptoms of chronic malnutrition among both children and adults. Household-level food insecurity is a persistent problem of a subset of households in both environments. For instance, in The Gambia, about one-third of households fell continuously below calorie requirements over two observed seasons, whereas in Rwanda, this applies to about 46 per cent of households. In the latter, a quasi-landless rural population has emerged over the past three decades.

3.2. Different Community Patterns: Different Social-Security Systems

In the West African setting, an important example of an institutionalized system of community-level food security and welfare can be found in the *Zakat* system, under which a tax (10 per cent delivery obligation of staple food to the mosque) is redistributed to the poor and the needy in the village communities through the Imam. The *Zakat* system highlights the fact that society-wide social-security spending is much underestimated when only government expenditures are taken into account (as in Table 9.1). Village-level savings societies and work groups along age and gender lines further contribute to the pooling and spreading of economic risks. Such groups are active in eight out of ten surveyed villages in The Gambia. Due to the existence of such village institutions, at least in smaller rural communities, a substantial degree of shared decline and shared improvement in social security can be observed. For example, the village of Tubanding on the bank of river Gambia suffered from three consecutive droughts in the 1980s. Calorie consumption in most households of this village dropped far below requirements. Drought can, in The Gambia, prevail quite locally. The village of Sarre Balla, only about 20 kilometres away was luckier and had favourable rains in the third year. Calorie consumption at household level recovered in Sarre Balla from low levels in most households in that third year whereas deficiencies remained widespread in Tubanding (von Braun, *et al.* 1989: 81). The localized, dispersed, and versatile nature of economic risks makes any targeting of interventions (such as food and income transfers) an administratively difficult task (say to discontinue transfers to Sarre Balla in year 3, and continue to target Tubanding—which by the way recovered in year 4). However, the nature of intra-village communal systems of social security make household-level targeting less of a necessity. Links between the community and local government require strengthening to cope with local hunger and welfare insecurity in these settings.[11] Investment in information and communication is as important as public capacity to respond to the food and health crises at village level.

Very different from that in The Gambia is the nature of community-level social security and related systems in Rwanda. There, settlements are largely

---

[11] This applies not only to the problem of acute food problems but also to local epidemics.

in the form of individual and scattered farms. Villages do not exist in rural Rwanda. Communities are clearly defined administrative units ('communes'). 'Community'-based social-security systems here are already to a large extent connected to the State. Elimination of the quasi-feudal system was followed by expanded State social-security provision in the 1960s. The strong role of the State is exemplified by public works (every adult has an obligation to work for the community for one day per week), and the system of rural health and nutrition centres. Also, formal rural financial institutions already have a significant role in the credit market, which permits some intertemporal spreading of risks.

3.3. Food Insurance, Transfers, and Labour Exchange for Social Security

In both contrasted settings, rural households attempt to run food insurance schemes. These schemes operate, however, very differently. While in The Gambia, large household units (compounds) comprising 10–100 people (16 on average) allocate labour time and land to produce food for the whole unit (the 'maruo' crop), food insurance at the household level in Rwanda is confined to the nuclear family unit. Cash and kind transfers between households are, on average, larger in the land-scarce setting of Rwanda than in the West African setting.[12] However, in the food-scarce pre-harvest season, transfers are quite important for the poorest in The Gambia, too (Table 9.4). The lowest income quartile in The Gambia obtained about 16 per cent of real income out of

Table 9.4. Value of cash and kind transfers received by rural households in The Gambia and in Rwanda by income classes (1985/6)

	Transfers as % of annual income			
	The Gambia			Rwanda
	Pre-harvest	Post harvest	Annual	Annual
Bottom quarter	15.6	2.9	5.5	16.8
Second quarter	9.5	2.7	4.4	7.9
Third quarter	10.8	3.1	5.4	6.9
Top quarter	16.8	3.4	6.5	14.2
Average	13.2	3.1	5.7	11.4

Sources: For The Gambia, joint survey by the IFPRI and the Planning, Programming and Monitoring Unit of the Gambian Ministry of Agriculture; for Rwanda, IFPRI survey.

[12] Note that income transfers relative to household income between small households (Rwanda) and large households (The Gambia) are not strictly comparable, as significant transfers occur within the large households in The Gambia between nuclear families and gender groups which would appear as interhousehold transfers in Rwanda's small household setting.

transfers and gifts in this 'hungry' season. In both settings, the lowest and the highest income quartiles obtained the highest transfers relative to income. Among the poorest, this may relate to welfare and charity, but it is (foreign) remittances reaching the higher-income groups which explain part of this similar pattern in both settings at the upper end of the income distribution.

Cash and kind transfers between households for food security is only one element of community-based social-security systems. At least as important are 'labour transfers', that is, making labour time available to the community or the extended family to achieve mutual food security. In The Gambia, this is mainly happening within the compound and to lesser extent at the village level. The labour input into compound (common) food production accounts for 56 per cent of total labour (von Braun and Webb, 1989). In Rwanda, labour-sharing occurs between individual farms. Of total farm labour input, about 30 per cent is non-family labour and 78 per cent of this is labour exchange without cash or in-kind payments involved, which means that 23 per cent of total farm labour is in the form of unpaid mutual help (von Braun et al. 1990b). While sizeable, this suggests that the labour transfer in Rwanda (23 per cent) is only about half of that observed in The Gambia (56 per cent). The aggregate resource transfers between households in Rwanda are thus much lower than in The Gambia, despite the somewhat higher income transfers received by Rwandan households.

The consequence of this for social security, however, needs to be seen in the context of the riskiness of the economic environment. Inter-annual crop production risks (fluctuations) are much lower in Rwanda than in The Gambia, as there are two cropping seasons in Rwanda. Yet, as manifested in the 1985 general food shortage situation in Africa, a minor drought in Rwanda combined with rising food prices in neighbouring countries transmitting into Rwanda resulted in rapid increases in severe child malnutrition: prevalence rates increased to 11 per cent in the study area whereas they are 2–4 per cent in normal years (von Braun et al. 1990). More than in The Gambia, specific social groups (especially the landless) rather than specific communities were affected. In Rwanda, State action for social security in the form of open-ended public works could be operated much more effectively than in The Gambia, given population concentration, a relatively large rural wage labour population, and an already existing system of public works (in the form of community work obligation without pay). At least in the 1985 situation, food availability would have had to be expanded jointly with food demand creating public works. Otherwise, further local food price inflation would have followed, adversely affecting poor food purchasers not being reached by such public works.

Open-ended public works, so effective in reducing famine vulnerability in India (Drèze 1988), are underutilized in the densely populated areas of sub-Saharan Africa. As pointed out above, helping each other in food crop production ('labour transfer') is a most important element of community-based social-security systems, frequently more important than the actual sharing of food or cash. Better understanding of these labour transfer systems in their specific contexts may be a key to a creative use of public works at the community level. Potentials for community participation in social development must not be overlooked but appropriately utilized to provide cost-effective social security with a broad coverage of the poor and at-risk population (Midgley 1986).

3.4. Intrahousehold Systems Failures

State-based and community-based social-security systems both have their elements of failure, inefficiency, and injustice. This not only relates to large insurance schemes but also to the very micro-level. Least understood are insurance market failures in community-based systems, and particularly at the intrahousehold level.

In several African languages, the common word for 'poor' implies lack of kin and friends. Iliffe, however, also documents in great detail the importance of the kind of family structures and support systems, since different kinds had their particular points of weakness and particular categories of unsupported poor—orphans in one case, barren women in another, childless elders in a third (Iliffe 1987). Platteau's review in this volume—not limited to Africa— shows that traditional social-security systems in village societies were and are far from being perfect hunger insurance mechanisms. One of the possible imperfections involved relates to intrahousehold divisions of resource control.

A traditional social-security system that, for instance, protects household consumption from falling below a certain level of average per capita food consumption in times of community-wide or individual household crises, but which does so with unequal treatment of types of household members relative to needs, fails to provide insurance to all. This would represent a coverage problem of social security due to intrahousehold systems failures. For instance, intrahousehold distribution of nutritional welfare is not found to be equal in the two contrasted environments of The Gambia and Rwanda when systems are under stress. While in both settings, no systematic discrimination against girls is found—in fact girls show up with better nutritional status than boys— other indications of intrahousehold conflict exist. Children of compound heads in The Gambia have a significantly better nutritional status than other children in the same households, controlling for age, sex, birth order, and other relevant characteristics (von Braun et al. 1989). The difference widens in situations of food insecurity, namely, in the pre-harvest stress situation of poorer households.

In Rwanda, spending from women-controlled income—holding total income per capita constant and controlling for household demographic characteristics—is more food-oriented than that from men-controlled income in the lowest-income group, but not so in the higher-income groups. This may indicate a latent intrahousehold conflict over resource allocation to food at low income levels in this setting.

We refrain from generalizations here. Understanding failures of traditional social-security systems at the intrahousehold level, however, has important implications for identifying the potential scope for State action. Scope for State action exists not only where a specific social-security good can be delivered at lower cost through public systems (for example, because of increasing returns to scale, or the advantages of pooling and spreading risks widely), but also where community-based systems show a risk of failure at the final element of the chain—inside the household. State action may have a special role in protecting children, the aged, women, or any specific group.

3.5. *The Aged*

Social-security systems in high-income countries are increasingly focused on the support of the old, while welfare improvement in low-income countries is much concerned with the very young. This is partly a reflection of the structures of current age pyramids. However, the small proportion of old people in the population of low-income countries—3–5 per cent over 60 in our Rwandan and Gambian samples—is a result not only of high birth rates but also of short lives because of high risk to survival at older age. Thus, there are few old people because social-security provisions are so limited. The absolute and relative growth of the aged population which is now emerging poses a challenge but must not be viewed as a burden in Africa. The aged will increasingly be able to contribute to home goods production and child welfare. Supply of child care time per child can increase. In such settings as The Gambia or Rwanda, given gender divisions of work, this will free younger women's time for work in fields and off farm. The African Conference of Gerontology recently urged that the aged be put on the policy and research agenda.[13] A key recommendation was to include ageing persons in the development process through participation in community activities, including organization of health care and the working of health care services.

3.6. *Complementarities of Community-Based and State-Based Systems*

Community-based and State-based social-security systems each have their strengths and weaknesses. These need, in the context of a specific country, to be explored to determine optimal system mixes which also change over time in the development process. The assessment of the cost-effectiveness of system elements and system mixes taking scale economies of State-based and com-

---

[13] On the deficiencies of knowledge and problems of social security for the aged, see for instance International Centre of Social Gerontology (1984).

munity-based systems into account is an important aspect of policy and programme design. However, interactions between the two types of systems may be both competitive and complementary. For instance, State-based systems may undermine community-based systems by reducing the incentive and solidarity to maintain their support, and in a situation of crisis the collapse of a State based system may leave the community worse off if the community-based system had deteriorated earlier due to State action. But there may also be complementary effects, for instance when the support of State systems during a crisis would prevent the collapse of community support—or even the collapse of whole communities forced into distress migration in a famine situation as in parts of Sudan and Ethiopia in the mid-1980s.

Complementarity and competition between State-based and community-based systems are specific to the social-security good they are to deliver, to the abilities of the State and the communities, and to the socio-economic environment. The Gambia–Rwanda contrast has highlighted the latter in particular. In terms of goods, there is in general probably much less scope for community-based systems to provide health (vaccination, curative services) than sanitation and food security. Weak local governments may find they have a complementary part to play in strengthening (subsidizing) existing community-based systems and initiatives. In any case, a knowledge and an appreciation of community-based systems are pre-conditions for their effective utilization for improved social security.

4. CONCLUSIONS

In view of the fact that nutritional and health improvement in Africa is not only an objective in itself but also a precondition for development, this chapter argues for 'social security before and with growth'. The massive human welfare problem in rural Africa on the one hand, and the resource constraints and weak public institutions on the other, pose a dilemma for State-based social-security systems. But while Africa is poor in State institutions, it is rich in community-based institutions which should be viewed as an asset. Public-sector resource constraints and the existence of effective elements in traditional systems of social security suggest the need to consider creative combinations of State-based and community-based social-security systems, rather than the adoption of Bismarckian systems which could only provide social security for a few.

The need for social-security expenditures by the state is much influenced by development strategy. A rurally biased development strategy reducing the rapid growth rates of urbanization might help to reduce the fiscal and economic costs of social security, as greater reliance could be placed on elements of functioning community-based systems in rural areas.

African countries as much as other low-income countries exponentially expand their State social-security expenditures with rising per-capita income. Thus, revitalized growth in Africa would expand public spending on social security to a considerable extent. The critical policy questions will be the setting of priorities within social-security spending, and the direction of social security toward the truly needy, that is, the food and health insecure. Health of the work-force, technological change in agriculture, and improved market integration are critical foundations for the sustainability of improved social security.

Insecurity of livelihood in rural Africa relates closely to fluctuations in crop production and income, and to low levels of productivity in agriculture. Food security remains a crucial aspect of social security. The latent demand for public involvement in the provision of food security may be greater in the land-scarce, more densely populated areas, where proportions of non-agricultural income are already high but income levels in general are low, and where community-based systems of food security provision are constrained. The growing non-agricultural self-employed and wage labour population has only a reduced chance of food insurance at household and community level based on own food production and stockholding. Thus, as land scarcity is emerging in increasingly large parts of rural Africa, the need for expanded State involvement in social-security provision is increasing.

Famine prevention remains a key task for social security in sub-Saharan Africa. The lack of availability of food in famine-prone areas has often resulted in drastic price increases which limit the impact of programmes for income transfer that do not provide a simultaneous expansion of food availability. Employment-expanding and asset-creating public works for famine prevention appear so far to be underutilized in Africa. Especially in the more densely populated areas, public works could become an important instrument. In this context, it is noteworthy that food and cash redistribution is frequently less important in traditional community-based systems than making labour time available.

There is a great deal of scope to seek creative combinations of State-based and community-based systems for social security. Optimal mixes of these may take very different forms in land-rich and land-poor environments. In order to capitalize on community-based systems, a better understanding of their strengths and weaknesses is required. Basic differences in community-based systems as identified in a land-rich setting (The Gambia) and a land-scarce setting (Rwanda) call for a careful assessment of the scope for State-based social-security systems to achieve optimal system mixes for specific settings and stages of development.

References

Binswanger, H. P., and McIntire, J. (1987), 'Behavioural and Material Determinants of Production Relations in Land-abundant Tropical Agriculture', *Economic Development and Cultural Change*, 3611.

Clarke, D. (1977), *The Economics of African Old Age Subsistence in Rhodesia. A Report to the School of Social Work*. Salisbury: Mambo Press.

Curtis, D., Hubbard, M., and Shepherd, A. (1988), *Preventing Famine: Politics and Prospects for Africa*. London: Routledge.

Downing, T., Gitu, K., and Kamau, C. (eds.) (forthcoming), *Coping with Drought in Kenya: National and Local Strategies*. Boulder, Colo.: Lynne Rienner.

Drèze, J. (1988), 'Famine Prevention in India', Discussion Paper No. 3, Development Economics Research Programme, London School of Economics; to be published in J. P. Drèze and A. K. Sen (eds.) (1990), *The Political Economy of Hunger*. Oxford: Oxford University Press.

—— (1989), 'Famine Prevention in Africa', Discussion Paper No. 17, Development Economics Research Programme, London School of Economics; to be published in J. P. Drèze and A. K. Sen (eds.) (1990), *The Political Economy of Hunger*. Oxford: Oxford University Press.

—— and Sen, A. (1989), *Hunger and Public Action*. Oxford: Clarendon Press.

Glantz, M. (ed.) (1987), *Drought and Hunger in Africa: Denying Famine a Future*. Cambridge: Cambridge University Press.

Hay, R., Burke, S., and Dako, D. Y. (1986), 'A Socio-Economic Assessment of Drought Relief in Botswana', report prepared by UNICEF/UNDP/WHO for the Inter-Ministerial Drought Committee, Government of Botswana, Gaborone.

Iliffe, J. (1987), *The African Poor: A History*. Cambridge: Cambridge University Press.

International Centre of Social Gerontology (1984), 'Proceedings of the African Conference of Gerontology', Dakar, Senegal.

ISSA (International Social Security Association) (1985), Eighth African Regional Conference, Lusaka, 17–21 Sept. 1984, Social Security Documentation No. 7, Geneva.

Kumar, S. (1987), 'The Nutritional Situation and its Food Policy Links', in Mellor *et al.* (1987).

Mellor, J. (1976), *The New Economics of Growth: A Strategy for India and the Developing World*. Ithaca, NY: Cornell University Press.

—— Delgado, C., and Blackie, M. (1987), *Accelerating Food Production in Sub-Saharan Africa*. Baltimore: Johns Hopkins University Press.

Midgley, J. (1986), *Community Participation, Social Development and the State*. London: Methuen.

Mitchell, J. C. (1987), *Cities, Society and Social Perception, A Central African Perspective*. Oxford: Clarendon Press.

Mouton, P. (1975), *Social Security in Africa*. Geneva: International Labour Office.

Sen, A. (1981), *Poverty and Famines: An Essay on Entitlement and Deprivation*. Oxford: Clarendon Press.

Torry, W. (1987), 'Evolution of Food Rationing systems with Reference to African Group Farms in the Context of Drought', in Glantz (1987).

Vaughan, M. (1987), *The Story of an African Famine: Hunger, Gender and Politics in Malawi*. Cambridge: Cambridge University Press.

von Braun, J., de Haen, H., and Blanken, J. (1990), 'Commercialization of Agriculture Under Population Pressure: Production, Consumption, and Nutritional Effects in Rwandar', International Food Policy Research Institute Research Report, Washington, DC.

—— Puetz, D., and Webb, P. (1989), 'Irrigation Technology and Commercialization of Rice in The Gambia: Effects on Income and Nutrition', International Food Policy Research Report No. 75, Washington, DC.

—— and Teklu, T. (1988), 'Food Policies for Drought Affected Areas in The Sudan', mimeo, International Food Policy Research Institute, Washington, DC, and the Ministry of Finance and Economic Planning of the Republic of Sudan.

—— and Webb, P. (1989), 'The Impact of New Crop Technology on the Agricultural Division of Labor in a West African Setting', *Economic Development and Cultural Change*, 37.

Watts, M. (1983), *Silent Violence: Food, Famine and Peasantry in Northern Nigeria*. Berkeley: University of California Press.

Webb, P., and von Braun, J. (1989), 'Drought and Food Shortages in Ethiopia: A Preliminary Review of Effects and Policy Implications', mimeo, International Food Policy Research Institute, Washington, DC.

World Bank (1987), *World Development Report*. Washington, DC: Oxford University Press.

—— (1988), World Development Report. Washington, DC: Oxford University Press.

10

Social Security in the SADCC States of Southern Africa: Social-Welfare Programmes and the Reduction of Household Vulnerability[1]

Richard Morgan

1. INTRODUCTION

The 'SADCC' countries are defined by their membership of the Southern African Development Co-ordination Conference, established following the independence of Zimbabwe in 1980 as a body aimed at regional co-operation with the purpose of reduction of economic, technological, and transport dependence on South Africa. The body is not a trading block—the Preferential Trade Area (PTA) exists to promote and facilitate trade among a large number of central and southern African countries—but an alliance of countries with a disparate set of political, economic, and historical characteristics which have recognized a common interest in reducing their dependency on the dominant sub-regional power. The fact that the SADCC has been successful in the mobilization of international donor funds for projects with a regional character or for national projects with potential regional benefits, in a wide range of economic sectors, has increased its attraction for the member States, each of which have co-ordinating responsibilities for specific sectors.

For the purposes of discussion of social-welfare policies and programmes, the SADCC programme *per se* is of limited relevance (with the main interest being in the Food Security Programme co-ordinated by Zimbabwe). The nine SADCC countries[2] do not present a coherent set of features for easy common analysis: there are two lusophone members which achieved independence in 1975 through a liberation war, one anglophone member which achieved the same in 1980, three former British Protectorate territories which became nation states peacefully in 1966 and retain close economic relations with South Africa including membership of a common Customs Union, and three anglo-

[1] Acknowledgement is made to UNICEF for permission to devote time to the paper on which this chapter is based and for use of the periodic Situation Analyses of Children and Women produced jointly with national governments, which form a major data source for the paper. The views expressed are however attributable to the author alone, writing in a personal capacity. Thanks are due to John Hills, Michael Lipton, and Joao Donato for their comments and assistance on earlier drafts, and to Reg Green and Roger Hay for general inspiration on the subject matter in recent years.
[2] Angola, Botswana, Lesotho, Malawi, Mozambique, Swaziland, Tanzania, Zambia, Zimbabwe.

phone central and east African states which became independent in the 1960s, whose relations with South Africa range from close to reluctant to virtually non-existent (Malawi, Zambia, and Tanzania respectively).

Economic indicators also suggest a massive disparity within this geo-graphically almost-contiguous block (Fig. 1). Table 1 shows a range of per capita GNP from US$840 in the case of mineral-rich Botswana to US$160–70 for landlocked, crowded Malawi and war-torn Mozambique. Variations in health and welfare outcomes, and their relation with economic indicators such as these, are discussed later in this chapter. Natural conditions including fertility of land, water availability, proximity to sea routes, as well as internal political configurations and economic policies are also highly disparate between these countries.

Table 10.1. SADCC members: Basic data

	Population (millions)	Area (000 sq. km.)	GDP ($ million)	GNP per capita ($)
Angola	8.8	1 247	5 700	690
Botswana	1.1	600	830	840
Lesotho	1.5	30	260	470
Malawi	7.0	118	970	170
Mozambique	13.8	802	3 230	160
Swaziland	0.8	17	590	670
Tanzania	22.2	945	5 600	290
Zambia	6.7	753	2 330	390
Zimbabwe	8.4	391	4 530	680
TOTAL	70.3	4 903	24 040	

Note: Data refer to 1986, except GDP for Angola and Mozambique which are 1984.

Sources: World Bank, *World Development Report 1987* (Washington, DC: World Bank); SADCC, *Macro-Economic Survey 1986* (Gaborone: SADCC); EIU, *SADCC: Progress, Projects and Prospects* (London: Economist Intelligence Unit, 1984) (GDP Angola and Mozambique).

However, the premiss of this chapter is that the greatest single factor now affecting the development and effectiveness of social-welfare policies and programmes in the SADCC States is the external one of South African military aggression and promotion of military/economic destabilization. The degree of impact of this factor, present in some form for all SADCC countries, has become a major constraint on the extent to which social-service programmes could be developed and implemented, at any given level of policy commitment and enthusiasm. Combined in many cases with the effects of severe droughts and unfavourable external economic circumstances, the destabilization phe-

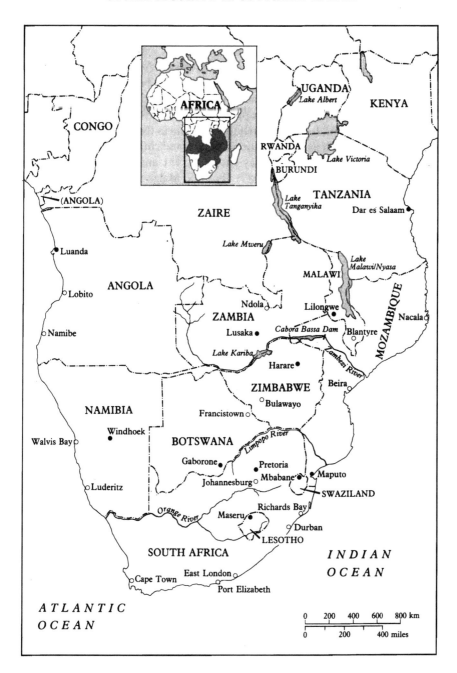

Fig. 10.1. SADCC member States.

nomenon affects social services particularly through the medium of reduced resource availability to finance such programmes—whether due to absolute resource loss or the pressure to divert to types of expenditure designed to bolster security and protect trade routes. In the cases of Angola and Mozambique (and to a lesser extent Zimbabwe) social assets have been directly destroyed and programmes massively disrupted by externally backed insurgents, whilst the displacement of millions of people within and across national borders has increased the demand for urgent welfare provision in these countries and their neighbours. Over half a million additional infant and child deaths are estimated to have been caused by insurgency between 1981 and 1986 in Angola and Mozambique alone (Green *et al.* 1987). By 1988, Malawi was accommodating a number of displaced Mozambicans reaching almost 10 per cent of its own population.

The undermining effect of South Africa's regional destabilization policy on the SADCC States, documented in particular detail in Hanlon (1986), has been interlinked with a series of natural events which combined to increase vulnerability of (particularly) rural households in the region in the first half of the 1980s. The period 1981–5 was characterized by rainfall insufficiencies of historically severe proportions, lasting in most cases for more than one year, in all the SADCC States. The resultant reductions in food and livestock production and access, when coupled with disruption of rural society and transport and trading links due to war, turned 'normal' hungry seasons into droughts, and in the countries worst affected by both phenomena, to famines. Whilst drought receded as a widespread occurrence after the 1985/6 agricultural season, and food production and flows in most countries began to recover, the destabilization wars have tended to intensify. In the last few years, most of the larger SADCC countries have also adopted economic 'adjustment' programmes, which, although the initial record is mixed, have tended further to reduce the share of national resources allocated to social-service sectors.

For many countries, the experience of the 1980s represents a sharp reversal of earlier progress. Significant economic growth in the late 1960s and through most of the 1970s, despite for some countries declining terms of international trade, coupled with post-independence inflows of donor funds specifically for social-sector programmes, allowed even the weakest economies in the region to support a rapid build-up of social-service coverage. This was sometimes associated with community-level mobilization policies achieved through political channels and the use of literacy programmes and health education activities. Voluntary labour mobilization was in some countries a contributory factor in extending access to social infrastructure, and settlement policies encouraging rural concentration took this process further (Tanzania is an example). In some countries (Botswana, Lesotho, and later Zimbabwe), the social infrastructure facilities put in place during this period were able to support the implementation of nutrition-based food and income supplementation programmes in rural areas, which were introduced or expanded in times of stress to support vulnerable groups and households.

Following the achievement of Zimbabwean independence under a regime unfavourable to South African interests, and the realization of the SADCC 'project', South Africa's regional policy became increasingly militarized and a 'contextual shift' took place for development work in the entire region. With hindsight, the question for the subsequent period increasingly became one of how the gains in promotion of greater social security could now best be protected (rather than one of rapid expansion): a question posed in domestic economies affected by a hostile external military environment and a partly unfavourable international trading context. The question of protection of welfare gains is posed, for the most thoroughly destabilized countries, by the need to respond to deliberate and direct targeting of welfare programmes themselves, through attacks on health posts and schools, kidnap, murder and mutilation of the professionals who staff them, and attacks on the vehicles that conduct their mobile programmes, deliver relief food, and facilitate water-point maintenance.

This chapter proceeds with a review of social-service policies and programmes in the post-independence SADCC States, goes on to discuss the discernable impact of these programmes using health indicators of welfare, and then looks at the characteristics of the main target groups for these programmes, the poor and vulnerable. Case-studies are presented of State responses to external welfare-threatening events which occurred in the 1980s in two countries, one relatively at peace (Botswana) and one thoroughly subjected to war conditions (Mozambique), and some generalized conclusions from these studies and the review as a whole are drawn for the prioritization and design of welfare policies in the region.

2. SOCIAL-WELFARE PROGRAMMES IN SADCC STATES

The definition understood here of programmes adopted by the State to promote or increase family welfare (or the welfare of specific groups within families) is broader than that of not directly productive 'social sectors', principally health, education, and water. Also included are interventions and policies established by the State to promote or regulate production by families, and to influence access to 'basic' household items (those necessary to healthy life and social dignity) and to incomes. Such definition is largely based in a rural area perspective, where more than 70 per cent of the SADCC population are still found, mostly engaged in some form of agriculture, even if this may not comprise the largest source of their income.

2.1. *Broadening Access to Primary Health Care*

Having inherited health care systems biased towards urban facilities and high-cost, curative treatments, the SADCC countries have since independence shown a strong recognition of the importance of extending health services to the mass of their populations. Some convergence of health sector strategies, at least in terms of officially stated intentions, can be seen. In most countries, the rate of construction of lower-level health facilities was greatly increased in the years after independence, training of nursing staff and paramedical personnel expanded, and greater shares of generally increasing health sector expenditures allocated to preventive programmes.

This shift of emphasis accorded with the desire to bring greater proportions of rural and poorer populations within the coverage of the health network. Generally, the adoption of a primary health care (PHC) approach to health service provision allowed much greater numbers to be reached without impossibly large budgetary implications, especially to the extent that different types of programmes could be integrated (for example, public and personal health programmes). Typically, PHC has as its main elements: training and posting of frontline village health workers, community mobilization (for example, though village health committees), establishment of referral systems, mother–child health care, communicable disease control, young child growth monitoring, treatment of common diseases, child immunization, and water supply and environmental sanitation programmes.

Progress in these areas has however been highly variable between countries and regions. Some countries (Malawi, Swaziland) continue to show marked bias towards higher-level, urban-based curative facilities in their health sector expenditure patterns. In most PHC programmes, community involvement and village-based health activities have been weak in practice, and the roles of community health workers often unclear. Shortages of transport, medical equipment, fuel, and drugs, have played havoc in some areas with efficient delivery of services. None the less, the picture presented in the region is one of highly expanded coverage of physical facilities (subsequently reduced by war in Mozambique and Angola), with a less than consistent pattern of improvement in their efficiency of operation and rates of usage.

The health sector in SADCC States generally received some 5–8 per cent of total central government expenditure over the 1972–83 period (World Bank 1986), and the percentage in Mozambique was until recently considerably higher. However, despite the ability of health expenditures in most countries to retain their shares, the real values of expenditures have tended to fall in several cases as financial stringency affected the entire government budget (Mozambique since 1986, Zambia and Tanzania since the late 1970s, and Zimbabwe to some extent since 1982). This has resulted in substantial cuts in construction programmes in particular. On the other hand, the implications for poorer groups are counterbalanced to some extent where increasing emphasis is being given within health sector budgets to PHC programmes (as, for instance, in Tanzania and Zimbabwe). Finally, without consideration of relative cost-effectiveness in health programme delivery, the absolute financial base of governments is also a major determinant of the real value of services provided: despite devoting a higher proportion of the total budget to health, Lesotho in the mid 1980s spent about US$3 per person per year, and Mozambique US$4, compared to Botswana's roughly US$18.

Some degree of cross-country comparison is possible for one of the central PHC programmes under implementation in all SADCC countries, child immunization (although the data are not complete or fully consistent). As shown in Table 10.2, progress has been registered in immunization coverage over recent years in almost all countries, with particularly good results achieved in Lesotho and Botswana. The Zimbabwean coverage figures are also higher on aggregate than indicated here, and have increased rapidly since

Table 10.2. Estimated child immunization coverage rates for various SADCC countries in recent years (% coverage)[a]

	Vaccination				
	BCG (Scar)	DPT (3rd)	Polio	Measles	Full immunization coverage
Zimbabwe[b] 1982/84	53/76	32/66	31/66	51/53	25/42
Malawi 1977/81	97/80	46/60	23/53	11/60	n.a./55
Lesotho 1982/86	76/86	56/82	54/80	49/73	40/65
Swaziland 1982/84	n.a./72	31/43	22/43	31/37	n.a./24
Zambia 1984	68	44	44	55	35
Botswana 1985	68	68	67	68	68
Mozambique 1983/85	59/47	38/29	38/25	51/39	n.a.

[a] Of children up to one year, except Zimbabwe 12–32 months, Lesotho and Zambia 12–23 months.
[b] Zimbabwe, rural children only.
Sources: UNICEF, Situation Analyses; Mozambique Ministry of Health (unpublished data).

independence. Mozambique too made rapid progress up to 1983; since then, war-related insecurity has dictated concentration of vaccination programmes in towns and easily accessible rural locations only, where they have been highly successful.

In countries with relatively low rates of full vaccination coverage, such as Zambia and Tanzania, shortages of fuel to maintain the cold chain and of transport for outreach purposes are major constraints on these programmes. Basic drugs are often generally in short supply in these countries, particularly at the periphery. With depreciating currencies, costs of items not produced locally or supplied directly by donors have been rising rapidly, further constraining supplies to the health sector.

2.2. Widening Access to Education

Most SADCC nations have since independence rapidly expanded the primary-education system in an effort to provide universal access. Although qualified by the inclusion of over-age pupils, Table 10.3 suggests that this coverage is virtually achieved in Lesotho, Zimbabwe, and Swaziland, and nearly so in Botswana and Zambia. Zimbabwe is particularly notable for an annual increase of over 20 per cent between 1979 and 1985 in numbers attending primary school, and Tanzania and Mozambique have also made substantial advances from very poor colonial bases.

It is noteworthy that, in similar manner to the health sector, these indicators show Malawi lagging behind. In the case of Mozambique, rapid expansion

Table 10.3. Numbers enrolled in primary school as percentage of relevant age group[a]

	% Enrolment overall		% Enrolment of girls	
	1965	1983[b]	1965	1983[b]
Angola	39	n.a.	26	n.a.
Botswana	65	96	71	102
Lesotho	94	110	114	126
Malawi	44	63	32	52
Mozambique	37	79	26	68
Swaziland	n.a.	106	n.a.	105
Tanzania	32	87	25	84
Zambia	53	94	46	89
Zimbabwe	110	131	92	127

[a] Most countries include significant numbers of over-age children in enrolment.
[b] Some years differ (±2).

Sources: World Bank 1986; UNICEF Situation Analyses.

since independence has been followed by war-related decline: the numbers of children enrolled and primary schools operating rose by 122 per cent and 37 per cent respectively between 1975 and 1979, and then fell by 2 per cent and 37 per cent respectively from 1982 to 1987 (Mozambique Ministry of Education). A similar trend has probably occurred in Angola. 'Universal access' as a target cannot however be taken as referring to enrolment alone, and indications are strong that the quality of education tends to fall far short of functional levels in many regions. Retakes and drop-outs are common. In Mozambique less than 20 per cent of entrants complete their primary education (Grades 1–4) and less than 5 per cent graduate in the minimum number of years (Johnston et al. 1987). In Swaziland only 50 per cent of children entering Grade 1 complete Grade 7 and only 21 per cent of entrants do not retake a Grade during primary education. Conditions of education contribute to poor results, with overcrowded classrooms and shortages of textbooks and classroom materials being common, particularly in countries with severe budgetary constraints. Shortages of teachers in Malawi and Mozambique, for example, led to recent pupil–teacher ratios of over 60 : 1, and even in those countries better endowed, qualified teachers are often in short supply.

In contrast to primary-education coverage, pre-school child care and educational institutions are few in number and low in coverage; only in Swaziland do they cater for more than 5 per cent of 3–5 year olds, and here, as elsewhere, the bias is strongly towards urban areas and parents who can afford fees. This area has not been a conspicuous priority for SADCC States, despite the potential benefits to working mothers.

Expansion of secondary-education facilities has also tended to take a lesser priority than the achievement of universal primary access, but some countries have expanded rapidly in this area (Table 10.4). Zimbabwe has been able to build to some degree on an inherited base, whilst Botswana is now adding quickly to its stock of junior secondary schools. Even so, a relatively low percentage of secondary school age children in these countries, and even lower proportions elsewhere, are able to enter secondary education. Although this is slightly compensated by the existence of small-scale vocational or 'education with production' training organizations in some States, the SADCC countries face an overall 'primary school leaver' problem of substantial proportions, and a rapidly growing incidence of secondary school leaver unemployment as well.

Improvement in adult literacy rates has proceeded extremely rapidly where State policy has given priority to this objective (most notably in Tanzania). Recent estimates of adult literacy are given for some countries in the UNICEF Situations Analyses (Table 10.5).

Table 10.4. Numbers enrolled in secondary schools as percentage of the relevant age group

	Enrolment as % of age group	
	1965	1983[a]
Angola	5	12
Botswana	3	21
Lesotho	4	19
Malawi	2	5
Mozambique	3	6
Swaziland	n.a.	n.a.
Tanzania	2	3
Zambia	7	17
Zimbabwe	6	39

[a] Or nearby year.

Sources: World Bank, 1986; UNICEF: Situation Analyses.

Table 10.5. Estimates of adult literacy rates, recent years

	% of all adults literate	% of women literate
Botswana	40	n.a.
Malawi	27	13
Mozambique	27	12
Zambia	59	53
Tanzania	85	80

Source: UNICEF, Situation Analyses.

2.3. *Water Supply Provision*

Lack of access to 'safe' or improved water supplies is a major health hazard in SADCC countries, as suggested by the high incidence of diarrhoeal diseases and skin, eye, and parasite infections. A further dimension is that of the many hours of work and rest forgone due to long walking distances from home to natural water sources in rural areas. This affects women and children particularly: the UNICEF Zimbabwe Situation Analysis estimates that, in 1984, 73 per cent of rural water collectors were women and 25 per cent children.

Despite substantial public-sector investments in most countries, it has proven difficult rapidly to increase the access to improved water sources of rural populations in SADCC. Botswana, with its concentrated rural settlements and large expenditures on relatively expensive borehole-drilling for village water supplies, is the exception to this rule (Table 10.6).

A variety of technologies, from high-cost borehole-drilling to shallow wells fitted with handpumps, gravity systems, and protected springs, have been used in the region, with a tendency towards lower-cost solutions in recent years. Maintenance capacity has been a further important consideration, both in choice and design of system, and in the creation of back-up facilities and technical capability, whether in local authorities or among communities themselves. Experience has shown that switching water utilization to high-technology systems without ensuring local maintenance capability can leave communities highly dependent and in a worse position than before. Unfortunately, resources, whether national or international, to ensure the functionality of water systems have been given less priority in water supply programmes than those for the initial investment in construction.

Table 10.6. Estimates of percentage of rural population without access to improved/protected water source or latrine

	% without access to improved water	% without access to latrine
Angola	n.a.	n.a.
Botswana (1981)	23	77[a]
Lesotho (1984)	76	89[b]
Malawi (1977)	75	47[c]
Mozambique (1987)	87	n.a.
Swaziland (1983)	70	73
Tanzania (1981)	61	n.a.
Zambia (n.s.)	67	70
Zimbabwe (1983)	61–7	75

[a] Figure refers to 1983/4.
[b] Recent figure.
[c] National figure for 1982.
Source: UNICEF, Situation Analyses and country offices.

A similar problem of technical design appears to retard the adoption of improved sanitation methods, as indicated by the low latrine availability in rural areas. However, some latrine construction programmes have been usefully based on the provision of materials by the state, with labour and local material inputs contributed by the household (or community) concerned.

2.4. *Agricultural Programmes for Enhancing the Productivity of the Poor*

A wide range of policy approaches towards the agricultural sector, in which the majority of the region's population is still engaged, exist in the SADCC countries, with objectives of support to family-level producers and improvement of rural incomes often less than fully reconciled with concerns for improved levels of national self-sufficiency in food. As explored in Section 4 below, food security at the household level is, for much of the region, a question of stabilizing and improving levels not only of domestic production but also of off-farm incomes. Some development policies in the region have recognized this feature, with attention being paid to income diversification through small-scale irrigation and horticulture, cattle and small livestock raising and marketing projects, and craft or small industry promotion, as well as off-season household income supports introduced through public works and other means (see discussion of food and income support below).

In the areas of relatively high and reliable rainfall, agricultural development programmes have tended to adopt an approach designed to increase output of cereals, notably maize, through a combination of extension advice, small-scale credit provisions, and input distribution (improved or hybrid seed, fertilizer). The more successful of these in terms of raising short-term outputs, particularly Zimbabwe and Malawi, have combined such packages with substantial price increases and the effective extension of marketing points to smallholder areas.

In Zimbabwe, success in the 1980s in raising overall levels of small-scale farm maize output and marketing has been particularly rapid, one explanation being the extent of pre-independence investment in research on breeding and use of hybrid maize varieties and fertilizers in high rainfall areas. Only after independence in 1980 were these technologies made extensively available to smallholders (Rohrbach 1987). In other countries, notably those with labour constraints to increases in smallholder crop production, efforts have been made to promote the use of hired or government-provided tractors for land preparation and sowing (Botswana, Lesotho, and Swaziland), on the grounds that this ensures timely use of soil moisture. A further variant has been the use of area-based development programmes, incorporating community development activities and the construction of roads and social service infrastructure (such as the Swaziland Rural Development Areas). The example of Zimbabwe, however, suggests strongly the importance of sustained investment over time in agricultural research, with the emphasis on technological enhancement of the productivity of existing mass small-farmer production systems, whether in high rainfall or drought-prone conditions. Raising efficiency of soil moisture use, development of drought-tolerant foodcrop varieties, low-cost irrigation, and soil fertility improvements are among the research areas which have tended to remain neglected.

In three countries, where the rural production and income base is under threat from war (Angola and Mozambique) and severe drought (Botswana), a more 'minimalist' technical approach has been taken to try to avoid large-scale detachment of rural families from the land. In the first two countries, the provision of basic seeds, handtools, and consumer goods as production incentives, has been given increasing prominence in recent years. In Botswana, seeds have also been provided on a yearly basis to all farmers, as well as field clearance grants, and subsidies on the cost of basic farming implements and fencing materials.

Agricultural and rural development policies have in some nations been integrated with programmes aimed at social reorganization and the restructuring of production systems: the formation of communal villages and promotion of village-based co-operatives for the purposes of marketing and input provision in Tanzania, Mozambique, and Angola are examples. For various reasons, no great success in production terms can be claimed for these programmes, but by concentrating rural settlement patterns, they have facilitated a much wider access to social services than was possible previously. In Mozambique too, the formation of new village settlements has improved the security of some populations and facilitated the resettlement of displaced people. In Zimbabwe, resettlement in commercial farming areas, although so far relatively small in scale (involving some 32,000 families by 1986), has been a basic strategy to relieve land pressure in the 'communal' areas.

The drought period of 1982–5, coupled with concerns about national food security and with increasing international criticism of policy bias in favour of large-scale State farms, parastatal marketing systems, and export crop producers, led to some important shifts in policy in certain of the SADCC countries. It has become increasingly recognized that 'drought-staple' food crops play an important role in improving household food security. Hence price rises (in some cases through lifting of controls) have been effected for relatively drought-resistant crops such as sorghum, millet, and cassava. Research on seed-breeding and variety-testing for such crops has also been given greater priority in national programmes and by SADCC. A further realization has been that both production incentives through pricing policies effective at the farm level and the guaranteeing of the conditions to ensure productive potential through access to seasonal inputs and farming equipment are needed for sustained and broad-based increases in output. To make price incentives effective has required, in turn, simultaneous improvement in the efficiency and coverage of marketing systems, in some cases by allowing a greater role for co-operative and private sector agents alongside dominant parastatals, and also the provision of basic consumer goods in village shops or in direct exchange for agricultural products, to make marketing worthwhile. For economies with extensive shortages of foreign exchange, donor assistance in the provision of such goods has been an important condition for the realization of incentives to revive agricultural output.

Efforts to achieve this combination of apparently necessary conditions for increases in small farm production have been frustrated by several factors. In Tanzania, Zambia, Mozambique, and Angola, poor infrastructure and long distances coupled with fuel and transport shortages have hindered the delivery of already inadequate quantities of inputs and equipment. The reintroduction in the former two countries of co-operative and private marketing agents in 1985/6, with a reduction in the roles of the respective parastatals, has also not proceeded smoothly, although it appears likely that the trends towards increased competition within marketing systems will be maintained. Moreover, whilst most governments have recognized the economic potential and social benefits of providing more favourable producer prices for small farmers' products, some are highly constrained in their ability to do so, particularly for internationally traded crops where important parity prices (for example, from South Africa) or limited export market possibilities (such as for white maize) have to be observed.

In conjunction with the SADCC Food Security Programme, and based on agricultural, meteorological, and nutritional surveillance information systems already in place or being developed, attempts are being made to improve monitoring systems for national and household food security in the SADCC countries. These early warning systems have the potential to assist more effective crisis management and response by governments in the region, but thus far they suffer from a number of limitations. They are primarily concerned with aggregated food supply, crop, and rainfall data, which are not directly useful for monitoring stress among the food-deficit households dependent substantially on non-agricultural sources of income which, as described below (Section 4) are among the most vulnerable. Data systems to provide information on such indicators as local market prices, household food stocks, and the nutritional status of vulnerable group populations, whilst increasing in scope and coverage, are as yet incorporated into national monitoring systems in relatively few countries. Further, the systems in place tend to operate mainly at national level, reducing the scope for decision-making and timely response by provincial or district-level authorities to specific, localized problems. Even at national levels, existing early warning systems seldom feed directly into established structures for policy analysis and decision-making, meaning that much of the effort put into data collection and preliminary analysis may be wasted. None the less, the importance of sustained investment in the development of 'wide' information systems, including local and informal indicators of household economic status and activity, is increasingly clear in view of the complex and structural nature of household vulnerability in the region.

2.5. *Food and Income Support Programmes for Vulnerable Groups*

Despite the weakness of the data base for programme design and monitoring, a range of interventions directed to high-risk areas, groups, or households are carried out by SADCC governments in addition to programmes of agricultural output promotion, primary health care, and other social services. These are essentially direct income and welfare transfers, in recognition of special problems of poverty, food shortages, and low income, or in response to normally short-run emergency situations. The main types of programmes in operation are:

(1) Institutional feeding and food distribution for nutritionally at-risk groups. These operate typically through social-service facilities and are active on some scale in almost all the SADCC countries. They break down into four basic types: (i) feeding programmes in education and training establishments, including primary schools (notably the BLS countries, Botswana, Lesotho, and Swaziland); (ii) provision of take-home rations at health facilities for selected vulnerable groups (women, undernourished children, TB patients, and so on), also widespread in Botswana and Lesotho, and to a lesser extent in Swaziland and Malawi; (iii) rehabilitative, often 'on-site' feeding of actually mal-nourished children at health facilities, which operates in Zimbabwe (Child Supplementary Feeding Programme), Botswana, and in Malawi and Mozambique to some extent; and (iv) distribution of supplementary rations to families in situations of drought or other emergency. By the mid-1980s this was confined to Botswana (with some 270,000 additional beneficiaries), Mozambique (where the total number of 'affected' and displaced people eligible for free food distribution stood at some 3.2 million in 1988), and Angola. Drought-hit areas of Zimbabwe also retained a limited food distribution programme of this type during 1986/7. In other countries, such operations have largely been phased out since the severe drought periods of the early 1980s.

(2) Village-level food-for-work projects, which are most extensive in Lesotho, with about 17,000 participants per year, but also in limited operation in Tanzania and Malawi. In Mozambique, both food-for-work and com-modities-for-work projects have been undertaken on a small scale, as well as food sales for workers in agricultural state enterprises.

(3) Seasonal rural employment creation on public-works projects at basic wage levels, undertaken in order directly to boast household income levels. These have been extensive since 1982 in Botswana, where they complement the food relief element of the government's response to drought (see Section 5). Such public works were also used extensively in Zimbabwe in 1983/4, and on a lesser scale in 1986/7.

(4) Market intervention sales of food in order to stabilize or reduce prices in urban areas, undertaken by Grain Marketing Boards. These were used until recently in Tanzania to protect real incomes of the urban poor.

An emerging issue with regard to such programmes, explored further in Section 5, is their role not merely as short-term buffering mechanisms for emergency-affected households, but also in relation to strategies for more sustained attacks on poverty and vulnerability, through such mechanisms as community mobilization, creation of permanent income-generating opportunities, and income-protection during medium-term economic adjustment policy implementation. These potentials have not yet been fully realized in either policy formulation or practice in the region (although the trend to adoption of intersectoral food and nutrition strategy perspectives in some countries is encouraging). A particularly weak linkage has been with the area of pricing and subsidy policy, one with major implications for the welfare status of the urban poor.

2.6. Consumer Pricing and Subsidies

Some governments in the region have used a policy of subsidizing extensively the costs to consumers of basic food products, particularly staple cereals. This has been the case in countries with large urban populations: in Mozambique and Angola through city rationing systems, and in Zimbabwe, Zambia, and Tanzania through covering losses of Grain Marketing Boards and/or payments to milling companies to limit the mark-ups passed on to the consumer. Since the sales of these Boards and companies have been concentrated in urban areas, such policies have tended to benefit the urban poor, who devote a high proportion of their household budgets to purchase of staple commodities.

Levels of subsidization have not proven sustainable in the 1980s, with state finances under pressure from the effects of worsening international terms of trade and military destabilization. Mozambique's urban rationing system for basic commodities has come to rely almost entirely on external donations, and the low-price consumer policy was abandoned in steps during 1987/8 as part of the economic adjustment programme, which envisaged rapid elimination of consumer subsidies. In Tanzania, due to the poor performance of the official internal marketing system, urban sales of maize meal and other cereals (rice and wheat) have relied increasingly on commercial imports, difficult for the country to afford, as well as food aid donations. Urban demand at relatively low prices has tended to outstrip supply, causing shortages of basic products and rationing by parallel markets, with negative implications for the poor. It is probable that such policies have also influenced consumer preference in favour of less nutritious, highly refined blends of maize, as well as cereals in which countries have no immediate prospect of self-sufficiency (wheat, rice), leading to further import dependence. Most seriously, however, for all three countries which have used parastatal marketing boards to implement these subsidies, the costs of the programmes have taken up increasing proportions of government budgets otherwise under stress. This factor above all has led to their curtailment (Zimbabwe in 1982–3, Tanzania in 1984, Zambia over the period 1984–6), in an effort to reduce losses sustained and the often inflationary borrowing associated with such deficits.

3. THE IMPACT OF WELFARE POLICIES ON HEALTH AND NUTRITION

Health indicators of the success or otherwise of the range of welfare policies and programmes adopted in SADCC countries can only give rough measures of overall changes in well-being: this is also true for sectorally based information of other kinds. However, allowing for variations in average income levels between countries, health sector indicators, for all the recognized difficulties of cross-country comparison and the poverty of data series, do provide some convenient, broadly comparable measures of impact. They are also useful in focusing the argument on those groups within the population facing the greatest vulnerabilities from a welfare point of view.

UNICEF estimates of infant and under-5 mortality rates for the years 1960 and 1986 and for life expectancy at birth for 1986 are shown in Table 10.7. The most significant achievements in life expectancy, on these estimates, have been made in Tanzania, Zambia, Zimbabwe, and Botswana, where high commitment to the health and other welfare sectors in public policy, and in the case of the latter two countries, rapidly rising income levels, have been apparent. In the two countries most affected by destabilization wars (Angola and Mozambique), and in low-income Malawi, life expectancy (for both sexes) remains under 50 years.

A similar pattern is clear, broadly, for changes in infant mortality rates (IMRs) over the same period. All countries achieved falls of 20 per cent or more, except for Mozambique and Angola where rapid improvements in welfare services after independence were reversed by the effects of war since the early 1980s. As argued in Green et al. (1987) rates of 200 per thousand for the IMR and of 325–75 for child mortality are realistic, and accord with recent if limited survey evidence. Such rates are not unknown even in parts of the region not directly affected by war: certain districts of Malawi are also estimated to have IMRs above 200 per thousand.

Fig. 10.2 shows a close relationship between GNP per capita (estimated for 1985 except Angola, 1980) and national IMRs (estimated for 1986). The impact of war on mortality in low-income Mozambique and middle-income Angola is clearly seen. Also of interest is the relatively poor performance of

Table 10.7. Infant and under-5 mortality rates, and life expectancy in SADCC countries, 1960–1986

	Infant mortality rate (deaths per 1000 live births under one year)		% change in infant mortality rate 1960–86	Under-5 mortality rate (deaths per 1000 live births under five years)		Life expectancy at birth (years)
	1960	1986		1960	1986	1986
Angola	208	200[a]	−4	346	–[b]	44
Botswana	119	69	−42	174	96	56
Lesotho	149	102	−32	208	140	51
Malawi	206	153	−26	364	270	47
Mozambique	174	200[a]	+15	302	–[b]	47
Swaziland	152	120	−21	227	178	50
Tanzania	146	107	−27	248	179	53
Zambia	135	82	−39	228	132	53
Zimbabwe	110	74	−33	182	118	57
South Africa	135	75	−44	192	101	55

[a] These figures only from Green et al. (1987).
[b] Estimated by Green et al. to be in range of 325–75.
Source: UNICEF (1988) except as indicated in note above.

non-war-affected Malawi and middle-income Swaziland, in relation to other countries with similar characteristics.[2]

Figure 10.3 relating life expectancy to GNP per capita gives similar indications. The directly war-affected countries perform least well; Malawi and particularly Swaziland appear somewhat below trend; whilst considerable achievements in increasing life expectancy at respective levels of resource availability are suggested in Tanzania and Zimbabwe. As stated above, however, care needs to be exercised in drawing even limited conclusions from these data.

An 'intermediate' set of welfare indicators from the health sector are shown in Table 10.8, involving measures of access to and utilization of health services.

Whilst here again the higher-income countries such as Botswana, Zimbabwe, and Zambia tend to have the most favourable results, rural–urban and inter-provincial disparities in access within countries are likely to be almost as great as those between them. Such figures also do not reflect the existence of medical and healing services outside the State sector (namely, the significant private medical sectors in Botswana, Zimbabwe, and Swaziland, and the 'traditional

[2] South Africa's failure to improve on the IMRs achieved by Zimbabwe and Botswana with per capita GNP 2.5 to 3 times higher than those countries is also noteworthy in the regional context.

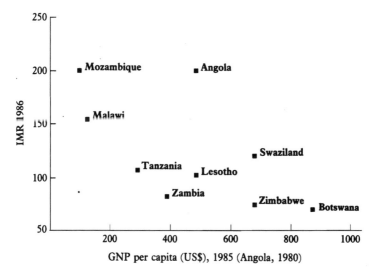

Fig. 10.2. GNP per capita against infant mortality rate.
Note: Infant mortality rate figures represent annual deaths of children under 1 year per 1,000 live births.
Sources: World Bank and UN Population Division estimates quoted in UNICEF (1988), except Mozambique and Angola IMRs, re-estimated in Green *et al.* (1987) to take account of effects of war.

healers' who are widespread in the region). The impact of policy, however, is particularly apparent in the case of Tanzania, where extraordinarily high levels of ante-natal coverage and institutional births have been achieved for a country so populous and poor.

Improvements in nutritional status and reduction in the incidence of common diseases are both more difficult to measure and more complex to achieve. Rising real levels of personal incomes and per capita health expenditures by the State are not necessarily enough to effect these improvements, since disease and nutrition patterns tend to reflect underlying conditions of household and communal poverty, which require to be addressed by specific intervention in a range of sectors, even as incomes rise.

Diarrhoeal diseases, and intestinal infections generally, remain a common cause of death in young children throughout the region, and acute respiratory infections are also still prevalent. Measles has not yet been eradicated as a cause of death in all countries, and malaria is endemic in most of the central SADCC area. Perinatal complications and infections are prime contributors to high IMRs. Bilharzia and tuberculosis remain problematic in countries such as Botswana and Swaziland, despite rising income levels; and sexually transmitted diseases, including AIDS, exist throughout the region and appear to be increasing rapidly.

Table 10.8. Indicators of access to and use of health services

| | Population (000) per | | | | Estimated % of births in health institutions | Estimated coverage of pregnant women by ante-natal care services (%) |
| | Physician | | Nurse | | | |
	1965	1981	1965	1981		
Angola	12	n.a.	4	n.a.	n.a.	n.a.
Botswana	22	9	16	1	66	89
Lesotho	23	13[a]	5[a]	3[a]	51	61
Malawi	47	53	49	3	35	n.a.
Mozambique	22	33	5	6	28	46
Swaziland	n.a.	7	n.a.	n.a.	30	86
Tanzania	22	19[b]	n.a.	5	58	96
Zambia	11	7	6	2	43	80
Zimbabwe	5	7	1	1	67	89

[a] These figures from UNICEF Situation Analyses, 1983/4.
[b] This figure is for 1984.

Sources: For columns 1–4, World Bank (1986), except as indicated in note above. For columns 5–6 UNICEF Situation Analyses.

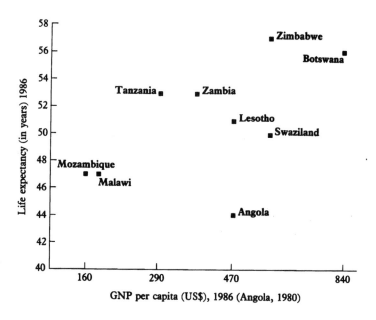

Fig. 10.3.   GNP per capita against life expectancy.
Source: UNICEF (1988).

In consideration of trends in the nutritional status of children, insufficient and often inconsistent time series surveillance or survey data in almost all countries permit not more than a sketching of broad characteristics. It is clear that undernutrition is widespread throughout the region, and is largely structural and poverty-related in nature, tending to be higher in remoter areas such as the Western Kalahari and Lesotho Highlands, in small villages, among families of low-waged workers on agricultural estates, and in some cases in newly settled peripheral urban areas. Widespread stunting (low height for age) is mainly the result of growth faltering during the weaning period (normally the second year of life), associated with abrupt termination of breastfeeding, poor feeding practices, and lack of protein supplements. Despite this, breast-feeding practices, promoted by most governments, remain favourable in most countries, with little decline associated with urbanization. Whilst the lowest incidence of breastfeeding is found amongst the most highly educated women, these are often the best weaners. In general, a strong inverse relationship is found in nutrition research in the region between the mother's educational attainment and the incidence of young child malnutrition. The 1983 Swaziland Nutrition Survey also found negative associations between child stunting and household ownership of consumer durables as well as access to improved water supplies (UNICEF, Swaziland Situation Analysis, 1987).

Since few countries carry out regular monitoring of nutritional status from a reasonably consistent sample population, trends in this indicator are difficult to determine. The case of Botswana, with a national surveillance system in place since 1978, indicates a major worsening of young child nutritional status in the early 1980s, coinciding with the onset of repeated drought years, and a stabilization and subsequent dramatic improvement after 1984 coinciding with the implementation of large-scale drought relief measures (see Section 5 and Fig. 10.5 below; and Cornia et al. 1987: vol. ii). In Lesotho, however, rural area monitoring of child weights at clinics with food distribution by the Catholic Relief Service over the period 1980 to 1986 showed that initial improvements up to 1983 in the percentage of children found underweight were rapidly reversed by 1986, despite the lessening of drought conditions and continued growth in imports of food aid (Food Studies Group 1988). Admissions and deaths in the main central hospital associated with protein energy malnutrition also rose over the period. Possible determinants of these phenomena in Lesotho include declining crop yields, land access, and work opportunities for rural families in the 1980s, and rises in the price of the main staple food, maize, relative to other commodities (ibid).

Survey data elsewhere show high levels of chronic malnutrition persisting in the low-income countries (Malawi, Mozambique, and Tanzania). In Malawi, a 1981/2 national survey found over 50 per cent of pre-school children to be stunted (below 80 per cent of expected height for age) (Quinn 1986), whilst in Mozambique, limited surveys suggest stunting in the range of 35–55 per cent in rural areas. In other SADCC countries, the available indicators show levels of stunting or low weight in the 25–30 per cent range.

Severe weight loss is found to reach levels of up to 11 per cent in children of recently displaced families in Mozambique and in areas of recent conflict (see 1987 Bulletins of the Nutrition Section, Ministry of Health, Maputo). Whilst this phenomenon can be quite extensive also in Tanzania, it is by contrast relatively rare in Botswana and Swaziland (usually 1–2 per cent). Surprising anomalies still exist, however, cautioning against aggregation to the national level for comparative purposes: despite a relatively low IMR and high per capita income and food production levels, widespread undernutrition appears to persist in Zimbabwe, and various surveys between 1980 and 1982, before the onset of drought, suggested that some 9 per cent of children were severely underweight (data summarized in Davies and Saunders 1987). There is little evidence of a consistent pattern in nutritional trends in Zimbabwe since independence, although young child rates of mortality and perhaps morbidity have been reduced in association with the rapid expansion of primary health care programmes and implementation of relief measures in response to drought reviewed above.

As posited by Davies and Saunders, and suggested by the existence of widespread undernutrition in other relatively high-income SADCC countries, selective approaches to welfare, including health care, are not sufficient to address the root causes of these and other aspects of child (and vulnerable group) ill-health. As described in the next section, such causes are found also in the systematic patterns of household vulnerability, dependence, and income insecurity that persist in wide areas of all SADCC countries.[3]

4. VULNERABILITY OF SADCC HOUSEHOLDS TO FOOD DEFICITS, DROUGHT, AND DEPENDENCE

4.1. *National and Household Food Security*

A clear characteristic of food and especially cereal production in the region is that of large year-to-year fluctuations in both marketed and, to a lesser extent, total output, associated with apparent medium-term declines in production per capita. At the height of the recent droughts, in 1983, total cereal production in the nine countries fell to some 7.3 million tonnes as against pre-drought levels of 8–10 million, and in Botswana, Lesotho, and Mozambique (the latter partly due to war), cereal imports exceeded estimated levels of internal production. At the country level, Zimbabwean maize production fell by over 70 per cent between 1980 and 1983, turning the group's major cereal exporter into a food aid recipient (Morgan 1986*b*).

---

[3] This is not to suggest either that increases in household income, taken alone, are necessarily cost- (or otherwise) effective in leading to rapid improvement in child nutritional status.

By 1985, however, the group as a whole had recovered an overall surplus production position relative to basic estimated requirements; this surplus was largely due to Zimbabwe and Malawi cereal output, which formed about 45 per cent of the total. Through the intermediary of foreign-exchange backed donor purchases (or swap arrangements providing wheat for maize), these two countries became major suppliers to relief programmes in the neighbouring States, particularly Mozambique. This is one of four countries in SADCC persistently unable to meet internal needs for staple cereals. Like Angola, the major reason is that of war and destabilization, whilst Botswana and Lesotho are able to compensate for their increasing structural food deficits through commercial imports based on diamond and migrant labour earnings, topped up with food aid receipts targeted mainly to nutrition-oriented programmes.

War has therefore now superceded drought as the primary factor threatening the region's food supply position: progressive collapse of cereal and probably cassava production in both Mozambique and Angola, and growth of the non-agricultural population (largely the displaced and the urban dwellers) reliant on food aid imports to meet basic supplies, have led to a current annual food aid requirement of more than one million tonnes for the two countries. This is associated with the war-related collapse of foreign exchange availability, and, in the case of Angola, with falls in the price of oil, its main export. In 1987/8, Malawi also became a large-scale recipient of food aid, mainly due to the presence of some 400,000–600,000 Mozambicans within its borders, displaced by insurgency.

Whilst the highly precarious access to food for households in the war-affected parts of the region is clear, indicators of such access in other areas are more difficult to establish, and are not necessarily provided (as seen in the review of nutrition data above) by degrees of food production self-sufficiency at national level. Although measures of calorific supply per capita against basic requirements are some guide, and show even before the droughts and intensified warfare of the mid-1980s that most SADCC countries had serious shortfalls (Table 10.9), they provide little sense of disaggregated and household level food access.

The need to consider overall incomes, multiple sources of food supply, access to services which help increase the efficiency of intake and use of food (such as elimination of internal parasites through health and sanitation programmes), and possibilities for fallback strategies such as migration and livestock sales in times of stress, vastly complicate analysis of household vulnerability to food shortage. That such elements are important, in a region where some 25 million or more people live in normally food-deficit or drought-prone rural areas (see Fig. 10.4; also Morgan 1986b), can be briefly illustrated by two countries:

(1) Malawi was cereal self-sufficient and produced modest export surpluses during much of the 1980s. Most cereal production came from small

Table 10.9. Some estimates of calorie availability per capita in SADCC countries (per day)

	FAO estimate of daily calorie needs per capita	Average calorific supply per capita		Calorie supply 1981–83 as % of estimated need
		1979–80[a]	1981–3	
Angola	2 350	2 093	2 204	94
Botswana	2 320	2 242	2 180	94
Lesotho	2 280	2 248	2 313	101
Malawi	2 320	2 185	2 237	96
Mozambique	2 320	1 885	1 725	74
Swaziland	2 320	2 510	2 618	113
Tanzania	2 320	2 004	2 502	108
Zambia	2 310	1 981	2 000	87
Zimbabwe	2 390	1 944	2 154	90

[a] Quoted from FAO Food Balance Sheets in 'SADCC Regional Food Reserve, Pre-Feasibility Study, Main Report', Technosynesis, Rome, Jan. 1984.

Note: Supply is estimated after allowance for usage for seed, animal feed, wastage and industrial purposes, as well as stock changes. No account is taken of the possible extent of maldistribution of access to food between families, population groups, etc. Given this, and other factors such as pricing, special distribution schemes, etc., these figures should be taken as broad indicators only.

Source: Calculated from FAO Food Balance Sheets (FAO, Rome, mimeo).

farms. Yet, partly due to maize pricing policies, and the small size of farm holdings, farming families continue to rely heavily on off-farm income, including remittances from South Africa and from seasonal work on commercial estates. As seen earlier, infant mortality and malnutrition rates are among the highest in the region.

(2) In Botswana, crop production plays a small role in the national economy and rural incomes rely heavily on casual employment, remittances, and, for a minority of households, sales of livestock. Although repeated droughts have reduced agricultural sector incomes, large-scale state transfers financed from diamond revenues and aid programmes have not only compensated for the effects of drought, but have also greatly widened access to health, water supplies, and other services, with notable effects on welfare outcome indicators.

4.2. Income and Migration Dependence

The contrast drawn above is between countries each with low rural household incomes, one with a strong State redistribution policy and the means to effect

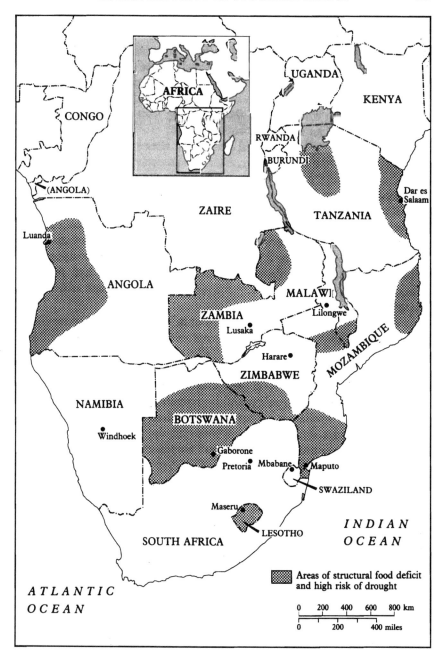

Fig. 10.4. High-risk food security areas in SADCC member States.

it, through both 'development' and 'emergency' programmes, and the other without these conditions. Even if through the medium of the State, therefore, a general relation can be assumed in broad terms for SADCC households between total household income access and degree of food security, or, alternatively, of vulnerability to collapse of food entitlement. The problem of vulnerability is related closely also to the instability of the various sources of income themselves, within which those deriving from the State, directly or indirectly, can play an important buffering role.

Whilst droughts and other natural disasters, as already noted, have powerful short-term, and often more lasting, effects on household incomes, a further area of vulnerability in wide areas of SADCC is the reliance of families on remittance earnings from migrant workers in South Africa. Recruitment of foreign workers by the South African mining and farming sectors has been a feature of the region since the late nineteenth century. Modern-day Lesotho, Botswana, Swaziland, southern Mozambique, and Malawi provided successive generations of workers to the dominant economy, under the supervision of the British and Portuguese colonial regimes, a process which had profound consequences for the semi-subsistence agricultural sector and assisted the penetration of the cash economy.

As dependence on incomes derived from migrant earnings has persisted, States in the region facing constraints on economic growth and employment generation also remain substantially reliant on this migration as a source of jobs and of foreign exchange. The most prominent cases are Lesotho and Mozambique, where remittances form the largest single source of export earnings. In Mozambique, the reductions by South Africa of the numbers of mine-workers recruited has already had serious consequences for household incomes and national revenues in the period since 1975. By late 1987, the number of Mozambicans employed in the South African mining sector had fallen to some 40 per cent of 1975 levels. This fall in recruitment has deprived the families of mine-workers, concentrated in the largely semi-arid three southern provinces of Mozambique, of basic, long-established means of economic survival. Income and job losses have been further increased by South African repatriation of unregistered Mozambican migrant workers.

Lesotho presents a picture of even greater dependence on, but also of sustained and increasing benefit from, migrant workers in South Africa. With 80 per cent of households relying directly or indirectly on employment and incomes generated by South African mine employment, and over 85 per cent of foreign exchange earnings derived from remittances, the number of Basotho mine-workers in South Africa has shown only slight declines in the 1980s, whilst average earnings grew some 16.5 per cent in real terms between 1979 and 1985 (Food Studies Group 1988). With cereal production showing a decline over the same period, the vulnerability of Lesotho households to the effects of possible changes in South African labour import policies has reached extreme proportions.

Other countries are now far less vulnerable, although Botswana and Swaziland (with about 25,000 and 17,000 migrants respectively) still have significant proportions of their work-force employed in South Africa. Malawi also retains a similar number of migrants in that country, much reduced from levels of the early 1970s. All national States, except perhaps Botswana, would face difficulties in helping affected families to ease the transition to other sources of income, were the bulk of these migrants to be suddenly repatriated.

4.3. Characteristics of the Rural Poor

Little comprehensive information is available on the nature and scale of rural poverty in the SADCC region, and the data base on levels, sources, and distribution of incomes is particularly poor. The wide differences in per capita GNP levels already noted give no more than a first indication of family-level welfare, tending to mask, for example, the relatively good access of Tanzanian rural households to basic services, and understating heavily the levels of rural poverty in countries like Botswana and Angola, where much of national income arises from enclave extractive industries which generate little local employment.

Rural areas in SADCC are generally characterized by low yields, by world standards, in arable farming, ranging from under 150 kg to slightly over 1 tonne per hectare for cereals. Use of fertilizers and improved seed is confined to a minority in all countries (Swaziland and Zimbabwe are growing exceptions), and in the most populous countries (Mozambique, Angola, Tanzania, and Malawi) cultivation is almost exclusively by (female) hand, limiting areas which can be planted. Chronic shortages of handtools exacerbate this problem. Land access is overall very high, a major advantage for the poor in the region, but is becoming limited in some States, with Malawian farm size averaging about 1.2 hectares, and some 20 per cent of rural Lesotho households estimated to have no land access. In Botswana, poverty of soils and cattle damage to crops are major obstacles to production, whilst in Zimbabwe the historically determined distribution of land between large commercial farms and the mass of 'communal' farmers—concentrating the latter in areas of poorer soils and less reliable rainfall—remains fundamentally unchanged.

Access to livestock, particularly cattle, is low in many areas, and has been reduced by droughts and decimated (in Mozambique) by warfare. Where average cattle numbers per family are high, as in Botswana, distribution tends to be highly uneven, and least favourable for households managed by women. Such households in turn are common (at least 25 per cent in rural areas in most countries, and as high as 40–60 per cent in Botswana and Lesotho), due in significant measure to the labour migration phenomena already described.

Resulting from these circumstances, a substantial proportion of rural households are unable to obtain a basic means of livelihood from agricultural activities alone, and are obliged to seek off-farm sources of income. Many of these are seasonal in nature (weeding, bird-scaring, grass collection), yield low returns (sewing, handicrafts), and are liable to sudden downturns during droughts. For poor rural families, therefore, the effects of local economic and climactic stress are often highly cumulative and interactive, leading to sudden income collapse.

Internal migration opportunities exist in most countries, but tend to be associated with the perpetuation, rather than alleviation, of poverty. Adequate data exist in Botswana and Zimbabwe to indicate that some of the most widespread child malnutrition is found among families of employees on freehold ranches in the former, and commercial farms in the latter.[4]

Further groups to be considered as characterized by poverty are those living in remote areas: the Lesotho Highlands, the Kalahari in Botswana, western Zambia, and Tanzania, and interior areas of Mozambique and Angola. Such areas are not only relatively lacking in social-service access and tend to have lower than average incomes and higher than average incidence of child malnutrition, but are often associated with low agricultural potential and unreliable rainfall.

Such surveys on rural incomes as have been undertaken bear out this picture of a large minority of households existing in a structurally reinforced condition of poverty. The Botswana Rural Income Distribution Survey (RIDS), possibly the most comprehensive of its kind, has already been referred to. A study of one of the largest villages in the country in 1984 (Mahalapye) illustrated further the high dependence of lower-income families on transfers compared to production, and also the seasonality of incomes (UNICEF Botswana Situation Analysis). In Swaziland, the Rural Homestead Survey of 1978/9 found that 56 per cent of total income came from cash earnings, mainly from wage employment; again, the poorer households were more dependent on remittance transfers, which were highly erratic in nature (UNICEF Swaziland Situation Analysis). The UNICEF Lesotho Situation Analysis identifies the 'rural poor' as the members of the 67 per cent of rural households which in 1985 had no migrant, the 20 per cent who had no land, the 60 per cent which were female-managed and the 47 per cent of the farming households which had no livestock. Given the great overlap between these categories, the picture of poverty that emerges is of widowed or abandoned mothers with young children owning few productive assets and with low-yielding, unreliable sources of income.

Estimates of the extent of rural poverty in other SADCC countries are even

[4] In Botswana's 1974 Rural Income Distribution Survey (RIDS), for example, 72% of families based on freehold farms were found to have incomes below the calculated poverty datum line, compared with 55% in small villages and 45% among rural families overall.

harder to come by. Very few rural Angolans and Mozambicans probably now escape conditions of serious poverty, other than those able to gain employment on State farms, where at least some degree of security of income and food supply is present (even rural civil servants experience great difficulty in the purchase of food and basic goods). In the current circumstances, probably only a small proportion of farming families are relatively self-sufficient in food, and manufactured products are scarce. Large-scale displacement due to banditry has caused collapse of family production systems. In Tanzania, where conditions both in terms of family farm production and access to social services are relatively much better, and cash earnings are derived from a number of export crops (although consumer goods are also scarce), it has been estimated that some 25–30 per cent of rural people remain below an assumed poverty line. In Zambia, an ILO study of basic needs in 1981 estimated that 80 per cent of rural households were 'poor or very poor' based on an estimation of minimum needs and projections from the 1974–6 Household Budget Survey. Perhaps more importantly, the 1980 Census in Zambia found almost 31 per cent of households without an economically active member (see UNICEF Situation Analyses of Tanzania and Zambia).

4.4. Urban Poverty in SADCC

Consideration of urban poverty also proceeds from an inadequate data base, with little reliable information available on the generally fast-growing urban and 'urban marginal' (or peri-urban) settlements in the region. Again, Botswana provides one of the better sources. The national Nutritional Surveillance system has over the last few years found consistently above average levels of undernutrition in children attending health facilities in low-income and recently settled urban areas. These phenomena may be closely related to migration and economic stress caused by the continuing drought. Earlier information, from a poverty datum line (PDL) study carried out by the government of Botswana in 1976, found that some 36–47 per cent of urban dwellers in the four main towns fell below the PDL, although average monthly household income exceeded it. By contrast, a PDL survey in Maseru, capital of Lesotho, carried out in 1984, found that some 60 per cent of households fell below the PDL, including all those with 'single person breadwinners' (UNICEF Botswana and Lesotho Situation Analyses).

Available information on poor urban households indicates that their income derives from casual sources, short-term and unskilled employment, as well as activities such as hawking, marketeering, and the running of 'shebeens' (beer parlours). The picture is similar to that of the rural poor in some respects, with the emphasis more on the periodic selling of goods rather than (but not excluding) labour. Such incomes are clearly vulnerable to sudden downturns in the local economy. Added to the high density and often inadequate servicing of newly settled urban areas, and the shortages of low-cost housing, the low and fluctuating levels of income for household without full-time wage earners are associated with widespread problems of health and sanitation.

Those families with members in full-time employment are also not isolated from economic stress. In Zimbabwe, Mozambique, Zambia, and Tanzania, real urban minimum wages have been eroded by rising official prices for basic food items and consumer goods (but see subsection on trends below). In Tanzania this process of reduction of the real minimum wage value started as long ago as 1974, and has probably been accelerated since the removal of maize meal subsidies in 1984. In Zimbabwe there were initial gains in the early post-independence period, which were somewhat eroded by wage freezes and removals of subsidies beginning in late 1982, as well as by general inflation. Real wages in Zambia have been declining since about 1977, in association with various adjustment measures taken in response to the collapse of copper export earnings in the mid-1970s. The reduction in purchasing power amongst low-income wage earners in these countries doubtless reduced in turn the demand for the services provided by the informal sector.

Net reductions in urban employment have not yet occurred on a large scale in SADCC urban areas except, to some extent, in Zambia. However, the types of economic adjustments being adopted by some countries in association with IMF/World Bank loan packages will certainly involve temporary losses of urban employment, particularly in the State and parastatal sectors; it is not yet clear how households would be expected or assisted to cope with the consequences of this.

4.5. *Trends in Household Incomes and the Impact of 'Adjustment'*

Four distinct factors mentioned above combine to indicate a relatively gloomy short-term outlook for household incomes in the SADCC region, and for the welfare of vulnerable groups in turn, despite advances made in the coverage of welfare services. First, the drought conditions of the early 1980s which affected most of the region not only continue in certain areas, but probably worsened income differentiation and permanently lowered the productive capacity of some of the very poor.[5] Secondly, growth of national income is in most SADCC countries not now exceeding that of population, indicating no prospect of general, widespread increases in welfare, particularly where little scope exists for redistribution of land, income, or State spending. Thirdly, external factors including low prices for major exports (oil in Angola, sugar in Swaziland, copper in Zambia, and so on), rising transport costs for imports (due partly to sabotage of the Mozambican sea routes), increased defence commitments, and high debt service obligations, have combined seriously to

---

[5] For example, cattle death rates in Botswana during the 1980s drought were strongly inversely related to the size of herd holdings (Botswana Ministry of Agriculture/CSO 1986: 37).

undermine the budgetary position of several governments. This in turn has led to cutbacks in expenditures on areas of importance to the poor, and to currency depreciations which have further disadvantaged urban consumers. Economic decline in Zambia, Tanzania, and Mozambique has reduced the efficiency of agricultural services in rural areas, leading to virtual breakdowns by the mid-1980s in marketing systems and the timely delivery of inputs. Although the new emphasis on price incentives to smallholder farming associated with structural adjustment policies may enable real farm incomes to increase for certain strata of net surplus producers, even these gains may prove short-lived: real prices for maize have been falling back in Zimbabwe and Malawi following increases in the early 1980s once these countries were faced with surpluses that could only be stored at high cost or exported at a loss. Finally, the massive destabilization of the two former Portuguese colonies has left economic and social turmoil and instability that will probably take decades to overcome, whilst the burden of these costs shows no sign of diminishing, and may spread to other countries as well.

This discussion, perhaps controversially, does not locate a major responsibility for recent depression of household incomes or access to welfare services in the region with the various 'structural adjustment' programmes now in force. It assumes that the important questions are related to the management of the adjustment process, seen to be inevitable in some form, rather than whether it is consciously undertaken at all. In a war-torn economy such as Mozambique's, the impact of expenditure cuts in social sectors, and of the reduction of credit provision to State enterprises leading to employment losses, has almost certainly been minor since the introduction of such measures in January 1987 in comparison with the continued closure of rural schools, health posts, and agricultural units due to direct attacks, and with additional employment losses for Mozambicans in South Africa. Urban consumers with semi-indexed wages may be at least no worse off as increases in official prices divert goods from illegal channels, thereby bringing down prices facing consumers overall. Meanwhile, adjustment programmes have generally been associated, as in Mozambique, with greater inflows of international resources for rehabilitation of productive sectors, and for commodity imports of raw materials and basic goods, although not necessarily at a rate quick enough tolerably to offset the effects of reductions of demand.

The effects on sustainability of welfare services of 'adjustment', however, may be more difficult to justify, particularly in the absence of major distortions due to destabilization and resource diversion to defence. The 'alternative approach' developed by Cornia, Jolly, and Stewart in *Adjustment with a Human Face* is based on the argument that negative effects on nutritional levels, educational access, and low-income households are likely to occur, and to prejudice medium-term economic growth, unless careful intervention measures to protect the more vulnerable are designed and implemented during the transition period whilst sustainable growth is being restored. Specifically, adjustment programmes concerned solely with the rectification of domestic and external monetary and trade balances are shown not necessarily to result in the restoration of economic growth. Additional resources need to be dedicated to the avoidance of steep declines in levels of household consumption and health and nutritional status, both through targeted welfare interventions and through production sector investment and rehabilitation, if such adjustments are to be sustainable. Very often, the timing of implementation of such measures has been a crucial and neglected policy question.

Most countries in SADCC have already in place some 'targeted welfare interventions', usually with nutrition-related objectives. These, particularly as concerned with temporary income-creating employment schemes and food distribution programmes, are discussed in more detail later. Measures to 'stretch' available resources in the social sectors, by increasing cost efficiency and equity in service provision, furthering auto-financing by selective user fees among groups which can afford to pay, and encouraging self-management by communities, are less common. A potential benefit of adjustment programmes, which may be overlooked, is the provision of an environment of greater incentives for social-service managers and decision-makers to consider such possibilities, which may promote greater long-run sustainability of services.[6]

5. CHOICES IN STRATEGIES FOR WELFARE PROTECTION TO VULNERABLE GROUPS UNDER STRESS: TWO CASE-STUDIES

The twin devastations of war and drought, their effects on vulnerable groups and families, and the responses by States whose own access to resources is differently affected by these circumstances, are illustrated by the cases of Mozambique and Botswana. Whilst the latter country, although affected by severe drought in successive seasons from 1981/2 to 1986/7, has abundant national access to financial resources by which to effect compensatory measures, the former has had to make more careful and difficult choices among types of programmes, possible beneficiaries, and limited means of implementation, given an economy in crisis. In doing so, it has been unable to rely on the economic mechanisms that have continued to function in Botswana, ensuring there the physical presence of food and consumer goods in local shops even in remote areas, and providing the possibility of using private-sector transportation,

---

[6] Budget and expenditure maximization in themselves are clearly questionable as primary social-sector objectives when, for example, high-cost hospital care for the few, and teachers' or nurses' salaries make up large proportions of such expenditure, whilst basic drugs and school material remain widely unavailable. Use of low-cost technologies (e.g. for oral rehydration treatment of diarrhoea), bulk procurement policies for a reduced list of priority medical and school supplies, and community-based approaches to service delivery are among the measures proposed by Cornia et al. (1987) as appropriate adaptations to a highly resource-constrained social-sector environment.

storage, and food-processing facilities. The main common factors facing the two countries in designing responses to 'emergency' have been simply the persistent and structural nature of the vulnerabilities that lead to repeated crises in rural society, and the scarcity of relevantly trained and experienced nationals who can be mobilized for programme implementation.

5.1 Botswana: Addressing Drought and Structural Poverty

Although Botswana is ecologically a semi-arid land where arable farming is marginal in the best of years and livestock, particularly cattle, provide the main source of rural incomes, about 70 per cent of rural households engage in rain-fed crop production. By contrast, 45 per cent or less of such households are owners of cattle (RDC 1985). Rural income surveys quoted above have shown a very high dependence among poorer families on casual employment and remittances. None the less, the loss of self-provisioning capability and opportunities for seasonal work on fields caused by drought conditions, particularly repeated over several seasons, leads to an intensification of poor health and nutritional status. Whilst between 1978 and 1984 cereal production fell from about 50,000 tonnes to some 7,000 tonnes per year, malnutrition rates in children under 5 rose from a yearly average of 25 per cent to 31 per cent in the respective years (percentage below 80 per cent of expected weight for age, based on monthly weighing at all health facilities). Income from crops per household actively engaged in agriculture fell from about 275 Pula (about US$138) in 1981 to some 39 Pula in 1984. In this period of the early 1980s, overall cattle numbers were reduced from almost 3 million to about 2.3 million, with losses concentrated disproportionately in the smaller herds, namely those of lower income households (see Morgan 1986a).

None the less, Botswana during the period 1984–6 managed to reverse the deteriorating nutritional status of children associated with the drought (Fig. 10.5), even improving on the original pre-drought position (although changes in the recording system at health units in 1985 throw some doubt on the extent of this). It was also possible to avoid a mass exodus from rural areas to the prosperous urban centres which had sprung up around mining, meat-processing, and civil service activities, and which remain largely free of 'slum' areas. Equally, despite repeated harvest failures over a period of several years, the numbers of households planting crops fell only some 25 per cent at most, and recovered to near pre-drought levels by 1986. Starvation, even among extremely isolated communities, was entirely averted during the droughts.

Supported by a budget surplus and extensive foreign exchange reserves, plus a level of food aid donations per capita which stands at one of the highest in Africa (in 1983/4, for example, between 24 and 30 kg per person; see RDC 1985), the Botswana government has run a nationwide Drought Relief Programme since 1981 which simultaneously addresses income losses experienced

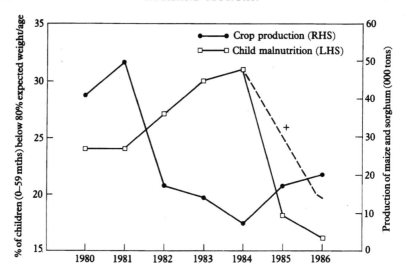

Fig. 10.5. Child malnutrition and crop production in Botswana, 1980–1986.
Note: Broken line shows estimated malnutrition incidence adjusted to take account of
changes in recording system in 1985.
Sources: Cornia *et al.* (1987); Botswana Ministry of Agriculture (1986).

by rural households, targets food supplies to non-able-bodied groups presumed
most vulnerable, and provides the means for agricultural recovery in the small
farm sector. The basic elements of the programme have been:

(1) Distribution of free food as take-home rations on a monthly basis,
    through the extensive national network of health facilities, to all pregnant
    and breastfeeding women, all children under 5 years, and registered
    destitutes and tuberculosis patients (6 kg per month of cereals plus
    cooking oil).
(2) Maintenance of a school feeding programme for primary school children.
(3) Therapeutic feeding on a daily attendance basis to actually malnourished
    children at health facilities.
(4) A special trucking operation to supply maize to roughly 2 per cent of the
    population classified as 'remote area dwellers', in areas which tend to
    show the highest rates of malnutrition among children.
(5) Public works programmes with payment on a cash basis for days
    worked, employing between 50,000 and 70,000 people at some time
    during the year. This has involved work in labour-intensive projects
    selected by village committees, such as dam construction, building of
    traditional houses for extension workers, of communal kraals, and of

local roads. A special programme has employed some 4,000 women per year to handstamp the sorghum used in the school feeding programme.

(6) Provision of seeds (usually 20 kg per family per year) to farming households, as well as grants to allow for local hiring of tractors and of labour for clearance of fields before ploughing. In 1985/6, a weeding subsidy was introduced (these forms of assistance now form a major component of Botswana's Accelerated Rainfed Arable Programme aimed at promoting post-drought recovery in the late 1980s).

A series of additional measures financed within the Drought Relief Programme included the expansion of water-drilling and maintenance capacity at national and district levels, and the purchase and distribution of stock-feed and vaccines for cattle farmers. Cattle-marketing possibilities were extended by grants to district councils for purchase of animals to be used in school-feeding.

Although the programme at its height has taken up some 12 per cent of the government's development budget (Holm and Morgan 1985), its implications in terms of additional personnel and institutional resources have been very light. Implementation of the measures described above has been based almost entirely on existing health, agricultural extension, and local council service structures. The food distribution programmes, which use village-level health posts and schools as final distribution points, are based on an expanded version of an earlier nutrition promotion project supported by the World Food Programme. The public works schemes depend largely on community-level supervision and very limited technical support from the district councils which effect payment to workers once a month. The main additions to available cadres for these measures, which amount to a significant extension of Botswana's Welfare State, have been the recruitment of a dozen 'Western' volunteers as technical officers for public works, and of a similar number of district-based drought relief co-ordinators, usually retired civil servants.

In designing this programme, however, the Botswana State decided to take full advantage—drawing on the experience of earlier, less effective drought relief campaigns in the late 1970s—not only of its existing local institutions, but of national monitoring systems gradually being developed in the fields of nutritional surveillance, agro-meteorology, livestock and grazing conditions, and food availability (Morgan 1985). The early warning system, which was established in early 1984 based on these data sources, initially as a review committee making recommendations for resource allocation to a parent Interministerial Drought Committee, was able, in compiling short-term indicators, to provide the beginnings of a national targeting mechanism for such allocations.

Furthermore, the State was not ideologically constrained from contracting out certain functions involved in the implementation of programmes to private enterprise: indeed, this was increasingly seen as attractive to political decision-makers, often owners themselves of trucks and tractors eligible for hire. The country's (then) only maize mill, South African owned, received a steady flow of contracts for the milling and mixing of maize and milk powder for clinic distribution. In a perhaps healthy division of labour, rural women and, for urban areas, co-operative millers, continued to process sorghum for primary-school feeding.

Along with its political attractiveness to richer farmers and entrepreneurs, the programme—distributing food to over 60 per cent of the rural population as direct beneficiaries, seeds to almost all rural households, and employment to many others—has become a major election plank for the ruling Botswana Democratic Party (BDP), to the point where the (nominally socialist) opposition complained during the 1984 election campaign of unfair buying of votes. Given the opposition's dominance of the small number of urban constituencies, and the BDP's reliance on the majority rural electorate, there will be a strong political incentive, based on a coincidence of economic interest between the rural élite and the rural poor, for the government not to reduce drastically the scale of these welfare measures as climatic conditions improve. This will be the case even if donated food aid volumes decline, assuming that the budgetary position of the State remains in sufficient surplus to allow it to compensate.

As implied already, Botswana's budget surplus and foreign exchange reserve positions, coupled with donors' willingness to provide relatively high levels of food aid to an efficient distribution system, have enabled it to avoid certain hard choices in the design and targeting of its drought relief measures. At certain points in the budgetary process, the only apparent limitations on resource allocations in the past few years have been the implementation capacities of local government institutions and the ability of communities to identify projects not evidently absurd. The public-works programmes have proven an efficient and speedy way of redistributing mining sector State revenues directly to the rural poor in cash, thus bolstering their incomes in times of stress. The setting of a daily wage-rate high enough to provide a meaningful return but low enough not to attract members of relatively well-off families to manual work on the schemes has proven an administratively simple targeting device (from personal experience of these projects, over 80 per cent of participants have normally been women). Similarly, women from well-off rural families are less likely to join the monthly queue at health posts to have their children weighed and collect a take-home ration. The apparent effectiveness of the 'self-selecting' mechanisms used is partly assisted by the fairly clear wealth division prevalent in rural Botswana, between a large-herd-owning minority on the one hand, and the mass of few- or no-cattle-owning families on the other. A further contributory factor has been the significant involvement in local drought relief operations of village-based organizations—for example, the Village Development Committees in the identification of projects and selection of participants, and the Parent–Teacher Associations in school feeding and food preparation.

Economically, however, the programme has inefficiencies that a less well-endowed national State would have been forced to address. Little productive or permanent infrastructure has resulted from the US$5 million (equivalent) or more spent yearly on public works under drought relief since the early 1980s, and labour productivity on most such projects has been low. Furthermore, the opportunity to use these resources as an initial community investment in what might later develop into much needed additions to permanent rural employment has largely been missed. It is also argued that disincentive effects on agricultural production have resulted from the high levels of free food distribution (an assertion unproven and belied by the only small reduction in the number of households planting) and that—more plausibly—understanding of health facilities among the rural population as a service for disease prevention has been undermined by their use in a food distribution role. Finally, the programme has done little to address the structural aspects of rural poverty which tend to provoke a high demand for relief intervention in drought years: the very limited access to cattle and draught animals, which form the main repository of rural wealth, and high reliance on remittances, casual employment, and low-yielding, high-risk arable farming. It is not apparent either that Botswana's 'Drought Recovery Programme', coming into effect following generally good rains in 1987/8, will directly address these problems.

5.2. Mozambique: Management of Acute and Structural Crisis

Mozambique provides as different a picture as can possibly be imagined from Botswana for two countries in such geographical proximity. Emerging from a highly repressive colonialism and inheriting the remains, often sabotaged, of a notoriously inefficient State and formal sector economy, the Mozambique liberation movement FRELIMO continued to be involved with a regional war against white minority rule, first in Southern Rhodesia from 1975–80, and later, until it reduced its role under the 1984 Nkomati Accord, in support of the African National Congress in South African. With the flight of about 90 per cent of the Portuguese settler population in the mid-1970s, and as a result the virtual disappearance of the commercial sector and managerial class which had been dominated by it, the State was obliged (whether eagerly or not) to assume much of the responsibility for the running of the country's economic enterprises, large and small. This it was very inadequately equipped to do. None the less, after the initial disruptions of the independence process, modest economic growth from very low levels of per capita income were achieved until 1981. At this point, widespread, externally supported insurgency began to affect several provinces, eventually extending its destructive effects to all districts in some form. The strategy of this insurgency focused initially on the closure of the main transport routes to the sea used by Mozambique's SADCC neighbours, and extended to attacks on all types of productive units as well as the social and commercial sectors. Coupled with production falls due to drought, the Mozambique economy contracted by some 33 per cent in real terms between 1981 and 1985, with modest growth resuming thereafter. Meanwhile, South Africa intensified its economic sanctions against Mozambique, reducing its use of Maputo port for international trade by over 80 per cent from 1975 to 1987, and recruitment of Mozambican mine workers by about 60 per cent over this period—thus intensifying the shortages of foreign exchange and problems of employment and income in southern Mozambique.

Without a widespread and well-endowed State structure to offer social protection, the effects of the intensified crisis on rural households in Mozambique became dramatic by 1983/4. In that period, it is commonly accepted that some 100,000 people may have died due to drought, coupled with inaccessibility and displacement caused by insurgency, and the failure of international food aid donors to provide timely support. Whilst since that time famine has not been widespread, displacement and loss of household assets and the family production base have become commonplace, with probably several million Mozambicans forced to flee their home areas. At the time of writing, roughly one million citizens are estimated to have been recently displaced within the country, and a further million are in neighbouring countries (adding to demands on Zimbabwean, Zambian, Malawian, Tanzanian, and Swazi State welfare systems in the process).

The household level crisis is indicated, as described earlier, by extremely high levels of infant and child mortality, as well as extensive chronic malnutrition (stunting) in children, high levels of acute malnutrition (wasting) in recently displaced communities, increasing incidence of low birth weight, and out-breaks of preventable infectious diseases. In contrast to Botswana, the largely externally induced crisis has not only affected welfare status at family level, but has drastically eroded the already weak financial and institutional capacity of the state to mount responses to mitigate the effects on the most vulnerable.

Alliances with what remained of the private sector after independence in operational terms have also been largely unavailable as options to assist responses. Although ideological considerations deterred this for several years, the main impediment has been the destruction of rural shops and breakdown of private transport capacity due to extreme scarcities of spare parts, servicing, and fuel.

The State has been faced with a further complicating factor: the need to intervene to secure at least minimum food supplies for urban populations, following the collapse of internally marketed food production and the inability of private channels to provide significant imports (Fig. 10.6). By 1984, the main towns (containing 2.0 to 2.5 million people) were largely dependent on food aid deliveries, supplied through rationing systems, to meet basic food needs, particularly for cereals, salt, sugar, and cooking oil. This presented the State with the constant need to make allocative decisions with inadequate

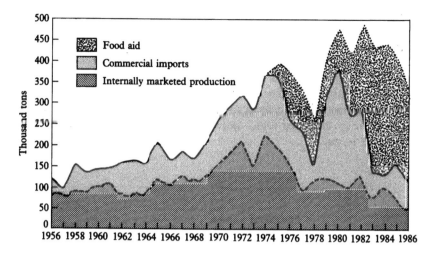

Fig. 10.6. Cereal market supply in Mozambique, 1956–1986.
Source: Food Security Department, Ministry of Commerce, Mozambique.

resources, between the urban population with some levels of local currency purchasing power but no food to purchase, and the rural population extensively affected both food and income shortages due to the emergency. Whilst local transport costs for supplying the urban populations are in most cases relatively low, the administrative costs of operating rationing systems for hundreds of thousands or urban families are high, not least given the State's limited managerial capacity.

Despite these costs, urban rationing is administered fairly and effectively in Mozambique when food is available. In the rural areas, delivery of all basic services and needs, ranging from food to health care, clean water, and clothing, is inhibited by a wide range of physical constraints. Firstly, negligible investment in transport infrastructure during the colonial period, except in the export 'corridors' serving neighbouring countries, has not yet been compensated for. This implies reliance on a complex combination of transport means, including road, rail, air, and sea, depending on the locality. Secondly, poor telephone and radio connections make co-ordination of delivery systems more difficult. Most importantly, the danger of attacks on road and rail traffic, including relief deliveries, necessitate travelling in convoy with military protection in many districts, a process which is both time-consuming to arrange and usually costly in terms of the value (if not the benefits derived from) the commodities delivered.

Social-service provision has been reduced to an extraordinary degree by systematic destruction of physical units, looting of supplies in stock, and attacks on state employees. Some 31 per cent of rural health facilities (Fig. 10.7) and 36 per cent of primary schools existing in 1981 were by 1988 not functioning for these and related reasons, depriving some 2–3 million people of access to primary health care, and roughly half a million school age children of education. Also serious has been the impact on service provision of reductions in the real value of the State budget both overall and for the functioning of social-sector programmes—although this has been partly compensated for by increased donor assistance in kind (medical supplies, school books, and so on).

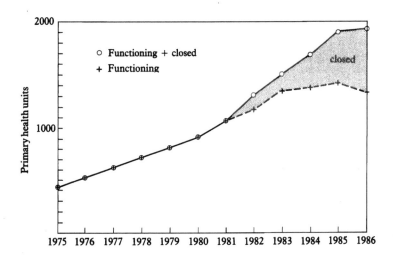

Fig. 10.7.   Numbers of primary-level health units functioning and not functioning due to closure in Mozambique.
Source: Noormahomed and Cliff (1987).

The response of the Mozambique State to the increasing pressures generated by the emergency, and the willingness of international aid agencies to provide resources under an 'emergency' label, was initially modest. A national relief agency, the Department for Prevention and Combat of Natural Calamities (DPCCN) was established under the Ministry of Co-operation in 1981, in response initially to problems caused by floods and cyclones. However, it took several years before a reasonable logistical delivery capacity was established by DPCCN reaching to district level, and the management resources provided to its national and provincial offices were initially poor. The DPCCN also failed to establish regular operational links with other sectors of government and with donor agencies, although co-ordination meetings were held monthly with non-government organizations (NGOs). Until 1987, DPCCN had developed no planning information or monitoring capability, nor had it recognized a need to do so. The concentration on delivery of relief goods without attention to co-ordination, establishment of priorities, and development of a 'prevention' or post-emergency strategy, was consistent with the orientations of some of the agencies supplying goods for the relief effort.

In the first half of 1987, however, the government adopted a different approach, one much more consistent with the economic adjustment programme adopted at the beginning of that year. Emphasis in strategy for emergency response began to be laid on the need to integrate this at the community level with medium-term rehabilitation and recovery measures, in order to avoid a condition of permanent crisis. Interventions were made to promote productive activities in areas of resettlement of displaced people, and low-cost rehabilitation of social-service facilities began to be undertaken, to provide a socio-economic base for rural recovery.

As a result, a multisectoral approach to the emergency became essential, and this resulted, in terms of institutional arrangements, in the creation of a National Executive Commission for Emergency (CENE) with co-ordinating responsibilities for the rehabilitation programmes which now began to be developed in the technical ministries responsible for social services and rural production. During 1987, Provincial Emergency Commissions were established along similar lines, under the political authority of the governors (with ministerial rank). At both national and provincial level, DPCCN's role was broadened to include not only the distribution of food and relief items, but also to provide logistical services to the rehabilitation programmes initiated by the technical ministries. DPCCN was allowed to sell services to ministries and to private traders, thereby accumulating local currency which remained at the disposal of the emergency programme for support to rehabilitation projects.

Apart from the incorporation of multisectoral elements and medium-term perspectives into its emergency programme, the CENE has also begun to rationalize the involvement of by now large numbers of international agencies providing resources. NGOs and some multilateral agencies such as UNICEF and the EEC have been encouraged to focus on specific geographical areas, usually one or more of the 120 districts, to provide sustained institutional support to local structures, relief items for displaced families, agricultural inputs, and assistance in the recuperation of social services for the entire area. Although this 'district adoption' approach has both political and technical drawbacks, it simplifies the co-ordination tasks of national and provincial State structures, and encourages agencies to adopt multisectoral, recovery-oriented perspectives consistent with local conditions and security constraints.

A further development of the government's emergency policy has been that of conscious limitation of free food distribution in rural areas, in order to avoid disincentive effects perceived to result. The CENE has requested food aid agencies to provide flexibility to enable food aid to be sold in any local situation where people can apparently afford to buy it (which, if accepted by donors, gives the State more leeway in making adjustments in allocations between agricultural and non-agricultural or urban areas). Limitations on the periods for which, and areas within which, food can be distributed free have also been introduced, with the preference to be given to recently displaced people. Such people normally receive land allocations from the local authorities and agricultural inputs through the Emergency Programme, and are expected, in the absence of drought conditions, not to require food aid after the first or second harvest period. In this way, the government hopes to avoid a self-perpetuating food crisis in the countryside. The establishment of new settlements due to displacement is also taken as an opportunity to introduce irrigation on a co-operative basis, particularly in the vicinity of urban settlements (constituting so-called Green Zones). Further initiatives, aimed at the revitalization of local economies and trading relationships, have been undertaken using food aid as a 'financial' resource: donated commodities may be sold within enterprises to finance labour hiring, or exhanged with local producers for export crops such as fish and cashew.

A final characteristic of the Mozambique government's emergency response has been its recognition of the limitations of its lower-level structures and unwillingness to place undue demands on them. Reporting obligations for food distribution, for example, extend only as far as the district level, and local decision-makers are left to determine priorities for lower administrative units. Health units have been required only to feed people who suffer from acute malnutrition or related illnesses, and require internment as a result. By simplifying procedures, and not overloading limited administrative capacities, the opportunity costs in diversion of personnel from other public sector programmes have been kept low. Conversely, very limited targeting of emergency programmes exists, beyond broad geographical areas and to concentrations of displaced people where these are apparent. Given the still fragmented nature of socio-economic data on emergency-affected areas and vulnerable groups, there exists little basis as yet on which systematically and explicitly to prioritize the allocation of emergency goods; however local political or State structures provide some articulation of popular 'needs', and can be effective in responding to them, within the limits of their human and material resources.

6. SOME GENERALIZED CONCLUSIONS

6.1. *The Regional Context for Protection of Household Welfare*

A predominant feature of welfare status in the Southern African region which has emerged from this review is that of insecurity of access at household level to necessities, and of household food production. As has been seen, this insecurity is provoked by both historical and/or underlying factors and by welfare-threatening shocks such as drought and the effects of war. A further problem is the tenuous sustainability of State services in many countries of SADCC in circumstances of economic decline related to exogenous factors, adjustments of State expenditure levels and intersectoral allocation, and in the case of two (or possibly more) particular countries, warfare. Exacerbating these insecurities are the increases in demands on natural resources and State services resulting from an overall growth in SADCC population of the order of 3 per cent per year.

The common themes concerning the choice of strategies for welfare protection in times of stress or crisis, as discussed in the case studies and earlier review, suggest and emphasize (1) the need for co-ordinated, multisectoral strategies defined at national political levels; (2) the building over time of institutional capacity in the various levels of the State to implement extraordinary as well as ongoing welfare programmes, the former preferably on the basis of the latter; and (3) the range of options already available and for which experience exists within the region, to be adapted to local circumstances and the current nature of the crisis to be addressed.

The regional phenomena of structural poverty, chronic malnutrition, and shortages of trained personnel, features of the historical processes of colonial domination, labour migration, and dependency, in addition to the relative weakness both of the post-independence States and of rural communities as a result of these factors, suggest and necessitate a political element to the protection of the most vulnerable. The development of a popular politics around the process of creation of welfare-providing infrastructure, income-enhancing projects, and poverty-oriented programmes, by communities in alliance with the State, can, as shown in the early years of the FRELIMO movement and still in Mozambique today, help to reduce the need for capital- and import-intensive, and skill-demanding, programme designs, at least in the early stages of establishing or restoring mass welfare provision. In health and other areas, low-cost technologies to support this—oral rehydration treatment, child growth monitoring, community-built classrooms, and low-cost hand-pumps and latrines—can often be secured. As Botswana has shown, where the State is dependent for its political legitimacy on a regular electoral process, mass demands for welfare provision by an overwhelming poor and rural electorate are influential in determining resource allocation priorities. Further-more, the extensive measures taken by the Botswana State to prevent economic collapse in rural areas in times of drought, indicate the potential of an effective alliance of interests between the different rurally based economic classes. By contrast, it seems no accident that those SADCC countries with the least populist, or most autocratic, political regimes are those which perform least well on a range of welfare achievements, both promotive and protective, taking into account levels of income per capita.

Examples have been given of the relation between political and social objectives in the process of establishment of and access to welfare programmes in Southern Africa, as a region faced with the military and economic dominance of a white minority regime. These include Mozambique and Zimbabwe's prioritization of community health and primary-education programmes; the targeting by insurgents in both countries of the very infrastructure created and personnel trained for those programmes; South Africa's interference with the food and fuel supply flows of its neighbours (and threats to do so); and disparities in welfare-spending, child mortality, and life expectancy rates between legally designated racial groups in South Africa itself (Green *et al.* 1987: pt. 2). Such factors all attest to the existence of this context. As put by the governor of a Mozambican province, 'we can only win this war if we help the population to build something worthwhile to defend.' Such a statement contains a degree of relevance for most countries of the region, and suggests the need for further investigation of how the poor can be assisted to adapt to situations of displacement and military unrest.

6.2. *Common Strategies and Approaches to Welfare Protection and the Reduction of Household Vulnerability*

Against this background, the following common approaches are suggested as important for the development of more effective welfare protection measures in the region as a whole:

1. Prevention of crisis is related to the development of institutional bases in the State for the design and implementation of assistance programmes and the monitoring of vulnerability amongst families. Such bases have enabled the Botswana government to deliver effective compensatory measures for households during the 1980s' droughts, without significant recourse to external agencies for implementation. The question relates also in part to the development of formal 'early warning systems', to inform decisions about such interventions; but also to the enhancement of analysis and understanding of the structural aspects of underdeveloped, dependent, and vulnerable local economies. 'Early warning' can equally be provided through the strengthening and harnessing of local political structures (such as FRELIMO Party's village cells in Mozambique) or processes (such as Botswana's liberal-democratic national and local electioneering which retains pressure on a rurally based ruling party). These in turn need to generate the political demands for effective action on behalf of the rural poor that are weak in some parts of the region.

2. The development of multisectoral welfare strategies and co-ordination bodies to implement them within the State, linked to the productive sector ministries and overall resource allocation and economic decision-making bodies, can help ensure a sustained approach to welfare requirements. Few countries in the region have even begun to achieve this (with the result, for

example, that nutritionists and their priorities remain isolated even within their health sector ministries, unable to influence choices in agricultural research, crop, or food-pricing policies). Again, Botswana provides something of an exception, incorporating ongoing nutrition sector, drought relief, and early warning activities into a National Food Strategy (RDC 1985), published as a 'White Paper' and incorporated, both as a strategic component and as a loose set of expenditure plans, into the Sixth National Development Plan (1986–91). The strategy is monitored by a working group, based in the Rural Development Unit of the central Ministry of Finance and Development Planning, which reports on progress and issues requiring resolution, to a group of top civil servants headed by the vice-president. Such a machinery ensures the possibility of bringing household food security and nutrition-related questions to high-level decision-makers in a coherent policy context.

3. Whilst cost-effectiveness considerations vary in their prominence from country to country, all states in the region still face some degree of shortage of trained personnel for the implementation of social-welfare programmes, and in most cases are particularly ill-equipped to provide the types of staff required for implementation of responses to crises. Strengthening of response capacity is often conceived, firstly, narrowly in terms of food provision (usually relatively easy to obtain from donors), and, secondly, in terms of financial outlays to complement delivery. Opportunities exist, however, for the process of extending welfare programmes as a development objective to incorporate routine training for the design and implementation of 'emergency' measures, partly by actually carrying out such measures on a smaller scale as part of a poverty alleviation programme. A range of options, depending on local economic and social circumstances, is available and tested for income supplementation in crises (food-for-work, consumer goods-for-work, commodity exchange programmes, cash-for-work, and so on), which also has relevance to households with low productivity in farming or in the informal sector in 'non-crisis' periods. Such activities, organized at the village level and supervised or monitored by the lower levels of local government, can be linked to community health and nutrition programmes, as well as to the improvement of 'village assets' such as water points and schools. Regular programmes of this sort would refine skills and organizational experience available to carry expanded income-enhancing and welfare-defending interventions, following harvest failure, an insurgent attack, or the influx of displaced people from a neighbouring district or country.

4. Given actual or plausible future situations of State budgetary constraints and foreign exchange shortages which impinge on sectors concerned with welfare provision, including those arising from 'forced' diversion of resources to defence and security, welfare programme design in SADCC should favour increasingly the identification and development of cost-effective means of welfare provision and an increased degree of community responsibility for

operation and maintenance. Programme design has tended to neglect the possibilities for achieving greater sustainability of capital investments, and coverage of recurrent costs, that may exist with 'recipient' communities, even when themselves under economic stress. With the opening up of opportunities for local-level expression of welfare priorities, and of channels and incentives (matching or otherwise) for community labour, cash, skill, organizational and material contributions, access to services at actual constrained levels of State budgetary provision can be improved. Use of decentralized management and investment decision-making, and of control over revenue-raising and expenditure may also (depending on the nature of the decision-making bodies) be a complement to this trend. Donor aid, including food aid in kind, should also seek to provide necessary resources for increased community (or group-specific) responsibility over welfare services.

5. Technology and building standards chosen for social investment projects, and techniques used in service provision, apparently need to be subjected to more systematic tests of cost-efficiency and relevance than is usually the case in social-sector ministries. This is certainly increasingly recognized by governments in the region, but largely under increasingly rigorous conditions of resource shortfall, and in the context of economic adjustment programmes. The tendency still exists for welfare programme design to assume that provision is an end in itself; that future maintenance and rehabilitation costs need not be built into investment analysis; that benefits (in terms of expected improved health status, additions to community or national human capital stock, and so on) need not be subject to estimation; and that the efficiency of resource use in achieving such benefits need not be examined. This tendency is encouraged by the availability, in many places, of 'free' international resources lobbying, and often competing, to be accepted. Whilst such characteristics have been more typical of the initial post-independence periods than of today, State expenditure patterns in some countries still seem slow to adjust to accumulated experience: for example, although the Zambian education system has recently been willing to consider cost-efficiency promotion and the transferral of some expenses to users and parents, such costs are kept unnecessarily high by the continued training of fairly large numbers of new teachers, whilst the greater need is for upgrading and retraining of existing teaching staff to improve the efficiency of educational output, and to free resources for expenditure on school books and materials (Johnston *et al.* 1987). Indeed, for the countries which now face the greatest limitations on public-sector resources, the national objective of provision of universal access to primary (and in some cases junior secondary) education for a rapidly growing school-age population may itself come under increasing scrutiny.

6. 'Economic adjustment programmes', implemented as financial and fiscal review and reallocation mechanisms, can, in a receptive political and administrative climate, be viewed and used as opportunities for increasing the

incentives to welfare policy-making and programme implementors to improve methods for cost-efficiency analysis in their sectors, thereby increasing the medium- to long-term sustainability of these programmes. Such measures, far from being necessarily detrimental to welfare access, may in fact prevent future drastic and disruptive reductions in service provision should export earnings from mining (Zambia, Botswana), oil (Angola), or agricultural (Malawi, Zimbabwe, Zambia) sectors fall; when migrant labour opportunities are suddenly reduced (Mozambique, Lesotho); when international transport costs for landlocked countries are inflated due to sabotage of low-cost routes; and when defence expenditure growth under external threat is suddenly high.

7. Regional and international experience with programmes to reduce household food and income insecurity needs rapidly to be drawn together and made available to policy-makers and programme designers. The SADCC Food Security Programme based in Zimbabwe is the obvious body to do this, on behalf of the region. SADCC has already instituted a number of important research activities in areas relevant to this concern, such as land and water management for eroded or semi-arid areas, improvement of small grain and other drought-tolerant crop varieties, and livestock and veterinary programmes. Further work is needed, however, in documenting and analysing experience obtained in SADCC and other States (such as India), in the design and implementation of income-buffering measures, particularly in response to emergency-induced stress, but also as a more sustained approach to the reduction of structural poverty related to low household access to productive assets (including land, livestock, and labour).

8. In particular, as described in the Botswana case above, further attention needs to be focused on ways in which responses to short-term stresses and household income fluctuations can be designed so as also to promote reduced vulnerability in future to such stresses, particularly through diversification of income sources. The use of food or cash injections in drought- or war-affected areas to provide start-up funds for household income-earning activities, not just consumption, is one example. Such inputs need to be complemented by the provision of incentives to improve local skills and community infrastructure in order to increase viability of household production (roads for marketing, dams for livestock and crop watering); by the distribution of scarce tools and equipment; and by a macro-economic climate which increases economic opportunities for participating households. As suggested by Hay (1986), post-relief phases need to do more than merely replace lost household assets: they need to apply resources simultaneously to prevent future collapses of income and reverse the increasing trend to vulnerability. The earlier review of the nature of rural poverty also suggests that sustained policies to pre-empt the strains caused by short-term insecurity will need to focus particularly on investment in technology development for smallholder farming (raising yields

and effective water availability), as well as broadening income sources and access to productive assets. Interestingly, despite the extreme collapse of incomes in much of rural Mozambique, the national consensus in that country for the strategy of an appropriate response is now one of the most advanced in the SADCC region, in its insistence on the integration of rehabilitation and development, both conceptually and practically, with relief responses (see Government of Mozambique 1988).

9. Related to the above point, 'traditional' (namely, persisting and proven) community and household coping systems in times of stress need to be better understood in Southern Africa, and should not be undermined by larger-scale response mechanisms financed by national or international resources. Village-based welfare strategies and adaptations, ranging from deployment of extended family connections, resort to hunting and veldfood gathering, use of medicinal herbs and healers, running down through local sales of livestock holdings, to migration in search of casual employment, are among the mechanisms long used in the first instance following income losses. Environmental changes and certain State policies in both colonial and more recent times tended to reduce possible recourse to such buffering mechanisms (via, for example hunting regulations, overexploitation of grazing resources, land alienation, discouragement of drought-resistant crops, restrictions on population movements). Examples of current dilemmas exist within the programmes reviewed in the previous case-studies: the feeding of people declared destitute by their communities under the Botswana Drought Relief Programme has, in the view of many local observers, tended to reduce family willingness to take responsibility for older, poorer members; whilst the Mozambique government, faced with the problem of large numbers of children either orphaned or out of contact with their parents due to war, has opted quite successfully for the promotion of fostering of such children by new families within displaced communities.

10. For improved welfare programme management and implementation, further attention is needed to human resource development in this as a specialized area. This is particularly required as methods of financing for welfare delivery become more highly decentralized, and as maintenance and rehabilitation take increasing priority over initial capital investment in infrastructure. The accountants and budget managers, supply and logistics officers, hospital, school, and training institute directors, vehicle maintenance and fleet management specialists, all of whom are needed to improve the efficiency of working conditions for the doctors, nurses, teachers, water engineers, and relief programme co-ordinators, seem to be in chronic short supply across the region. Equally, the patchiness and poor quality of data collection and analysis, in areas which would provide resource allocators in welfare-related sectors with indicators of priorities and results of their decisions, are prevalent constraints—in some countries, information systems themselves are the victims

of destabilization. Without improvements on the basis of training in information collection, communication, and use, from the household or community level upwards, more efficient design and implementation of welfare programmes, and more timely response to situations of stress and emergency, even in the presence of effective political demands, can hardly be expected.

References

Botswana Ministry of Agriculture/Central Statistics Office (1986), *Botswana Agricultural Statistics*. Gaborone: Government Printer.

Cornia, G., Jolly, R., and Stewart, F. (1987), *Adjustment with a Human Face: Protecting the Vulnerable and Promoting Growth*, 2 vols. Oxford: Clarendon Press.

Davies, R., and Saunders, D. (1987), 'IMF Stabilisation Policies and the Effect on Child Health in Zimbabwe', *Review of African Political Economy*, 38.

FAO (Food and Agriculture Organization) Food Balance Sheets (1984), Rome: FAO (mimeo).

Food Studies Group (1988), 'Lesotho, Food Aid, Food Security Disincentives and Dependency', mimeo, Oxford University.

Government of Botswana (1974/5), *Report on the Rural Income Distribution Survey*. Gaborone: Government Printer.

Government of Mozambique (1988), *Rising to the Challenge*. Maputo: National Executive Commission for Emergency (CENE/DPCCN).

Green, R., Asrat, D., Mauras, M., and Morgan, R. (1987), *Children on the Front Line, the Impact of Apartheid, Destabilisation and Warfare on Children in Southern and South Africa*, (pt. 1). New York: UNICEF.

Hanlon, J. (1986), *Beggar Your Neighbours*. London: James Curry.

Hay, W. R. (1986), 'Food Aid and Relief: Development Strategies', *Disasters*, 10/4.

Holm, J., and Morgan, R. (1985), 'Coping with Drought in Botswana: An African Success', *Journal of Modern African Studies*, 23/3.

Johnston, A., Kaluba, H., Karlsson, M., and Nystrom, K. (1987), *Education and Economic Crisis: The Cases of Mozambique and Zambia*. Stockholm: Swedish International Development Authority, Education Division.

Morgan, R. (1985), 'The Development and Application of a Drought Early Warning System in Botswana', *Disasters*, 9/1.

—— (1986a), 'From Drought Relief to Post-Disaster Recovery, the Case of Botswana', *Disasters*, 10/1.

—— (1986b), 'Calculation of Size of Regional Reserve Stocks: Working Paper, Regional Reserve Study Part I', mimeo, Vakakis and Associates/SADCC Regional Food Reserve/Food Aid Study.

Noormahomed, A. R., and Cliff, J. (1987), 'The Impact on Health in Mozambique of South African Destabilisation', 2nd edn., mimeo Ministry of Health, People's Republic of Mozambique.

Quinn, V. (1986), 'Malawi: Agricultural Development and Malnutrition', mimeo, UNICEF, Nairobi.

Rohrbach, D. (1987), 'The Growth of Smallholder Maize Production in Zimbabwe 1979–1985: Implications for Food Security', paper presented at Third Annual Conference on Food Security in Southern Africa, University of Zimbabwe, Harare.

RDC (Rural Development Council, Republic of Botswana) (1985), 'Report on the National Food Strategy'. Gaborone: Ministry of Finance and Development Planning.

UNICEF (1988), *State of the World's Children, 1988*. Oxford: Oxford University Press.

UNICEF: Situation Analyses of Children and Women (variously titled, published jointly with national governments): Zambia (1986), Zimbabwe (1985), Botswana (1986), Lesotho (draft, 1986), Mozambique (1983), Malawi (1983), Swaziland (draft, 1987), Tanzania (1985, 2 vols.), Angola (draft, 1986), available from respective UNICEF country offices.

World Bank (1986), *World Development Report 1986*. Washington, DC: World Bank.

INDEX